T0228874

Praise for *Embedded Computing: A VLIW Approach to Architecture, Compilers and Tools*

There is little doubt that embedded computing is the new frontier of computer research. There is also a consensus that VLIW technology is extremely powerful in this domain. This book speaks with an authoritative voice on VLIW for embedded with true technical depth and deep wisdom from the pioneering experiences of the authors. This book will find a place on my shelf next to the classic texts on computer architecture and compiler optimization. It is simply that good.

Tom Conte Center for Embedded Systems Research, North Carolina State University

Written by one of the field's inventors with his collaborators, this book is the first complete exposition of the VLIW design philosophy for embedded systems. It can be read as a stand-alone reference on VLIW — a careful treatment of the ISA, compiling and program analysis tools needed to develop a new generation of embedded systems — or as a series of design case studies drawn from the authors' extensive experience. The authors' style is careful yet informal, and the book abounds with "flames," debunked "fallacies" and other material that engages the reader in the lively interplay between academic research and commercial development that has made this aspect of computer architecture so exciting. Embedded Computing: A VLIW Approach to Architecture, Compilers, and Tools will certainly be the definitive treatment of this important chapter in computer architecture.

Richard DeMillo Georgia Institute of Technology

This book does a superb job of laying down the foundations of VLIW computing and conveying how the VLIW principles have evolved to meet the needs of embedded computing. Due to the additional attention paid to characterizing a wide range of embedded applications and development of an accompanying toolchain, this book sets a new standard both as a reference and a text for embedded computing.

Rajiv Gupta The University of Arizona

A wealth of wisdom on a high-performance and power-efficient approach to embedded computing. I highly recommend it for both engineers and students.

Norm Jouppi HP Labs

Praise for *Embedded Computing*   continued

Josh, Paolo, and Cliff have devoted most of their professional lives to developing and advancing the fundamental research and use of VLIW architectures and instruction level parallelism. They are also system-builders in the best and broadest sense of the term. This book offers deep insights into the field, and highlights the power of these technologies for use in the rapidly expanding field of high performance embedded computing. I believe this book will become required reading for anyone working in these technologies.

Dick Lampman HP Labs

Embedded Computing *is a fabulous read, engagingly styled, with generous research and practical perspective, and authoritative, since Fisher has been responsible for this paradigm of simultaneously engineering the compiler and processor. Practicing engineers — both architects and embedded system designers — will find the techniques they will need to achieve the substantial benefits of VLIW-based systems. Instructors will value the rare juxtaposition of advanced technology with practical deployment examples, and students will enjoy the unusually interesting and mind-expanding chapter exercises.*

Richard A. Lethin Reservoir Labs and Yale University

One of the strengths of this book is that it combines the perspectives of academic research, industrial development, as well as tool building. While its coverage of embedded architectures and compilers is very broad, it is also deep where necessary. Embedded Computing *is a must-have for any student or practitioner of embedded computing.*

Walid Najjar University of California, Riverside

Embedded Computing

A VLIW Approach to Architecture, Compilers and Tools

Embedded Computing

A VLIW Approach to Architecture, Compilers and Tools

Joseph A. Fisher

Paolo Faraboschi

Cliff Young

AMSTERDAM • BOSTON • HEIDELBERG • LONDON
NEW YORK • OXFORD • PARIS • SAN DIEGO
SAN FRANCISCO • SINGAPORE • SYDNEY • TOKYO
Morgan Kaufmann is an imprint of Elsevier

Publisher	Denise E. M. Penrose
Publishing Services Manager	Simon Crump
Senior Production Editor	Angela Dooley
Editorial Assistant	Valerie Witte
Cover Design	Hannus Design
Cover Image	Santiago Calatrava's Alamillo Bridge
Text Design	Frances Baca Design
Composition	CEPHA
Technical Illustration	Dartmouth Publishing
Copyeditor	Daril Bentley
Proofreader	Phyllis Coyne & Associates
Indexer	Northwind Editorial
Interior printer	The Maple-Vail Manufacturing Group
Cover printer	Phoenix Color, Inc.

Morgan Kaufmann Publishers is an imprint of Elsevier. 500 Sansome Street, Suite 400, San Francisco, CA 94111

This book is printed on acid-free paper.

Cover image: Santiago Calatrava's Alamillo Bridge blends art and engineering to make architecture. While his design remains a modern, cable-stayed bridge, it simultaneously reinvents the category, breaking traditional assumptions and rearranging structural elements into a new form that is efficient, powerful, and beautiful. The authors chose this cover image for a number of reasons. Compiler engineering, which is at the heart of modern VLIW design, is similar to bridge engineering: both must be built to last for decades, to withstand changes in usage and replacement of components, and to weather much abuse. The VLIW design philosophy was one of the first computer architectural styles to bridge the software and hardware communities, treating them as equals and partners. And this book is meant as a bridge between the VLIW and embedded communities, which had historically been separate, but which today have complementary strengths and requirements.

ADVICE, PRAISE, AND ERRORS: Any correspondence related to this publication or intended for the authors should be addressed to FFY@VLIW.org. Information regarding error sightings is also encouraged and can be sent to mkp@mkp.com.

Library of Congress Cataloging-in-Publication Data
ISBN: 1-55860-766-8

For information on all Morgan Kaufmann publications,
visit our Web site at www.mkp.com or www.books.elsevier.com.

Printed and bound by CPI Group (UK) Ltd, Croydon, CR0 4YY

Transferred to digital print 2012

About the Authors

JOSEPH A. FISHER is a Hewlett-Packard Senior Fellow at HP Labs, where he has worked since 1990 in instruction-level parallelism and in custom embedded VLIW processors and their compilers. Josh studied at the Courant Institute of NYU (B.A., M.A., and then Ph.D. in 1979), where he devised the trace scheduling compiler algorithm and coined the term *instruction-level parallelism*. As a professor at Yale University, he created and named VLIW architectures and invented many of the fundamental technologies of ILP. In 1984, he started Multiflow Computer with two members of his Yale team. Josh won an NSF Presidential Young Investigator Award in 1984, was the 1987 Connecticut Eli Whitney Entrepreneur of the Year, and in 2003 received the ACM/IEEE Eckert-Mauchly Award.

PAOLO FARABOSCHI is a Principal Research Scientist at HP Labs. Before joining Hewlett-Packard in 1994, Paolo received an M.S. (Laurea) and Ph.D. (Dottorato di Ricerca) in electrical engineering and computer science from the University of Genoa (Italy) in 1989 and 1993, respectively. His research interests skirt the boundary of hardware and software, including VLIW architectures, compilers, and embedded systems. More recently, he has been looking at the computing aspects of demanding content-processing applications. Paolo is an active member of the computer architecture community, has served in many program committees, and was Program Co-chair for MICRO (2001) and CASES (2003).

CLIFF YOUNG works for D. E. Shaw Research and Development, LLC, a member of the D. E. Shaw group of companies, on projects involving special-purpose, high-performance computers for computational biochemistry. Before his current position, he was a Member of Technical Staff at Bell Laboratories in Murray Hill, New Jersey. He received A.B., S.M., and Ph.D. degrees in computer science from Harvard University in 1989, 1995, and 1998, respectively.

Foreword

Bob Colwell, R & E Colwell & Assoc. Inc.

T here are two ways to learn more about your country: you can study it directly
by traveling around in it or you can study it indirectly by leaving it. The first
method yields facts and insights directly in context, and the second by contrast.
Our tradition in computer engineering has been to seldom leave our neighborhood.
If you want to learn about operating systems, you read an OS book. For multiprocessor
systems, you get a book that maps out the MP space.

The book you are holding in your hands can serve admirably in that direct sense. If
the technology you are working on is associated with VLIWs or "embedded computing,"
clearly it is imperative that you read this book.

But what pleasantly surprised me was how useful this book is, even if one's work
is not VLIW-related or has no obvious relationship to embedded computing. I had long
felt it was time for Josh Fisher to write his magnum opus on VLIWs, so when I first heard
that he and his coauthors were working on a book with VLIW in the title I naturally and
enthusiastically assumed this was it. Then I heard the words "embedded computing"
were also in the title and felt considerable uncertainty, having spent most of my professional career in the general-purpose computing arena. I thought embedded computing
was interesting, but mostly in the same sense that studying cosmology was interesting:
intellectually challenging, but what does it have to do with me?

I should have known better. I don't think Josh Fisher can write boring text. He
doesn't know how. (I still consider his "Very Long Instruction Word Architectures and
the ELI-512" paper from ISCA-10 to be the finest conference publication I have ever read.)
And he seems to have either found like-minded coauthors in Faraboschi and Young or
has taught them well, because *Embedded Computing: A VLIW Approach to Architecture,
Tools and Compilers* is enthralling in its clarity and exhilarating in its scope. If you are
involved in computer system design or programming, you must still read this book,
because it will take you to places where the views are spectacular, including those
looking over to where you usually live. You don't necessarily have to agree with every
point the authors make, but you *will* understand what they are trying to say, and they
will make you think.

One of the best legacies of the classic Hennessy and Patterson computer architecture
textbooks is that the success of their format and style has encouraged more books like
theirs. In *Embedded Computing: A VLIW Approach to Architecture, Tools and Compilers*, you will find the pitfalls, controversies, and occasional opinion sidebars that made

H&P such a joy to read. This kind of technical exposition is like vulcanology done while standing on an active volcano. Look over there, and see molten lava running under a new fissure in the rocks. Feel the heat; it commands your full attention. It's immersive, it's interesting, and it's immediate. If your Vibram soles start melting, it's still worth it. You probably needed new shoes anyway.

I first met Josh when I was a grad student at Carnegie-Mellon in 1982. He spent an hour earnestly describing to me how a sufficiently talented compiler could in principle find enough parallelism, via a technique he called trace scheduling, to keep a really wild-looking hardware engine busy. The compiler would speculatively move code all over the place, and then invent more code to fix up what it got wrong. I thought to myself "So *this* is what a lunatic looks like up close. I hope he's not dangerous." Two years later I joined him at Multiflow and learned more in the next five years than I ever have, before or since.

It was an honor to review an early draft of this book, and I was thrilled to be asked to contribute this foreword. As the book makes clear, general-purpose computing has traditionally gotten the glory, while embedded computing quietly keeps our infrastructure running. This is probably just a sign of the immaturity of the general-purpose computing environment (even though we "nonembedded" types don't like to admit that). With general-purpose computers, people "use the computer" to do something. But with embedded computers, people accomplish some task, blithely and happily unaware that there's a computer involved. Indeed, if they had to be conscious of the computer, their embedded computers would have already failed: antilock brakes and engine controllers, for instance. General-purpose CPUs have a few microarchitecture performance tricks to show their embedded brethren, but the embedded space has much more to teach the general computing folks about the bigger picture: total cost of ownership, who lives in the adjacent neighborhoods, and what they need for all to live harmoniously. This book is a wonderful contribution toward that evolution.

Contents

CHAPTER 5

Microarchitecture Design

CHAPTER 6

System Design and Simulation 231

Preface

Welcome to our book. We hope you enjoy reading it as much as we have enjoyed writing it. The title of this book contains two major keywords: *embedded* and *VLIW* (very long instruction word). Historically, the embedded computing community has rarely been related to the VLIW community. Technology is removing this separation, however. High-performance techniques such as VLIW that seemed too expensive for embedded designs have recently become both feasible and popular. This change is bringing in a new age of embedded computing design, in which a high-performance processor is central. More and more, the traditional elements of nonprogrammable components, peripherals, interconnects, and buses must be seen in a computing-centric light. Embedded computing designers must design systems that unify these elements with high-performance processor architectures, microarchitectures, and compilers, as well as with the compilation tools, debuggers, and simulators needed for application development.

Since this is a book about embedded computing, we define and explore that world in general, but with the strongest emphasis on the processing aspects. Then, within this new world of embedded, we show how the VLIW design philosophy matches the goals and constraints well. We hope we have done this in a way that clearly and systematically explains the unique problems in the embedded domain, while remaining approachable to those with a general background in architecture and compilation. Conversely, we also need to explain the VLIW approach and its implications and to point out the ways in which VLIW, as contrasted with other high-performance architectural techniques, is uniquely suited to the embedded world.

We think this book fills a hole in the current literature. A number of current and upcoming books cover embedded computing, but few of them take the combined hardware–software systems approach we do. While the embedded computing and digital signal processing (DSP) worlds seem exotic to those with general-purpose backgrounds, they remain *computing*. Much is common between general-purpose and embedded techniques, and after showing what is common between them, we can focus on the differences. In addition, there is no standard reference on the VLIW approach. Such a book has been needed for at least a decade, and we believe that a book explaining the VLIW design philosophy has value today. This book should be useful to engineers and designers in industry, as well as suitable as a textbook for courses that aim at seniors or first-year graduate students.

While considering the mission of our book, we came up with three different possible books on the spectrum from VLIW to embedded. The first is the previously mentioned book, purely about VLIW. The second is a book about high-performance approaches to the embedded domain, with equal emphasis on VLIW, Superscalar, digital signal processor (DSP), micro-SIMD (Single Instruction Multiple Data), and vector techniques. Our book (the third option) strikes a balance: it focuses on the VLIW approach to the embedded domain. This means we give lighter treatment to the alternative approaches but spend additional effort on drawing the connections between VLIW and embedded. However, large parts of the information in our book overlap material that would go into the other two, and we think of this book as valuable for those with a strong interest in embedded computing but only a little interest in VLIW, and vice versa.

Along the way, we have tried to present our particularly idiosyncratic views of embedded, VLIW, and other high-performance architectural techniques. Most of the time, we hope we have impartially presented facts. However, these topics would be terribly dry and boring if we removed all controversy. VLIW has become a significant force in embedded processing and, as we make clear, there are technical and marketing reasons for this trend to continue. We will wear our biases on our sleeves (if you can't tell from the title, we think VLIW is the correct hammer for the embedded nail), but we hope to be honest about these biases in areas that remain unresolved.

Content and Structure

When we first wrote the outline for this book, the chapters fell into three major categories: *hardware*, *software*, and *applications*. Thus, the outline of the book correspondingly had three major parts. As we have written and rewritten, the organization has changed, pieces have migrated from one chapter to another, and the clean three-part organization has broken down into a set of chapters that only roughly matches the original tripartite structure. The unfortunate truth of modern computer architecture is that one cannot consider any of hardware, software, or applications by themselves.

This book really has two introductory chapters. Chapter 1 describes the world of embedded processing. It defines embedded processing, provides examples of the various types of embedded processors, describes application domains in which embedded cores are deployed, draws distinctions between the embedded and general-purpose domains, and talks about the marketplace for embedded devices. The second introductory chapter, Chapter 2, defines *instruction-level parallelism* (ILP), the primary technique for extracting performance in many modern architectural styles, and describes how compilation is crucial to any ILP-oriented processor design. Chapter 2 also describes the notion of an architectural style or design philosophy, of which VLIW is one example. Last, Chapter 2 describes how technology has evolved so that VLIW and embedded, once vastly separate domains, are now quite suited to each other.

Chapters 3 through 5 constitute the purely "hardware"-related part of the book. Chapter 3 describes what we mean when we say architecture or instruction-set architecture (ISA), defines what a VLIW ISA looks like, and describes in particular how VLIW architectures have been built for embedded applications. Chapter 3 also describes instruction set *encoding* at two levels. From a high-level perspective, Chapter 3 revisits the notion of design philosophy and architectural style with respect to how that style affects the way operations and instructions are encoded under each design philosophy.

At a detailed level, Chapter 3 describes the particular issues associated with VLIW operation and instruction encoding.

Chapter 4 might be seen as a continuation of the previous chapter, but instead of describing ISA design as a whole (with a view across various ISA styles), Chapter 4 examines the hardware structures (such as the datapath, memory, register files, and control units) necessary to all modern processors. Chapter 4 pays particular attention to how these structures differ in the embedded domain from their general-purpose counterparts.

The next chapter explores microarchitecture, the implementation of techniques within a given ISA. Chapter 5 can be seen as largely paralleling Chapter 4 in subject matter, but it considers how to *implement* each piece of functionality rather than how to *specify* that work be done within an ISA. Chapter 5 is informed by the technological constraints of modern design; that is, wires are expensive, whereas transitors are cheap. The chapter also (very briefly) considers power-related technological concerns.

Chapter 6 fits poorly into either the hardware and software categories, as both topics occur in each of its sections. Chapter 6 begins with a description of how a system-on-a-chip (SoC) is designed. Most modern embedded systems today are designed using the SoC methodology. Chapter 6 continues with how processor cores integrate with SoCs. Then it describes simulation methodologies for processor cores, followed by simulation techniques for entire systems. Last, Chapter 6 describes validation and verification of simulators and their systems. It might be best to view Chapter 6 as a bridge between the hardware and software areas, or perhaps its integration of the two serves as a good illustration of the complexities involved in building hardware/software *systems*.

The next three chapters emphasize the software area, although reading them will make it clear that they are infused with hardware-related topics in a number of ways. Chapter 7 describes the entire *toolchain*: the suite of software programs used to analyze, design, and build the software of an embedded system. Chapter 7 also describes a number of embedded- and DSP-specific code transformations.

Chapter 8 describes a subset of the compiler optimizations and transformations in an industrial-strength ILP-oriented compiler. This book is not a compiler textbook. Our goal in this chapter is to paint a balanced picture of the suite of optimizations — including their uses, complexities, and interactions — so that system designers will understand the nature of compilation-related issues, and so that compiler designers will know where else to look.

Chapter 9 covers a broad range of topics that often fall between the cracks of traditional topics, but are nonetheless important to building a working system. Chapter 9 details issues about exceptions, application binary interfaces (ABIs), code compression, operating systems (including embedded and real-time variants), and multiprocessing. Many of these topics have a strong software component to them, but each also interacts strongly with hardware structures that support the software functionality.

The last two chapters focus on applications. Chapter 10 begins by discussing programming languages for embedded applications, and then moves on to performance, benchmarks, and tuning. Then it continues to scalability and customizability in embedded architectures, and finishes with detail about customizable processors.

Chapter 11 visits a number of embedded applications at a variety of levels of detail. We spend the most time on digital printing and imaging, and telecommunications, and less time on other areas, such as automotive, network processing, and disk drives.

While writing this book, it became clear that there are a large number of terms with overlapping and conflicting meanings in this field. For example, *instruction* can mean operation, bundle, parallel issue group, or parallel execution group to different subcommunities. Wherever possible, we use the terms as they are used in the architecture field's dominant textbook, John Hennessy and Dave Patterson's *Computer Architecture: A Quantitative Approach*. The Glossary lists alternate definitions and synonyms, and indicates which terms we intend to use consistently.

The VEX (VLIW Example) Computing System

Lest we be accused of writing an armchair textbook (like those scientists of the nineteenth century who deduced everything from first principles), our book ships with an embedded-oriented VLIW development system. We call this system VEX, for "VLIW Example." We hope it is even more useful to our readers than its textbook ancestors, MIX and DLX, were for their readers. VEX is based on production tools used at HP Labs and other laboratories. It is a piece of real-world VLIW processor technology, albeit simplified for instructional use.

VEX is intended for experimental use. It includes a number of simulators, and its tools allow hardware reconfiguration and both manual and automated design-space exploration. Code, documentation, and samples can be downloaded from the book's Web site at *http://www.vliw.org/book*. VEX examples and exercises occur throughout the book. The Appendix describes the VEX instruction set architecture and tool chain.

Audience

We assume a basic knowledge of computer architecture concepts, as might be given by some industrial experience or a first undergraduate course in architecture. This implies that you know the basic techniques of pipelining and caching, and that the idea of an instruction set is familiar. It helps but is not a requirement that you have some background in compilation, or at least that you believe an optimizing compiler might be useful in producing fast code for modern machines. For reasons of space, we touch on those fundamentals related to this text and for more basic information refer you to more basic architecture and compilation textbooks. Patterson and Hennessy's undergraduate architecture textbook, *Computer Organization and Design*, and Appel's polymorphic set of undergraduate compiler books, *Modern Compiler Implementation in C, Java*, and *ML* are fine places to start.

There are four likely types of readers of our book. For those trying to bridge the embedded and high-performance communities, we believe this book will help. Designers of general-purpose systems interested in embedded issues should find this book a useful introduction to a new area. Conversely, those who work with existing embedded and/or DSP designs but would like to understand more about high-performance computing in general, and VLIW in particular (as these technologies become a central force in the embedded domain) are also part of our audience. Third, the book should serve well as a general reference on all aspects of the VLIW design style, embedded or general-purpose. Last, this book should be usable in a senior undergraduate or graduate-level computer architecture course. It could be the main textbook in an embedded-specific course, and it could be used to supplement a mainstream computer architecture text.

Cross-cutting Topics

From the chapter organization of our book, you can see that we have organized it horizontally, in effect by different traditional layers between fields: hardware versus software, with various chapters dealing with issues within the hardware area (such as ISA, microarchitecture, and SoC). However, some ("vertical") topics cut across multiple layers, making them difficult to explain in a single place, and unfortunately necessitating forward references. These topics include clustering, encoding and fetching, memory access, branch architecture, predication, and multiprocessing and multithreading. This section points out where the cross-cutting topic threads can be found, so that readers can follow a single thread through multiple layers.

Clusters, or groupings of register files and functional units with complete connectivity and bypassing, are described from an instruction-set encoding perspective in Section 3.5, "VLIW Encoding," as a structure in hardware design in Section 4.2, "Registers and Clusters," with respect to branches in Section 4.4, "Branch Architecture," from an implementation perspective in Section 5.1, "Register File Design," as a compiler target in Section 8.2, "Scheduling," and with respect to scalability in Section 10.3, "Scalability and Customizability."

Encoding and its dual problem of decoding occur as general topics in Chapters 3 and 5. However, the specific physical issue of dispatching operations to clusters and functional units is treated more specifically in Sections 3.5, "VLIW Encoding" and Section 5.3 "VLIW Fetch, Sequencing and Decoding." There are also correspondingly detailed discussions of encoding and ISA extensions in Sections 3.6, "Encoding and Instruction Set Extensions" and Section 5.3 "VLIW Fetch, Sequencing and Decoding."

The architectural view of predication is introduced in Section 4.5.2, "Predication." Microarchitectural support for predication, and in particular its effect on the bypass network, is described in Section 5.4.4, "Predication and Selects." Compiler support for predication is discussed throughout Chapter 8, and in particular appears in Section 8.2.1, "Acyclic Region Types and Shapes," in Section 8.2.5, "Loop Scheduling," and in Section 8.4.2, "Predicated Execution."

Multiprocessing, or using multiple processor cores (either physical or virtual) in a single system, is discussed as a pure memory-wiring problem in Section 5.5.4, "Memories in Mutliprocessor Systems," with respect to SoC design in Section 6.2.2, "Multiprocessing on a chip," and with respect to the run-time system in Sections 9.4.3, "Multiple Flows of Control" and Section 9.5, "Multiprocessing and Multithreading."

How to Read This Book

The most obvious reading advice is to read the book from cover to cover, and then read it again. This is not particularly useful advice, and thus the following outlines how we think various types of readers might approach the book.

To use this book as the main text in a senior or graduate course, we recommend using each chapter in order. The other possibility would be to jump immediately to the software section after a prerequisite in hardware from another course. If the book is supplementary material to another architecture or compilation textbook, various chapters (e.g., those on microarchitecture, simulation, and application analysis) will be especially appropriate as selective reading.

If you already know a lot about VLIWs, much of the introductory chapter on VLIWs (Chapter 2) and most of the compiler details in Chapters 7 and 8 will be familiar. We recommend focusing on Chapters 3 through 5 (on ISA, structure, and microarchitecture, respectively), and also scanning for topics that are unique to embedded systems. The information about other parts of the development toolchain in Chapter 7 will still be relevant, and the application-related chapters (10 and 11) will be relevant in any case.

If you already work in an embedded or DSP-related field, the embedded-specific parts of the hardware-oriented chapters (3 through 5) will be familiar to you, and some or all of the application examples in Chapter 11 will be familiar. Depending on your specialization, the SoC part of Chapter 6 may be familiar, but the simulation and verification parts of that chapter will be especially valuable. Pay close attention to the importance of ILP compilation and the pitfalls associated with compilers, covered in Chapters 7 and 8.

If you have a general-purpose architecture background, many parts of Chapters 3 through 5 will be familiar, as will the sections on the software development toolchain in Chapter 7. Try reading them, and skim where it seems appropriate. Parts of Chapter 8 (on compilation) may be skimmed, depending on your particular expertise. The final chapter, dealing with application examples, pulls together many of the principles of the book, so they're worth spending the time to read.

We greatly admire the textbooks of Dave Patterson and John Hennessey, and we adopted some of their organizational ideas. Like them, we include sidebars on "fallacies" and "pitfalls." We also added sidebars we call "controversies." These comment on issues too unsettled to fall into one of the former categories. Our equivalents of their "Putting It All Together" sections have been grouped in Chapter 11. These application examples play the same role in our book that example instruction set architectures such as MIPS, the Intel x86, the DEC VAX, and the IBM 360/370 play in Hennessy and Patterson [2004].

Because our book emphasizes embedded processing, there are sections and sidebars that focus on "embedded-specific topics." As in general-purpose work, performance remains a central theme, but the embedded world adds additional optimization goals for power/heat, space/size, and cost. Each of these topics receives special emphasis in dedicated sections.

The book does not cover the entire space of embedded systems and tries to remain within a rather fuzzy set of boundaries. On the hardware and modeling side, we never descend below the architecture and microarchitecture level, and only provide pointers to relevant literature on ASIC design, CAD tools, logic design techniques, synthesis, verification, and modeling languages. Although reconfigurable computing is of increasing importance in the embedded domain, of necessity we give it less time than it deserves. In the chapters dedicated to compiler technology, we focus largely on VLIW-specific and embedded-specific techniques for regular architectures. For example, we do not cover front-end-related issues (lexical analysis, parsing, and languages) nor "traditional" scalar optimizations, both of which can be found in the abundant compiler literature. When talking about system software and simulation, our boundary is the operating system, whose role we discuss but whose technology we only skim (this also applies to programming languages). We spend very little of the book discussing real time. Finally, in the application sections, we cover only the most relevant aspects of some of the underlying algorithms, but always with an eye to their computing requirements and the interaction with the rest of the system.

Each chapter is accompanied by a set of exercises. Following widespread practice, especially difficult exercises are marked with chili pepper symbols. A single 🌶 means that an exercise requires some materials not included in this book. Two 🌶🌶 indicate that the exercise is something of a project in scope. Three 🌶🌶🌶 mark those places where we weaseled out of writing the section ourselves, and left the actual work to the reader.[1] Throughout the book we use several well-known acronyms, whose definitions and explanations we collect in the glossary.

---

1. If you do a good job, please send us your text for our next edition.

Figure Acknowledgments

Figures 1.3, 6.9 adapted from Texas Instruments Incorporated.

Figures 2.4, 11.1 courtesy, Hewlett-Packard Company.

Figure 5.11 adapted from Montanaro et al. *IEEE Journal of Solid-State Circuits*, volume 31, number 11, November 1996, pages 1703–1711.

Figure 5.12 adapted from Sukjae Cho, University of Southern California, Information Sciences Institute, *http://pads.east.isi.edu/presentations/misc/sjcho-pm-report.pdf.*

Figure 6.2 adapted from Cirrus Logic, Inc.

Figure 6.4 adapted from Cadence Design Systems, Inc.

Figure 6.5 adapted from IBM Corporation and ARM Ltd.

Figure 6.8 courtesy of Altera Corporation. Altera is a trademark and service mark of Altera Corporation in the United States and other countries. Altera products are the intellectual property of Altera Corporation and are protected by copyright laws and one or more U.S. and foreign patents and patent applications.

Figures 11.3, 11.4 adapted from Kipphan, Helmut. *Handbook of Print Media: Technologies and Manufacturing Processes.* Springer-Verlag, 2001.

Figure 11.18, courtesy of Siemens VDO Automotive.

Figure 11.19 adapted from Balluchi, Andrea; Luca Benvenuti, Di Benedetto, Maria Domenica; Pinello, Claudio; Sangiovanni-Vincentelli, Alberto Luigi. *Automotive Engine Control and Hybrid Systems: Challenges and Opportunities. Proceedings of the IEEE,* 88(7):888–912, July 2000.

Figures 11.21, 11.22 adapted from Intel Corporation.

Acknowledgments

Our first praise and thanks must go to our editor, Denise Penrose, of Morgan Kaufmann Publishers (a division of Elsevier). She has happily, patiently, and diligently assisted us through the various stages of writing, and she has tolerated missed deadlines, slipped schedules, and annoyingly inconvenient phone calls beyond all reason. We also thank the rest of the enormously talented team at Morgan Kaufmann (Elsevier) — both the folks behind the scenes, and Angela Dooley, Emilia Thiuri and Valerie Witte, who we had the pleasure of dealing with directly.

Next, we thank our reviewers: Erik Altman, IBM; Eduard Ayguade, Universitat Politècnica de Catalunya; Alan Berenbaum, Agere Systems; Peter Bosch, Bell Labs; Dan Connors, University of Colorado; Bob Colwell, R&E Colwell & Assoc. Inc.; Gene Frantz, Texas Instruments; Rajiv Gupta, University of Arizona; John Hennessy, Stanford University; Mark Hill, University of Wisconsin-Madison; Tor Jeremiassen, Texas Instruments; Norm Jouppi, HP Labs; Brian Kernighan, Princeton University; Jack Kouloheris, IBM Research; Richard Lethin, Reservoir Labs, Inc.; Walid Najjar, University of California, Riverside; Tarun Nakra, IBM; Michael D. Smith, Harvard University; Mateo Valero, Universitat Politècnica de Catalunya.

They constructively criticized our work, sometimes contributing technical material themselves, and they vastly improved both the details and the overall shape of this book. The turning point in our work came when we first saw the reviews and realized that despite assigning us much more work to do, our reviewers believed we were building something good. We thank them also for their patience with the early and incomplete versions we shipped them. Bob Colwell deserves special mention. His combination of precision, technical mastery, and willingness to flame made his reviews both a delight to read and a major source of improvements to our book.

Two other people helped to better tie our book together. Kim Hazelwood performed redundancy elimination and cross-linking on our text. Mark Toburen compiled, sorted, and double checked our bibliography and bibliographic references.

Many other individuals helped with specific technical points. Peter Bosch and Sape Mullender helped with the history of real-time schedulers. Andrea Cuomo and Bob Krysiak educated us about the embedded marketplace. Giuseppe Desoli's work at HP Labs inspired us in many ways when discussing applications analysis, optimization, and fine-tuning techniques. Gene Frantz helped us with the standards battles in DSPs using saturating arithmetic. Stefan Freudenberger designed and wrote the run-time architecture of the Lx/ST200, the starting point for the VEX run-time architecture.

Fred (Mark Owen) Homewood helped us with his insightful views on microarchitecture and VLSI design. Dong Lin checked our work describing networks and network processors. Josep Llosa gave instrumental advice about the discussion of modulo scheduling. C. K. Luk gave us advice on the state of the art in compiler-directed prefetching. Scott Peterson was an invaluable source of information for anything related to the legal aspects of intellectual property and the complex legal ramifications of open-source licenses. Dennis Ritchie improved our discussion of C99. Miami Beach architect Randall Robinson helped us with the role of design philosophies as seen by true architects (i.e., those who build buildings and landscapes, not those who build chips). Chris Tucci informed us about the economics of monopolies, and their effect on innovation. Bob Ulichney reviewed our various descriptions of image-processing pipelines. Gary Vondran and Emre Ozer helped us with their evaluations of code compression and code layout techniques.

A special mention goes to Geoffrey Brown, who was one of the originators of the idea of this book, and who made significant contributions to the initial definition of the book's topics. As we were starting to write the book, Geoff decided to follow other career paths, but many of his initial ideas are still reflected in the book's organization and content.

At the beginning of this project, a number of computer science authors gave us extremely useful advice about how to write a book. Al Aho, Jon Bentley, Brian Kernighan, Rob Pike, and Dennis Ritchie gave freely of their time and wisdom. Their suggestions (especially about carefully choosing coauthors) were invaluable to us. Arthur Russell and his associates reviewed our contract, and Martin Davis helped us with his experiences with publishers.

A number of individuals and organizations loaned us infrastructure while we were writing this book. Glenn Holloway, Chris Kells, John Osborn, Chris Small, and Michael D. Smith variously loaned us machines and conference rooms in which to work. We also drew on the resources of Bell Labs in Murray Hill, HP Barcelona, HP Labs Cambridge, HP Cambridge Research Laboratory, and HP Glastonbury.

Our enlightened and flexible managers at Bell Labs, DE Shaw, and HP deserve particular thanks. Al Aho, Wim Sweldens, Rob Pike, and Eric Grosse continued the Bell Labs tradition of allowing authors to write as part of their day jobs. Dick Lampman, Patrick Scaglia, and Rich Zippel supported Josh and Paolo's work on the book, in the tradition of fostering technical excellence at HP Labs. Ron Dror and David Shaw gave Cliff the flexibility to complete this work.

Last and most important, we thank our wives, Elizabeth, Tatiana, and Joyce, for their support, encouragement, tolerance, and patience. Elizabeth has long been used to life like this, but Paolo and Cliff are particularly amazed that Tatiana and Joyce (respectively) married them *while we were working on the book*. We question their judgment, but we are grateful for their grace.

1

An Introduction to Embedded Processing

If you round off the fractions, embedded systems consume 100% of the worldwide production of microprocessors.

—Jim Turley, Editor, *Computer Industry Analyst*

Moore's law states that transistor density doubles roughly every 18 months. This means that every 15 years, densities increase a thousandfold. Not coincidentally, computing undergoes a "generation shift" roughly every 15 years. During such a shift, the winners of the previous battle risk being pushed aside by the products and companies of the next generation. As Figure 1.1 indicates, the previous generations include mainframes (one per enterprise), which were displaced by minicomputers (smaller, but one per department), which in turn were displaced by personal computers (smaller still, but one per person). We have reached the next generation shift, as we move to multiple, even smaller, computers per person. In 1943, the chairman of IBM predicted a world market for no more than five computers. Today, five computers seems too few for one individual.

The next computing generation has been termed various things, including embedded processing, the post-PC era, the information age, the wireless age, and the age of information appliances. Most likely, the true name will only become apparent over time; such things matter more to historians than to technicians. What is true, however, is that a new generation of smart, connected (wired or wireless), powerful, and cheap devices is upon us. We see them as extensions of traditional infrastructure (e.g., cellular phones and personal digital assistants) or toys of single-purpose utility (e.g., pagers, radios, handheld games). But they are still computers: all of the old techniques and tricks apply, with new subtleties or variations because they are applied in new areas.

System class:	Mainframes	Minicomputers	Desktop systems	Smart products
Era:	1950s on	1970s on	1980s on	2000s on
Form factor:	Multi-cabinet	Multiple boards	Single board	Single chip
Resource type:	Corporate	Departmental	Personal	Embedded
Users per CPU:	100s–1,000s	10s–100s	1 user	100s CPUs/user
Typ. system cost:	$1 million+	$100,000s+	$1,000–$10,000s	$10–$100
Worldwide units:	10,000s+	100,000s+	100,000,000s	100,000,000,000s
Major platforms:	IBM, CDC, Burroughs, Sperry, GE, Honeywell, Univac, NCR	DEC, IBM, Prime, Wang, HP, Pyramid, Data General, many others	Apple, IBM, Compaq, Sun, HP, SGI, Dell, (+ other Windows/UNIX)	?
Operating systems:	By manufacturer	By manufacturer, some UNIX	DOS, MacOS, Windows, various UNIX	?

FIGURE 1.1   **The "center of gravity" of computing.** In the last 50 years we have witnessed a constant downward shift of the "center of gravity" of computing, from hundreds of users per CPU to hundreds of CPUs per user. We are now entering a new era of pervasive *smart products*. Note that each paradigm shift in the past had its victims, and only a few of the major players managed to adapt to the transition to the next phase. To our knowledge, IBM is the only company that successfully adapted their business model from mainframes to desktop systems. Who will be the major players in the new era? This characterization is due to Bob Rau and Josh Fisher.

Whatever you term the next generation of computers, this book is about them. For our purposes, we will call them embedded computers, although the connotations of this term are more limiting than does the field justice. Just as PCs grew out of toy machines and chips that no "real" computer designer took seriously, embedded devices seem small compared to the latest power-ravening x86. We have no doubt that such toy devices will become the bulk of the market and the area where the most interesting work takes place in the decade to come.

The field of embedded systems is itself undergoing dramatic change, from a field dominated by electrical and mechanical considerations to one that far more closely resembles traditional computing. In traditional embedded systems, processors were commodity parts and the real art was the "black art" of assembling the system, where the system comprised nonprogrammable components, peripherals, interconnects and buses, and glue logic. Our view is much more processor-centric, which is why our title includes the term embedded *computing* rather than embedded systems. We believe the future will be much like the past: as (embedded) processors gain capabilities and power, many functions previously handled in special-purpose, implementation- and application-specific hardware held together with baling wire and spit will now be handled as software in the processor core. Figure 1.2, while facetious, makes this point: the seven-segment display is no longer an important thing to learn about; the processor behind it is.

To gain a good grounding in embedded computing, it is important to understand both what is underneath it (processor architecture, microarchitecture, compilers) and how that is used for application development (compilation tools, debuggers, simulators). We cover these topics in great detail.

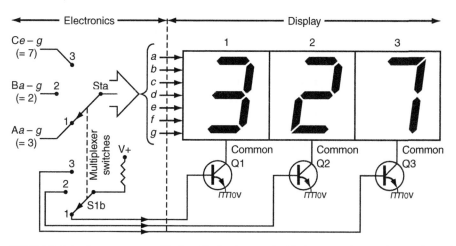

FIGURE 1.2 **Seven-segment display.** No book on embedded systems is complete without the picture of a seven-segment display. Here it is. Now, let's move on to embedded computing.

This book is also about a particular way of building processors, called VLIW (very long instruction word), which is well suited to the requirements and constraints of embedded computing. The term *VLIW* is a pithy summary of a superficial feature of the architectural style. The rest of this book goes into much more detail about the substantial features of VLIW, including its emphasis on instruction-level parallelism (ILP), its dependence on compilers, its high degree of scalability, and its high performance and performance/price characteristics. The remainder of this chapter defines and describes embedded computing; the next chapter introduces architectural design philosophies and VLIW.

1.1 What Is Embedded Computing?

The simplest definition is that embedded is all computing that is not general purpose (GP), where general-purpose processors are the ones in today's notebooks, PCs, and servers. This is not to say that general-purpose processors are not used in embedded applications (they sometimes are), but rather that any processor expected to perform a wide variety of very different tasks is probably not embedded. Embedded processors include a large number of interesting chips: those in cars, in cellular telephones, in pagers, in game consoles, in appliances, and in other consumer electronics. They also include peripherals of the general-purpose systems: hard disk controllers, modems, and video cards. In each of these examples, the designers chose a processor core for their task but did not pick the general-purpose processor core of the time.

Reasons for non-general-purpose processor choices vary and include not just the usual metric of performance but also cost, power, and size. Many embedded processors have less performance than general-purpose processors; a less ambitious device suffices. However, a significant number of embedded processors (e.g., digital signal processors

[DSPs] and network processors [NPs], as explained later) offer *more* performance on specific applications than a general-purpose processor can provide. Cost is obvious: even the cheapest Pentium processor costs more than many consumer electronics items. Power is increasingly important, especially in portable applications: the batteries and cooling required to make a general-purpose processor perform cellular phone functions would be prohibitive. And many embedded *devices* are smaller than general-purpose chips and modules. For example, in 2002, a typical cellular phone was smaller than a Pentium Xeon processor module. In processing, one size does not fit all.

If embedded computing involves *processing*, we must also contrast processing (either general-purpose or embedded) with nonprocessing alternatives. ASICs (application-specific integrated circuits) are today's custom logic, incorporating functions formerly performed by many low-scale integration components into a single chip. Designing an ASIC is complicated and expensive. It requires hiring hardware designers and admits very little flexibility if requirements or standards change. ASICs may be the only way to solve a particular problem, especially at the highest end of performance (e.g., gigahertz radio or fiber optic transceivers). However, if a software-programmable device has adequate computational power to accomplish the desired task, a programmable core with software may enable a much cheaper design. Further, many such processor cores can be shared across different projects, allowing economies of scale in production. And a software solution can allow changes, even in the field.

At the beginning of the 1990s, electronic systems were built by assembling components in board-level assemblies. A processor took up an entire chip; other chips or "random logic" provided memory, control, and I/O. Moore's law has transformed this style of construction: what used to take up a board now fits on a single chip. This has given rise to a new term, the System-on-a-Chip (SoC). A processor (or "core") is the computational part of an SoC, but because the processor no longer takes up the entire chip, other functions have migrated on-die.[1] This higher level of integration lowers overall costs, both in construction and in design. SoCs can contain multiple processors that cooperate. For example, today's cellular phones sometimes contain two processors: a DSP (see following) that compresses and decompresses speech and a general-purpose embedded processor that runs the phone's display. Many processors are available as "soft cores" described by relatively high-level hardware description languages so that they can be integrated with some effort into SoC projects.

1.1.1 Attributes of Embedded Devices

From the point of view of this book, an embedded system is something that was *not designed to be general purpose*. For example, we do not consider desktop personal computers or laptop computers in this category. Systems that contain a microprocessor largely invisible to the user and systems in which the user is never, or rarely, expected to load a program are examples of embedded systems. Note that we say "never, or rarely,

---

1. Even general-purpose cores have followed this trend. Often more than 50% of general-purpose processor dies are devoted today to cache memory.

expected to load a program." This is because patching the firmware to work around problems or upgrading firmware to add features are the types of common tasks we normally imagine, and these often happen invisibly (e.g., in satellite-television tuners). This is even truer in a world in which the networking infrastructure becomes pervasive and always available.

Other possible definitions of embedded devices are more sophisticated but do not necessarily cover all of the embedded space. Most embedded devices *embody the capability* they perform. For example, appliances typically serve a single purpose; that is, we do not expect a software upgrade to our washing machine to enable us to wash dishes. In a general-purpose system, we load new software to increase or change the capabilities. In fact, the integration of embedded computers into embedded devices is seamless. Few people are aware that embedded microprocessors are part of virtually every household appliance bought in the last ten years.

The converse of embodying the capability is *versatility*, or lack thereof. Embedded devices are usually tuned for one or a few applications, rather than attempting to be useful for all tasks, as does a general-purpose device. This particular distinction has become rather fuzzy. The evolution of cellular phones provides an obvious counterexample, as phones have gradually incorporated several other functionalities, such as games, calendaring, e-mail, and cameras. However, all of these enhancements are secondary. Few would purchase a cellular phone for its gaming capabilities (although networked games running on phones are a bigger incentive than standalone games).

Another aspect of versatility has to do with interfaces to peripherals and to device drivers, the software that manages those peripherals. Whereas general-purpose software systems must be able to handle a wide variety of devices (and in the case of Microsoft Windows, virtually the entire history of PC peripherals), a typical embedded system has very few devices to support.

Embedded systems are often *commodities* (or commodity parts of capital items) rather than capital items themselves. This implies a different marketing model and lower prices. Traditionally, sales channels for embedded devices are different from channels for computers, although this separation has progressively blended, as desktop computers have become more of a commodity item.

In terms of *intended use*, embedded systems are devices users purchase for a reason that is not thought of as "computing." This is probably what everyone agrees upon: when you purchase a car or a microwave oven, you buy it for its intended use, and the fact that it might include a better computing system may be a plus but it is probably not the highest priority among your purchasing criteria.

If we look at the spectrum of products offered in the market today, obvious examples of embedded systems include the electronics in items such as cars, cellular phones, printers, home audiovideo entertainment systems, and home appliances.

1.1.2 Embedded Is Growing

Pundits believe the next generation of tiny computers will provide unimaginable benefits, perhaps on the same scale the Second Industrial Revolution (driven by electricity, and allowing electric lighting and electric motors) did in the nineteenth century. In some cases, these benefits are difficult to imagine. In other cases, the benefits are immediate and concrete: without today's automotive microprocessors, features such as antilock braking, traction control, all-wheel drive, "smart" airbags, and situation-sensitive automatic transmissions would be impossible or much more expensive. One version of this future includes a world of smart devices, in which virtually any product contains its own processor. Computing will become a seamless and ubiquitous part of the world, like writing and electricity before it.

Along with the vision of cores everywhere comes a belief that most of these devices will be linked by some sort of data networking capability. This makes the vision more plausible. For example, a refrigerator that can reorder when one runs out of orange juice might be useful. One can imagine replacing almost any object X with the intelligent, networked X, and a variety of benefits might come from this. As we write this book, wireless communities are forming that permit one to walk for many blocks in major cities and always have a high bandwidth connection to the Internet, and chains of coffeeshops are providing their customers with similar wireless access. We expect that this phenomenon will become widespread.

Affordable, ubiquitous computing power enables interesting new applications. Today's digital cellular phones require large processing power, and the DSPs that power them are remarkably powerful, cool, compact, and energy efficient. In the future, richer and more dynamic media (including audio, still images, and video) will be made available in more places. We have already mentioned networking. In addition, customer requirements ensure that all of the technologies previously discussed are provided securely and privately. Tasks that once required a supercomputer can be performed everywhere. High performance is now cheap enough.

1.2 Distinguishing Between Embedded and General-Purpose Computing

To understand what falls into the category of embedded computing, it is instructive to note what is *not* a requirement for embedded devices. Lifetimes of embedded devices are very different from the three-year obsolescence cycle of general-purpose machines. Some devices are nearly disposable: the average Japanese cellular phone is replaced in less than one year. At the opposite extreme, infrastructural devices such as telephone switches depreciate on a 30-year schedule.[2] These lifetime differences have concrete effects on *upgradability* and *backward compatibility*. Few embedded devices have upgrade requirements. For example, avid automotive enthusiasts change the chips in their cars, but these are usually ROMs, not processors. Most consumer items (e.g., cellular phones and pagers) are replaced, not upgraded.

Backward compatibility is seldom an embedded requirement, as software does not migrate from one device to another. (An interesting exception is game consoles: to

2. Depending on your regulatory authority, the actual number varies from 28 to 42 years.

Pitfall: Thinking There Is a Sharp Line Between Embedded and General-Purpose Computing

For the most part, it is easy to distinguish between systems used for the sole purpose of computing (e.g., a mainframe or a desktop computer) and systems that use computing as a means to achieve another primary task (e.g., a microwave oven, a camera, a car, or an airplane). Historically, computing power was a distinguishing factor, in that embedded electronics were mainly deployed to control the appliance in which they were embedded. Such applications had small requirements for speed or generality.

More recently, several trends have produced devices that are not clearly in one camp or the other. First, microprocessors became commodities. It is often possible to find a microprocessor with a performance/cost that outperforms a solution based on ad hoc electronics. VLSI technology, largely driven by desktop computers, has lowered the cost of silicon so much that microprocessors have become cost effective for most consumer-priced products. One can now purchase 8-bit, 16-bit, and 32-bit embedded processors at prices that range from a few cents to a few dollars.

Second, massive computing capability became pervasive. Telephones, consumer electronics, cars, and entertainment systems are just a few examples of areas that today run compute-intensive tasks that not long ago would have challenged a supercomputer.

Third, mobile computing emerged as an important area. Road warriors continually demand personal devices with more performance, longer battery life, and less weight. Although it is fair to classify laptops as "computers," how do we classify a general-purpose palm-sized device?

These three trends are not likely to stop, and it is already easy to find devices that defy our definitions. Such products are typically in the middle of an evolutionary change.

For example, PDAs (personal digital assistants) evolved from being calculators with a phone book to full-blown computers powered by 32-bit high-clock-rate general-purpose microprocessors. Similarly, set-top-box devices transformed from simple descramblers of analog signals to Internet-enabled web browsers, following a very similar trajectory in terms of computing capabilities. In both cases, these systems are very close to the frontier between general-purpose and embedded and are likely to escape any classification attempt.

Game consoles are another confusing domain. For many generations, game consoles were clearly dedicated to one specific task, gaming, but the more recent generation of products often skirts the boundary of general-purpose computing, as they incorporate features such as networking, web browsing, and keyboards, and as they incorporate download support to programs that add functionality not planned at product design time. As an extreme example, in 2003 the National Center for Supercomputing Applications assembled an effective supercomputer out of $50,000 worth of Sony Playstation 2 components!

One might imagine that in these boundary areas only a few product concepts will survive to become the "standard" in mobile computing or the "standard" in home entertainment. Such a "narrowing of diversity" has happened in many marketplaces (e.g., desktop personal computers, videotape formats, and rail gauges). Economists are unresolved as to whether such narrowings reduce competition and innovation or provide standardization that fuels wider benefits.

maintain compatibility, later console chips must be capable of being exactly as fast as the early versions despite changes in underlying process technology. In consoles, backward compatibility is often implemented by putting a *complete copy* of the previous-generation console in one small corner of the next-generation die.) Because many embedded designs need not be backward compatible with previous implementations, designers are free to switch designs with each product generation. Consequently, there is less emphasis on the distinction between architecture and implementation. If a new version of a chip is slightly incompatible but much better than its predecessors, designers may still be willing to use it.

Designers of embedded devices face more constraints than designers of general-purpose devices. Power, energy efficiency, cost, and physical dimensions usually have a much bigger role in embedded systems. This is not to say that embedded devices are more difficult to build than general-purpose devices; the latter tend to have high overall performance goals and huge compatibility requirements. But the overall priorities and the balance among them are different for embedded devices.

1.2.1   The "Run One Program Only" Phenomenon

As we previously discussed, embedded devices normally embody the functionality they implement. In other words, they are designed to run one program (or just a few) with a predictable usage pattern. This is in clear contrast to general-purpose systems for which programs and usage are rarely known at design time and for which these parameters can only be inferred based on statistical information about the installed base.

Nonetheless, the spectrum of variability in the general-purpose capabilities of an embedded device is quite broad, from truly single-function devices to completely versatile PDAs. In particular, the emerging ubiquitous networking infrastructure is making it much more likely that devices will have multiple functions and more general-purpose functionality. For example, the job of keeping up with networking is itself not a fixed task: protocols and standards evolve continuously and networking systems need programmability to avoid earlier-than-necessary obsolescence. Even in areas for which networking was previously considered impractical or too expensive, new technologies are starting to bridge the gap. For example, *Bluetooth* (a short-range wireless protocol) is successfully attacking the domain of *personal area networking*. New generations of cellular technology (GPRS, 2.5G, or 3G) are making transparent connectivity for noninteractive devices a reality, and between these two, medium-range standards such as *802.11* are becoming popular.

Once devices become transparently connected network nodes, the operation of downloading a new program to them becomes much easier. This functionality is already being used in various forms for diagnostics and accounting (vending machines), maintenance and upgrades (set-top boxes), or selective support of new algorithms (cellular base stations).

In spite of this, there are still many applications in which the "run one program only" phenomenon dominates. In these areas, radically new devices can sometimes turn around quickly from concept to product, because of shorter development time opportunities. A device that runs only one application requires less system development than a workstation with a new CPU or OS (operating system) because, for example, such single-program devices need not support legacy applications.

1.2.2 Backward and Binary Compatibility

The problem of having to seamlessly support legacy applications written for previous generations of the same device is known as *backward compatibility*. In the general-purpose domain, the only successful approach to this problem has been through **binary compatibility**, whereby successive generations of microprocessors and systems run previously compiled binary programs without modification. Testimony to this fact is the undisputed market supremacy of the standard PC platform (programs written for Windows OS running on x86-compatible CPUs). Even within a largely binary-compatible market, evolution still happens, although at a very slow pace. For example, successive generations of x86 CPUs gradually introduced small but significant binary-incompatible features, such as floating point instructions in the 486 family, or matrix math extensions (MMX) in Pentium processors. With time, application programmers and compilation tools gradually catch up, and in the time frame of a couple of generations the majority of the code base migrates to adopt the new features. Of course, *backward binary compatibility* is necessary to avoid a forced migration that would disrupt the market.

In the embedded domain, binary compatibility in the way we just described it is rarely as large an issue. Embedded applications are recompiled for each new product. The development of a new electronic platform always implies some changes with respect to the previous generation: in the processor, peripherals, memory system, and firmware (of course, where these do not change, it is desirable to be able to reuse code). New changes require a different code base, and recompilation is always taken for granted. Even most embedded operating systems are recompiled for each individual product platform (there are notable exceptions, though; PocketPC being one of them). This phenomenon is more evident in more rigid embedded systems. It would be less applicable to a PDA — PDAs being at the boundary of the general-purpose domain. However, as the complexity of embedded applications grows, other forms of compatibility constraints limit the rate of introduction of radically new platforms.

> **Feature compatibility** becomes important when developers write applications with assumptions about the availability of certain hardware resources in mind. For example, an application that assumes the existence of floating-point hardware support in the CPU is likely to be locked into using floating-point CPUs, in that the performance degradation of emulated floating point would be too big, and the effort to migrate to a fixed-point source base is usually rather large. Other examples are: code written for a big-endian or little-endian platform only, code written with extensive use of nonstandard instructions, and code using architectural extensions (such as MMX).
>
> **Source compatibility** becomes important when either the complexity of an application or the engineering cost to make it portable overshadows the benefits of adopting

new technologies. A good example of this is the DSP domain, where programmers hand code in assembly, resulting in applications that are very difficult to maintain. In this case, migrating to a new platform is a major task, often comparable to rewriting the entire application from scratch. Using high-level programming languages can sometimes help, but it still does not completely resolve the issue. In many cases, embedded implementations of high-level languages introduce nonstandard features that become a burden for future generations.

Tool compatibility issues arise when products strongly depend on the availability of a certain set of tools. The choice of a programming language is a very delicate decision that potentially impacts many generations of a product lifetime. The mainstream programming language for embedded systems today is C, and it is reasonable to expect any new platform to support it. When it comes to other languages (C++, Java, Eiffel, and so on), their support in the embedded world is spotty, and often only partial implementations are available. Deciding to use a nonmainstream language may impact the ability to change to other hardware platforms because of the absence of the necessary tools.

OS compatibility becomes an issue when the application relies on the existence of a certain OS. Embedded applications that only require limited operating system support (or none at all) are less sensitive to this. Many microkernels are easily portable, and for "simple" embedded OSs (such as Wind River's *VxWorks*) the porting effort to a new platform is straightforward, given a minimal set of tools (basically, just a C compiler). For other "complex" OSs the picture is quite different. Contrary to popular belief, embedded Linux is quite demanding for the underlying hardware and software platform: the availability of *gcc* (the GNU C compiler) for the new CPU is necessary, and virtual memory (VM) support is a strong preference. On the positive side, porting Linux — and *gcc* — to a new platform is a "simple matter of engineering," and acquiring licensing rights is not an issue, in the spirit of Open Source development. At the other extreme, Microsoft's PocketPC is a proprietary system. Only Microsoft ports PocketPC to new hardware platforms. Additionally, Microsoft requires that their own proprietary compilers support the platform CPU. This implies that specific business negotiations are necessary, in addition to the large up-front engineering effort, to convince Microsoft of the benefits of porting to a new platform.

To summarize, binary compatibility in its strict definition is less of a concern than in general-purpose systems. However, we should not underestimate the subtle compatibility issues of an industrial design environment and large code bases. The cost of switching to a new platform can be overwhelming, and it may depend on factors beyond developers' control, such as tools or third-party components.

1.2.3 Physical Limits in the Embedded Domain

Design constraints are another way of differentiating embedded processing from the desktop and workstation domains.

Cost is probably the single most important factor in the design of an embedded system. A hypothetical consumer product with a street price of $199 usually requires the manufacturer to limit the build cost to less than $100. This further lowers the cost of the entire electronic system to the $30–50 range, and does not leave much room for the processor itself. Luckily, advances in VLSI technology enable the integration of several system blocks and microprocessors in the same piece of silicon (*SoC*), yielding significant cost reduction opportunities.

Power consumption and energy efficiency are strictly related, but not always equivalent. The power characteristics of a system drive cost, capacity, and power supply size, as well as the thermal dissipation strategy. For example, top-of-the-line general-purpose microprocessors reach instantaneous power consumptions in the hundreds of watts. This adds pressure to the design and cost of the power supply, of the microprocessor package (as we write this, ceramic packages are being displaced by plastic packages, which have competitive thermal dissipation but are cheaper), and many other system components (micro-ventilators to improve the air flow, expensive heat sinks, and even more exotic technologies). On the other hand, the energy efficiency characteristics of a system impact how long it will operate via a fixed energy source (e.g., a battery).

It is becoming common to express merit figures of efficiency for embedded microprocessors in Watts/MIPS, where the idea is that efficient processors should also optimize the amount of energy necessary to run a given task in a certain amount of time.

Physical dimensions (volume, weight, and form factor) are growing in importance as embedded systems become mobile. A very visible example of this trend is the astonishing progress of cellular phone technology, where telephony, calendaring, e-mail, and wireless web interfaces are packed in a few ounces and run for days between recharges.

There are notable exceptions to each of these, however, and readers should keep in mind that not all embedded systems are necessarily low cost, small, and power efficient. Cars, airplanes, the networking infrastructure, and medical imaging devices are among the many examples of embedded systems that violate one or more of the guidelines we presented as characterizing the embedded domain.

However, cost and power are among the most important constraints an embedded system designer must face. Consequently, in the embedded computing world power consumption and cost are emphasized in addition to the more traditional general-purpose metric of speed-based performance.

1.3 Characterizing Embedded Computing

Our definition of embedded computing is based on *what it is not*, rather than *what it is*, making it difficult to describe concisely the space of embedded systems. In trying to do so, it is valuable to categorize embedded processors by their use, but even that is deceptive in its complexity. "Use" might refer to the application market the processor is being sold in; or it might mean the characteristics of the workload the processor will run; or it might even refer to the structure of the processor itself, in that its intended use is reflected in how the computer architects designed it, however it turns out the processor is eventually used. Even though these perspectives are not independent of one another, we find it valuable to look at embedded processing from the point of view of all of them, and in this section we do so.

1.3.1 Categorization by Type of Processing Engine

Any computing system requires a processing engine. These processors, or cores, span a range from tiny bit-sliced or serial devices to wide-word systems with clustered, parallel, pipelined functional units. Although most of us think of a "computer" as a system such as a PC, there are many types of embedded computing devices deployed today. Market analysts break processor cores into four broad categories based on industry sectors and usage patterns.

1. **Computational micros** are general-purpose processors, usually adopting a 32- or 64-bit datapath, and typically deployed as the central processing engine of a mainframe, workstation, PC, or high-end portable device (such as a PDA). Most off-the-shelf, high-end RISC and CISC engines (x86, PA-RISC, PowerPC, SPARC, Alpha, and so on) fall into this category.

2. **Embedded general-purpose micros** are components designed for a wide range of applications (especially consumer and communications), usually with a 32-bit datapath. These are often scaled-down versions of existing computational micros (or micros abandoned by the workstation market). Some of the primary architectures in this space include ARM, PowerPC, MIPS, 68K, x86, and SH, although in recent years ARM has seized the lion's share of the market. Most vendors have recently started offering versions of these micros as embedded cores, to be integrated into larger dedicated systems. We refer to systems that use such embedded cores as *core-based ASICs*.

3. **Digital signal processors** differ from general-purpose micros in their focus on the very efficient execution of arithmetic operations in tight loop-oriented kernels. Processors from Texas Instruments (TI), Motorola, Agere (formerly Lucent, which was formerly AT&T), and Analog Devices are the market leaders in the DSP domain. TI has been the dominant player in the DSP market for several years. DSPs are one of the fastest growing sectors in the computational semiconductor market.

4. **Microcontrollers** are the workhorse of industrial electronics. Typically designed for standalone operation, they include memory, I/O, buses, and peripherals in addition to a simple processing unit. Many microcontrollers are descendants of successful architectures from the 8-bit and 16-bit microprocessor generations.

From a programmer's point of view, the first two of these categories, computational micros and embedded general-purpose micros, will be familiar to anyone who works with computers, as would microcontrollers (albeit limited in bus width). However, the remaining category—DSPs—deserves further treatment. This section also discusses network processors (NPs), a recent class of computational device that includes aspects of both embedded general-purpose micros and microcontrollers in a single chip.

Digital Signal Processors

Despite the strong growth of the DSP market, it is our belief that DSPs, per se, will not long continue to be a force in the embedded market. Classic DSPs (see Figure 1.3) will migrate into something that is much closer to VLIWs (even though they might still sometimes have the tag *DSP*). That migration is already under way, and seems inevitable. Thus, this book does not cover DSPs in depth, as these have been known for decades. Instead, VLIW is one of its central themes. We believe that learning about VLIWs will teach you the most important things you need to know for the future of DSPs. Nonetheless, today's DSPs have their own characteristics, which are worth noting.

DSPs are processor cores designed specifically to perform well on the family of signal processing algorithms. Superficially, general-purpose processors and DSPs are similar. Both have the usual processor trappings: registers, functional units, buses to memory, and a control mechanism (microsequenced or hardwired) that determines how everything operates. DSPs differ because signal processing has peculiar numerical requirements. The distinguishing feature of most DSPs is the ability to rapidly (typically in one clock cycle) perform a fixed-point arithmetic multiply-accumulate operation. Multiply-accumulates are common in signal processing because most signal-processing algorithms (often filters of various sorts) map to standard vector and matrix operations. Computing elements of result vectors or matrices involves dot products, and these are efficiently implemented by multiply-accumulates within a loop. Fixed-point computation was originally believed to simplify hardware implementation at the cost of more complex software design, but floating-point DSPs have also begun to appear. By contrast, most general-purpose processors require multiple cycles to perform a multiplication, and only a few can combine the multiplication with an addition into an existing sum. DSPs are typically weak at traditional general-purpose computation, having few registers, low clock rates, and complex and slow control mechanisms. These differences mean that DSP and general-purpose cores are not strictly comparable: each device is better than the other in certain ways. For some applications, DSP and general-purpose cores are paired.

Historically, DSPs and general-purpose cores have very different origins. The seminal work of Eckert, Mauchly, and Von Neumann fueled the progress of general-purpose computers. Conversely, DSPs can be considered an evolution of *analog signal processors*, which use analog hardware (such as banks of operational amplifiers) to transform physical signals. Different history and different applications led to different terms and metrics in the DSP world.

The Structure of DSPs. DSP designers are very concerned about energy and cost (including code size), and this is reflected in the extreme degree to which pipeline and hardware control are exposed to the programming interface. DSP programs are traditionally coded

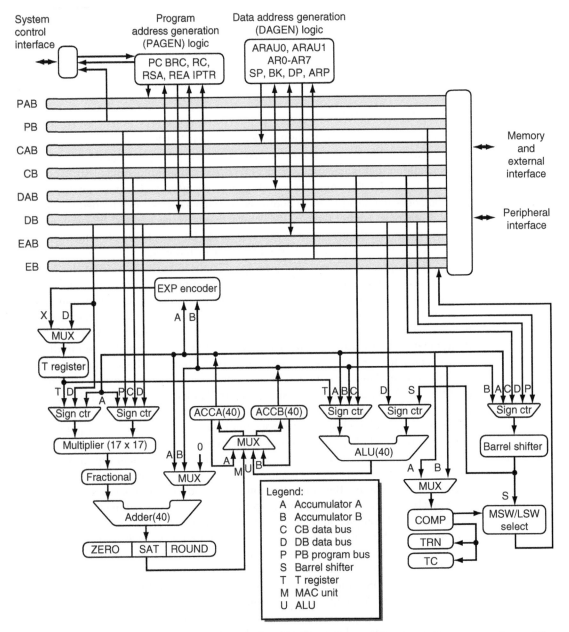

FIGURE 1.3 A typical DSP architecture. The diagram shows the structure of one of the most popular DSPs: the Texas Instruments C54x family. The architecture includes a multiply-accumulate (MAC) unit, two accumulators, an ALU, and a barrel shifter, together with several buses for data and control. The C54x has a very specialized nonorthogonal ISA that is a perfect match with typical DSP algorithms, achieving very small code size and excellent energy efficiency.

in assembly language, and thus it should not come as a surprise that DSP architectures are not good targets for high-level language compilers.

DSPs are often used to execute a single program, and consequently typical DSP operating systems are much simpler, requiring no virtual memory, memory protection, or true multitasking. Often, DSPs are deployed to run *hard real-time* applications, wherein the task scheduler has to account for anything that could happen within a time slot. For example, a real-time application would have to reserve the time necessary to service all possible interrupts or exceptions, and subtract their worst-case collective time from the time slot.

DSPs often process an "infinite" continuous data stream, which a "background" engine loads to a memory buffer available as random-access memory (RAM) for the DSP. This stream has to be processed in real time, and this usually involves intensive arithmetic processing with a low amount of loop control and branching. This way of operating also implies massive amounts of I/O with the analog interface of the product.

To scale performance, high-end DSPs often adopt multiprocessor system designs with *arrays of DSPs*, usually arranged as a loosely connected multiprocessor. The individual DSPs are often unaware of the presence of other DSPs cooperating to the same task, and the job of partitioning the workload is left to programmers and system designers.

The biggest markets for DSP processors today include digital cellular phones and pagers, modems, speech and audio compression, filtering (modulation and demodulation), error correction (coding and decoding), servo control (including disk drives), audio processing (surround sound, noise reduction, equalization), signaling (dual-tone multifrequency [DTMF] detection), speech recognition, and signal synthesis (music/speech).

Because of their separate evolution, DSPs often reflect further tweaking to benefit particular signal processing algorithms. These tweaks come in a variety of forms, including saturating arithmetic modes, extra-wide accumulators, bit-reversed and cyclical (modulo) addressing, reuse of program memory for filter coefficient storage, zero-overhead looping constructs, very efficient and nonorthogonal instruction encodings, eschewing of caching to ensure deterministic timing, bit-oriented instructions, explicit I/O operations, and on-chip caches that can be reused as fast local memory.

Recently, several DSPs appeared claiming to perform well for domains outside traditional signal-processing applications. Conversely, DSP territory is being encroached upon by various general-purpose (x86) and embedded (ARM, MIPS) architectures. The various media-oriented x86 instruction set extensions (MMX and streaming-SIMD extensions [SSE]) have instructions with DSP-like flavors. ARM and MIPS have each announced DSP-specific extensions to their architectures, and have made cores available incorporating these extensions. It will be interesting to see where the market goes.

DSPs can be awkward to use. Their idiosyncratic design makes it very difficult to build optimizing compilers for them, necessitating hand coding to produce correct and efficient programs. In the DSP marketplace, this has historically been acceptable because "design wins" involved large numbers of devices being sold by a supplier (the supplier typically threw in the software design as part of the deal). However, one should not just write off DSP compilers, as the size of applications is rapidly increasing. It may be sufficient to hand code the frequently used parts of applications, but a good DSP compiler is still required to ensure that the rest of the code also runs well.

Our earlier definition of "embedded device" includes DSPs. Programmability is required, but general-purpose processors are today too expensive and not powerful enough for the task DSPs solve. General-purpose processors are surprisingly bad at DSP tasks. A multiply-accumulate operation takes multiple clock cycles on most general-purpose processors, negating the clock rate advantage of the general-purpose chip. The idiosyncratic instruction set extensions listed previously are difficult to emulate (achieving the same benefits requires rewriting code, often in assembly language). Last, general-purpose cores tend to be much bigger than DSP cores, simply because they are general (many general-purpose mechanisms, and their accompanying transistors, are simply omitted from DSP chips).

Network Processors

In the last few years, chip vendors (notably Intel, Motorola, IBM, AMCC, Agere, and Vitesse) have announced and shipped products called "network processors" (NPs), which are designed to be used in data communications devices such as routers. These devices are very similar in spirit to DSPs, having exposed, application-specific pipelines and incomplete connection networks. They are typically programmed in assembly language, and compiling to them is extremely difficult. However, NPs target protocol processing and data movement instead of signal processing.

Beyond just moving data, network infrastructure devices make routing decisions, deciding *where* in the network to send data at each hop. Data moves across networks in *packets*, which can be thought of as envelopes that contain user data. Each packet includes a *header*, which is analogous to the label on the envelope. Depending on the communications protocol, a header might include a destination address (as is the case for the Internet Protocol[3]) or contain a virtual circuit identifier (as is the case for Asynchronous Transfer Mode, ATM, another networking protocol), which names a path from source to destination. When a networking device receives a packet, it examines the header of the packet, then looks up some of the header information in a table (sometimes multiple tables), then uses the information from the table to decide where to send the packet for the next step of its journey. Routing tables can be very large data structures, as they may need to describe virtually any destination on the planet.

One key feature distinguishes the routing process from other computational tasks. For the most part, routing decisions are *independent* across packets. The destination of one packet does not directly affect the destination of another packet.[4] Network processors

---

3. While the Internet Protocol is frequently referred to as IP by computer scientists, we reserve that acronym for intellectual property in this text.

4. This is not strictly true, as feedback mechanisms in the network attempt to adjust routes in response to congestion. However, the timescale for these adaptive mechanisms is usually measured in minutes, whereas the timescale to make a routing decision is typically microseconds. From the perspective of individual routing decisions, we can treat the routing tables as invariant.

exploit this independence in their designs, employing both multiprocessing and multi-threading. Rather than having a single fast processor attempt to keep up with a full-rate data link, NPs deploy multiple, separate processing engines and divide the incoming packets among these multiprocessing engines. Because packet decisions are independent, the engines need not communicate much with each other, if at all. Further, each processing engine supports multiple hardware threads. Only one thread uses the shared core at a time. However, instead of stalling on a slow access to memory, a thread can yield to another ready thread, allowing efficient use of hardware resources despite the long memory access time. The multiple threads look like multiple "virtual" processors per physical processor, further increasing the number of packets that can be processed at once.

Network processors are very good examples of SoC, integrating many heterogeneous components onto a single die. Most NPs have a variety of specialized processors linked with purpose-built communication networks, some sort of embedded general-purpose processor to serve as overall system controller, and high-speed interfaces to off-chip RAM, communications framers, and other NP chips. Throughput figures for NPs in terms of operations per second can be staggeringly high because of the large number of independent cores integrated into one chip. Bandwidth figures for NPs also tend to be quite high, because the NPs must be able to process the data stream from many simultaneously active communication links.

The network processor marketplace has already narrowed during its brief history. IBM and Vitesse have decided to exit the marketplace, and only Intel appears to be gaining market share.

Unlike DSPs, we are not convinced that network processors will evolve toward a VLIW-style approach. Networking applications do not have obvious instruction-level parallelism, making them poor matches for VLIW architectures (although it is interesting to note that at least one NP vendor claims in its marketing literature to use VLIW execution cores in its network processor devices). As we did for DSPs, we also choose not to cover NPs in great depth during the course of this book. A somewhat more detailed description of how network processors are built and used can be found in Chapter 11. That discussion also describes how the processing in network switches has evolved *away* from general-purpose cores.

1.3.2 Categorization by Application Area

This section paints a broad-brush picture of embedded computing applications. Looking at 16-bit and wider processors, we illustrate embedded applications with examples from three major embedded computing markets.

1. **The image processing and consumer market** includes printers, audio, video, cameras, and home entertainment.

2. **The communications market** includes telephony and data networks.

3. **The automotive market** includes safety, engine control, navigation, and brakes.

The first two markets in particular are fast-growing segments (as far as processors are concerned), implying a tremendous push in performance demands, as well as power and cost requirements for the processing engines that will drive these market segments. There are plenty of other embedded application areas, such as medical, military, industrial control, and avionics.

Each of these areas has different fundamental characteristics, including the computation mix, presence or absence of real-time constraints, and workload. The following examples illustrate the spectrum of diversity in the embedded world.

The Image Processing and Consumer Market

Consumer electronics devices usually manipulate *media* in one form or another, such as audio, video, or still images. Manipulation functionality ranges from playback (such as an MP3 player or TV set), to capture (digital still and video cameras, scanners), and transduction (printers, projectors). The time needed to access, compute, and transform the media data dominates the typical workload of such systems. Progress in the technology for capture, transformation, and output of media data produces massive amounts of data that have to be moved throughout the embedded system.

Printers. A good quality thermal-inkjet imaging printer today produces pictures with a resolution of 1200 dots per inch (*dpi*). For a standard letter-size page (8.5 × 11 inches) filled 80%, this translates into approximately 100M dots to be emitted per page. If we need 3 bytes per dot to represent the entire color space at any point in the printer pipeline, we have to design the system to be able to cope with about 300 MB of data per page. If our target speed is one page per minute, we can only spend about 600 ns of CPU time per dot, translating to 120 cycles for a 200-MHz processor. In this very short amount of time, the printer's imaging pipeline has to decompress the image (usually from a JPEG format), convert the color space from RGB (red-green-blue) to CMYK (cyan-magenta-yellow-black, the set of additive colors used by most printers), and dither the image to accommodate a small number of color levels (usually two or four) supported by the print heads. Dithering itself (also called *halftoning*) is a computationally intensive sequential operation that requires examining a neighborhood of pixels to produce the next value. In many cases, the printer does not need to produce the entire page before starting to print (although some of the high-end large-format printers include a hard disk exactly for this purpose). The printer usually renders slices of the page (called *swaths*) to a memory buffer, which the print-head electronics read through a direct memory access (DMA) operation. This mode of operation has a double advantage: the printer can operate with less memory than for an entire page and the real-time component of the task (firing up the printer's nozzles) is decoupled from the main computational pipeline.

Cameras. The imaging element in a consumer-grade digital camera is a *charge-coupled device* (CCD). A typical CCD matrix produces 2 to 4M pixels per image. CCD elements are essentially monochromatic and need to be arranged in regular patterns of red, green, and blue sensors to be able to capture color images. In other words, the raw data captured by the CCD sensor is a *mosaic* of red, green, and blue pixels. Before being stored in a standard format, the camera must filter the pixels with an operation called *demosaicing*, to interpolate the spatially interleaved pixel data of the mosaic. Demosaicing usually involves a 2D convolution with a large mask and is a very compute-intensive task. In addition, this is not the only operation required to produce a quality image. Before demosaicing, the electronics in the camera have to compensate for various imperfections of the sensors, such as misalignment, optical distortion, and nonuniform image intensity, focus, and exposure. After demosaicing, the camera resizes the image to the desired size (another form of interpolation), equalizes colors, and finally compresses it — typically emitting a JPEG format. Without getting to the details, it should be evident that each of these steps requires applying some form of compute-intensive nontrivial transformation on all pixels of the image.

In addition to the CCD, today's digital cameras include a standard amount of RAM (16 MB of synchronous DRAM [SDRAM] in some examples) and an integrated processing chip that includes a general-purpose processor (e.g., ARM), a DSP, or both. CCD and computation are not yet integrated on a single chip because of different process technologies used to fabricate each.

In this media-oriented, consumer domain, a small number of characteristics dominates all applications. First, processing involves a large data structure, often with limited temporal locality. This data structure may have to stream multiple times through all parts (CPU, caches, main memory, secondary storage/flash) of the system. This data structure mandates that computationally intensive, loop-oriented integer applications dominate the workload. Finally, the speed of the electronics determines the speed of the device. In other words, the mechanical components of the device are faster than the computational components, and thus the power, performance, and price performance of the computational elements drive the pricing structure. This last observation is true not just for cameras but for many other embedded devices, including printers and hard disk drives.

Digital Video. DVD gave consumers their first taste of digital video in 1997, using disks that store 5 to 12 GB of data and transfer information at up to 10 Mbit/s, giving significantly higher quality than VHS tapes or even analog broadcast. More recently, digital video has been deployed over cable systems, and high-definition (HD) video broadcasts have begun over the airwaves and through cable and satellite systems. More recently still, personal video recorders (PVRs), such as Tivo and ReplayTV, have been offered as high-value, high-quality alternatives to user-programmed VCRs.

The common technology behind all modern digital video is digital video compression. Most video compression is based on the work of the MPEG group, which builds upon the JPEG standard for still image compression. Details about video compression can be found in Chapter 11, but the most important overall point is that video compression, like any compression scheme, makes a storage-computation tradeoff, whereby better compression ratios can be achieved by applying more processing power to both encoding and decoding stages. North American HDTV was enabled by simultaneous advances in compression algorithms and integrated circuits that allowed a decoder to fit on a single chip. Consumer electronics manufacturers have recently been debating the format for HD video disks, with much higher capacities based on blue lasers. However, Microsoft has "scooped" the hardware manufacturers. The Microsoft Windows Media 9 format (WM9), which uses more aggressive compression and requires more computation than prior formats, can encode a 2-hour HD movie in the space of a regular DVD.

Cost makes general-purpose processors unsuitable for most consumer items. Many consumer electronic devices sell for less than the cheapest Pentium-family processor. Size and power constraints are also important determinants for the processors in portable consumer electronics devices. And although one might expect the WM9 format to be decodable only on PCs, at least one manufacturer has announced plans to build a WM9 DVD player around the Sigma Designs EM8620L digital media processor chip.

The Communications Market

Systems involved in the telecommunication and networking infrastructure manipulate digital circuits and/or digital packet data, and depending on the protocol level they operate in are responsible for initiating, servicing, routing, transporting, and terminating network connections. Equipment at the periphery or edge of the network is often very different from equipment at the core of the network, which is true for wired telephones, cellular phones, and the data network.

Wired Phone Networks. Today's wired telephone system is designed for cheap handsets and expensive core components. The *local loop*, the copper wire between the handset and the central office (CO), uses analog signals that are ingeniously encoded using only one pair of signal wires per connection. CO telephone switches are large parallel computing systems that support huge numbers of low-bandwidth lines. At the CO, analog-to-digital and digital-to-analog conversion are performed, and the actual data shipped in the core network is entirely digital. Most wireline voice is sampled at 8-bit resolution at 8-KHz rates, giving a 64-Kbit/s data rate for a standard voice call. Central office switches connect to a wide variety of other types of devices that form the core telephone network. All core network devices in the phone system are synchronized to a single global clock, and all data connections between COs are driven by the same global clock, like a continually meshed global system of gears. This nationwide (even worldwide) synchronization allows the phone system to use time-division multiplexing (TDM) to combine small 64-Kbit subscriber lines into larger trunks. Placing a call involves reserving a time slot on each link between the two endpoints and getting the infrastructure to move bytes from time slot to time slot at each switch along the path.

Cellular Networks. The cellular network builds on the technology of the wired network (using some of the same types of telephone switches) but uses entirely different technology for the wireless hop from handset to base station. A variety of radio standards are used throughout the USA (analog or AMPS, TDMA, CDMA, and GSM), whereas the rest of the world (with the notable exception of China) uses GSM. A typical GSM voice stream is compressed to a rate near 24 Kbit/s. Standby power for today's cellular phones is a few milliwatts, but transmit power is much higher, in the hundreds of milliwatts. Various encoding and protocol techniques mean that even a cellular phone with an active conversation is at transmit power levels one-eighth or less of the time. Typical batteries today hold between 500 and 1,000 milliamp hours, leading to the various standby and talk time ratings claimed by manufacturers.

Cellular Telephones. The inside of a modern cellular phone is a marvel of integration. Although a phone does not yet fit onto a single chip (differences in analog and digital circuit processes currently prevent this), typical phones hold between five and fifteen integrated circuits. A typical phone might have both an embedded microprocessor (such as an ARM) and a DSP, such as a TI C54x or Agere 16000. Such processors are implemented in relatively unaggressive silicon processes (0.25 micron in 2001, compared to 0.13 micron in some desktop computers) and run at mild clock rates (about 100 MHz in 2001, compared to 1 to 2 GHz in desktops). The DSP and processor cores also typically include on the order of 256 KBytes each of RAM and ROM.

Routers. A typical "backbone" router (e.g., those owned by MCI and Sprint) has between 16 and 32 interfaces, each running at OC-192 rates, which is roughly 10 Gbit/s. Packet sizes over the backbone are bi-modally distributed, at either 64 bytes (minimum to carry a keystroke or TCP acknowledgment) or 1500 bytes (Ethernet minimum transfer unit [MTU] size) per packet. At the smaller packet size, that translates to 160M routing decisions per interface per second. Routing decisions are made by looking up information in routing tables. The typical routing table has on the order of 50,000 entries, but they are not organized for quick access. Tree-based traversals or content-addressable memory (CAM) approaches are used to implement the access in time. All datapath functions are handled by ASICs or FPGAs.[5] Control processors update the routing tables and are typical general-purpose devices running, say, Cisco's networking operating system. Data buffer size in packet routers is proprietary information. Rumors claim either on the order of 100 packets for the *entire router* (i.e., zero buffering) or on the order of 100 ms of buffering, which is 250 Mbit or 30 MBytes of storage per interface card.

For the wired phone network, history plays a part in the lack of general-purpose microprocessors. Digital phone networks were deployed in the 1970s, long before many of today's microprocessor families had been invented. Reengineering efforts within the Bell System and its descendants have replaced many of the proprietary processors of that earlier age, but economics keep the job from being completed. General-purpose processors play a signaling, controlling, and database management role in modern cellular networks, but the vast majority of processing is performed by racks of DSPs. And although early routers were built from general-purpose computer chassis, designs rapidly became specialized in later generations (see Chapter 11 for a somewhat more detailed description of this evolution).

---

5. Note that the terms *FPGA* (*field-programmable gate array*) and *PLD* (*programmable logic device*) are often used interchangeably. They historically derive from the fundamental technologies that differentiate the two major competitors in the arena: *Xilinx* with FPGA, and *Altera* with PLD. In this book, we (incorrectly) often use the term *FPGA* without vendor-specific connotations, to indicate a generic programmable hardware device.

The Automotive Market

Even the traditionally conservative world of control systems has witnessed a dramatic escalation in the complexity of the electronics components, as well as in the algorithms they implement.

In the automotive control world, consumer demand for enhanced safety features and entertainment systems, and emissions control regulations, have fueled a tremendous growth of the role of computing components. It is common to find about 50 microprocessors in today's luxury vehicles, and about 10 to 15 in economy cars. Several factors contribute to this growth. The complexity of the systems themselves and the algorithms used to drive them is increasing, and each subsystem is starting to share data in real time, thus opening up opportunities for better control. For example, cars are starting to integrate information coming from the braking, steering, suspension, and powertrain systems. Communication among the various electronic control units (ECUs) is becoming a standard, usually partitioned across separate controller area networks (CANs), such as instrumentation and body, powertrain and transmission, steering-braking-suspension, entertainment, and safety. The sensors that provide information have transformed as well, from simple analog devices to *smart nodes* (sensors equipped with a small dedicated CPU) that communicate through a digital bus. When a mechanical backup is available (such as hydraulic brakes for the ABS electronics), most of these systems must operate in *fail-safe* mode (detect errors and default to the backup system). When the presence of a digital bus makes brake-by-wire or steer-by-wire possible, these systems must also include *fault-tolerant* features (must continue to work even in the presence of errors). All of this significantly increases the complexity of the design.

An example of a high-end microprocessor for the next-generation automotive world is the Motorola MPC555. The MPC555 is based on the PowerPC RISC architecture (over 6.7 million transistors in a 0.35-micron process), with multiple execution units, floating point, separate instruction/datapaths to memory, 448 KB of electronically erasable programmable read-only memory (EEPROM), and 26 KB of RAM. In addition, this SoC includes peripherals to deal with 32 analog signals, 48 timer-controlled I/O channels, and two CAN serial communication interfaces to talk to the other electronic subsystems of the vehicle. Such a system is more than two orders of magnitude more complex (in terms of memory, connections, and bandwidth) than systems deployed in cars less than a decade ago. And although the processor core in an MPC555 is a general-purpose computing core, it is very different from its high-performance relatives, running at a relatively low clock rate (40 MHz). The overall package of core and peripherals is what provides value to automotive designers. Replicating the same functions with a general-purpose processor and separate logic would be much more expensive.

1.3.3 Categorization by Workload Differences

Workload differences fundamentally affect the design of the entire system. It is difficult to identify a typical workload in a general purpose system; this is much easier to do in an embedded product, and the entire system can be tuned to match that specific workload. As we saw in Section 1.3.2, we can break down the most important embedded markets into a few significant areas. In a similar way (although the correspondence is not one-to-one) we can distinguish a few basic workload styles.

Controlling is the traditional workload of the embedded market. Control-dominated applications usually imply a rather strong real-time component (hence, a real-time OS or microkernel), fairly light computational requirements, a simple memory system, and a tight coupling with a rich set of peripherals and sensors. This is the kingdom of 8-bit and 16-bit microcontrollers, which occur abundantly in appliance, automotive, and industrial environments. Control applications are well studied and represented in the literature and are not the focus of this book.

Switching and routing can be seen as control applications that coordinate streams of data — typically found in networking applications. In addition to the real-time component common among pure control applications, networking workloads involve quickly moving large amounts of data. This adds significant pressure on the memory system and heavy requirements on its buffering capabilities. In addition, the fact that the system needs to process multiple independent streams concurrently complicates the software infrastructure with efficient multithreading support. At the same time, the amount of "computation" being performed by the system is still within reach of a today's scalar CPUs.

Media processing stretches the computational capabilities of the system to the limit. A seemingly innocuous task, such as decoding an MPEG2 stream for digital television, is already beyond the reach of most of today's embedded CPUs and requires dedicated hardware support. Adding encoding, networking, interactivity, and security functions adds one or two orders of magnitude of complexity. Media processing stresses every component of the system. Again, if we look at video *codecs* as an example we have to deal with real-time restrictions to match acceptable frame rates, heavy computational workloads to compress and decompress video streams, and large memory bandwidth and capacity requirements.

1.4 Embedded Market Structure

This last section of the introductory chapter contains a number of different topics that can be lumped under the loose description of business or market related. Unlike the majority of this book, which addresses technical topics, this section is all the space we can spare to talk about how embedded processing fits into society and into the economy. Beyond applications and users, these are the ultimate "top level" engineers must consider.

Our survey of markets and businesses begins by describing the market for embedded processor cores as our book goes to print. Readers should not be surprised that our chapter holds that virtually all processors sold today are embedded processors. The next two subsections (1.4.1 and 1.4.2) describe the interactions between business and technology. In Section 1.4.2 we contrast the cost and yield issues of general-purpose processors with their embedded brethren. In Section 1.4.3 we broaden the discussion from the processor die to the development of the entire system, including tradeoffs among the various computational styles that go into a design.

The next three sections describe issues shared by, but sometimes handled differently within, the general-purpose market. Section 1.4.4 talks about how software is becoming unbundled from development in embedded systems, following the mainframe trend of twenty years ago. Section 1.4.5 discusses the role of industry standards (both *de facto* and official) in embedded designs, and Section 1.4.6 describes how the lifetimes of embedded systems vary widely, unlike the rapid obsolescence of the general-purpose market.

The last two parts of this section look to the future. In Section 1.4.7 we describe the most recent effect of Moore's law: the integration of entire computing systems onto a single chip, and the implications for generality, specialization, volume production, and cost that this trend implies. The last section, 1.4.8, speculates about where embedded computing, and computing in general, will go.

1.4.1 The Market for Embedded Processor Cores

Earlier in this chapter we described how processor cores can be divided into four major categories: computational microprocessors (32-bit or more architectures), embedded general-purpose microprocessors (typically 32-bit architectures), microcontrollers (8- or 16-bit), and DSPs.

We are used to hearing about phenomenal growth in the computational microprocessor market, although recent revenue reports from Intel and AMD suggest that growth in this market is finally leveling off. The interesting story is that although *volumes* of computational micros are still growing, revenues have been flat. Arguably this is not due to competition, but rather because general-purpose microprocessors have finally become "fast enough," as consumers perceive very little difference in performance between the most and least expensive x86-compatible processors.

However, computational micros are just one part of the larger processor market. In 2001, computational micros accounted for less than 2% of the volume of processors shipped. Embedded general-purpose micros constituted about 11% (8% of the total volume were core-based ASICs) of total volumes. DSPs accounted for 10%, and microcontrollers an overwhelming 80%. The revenue story is roughly inversely proportional to volumes. Computational micros constituted 51% of core-related revenues in 2001, whereas embedded general-purpose micros accounted for 8% and DSPs for 13%. The remaining 28% of revenue came from microcontrollers. Growth in embedded general-purpose micros, DSPs, and microcontrollers is expected to outstrip growth in computational micros in both volume and revenue for the foreseeable future.[6]

Small 8-bit CPUs still dominate the market, representing about two-thirds of microcontroller shipments (and about 70% of overall processor shipments). Higher-end applications (for example, those with addressing requirements beyond 64 KB of memory)

---

6. Source: Gartner Dataquest, Jan. 2001. For more information about market structure, see the book web site at *http://www.vliw.org/book*.

often use 16-bit microcontrollers, in many cases implemented as an evolution of a successful 8-bit instruction set. 32-Bit microcontrollers have a minor role (constituting a $1B market), and are under increasing competition from established 32-bit general-purpose RISC processors.

1.4.2 Business Model of Embedded Processors

The economics behind designing a processor (or processor core) for a typical embedded system are very different from the workstation and PC worlds. Among the most perceivable deviations, the difference in margins on units sold has a great effect on both business models and design practices. Higher sales margins on workstation and PC processors usually justify larger development costs, lower yields, and speed-binning of parts. In the extreme, when proprietary processors are embedded in proprietary workstations (such as most of today's UNIX systems) the cost of these processors is bundled with the cost of the entire system that gets passed on to the final customer. This business model is what drove the design of most UNIX-class RISC processors, such as Sun SPARC, HP PA-RISC, IBM PowerPC, and DEC Alpha.

For consumer appliances, the model is very different. In an SoC, parts can be designed by multiple parties and integrated by a third party; the third party purchases intellectual property (IP) in the form of IP blocks (licensed hardware designs) from the other designers. The IP model is an attempt to build standardized parts for digital design, but this approach is still maturing, increasing the complexity of the task. The owner of the processor IP is different from the silicon manufacturer; the silicon manufacturer is different from the system integrator. If we couple this with the inherent lower average street price of most typical appliances, it is obvious that profit margins are much more constrained.

From the design standpoint, thinner margins mean that embedded silicon manufacturers have to keep costs under severe control. The absolute number of dies produced by a single wafer contributes to unit cost. Smaller dies give more dies per wafer, which gives lower cost per die. Other factors that contribute to costs include the packaging, the number of pins, the number of wire bonds or solder bumps, the number of decoupling capacitors, power supply requirements, and the number of layers required in the printed circuit board to support a chip. Stringent control over costs implies targeting much higher yields, higher absolute part volume, and smaller development costs, as well as rigid area limitations, power thresholds, and simple testing strategies. In the following, we briefly cover some of these issues.

Getting a Better Yield. The ratio between working and defective parts depends on manufacturing factors that are largely design independent, and on some basic design choices. Manufacturers characterize processes with best, average, and worst-case parameters, for both environmental (such as temperature and voltage) and process variations. Speed *derating factors* between best and worst case of 2–4x are not unusual, but designing for a worst-case scenario greatly improves the chances of getting working parts (albeit at a lower frequency).

Controlling Area and Power Consumption. The typical cost of a state-of-the-art piece of silicon usually scales with the cube of its area. As a consequence, it is extremely important to stay below the knee of the curve for any given process technology and wafer size. For example, although it is not uncommon to find general-purpose processors that use up to 300 to 400 mm^2 of silicon real estate, few embedded components go over 40 to 50 mm^2 in an equivalent process. On the other hand, peak power consumption is what determines the choice of the chip packaging. Again, top-speed designs use much higher currents, requiring packages (increasingly plastic rather than ceramic) that can dissipate more heat.

Testing Costs. These cover the amortization of the testing equipment for a given part throughput. On first approximation, this is proportional to the time it takes to test a component in isolation. To improve the testability of a component, we have the choice of increasing the number of test patterns (which increases test costs) or augmenting the component's observability and self-test capabilities. This is the reason practically all embedded components are *fully scannable* (i.e., it is possible to access all internal state elements through a few serial *scan chains*), and why they include BIST (*built-in self-test*) circuitry for regular structures, such as embedded memories. Unfortunately, *design for testability* has a negative impact on the achievable speed.

Finally, we note that testing, power, and yield issues are intimately intertwined in a very complex relationship that goes beyond the scope of this book. For example, in many environments testing each component in isolation is not sufficient to guarantee a working product. Given the skyrocketing costs of testing equipment, some customers may prefer to get only partially tested parts, integrate them, and only exhaustively test the final system. This means that a defective part implies wasting a part of the system much larger than the individual part. Such a scenario puts much greater pressure on silicon manufacturers to improve product quality (which is rated in good parts per million, or PPM).

1.4.3 Costs and Product Volume

In a simplified view, we can split the cost of an electronic product into two components: *part cost* and *NRE cost*. Part cost is the cost of building, testing, and assembling the device itself. NRE (*non-recurring engineering*, or tasks that only need to be performed once) costs include design activities, equipment amortization, and one-time fabrication costs (such as the cost of producing the VLSI masks for a semi-custom design).

Traditionally, part cost is what dominates embedded products. The impact of NRE diminishes with increasing volume, and for high-volume products (tens of millions of parts per year) it quickly becomes negligible. However, some new factors are changing this scenario.

As VLSI devices become more complex and start absorbing other product-specific specialization, their volume decreases. For example, a standalone processor core that can be sold to several markets for a long time can justify a high development effort.

For a dedicated SoC (perhaps including a soft version of the same CPU together with other product-specific blocks), only the product volume matters.

The cost of fabricating a die has become a relatively small portion of the total NRE cost when we consider design time, testing, a few redesigns, and package costs. For complex SoC designs, manufacturing costs can be enormous (figures of about $500,000 for mask sets alone are not uncommon). Smaller process geometries and more mask layers make this trend even worse. In addition, we need to account for the additional costs of a few redesigns, and the matching silicon respins.

The capacity of state-of-the-art silicon fabs is limited, and is filling up quickly. Consequently, most ASIC manufacturers only accept designs with minimum volume guarantees of hundreds of thousands of units.

ASIC design teams are difficult to build from scratch, in part because of the wide variety of skills involved. Not many experienced ASIC design teams exist, sophisticated CAD tools are very expensive, and the tools are usually associated with a very steep learning curve. Design, and especially verification, of complex semi-custom devices works against time-to-market and flexibility, and can cause significant opportunity losses.

An interesting example that illustrates the importance of cost/volume/NRE considerations is the success of programmable hardware devices. Because of many of the factors we highlighted, FPGAs have become promising alternatives for low- and medium-volume products. In every embedded product design there is a point at which volume, cost, and time considerations mandate the choice between semi-custom (ASIC) and programmable solutions. For a low-volume, time-critical product such as a high-performance router, an FPGA design is usually the best choice. FPGAs can have a major impact on reducing the NRE of a product. They can be reworked very quickly and cheaply, and are tolerant to evolving standards and last-minute changes to future sets. A few other trends favor FPGA adoption.

It has become significantly more difficult to obtain access to deep submicron manufacturing processes for low- to medium-volume designs. Many of the traditional ASIC vendors stopped at 0.35μ processes. On the other hand, the high volume of a single FPGA part (which can be sold to many different designs) justifies the investment into deep submicron technologies. This tends to level the playing field in terms of speed and density.

Validation and verification of a complex design take up the overwhelming majority of time to complete a semi-custom project. FPGA devices remove a large part of this, their silicon having been preverified and their programmability lowering the impact of functional mistakes.

Hybrid circuits that include a "chunk" of FPGA logic and other standard IP blocks are becoming available. Again, due to ever-increasing densities one can now purchase high-end FPGA parts that include supplemental logic (RAM, multipliers, and even entire processor cores!) and standard peripherals (Universal Asynchronous Receiver Transmitters [UARTs], memory controllers, and high-speed I/O connections) together with a large amount of uncommitted logic blocks. Recently, some vendors have begun to offer *System-on-a-programmable-Chip* (SopC), which includes a microprocessor core in addition to the functions previously cited.

SoCs and SopCs illustrate how cost/volume/NRE considerations drive technology choices in an embedded product. In addition, it is important to remember that trade-offs continuously evolve, which need to be reevaluated carefully. This is especially true when technological breakthroughs (FPGA), sudden drifts in market demands (evolving standards), and changes in manufacturing scenarios (fab pressure) occur.

1.4.4 Software and the Embedded Software Market

The cost of software in an embedded system should not be underestimated. The fully integrated processor cost of the SonicBlue RIO MP3 player was $9[7], whereas the software cost amortized per unit was $12. This can be as much as 30 to 40% of total cost. Worse yet, software programmer productivity is growing much less quickly than hardware designer productivity, as indicated in Figure 1.4.

Manufacturers of embedded systems used to charge only a minimal amount for related software products. Recently, this trend has reversed, and embedded systems users are becoming accustomed to paying royalties for software intellectual property. For example, typical royalties for a deeply embedded OS are on the order of 2 to 3% of the cost of the core itself. Similar royalty-based considerations apply to other IP software blocks, such as protocol stacks and device drivers.

On the other hand, embedded software tools (such as compilers) are almost free, or at least seemingly so, their cost being invisibly folded into the cost of silicon itself. Maintenance, training, and consulting services remain fee-based. The total market for embedded tools (excluding semiconductor companies) was about $1.1B in the year 2000, and it is predicted to grow to about $2.6B in the year 2005, with an 18.7% compound annual growth rate (CAGR).[8]

New categories of embedded software tools are emerging in the area of *customizable processors* (such as the *Tensilica Xtensa* platform or the family of *ARC* cores). In this domain, customers specialize a processor to their intended use by changing an architecture template within certain restrictions. For example, currently available systems allow adding special instructions or changing the sizes and parameters of local memory and caches. Here, tools to help make design decisions (retargetable compilers, simulator and analysis programs) become critical for the success of these new types of products.

1.4.5 Industry Standards

Another factor that influences the design of embedded systems is the strong role of industry standards. By this, we mean not only officially endorsed standards (such as ISO communication protocols, compression methods, and so on) but *de facto standards*: common practices that strongly favor certain designs.

Until recently, embedded devices were dedicated to one (or a small number of) specialized function. As a device becomes more specialized in function, the

---

7. Source: Andy Wolfe, former SonicBlue CTO, Micro-34 keynote speech, 2001.

8. Source: Venture Development Corp.

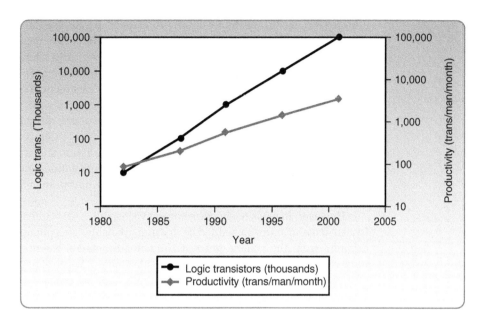

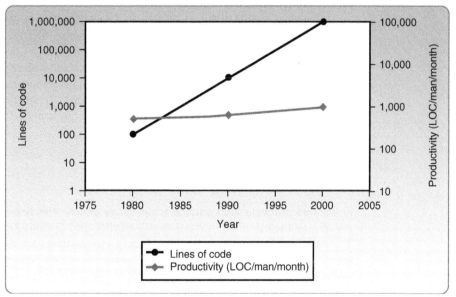

FIGURE 1.4 **Productivity growth for hardware designers and software programmers compared.** The top chart shows the 21% CAGR for hardware designers (source: Sematech); the bottom chart shows the corresponding 3 to 7% CAGR for software developers (source: IEEE, Applied software measurement [Capers Jones]).

cost/performance tradeoffs favor a more dedicated implementation direction. In other words, a greater percentage of special-purpose circuitry becomes practical when doing one standard thing most of the time. This is the reason ASICs have been—and still are, in many areas—the most widely adopted design philosophy. The primary justification for hardwired functionality is a greater return on investment. The performance/cost of dedicated logic can outperform an equivalent programmable solution by more than one order of magnitude. However, this comes at a much higher design cost and lack of flexibility. Once a standard emerges for a specific functionality (for example, an RS232 serial port or a VGA controller), flexibility ceases to be an issue, and we can easily justify the higher costs with the opportunity of reuse. In the workstation domain, similar considerations have driven increasing uniformity in the periphery, such as with devices, buses, and memory.

However, in areas of changing (or not yet established) standards, the lack of flexibility can make an entire embedded device unmarketable. This phenomenon is significantly different from the general-purpose domain (the market might still accept a general-purpose product when one capability is substandard, because of the intrinsic versatility of a general-purpose platform). For example, laptops typically have lower-resolution screens than desktops, and many business desktops have limited graphics or sound capability. For the more limited and dedicated functionality of an embedded product, a substandard component is usually not acceptable.

If we look at some of the most promising embedded areas, we can observe an acceleration of adoption of new technologies. Digital video and telecom applications are two of the most visible examples. Here, the need for quick turnaround—such as the time to market after the emergence of a new technology—becomes much more important than the absolute best cost/performance ratio. Lost opportunities and market share due to the late introduction of a product usually dwarf any other considerations. This is where high-performance software solutions become fundamental, even in the embedded domain.

1.4.6 Product Life Cycle

Embedded products span a much wider range of activities than general-purpose computers, and their product lifetimes, serviceability, and upgradeability differ accordingly. Typical general-purpose products (such as PCs or laptops) have three-year expected lifetimes, after which they are replaced by newer, faster models. PCs are designed with replaceable modular components, which allows component-wise fault isolation and replacement (few PC components can be serviced in the field). Modular components also allow owners to upgrade their PCs to lengthen the useful lifetime of the product, but such upgrades are not often cost effective when the bundled savings of complete replacement are considered.

Embedded products have a wider range of lifetimes than general-purpose products. At the short end of the cycle, cellular phones are replaced frequently by their users; more at the dictate of fashion than of technology. On the long end, embedded devices in public infrastructure are designed to age slowly. For example, telephone switches depreciate over decades, and nuclear reactors are designed for 40 to 60 years of service.[9]

Depending on the cost and size of the embedded device, service may or may not be possible during its lifetime. Inexpensive consumer products (e.g., VCRs, CD players, and portable phones) are replaced rather than repaired (the repair cost would be higher than the cost of a new device). Larger devices are, like their general-purpose counterparts, built with modular parts (service also involves replacing damaged parts). In certain extreme cases, service is not possible at all. For example, deep space probes enjoy no direct "customer support." Engineers must build redundant systems and paths for working around failed components.

Hardware upgrade patterns in embedded devices follow similar patterns concerning serviceability. Low-end devices are replaced rather than upgraded. Larger, modular devices may be upgraded piecewise (for example, cards can be replaced in cellular base stations to vary the mix of protocols supported).

It is interesting to note that *software* upgrades have enabled dramatic functionality changes in embedded devices. Returning to the previously mentioned deep space probes, image-processing algorithms developed after the spacecraft were launched allowed the Voyager missions to return more and better data than originally planned by the designers. Saturn vehicles with automatic transmissions and the antilock brake option get traction control "for free." That is, because all of the necessary hardware inputs and outputs (engine management, traction sensors, and brake modulation) were controlled by the same computer, traction control became a software upgrade. It has been reported that the managers of the DirectTV satellite television system, frustrated with hackers, gradually downloaded a new security scheme over the course of months, and then activated the new system all at once, disabling virtually all hacked devices one week before the 2001 Super Bowl.

1.4.7 The Transition to SoC Design

Yesterday's circuit boards are today's SoC. Current VLSI manufacturing processes allow the integration of very complex functionalities in the same piece of silicon in a very cost-effective manner. We can now fit into a single die what yesterday took many individual integrated circuits and boards, with dramatic improvements in cost, performance, and time-to-market. The challenge for engineers has shifted from minimizing gates to finding ways to use all available gates at a given cost, and to worrying about wires rather than about transistors.

High-volume SoCs today include blocks such as microprocessor cores, DSPs, memories, buses, and peripherals. A huge enabler for the proliferation of SoC designs is the success of the consumer electronics and wireless market, in which complex system chips are now necessary for any semiconductor company that wishes to remain a significant player. For example, next-generation cellular phones will integrate the entire baseband

---

9. Thirty years is typical for nuclear power plants, but Japan is considering stretching the lifetime of its plants to 60 to 80 years.

	97–98	98–99	99–00	00–02
Process Technology	0.35μ	0.25μ	0.18μ	0.13μ
Cost of Fab	1.5–2.0 B$	2.0–3.0 B$	3.0–4.0 B$	4.0–5.0 B$
Design Cycle	18–12 mos.	12–10 mos.	10–8 mos.	8–6 mos.
Design Complexity	200–500K gates	1–2M gates	4–6M gates	8–10M gates
Intellectual Property Sources	Intragroup	Intergroup	Inter-company	Inter-company
Applications	Cellular phone, Simple PDA, DVD	Set-top box, wireless PDA	Internet appliance, multifunction device	Digital video recorder, video conferencing

TABLE 1.1   Technology trends for SoC designs. Increases in design complexity, driven by Moore's law, make it uneconomical to embrace new SoC designs from scratch. Absorbing intellectual property blocks from other groups or companies is unavoidable. Thus, *authoring* and *integration* of intellectual property blocks are often carried on as separate activities by different teams. New methodologies for SoC design are needed (*source: The Transition to System-on-a-Chip* by L. Todd and A. McNelly).

subsystem (codec, vocoder, baseband processor, interfaces, and system microcontroller), as well as the radio frequency subsystems, into a single chip.

The increased complexity of SoC designs has deep repercussions on the entire design process. As we can see in Table 1.1, SoC projects are shifting from single-team designs to multi-team (and, sometimes multi-company) activities. Concurrently, the time-to-market window for a new product is shrinking to 8 to 10 months, and the density of the design increases with Moore's law. In other words, although the advantages are many, designing SoCs in a timely and efficient manner poses very significant challenges even for large companies. Now, we briefly present the challenges and strategies that increase the probability of a successful design.

The first challenge for SoC designers comes from design tools. The improvement of EDA (electronic design automation) tools in the 1990s lagged behind the increase in design complexity. In addition, the interaction of EDA tools within a complete design workflow is still an open question. Industry-wide standards are struggling with proprietary tools, legacy issues, and a traditional resistance to change in engineering teams. Finally, the need to integrate IP blocks from different groups, or even different vendors, poses very significant challenges to the overall verification strategy for SoCs.

Controversy: Silicon Will Be Free

Because silicon densities have grown exponentially throughout the history of micropro-cessors, design elements aimed at saving silicon can seem worthless or even silly just a few years later. Saving silicon often involves tricks that complicate a system, and thus designers sometimes advise that because silicon is almost "free" (that is, a given amount of it will soon cost very little compared to what it used to cost) these tricks should usually be avoided.

This advice has become the conventional wisdom, and it is usually good advice. Sometimes it is bad advice, however, and there is good reason to believe it could become worse advice as times goes on. As this book is being written, a new barrier is being approached: high performance is going portable, due to a combination of silicon densities and battery technology. The significance of this is that although the engineering cost of saving small amounts of microprocessor silicon may not be justified for plugged-in devices, for portable devices it can make an impractical product practical. A portable device needing a high-performance microprocessor may not be able to afford the power and silicon cost budget required to attain the needed performance. However, the saving of silicon, of some of the "free silicon," might well make the product practical.

This advice generalizes. There is no size too small for the requirements of some of the applications computer visionaries foresee, from wearable computers to "smart dust." The availability of high performance can practically enable those applications, making silicon cost the barrier to overcome. There is every reason to believe that the need to save silicon will always be with us in some important environments.

Inadequate tools and poor collaborative working practices cause projects to slip. Project delays often mean that specifications change to adapt to new market requirements, and projects slip even further. If we compare this to more stable designs using off-the-shelf components, it becomes clear that SoCs are only a win if they can hit the market opportunity window in time, and that the risks of missing the window are much higher than in the past.

A successful SoC development requires approaching the project with a system perspective that combines hardware, software, and marketing. Traditionally, semiconductor companies have not excelled as system companies (they rarely had to write their own software), and only recently have they started emphasizing complete solutions that encompass both hardware and software.

It is now unanimously recognized that the most difficult aspect of SoC design is verification. Even the most experienced semiconductor companies fight daily with the complexity of verifying large designs. As we have noted, tools are behind, and the winning approach always involves discipline and an early definition of the verification strategy. The definition of a test suite for a complex SoC is often more difficult than the hardware itself, due to the limited observability of the internal signals of the chip, and the development of a suite often involves developing ad hoc tools, such as *assembler generators* for processor cores. Companies routinely spend more than 60% of SoC development time and resources in verification.

The nature of processor-based SoC designs implies a tight cooperation between hardware and software teams. The debugging strategy must be an integral component of the overall architecture, and one that engages tools, compilers, and system firmware. Hardware, software, and test engineers once had little need to interact on a daily basis. Successful SoC designs involve cross-functional teams and call for participation of groups with very diverse expertise and working habits.

Effects of SoC on the Business Model

When systems were assembled through a collection of off-the-shelf discrete VLSI components, the optimized implementation and the volume of each component were the dominant aspects of the business model. The success of a given component (such as a microprocessor) was proportional to the cumulative volume of parts for all designs that used it. As the volume grew and successive generations appeared, semiconductor companies could slowly tune the process and tweak the design to produce better, faster, and cheaper parts. This was, for example, part of the recipe of the success of Intel (with the x86 general-purpose family) or TI (with the C54x DSP family and its ancestors).

In such an environment, attempting to introduce a new instruction set, or even a new hardware implementation for an existing instruction set was an almost impossible task. New designs require time to mature. The first implementation of a new design is usually much behind the design of a component that has already seen a few generations of predecessors. Design teams learn from previous mistakes, and VLSI manufacturing processes can be tuned to optimize the production of a given component in high volumes.

With the advent of SoC, the silicon itself is produced as a platform for a single use. In other words, different products will always use a different piece of silicon than other products (and often even ancestors in the same product line). Once the economic trade-offs mandate making new silicon for each generation, designers can change to a mode that makes modifications with each successive generation.

This is a major paradigm shift for the silicon manufacturing industry, in that it allows changes to a microprocessor that is part of an SoC design with different effects from similar changes to a standalone microprocessor (where such changes would be devastating to the yield and NRE costs of the design). In this scenario, *customization* becomes a much more practical thing to consider, and part of the balance of the value of a processor shifts from physical implementation and volumes to its intrinsic intellectual property value.

For these reasons, SoC techniques also complicate accounting for the various parts of the system. It used to be easier to identify volume, revenue, and market trends for microprocessors, microcontrollers, and DSPs implemented as discrete components. *Super-integration* (integration of a processor core together with dedicated logic in a single application-specific SoC) makes this task virtually unachievable. For example, in many cases, what CPU core is used in a complex SoC is proprietary information not available to analysts. Even concerning revenue figures, it is difficult to understand the relative contribution and value added of a processor core within a larger system. The typical problem is: how can we break down the cost of a highly integrated $20 SoC component? We could consider, for example, a contribution of the CPU core to be $5 based on silicon area, but then we would need to add the value of the intellectual property of the core itself; and quantifying this is even more challenging. In other words, a precise partitioning is practically impossible.

Centers of Embedded Design

A similar effect has changed the center of design of many embedded systems, and particularly those built on SoC technology. Consider the relationship between the manufacturer of a product using embedded processing (for example, a cellular phone) and the manufacturer of the electronic platform for that product. Before SoC, the electronic platform was a board containing several different critical components. Some of these were quite specialized computational components. This IP either came from outside suppliers or was supplied by the product manufacturer itself and was integrated into the electronic platform by a lower level supplier, not necessarily at all skilled in the application area of the product manufacturer.

Now that SoC has entered the picture, the IP itself has to be integrated much more carefully into the SoC, and IP has to fit the constraints of the system. Typically, the manufacturer of the product does not have all the skills necessary to specify and produce an SoC. Now it is much more likely to be the supplier of SoCs who is the focal point of the design. Many of the SoC suppliers have specialized in gathering large libraries of IP blocks that fit their systems in several different application areas, as described in Section 1.4.2. The gathered critical mass of IP plus SoC expertise makes it more attractive for a product manufacturer to outsource the entire electronic platform (consisting largely of the SoC itself). This in turn makes it economically viable for the SoC vendor to amass not only IP but application expertise in the given application area. In a world dominated by ASIC designs and awkward DSP programming, a large investment in the ability to manage complex systems built of highly specialized devices can be very valuable. This investment can be leveraged against many customers of the SoC manufacturer. Thus, SoC vendors are becoming centers of embedded design.

Although this trend will undoubtedly continue to an extent, we believe it will become less of a factor once processor cores containing greater amounts of ILP become available. Greater amounts of ILP will enable more and more IP in the form of programs written in high-level languages, and manufacturers of products using that IP will have greater freedom to control their own destinies, rather than purchasing the most important parts from third parties (in that it is far easier to fit a piece of code into an application than an IP block into an SoC). As this trend continues, it will be easy for product manufacturers to specify SoCs containing powerful processors and standard peripheral IP blocks, without relying so greatly on the SoC manufacturer to supply the IP that is core to the product manufacturer's business. In the face of the opportunity to own the most critical IP in their own business, product manufacturers are likely to welcome this model.

1.4.8 The Future of Embedded Systems

Pundits and futurists are almost always wrong. In this section of the book, we make ridiculous future predictions. Undoubtedly, we will be off the mark in major and minor ways. What might be useful is if any of this discussion stimulates thought or discussion about what the future might look like. We can't exactly predict the future, but understanding what is likely makes it more likely we will live in a future we want to live in.

We have already discussed how the world is moving to multiple computing devices per person. For all but a few applications, processing power will cease to be an issue. Already, today's personal computers offer more processing power than the average user can employ. Cost-effective performance will be much more important than absolute performance. Most people commute in Hondas, not Ferraris. In addition, connectivity, administration, and state will become increasingly important. Today's solutions for these issues are frustratingly inadequate.

Connectivity: Always-on Infrastructure

Embedded devices are increasingly connected, and this makes them fundamentally different from standalone devices. Connectivity enables new applications. For example, a connected device can order its own service (e.g., the latest copiers) or report its own status (e.g., automotive accident-notification systems such as General Motors' OnStar). Connectivity enhances value through network effects. For example, a remote-controllable stereo component adds its utility to all rooms in a multiroom sound system; remote-less components work only in one place.

Obviously, connectivity will get better. Both wired and wireless solutions are spreading throughout the modern world. Bandwidth, latency, and wireless coverage are all expected to improve. In twenty years, no one will say, "I can't get a signal," even in the most remote parts of the world. Networking costs will drop so low that virtually all electronic devices will export some sort of networked interface. How these interfaces end up being used remains to be seen.

The downside of connectivity is that formerly simple components now participate in a complex system. Continuing the stereo analogy, no one has found a good solution to the "pile of remotes" problem, that is, the more components one adds the more different buttons in different places one has to push. Systems allow complex and mysterious failure modes. Engineers beware.

State: Personal Storage

Technology trends are making storage cheaper, physically smaller, and informatically more capacious. New storage technologies are changing the shapes and constraints on various devices. Flash memory today allows tiny MP3 players, flash and micro-drives make CCD devices into attractive alternatives to film cameras, and computing devices such as laptops and palmtops now have storage capacities comparable to desktop machines.

State and connectivity interact in complex ways. In some ways, one compensates for the other. For example, laptop users can carry their entire computing environment without needing to connect with the office, and web browsers are connected to a remote state larger than any single machine could hold. In other ways, connectivity and state work together. HotSync is the feature that made Palm connected organizers successful. Previous organizers had poor backup (or no backup) and no way to transfer state to other devices.

Proliferation of storage also has its downside: every device with state is its own sovereign world. In a world with multiple devices, managing and keeping state up to date can be very complex. Already users need to worry about where copies of files live: on the office network, the home machine, or the laptop. A world with tens or hundreds of devices per person could become unmanageably complex. Maintaining consistency across many devices and performing backups (at all) will remain difficult and expensive problems to solve.

Administration

Storage proliferation is one example of an administrative problem. More generally, smart, connected devices need to be set up to work, and they may need to be reconfigured to continue working. Viable consumer devices can't be like personal computers; they need to work with a minimum of user "futzing."

Better and cleaner user interfaces will also need to be designed, to match the needs of future connected, multiple-device environments. Today's pile of remote controls is indicative of a difficult systems problem waiting to be solved. Tomorrow's personal network of devices will become incredibly frustrating without a move toward simpler, consistent interfaces.

Security

Although security is *au courant* as this book goes to press, we predict that the major *technical* security-related problems will be solved adequately, if not elegantly, for all practical purposes within a decade. The major technical issues are *authentication* (determining that the person with whom you are communicating is who they say they are), *encryption* (preventing eavesdroppers on a communication) and *trust* (establishing to what extent you trust the other party). The major societal issues associated with computer security (what to deploy, and where) will be hashed out in the marketplace and the political sphere, for which we claim no expertise.

The Next Generation

What comes after the embedded computing generation? It's difficult to guess, although it's safe to say that it will involve even more computers and communication than anything we can imagine today. Researchers and science fiction writers have already proposed "smart dust," whereby dust-sized particles would compute and communicate with their neighbors to make a compute-rich physical environment. A world full of smart dust obsoletes the traditional boundaries between public and private spaces. Perhaps more transformative is the fact that an entire person's life will soon be recordable in a variety of media on a single hard disk. If e-mail lasts forever today, might casual utterances or momentary indiscretions be recorded forever tomorrow? Or on the optimistic side, might we never forget or lose anything in the future?

Another source of the "next wave" might be an unexpected advance in a nontraditional area near computing. MEMS (micro-electrical mechanical systems) have shown promising applications in airbag motion sensors and in "light-processing" devices for video projectors, but have not broken open into a diverse field with many applications. At an even smaller scale, nanotechnology holds up the promise that we will manipulate single atoms with the same dexterity we manipulate single bits today. Alternate computing technologies, such as biological computing and quantum computing, might become practical through the construction of a breakthrough device, fueling another exponential growth curve along the lines of Moore's law.

The most interesting cause of the next wave might be the long-anticipated end of Moore's law. We observe wryly that *no one* has gotten rich by successfully predicting the end of Moore's law, but those who have profited handsomely from its continuation (notably the SIA and Intel) are now among those anticipating its demise. Fundamental physical limits, such as the number of atoms required to form an insulating layer, are on the horizon, if not on the doorstep.

A world without Moore's law would be very interesting indeed. With a maximum achievable areal transistor density, research and development funding would reinvigorate areas such as distributed systems, parallel machine design, and 3D transistor fabrication. Software would change significantly, too, as the headroom for code bloat would disappear.

We'll stop speculating now, and return to today's world, with the marvels we already know how to construct.

1.5   Further Reading

It is not easy to capture the entire field of embedded systems in a concise list of references, because the breadth of topics ranges from architecture to components and systems, from programming guidelines to compilers, tools, and application-specific knowledge.

There are very few good attempts at defining the term *embedded*. For a definition of embedded computers as systems that must interface with the real world, see Lee [2002]. A better sense can be found by reading trade magazines and web sites that track the embedded marketplace. We recommend *Embedded Processor Watch* (*http://www.mdronline.com/publications/e-watch.html*), *Design and Reuse* (*http://www.design-reuse.com*), *EE Times* (*http://www.eet.com*), and *Embedded.com* (*http://www.embedded.com*). Embedded Processor Watch focuses mostly on processor chips and cores, whereas the others are good starting points for understanding embedded systems and SoCs. (Since URLs are always changing, please see the book's website, *http://www.vliw.org/book* for a page of references to current information.) An interesting reference is also the recent *Embedded System Dictionary* by Ganssle and Barr [2003], covering a few thousand words and definitions of the embedded system universe.

Everything starts with the underlying silicon technology. For decades, the Semiconductor Industry Association (SIA) has provided self-fulfilling prophecies (called "roadmaps") of the future size and speed of transistors. Their site is found at *http://www.sia-online.org*.

Chinnery and Keutzer [2002] investigate the differences in speed between application-specific integrated circuits and custom integrated circuits when each are implemented in the same process technology. The book attempts to account for the elements that make the respective performances different, and then examines ways in which tools and methodologies may close the performance gap between application-specific integrated circuits and custom circuits.

Todd and McNelly's [2001] technical report is a good general introduction to SoC design. For a good overview of component-based design, the book by Wolf [2000] provides the foundations as well as some real practical examples, centered on the use of UML for embedded system modeling. Another textbook by Wolf [2002] provides a similar introduction to many aspects of SoC design. The book by Barr [1999] is a general introduction that focuses on development and compilation aspects, targeting readers that have some familiarity with C and C++. Barr [2003] also provides an extensive online "Embedded System Bibliography," which is regularly updated with new book and journal reviews. The books by Simon [1999] and Moore, Grehan, and Cyliax [Grehan et al., 1998] also cover real-time OS aspects of embedded systems.

Embedded computing turns up in unexpected places. The "top 500 list" of supercomputers, maintained at *http://www.top500.org*, recently included a "supercomputer" built from Sony Playstation 2 processors. That project is documented at *http://arrakis.ncsa.uiuc.edu/ps2*. The Linux port to the Playstation 2 further confirms the blurring of boundaries between general-purpose and embedded. That community's web site is found at *http://playstation2-linux.com*. Putting the shoe on the other foot, MAME (the Multiple Arcade Machine Emulator) can be found at *http://www.mame.net/*. MAME is a software emulator for a wide variety of console arcade games (those that require quarters to operate) that run on modern PCs. Using MAME involves copyright issues. That is, the content of the ROMs of the original arcade games is required to emulate a game.

For background on digital signal processors, BDTI (Berkeley Design Technology, Inc.) publishes the "comp.dsp" meta-list of books on DSP at *http://www.bdti.com/faq/1.htm*. Orfanidis's *Introduction to Signal Processing* [Orfanidis, 1995] gives an accessible introduction to the topic, whereas the definitive reference on the topic remains Oppenheim and Schafer's *Digital Signal Processing* [Oppenheim and Schafer, 1975]. As usual, manufacturers' web sites are the best sources for up-to-date information. Texas Instruments' site is *http://dspvillage.ti.com*, Analog Devices' site is *http://www.analogdevices.com/processors*, and the DSP Group's site is *http://www.dspg.com*.

For more details on embedded applications, see our own "Further Reading" section in Chapter 11.

For a deeper dive into hardware design for embedded systems and ASICs, the book by Thomas and Moorby [1998] is the reference for the Verilog programming language, and the book by Ashenden [1995] is the counterpart for VHDL. The description by Balarin et al. [1999] of the POLIS academic tool for the synthesis of automotive controllers is a good place to start to understand some of the commercial synthesis tools, such as Cadence VCC (which was heavily inspired by POLIS itself).

On system modeling, and in particular the use of Petri nets in embedded, good reads are the initial parts of the book by Thoen and Catthoor [2000], as well as the work of Gajski et al. [1994, 2000], both of which also cover hardware/software co-design aspects. For a better understanding of real-time issues (scheduling, OS implications, prediction of execution time), the book by Shaw [2001] provides in-depth theory and practical examples.

On embedded software, it is much more difficult to find books that are not completely out of date, because of the speed in which the sector changes. A couple worth mentioning are the book on debugging embedded software (a rather challenging endeavor), and the book on the interfacing of embedded systems to the analog sensors that make them talk to the external world, by Ball [1998, 2001].

Finally, this chapter also skirts some areas at the intersection between computer science, business practices, society, and economics. Schumpeter was the first to explore the interaction between monopoly and innovation in his book *Capitalism, Socialism, and Democracy*. Another excellent source on this topic is Freeman and Soete's *The Economics of Industrial Innovation*, which also has extensive references. For the specifics of the PC marketplace (and the alliance between Intel and Microsoft that is pejoratively known as "*Wintel*"), see Nick Economides' web pages (*http://www.stern.nyu.edu/networks/site.html*) for the pro-Wintel argument, and Rebecca Henderson's [Henderson, 2004] testimony in the Microsoft antitrust trial for the anti-Wintel argument.

1.6 Exercises

1. On a scale of 1 to 5, where 1 is general-purpose and 5 is embedded, rate the following devices: laptop computers, palmtops, web TVs, game consoles, cellular phones, java-enabled phones, printers, desktop computers, servers, mainframes, calculator watches, set-top boxes, Internet kiosks, and antilock brake systems. For each device rated 3, justify your answer.

2. On a scale of 1 to 5, where 1 is general-purpose and 5 is embedded, rate the following processors: Itanium, x86, 80286-embedded, 68030, 68K-series (Coldfire, DragonBall), PPC-G4, PPC-405, StrongARM, XScale, Transmeta Crusoe, C54x, C60x, TriMedia, HP/ST Lx(ST200), MIPS 5400, and I/O chips.

3. In general-purpose devices, upgradeability is sometimes accomplished by reinstalling the software on your hard disk. Describe other ways in which embedded devices might support upgradeability.

4. Why is backward compatibility less important in an embedded device than in a general-purpose device? In what ways might it still be important?

5. What was the last ISA that appeared (and when) with all of the following properties: it was incompatible with all existing ISAs, it was put forward by a company that was not yet a major force in the computing industry, and it made a major dent in the general-purpose computing market? What about in the embedded computing market?

6. As a rule of thumb, a $99 appliance implies that the cost of electronics is about $5. Using whatever resources seem appropriate, estimate how much processing power (in MIPS) and memory (in Bytes) was available for $5 in the years 1980, 1990, and 2000. Predict what will be available in 2010.

7. Using whatever resources seem appropriate, draw a graph that plots the energy efficiency of the most popular general-purpose and embedded processors (five each) in peak mW/MIPS. Do the same for cost performance in MIPS/$.

8. Using Table 1.1, compute the fraction of a typical SoC design occupied by a 100K gate CPU core in each technology generation. Extrapolate to the years 2005 and 2010.

9. List three distinguishing features of digital signal processors (DSPs).

10. Diagram the pipeline of the printer described in the text, with data/computation rates on the edges and blocks. Do the same for a digital camera.

11. Describe the data bandwidth associated with each stage of printing an 11 × 8.5-inch page at 600 dpi on a color inkjet printer. The stages are JPEG decompression, rescaling to printer resolution, and dithering. Assume that the page contains one 7 × 10-inch JPEG image with 1600 × 1200 resolution, that the printer produces four pages per minute, and that the JPEG algorithm compresses at approximately 10:1. If each stage takes about the same amount of time, calculate the bandwidth through the cable going to the printer, the bandwidth through memory after decompression, the bandwidth required to move the image after scaling, and the bandwidth to the print heads after dithering.

12. Next-generation (3G) cellular phone systems claim a peak bandwidth per user of 2 Mbps. A typical metropolitan area of 1 million people is served by a network of about 200 cells, each of which can carry 48 calls at a time. What is the maximum number of minutes per day per person of data traffic, on average, such a network can support? What is the peak bandwidth of the entire metropolitan area network? Do you believe that wireless data transport will replace wired broadband connections during your lifetime?

13. Research how modems find the bit rate of the underlying voice line and use the underlying digital connection to reach data rates as high as 56 Kbps.

Explain why you can only get 56.6 Kbps instead of 64 Kbps from the modem. Draw a diagram of the system, and estimate the processing power required by the endpoint modems to "second-guess" the underlying telephone network.

14. Consider a 2M-pixel digital camera with 24 bits per pixel, 8 Mbytes of memory, and a 128-Mbyte flash card. Assuming computation is instantaneous, with a 10-ns word-addressed memory, how many pictures per minute can you take, and after how many pictures does the camera stop to write the pictures to flash? How does this change for a 3M-pixel digital camera with all of the other parameters held constant?

15. Take a digital photograph of your choice. Using JPEG manipulation software, compress the photograph minimally and maximally. Print out the results, and compare the results visually. Can you find any JPEG artifacts? If so, describe them. How big are the resulting images?

16. Suppose you had to store 400 pictures in 128 Mbytes of flash memory. Experiment with various tradeoffs of compression level and reduced picture resolution through rescaling. In your visual opinion, would you be better off using a 3M-pixel camera and more compression or a 2M-pixel camera and less compression? Which resolution and compression combination would you use?

17. Mercedes-Benz claims that the active suspension components in its newest vehicles analyze and respond to road conditions on average every 2.5 cm at 100 kilometers per hour (1 inch of highway travel at 60 mph). How many decisions per second is this? If the microcontroller runs at 25 MHz, how many operations can be processed per decision?

18. Pick a non-GNU program with source code available. Port it to a different platform, with at least a different operating system and compiler. How many source changes (including makefiles) were necessary to make the program work? What fraction of the lines of code of the program is this? How long did it take you to perform the port? Comment on the likely usefulness and impact on productivity of different levels of compatibility: feature, source, and tool.

19. Assume that masks cost $300K, and that in ASIC technology each part of a custom design costs $8.50. If you can implement the same circuit at the same speed on an FPGA that costs $70 per part, what is the break-even volume for switching over? Chart the two curves.

20. Suppose that design time for an ASIC is on the critical path to shipping a product, and that each month of delay to market has an opportunity cost of $XXX in revenue. Assume ASICs add six months to the time-to-market. Calculate the cost and revenues (as a function of volumes per month) of the ASIC-only approach, the FPGA-only approach, and the hybrid approach that initially deploys FPGAs and then switches over to ASICs later in the

production run. Repeat the exercise for XXX = $100K, XXX = $1M, XXX = $10M, and comment on the results.

21. In 2002, the Pentium 4 reached clock rates of 2.4 GHz, whereas Xscale reached only 400 MHz. They are implemented in the same silicon process, by the same company. Explain the differences between these figures (hint: consider yield, design team size, cost, design maturity, synthesizability versus full-custom design, profitability, target market, global warming, tectonic stability of fabs, and so on).

22. Consider a processor core that sells for $10. Assuming that the cost of an engineer/year (EY) is $200,000, how many parts do you have to sell in five years to pay for the cost of a five-person engineering team that takes 18 months to develop the processor core? A ten-person engineering team? Assume a sales and marketing overhead of 27% of the sales cost, a build cost of $3.50 per part, and ignore the time value of money.

2

An Overview of VLIW and ILP

A fanatic is one who can't change his mind and won't change the subject.

—[attributed to] Sir Winston S. Churchill, 1874–1965, *British Prime Minister* [1941–1945, 1951–1955]

Computer systems are said to embody instruction-level parallelism (ILP) when programs running on them go faster because multiple operations (such as adds, multiplies, and loads) execute at the same time, even though only a single stream of execution was presented to the system. Being an architectural technique, it is largely independent of improvements in hardware technology, such as circuit speed and power reduction.

ILP can have a significant effect on performance, and thus its use has become the norm in processors designed for desktop and server use. Because performance is critical in embedded systems as well, ILP is becoming more prevalent now that circuit density is becoming sufficient to use it. Additionally, ILP can offer the designer of embedded systems an important form of power saving. A designer of portable embedded systems may use ILP to increase performance beyond that required by the system, and then give back some or all of the extra performance by slowing the clock. Since reducing clock cycle time is one of the most effective ways to reduce power usage, this can have a significant effect on total consumption. And because power consumption is usually critical in portable embedded system design, ILP may assume an even greater role there than it has in larger systems, for which power consumption is less important.

When a system offers ILP, its speedup gains are largely transparent to users, requiring little (if any) change in source programs. The opposite is usually true of systems that speed up programs by running multiple streams of execution in parallel. A processor using ILP has the same type of execution hardware as a normal RISC machine. In the case of a processor using ILP, however, the expected hardware may operate in parallel, or there may be more of that same execution hardware, or a greater variety of hardware, thus enabling more parallelism. Sometimes additional hardware is used to arrange the parallel operations while the program runs; other times programs are presented to the hardware with the parallelism already arranged and specified in the programs.

This chapter has five sections. The first section explores the semantics of how programs execute on a machine, with particular focus on parallelism and sequentiality. Section 2.2, "Design philosophies," introduces the concept of an architectural design philosophy, of which VLIW is one example. Section 2.3, "Role of the compiler" describes the high-level structure of a modern optimizing compiler and the role it plays in extracting performance. Section 2.4, "VLIW in the embedded and DSP domains," describes how VLIW and the embedded domain are well suited to each other. This chapter also contains the section "Historical Perspective and Further Reading" (Section 2.5), which discusses the origins and evolution of VLIW.

2.1   Semantics and Parallelism

This section begins with "standard" sequential semantics, and then explores variations on the theme of using parallelism. Most of these forms of parallelism examine the relationship between instructions in improving performance, but we also discuss thread-level and loop-level parallelism as part of this section.

2.1.1   Baseline: Sequential Program Semantics

A typical RISC processor tries to issue an operation every clock cycle. In the slowest designs, processors wait until the previous operation is completed before issuing the next, and execute every operation in the order in which the code was written or produced by a compiler. Human programmers often think of the programs they read or write as operating that way, and we say that the program we hand to the computer, or to a compiler, has "sequential semantics." In practice, a computer designed to operate this way would not be expected to issue an operation every cycle or even come that close to it, since some operations will have a latency longer than one cycle, and branches will interrupt the expected flow of control.

A rough measure of the ILP attained when a program executes is *instructions per cycle* (or IPC). It is simply the number of operations performed per cycle of execution. In a processor that has strict sequential semantics, one might expect to see an IPC of about 0.3 or less, depending on the instruction mix, the memory latency, and various similar factors.

To illustrate sequential semantics, consider the snippet of code labeled "Sequential VEX" in Figure 2.1. It is written in the machine language VEX (for VLIW Example), the processor-level language we will use for our low-level code examples. Appendix A, "The VEX System" is a full reference to the language VEX. Although we will incorporate ILP into VEX shortly, we will ignore that for now and use VEX to illustrate simple sequential semantics. Because there are 18 VEX operations taking 33 cycles to execute, the IPC of this simple system is only 0.55.

IPC or CPI?

In this book we use IPC to characterize the execution efficiency of a processor when running a given program. Although both IPC and CPI are used, the computer design literature more commonly refers to the reciprocal of IPC; namely, cycles per instruction (CPI). This was more common in the period before ILP became pervasive because getting to where a processor could perform an operation every cycle was the "Holy Grail." Manufacturers bragged about achieving it, and researchers studied the quest for a CPI of only 1 (especially Douglas Clark at DEC and his colleagues, and particularly the classic paper by Emer [1984]). In practice, the CPIs one saw were well above 1, and speaking of CPIs in that range was more satisfying and intuitive than talking about small fractions. Now the situation is reversed. We will see that due to ILP, IPCs about or considerably above 1 are common and are the more interesting quantities. We believe that given the pervasiveness of ILP the computer architecture community will eventually settle on IPC.

In the terminology used in this book, we refer to "operations," not the badly overloaded term *instructions*, as the fundamental things being counted for CPI (see Table 3.3). However, we will stick with using the term *instruction* as part of the acronym IPC, since that term has such wide use in computer science.

2.1.2 Pipelined Execution, Overlapped Execution, and Multiple Execution Units

In practice, operation execution in any modern processor, especially if it embodies ILP, is significantly more complex than the model shown in Figure 2.1, and these complexities play a large role in ILP and in performance considerations in general. First, operations are subdivided into execution stages within a single machine cycle; second, longer-than-one-cycle operations are often divided into stages of one cycle apiece; third, operations often can be overlapped, or even issued together, because they use completely disjoint hardware functional units; and, fourth, aspects of the flow of control of operations often cause timing changes that are important for ILP. For now, we will not discuss the first factor: the execution stages of an operation. They appear in the processor's microarchitecture and are discussed in detail in Chapter 5. They are not visible in VEX listings (which capture the "instruction-set architecture" level of the processor). It is worth noting that the following discussion of pipelining involves concepts similar to the execution-stage concepts discussed later.

Some operations that take longer than one machine cycle to execute use hardware resources exclusively, preventing other operations that would use those same resources from executing until the first operation has completed. Other times, an operation is *pipelined*; that is, a later operation can share some or all of the resources the first operation (still "in flight") used in previous cycles. When this happens, we also say that the shared hardware is pipelined, and the entire process is called pipelining. Thus, pipelining offers us the ability to overlap parts of operations that use the same execution

What it implements:

```
    ⋮
if (B0 == 0)  break;
j = j + (A0-B0) ;
if (B1 == 0)  break;
j = j + (A1-B1);
if (B2 == 0)  break;
j = j + (A2-B2);
    ⋮
```

To implement these two lines, on the default VEX
system we have to do the following:

— Load B0 (3 cycles)
— Compute the condition (2 cycles before use)
— Test the condition and branch if true
— Load A0 (3 cycles)
— Subtract B0 from A0
— Accumulate in J the result of the subtraction

This requires 11 cycles, and thus all six lines
require a total of 33 cycles, as indicated at right.

Sequential VEX (33 cycles):

```
ldw   $r20 = 0[$r10]
nop
nop
cmpeq  $b0 = $r20, 0
nop
br $b0, DONE
ldw $r23 = 0[$r13]
nop
nop
sub $r23 = $r23, $r20
add $r4 = $r4, $r23
ldw $r21 = 0[$r11]
nop
nop
cmpeq  $b1 = $r21, 0
nop
br   $b1, DONE
ldw $r24 = 0[$r14]
nop
nop
sub $r24 = $r24, $r21
add $r4 = $r4, $r24
ldw $r22 = 0[$r12]
nop
nop
cmpeq  $r2 = $r22, 0
nop
br $b2, DONE
ldw $r25 = 0[$r15]
nop
nop
sub $r25 = $r25, $r22
add $r4 = $r4, $r25
```

FIGURE 2.1 VEX example. This "snippet" of six lines of C would be executed in 33 cycles
by a VEX CPU that overlapped nothing whatsoever. The snippet of code might appear within
an unrolled loop, where the original loop the compiler unrolled was:

```
while (B[++i] != 0) j=j+(A[i] - B[i]);
```

The variables A0, A1, A2, B0, B1, and B2 are precomputed locations containing what had
been array references in the original loop (A[i], A[i+1],...B[i+2]); these are precomputed
in order to remove a sequential data dependence that would slow down their access once we
consider ILP (as we will soon). When the snippet is encountered, the following register
assignments are in place: B0 through B2's addresses are r10–r12; A0 through A2's addresses
are r13–r15; and j is found in r4, and remains there after the snippet. We are assuming a
single-cluster VEX system, and so for clarity the cluster modifiers (see Appendix A) are not
written in the sequential VEX code.

hardware, at least partially. The usual analogy is to a factory floor assembly line, in which
a product advances down the line having different things done to it at each station of
the assembly line. Each station does not have to wait until the object being processed
completely finishes before contributing to the process again. In a processor, hardware

that carries out a 32-bit integer multiply in two cycles can be built in such a way that a new multiply operation can be started each cycle, with the result always popping out of the pipeline two cycles later. The hardware used for the first half of the operation is completely freed up after one cycle and may be used for the next relevant operation on the very next cycle.

Pipelining speeds up programs by allowing parts of the execution of that program to occur in parallel in a way that goes beyond the most simple-minded view of what the program does, and the resulting speedup is a form of ILP. However, when people think of ILP they tend to think of two other factors that speed up programs: *multiple issue* and *extra functional units*. Both of these typically allow different operations to overlap their execution on disjoint functional units. If a three-cycle floating-point add is issued, for example, a following one-cycle integer add could be started in the very same cycle, rather than waiting for the floating-point operation to finish. (We will ignore until Chapter 5 details involving a potential clash of such operations in other parts of the datapath, such as when their results are written in a register bank.) Similarly, the hardware may contain extra functional units. This could allow operations that otherwise would have shared hardware resources to be executed in parallel. When there are extra functional units, often processors are designed to issue multiple operations at once. It is common, for example, for systems featuring ILP to be able to issue more than one integer add per cycle, each dispatched to its own integer-add functional unit, which in turn can use a path to the register bank that is disjoint from any other operation's path.

Thus, we can identify several aspects of a processor's hardware that enable ILP:

1. Different multicycle operations may share the same hardware by using different parts of it in different cycles. This allows different operations to be "in flight" at the same time. (For example, some multicycle floating-point functional units can issue a new operation every cycle. Another example is shown in Figure 2.2, where we issue a memory operation in each of the first six cycles.)

2. Operations may be executed using different parts of the execution hardware found in the processor. (For example, a multicycle floating-point operation or a multicycle memory operation may overlap with an integer add. Another example is shown in Figure 2.2, where we issue a load, a compare, and a branch in cycle 6.)

3. More than one operation might be issued in a given cycle. (For example, one commercial VLIW processor, the Multiflow TRACE [Lowney 1993], could issue 28 operations in each cycle. The system shown in Figure 2.2 can issue four operations in each cycle.)

4. New or replicated functional units may be added, allowing different operations to be overlapped. (For example, a processor might have two integer-add functional units, as it does in Figure 2.2, where we perform both an addition and a subtraction, requiring two integer functional units, identical in this case.)

In Figure 2.2(a), we see that the code snippet, which took 33 cycles to execute on the most sequential-possible system, can be executed on this modest VLIW in 10 cycles. This is a 3.3x speedup over that simple system, yielding an IPC of 1.8 (since there were 18

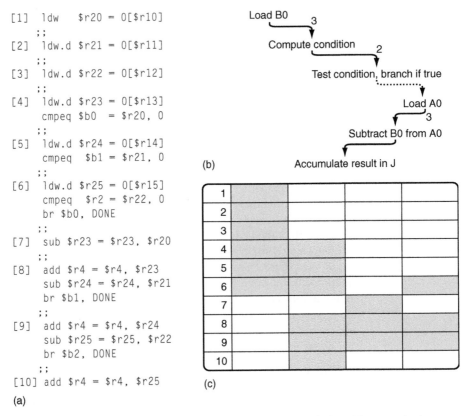

```
[1]  ldw    $r20 = 0[$r10]
     ;;
[2]  ldw.d  $r21 = 0[$r11]
     ;;
[3]  ldw.d  $r22 = 0[$r12]
     ;;
[4]  ldw.d  $r23 = 0[$r13]
     cmpeq  $b0  = $r20, 0
     ;;
[5]  ldw.d  $r24 = 0[$r14]
     cmpeq  $b1  = $r21, 0
     ;;
[6]  ldw.d  $r25 = 0[$r15]
     cmpeq  $r2  = $r22, 0
     br $b0, DONE
     ;;
[7]  sub $r23 = $r23, $r20
     ;;
[8]  add $r4  = $r4, $r23
     sub $r24 = $r24, $r21
     br $b1, DONE
     ;;
[9]  add $r4  = $r4, $r24
     sub $r25 = $r25, $r22
     br $b2, DONE
     ;;
[10] add $r4  = $r4, $r25
```

(a)

(b)

Load B0

Compute condition   2

Test condition, branch if true

Load A0   3

Subtract B0 from A0

Accumulate result in J

(c)

FIGURE 2.2 A compacted snippet. In (a), the "snippet" of code from Figure 2.1 is shown scheduled for the VEX default system (see Appendix A). This system, which has 64 general-purpose 32-bit registers (GRs) and eight 1-bit branch registers (BRs), can issue up to four operations in each cycle. However, it cannot issue more than one memory operation at a time. In (b) we see a data-dependence graph (or *DAG*, for *directed acyclic graph*) representing one iteration of the loop. The numbers on the edges are the latencies of the dependence. The dotted edge represents a control dependence, and the solid lines represent data dependences. The diagram in (c) is a way of representing the program that gives the system designers a way to visually get a sense of the ILP being extracted (it corresponds to the snippet, but is not as detailed as would be those which come from the VEX tool that produces these).

original operations). This speedup derives from all of the factors described previously, and from scheduling past branches (as described in the following).

A complexity very important to ILP occurs when programs branch. Typically, processors are built in such a way that the operation that follows an untaken branch operation can be executed in the next instruction cycle. When a branch is taken, however, a break in the execution of the pipeline occurs that results in a delay while the processor prepares to execute the correct next operation. That break is referred to as a "bubble in the pipeline," and typically ranges from two to as many as 15 or 20 cycles.

ILP can often be enhanced if program execution is rearranged in such a way that the branch direction is determined earlier than it was in the original sequential semantics. The enhancement occurs because the operations that used to be immediately before the branch are now after it, and must be executed either way the branch goes. We thus could perform these operations during the "bubble." Some processors are built to allow this form of ILP, referred to as *filling the delay slot* or *filling the pipeline bubble*.

Pipelining and filling delay slots are techniques not often classified as ILP, since they are commonly used in RISC processors to try to bring the IPC up to 1 (the "Holy Grail" of RISC processor architectures), and because many people picture ILP in terms of multiple issue. However, these techniques fit the definition and spirit of ILP, and we regard them as such. Nevertheless, it is only after we add multiple issue that we can obtain IPCs in excess of one, the expectation for processors offering ILP.

2.1.3 Dependence and Program Rearrangement

Hardware manufacturers have repeatedly built processors that offered ILP in the form of pipelining, delay-slot filling, and more recently multiple-issue and replicated functional units. At first, it was common for these processors to be disappointing in the IPC they attained. The problem was related to a factor that must be considered when operations are overlapped; namely, "operation dependence." Operation dependence refers to the fact that sometimes an operation cannot be issued until a previous operation has completed. If one executes using the simplest sequential semantics, there is no problem. However, if you overlap operations there is the chance an operation you would like to issue next cannot be issued because a previous operation is not finished and, for example, the data it produces is required for the operation you would like to issue. In this case we refer to the operation dependence as *data dependence*. Usually, when an operation cannot be issued because of data dependence there are independent operations later on that could be issued immediately, if only the hardware were offered an opportunity to do so. To solve this problem, programs must (while running or earlier) be rearranged from their original sequence of execution but still give the same results as the original program. Without such rearrangements, we cannot expect IPCs much above 1.

A second form of operation dependence occurs when we would like to issue an operation when a prior branch has not resolved. In that case, the limitation occurs because not knowing which direction the branch will take means we cannot be sure whether it would be correct to issue the operation we would like to issue. We refer to this as *control dependence*.

Because operation dependence is such a major limiter of IPC, much of the research and development effort in ILP has been devoted to methods of rearranging programs so that more operations can be issued per cycle, but with the same results as would have been obtained following sequential semantics. Where and when these rearrangements are done — whether in hardware as the program runs or in software either in advance or as the program runs — are the major distinguishing characteristics among processor types and design styles. The effects of program rearrangements are quite subtle, and involve such factors as whether seemingly commutative operations are indeed commutative when implemented in hardware; what the state of a computation is, in terms of the original sequential semantics; when an interrupt occurs; and when the operation of the program is observed by a programmer using a source-level debugger.

However, as will be explained in detail as a running theme in this book, a great deal of ILP is enabled by our ability to move operations beyond control dependences, using the critical technologies of trace scheduling (and its successors) and software pipelining (see "Global Instruction Scheduling" later in this chapter, and Chapter 8 "Compiling for VLIWs and ILP"). These are both examples of *speculative* techniques, in which operations are executed before they would be under sequential semantics (and thus corrective measures are required to ensure program correctness). A related technique called *predication* also enhances scheduling freedom, by converting control dependences into data dependences. In an architecture that supports *full predication*, every operation includes an extra 1-bit "predicate" operand to guard the execution of the operation (the operation only takes effect if the predicate is true). As we discuss in Section 4.5.2, "Predication," there is also a poor-man's version of predication called *partial predication*. In an architecture that supports partial predication, we can use multiplexer-style operations (an operation called a *select* or a *conditional move*) to choose between two values to store as the result.

The snippet shown in Figure 2.2 is an example of code in which the ability to move operations above branches is critical in attaining ILP. We will see that there are problems with moving memory operations past control dependences, and in the scheduled snippet five of the loads become speculative and their opcodes change from ldw to ldw.d. Due to their speculative nature, they have each become *dismissable loads*; that is, a load for which an exception must receive special treatment because it is possible it would never have executed and raised the exception. (The history of the term *dismissable loads* is interesting. At Multiflow Computer, the VLIW pioneer first to use these loads in this form, they were called *dangerous loads* while the first computers were being developed. Once Multiflow had customers, it became obvious that a different term would be better, but the "d" was already immortalized in the opcode *dld*. Thus was born the term *dismissable*.)

2.1.4　ILP and Other Forms of Parallelism

ILP is often contrasted, and often confused, with other forms of processor parallelism. When these other forms of parallelism are effective, sometimes the parallelism they achieve lowers the ILP available, and sometimes the successful use of ILP lowers the parallelism available via these other methods. Others of these forms of parallelism tend to be relatively independent of ILP.

The most popular form of processor parallelism during the 1970s and 1980s was *vector processing*. A vector processor has dedicated hardware for long vectors. The instruction-set architectural view of a single machine-level vector operation is that it sets off a process whereby vector operands are operated upon as a whole. For example, a VECTOR ADD operation might bring two long streams of data in from memory, add them in pairwise fashion, and store the resulting long stream of sums in memory.

Vector operations are mixed with normal (scalar) operations in the code executed by the vector processor. When vector processors first appeared, these operations were usually placed there by a hand coder or a human user of vector library calls. By the end of the 1980s, however, compilers were doing a better job of this than humans, except for the most painstakingly handcrafted vector code. Vector processing was most popular in scientific simulations and in other domains in which long numerical vectors dominated, and remains popular in that environment.

Vector systems usually find parallelism that is also available via ILP. The ILP compiler techniques of software pipelining and loop unrolling work best on code that is vectorizable. Generally, vector hardware works better than ILP on very regular code containing long vectors, whereas ILP techniques and hardware tend to work better than vector processing when the structure of the code is somewhat more irregular, and when vectors are short. In addition, ILP offers the advantage that the same hardware can be used on the parts of code that are not vectorizable, whereas vector hardware is dedicated to vector use only.

Multiprocessing and *multithreading* are terms used inconsistently in computing. Both involve running different programs, or parts of programs, at the same time — either literally together on multiple processors or alternately stopping one to run the other for a period. Sometimes the motivation for multiprocessing is to allow more than one program to share a system, thus showing progress on several programs at once. Other times multiprocessing is used when there are multiple processors within a single computer system. When these techniques are used to speed up a single program, that program is divided into relatively independent (in the sense of needing little data communication among them) processes. These are then either run on separate processors in order to effect parallelism, or possibly swapped in and out of a single processor to hide the latency of a processor waiting for something (for example a fetch) to complete. Often, special processor hardware facilitates this. Usually, when people refer to multithreading they mean a system in which the independent processes, called threads, are very *lightweight* or are not very self-contained. They are usually small fragments of the computation having little state beyond the current state of the program they are part of. Thus, the cost of switching from one to another can be quite low, and the performance gain does not have much overhead to amortize. A technique called *simultaneous multithreading* (SMT) allows different threads to be active in the processor at the same time, often having their own private registers or hardware instruction register but sharing functional units and other hardware. This old idea (first appearing in the CDC-6600 peripheral hardware in the early 1960s) had a resurgence starting in the 1990s, and it is now used within the main CPU of some processors.

Like vector processing, these techniques sometimes share the parallelism available to ILP. When that happens, it is usually the case that the code being multiprocessed is also vectorizable, and all three techniques work, each to the exclusion of the others. Other times, these techniques find completely independent parallelism, and they and ILP may provide a multiplicative reduction in compute time.

Micro-SIMD (for "single instruction, multiple data") involves new operations that, although they operate on standard-sized architecture registers, treat each register as a collection of smaller pieces, and thus work on data that has word size shorter than the basic data size of the processor. These short pieces of data are grouped into single data words and then operated upon simultaneously by functional units specially built to do this. For example, a single 32-bit data word might really consist of four 8-bit data quantities, and micro-SIMD hardware might add two such words in a single cycle (performing, in effect, four operations in one). Most micro-SIMD parallelism is independent of ILP, and can be exploited in an ILP processor. We return to micro-SIMD instructions in later chapters, in particular in Section 4.1.4 and Section 5.4.1, where we discuss how micro-SIMD units are implemented.

2.2 Design Philosophies

In the short (25-year) history of VLIWs, there has been a lot of confusion about what class of "thing" a VLIW is. Is it "an architecture"? An "implementation technique"? Or "a machine"? These questions seemed confusing when VLIWs were first proposed, and the debates were not always so academic. Early investors in VLIW computer companies wanted to know what they were getting. Was there, for example, some form of intellectual property they would own that characterized all VLIWs? Similarly, even established computer companies doing deals with VLIW companies wanted to put boundaries around what was or was not part of the deal. Debates occurred with regularity about what exactly VLIW was. Even today, people debate whether the Intel IPF architecture,[1] the heir presumptive to the Pentium line, is or is not a VLIW. It is instructive to understand the answer to the question "What does it mean to say something is a VLIW?" Doing so will add clarity to many of the discussions that follow, and many of the concepts we describe are clearer when seen through the lens of this understanding.

So what is VLIW? Although VLIW is often referred to as an "architecture," it is most accurate to say that VLIW is an *architectural design philosophy* or a *design style*. A design philosophy is, in essence, an informal set of guidelines, principles, and common building blocks that distinguish one processor design from another. There is no easy litmus test that tells you whether a given processor was built following a given design philosophy, since this is rarely a black and white issue. However, people experienced in the field of computer architecture will agree on whether it was, and to what extent.

The concept of computer architecture design philosophies maps very well to the concept of building architecture design philosophies. For buildings, this is a well-known concept. See the book by Poppeliers and Chambers [1993]. For example, some buildings are described as following the Victorian design philosophy, whereas others might be following modernism, art deco, or gothic. And just as we refer to a house as a contemporary house, we say that a processor is a VLIW processor or just "a VLIW," all being

---

1. When we began writing this book, the 64-bit EPIC architecture developed by Intel and HP was still called IA-64 (for "Intel Architecture" with a 64-bit word length). The first commercial implementation of that architecture was dubbed "Itanium," and Intel has since renamed the architecture IPF, for "Itanium Processor Family."

What Does It Mean to "Invent" a Design Philosophy?

In writing a book of this nature, we often need to cite the source of a concept or piece of technology. In some instances that source is muddy or controversial. The RISC architecture style is an instance in which it is controversial. We have heard many debates on who invented RISC. A simple web search reveals:

- *"Cray also invented RISC, Reduced Instruction Set Computing, a technology that allows desktop computers to process tasks more quickly."* (From the CNN obituary of Seymour Cray dated October 5, 1996, referring to the design of the CDC-6600 or perhaps its predecessors.)
- *"I mean, there is no question that even though we invented RISC..."* (From a speech by Lou Gerstner, IBM CEO, February 14, 1996.)
- Other attributions to John Hennessy, John Cocke in 1979, earlier (1960s) IBM designs.

These debates are a perfect example of the difficulty of this sort of attribution. In this book, we cite David Patterson, and to a degree John Cocke and John Hennessy, as the inventors of RISC. However, their invention of RISC happened in the early 1980s, whereas there were RISC-style CPUs designed as early as the 1960s, if not earlier. To us, this is completely consistent: the "invention" of a style is not quite the same as, say, the invention of the cathode ray tube or a new sorting algorithm. The invention of a style occurs when someone frames the idea, lists its attributes, points out the alternatives, and probably gives it a name. This is what Patterson did, quite energetically, in the early 1980s. He framed the RISC-versus-CISC debate (no one used those terms before that), and he made the entire community aware of the distinction. Before Patterson, there was no framework in which to have the debate, although many people preached simplicity in architecture (just as right-thinking people do in virtually all aspects of computer systems). And once the RISC/CISC debate was framed, a great deal of measurement followed, one of the main positive effects of this debate.

Patterson did not even invent the term RISC. Carlo Sequin did during a discussion with Patterson in a car while they were trying to think through a contract proposal. (Patterson says they were attracted to the word because the funding agency liked risky projects.) But in our minds Patterson deserves to be regarded as the "inventor" of RISC; or perhaps the trio of Patterson, Cocke, and Hennessy, all of whom popularized it.

We are reminded of the very relevant joke about two historians debating whether Christopher Columbus or Leif Erickson was the first European to "discover" America. The two argue back and forth for some time, quite heatedly, with the Erickson advocate saying "but we've found the ancient settlements, and there are written records, and..." until the Columbus advocate, in disgust, slams his fist on the table and screams "but, dammit, when Columbus discovered America it STAYED discovered." The attribution of the invention or discovery of a style is very much like that.

shorthand for "following the philosophy of." This is different from referring to a house as an Eichler or Gaudí (referring to the builder or architect), just as it is from referring to a Hewlett-Packard or Seymour Cray processor (referring to the builder or architect).

We'll now briefly compare five important design philosophies, in pairs: RISC versus CISC, VLIW versus superscalar, and VLIW versus DSP. We do this to illustrate the concept of design philosophies and because these particular philosophies are important to the content of this book.

2.2.1 An Illustration of Design Philosophies: RISC Versus CISC

In the early 1980s the design philosophy of *Reduced Instruction Set Computing*, or RISC, emerged. Popular processors had been built that followed the RISC philosophy (some were built 20 or more years earlier), but the debate over whether RISC was a good design philosophy, as well as the terminology in which one might have this debate (including the term *RISC* and its alternative, *CISC*), did not occur until the 1980s, largely as a result of the popularization of it by David Patterson of UC Berkeley and, to a degree, by John Cocke of IBM Research and John Hennessy of Stanford University. The RISC philosophy can be stated as: build hardware in which almost all of the operations are simple, fundamental operations, operating on simple data kept in registers, plus load and store operations. The alternative philosophy, complex instruction-set computers (CISC), advocates the use of complex operations in addition to simple instructions. The classic example of a complex instruction is a STRING MOVE, in which a stream of characters stored in memory is moved to another location by being loaded to and then stored from the registers, and set off by a single operation. The debate arose after CISC-style computing became very popular in the 1970s. It was aided by the emergence in the 1960s of programming languages, notably PL/1 and Algol 68, containing many complex operations as primitives of the languages. One motivation behind the CISC design philosophy was that the compiler could, in principle, map these operations to similar complex operations in the hardware, thus, as it was said, "reducing the semantic gap between programs and hardware." Indeed, it was hoped that compilers could synthesize these operations even when the programmer had not expressed them directly. (Vector operations and their corresponding hardware are excellent examples of the CISC philosophy, and in that limited domain compilers did ultimately get good at synthesizing vector operations even when they were not explicitly expressed.) Commercial compilers never got good at finding CISC operations, and the value of CISC-style architectures lay in more subtle factors, not least of them being the market position of existing CISC architectures.

Today, the RISC/CISC debate is over. With the introduction of Pentium Pro, Intel proved to the world that an implementation of a CISC ISA could apply all of the same techniques used in RISC processors. Most of the manufacturers of RISC processors have exited the market. IBM's Power/PowerPC architecture seems to be the sole remaining healthy contender. For our purposes, what is important is the concept of an architectural design philosophy, and the ways in which such philosophies can be compared and analyzed.

An interesting way of looking at the RISC/CISC design philosophy debate is to consider what is exposed to the machine-level program (or, looked at another way, to the compiler). In a RISC system, the machine-level coder or compiler can see all of the simple operations the processor is capable of. The operations will then be executed only when they are explicitly set off in the code. In a CISC system, the hardware itself sets off simple operations — the very operations that compiler might have seen — but the hardware hides them from the compiler in the course of carrying out a complex instruction. In a STRING MOVE, for example, there are many loads and stores (and even an end-of-string test to check whether it is finished) that the compiler is not aware of. The generated code says something higher-level, and then the processor manipulates the simple operations on its own. Thus, we say that the operations of a RISC processor are "exposed to the compiler" or just "exposed." (This has led to the suggested other meaning of the acronym RISC: "Relegate the interesting stuff to the compiler.") There are at least a half-dozen major characteristics a processor might have that would make it simple rather than complex. Few processors fall on the RISC side of all of these characteristics. It is thus clear that this distinction is one of "general philosophy followed" rather than anything more precise.

2.2.2 First Definition of VLIW

Since VLIW is an architectural design philosophy, it is more of a loosely connected set of guidelines and beliefs than a precisely defined methodology. A succinct statement of the VLIW philosophy might be: "Expose instruction-level parallelism in the architecture." This statement applies to many levels of the system, including the microarchitectural hardware, the instruction-set architecture, and the compiler that targets the architecture and microarchitecture. Parallelism refers to the opportunities in a program to find independent tasks and perform them separately rather than sequentially. ILP focuses on the instructions in the processor's control stream. In an ILP machine, multiple operations can be executed in the same clock cycle, which is accomplished by explicitly encoding this execution parallelism into the instruction-set architecture and the machine implementations. ILP has fueled much of the architectural performance gains of the microprocessor revolution.

VLIW has historically been a high-end general-purpose architectural technique. For a long time VLIW implementations required too-high transistor budgets and connectivity, and VLIW compilers were too fragile to use outside a relatively narrow range of supercomputing problems. However, improvements in transistor budgets and refinement of ILP compilation techniques have closed this formerly large gap. It is now possible to envision (and deploy) VLIW machines that target embedded-processing performance, cost, power, and size. VLIW machines currently occupy the high end of the embedded space, but over time they will become increasingly attractive and useful for all embedded applications.

Like any other engineering choice, VLIW makes tradeoffs. VLIW architectures tend to have plentiful registers, simple encodings, and manageable resource requirements, making automated compilation for them possible. Indeed, getting performance from

Pitfall: Confusing the Aspects and Performance of a Design Philosophy with Its Early Implementations

A great deal of attention surrounds new types of processors, especially when they espouse a new design philosophy. There are two ways in which this attention may paint an inaccurate picture of the design philosophy. First, outstanding characteristics of the processor can be seen as hallmarks of the design philosophy. An example in the emergence of the RISC philosophy was "register windows" on the Sun SPARC architecture. This was a processor feature that had nothing to do with the RISC philosophy. However, because this was a well-publicized early RISC implementation, many people, including some quite sophisticated about computer architecture, came to the conclusion that this was a RISC feature. A second factor is that new processor implementations are immature, and have not yet been tuned for performance in the way more mature implementations are. Thus, the performance of a new processor that follows a new design philosophy will often be slower than the designs it is compared with, or at best no faster, adding to the natural skepticism of the new design philosophy. This effect applies to new technology in general, and is described well by Clayton Christensen in *The Innovator's Dilemma* [Christensen, 1997].

An interesting demonstration of this second effect occurred during the period 1999 to 2000, when information was being released about Merced, the first implementation of the VLIW-style Intel IPF (but dubbed "EPIC Style" by Intel). The frequency of this first implementation, 800 Mhz, was unimpressive when compared to contemporary x86 implementations and other mature designs. This prompted a lot of skepticism about the new processor family, as well as a five-page editorial largely on this subject in the well-thought-of "Microprocessor Report" by a highly respected researcher. The author wrote, *"One of the surprises about IA-64 is that we hear no claims of high frequency, despite claims that an EPIC processor is less complex than a superscalar processor. It's hard to know why this is so, but one can speculate that the overall complexity involved in focusing on CPI, as IA-64 [IPF] does, makes it hard to get high megahertz."* He then presented a very thorough and excellent analysis of many of the complex aspects of the IPF architecture. However, at no point did he mention, or seem to be aware of, the fact that he was talking about a first, experimental design of a complex architecture, built by a company and a design team more expert at implementing new versions of an existing ISA than innovating at all systems levels simultaneously. We do not know whether the complexity of the design will significantly slow the frequency of future implementations, but even a few years later the gap is narrowing considerably. We are sure, though, that complexity was a much smaller factor than the immaturity of the design. For a design as immature as that was, it might have been more accurate to conclude from its performance that IPF implementations would ultimately cycle very fast and perform very well.

an ILP-oriented machine requires a compiler (hand coding is expensive and difficult). Advocates believe that throughout their use VLIW machines have offered attractive price and performance compared to competing design styles. Implementations can have lower transistor count than other ILP designs, and these price, performance, and size efficiencies can be traded off to reduce power consumption. As drawbacks, VLIW architectures have always had a difficult time managing backward compatibility or upgradeability, because implementation details must be exposed in program code to enable high performance. Historically, VLIW machines were criticized for their dependence on compiler support, but this objection has faded as vector machines (and more recently, superscalars) have adopted aggressive compilation techniques to improve performance.

VLIW is orthogonal to a number of other performance-oriented techniques. Pipelining has become so ubiquitous and so basic that almost no implementation of any technique excludes it. Most forms of threading, including simultaneous multithreading (SMT), can be implemented on top of a variety of processors, VLIW included. In addition, multiprocessors can be built out of almost any type of uniprocessor core.

2.2.3 A Design Philosophy: VLIW

The VLIW processor design philosophy is to open up to the program not only the operations, as in RISC, but the ILP itself. Just as there are constituent parts of a CISC operation that are not visible in the program, superscalar ILP hardware can arrange the parallelism in ways not specified in the code. The VLIW design philosophy is to design processors that offer ILP in ways completely visible in the machine-level program and to the compiler.

Examples of the principles of VLIW design are: don't allow the hardware to do things you cannot see when programming; don't waste silicon on said hardware; avoid hardware that computes anything other than the intended computation on the critical path of every instruction; have only clean instructions; and don't count instruction bits. We will return to these types of guidelines in more detail in the next chapter.

VLIW Versus Superscalar

Recall the VEX snippet in Figure 2.2, showing how some code might execute on a modern high-performance desktop microprocessor. As we saw, there are several steps that must be carried out to determine which operations can be executed in a given cycle. For example, both data dependence and the availability of sufficient resources to carry out the operation must be considered. Often operations must be moved up above many other operations in the execution stream in order to gain significant performance from ILP, and the questions of data dependence and resource availability must be considered as the motions are made and as it is decided in which cycle an operation will be executed. A very important consideration, then, is when and by what means these questions of data dependence and resource availability are answered.

In some processors there is special control hardware that examines each operation as it comes from the instruction stream. That special hardware must answer the questions of data dependence and resource availability, and must potentially look at several operations before deciding what to issue in a given cycle. Such a processor is said to be *superscalar*; that is, we say it follows the superscalar design philosophy, and we refer to the special control hardware as superscalar control hardware. (See Figure 2.3, which compares VLIW and superscalar.) Note that in this case the ILP is

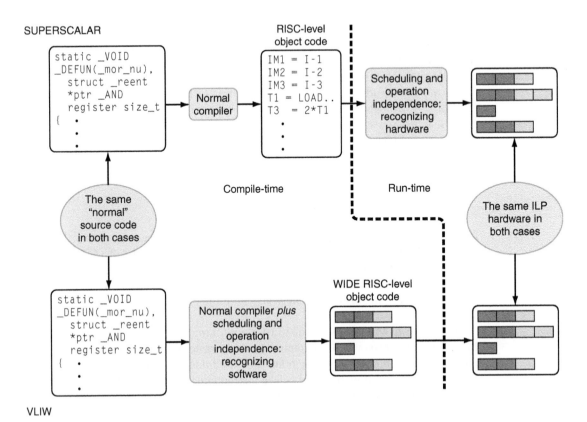

FIGURE 2.3 **VLIW versus superscalar.** The execution hardware of both methodologies is instruction-level parallel and approximately equivalent. The distinction is in the scheduling: superscalars perform this in hardware, whereas VLIWs let the compiler rearrange the code so that the hardware can execute it without changing it.

not exposed to the program. Instead, much as a CISC processor hides the execution stream of small operations carrying out a STRING MOVE, a superscalar hides the process of finding ILP. The ILP is nowhere to be seen in the program that was presented to the processor. (Historically, programmers and compiler writers, knowing in advance what a superscalar architecture will do, have used that knowledge as if it were a visible feature of the architecture, and have rearranged programs for better performance using that information.) Figure 2.4 depicts the HP PA-8000, a superscalar processor from the mid 1990s.

In contrast, a processor that follows the *VLIW* design philosophy makes the parallelism explicit as part of the program itself. Thus, the questions of data precedence and resource availability have already been answered in the code that is presented to the processor, at least in a design that follows the VLIW philosophy fully. Normally it is the compiler that has answered these questions, in the course of generating code, and

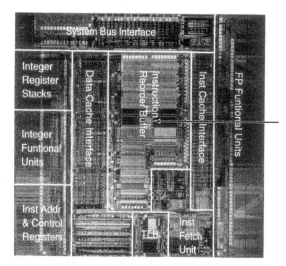

FIGURE 2.4 **An ambitious superscalar design.** The major functional blocks in the physical layout of the HP PA-8000, a four-way out-of-order superscalar designed in the mid 1990s (the die above was 347 square millimeters in size in the first such chips). The arrow points to the *instruction reorder buffer*, which is the heart of the superscalar engine, responsible for issuing operations to the execution units. From the size and position of the block, it is obvious that it occupies prime silicon real estate. In domains that are particularly cost sensitive (such as embedded), the first question that comes to mind is "What if you could do what this does transparently at runtime, even more effectively, without the reorder buffer?" This is why VLIWs are particularly appealing in such domains.

Fallacy: VLIW Controls Everything in Software

VLIW is an instruction-set architecture design style, not a dogma (at least we don't think so). The (building) architectural style Catalan Modernisme is very fanciful. Almost everything visible is very fanciful, with objects swooping everywhere, and everything very distorted. We sure hope the elevator mechanism isn't like that, though. Similarly, when we build the microarchitecture to implement a good, clean and exposed VLIW ISA, we expect that we will build dynamic mechanisms whenever that is the best technique to use. For example, VLIW architects are not shy about dynamic register bypassing, and various sorts of loosely coupled memory mechanisms. Indeed, some VLIW architectures even open a few dynamic features up to the ISA without losing their pedigree.

---

in the most extreme case code for a VLIW looks exactly like what is executed, step-by-step. Thus, the name "very long instruction word" processor (a program presented to the processor will look much like the code sequence shown in Figure 2.2).

In Chapter 3 we discuss in detail the relative advantages and disadvantages claimed for each design style. Briefly, it is often claimed that implementations that follow the

VLIW style have the advantage of requiring less hardware, lower power, and lower design cost and time. They are often easier to design and build than superscalars offering similarly complex instruction sets, and are more easily mutable than superscalars (i.e., one can take a design of a VLIW processor and change it to a new, similar VLIW with relatively little effort). All of these VLIW advantages arise from the absence of a superscalar control unit, which can be a complex, large, and power-consuming section of the processor design. Taken together, these advantages make it practical to contemplate VLIWs that offer far more ILP than a superscalar can. They also have the advantage of being easier to simulate the behavior of, since the hardware does not rearrange the execution sequence while the program is running in ways simulators have to predict. Superscalars have the advantage that because a sequential program can be presented to the processor different superscalar implementations of the same sequential ISA are *object-code compatible*. This is the benefit of superscalars that has made them overwhelmingly attractive in the general-purpose processor space. Because the ILP is exposed in a VLIW, programs typically must be changed if they are to run correctly when even small details of the implementation change. Superscalars are also able to adjust their execution sequence to dynamic changes (e.g., when a fetch takes a variable number of cycles) while the program runs, thus increasing performance. Finally, there is the fact that less compiling is required for a superscalar, since the hardware does part of the job. As we discuss in the sidebar "Fallacy: VLIWs Require 'Heroic Compilers' to Do What Superscalars Do in the Hardware" later in this chapter, we believe that this last claim is overstated and that in fact the great majority of the work involved in compiling for these processors is a function of the ILP achieved, not of the processor's architectural style. Figure 2.3 and Table 2.1 illustrate and summarize the comparison between the two styles.

VLIW Versus DSP

As we saw in "Digital Signal Processors" in Chapter 1, DSPs are very complex devices, often optimized in very idiosyncratic ways to be efficient on the tasks they were designed to perform well. As silicon has become denser, DSPs have added ILP for greater performance. Indeed, the entire modern history of DSP microprocessor engines mirrors that of older DSPs, called "array processors." Over time, those processors contained ILP as well.

Given the complexity of modern DSP devices, and given that they are already laboriously hand coded, it is not surprising that manufacturers adopted VLIW-style rather than superscalar-style ILP. However, do not take the word of any manufacturer that claims to have a VLIW DSP. When silicon budgets allowed the development of "dual-MAC (Multiply-ACcumulate)" DSPs (which could perform two multiply-accumulate operations in a single cycle), some manufacturers claimed that they were VLIWs, even though they kept the horrible instruction encodings, limited registers, and general uncompilability of the standard DSP style. Such devices are not VLIWs. To us, the VLIW architectural style means more than exposed ILP: we expect to be able to compile for VLIWs, we expect them to be able to run ordinary code, and we expect them to be the clean successors of RISC that modern VLIWs are. TI's (Texas Instruments') C6x DSP

	Superscalar	**VLIW**
Instruction Stream	Instructions are issued from a sequential stream of scalar operations.	Instructions are issued from a sequential stream of multiple operations.
Instruction Issue and Scheduling	The instructions that are issued are scheduled dynamically by the hardware.	The instructions that are issued are scheduled statically by the compiler.
Issue Width	The number of issued instructions is determined dynamically by the hardware.	The number of issued instructions is determined statically by the compiler.
Instruction Ordering	Dynamic issue allows in-order and out-of-order.	Static scheduling allows only in-order issue.
Architectural Implications	Superscalar is a micro-architecture technique.	VLIW is an architecture technique. Hardware details are more exposed to the compiler.

TABLE 2.1   Differences between superscalar and VLIW.

architecture follows these VLIW design principles, and thus has a truer claim to the VLIW title. Nonetheless, DSPs often embody enough of the VLIW design style that the boundary between DSPs and VLIWs is fuzzy, and many DSPs are referred to as VLIW DSPs.

2.3 Role of the Compiler

All compilers translate from high-level languages to the machine language of the target machine. The very first compilers performed no optimization (it was sufficient to show that the translation was possible at all). However, very soon after the first compiler was built for a high-level language designers noticed that additional effort by the compiler would yield better machine code. Formalization of these techniques gave birth to the field of compiler optimizations. All modern compilers perform some type of optimization. The difference between a "normal" compiler and an ILP compiler is not so much whether optimization is performed but the extent to which efforts are made to perform optimizations, and the presence of a few specialized optimizations.

2.3.1 The Phases of a High-Performance Compiler

Any high-performance compiler can be seen as consisting of three major parts, unglamorously known in the trade as the "front end," the "high-level optimizer," and the "back end." This holds true for ILP compilers as well. The front end is language specific, and

Controversy: Is EPIC Another Name for VLIW?

Intel took a large step in the direction of VLIW with the announcement of the Intel IPF architecture, developed jointly with Hewlett-Packard. Intel coined the term *EPIC* (explicitly parallel instruction computing) for the design style of this architecture, describing EPIC as building on VLIW but embodying enough new principles to deserve its own name as an architectural style. This has given rise to a small debate within the computer architecture community: Is EPIC VLIW? What separates the two? Was it more marketing considerations than technical that prompted the new name? Was Intel worried about the image of VLIW after the commercial failure of early VLIWs? Was this simply an instance of the "not invented here" syndrome? In short, do the differences between EPIC and the VLIW styles merit a new label?

There is no question that in designing this processor family HP and Intel added many features not found in previous commercial VLIWs. IPF goes farther than any prior VLIW in separating the ISA from the implementation. It exposes information so as to leave the hardware free to implement in its own way (for example, in extensive use of hints — in branch prediction, in memory latency registers, and in optional register windows). (All of these differences between EPIC and VLIW are largely there for compatibility reasons, and thus are somewhat less relevant in the embedded world.) Ironically, those searching for a distinction between EPIC and VLIW often assume it is speculation and predication that set EPIC apart — ironically because these were the hallmarks of Multiflow and Cydrome (the classic VLIW startups in the 1980s), respectively.

Ultimately, only the test of time will answer this question. Design styles are essentially art, and any real processor or architectural family will vary from the orthodoxy of any given design style (see "Fallacy: VLIW Controls Everything in Software" previously), just as any interesting painting or building will vary from the standard of a style. Whether a new variant deserves a name of its own is a subject hotly debated in many areas, as when linguists sometimes quip, "A language is a dialect plus an army plus a navy." (Given Intel's strength in the general-purpose processor market, this has some relevance.) In the art world, where movements with names seem to pop up daily, this subject can be most controversial. In that context and in ours, Janson's classic *History of Art* has apt advice: "It has always been easier to invent new labels than to create a movement in art that truly deserves a new name."

handles the task of recognizing and organizing the input language from human-readable form (i.e., ASCII/Unicode text) into a computer-manipulable form, or intermediate representation (IR). The high-level optimizer (sometimes called the "middle end") is responsible for machine-independent code transformations that improve performance. The back end is machine specific, and handles the task of translating from the IR into the bits and bytes of machine code for the target machine.

For all popular high-level languages, "off-the-shelf" front ends exist that can be adapted relatively easily to generate IRs of standard forms. Front ends may also include "high-level" optimizations or language-specific optimizations. For example, vector-oriented loop transformations or optimizations of virtual function calls in object-oriented languages can be found in some expanded front ends.

Intermediate representations are the source of many debates within the compiler-design community. As computer performance and memory capacity have improved, the trend has moved from simple, space-efficient IRs to more complex IRs that summarize more useful information but require more computation to build and more space to store. Compilers can have a number of IRs and optimizing compilers tend to have at least two: one corresponding to the syntactic structure of the source language and one corresponding closely to machine code.

In addition to translating from an IR to machine code, the back end performs most ILP-oriented optimizations. ILP considerations occur throughout back-end tasks, which include instruction selection, register allocation, instruction scheduling, and a variety of code rearrangements. Generic optimizations (sometimes called "machine-independent" optimizations) such as constant propagation, common subexpression elimination, and partial redundancy elimination also take place as part of back-end optimization. (We will return to compiler structure, front and back ends, optimizers, and IRs in Chapter 7.)

2.3.2 Compiling for ILP and VLIW

ILP compilers are similar to traditional high-performance compilers in many respects. However, the focus on ILP requires changes throughout the structure of the compiler. The back end must understand not just the encoding of individual operations but the implicit (superscalar) or explicit (VLIW) ways in which parallelism across operations can be encoded and expressed to the execution engine. More dramatic code reordering must be performed in order to capture this parallelism. This is typically performed by a global instruction scheduler, and to a lesser extent by code layout optimizations. The scheduler also interacts with other machine-specific optimizations. The interaction between the scheduling process and deciding which registers of the machine to use (register allocation) is an open research topic, as is the question of how to schedule for "clustered architectures," wherein there are groups of functional units and register banks and the compiler must decide which clusters to schedule on.

Unfortunately, ILP optimizations are not monotonically beneficial. Many of them trade one scarce resource (e.g., code space) for another (typically, performance). Tuning these tradeoffs remains an engineering black art; such information and experience is jealously protected by compiler developers. In addition to such tradeoffs, compiler engineering includes large-scale decisions for which no well-known answers exist, such as phase ordering choices (which comes first, register allocation or scheduling?), which IR to adopt at which phase, and how to represent profile information throughout compilation.

Global instruction scheduling is the key ILP-oriented optimization. An instruction scheduler finds and organizes operations that can be executed in parallel on the hardware

Fallacy: VLIWs Require "Heroic Compilers" to Do What Superscalars Do in the Hardware

It is often stated that a disadvantage of VLIW processors, as compared to superscalars, is that VLIWs need very ambitious compilers. In fact, here are two inarguably true statements:

1.   To use a VLIW processor well, one must use a very ambitious compiler.

2.   A compiler for a VLIW has to perform some things that instead are performed in hardware in a superscalar.

Logically, then, by having a superscalar control unit one avoids this heroic compiler. Well, not quite. The flaw in the logic is deducing from the previous statements that the ambitious part of a VLIW compiler is there to replace what the superscalar performs in hardware. It isn't. Indeed, the very fact that the job is performed in hardware every time an operation is issued by the control unit is already an indication that it isn't very difficult. In fact, the final rearrangement of code — the thing performed by the superscalar control unit — is relatively trivial, and compilers handle this without much effort (sadly misleading many compiler novices into thinking they have implemented something they always heard was very challenging).

Instead, there is a third statement one can make — a statement we and many others are confident of but one that was almost universally disbelieved in the 1980s and is still disbelieved by some.

3.   The effort required to compile good code for a VLIW or a superscalar is 99% a function of the amount of ILP it offers, not which architectural style it follows.

The reason for the belief that VLIWs require heroic compilers while superscalars do not is simply that VLIWs make much more ILP practical. Superscalars that issue many operations per cycle need heroic control units, with all of the disadvantages that implies. And then they need essentially the same heroic compilers that VLIWs need to boot!

---

of the target machine. In a *local* instruction scheduler, all of the operations under consideration belong to a single straight-line piece of code, and because programs typically have complex control structure this severely limits the scope of the scheduler. In contrast, the scope of a *global* instruction scheduler includes complex control flow in the program, expanding the ILP opportunities but complicating the analysis and transformation that must be performed to maintain program semantics.

Prior to 1979, practical scheduling techniques were limited in the amount of ILP they could find. Introduced in 1979, region scheduling (a form of global instruction scheduling) enabled a new generation of ILP-oriented processors. The basic idea, first elaborated in the region scheduling technique *trace scheduling*, is to select code originating in a large region (typically many basic blocks) before scheduling. One then schedules operations from the region as if it were one big basic block, possibly adding extra operations

Region Scheduling

A region-scheduling compiler typically follows this sequence in its scheduler:

Given the representation of the code being compiled in the compiler's intermediate form, pick a region from the as-yet-unscheduled code. The region is simply a set of operations originating in more than one basic block. Typically, but not necessarily, a region is a set of contiguous basic blocks. Sometimes a code transformation is performed prior to region selection, with the goal of enhancing the region selected (for example, by making it larger). Figure 2.5 shows an example of a typical code region.

Next, place the selected operations on a data-precedence graph. Sometimes the edges or the operations are decorated with additional information that is only important to region scheduling. In addition, some special edges may be added to the graph that prohibit illegal or undesirable code motions. These edges prevent code motions that would be illegal because they would imply a violation in flow control that cannot be compensated for when the schedule is produced. Such special edges are not required for local compaction, since there is no flow control to consider within a basic block.

Next, construct a schedule for the operations in the data-precedence graph for this region. This is an easier problem than scheduling an entire program, because the constructor is aided by the data-precedence graph and because the region is typically restricted in shape.

Finally, either along the way or in a post phase, perform any necessary fix-ups. Usually these fix-ups take the form of extra operations that mitigate what would have been an illegal transformation caused by the positions of the scheduled operations. For example, sometimes an operation is moved in such a way that it should have been executed along some path through the code but isn't. In that case, a copy of the operation is placed in the path from which it is missing. These added operations are often called *compensation code*.

Repeat until no unscheduled code remains.

This is the core algorithm of region scheduling, as specified in trace scheduling. There are many other region-scheduling algorithms that have appeared in the past 20 years, which vary from the trace-scheduling algorithm at any step but most of which follow essentially this framework. Typically, the algorithms vary in the region they select and in the complexity of the schedule construction pass.

so that the effect of the program remains unchanged. See the sidebar "Region Scheduling" for the core of the region scheduling algorithm.

Although region scheduling usually involves regions of loop-free code, most algorithms handle loops in some way. For example, many compilers unroll important loops to increase region size, but in that case the region actually scheduled is still loop-free.

Software pipelining is a set of global instruction-scheduling techniques that deal systematically with scheduling loops. Under software pipelining, operations from several loop iterations are gathered in a single new loop. The new loop intermingles operations

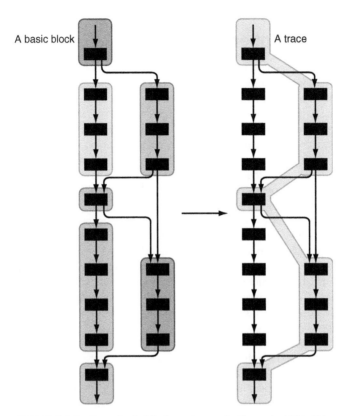

FIGURE 2.5 **From basic blocks to traces.** In the early 1980s it became clear that compacting only basic blocks (left) was exposing too few operations to fill all usable slots of instruction-level parallel hardware. New global techniques that consider larger regions, such as traces (right) emerged and opened up a new field of research.

from different iterations to fill slots. At the entrances and exits of the new loop, new code (analogous to the compensation code of region scheduling) is placed that allows original loop iterations that are not completed in a single iteration of the new loop to be completed. Software pipelining is covered in more depth in Section 8.2.5.

Profiling may be the largest area of stylistic distinction between traditional compilation and ILP-oriented compilation. Profiles have been used for decades by researchers interested in tuning programs, but ILP compilers use them exhaustively to determine where the "hot" regions of the program are and to focus aggressive optimizations within those regions. In traditional compilation, profiling was considered too operationally difficult to implement because of the complexities of having users implement the two-stage compile-profile-recompile stages. More recently, the arguments against traditional profiling have fallen away because of a number of technical and market changes. Technically, dynamic optimization and translation systems have blurred the line between compile time and run-time. Such systems continually update executable programs while they are running. In the market, users are increasingly willing to profile their preferred workloads, and the SPEC benchmarks began allowing profile-based optimization passes (and even supplying profile data sets) in 1995. In addition, particularly in the embedded market, applications and sample data sets are easy to find and use, and the additional design/compilation costs are acceptable when they improve unit cost and performance.

2.4   VLIW in the Embedded and DSP Domains

From the first introduction of ILP in embedded and special-purpose devices, exposed ILP has been the method of choice. For example, FPS built the AP-120b array processors used in GE CAT scanners, and AMD offered the bit-sliced building block family called the AMD 29000 (with VLIW-style ILP), which was used extensively in graphics boxes. This was a very natural trend. Designers were unlikely to build a complex superscalar for the small amount of code these systems were designed to run. Like today's DSPs, there was already the requirement that the systems be intricately hand coded, and it would have been a difficult job to build the superscalar hardware to control systems like that. In the end, it was easier to build simple execution hardware and to perform the equivalent of the superscalar control-unit job by hand while writing the code. Invariably, immediately after any of these products appeared someone wanted to sell the hardware as a more general-purpose scientific computer. "All we need is RAM instead of ROM, and some documentation. Oh, yeah, and a compiler."

Modern embedded microprocessors have repeated this trend. Though sometimes for slightly different reasons, as ILP has been added to embedded microprocessors, the ILP has followed the VLIW style, not the superscalar style. It is interesting to consider this in light of the claimed advantages and disadvantages of each style, some of which are controversial and subject to much debate. Consider, for example, the advantage VLIWs offer of requiring less control hardware than superscalars (and in the presence of a lot of potential ILP that can be a large amount of hardware). In a general-purpose microprocessor, with a very high volume of parts and less power and cost consciousness, the added silicon is less of an issue than in an embedded processor, for which the opposite of those factors is more often the case. Indeed, power consumption and small differences in cost are often the single most important factor in the selection of an embedded processor, and often present the designer with the firmest limits—the limits that cannot be broken no matter what. In contrast, even though these are still important factors in the general-purpose domain they are typically more flexible and somewhat less important.

Another factor that changes is the related pair of questions: how much ILP is available in the application, and how predictable is its structure in code that is running. Starting with VLSI processes with a feature size of 0.13 micron or less, as became available around the year 2001, there has been enough silicon available to build high-frequency processors offering significant amounts of ILP at low enough power to make them usable in embedded applications. Since these processors are pushing their frequency and power consumption to the limit that allows them to be practical in embedded domains, it is the most compute-intensive applications that are the limiters. However, those applications tend to be media codes and the like, unlike the systems programs that tend to have a greater relative importance on the desktop. These media codes, unlike systems programs, are very highly predictable and have a lot of ILP available. Thus, the attractions of a VLIW are increased, given the large amounts of ILP, and the ability of superscalars to adjust to dynamic changes in program behavior assume a lesser importance.

A third factor is object code compatibility. The need for each generation of a processor family to be object-code compatible with its predecessors—one of the main motivations of the superscalar style—is dramatically reduced in the embedded world, in which code and indeed entire systems are typically rebuilt for each new product. Although a dramatically new processor family will incur costs related to the port of operating systems and applications, this effect is far reduced because:

- In embedded processing, the narrowness of the functionality of the product containing the CPU means that customization of the entire system will pay off, and thus new processors are less likely to look exactly like their predecessors.

- The overwhelming importance of size and power also dominates design decisions. Thus, the alternative of keeping backward compatibility, which is not consistent with these goals, is less compelling.

- Similarly, the overwhelming importance of size and power also limits performance, and often performance goals must be met. Object code compatibility can incur performance costs that might be unacceptable.

Once it is apparent that object-code compatibility is not as big a factor in the embedded world, there is still the need to incur the design costs of new hardware. VLIW processors are much easier to scale and customize than superscalars, in that they consist of regular functional unit and register bank components, rather than the more ad hoc and difficult-to-design superscalar control units. Thus, customization itself becomes far more important in embedded processing, and VLIWs lend themselves far better to customization than do the alternatives.

When one considers the unique constraints of embedded applications (programmability, power, size, cost) in addition to their unique liberties (little need for backward compatibility, little need for upgradeability, and willingness to trade design/compile time for reduced production cost and complexity), VLIW seems like a close match for the embedded world. Further benefits can be obtained by tuning the VLIW instruction set to specific embedded applications.

Designers appear to agree with this argument. In the last few years, many VLIW cores have been announced and deployed in the embedded and DSP markets. Examples include the TI C6x family, the Agere/Motorola StarCore architecture, Sun's MAJC architecture, Fujitsu's FR-V, ST's HP/ST Lx(ST200), Philips' Trimedia, as well as Silicon Hive Avispa, Tensilica Xtensa Lx, Analog Devices TigerSharc, and many others.

2.5 Historical Perspective and Further Reading

As early as the 1960s, several groups were doing work related to what would eventually become ILP, but there was little consciousness of ILP as a subject. Before the 1980s, there was no organized attempt at a body of technology that addressed VLIWs and ILP (and the terms were not even used until then). However, there were hardware and software development efforts that were a preview of modern ILP.

2.5.1 ILP Hardware in the 1960s and 1970s

During the 1960s and 1970s, architectural trends in three different processor areas started the motion toward ILP. These areas were:

1. **High-performance general-purpose scientific computers**, which we would today say had superscalar characteristics. These were the supercomputers of their day.

2. **Attached signal processors**, or "array processors," which were the forerunners of today's DSP processors.

3. **Horizontal microcode**, which can be thought of as a RISC-like level of code, used to hardwire a program into the CPU that emulates a more complex instruction-set architecture's instructions.

In each case, an innovative CPU design allowed some degree of ILP, but in all three areas there was a perceived inability to automate (via a compiler) the production of very much ILP. The gap between the ILP that seemed to be available and what could be produced automatically led to a robust research area, and eventually to the modern era of ILP.

Early Supercomputer Arithmetic Units

The CDC-6600 [Thornton, 1964], the IBM research processor Stretch described by Buchholz [1962], and the IBM 360/91 [Tomasulo, 1967] were the scientific supercomputers of the 1960s. They embodied ILP by performing several arithmetic operations simultaneously. These processors were the prototypes for the scalar portions of the supercomputers of the 1970s and 1980s, and for the superscalar microprocessors of the 1990s.

The computer science community surrounding these early scientific computers was very aware of their instruction-level parallelism, and they already contemplated the question of whether ILP (though they did not yet use that term) could be exploited for still greater gains. It is remarkable to read: "If this approach is carried further in the coming years, processors may contain tens or hundreds of independent arithmetic units. The problem of efficient utilization of such a processor then becomes a major problem. Ultimately, the problem of efficiency will fall on the compilers and the compiler writers." [Stone, 1967]. The compiler experts, too, were aware of the potential, but saw the limitation: "In particular, stores must be inhibited while fetches are in progress, and vice versa. This feature makes it infeasible to extend this design to include parallelism on a very large scale." [Schwartz, 1966]. Compilers did do the job of finding ILP in short, straight-line pieces of code as early as 1964. Indeed, a discussion was reported in *Communications of the ACM* in 1964—involving such computer pioneers as Alan Perlis, John Backus, Robert Floyd, and Maurice Wilkes—after the presentation of a paper on the subject [Allard, 1964]. The summary of the discussion was that "The paper did present an ingenious method of rearranging the linear structure of a calculation and of departing from a linear structure and carrying out operations in parallel. The demanding bookkeeping required to assure that the proper operands enter into the calculation seemed, at least at first glance, to have been solved."

Unfortunately, the movement toward general-purpose ILP soon died out in this community. Anecdotally, it is believed that it was killed by a series of experiments to measure the maximum ILP available in programs (the first of the so-called "Maxpar" experiments), most notably experiments done by Riseman and Foster [1972]. Ironically, they found nearly unbounded amounts of ILP, but the straightforward hardware-oriented methods they imagined would be able to exploit it required impractical quantities of hardware. The community took this to mean that there was not much ILP available, rather than that it was there but they were not looking at the problem the right way.

Attached Signal Processors

The 1970s saw the development of what were called attached signal processors, or "array processors." The most famous of these were the Floating-Point Systems (FPS) AP-120b (introduced in 1975) and FPS-164 (introduced in 1980), though there were many others, offered by Numerix, Mercury, CDC, and Texas Instruments, among others. Charlesworth [1981] is a good summary of the FPS processors.

These processors were designed for scientific computing, but offered a greater amount of ILP (in a style that resembled VLIW) than the general-purpose scientific computers. Because the architectures were very idiosyncratic to begin with, and offered so much ILP, they were exclusively hand- and library-coded. Users always wanted to have compilers for these systems, and there were many efforts to build them, but even when compilers for these systems worked correctly they could not find much ILP. They were used strictly for low-frequency code, not the high-performance code the machines were acquired for.

These systems had architectures and applications very similar to today's DSP microprocessors. Although many were used as small departmental supercomputers, their greatest volumes were in embedded use.

Horizontal Microcode

Microcode, which can be thought of as a RISC-like level of code, is used to hardwire a program into the CPU that emulates a more complex instruction-level architecture's instructions. Some people describe RISC as being the microcode level of a CISC computer, cleaned up and simplified. The main difference between microcode and RISC is that microcode operations are at a somewhat lower and more detailed level than RISC operations, and are usually more idiosyncratic. Since typically only one program is to be written in it (the one program being the emulator of the ISA), the price of obscurity is not so high.

In microcode, it is very natural to allow several of the pieces of hardware to run in parallel, and then the microcode is described as being "horizontal." Sequential microcode is described as "vertical." Despite the small quantity of code production, there was a desire to make the code more manageable, which led to the research area of "microcode compaction," or the conversion of vertical into horizontal microcode. This was made more widely applicable by the prospect of "writable control stores" for microcoded CPUs, which were expected to lead to the production of far more horizontal microcode (but that did not happen). The extensive research on this topic, first appearing in the early 1970s and peaking by the end of that decade, is described by Landskov [1980] and Dasgupta [1979]. That research community, largely centered on the "Workshop on Microprogramming" (now the International Symposium on Microarchitecture), never produced technologies that led to the widespread use of compiled microcode, but the techniques developed there eventually enabled VLIWs. Thus, one can think of VLIWs as having sprung from that community.

2.5.2 The Development of ILP Code Generation in the 1980s

Before the early 1980s, there were no automated software techniques that found large quantities of ILP in programs and presented that ILP to the hardware. As a result, processors offering more than just a minimum of ILP were necessarily special-purpose devices, running handcrafted code, and relegated to highly specialized tasks. The change in ILP occurred when two different classes of code-generation technologies — region scheduling (for acyclic or nonloop code) and software pipelining (for loop code) — were proposed, put forward algorithmically, and developed into products. This made possible the use of ILP in much more varied applications, and eventually led to both general-purpose and embedded processors offering far more ILP than before. The change was brought about by compiler and architecture researchers and engineers in all three ILP processor domains, who often worked on these problems without knowing of the existence of the other domains. Today, rearranging code in ways that would have applied to all three domains, as well as modern VLIWs and superscalars, is seen as one problem.

Acyclic Microcode Compaction Techniques

The first acyclic techniques were referred to as "local compaction." These techniques tried to find ILP in code without branches. Research done at the time did not involve realistic implementation in actual products, and more difficult problems were largely ignored. For example, there was little consideration of issues such as the phase ordering with register allocation, operations with multiple-cycle latency, and complex underlying hardware structures.

Inadequacy of Local Compaction. Local compaction techniques were applied to a basic block because, intuitively, it did not make sense to schedule across branches. However, as these techniques were proposed and investigated researchers noticed that too many "slots" remained — too many in the sense that hand rearrangements still seemed to use more of what the hardware was capable of. This shortfall occurred because operations from other basic blocks could fill the slots in ways that considered branches and accounted for them. For example, one might shorten a schedule by moving an operation down past a branch, making a copy of the operation in both basic blocks that were targets of the branch. Sometimes this could eliminate a cycle in the earlier block, while not adding cycles to one or both of the target blocks. Many similar motions of this sort become evident after even a few minutes of working with a section of code.

Although these opportunities might seem small, experiments had indicated that most of the opportunity for shortening schedules lay beyond branch boundaries, and although few people in the field were aware of these experiments (they were done in an architecture context, not a software tool context) there was the broad realization in the research community that the boundary caused by branches was the largest limiting factor.

First Global Compaction Attempts. This realization motivated many new techniques. The first group of "global compaction" (beyond basic block) techniques could be described as "schedule-and-improve" techniques. These first techniques grew out of the microcode domain, in which producing microcode in horizontal format was very difficult, error-prone, and time consuming. Schedule-and-improve techniques appeared in the mid 1970s. The schedule-and-improve techniques worked roughly as follows:

1. The program is divided into basic blocks, each of which is scheduled (local compaction).

2. The scheduled program is then iteratively improved by moving individual operations from block to block.

These techniques gave researchers the intuitive feeling that they were mirroring what people were doing when they performed microcode compaction by hand. The best known of the early global compaction techniques was developed by Tokoro and his colleagues [Tokoro, 1977]. They built templates for each operation, in which the two-dimensionality of the template allowed a limited representation of the resources used by the operation. After local compaction, a search was performed to find candidate moves between blocks, based on the criticality of the operations. Then a catalog of potential legal moves, similar to those used for compensation code in region scheduling, was considered for the most critical operations. There was an additional facility for backtracking to avoid deadlocks that could occur when code motions left an operation no legal slot to occupy.

One fascinating schedule-and-improve technique took the fill-the-slots philosophy to the extreme. Nobel laureate Ken Wilson and his students, working with FPS CPUs in the attached processor domain, considered a scheme involving Monte Carlo techniques, which had been quite successful in particle physics. The basic idea was that after local compaction huge quantities of random legal code motions would be tried in search of improvements. Sometimes even bad code motions would be tried, so that hills could be climbed. At the time, some felt that compute time was a basic flaw in this idea.

The only report we know of on this work acknowledged: "It has not been determined yet how much computer time will be required to achieve effective code optimization by the Metropolis Monte Carlo procedures. If the Monte Carlo approach works . . ." [Jacobs, 1982].

Schedule-and-improve methods never became popular—nearly all ILP code generation techniques proposed and implemented during the last 20 years have instead involved some form of region scheduling.

Acyclic Region-Scheduling Techniques. A fundamental flaw in the schedule-and-improve techniques, as seen by some researchers at the time, was that too many arbitrary decisions were made when basic blocks were scheduled. Arbitrary local choices might be all wrong when operations from other blocks were considered. The easiest-to-see example of this is that operations within a block will be scheduled near the beginning of the schedule if possible, but far more critical sequences from later blocks may be the real processing bottleneck. Not starting the later sequences earlier may be an undesirable choice, but by the improve phase, there are no longer slots left in which to start the more critical sequences. Attempting to undo the earlier schedules to make new slots near the top of the blocks can result in impractical computational complexity. Nor does it make sense to reserve slots at the top of every block.

Region scheduling emerged in 1979 as an alternative to schedule-and-improve and has dominated global scheduling ever since. Region scheduling, in the form of the trace scheduling algorithm, was put forward by Fisher [1979 and 1981] and is implemented and described beautifully by Ellis [1985]. Although we have introduced region scheduling in the previous section "Global Instruction Scheduling," Chapter 8 contains a thorough discussion of region scheduling, its variants, and associated optimizations, and provides references for more advanced techniques.

Cyclic Techniques: Software Pipelining

As outlined previously and described more fully in Chapter 8, *software pipelining* is a set of techniques that deals systematically with enhancing ILP in loops. Some software pipelining techniques were developed before 1970 for the CDC-6600 Fortran compiler, although we know of no written description of those techniques. We would not be surprised to hear that they were also applied by the IBM compilers for the high-performance CPUs of the same era. We know of no sources that describe these techniques in any detail, though they are mentioned with respect to the slightly later CDC-7600 [Weis and Smith, 1987; Charlesworth, 1981]. Anecdotally, the basic idea in the 6600 Fortran compiler was to identify loops that fit a particular pattern. These loops performed a short string of binary operations in each iteration that were data dependent on each other and could not keep the functional units as busy as the issue rate theoretically allowed. The compiler essentially performed a patterned transformation of the loop into a new loop, as well as what are now called a prologue and an epilogue. The new loop would basically have its halves reversed; that is, in the new loop, the bottom half of the original loop from one iteration would be followed by the top half of the next iteration, allowing some overlap between the two halves. The prologue and epilogue maintained program correctness by executing the top of the first iteration and bottom of the last iteration, respectively. This strategy worked when the loop iterations were relatively independent.

Systematic Software Pipelining. In the early 1970s, more scientific approaches for dealing with pipelines began to emerge. The first important work was done in the area of recurrences and parallel processing in general [Davidson, 1971; Kogge, 1972, 1973], in which the general methodology was laid out and some important terminology, such as *initiation interval* [Patel, 1976] established.

More ad hoc work was done in the context of hand coding the Floating Point Systems AP-120b and FPS-164 array processors, and some understanding of the science of software pipelining (by hand) started to emerge [Kogge, 1977; Cohen, 1978]. In 1981, Charlesworth was the first we know of to use the term *software pipelining* [Charlesworth, 1981], laying out the beginnings of a more scientific approach. Shortly thereafter, Floating Point Systems produced a compiler that could do software pipelining [Touzeau, 1984].

In parallel with this, Rau, Glaeser, and Pickard [Rau, 1981, 1982] established the theory and algorithms used for software pipelining in production compilers today, laid out constraints under which their techniques could software pipeline successfully, and elaborated on hardware structures that would enable effective software pipelining. Their work is the essence of modern software pipelining. Although we have introduced software pipelining previously, Chapter 8 contains a thorough discussion, and provides references for more advanced techniques and further study.

2.5.3 VLIW Development in the 1980s

In the early 1980s, many startup companies attempted to deliver high-performance scientific departmental computers, using some form of parallelism as the enabling technology. The goal was to replace minicomputers with equally usable and low-cost systems that would give near-supercomputer performance. In 1984, two companies, Multiflow [Colwell, 1988, 1990; Lowney, 1993] and Cydrome [Rau, 1989; Denhert, 1993; Beck, 1993], used the recent progress in ILP compiling to deliver VLIW mini-supercomputers.[2] Before these companies, VLIW was regarded as something of a wild idea (the term was coined by Fisher [1983]). However, both companies delivered working systems, and the practicality (if not the desirability) of VLIW was never again challenged. Cydrome, started by Rau and his colleagues, had an architecture particularly suited to software pipelining, or *modulo scheduling*, as it was called by Rau and others who had turned it into a science. Although Cydrome's computer did work, no systems were delivered for revenue. Multiflow, started by Fisher and his colleagues, had an architecture that

---

2. A third minisuper company, Culler, also developed a processor that had some VLIW characteristics, but this had sprung out of the attached processor world (Culler was the architect of the FPS processors) and was never effectively compiled for.

was inspired by region scheduling. Multiflow had a lot of commercial success, and for a time was the performance/price leader in scientific computing, but eventually it folded as well. None of the many minisuper companies could withstand the onslaught of the microprocessor revolution. Not until 1990 would there be enough chip density for VLIWs on a chip, the first having been the Philips Life [Labrousse, 1990]. After their companies died, both Fisher and Rau joined Hewlett-Packard Labs and worked on the project that became the Intel IPF. Rau was much more influential in that project, and the IPF contains many artifacts reminiscent of Cydrome's technology.

It is interesting to note that both VLIW and RISC design styles came out of the world of microcode, and were in a sense a movement toward a more important role for compiling in processor style. Rau and Fisher were both a part of the microcode research world, and the main proponent of RISC, David Patterson, developed his ideas there as well. Patterson [1985] concluded his influential *Communications of the ACM* article "Reduced Instruction Set Computers" with, "Joseph Fisher, a Writable Control Store refugee like myself, is now working on compiling "normal" programming languages into very wide instructions (or horizontal microinstructions, depending on your perspective) for a high-performance multiple arithmetic unit computer."

Also, during the 1980s, and extending into the early 1990s, there were more "Maxpar" experiments, similar to those of Riseman and Foster. The first was conducted by Nicolau and Fisher [1981], seeking to replicate the earlier experiments from the point of view of showing a large quantity of available ILP. These were followed by a series of experiments; most notably, Jouppi and Wall [1989]; Smith, Johnson, and Horowitz [1989]; and Lam and Wilson [1992]. Each of these showed that ILP was limited to a small speed-up, but the pessimistic conclusion of the results failed to take into consideration potential improvements in compiling. Amusingly, though they were presented as upper bounds on ILP the results tended to go up over the years!

2.5.4 ILP in the 1990s and 2000s

A good overview of ILP can be found in the *Journal of Supercomputing* article by Rau and Fisher [1993], which was the introduction to the Multiflow and Cydrome articles from 1993 cited above. (There was also a shorter version by Fisher and Rau [1991] published in the journal *Science*.)

ILP compiling has progressed significantly during this period, and references can be found later in this book (in Section 8.6). In Section 2.1.4, we wrote briefly about micro-SIMD and other forms of parallelism. To get a sense of these alternatives, we suggest Burton Smith's [1985] article on HEP, one of the first thread-oriented machines; the ISCA paper by Tullsen, Eggers and Levy [1995] containing the first appearance of SMT; and the micro-SIMD article by Lee [1994]. For multiprocessing, a good reference is Culler et al. [1998].

In this chapter, we discussed the EPIC architectural style and its relation to VLIW. Schlansker and Rau [2000] give a good description of the ways in which IPF goes beyond the traditional VLIW design style.

2.6   Exercises

1. Enumerate the innovations EPIC provides over VLIW (as it was perceived in the mid 1980s). Attribute each innovation to the research group(s) that first proposed it.

2. Construct a table with architecture style in the rows (minimum four rows) and attributes that distinguish the styles in the columns. What is the minimal set of attributes that makes it possible to uniquely identify each style?

3. *Superpipelining* is a technique that builds pipeline stages that are significantly shorter than the shortest operation latency. For example, consider a machine that can issue a single operation every cycle, in which the latency of an integer *add* is four very fast cycles and all other operations take correspondingly longer. Consider two possible superpipelined architectures: one that performs dependence checking and stalls the machine when dependent operations require results from operations that have not yet completed, and one that does not. How do these two machines relate to VLIW and superscalar design styles? Justify your answer.

4. One advantage of measuring ILP using CPI is that performance penalty components are additive. For example, one can attribute some fraction of the CPI to the imperfections of the memory system (such as cache misses). In this book, we advocate the use of IPC over CPI. Is there an equivalent property for individual components of IPC? What computation is involved?

5. Interestingly, there has been an idea at the intersection of region scheduling and software pipelining. First suggested by Fisher et al. [Fisher, 1981], and developed fully by Aiken and Nicolau [Aiken, 1988], *perfect pipelining* unrolls loops an indefinite number of times, and then schedules (using some region scheduling technique) until a pattern becomes apparent. Then a software pipeline is set up using that pattern as the model of the new loop. Using a short loop inspired by the snippet shown in Figure 2.1, manually start scheduling it as if it had been unrolled infinitely many times. That is, start scheduling the unrolled loop but never consider a cycle completed if further unrolling would have provided new operations for that cycle. Keep going until a pattern emerges. From this pattern, deduce the *perfect pipeline*, the prologue, and the epilogue.

6. In Figure 2.2, we saw a DAG for one iteration of the unrolled loop of the "snippet" that appears in this chapter. Produce a DAG that shows all 18 operations in all three iterations of the loop, annotating the edges with dotted lines and latencies, as in the figure.

7. In Figure 2.2, five of the loads were changed from ldw to ldw.d. List all of the other operations, if any, that are scheduled above operations they were (directly or indirectly) control dependent upon in the original VEX code

shown in Figure 2.1. Why wouldn't those also change to a special opcode?

8.   Match design philosophies in column A with properties in column B. Any number of properties may apply. Expect philosophical debates over the answers to some of these questions.

A: Design Philosophy	B: Property
VLIW	Single instruction triggers complex behavior
Superscalar	Better for scientific applications
RISC	Dynamic conditions change behavior of instructions
CISC	Multiple issue is a distinguishing feature
DSP	Backward compatible
Vector	Independence information is encoded in the ISA

9.   Explain why supporting binary compatibility is problematic for VLIWs.

10.   Consider the following computational styles: DSPs, ASICs, FPGAs, VLIWs, and RISC processors. Rank them with respect to cost, peak performance, field upgradeability, and time-to-market.

11.   Amdahl's law states that if you speed up portions of a program eventually the parts you do not speed up will dominate the running time, and thus you reach the point of diminishing returns. Write a formula that mathematically represents this law. Consider a program in which the dynamic execution breakdown of operations (assume unit latency) is the following: 30% memory ops, 40% integer ALU ops, 13% branches, and 17% floating-point ops. What is the maximum theoretical achievable speedup (versus a sequential machine) for a VLIW machine with one branch unit (and unlimited other resources)?

12.   Assuming a target VLIW machine with two memory units, four integer units, two floating-point units, and one branch unit, what is the maximum achievable speedup (versus a sequential machine) for this VLIW machine on the program described in the previous exercise?

13.   Given the following sequential list of VEX operations, why can't operations A and B be scheduled in the same cycle?

```
A) add $r1 = $r2, $r3
B) mpy $r4 = $r1, $r4
C) shr $r5 = $r2, $r3
D) add $r6 = $r7, $r8
E) sub $r7 = $r2, $r3
F) add $r8 = $r2, $r4
```

```
G) mpy $r9 = $r2, $r4
H) add $r2 = $r2, $r5
I) sub $r7 = $r9, $r6
```

14. Suppose that operations A, B, and C of the previous exercise are assigned to the functional units that perform addition, multiplication, and shift, respectively. Which two can begin immediately?

15. Operation I cannot be scheduled ahead of operation E in the sequence of the previous exercise. Why? What could you do that would allow them to be scheduled in this order?

16. How many of the following sequential VEX operations can be scheduled simultaneously in the first cycle (assume infinite resources)?

```
shr $r3 = $r1, $r2
mpy $r7 = $r1, 2
add $r8 = $r1, $r3
add $r1 = $r1, 1
mpy $r6 = $r3, $r2
```

17. In an architecture that supports full predication, every operation includes an extra 1-bit "predicate" operand to guard the execution of the operation. The following simple C code

```
z = 2;
if (x > 0) {
    y = x + 2;
}
else {
    z = 3;
    y = x - 4;
}
```

corresponds to the following (sequential) VEX code:

```
    mov $r1 = 2          # z in $r1
    cmpgt $b0 = $r2, 0   # x in $r2
    br $b0, L1
    add $r3 = $r2, 2     # y in $r2
    goto L2:
L1:
    mov $r1 = 3
    add $r3, r2, -4
L2:
    ...
```

Assuming a fully predicated VEX extension, rewrite this code so that it does not contain any branch operations. Schedule the code (hint: assign operations to cycles) by assuming a 4-wide VLIW target that can execute any four of these operations in one cycle.

18. In an architecture that supports partial predication, we can use a select operation to choose between two values. Repeat the previous exercise by using select operations instead of predicates. (Hint: read about selects in Section A.1.4.)

3

An Overview of ISA Design

There are no rules of architecture for a castle in the clouds.

— G. K. Chesterton, *British author and journalist,* 1874–1936

This chapter covers some of the main issues the designer of an instruction set for an embedded processor (in particular for a VLIW processor) faces. We do not treat each topic exhaustively, assuming that readers have familiarity with the fundamentals of modern general-purpose RISC instruction sets. Instead, we highlight the considerations that are more specific to the use of VLIW engines in the embedded world. Although few readers will find themselves in a position to design new embedded VLIW ISAs from scratch, many will face the task of choosing one among the large choice of embedded processors for a given application. In this respect, we believe that understanding the rationale behind the design of an ISA is a key factor in the process of selecting a processor or core.

One of the underlying principles that should guide any architecture design is: *Make the compiler's life easy.*[1] The catch is that from a pure hardware design point of view it is often easy to design simple features that have very negative repercussions on the compiler. These designs are driven by the promise of saving a few gates or some code. Unfortunately, these seemingly innocuous features sometimes force compilers to behave much more conservatively, hurting performance across the board. This tension between hardware and compiler mentalities has been a constant factor in the majority of ISA designs, and finding the right balance is one of the most critical tasks for a processor architect.

In the embedded domain, it used to be true that minimizing gates was the most important consideration of an ISA design. This is what led to many of the idiosyncrasies

---

1. Some truly horrible architectural decisions have been made in the name of this principle! An important unstated subprinciple is: Make sure a talented compiler developer is part of the decision-making process.

of early DSP designs. Advances in VLSI technology have changed this, and most of the embedded world can now afford enough complexity to allow much more regular and orthogonal instruction sets, as the success of 32-bit RISC microprocessor cores (such as ARM and MIPS) testifies.

In the following sections, we consider several factors in the design of an ISA — including expressiveness and regularity of the instruction set, cost, relationship to the compiler, and design styles — for some of the most widely adopted choices. Readers who are familiar with RISC processors will find many similarities, as should be expected, given the close ties between RISC and VLIW. In deciding the areas to explore, we choose to cover more extensively what we think is more relevant to a modern embedded VLIW.

3.1 Overview: What to Hide

It is conventional architecture wisdom that architectures can both *hide* and *expose* key implementation details to the programmer or compiler. For example, the delay slots of the early RISC machines expose part of the original five-stage RISC pipeline in the hope that otherwise wasted cycles could be used. By contrast, the registers of many RISC and superscalar machines are treated as if they were updated instantly by each operation. Upholding this abstraction necessitates microarchitectural techniques such as bypass networks, renaming, and scoreboarding. What is often omitted from the conventional wisdom is that hiding and exposing flows both ways: an architecture can also hide or expose key *compiler* details to the implementations. A VLIW architecture requires and exposes a scheduler in the compiler; a compiler without a scheduler cannot hope to generate good code for a VLIW machine. A compiler for an architecture with branch delay slots will not produce good code without some delay-slot filling optimization. Conversely, a superscalar architecture hides the compiler's scheduler from the implementation: the implementation must assume that there are no hidden guarantees beyond sequential semantics embedded in the code passed down at compile-time.

This section explores what to hide and what to expose in order of implementation sophistication, starting with a baseline "sequential" machine model. The section then explores complications that expose increasing details of implementation (microarchitectural) design. Having considered these tradeoffs, we finally describe the set of choices that typify the VLIW design philosophy.

3.1.1 Architectural State: Memory and Registers

Today's architectures have converged on a view of architectural state that distinguishes between two types of storage: memory and registers. Historically, registers were fast, small, expensive, on-chip storage areas connected to specific pieces of on-chip logic. Memory was slow, cheap, big, off-chip, addressable, and not specialized (any memory location would do the same things as any other memory location). Recent technologies break with some of these abstractions (memory is now sometimes fast and sometimes on-chip; some registers can be addressable), but overall these characteristics continue to hold.

The abstraction of memory and registers informs both compiler and microarchitectural design. Optimizing compilers expect to perform register allocation (because register access is faster than memory access, moving frequently accessed values into registers tends to produce faster code). Modern implementations are designed around fast on-chip operations and relatively slower memory operations. So-called "*load-store architectures*," including most RISC and VLIW variants, divide their operations into two groups: computational and memory access. Architectures that allow combined memory access and computation do so by breaking such instructions into component operations (recent aggressive CISC designs such as the Pentium 4) or by performing memory access and computation operations in separate parts of the chip (most DSPs).

Excessive register specialization provided historical benefits that are less relevant with today's transistor budgets and circuit technologies. When transistors were expensive, dedicating an individual specialized register to the input of a computational block (e.g., ALU, memory system, or barrel shifter) made sense. Today, such constraints still save a modicum of silicon but make compilation much more complicated. RISC and VLIW machines tend to use a large pool of general-purpose registers; other register banks exist mostly to support alternate data representations such as floating-point or micro-SIMD. Specialization (like clustering, see Section 4.2) becomes important when wiring congestion and number of register file ports are the limiting factors to cycle speed.

Many implementation techniques provide the illusion of a particular number of registers or a flat memory address space while speeding up access to either. In many superscalar designs, register renaming simulates the architectural registers using a larger set of physical registers. The larger pool allows more operations to execute in parallel (more on this below). Caching is prevalent across memory system implementations, simulating a fast main memory with a small, fast cache fronting a large slow memory.

3.1.2 Pipelining and Operational Latency

The baseline execution model in many ISAs is *sequential execution*, in which each operation executes to completion before the next operation begins execution. One alternative to this is *pipelined execution*, in which the effects of an operation may not become visible until some number of clock cycles after the operation issues. Even though an operation has issued, the next operation may not necessarily see the effects of the prior operation.

Pipelining is parallelism in time because the execution of different operations reuses the same piece of hardware at different times. All modern machines use pipelined implementations because certain operations (e.g., loads from memory, floating-point divides) require multiple clock cycles to complete. However, it is a design choice whether the implementation of pipelining is hidden or exposed; that is, whether the implementation simulates sequential execution or is allowed to issue other operations during the time between the issue of the long-latency operation and its completion.

Pipelined implementations can be hidden in a number of ways, including bypass networks (which allow a value to be used before or at the same time it is being written back to the register file), scoreboarding (which prevents a dependent operation from issuing before its sequentially determined operands are available), and out-of-order execution (a generalization of scoreboarding that allows any operation in a window to issue if its sequentially determined operands are available). Architectures or implementations that expose pipeline delays make them visible in the machine model. In such cases, operations are known to take a particular amount of time, and are typically measured in machine cycles. Early RISC machines used bypass networks but partially exposed their pipelines through branch and load delay slots. Such delay slots removed the need for interlocking or scoreboarding techniques in those early implementations. However, because these delay slots were *architecturally* determined, later RISC machines ended up using scoreboards because of changes to branch and load latencies (e.g., the MIPS R4000, released in 1991). More modern RISC machines (such as the Alpha architecture, first implemented in 1992) chose to eschew delay slots entirely. Many DSPs enforce a uniform latency model, in which complex operations such as fixed-point multiply-accumulate operations occur in a single cycle. This decision increases the number of levels of logic in a pipeline stage, limiting the clock frequency of the device in a particular technology.

VLIWs have exposed pipelines to various degrees and operations may take more than a single cycle for their results to take effect.[2] However, within VLIWs, pipelines can be exposed at either the architectural or implementation level, leading to different implications for compilation and for handling interrupts and exceptions. We will return to these implications in the discussion of VLIW design principles later.

3.1.3 Multiple Issue and Hazards

The other major alternative to sequential execution comes through *multiple issue*, in which multiple operations are launched simultaneously and independently. Multiple issue is parallelism in space, requiring separate execution hardware for each parallel operation. Once again, it is a design choice whether multiple issue is exposed or hidden. In a superscalar machine, multiple issue is hidden, and thus the implementation must examine the instruction stream to find opportunities for multiple issue. This means that superscalars issue instructions in parallel only when a compiler has left parallelism for the implementation to rediscover or luck has placed the instructions in such a way that they do not conflict.

Exposing Dependence and Independence

To expose parallelism in space or time, the instruction encoding must carry some additional information. That information might be some information about which operations cannot be executed in parallel, which is called dependence information because it says

---

2. This is also known as the NUAL (*non-uniform assigned latency*) execution model.

Terminology: Instructions and Operations

Unfortunately, the seemingly straightforward term *instruction* has different meanings for different architectural styles, and even within variants of a style. In our discussion in this chapter, we use *instruction* to mean "fundamental unit of encoding." However, different styles use *instruction* to refer to either units or groups at all or any of the decoding, issuing, and execution levels. Throughout this book we will use *operation* to describe the fundamental RISC-like minimal unit of work, and we will use *instruction* to refer to a parallel set of operations.

The decoder level can be seen as the level at which instruction boundaries are found within a cache line or lines. Following IPF, we will call a memory-aligned encoding unit a *bundle*, but following VEX we will call the minimum-sized encoding unit a *syllable*. This follows the essentially syntactic (and therefore static) nature of decode-level features.

RISC and superscalar proponents use *instruction* to refer to operations at the issue and execution level. It is indicative of their priorities that there is no common term for a set of operations (again, they call them "instructions") that can issue or execute in parallel. The IPF architecture refers to "issue groups." Unfortunately, VLIW proponents have hardly done better. The instruction/operation split comes out of the Multiflow and HP Labs tradition, whereas TI calls operations "instructions" and instructions "execute packets."

---

what operations depend on each other. Alternatively, it might be some information about which operation may be executed in parallel (i.e., operations that do not depend on each other). Because the expression of a superscalar program displays neither of these, but rather shows just one sequential order in which the program semantics will be correct, we refer to superscalar architectures as *sequential architectures*. In a VLIW, however, multiple issue is explicitly exposed in the multiple operations that make up a VLIW instruction. An instruction still executes as a whole, but the pieces of the instruction go to separate, parallel hardware. In other words, VLIW architectures implicitly encode independence information about operations. That is, they are independent enough to be executed in parallel, in the form of multiple-issue instructions, and we refer to them as *independence architectures*. It is possible for a superscalar-like machine to encode dependence information by explicitly enforcing the dependences in the program, usually by reusing the same register name. Systems of that sort have been the subject of a great deal of study, with the most common variety being *dataflow architectures* (which we do not cover in this book). Since they encode dependence information in the program, we refer to them as *dependence architectures*. Table 3.1 sums up the essential differences among these three classes of architectural types.

Structural Hazards

Once an architecture has broken with sequential execution to embrace more parallel implementation techniques, something must ensure that the original sequential

	Sequential Architectures	Dependence Architectures	Independence Architectures
Example processor style	*Superscalar*	*Dataflow*	*VLIW*
Dependence information contained in the program	Implicit in register names	An exact description of all dependence information	A description of some operations that are independent of each other
How dependent operations are typically exposed	By the hardware's control unit	By the compiler (and they are embedded in the program)	By the compiler (and they are implicit in the program)
How independent operations are typically exposed	By the hardware's control unit	By the hardware's control unit	By the compiler (and they are embedded in the program)
Where the final operation scheduling is typically performed	In the hardware's control unit	In the hardware's control unit	In the compiler
Role of the compiler	Rearranges the code to make the parallelism more evident and accessible to the hardware	Replaces some of the analysis hardware that would be found in a superscalar	Replaces virtually all hardware that would be dedicated to parallelism exposure and scheduling

TABLE 3.1 Architectures that encode independence information are referred to as *independence architectures*, whereas those that encode dependence information are *dependence architectures*. *Sequential architectures* do not explicitly encode any dependence information. This classification is due to Rau and Fisher [1993].

semantics are preserved by the faster parallel or pipelined implementation. Preserving these semantics requires analyzing the *dependences* between operations. Dependences occur where reversing the order of the operations would lead to different execution results from their original sequential execution. Dependences come in a number of flavors, which we describe in more detail in Chapter 8. Of these flavors, there are three major cases: *true dependence, false dependence,* and *no dependence.* True dependence means that one operation actually uses the output of another operation; false dependence means that one operation does not use the output of the other, but reordering could still change the execution of the program; and no dependence indicates that the two operations can be freely reordered.

Designers have no choice whether to hide or expose dependences; that is, wherever storage can be read or written, dependences must be handled. However, many compiler and implementation features can help to remove dependences. *Speculative execution* can be performed either by the compiler or by hardware; speculation allows an implementation to gamble about the value of a true dependence and to complete its work faster if it gambles correctly. False dependences can be removed by a suite of techniques collectively called renaming. Compiler renaming moves or copies values into other registers, whereas hardware renaming keeps track of multiple sequential values of architectural registers in different physical registers. By copying and moving, both compile and hardware renaming remove false dependences and allow the program to execute as if the false dependence had not occurred.

Resource Hazards

Both pipelining and multiple issue allow multiple operations to be simultaneously active. This can lead to *resource hazards*, wherein two operations need to use the same piece of the machine. For example, in a pipelined machine two different floating-point operations might both need to use the floating-point rounding hardware, but because of different issue cycles and different operational latencies they end up requiring the rounding hardware in the same cycle. Or in the multiple issue case, two load instructions might not be able to issue at the same time because the cache has only a single read port. As before, resource hazards can be exposed or hidden. Machines that hide resource hazards must detect conflicts and delay conflicting operations; machines with exposed resource hazards require that the programmer or compiler guarantee that they do not occur.

3.1.4 Exception and Interrupt Handling

All modern architectures provide support for unexpected changes of control. These come in two major flavors: *exceptions* are raised when an operation encounters an unexpected condition (e.g., an illegal operation or a page fault), whereas *interrupts* happen externally to the processor core but require its attention. All of the architectural design choices listed above are complicated further when interrupts and exceptions are considered. In most cases, both interrupts and exceptions must be *resumable*, which means that the processor hardware and run-time software must have enough information to continue executing the interrupted instructions (and their constituent operations) where they left off.

There are a number of possible levels of support for handling interrupts and exceptions. In the sequential execution baseline, only a single operation is executed at a time, and thus all previous operations have completed and all subsequent operations have not yet begun when an interrupt occurs. In a pipelined machine, multiple operations can be in flight. When an interrupt arrives, the machine could choose to deliver the interrupt before the next instruction is issued, giving a "clean" interrupt point. Exceptions are more complicated, because they might arrive relatively "late" in the pipeline. Depending on how deeply pipelined the machine is, later instructions with shorter latencies may already have retired before the exception is detected. Such deeply pipelined machines are said to support an *imprecise exception* model, and these can require additional architectural state, special instructions, and special compiler support to repair and return from an exceptional condition. Some implementations (and especially superscalars with out-of-order execution hardware) support a *precise exception* model, in which the implementation uses its speculative hardware to squash or commit exactly the right set of operations to match the sequential execution case.

Interrupt and exception handling are even more complicated in multiple-issue architectures. First, any of the operations in an instruction can raise exceptions, and thus the architecture must be able to handle multiple outstanding exceptions in a single instruction. Second, all of the issues about which operations complete or fail get multiplied by the additional dimension of parallel issue (imprecise exception models require even more heroic architectural support, special instructions, and compiler support).

3.1.5 Discussion

Superscalar proponents value backward compatibility, and thus their architectural specifications often omit all details of issue width and execution unit latencies (such information can be found as tuning hints in product-specific optimization manuals). VLIW architectures encode issue and execution into instructions, making explicit the parallelism among independent operations. However, VLIW architectures are divided by whether to expose or hide functional unit latencies. Some encode delays into the architecture (e.g., TI C6x); others leave differences in delays to implementation choice (e.g., Multiflow TRACE). Many DSP architectures have implementations that are even more exposed than VLIWs: the programmer or compiler must manage details about which bus or functional unit performs a task, and often not all possibilities are encodable in instructions.

Each choice of what to hide or expose involves tradeoffs. Execution latency, mentioned previously, may be either an architectural parameter or an implementation choice. As another example, dynamic instruction scheduling (*out-of-order*, or *OoO, execution*) is compatible with both superscalar and VLIW architectures, but the two camps value out-of-order very differently. In the superscalar world, out-of-order allows an implementation to tolerate dynamic latency changes while preserving architectural backward compatibility. Few VLIW designers believe the incremental benefits of out-of-order evaluation to be worth the additional hardware costs. As an extreme example, some researchers have suggested exposing the bypass network of pipelined processors, saving some interconnect cost but complicating either issue hardware or compilation software. Few machines expose this low a level of implementation.

Perhaps the most fundamental tradeoff involves compilability. Compilers must always be aware of the architecture, since the architecture defines the compiler's target. Good optimizing compilers are also aware of the implementation, allowing implementation-specific optimization. Architectural choices affect the compilability of code and the quality of optimized code that can be generated. For both superscalar and VLIW machines, ILP-optimized code for a particular implementation can be generated. Such code will run correctly on only one of a family of VLIW machines, whereas it will run correctly on all of a family of superscalar machines but best on only the target machine. For traditional DSP architectures, so much is exposed that effective optimizing compilers are extremely rare. Hand coders end up tuning the kernels in DSP applications; compilers are used only for prototyping or for seldom-executed, lower-maintenance code.

No architecture ever perfectly abstracts away from implementation details. Inevitably, designers make architectural choices that later appear to have been motivated by particular implementation concerns. For example, the delay slots of the early RISC architectures were good engineering tradeoffs (from an implementation point of view) at a time when pipelines were relatively short and were single-issue. However, in today's world of deep pipelines and multiple issue delay slots are a historical appendage that complicate compilation and issue logic without providing commensurate benefits. The TI C6x architecture includes five-cycle load delays, which made sense on chips with off-chip memory. More recent chips in this family, such as the TI 64xx, have on-chip caches that can return results much more quickly. However, to maintain architectural compatibility the hardware must delay placing load results in registers until the requisite five cycles have passed.

3.2 Basic VLIW Design Principles

Every design philosophy has a set of principles that characterizes (or possibly caricatures) the style. This section summarizes these traits for VLIWs. In the case of VLIW, such a list is surprisingly difficult to produce, because it is much easier to say what *isn't* VLIW rather than what *is*. Such proscriptive techniques smack of orthodoxy and internecine feuding, rather than of recommendations for good engineering. Therefore, we strive to begin each described trait with a prescriptive, rather than proscriptive, statement. In refining the meaning of each prescription, we may sometimes give examples of techniques unlikely to be used by VLIWs. These should be viewed warily by VLIW designers but by no means should they be thrown out without consideration.

Enough methodological preamble! The following is a set of VLIW design characteristics. This set is not an acid test for "VLIWness," but rather a field guide. Minor variants on any of these might still describe a VLIW.

- **VLIW instructions consist of parallel operations**. These operations execute in parallel, on parallel hardware. The compiler guarantees that parallel execution of these operations is safe and correct (the implementation can assume the safeness and correctness of the choice of parallel operations). There is a 1:1 correspondence between syllables in the bundle and operations in the instruction.

- **Compiling to target a specific implementation is required for correctness**. Implementation operational latency, functional unit organization, and clustering are visible to the compiler. The compiler's job is to identify and expose parallelism through the parallel operations encoded into each instruction. As a corollary, recompilation may be necessary to target a different implementation.

- **Implementations execute the parallelism noted by the compiler**. The implementation *trusts* the compiler to produce fast and correct code. In particular, it does not double-check or second-guess what the compiler emits. Implementations do not have hardware that senses and prevents structural hazards, and may not even have hardware that senses and avoids resource hazards. Some highly successful implementation techniques translate the compiler's results into another hardware-level representation (e.g., CISC to *micro-op* translations in x86). Such techniques are dangerously close to second-guessing the compiler.

- **Expose power, and hide weakness** [after Lampson, 1983]. The microarchitecture and its implementations may choose to hide some details that are best handled by hardware; not everything is exposed to the compiler. Important examples include complete bypass networks and clean interrupt handling. Conversely, parallel execution units are exposed to the compiler, because the compiler can exploit that parallelism at compile-time.

Each of these rules indicates a choice about the boundaries between what is explicit (exposed) and what is implicit (hidden) in the VLIW design. The first three rules are fundamental identification points for VLIWs, and it is difficult to imagine a VLIW system that strays very far from them. The last rule is more of an elastic clause that says, "Make good engineering tradeoffs." If a combination of system design issues suggests that the bypass network be exposed, the resulting machine might still be considered a VLIW. Or one could imagine a design team that embraced a VLIW ISA but chose an out-of-order implementation, although one might question their wisdom.

We note in passing that VLIW operations also follow the same types of rules followed by RISC instructions: fixed-length encoding of the individual operations, large and regular register sets, and orthogonal instruction encodings. We do not count these choices as fundamentally VLIW because they are common across many design philosophies.

3.2.1 Implications for Compilers and Implementations

VLIW compilers must produce parallel instructions consisting of independent operations. Further, they must schedule operations so that structural and resource hazards are guaranteed not to occur. If the machine is clustered (for the moment, think of a clustered machine as having several groups of separate register files and associated functional units; we describe clusters in more detail in Chapters 4 and 5), the compiler must assign operations to clusters and generate the necessary moves or cross-cluster register references. All of these problems have been solved, although some have more satisfyingly closed-form solutions than others. All of the solutions require the engineering of an optimizing, ILP-oriented, production-quality compiler. Using a VLIW approach without a good compiler is not recommended.

Orthogonal encodings, plentiful and nonspecialized registers, bypassing, and interrupt support allow designers to build a relatively "clean" compiler, rather than having to build multiple passes that must adjust machine-specific code because of encoding-related limitations or idiosyncrasies.

Exposed parallel operations and pipeline latencies allow VLIW implementations to rely on guarantees provided by the compiler. VLIW code representations provide independence information, rather than its complement, dependence operation (the implementation knows a set of operations are safe to execute in parallel simply by finding them within the same instruction). No dependence checks need to be performed against prior or current operations.

The VLIW approach also discourages (but does not prohibit) certain implementation techniques. Because instruction scheduling must have been performed by the compiler, the marginal benefit or cost/benefit of dynamic scheduling must be carefully considered. Similarly, because registers are plentiful dynamic register renaming may be of less benefit than in other architectural styles.

3.2.2 Execution Model Subtleties

Even with the exposed pipelines of a VLIW, there remain execution model decisions that vary across VLIW families. These come in two major flavors — horizontal (within the instruction word) and vertical (across pipelined instructions) — and they unfortunately interact with the interrupt/exception model of the machine.

The first horizontal issue (see Figure 3.1) has to do with register access within a single instruction. A VLIW ISA must decide the semantics of execution when two operations read and write the same register within an instruction. There are three possibilities:

1. The read sees the original value of the register.

2. The read sees the value written by the write.

3. Instructions containing different operations that read and write the same register are illegal.

Virtually all VLIW ISAs choose the first approach, as it matches the underlying pipelining and register-file design techniques and allows a pair of move instructions to swap the

```
L0?3:
c0    mov $r0.1 = 1
c0    mov $r0.2 = 2
;;
c0    mov $r0.1 = $r0.2
c0    mov $r0.2 = 3
;;
```

| mov $r0.1 = 1 | mov $r0.2 = 2 |

| mov $r0.1 = $r0.2 | mov $r0.2 = 3 |

FIGURE 3.1   A contrived code example, the operations that make up the instructions for the example, and different possible horizontal semantics within an instruction. If a read sees original values, $r0.1 will have value 2 after these instructions execute. If a read sees the values of a parallel write, $r0.1 will have value 3 after these instructions execute. The second instruction is illegal for VLIW architectures that prohibit reading and writing the same register in a single instruction.

value of two registers. Both the second and third possibility make a subset of the instruction set into illegal encodings, in that a pair of operations that read and write a pair of registers in the second technique cannot be resolved. However, adopting the third model has one big appeal: parallel instructions *are not forced to execute in parallel*. For example, an implementation with a narrower issue width than what the compiler assumed can still execute the same binary correctly. This guarantees a restricted form of *binary compatibility*. The IPF architecture adopts a version of this rule, with the added complexity that only certain code sequences (in which the narrow- and wide-issue semantics are identical) are legal.

The second horizontal issue has to do with how operations within an instruction are completed if one of those operations causes an exception. One could imagine a number of possibilities, including "none complete," "all that can complete," "all operations *before* the excepting operation complete," and "free-for-all" (no guarantees). Each of these choices involves tradeoffs between implementation and compiler complexity. However, everything except "none complete" is a compiler and run-time train wreck,[3] as either the run-time must read special architectural registers to determine what remains to be fixed up (and then simulate the nonexecuted operations) or the compiler must constrain the code it emits to allow resumability after some subset of operations completes. However, implementers can (and have argued, in the RISC design years) argue for each of the other possibilities. The "none complete" model has the advantage that the run-time can "simply reexecute" the excepting instruction once the exceptional condition has been fixed. We will return to the subtleties of implementing various horizontal execution models when we discuss microarchitecture details in Section 5.6.4.

The vertical issue has to do with how pipeline latencies are exposed. Scheduling requires that the compiler understand the maximum latency an operation can take. However, it is possible for an operation to complete before its maximum latency has elapsed. The question is whether it is allowed to do so or must wait for the complete latency to pass. These two cases are called the *less-than-or-equals model* (LEQ) and the *equals* (EQ) model, respectively.[4]

EQ Model: In the EQ model, each operation executes exactly as its specified latency says. For example, we can rely on the fact that an operation will not write its destination register until the assigned latency expires. In this sense, the EQ model decreases register pressure, in that it allows registers to be reused while operations target them. On the other hand, as we will see later, the EQ model imposes heavy requirements on the exception model.

LEQ Model: In the LEQ model, an operation may complete in fewer cycles than its specified latency. For example, an operation can write its destination register at any point in time from the issue point up to the cycle corresponding to the assigned latency.

---

3. We mean this in the most precise technical sense.

4. This terminology was coined in a conversation among Bob Rau, Josh Fisher, and Rick Amerson at HP Labs during 1990 or 1991.

Although this may sound more complicated, this is a much more permissive model, simplifying the handling of exceptions and the implementation of precise exceptions and enabling a limited form of binary compatibility (for example, when latencies are reduced). (We will have more to say about interrupts and exceptions in Section 5.6.3.)

3.3 Designing a VLIW ISA for Embedded Systems

To this point, we have described ISA design and VLIW design styles without regard to how a machine or architecture might be used. However, this book is as much about embedded processing as it is about VLIW, and thus we now turn our attention to VLIWs in the embedded and DSP domains.

As we described in Chapter 1, the embedded domain differs from general-purpose computing in a number of important ways. Embedded devices have a single or limited number of purposes; that is, they run a limited, known set of code on a predictable set of input data. Most embedded devices are rarely repaired or upgraded; instead, they are replaced. Hardware and software are bundled together (there are rarely legacy binaries to support, and backward compatibility is much less of an issue than for general-purpose processors). Cost, power, and size can be as important as performance. Many of these aspects of the embedded domain play to the strengths of VLIWs, which has recently made VLIW a popular approach in the embedded and DSP areas.

Why are VLIWs popular today in the embedded domain, whereas they have yet to prove commercially successful as general-purpose processors? History tells us some of the story. Few people in the 1980s expected the VLIW startups, such as Multiflow and Cydrome, to produce working systems. Yet they did, and for several years Multiflow offered the best mix of performance and price performance available. Technical performance and traditional ease of use were not the barriers. Rather, these companies failed because of the economics of the microprocessor revolution, since processors built around ILP would not fit on a single chip at the time. They also failed because of compatibility factors:[5] binary compatibility (a barrier for all new ISAs, not just VLIW), support for legacy code, and the necessity of recompilation across variant implementations. Today, embedded VLIW microprocessors are common, and we have noted repeatedly that the compatibility barriers are much lower or entirely absent in embedded applications, making the overall VLIW package more attractive there.

Furthermore, the relentless advances in transistor density have recently given VLIW designs headroom in the other embedded goals of power, cost, and size. All processors have benefited from the lower voltages of recent silicon processes (such lower voltages allow lower overall power consumption). The other important power-related factor is clock frequency. VLIW designs have been shown to scale to very wide machines (up to dozens of operations per instruction) in many application domains. Superscalars have seldom exceeded quadruple issue or a dozen functional units, and DSP approaches are

---

5. Since 1983, no startup computer company that built general-purpose computers without a binary-compatible legacy code base has survived. Multiflow and Cydrome started in 1984.

limited by the number of distinct pieces of the DSP processor and by the limited and nonorthogonal encodings for parallel operations. VLIWs are thus easier to scale for ILP, which allows more work to be performed per cycle, which in turn can allow lower clock frequency and thus lower power.

What may have seemed a costly technology in an era of multiple-board computers built of low-scale-integration chips today occupies a small fraction of reasonable chip area, and memory/logic ratios have changed dramatically as well. This transistor-driven scaling also makes size less of a concern: all processor cores fit into part of an SoC (with the possible exception of the latest out-of-order superscalars).

Although binary compatibility and space are decreasing concerns in the embedded market, no project ever escapes the necessities of time-to-market. Idiosyncratic space-conservative approaches such as DSP extract their own cost in development time, as the lack of a compilable architecture requires expensive and time-consuming hand optimization. Without the space constraints, an architecture that extracts performance through automation (compilation) can reduce time-to-market, making for a more attractive package. The following sections discuss ISA design in three different embedded-processing contexts: application domain, ILP style, and microarchitecture.

3.3.1 Application Domain

In addition to all other considerations, some embedded applications have characteristics with direct effects on instruction-set architecture and implementations, such as *real-time* requirements and *numerical representations*. This subsection concludes by discussing scalability and customization, through which embedded processor designers allow their clients to modify processors to match their applications.

Few general-purpose systems have real-time requirements, although media types such as digital audio and video have brought streaming media to today's desktops. Digital media count as *soft* real-time applications, in that occasionally missing a deadline will lead to degraded service (and might not be acceptable if it happens too often) but will not be considered a failure by the user. In *hard* real-time applications, the system has failed if a task fails to meet its deadline. Many control systems have hard real-time requirements (e.g., it would be unacceptable for an antilock braking system to occasionally slip because software missed a deadline).

From an architectural standpoint, real-time constraints are most important when they interact with performance-enhancing techniques. Many such techniques, including caching and speculation, improve the average-case performance of the system without changing, or possibly even hurting, the worst-case performance. Some real-time system designers have thus been unwilling to adopt such techniques, because even though the average-case execution time of a real-time task is many standard deviations away from the timing bound the worst-case execution time cannot be shown to meet the bound. Computations of this worst-case time also tend to be unsophisticated and pessimistic at determining the likelihood of a hard real-time failure. In the most strict real-time applications, statistical, speculative, or caching techniques may not be acceptable, although the set of applications in which they are acceptable or in which designers have shown that the worst-case execution takes place with acceptably low probability continues to grow.

Many embedded applications use alternative data representations. General-purpose computer users are certainly familiar with integer and floating-point operations, whereby entirely separate hardware handles computations on various types of data. For a variety of reasons, many DSP applications also use *fixed-point* number representations, wherein fractional quantities can be represented but the value of each binary digit in the representation has a fixed power (general-purpose integers have fixed power as well, but cannot represent fractions, whereas the mantissa-exponent floating-point formats vary the power of the mantissa digits). Further complicating their computation hardware, some fixed-point representations use saturating arithmetic, wherein calculations that underflow or overflow are clipped to known minimum or maximum values. Many DSPs with fixed-point functional units also include special accumulator registers that have additional bits of resolution. These "extension" bits allow some types of overflow to be accounted for more gracefully than saturation allows.

Reasons for using fixed-point formats include cost, speed, and standards. A fixed-point adder or multiplier can be implemented in fewer levels of logic and can require fewer transistors than an equivalent-resolution floating-point unit. Standards may also mandate that a particular fixed-point arithmetic style be used (supporting such a computational style directly in hardware can reduce the instruction count of a program by a factor of 10).

Cautionary Tale: The Importance of Standards

The Texas Instruments C25 DSP, an architecture with a particular model of fixed-point saturating arithmetic, formed the basis for much of the work on the GSM cellular telephony standard in Europe. The GSM standard mandates *bit-exact* computations of voice-coded samples, because handset and base station vendors found that different implementations gave different coding artifacts, and that users perceived these artifacts as quality differences from one vendor to the next. Mandating bit-exact encoding ensured a form of level playing field among manufacturers.

AT&T's (later Lucent, and later still Agere) DSP division entered the cellular telephony market with a DSP supporting an incompatible fixed-point arithmetic model (emulating GSM-style operations involved as much as a factor of ten more instructions than on a TI C25). This incompatibility was not perceived as a major issue by U.S.-based design teams, as the American standards did not have the same bit-exactness requirements. Today, TI DSPs (led by the C54x family of DSPs, which debuted 5 to 10 years after the GSM standard was finalized) dominate the market for cellular (and not just GSM) phones. Evidently, Agere's not taking a real standard seriously had a major effect.

Many of the signal-processing algorithms that run on DSPs are initially envisioned in the real-number domain, and thus floating point would seem a more natural numerical representation than fixed point. Converting a floating-point program or algorithm into a fixed-point program is a complex job, typically involving careful analysis to determine where accuracy must be preserved and where it may be safely lost or approximated. This conversion task strongly resembles assembly hand coding in its manual intensiveness (it takes teams of experts months to perform such translations). In a further effort to remove this type of "hand-coding" effort from the development cycle, some manufacturers have begun offering both fixed- and floating-point versions of the same DSP. This allows faster time-to-market for the first product (using a floating-point processor), with possibly lower unit costs if product volumes increase and a fixed-point algorithm can be developed later.

The flip side of application requirements that affect processor designs occurs in the design of scalable and customizable processors, wherein designers intentionally leave space for application adaptation in a processor core or family. A *scalable* design is one in which the number of functional units or other resources can be easily varied within a processor family. A *customizable* design is one in which special functionality can be incorporated to provide additional features in an architecture.

The VLIW style lends itself to both scaling and customizability. Most other architectural styles can usually support customizability (because there is often space in their encoding schemes to add a few special-purpose opcodes), but many have difficulties with scaling. Scaling a superscalar design complicates the issue and execution logic, which may have to be expanded to handle the wider sets of instructions that can issue in parallel. Scaling a DSP typically involves encoding and naming a new architecture. For example, when DSP manufacturers moved from designs with a single multiply-accumulate (MAC) operation to dual MACs, they announced new product lines rather than claiming that the new machines were related to any previous design. (We will return to scaling and customization in Section 10.3.)

3.3.2 ILP Style

A particular ILP style can make it harder or easier to exploit ILP in an application. RISC architectures have no intrinsic ILP. Superscalar techniques can add ILP to baseline RISC architectures, but the superscalar issue and execution hardware can complicate microarchitectural implementation, adding to unit cost. DSP architectures encode ILP nonorthogonally, meaning that only certain combinations of parallel operations are possible (compiling efficiently to such irregular architectures remains an open research topic). Both superscalar and DSP styles still require scheduling to achieve ILP. The DSP may also incur interactions between scheduling and instruction selection to attain ILP, and some levels of ILP may be unattainable due to the nonorthogonality of the architecture. VLIW, with its combination of (relatively) simple hardware and straightforward ILP-oriented compilability, strikes a balance that focuses on maximizing ILP rather than maximizing backward compatibility or economizing on implementation transistors.

Using ILP to improve performance has been the subject of decades of research. We noted previously that VLIW designs have scaled as high as 28-issue (see Figure 3.2). We also discussed previously how a VLIW can trade clock frequency for issue width, allowing a lower clock rate and therefore lower overall power consumption. Cost and size are the remaining embedded targets. The VLIW approaches to reducing cost and

```
instr   c10 ialu0e st.64 sb0.r4,r3,zero
        c10 falu0 mpy.f64 lfb.r12,r4,r10
        c10 ialu0l dld.64 fb0.r14,r3,17#128
        c10 ialu1l cgt.s32 lilbb.r3,r32,6#3
        c10 falu1 mpy.f64 lfb.r46,r34,r42
        c11 ialu0e st.64 sb1.r4,r2,6#8
        c11 falu0 mpy.f64 lfb.r12,r4,r10
        c11 ialu0l dld.64 fb1.r14,r2,17#136
        c11 ialu1l cgt.s32 lilbb.r5,r32,6#2
        c11 falu1 mpy.f64 lfb.r46,r34,r42
        c12 ialu0e dld.64 fb2.r12,r2,17#144
        c12 falu0 mpy.f64 lfb.r0,r4,r10
        c12 ialu0l st.64 sb2.r4,r2,6#16
        c12 ialu1l cgt.s32 lilbb.r5,r32,6#1
        c12 falu1 mpy.f64 lfb.r46,r34,r42
        c13 ialu0e dld.64 fb3.r12,r2,17#152
        c13 falu0 mpy.f64 lfb.r0,r4,r10
        c13 ialu0l st.64 sb3.r4,r2,6#24
        c13 ialu1l cgt.s32 lilbb.r5,r32,zero
        c13 falu1 mpy.f64 lfb.r46,r34,r42
        c10 br true and r3 L9?3
        c11 br true and r5 L10?3
        c12 br true and r5 L11?3
        c13 br true and r5 L12?3
```

FIGURE 3.2 Scalability and VLIWs. A noncontrived, compiler-generated single instruction from the linear algebra routine DAXPY. This instruction, generated for a 28-operation wide Multiflow TRACE VLIW, contains 24 operations and is a good illustration of the scalability of VLIWs. Many embedded applications (e.g., signal processing and media) contain this much and more ILP. At the time we began writing this book, we knew of no one who had proposed such a wide CPU for embedded processors. However, a Philips-originated startup company, Silicon Hive, has recently proposed building 50-wide VLIW processors for embedded applications.

size are interrelated. Below a minimum implementation cost and size, VLIW designs are not possible because we cannot afford the parallel execution units. However, once we reach that minimum level VLIW designs are among the most economical in additional hardware, which directly affects cost and size. VLIW hardware is typically a subset of equivalent-width superscalar designs (both require bypass networks, whereas the VLIW decode, issue, and retirement hardware can be simpler). We have already discussed how other approaches scale.

Designers can obtain ILP through two mechanisms: pipelining and multiple issue. Each has advantages and disadvantages, and many designs use both to some degree. Deeper pipelining can allow shorter cycle times, but the shorter cycles also mean less work is performed per cycle. This can increase operational latencies, which although it can save power complicates scheduling. In addition, deeper pipelines require additional overheads in storing pipelined state, controlling the pipeline, and forwarding results within the pipeline. Although more instructions can be issued per unit of time, the latency to complete an operation will remain the same or even increase. Multiple issue rarely leads to shorter cycle times. The complexity of managing multiple pipelines and bypassing results across pipes tends to lead to overheads relative to narrower-issue machines. Depending on the application, the marginal benefit of additional parallel execution units can be small or negative, because few cycles allow all parts of a parallel instruction to be used.

Pitfall: Measuring Effective or Useful ILP

While designing an ILP-oriented architecture it is important to correctly measure ILP. It is easy to inflate the "apparent" ILP by adding instructions or diluting work across multiple instructions, but this does nothing to speed up the overall task. More seriously, many architectural or compiler features legitimately increase the number of instructions or operations generated. Speculation adds instructions that may later be ignored, predication provides for dynamically nullifying instructions from different control paths, and clustered designs require intercluster "copy" instructions that would be absent from a monolithic design. In all of these cases, we can define a revised metric of "useful ILP." Informally, it is the amount of work that is actually used (the committed instructions for speculation and predication, not the intercluster moves on a clustered design). The main thing is to be aware of such "useless ILP" in one's models and simulations, and to quantify it fairly when evaluating alternatives.

3.3.3 Hardware/Software Tradeoffs

Microarchitecture implementation techniques are properly the topic of Chapter 5, however, the choice of when and whether to use various microarchitectural techniques requires system-level evaluation. This subsection considers how VLIW and other architectural styles are suited to the embedded and DSP domains.

All microarchitectural techniques require hardware, which means that the cost of that hardware is part of the cost of every unit produced (economists call these *variable* costs, as they scale with the number of units produced). Compilation techniques, by contrast, are part of the fixed cost of developing an embedded application. Fixed costs are amortized over all units sold during the lifetime of the product; that is, the more units that are sold the lower the share of the fixed cost that must be covered by the price of each unit. This is not to say that fixed costs approach zero, only that they decrease per unit as the volume increases.

Many microarchitectural techniques have compile-time counterparts that perform essentially the same task and confer many of the same benefits (instruction scheduling and register allocation are only the most obvious examples). If designers can remove the cost of a dynamic technique from the system and obtain the same or nearly the same benefits from the related software technique, we have transformed a variable cost (which scales with the number of units) into a fixed cost (which gets amortized over all units). This tradeoff has been the source of a long-standing debate in the general-purpose community (for which performance is paramount) but it takes on added dimensions in the embedded domain (for which cost, power, and size also count). In performance alone we make tradeoffs between the cost of designing and building the hardware or software technique. In cost, we make tradeoffs between an increased unit cost that scales with volume and the fixed development cost that will be amortized. In both size and power, however, removing hardware unilaterally improves the end device. Because compilation takes place in the development laboratory (whereby size and power do not affect the end device), there is no longer a tradeoff.

Unfortunately, sophisticated compilation techniques *do not* come for free. Quite the opposite, in fact: engineering a production-quality, high-performance optimizing compiler is a work requiring person-decades and a great deal of sophistication. Building a new optimization is a time-consuming software development task that can easily fall on the time-to-market critical path. For these reasons, we recommend that VLIW designers start with the available *compiler*, not the available hardware, when considering the space of possible designs. Furthermore, one should expect that the compiler features available at the *beginning* of a development project are those that will be available when the first version of the product ships (we immodestly call this "*Fisher's law*"). Building a business plan on performance estimates of a soon-to-be-developed compiler's features is folly.

This is not to say that features cannot be developed during the design of a product. Modern computer design includes not just hardware designers but compiler builders and simulation/verification groups, and no project can succeed without active collaboration among all of these groups. It does little good to add features the compiler cannot use, or for the compiler to generate code sequences the hardware will inefficiently execute.

3.4 Instruction-set Encoding

The second half of this chapter discusses the topics of hardware, software, and architecture from a somewhat nonstandard perspective that focuses on *encoding* as the fundamental problem that bridges all three areas. The first section, "A Larger Definition of Architecture," introduces the metaphor we use in the remaining parts. Section 3.4.2 might be subtitled "Encoding in the Large," as it describes how encoding decisions relate to the larger topic of design philosophy (or architectural style). In contrast, Section 3.5 might be subtitled "Encoding in Detail," as it describes the particular details of encoding VLIW instruction sets and adding extensions to existing instruction sets. The first two sections have a very analytic tone, in part because few designers get to choose among design styles. The last section, about scalability and customizability, moves away from analytic discussion of encoding issues to a more empirical description of how an architecture can be adapted to particular applications and application areas.

3.4.1 A Larger Definition of Architecture

Scholars and designers have used a number of metaphors to describe the relationships among compilers, architectures, and implementations. Popular metaphors include interfaces (as used in Patterson and Hennessy's title, *Computer Architecture: The Hardware/Software Interface*), contracts (wherein the architecture is thought of as forming an agreement between software and hardware designers), and recipes (the object code is a recipe from which the execution of the program is built). What is common

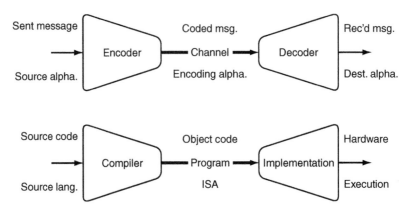

FIGURE 3.3 Analogy between information-theoretic channel codes and instruction sets.

to all of these metaphors is that each describes an abstraction layer, wherein various disciplines and skills meet and must cooperate.

To give us more descriptive precision, we choose a slightly more technical metaphor: programs are a communications *channel*,[6] with the ISA being the code for that channel. In communications theory, a sender and a receiver send *messages* through a *channel* (the channel is the sole means through which information passes). The sender and receiver must agree on what form (coding) valid messages can take. The device that translates from the original message to the coded message on the channel is called the *encoder*, and the device that translates the encoded message to the receiver's language is called the *decoder*. Source and destination language need not be the same, although they often are (the code on the channel typically differs from both). Stream-oriented examples of channels are common: telephone and telegraph lines, TCP/IP (Transmission Control Protocol/Internet Protocol) connections, and recorded music on tape or compact disc. However, channels can also transmit complex messages, books are channels between author and reader; a play forms a channel from author to director, cast, crew, and (hopefully) audience; and musical scores are channels from composer to performer. The upper half of Figure 3.3 illustrates the concept of a channel.

Program memory is a channel from the programmer to the execution hardware, wherein the ISA is the code in which messages are expressed. A program is a message (different programs have different semantics and lead to different execution behavior). In our analogy, the encoder is the compiler (or the unfortunate assembly language programmer). It translates from source language to a program in the ISA. The decoder is the implementation (also sometimes called *microarchitecture*). It translates from the program to its run-time execution. The bottom half of Figure 3.3 depicts this analogy.

---

6. More precisely, we mean an information-theoretic channel, but we do not plan to go into details of information theory at this point. Thus, the more intuitive description suffices.

This communications channel metaphor lends itself to engineering cost/benefit analysis. The instruction set (channel code) can be designed to meet a variety of criteria: compactness, completeness, orthogonality, fixed- or variable-length words, and so on. These choices then affect many aspects of the compiler (encoder) and implementation (decoder), including cost, size, latency, bandwidth, and efficiency (with very different meanings for each of these items for compiler and implementation). Further, the ISA (code) lends itself to multiple versions of compiler and implementation, tuned for various tradeoffs. A "production" compiler might be expensive, huge, and slow to compile but produce very compact code, whereas a "prototyping" compiler might be cheap and fast but produce inefficient code for the compile-edit-debug design cycle.

Variations in ISA design make for differing overall tradeoffs. For example, DSP architectures are idiosyncratically encoded and expose many details of a particular implementation's structure. The DSP approach restricts the range of possible implementations to a very small set, while requiring tremendous effort on the compilation and programming side. At the other extreme, one might imagine ISAs (codes) designed to simplify compilation as much as possible, making the ISA close to the source language (the "language-specific machine" movement of the 1970s typifies this approach). More concretely, ISAs today typically specify how instructions are encoded (fixed- or variable-length), the number and types of program-visible registers, and the types of operations that can be performed by the functional units of the machine.

Over the lifetime of an architecture, changes occur at all three levels: compiler, ISA, and implementation. Implementation changes are perhaps the most visible, as each new implementation technique is typically assigned a new name for marketing purposes. For example, x86 (the most popular general-purpose computing architecture) has enjoyed a long sequence of implementations, including the 4.77-MHz 8088 chip of the original IBM PC; the pipelined i486; the dual-issue Pentium; the out-of-order Pentium Pro, II, and III chips; and the most recent deeply pipelined trace-caching Pentium 4 chips. Throughout this sequence of implementations Intel has maintained architectural backward compatibility (today's Pentium 4 can still run programs designed for the original 8086). Similarly, the ARM (originally Acorn RISC Machine, but the acronym has become a name unto itself) architecture has had a number of implementations, from the original ARM2 of 1987 to the breakthrough (because they were high-performance yet low-power) 200-MHz StrongARM chips to today's 25–300-MHz ARM9/ARM11 and 600-MHz XScale variants.

Implementation techniques have wide latitude in how various hardware versions carry out instructions. These include the configuration of the processor pipelines (issue width, number of different paths, and number of stages), instruction evaluation methodologies (in-order versus various types of out-of-order), and the size and organization of caches. Depending on the ISA, implementations may have large or small amounts of freedom to use particular construction techniques.

Architectural evolution takes place more formally and less frequently, typically extending the ISA at the same time a new implementation is unveiled. In the x86 architecture, features such as floating point, memory management, and the media-oriented MMX and SSE instruction sets were introduced with the 8087 coprocessor, the 80286, the Pentium MMX, and the Pentium III, respectively. ARM architecture extensions include the Thumb compressed instruction set, support for vector floating-point arithmetic, and a number of attempts at DSP support.

Today, designers often leave "room to grow" in an instruction set architecture (growth can be either planned or organic). Texas Instruments' C6x series of processors had one more register encoding bit than early implementations required, and the later C64xx processors used that encoding bit to support twice as many registers. The designers of the first 8086 processors likely had no idea how far their architecture would stretch: from 16-bit registers to 64-bit (in AMD's latest ISA extensions) and from a 20-bit address space to 32-bit and even 64-bit. X86 architectural extensions are best described as "organic"; that is, some extensions have exploited unused values in the coding tree, whereas others have relied on new mode bits added to the architecture.

Compiler evolution over the lifetime of an architecture is often much less visible than ISA or implementation changes, which are typically tied to marketing announcements (All new! Pentium with MMX!). Only a few manufacturers have used compilers as a marketing point for their machines (IBM's optimizing FORTRAN compilers being perhaps the exception that proves the rule). However, compiler improvements occasionally make for marked improvements in processor performance. It is an unfortunate irony of optimizing compiler design that the best compilation is achieved toward the end of the useful lifetime of a particular implementation (just as the compiler gets good, the implementation becomes obsolete).

Our information-theoretic model of compilers, ISAs, and implementations allows us to better capture the notion of an *architecture*. In the academic ideal, the architecture is an abstract specification of a related set of computers, whereas an implementation is a particular computer that complies with the architecture. "Architecture" is also often used synonymously with "instruction-set architecture," which leaves out the broader issues of programmability and implementability. Another unfortunate phrase is that machines that share an architecture can all "run the same code." The problem with this statement is that it reflects a general-purpose mind-set, whereby all implementations of an architecture *must* run the same object code. Embedded architectures have more room to play. For example, even though the TI C62xx and C67xx series of chips are optimized to run fixed-point and floating-point code, respectively, they are undoubtedly part of the same architecture. By considering compilers, ISAs, and implementations as collectively constituting an architecture, we can capture the changing relations among them. Just as there are families of communication codes, with associated encoders and decoders, there are similarly families of processors, with associated compilers and implementations. Members of the same architecture may or may not be binary compatible, but they are still recognizable as relatives because they share compilers, subsets of their ISA, and even implementation techniques or functional blocks.

Computer architecture and implementation go hand in hand; it is impossible to discuss one without the other. Nevertheless, the preceding parts of this chapter tried to discuss architecture by itself. Chapter 5 explores implementation techniques in more detail, whereas this chapter discusses such details when necessary but attempts to focus on encoding and ISA design. The next section discusses ISA as an encoding problem, comparing and contrasting various design styles' choices about both how to represent instructions and what instructions represent.

3.4.2 Encoding and Architectural Style

Every instruction-set architecture has a manual that describes how all implementations of the architecture operate. Or more precisely, the manual describes the common aspects of operations across all implementations (there are of course implementation-specific variations). Such manuals are the codebooks of the architecture (like the codebooks of communications codes), explaining how to interpret various signals. The descriptions appear to dictate a particular hardware structure, typically describing an *architectural state* that consists of a number of registers and memory locations that can hold values, the *instruction set* that modifies the state, and an *execution model* for how instructions are sequenced and for how instructions update the state. Over the past half-century of machine design, styles have converged to a model with a single program counter (so-called von Neumann machines), registers, and memory.

Alternatives to von Neumann Machines

Machine styles without the usual notions of program counters and registers have been explored. They fall into two categories: radical (marginal?) designs that never proved they could be effectively deployed and designs that use von Neumann architectures as components.

The radical designs include architectures without registers (such as stack machines) and architectures without a traditional program counter, such as dataflow machines. Stack machines enjoy popularity as *virtual* machines (UCSD's *p-system* in the 1970s and the Java Virtual Machine today), but few commercial stack machine architectures exist (the Burroughs A-series mainframes being one of the few examples we know of). We leave stack machines and exotics such as dataflow machines out of our discussion, because they stray too far from our content.

Multiprocessors and multithreaded machines each have components that are traditional von Neumann machines in their own right. Multiprocessor and multithreading issues have a number of architecture-level implications, but most of them are handled transparently to the ISA. The few special-purpose process- or thread-related instructions tend to have the same flavor as other OS support instructions (they tend not to affect the overall encoding of the ISA).

The appearance of hardware structure in architectural descriptions is actually false. Implementations are free to build whatever structures they want to, as long as they *simulate* the architectural model. One of the most extreme examples of this is in virtual machine emulation, whereby a completely different implementation simulates the operation of another architecture. IBM pioneered virtual machine techniques on its System/360 line of machines during the 1970s. More recently, DEC's FX!32 system executed x86 programs on Alpha hardware, and Transmeta's Crusoe and Efficeon series of chips dynamically translate from x86 code to an internal VLIW implementation.

In describing various architectures and architectural models it helps to have an intuitive notion of the simplest unit of work that might be specified by an instruction. We call this unit an *operation*, which corresponds intuitively to the work performed by traversing a single implementation pipeline from beginning to end, or equivalently to the effect of a single, pure (i.e., no fancy addressing modes), RISC-style instruction. This definition has limitations, because every architecture also includes implicit side effects in its execution model that have to do with control and sequencing. Heretofore, we have used the terms *instruction* and *operation* somewhat intuitively. Now we can be crisper: *instruction* is the fundamental unit in which work is encoded, as opposed to the single or multiple *operations* into which that instruction translates when executed.

Returning to our explanatory metaphor, Instruction-Set Architecture is about *encoding*, or assigning meaning to different strings of bits in the instruction stream. We will return to the specific (and relatively mechanical) topic of VLIW instruction encodings in the next section. For now, we are concerned with the higher-level notion of what an instruction encodes, or represents. Let's consider design philosophies and their representative ISAs in terms of two questions. First, what is the basic encoding unit? Second, what happens at run-time as a result of a basic unit?

Virtually everyone calls the basic encoding unit an *instruction*, but what this means varies widely across architectural styles. Instructions can be fixed- or variable-sized. If variable, they can come in different sizes. In a CISC architecture, instructions are typically encoded in a variable number of bytes. The shortest instructions occupy only a single byte, whereas longer instructions with complex options and addressing modes may require tens of bytes. By contrast, the fixed-length 32-bit encoding of RISC instructions is a hallmark of the architectural style. Most DSP and vector instruction sets also use fixed-length encodings. VLIW *instructions* (in the sense we use in this book) may be either fixed- or variable-length. They typically consist of multiple 32-bit syllables, each of which represents an operation that resembles a single RISC instruction. Reaching farther afield, vector machines also typically use fixed-length instructions. Fixed-length encodings make for simpler decoding stages in implementations. Variable-length encodings can complicate decoding stages because of the levels of logic required to interpret where the instruction ends.

By "basic unit of encoding" we mean the natural unit considered by programmers or compiler designers. For superscalar machines (which exist in both RISC and CISC varieties), a group of parallel instructions in a program is *not* this natural unit. It is an important marketing point for such machines that correct single-issue code also operates correctly on more aggressive designs. Further, the superscalar performance guides provide "hints" for how to lay out instructions so that the decode/issue logic can find parallelism at run-time. Such hints indicate that tuning the code for ILP is an option, not a requirement for execution. In contrast, a VLIW instruction (comprising multiple, parallel operations) is the fundamental encoding unit of the architecture. VLIW compiler designers and even assembly language programmers must group parallel operations just to produce correct code.

Fallacy: VLIW Instructions Have Fixed Width

Early VLIW ISAs did indeed use fixed-width instruction encoding, in which an *n*-issue machine required an *n*-operation-wide instruction every cycle. This led early critics to attack the inefficiency of VLIW instruction words, as schedule slots would often hold many nops. This spurred alternate encodings, with straightforward names such as nop compression or vertical (multicycle) nops. Such schemes required more complicated decoding hardware, perhaps the most complex being the routing network required to match the operations in the compressed instructions to their target execution pipeline. We describe such techniques in detail in Section 3.5.

Continuing with the second question, the "meaning" of an instruction also varies according to architectural style. By "meaning" we mean the set of operations that results from executing the instruction. To explore various design philosophies and their instruction coding styles we now give concrete examples of various instruction sets and their meanings.

RISC Encodings

The meaning of a RISC instruction is perhaps the simplest to convey: in the purest RISC architectures, a single instruction corresponds directly to a single operation. Note that there are dilutions of this 1:1 correspondence. Many RISC instructions encode multiple actions (e.g., post-increment load instructions, branch-and-link instructions, or even the calculation involved in addressing modes), but the overall point remains that one RISC instruction usually corresponds to a single operation on a single pipeline. We might describe the RISC style of encoding as "1:1," meaning that a single instruction triggers a single operation.

This simplicity in the mapping from ISA encoding to hardware execution means that decoding RISC instructions is considered easy. Few RISC microarchitectures spend more than a single pipeline stage in decoding, and many combine decoding and register fetch into the same phase because decoding is so simple.

Compiling to RISC architectures used to be considered more complicated than compiling for other architectures because of RISC "features" requiring compilation support. The longest-lasting such feature is large register sets, which require good register allocation strategies to achieve high performance. Other such features include limited scheduling to fill delay slots and support for "pseudo-operations" that do not exist in the base architecture but that can be synthesized syntactically out of other instructions. We say "used to be" because effective compilation techniques for each of these problems were found during the 1980s, and these compilation features have migrated into general compilers. These features are considered required parts of standard machine-specific optimization today.

CISC Encodings

CISC instructions may translate to multiple hardware operations. At the simple end of the spectrum, all CISC machines have a "RISC subset" and these instructions are often those that run fastest on state-of-the-art implementations. At the complex end of the spectrum, canonically CISC instructions such as string copies or polynomial evaluations can translate to thousands of operations across multiple pipelines and cycles. As described previously, CISC machines take variable-length instructions. Coupling these variable-length instructions with the dynamically variable numbers of run-time operations leads to a characterization of CISC encodings as "*variable:dynamic.*"

CISC implementations pay for the complexity of their ISA with corresponding complexity in their hardware. For example, decoding even the simple "RISC subset" x86 instructions requires many pipeline stages in current implementations. The trace caching technique of Pentium 4 processors can be seen as an attempt to remove CISC decoding from the main processor pipeline. Executing CISC instructions is also complex. Many operations require special control units ("microsequencers") that take over and operate the pipelines of the processor to carry out instruction semantics.

Compiling to CISC architectures is similar to compiling for RISC architectures, with a few interesting subtleties. CISC architectures typically have fewer registers and sometimes have special-purpose limitations on register usage. This complicates register allocation but also limits the choices a register allocator must make. Instruction selection can be more complicated because there are multiple, functionally equivalent ways to perform the same task. Last, CISC compilation provides us with a cautionary tale about removing abstraction boundaries. One of the historical motivations for CISC instructions was to allow hardware to capture more of the semantics of high-level languages. CISC designers justified the complex string, polynomial, and call-sequence instructions by claiming that they would simplify the task of the compiler. However, shifting the work from software to hardware is not unilaterally a good thing. Clever compiler writers discovered that instruction sequences built up from the "RISC subset" instructions

---

Stylistic Exceptions

In our discussion of encoding styles, virtually every architecture contains instruction encodings that muddy the general boundaries we draw between styles. For example, some RISC architectures (PowerPC, ARM) have "load/store multiple" instructions that lead to variable numbers of operations. Other RISC architectures (PowerPC and HP PA-RISC) include "post-increment/auto-update" addressing modes that change the value of the address register in addition to the primary effect of the instruction. Such exceptions are subtleties rather than counterexamples. Taxonomy is not a precise science, and inflexible requirements that all examples fit the mold miss the point. However, stylistic exceptions come with a cost, and they generally make implementation more difficult.

often ran faster than the complex (but compact) instructions. The following question was one of many that motivated RISC designers: If the compiler doesn't use the complex instructions, why have them?

RISC and CISC encodings framed the architectural style debate of the 1980s. However, there are more possibilities between RISC's bare-bones "*1:1*" encoding and CISC's kitchen-sink "*variable:dynamic*" encoding. Other architectural styles that were less visible (but certainly used in real machines during the 1980s) represent other points in the design space.

VLIW Encodings

VLIW instructions at first seem like a "*variable:variable*" encoding (especially given that VLIW instructions can have variable length). However, as we noted previously, VLIW syllables look very much like single RISC instructions. These encoded syllables line up 1:1 with operations, which means that we can more precisely define VLIW instructions as "*n:n*" rather than "*variable:variable.*" The dynamic variability in CISC instructions (such as string moves) is absent from the VLIW case, making the effects of a VLIW instruction knowable at compile-time.

Like the RISC case, the 1:1 correspondence makes VLIW decoding and execution relatively simple. There are complexities beyond those in a RISC machine because multiple operations must be identified and routed to the correct pipeline, but many aspects of decoding and execution are similar to those in a RISC processor (more about this in Chapter 5).

Compiling for a VLIW also resembles compiling for RISC machines, with one major difference: instruction scheduling, which was of minor importance in filling RISC architectural delay slots (some early RISC machines even left filling delay slots to the assembler), is necessary to produce correct VLIW code. All commercial VLIW architectures include support for global instruction scheduling and/or modulo scheduling in their compilers. Such optimizations are necessary to extract performance. Other compiler optimizations also play a large role in compiling to VLIWs (the bulk of Chapter 5, on compilation, discusses these types of optimizations and the benefits they confer).

Why Not Superscalar Encodings?

Although many superscalar machines are based on RISC architectures, superscalar decoding is more like variable-width VLIW decoding (*n:n*) than simple RISC decoding (*1:1*). In the RISC-based superscalars, every legal RISC instruction stream is also a legal superscalar instruction stream, and vice versa. However, not every legal RISC instruction stream enjoys improved performance on the superscalar. Rather, the "efficient" superscalar instruction streams are a subset of the valid RISC instruction streams. As in the VLIW case, the compiler ends up with the job of generating an efficient program. Such a "compatible but efficient" program requires the same types of optimizations required for the VLIW case. The situation is even more complicated for the CISC-based superscalars, because typically only a subset of the CISC architecture's instructions will operate efficiently on a particular implementation. CISC superscalar compilers often target only the

"RISC" subset of the CISC architecture; or, even more complexly, they must model the decoding constraints of the target CISC machine to achieve high instruction issue rates.

On the implementation side, superscalar decoding and issue is more difficult than VLIW decoding and issue, because there is nothing explicit in the instructions that tells where a parallelizable group of operations starts or ends. Rather, the *implementation* has the job of determining where legal parallel operations can be found. Even though the compiler may have knowingly placed parallelizable operations in the instruction stream, the implementation still has to perform the check each time.[7] With respect to encoding, superscalarity should be considered an encoding technique overlaid on an existing design style, rather than a design style in itself.

DSP Encodings

On a DSP, instructions usually have fixed length, but they may translate to multiple actions in various parts of the processor. We claim that this is "*1:n*" because a single instruction triggers a fixed number of parts of the processor to perform specific operations. We say "*1:n*" rather than "*1:variable*" because the set of operations is not typically dynamically variable. Rather, one instruction triggers the addressing unit, multiply-accumulate unit, and buses to perform various operations in the same cycle.

Figure 1.3 in Chapter 1 depicts the hardware *architecture* of the TI C54x series of DSPs. There are a number of different functional units in which operations occur. These include the ALU, the multiply-accumulate unit, the shift/rotate unit, and the address-generation unit (AGU). The diagram also depicts a number of processor buses to memory, multiplexers that allow limited connections among the functional units, and the architecturally visible registers of the architecture, including two 40-bit accumulators (A and B). The structure of this diagram suggests that some operations are difficult or impossible to perform, which is further constrained by the limited encodings available (only certain combinations of operations on functional units and certain combinations of multiplexer settings are possible).

The ISA of the TI C54x basically determines its implementation. There is very little room for performance-enhancing microarchitectural techniques, given the degree to which the capabilities and connections of functional units are nailed down by the ISA.

Compilation to DSP-style processors is difficult. The additional constraints placed by the ISA complicate the engineering of traditional machine-specific optimizations. For example, the scheduler might wish to perform two operations in the same cycle that cannot be specified by any valid instruction. Either the scheduler must be made aware of the encoding restrictions or some other pass that understands these restrictions must be extended to perform scheduler-like work. Given the baseline complexity of schedulers, the revised pass seems even more daunting. Code generation for DSPs remains an open research issue (commercial compilers today are not capable of producing code that is as efficient as that produced by hand coding).

---

7. Or at least the first time, as trace caches do in the Pentium 4 microarchitecture.

VLIW-Style DSPs

Recent processors aimed at the DSP market have been fundamentally VLIWs in both ISA and design philosophy. Examples include the TI C6x family of processors and the Motorola/Agere StarCore processors. Although such processors retain some DSP-oriented data representations (most notably, fixed-point support), their encodings, implementations, and compilers use instructions consisting of compiler-selected independent operations. Such processors belong in the VLIW part of our taxonomy, not the DSP part. We will treat them as VLIWs from here on.

Vector Encodings

Vector instruction sets have a "*1:variable*" flavor. Vector instructions have historically been fixed-sized, but a single vector instruction can specify a dynamically variable number of operations. This dynamic variability is not necessarily visible in the register set (vector registers have a fixed, known size) but is captured in the architectural state through vector loop counters and vector mask control registers.

Vector machines were built with technologies wherein computational logic was relatively expensive compared to memory or register storage. Consequently, vector machines typically had a single ALU and a "streaming" mechanism for performing vector instructions, wherein each element of a vector would be handled by the single ALU in a different machine cycle. Vectors multiplied the power of individual instructions, allowing impressive speedups in limited (typically, scientific) workloads. This multiplicative effect also enables some power savings in control logic, as a single instruction translates into many dynamic operations. Because the memory footprint of a vector load or store instruction could be determined reliably by the hardware, vector machines rarely had cached memory systems. Instead, they used multiple banks, triggering them at just the right time to supply or accept data. Modern vector machines perform vector operations in a temporally parallel manner, using n ALUs to operate simultaneously on data. Each ALU is said to have its own *lane*, and the vector machine is said to have multiple lanes.

Vector compilers became quite effective at identifying loops that could be efficiently executed on vector hardware and transmuting them into efficient vector code. Such techniques involved sophisticated loop analysis and a large set of loop-oriented transformations (e.g., index transformations, loop fusion, strip mining, and unroll-and-jam) that enabled the innermost loop to be phrased as a well-conditioned vector instruction. Such technologies remain in use today in a number of high-performance compilers. See Kennedy and Allen [2001] for an exhaustive treatment of these approaches.

Table 3.2 summarizes the various options for encoding instruction size versus the number of run-time operations launched. "Single" really means a single unit (either a single, fixed-sized instruction encoding unit or a single operation), whereas "variable" means possibly more than one but not dynamically changing. "Dynamic" means dynamically variable, whereby run-time values determine the number of operations performed.

Instruction Encoding Size	Number of Run-time Operations		
	Single	Variable	Dynamic
Single	RISC	DSP	Vector
Variable	(compressed RISC)	VLIW	CISC

TABLE 3.2 Summary of mappings from encoding instruction size to run-time operations launched.

There is no "Variable" row in the table because there are no instruction sets with dynamically variable-length instruction encodings. Except for the "compressed RISC" style, to which we will return later, each possibility is one which we have discussed above.

Few designers have the luxury of choosing the architectural style in which they work. The main point of this section was to explain the space of possible alternatives and the encoding-centric view of how they differ. We now switch from the wider perspective of "encoding in the large" to the detailed topic of encoding VLIW instructions out of RISC-like operations.

3.5 VLIW Encoding

This section returns to the topic of instruction encoding, whereby an ISA assigns interpretations to specific patterns of bits. Although we use the term *encoding*, we are really referring to two problems: encoding and decoding. Encoding is about building the program, a stream of bytes in memory that represents what the processor should do at run-time. Decoding is just the reverse: figuring out what the processor should do from the stream of bytes coming from memory. Decoding can be thought of as a microarchitectural problem, and we will indeed return to it in more detail in Section 5.3. However, the two problems must be solved together to produce efficient solutions.

Before proceeding, let's define some terms we will use throughout this discussion and for the rest of the book. We have already defined *instruction* to be the fundamental architectural unit of encoding, and *operation* to be the equivalent of a RISC instruction-like unit of work. An instruction is thus an architectural (or ISA-level) concept, whereas an operation is much more closely bound to the pipeline, or implementation level. To these we add two encoding-level concepts: the syllable and the bundle. We define a *syllable* as the smallest amount of memory by which an encoding can vary, and a *bundle* as the unit of encoding that aligns naturally with memory boundaries, regardless of instruction or operation boundaries. For most of the VLIW- and RISC-style encodings we discuss there is a 1:1 correspondence between syllables and operations. However, this is not the case for CISC-style encodings such as x86. Table 3.3 lists how architectural terms and sizes map from some popular architectures to our terminology.

Architecture	Instruction	Bundle	Operation	Syllable
MIPS	Instruction, 32-bit	No term	Instruction, 32-bit	Instruction, 32-bit
Alpha	Instruction, 32-bit	No term, but cache-line sized	Instruction, 32-bit	Instruction, 32-bit
Transmeta	Molecule, ?-bit	?, 128-bit	Atom, 32-bit	Atom, 32-bit
IPF	Group, variable-length	Bundle, 128-bit	Instruction, 41-bit	No term, 41-bit
x86	Instruction, variable-length	No term	Instruction, variable-length	No term, 8-bit

TABLE 3.3 Encoding terminology across various architectures. Each column is headed by a term used by this book. The equivalent term in the language of another ISA is listed in the body of the table.

3.5.1 Operation Encoding

Instructions in modern architectures fall into four major categories. *Computational* instructions perform calculations. These include the usual integer, floating-point, and fixed-point operations, as well as comparison, logical, bit-shift (or bit-select), and conversion operations. *Memory* operations move data from register to memory. Many architectures also include fancy addressing modes that allow address calculations to be folded into particular instructions. Many architectural styles blur the distinction between computational and memory operations by allowing some operands of computational instructions to be specified by memory-addressing modes. *Branch and control* operations redirect program control. These include conditional and unconditional branches, calls, and return. Last, all architectures include *maintenance* instructions that do not easily fit into the categories previously discussed. They are typically privileged instructions executed only in supervisor mode. Examples of maintenance instructions include TLB and cache flushes for consistency, and returns from interrupts. Chapter 4 provides concrete details about the structures that support each of these categories of operations.

Encoding RISC-style instructions, or VLIW-style operations, is relatively straightforward. Typically, known ranges of bits within a 32-bit syllable correspond to operation codes (opcodes), register specifiers, and immediate values. There may be additional interpretation of some ranges, depending on the value of the opcode. RISC encodings are described in many basic architecture textbooks. In this section we assume an underlying RISC-style encoding into syllables, and we consider how to represent VLIW instructions in program memory.

3.5.2 Instruction Encoding

The "very long" nature of VLIW architecture has two immediately obvious consequences: programs made of "very long" instructions may end up being very long themselves, and fetching the "very long" instructions from memory may require high memory bandwidth. These are bad characteristics in any environment, but because "long" directly affects power, cost, and size they are especially bad in the embedded world. VLIW ISAs for embedded systems must consider ways to compactly encode programs. Such techniques include both clever encoding and compression.

Note that compacting or compressing the instruction encodings works against implementation simplicity. We observed previously that VLIW architectures have "*n:n*" encodings, whereby one syllable translates to one operation. At one extreme, the simplest VLIW encoding scheme would align operations 1:1 with the functional unit slots in memory. Such an extreme encoding (unfortunately the model VLIW critics often hold in their heads) wastes memory, encoding nops in those cases for which the compiler does not use a functional unit. In other words, uncompressed VLIW instructions are often excessively wide. Compilers do not always fill all functional units in all cycles. It is hoped they do a good job in the critical sections of code relevant to performance, but the encoding also has to consider the large parts of applications with limited amounts of ILP.

How do we reduce size requirements for VLIW instructions? We will return to system-level code compression techniques in Section 9.3. Here, we consider ways to simply remove nops from a VLIW encoding. We can distinguish two types of nops: *vertical* and *horizontal*. Vertical nops appear as an effect of exposed latencies, when the compiler is unable to fill latency cycles with other useful operations. Removing vertical nops is straightforward, and the most common way is through *multicycle nop* instructions (see Figure 3.4). A multicycle nop fills the machine pipeline with nops for a given number of cycles. However, even if the technique is simple, its effectiveness depends on how efficiently we can encode the *multicycle nop* directive. For example, if we can "steal" a few bits from the encoding of an individual syllable, we can implement a (virtually free) multicycle nop that can completely hide vertical nops.[8] If, on the other hand, we need to spend an extra syllable for the multicycle nop, its effectiveness drastically diminishes. For example, it is only useful to encode sequences of two or more nops.

Horizontal nops appear as an effect of the inability of the compiler to use all functional units in the machine in a single cycle. Removing horizontal nops is more challenging, since it impacts the overall decoding strategy. Researchers have traditionally approached the problem of removing horizontal nops in two ways. Representing the removed nops requires bits, and the bits can be either fixed (per instruction) or variable (per operation). In a fixed-overhead (or *compressed format*) encoding, some number of bits is dedicated per instruction to representing the nops. Compressed formats often use a form of run-length encoding, templates, or mask bits. In a variable-overhead encoding, a bit per operation (either a "start bit" or "stop bit") indicates the beginning or end of the instruction.

---

8. Incidentally, this is the model adopted by VEX.

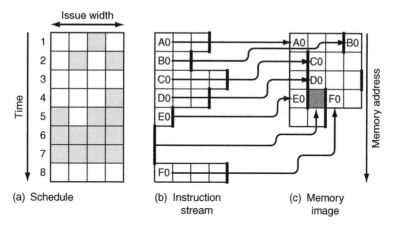

FIGURE 3.4 **How a VLIW schedule can be encoded compactly using horizontal and vertical nops.** This example shows a schedule for a 4-wide VLIW machine over eight cycles. In (a), gray boxes indicate nops in the original schedule. (b) shows the temporally equivalent instruction stream (made up of 0 to 4 operations per instruction) with variable-width instructions. Instruction length might be encoded using start bits, stop bits, or templates in each case. Darkened vertical bars show the end of each instruction. (c) shows the corresponding memory image for this instruction stream. Cycles 6 and 7 are nop cycles, and thus are replaced by a vertical nop instruction, represented by the gray box in (c) between operation EO and operation FO. Instruction boundaries are still portrayed in the memory image, although they are of course encoded within the constituent instructions and operations.

Fixed-overhead Encoding

Fixed-overhead encoding is a fixed-overhead compressed format for VLIW instructions. It was used in first-generation VLIW machines, such as the Multiflow TRACE. It involves prepending a syllable-sized bit mask to all instructions, to specify the mapping between parts of the instructions and slots in the instruction buffer. The main advantage of this approach is its simplicity. The main disadvantage is the fact that shorter formats need to pay the price (in terms of mask bits) for the longest possible VLIW instruction. Figure 3.5 shows an example of mask-based encoding.

Distributed Encoding

Distributed encoding is a variable-overhead method of encoding VLIW instructions by explicitly inserting a *stop bit* to delimit the end of the current instruction (or a *start bit* for the start of the next instruction). Compared against mask encoding, variable-size encoding has the advantage of having a distributed and incremental encoding cost that does not penalize the shortest instructions. In addition, there is no need to explicitly encode the "next PC," as it is obvious from the presence of the start or stop bit. On the negative side, it does require a more complex decoding scheme and a more complex sequencing scheme (for example, it is necessary to "look ahead" for the next stop bit to find the next PC). An equivalent alternative to the use of start/stop bits uses the concept

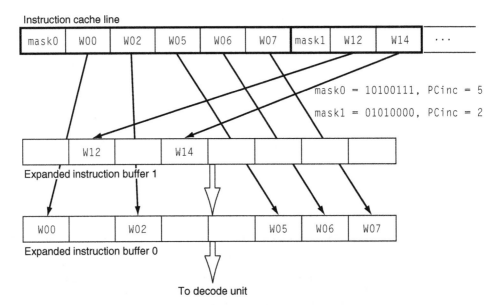

FIGURE 3.5 **Example of mask-based VLIW encoding.** The idea behind mask-based encoding is to add "mask bits" (or templates) to a VLIW instruction to identify "what goes where" in the expanded instruction buffer (containing all nops), and at the same time to precompute the address of the "next PC" so that we can keep filling the pipeline. In the example, the "mask" field contains both the dispersal information and the information to compute the next PC (expressed as number of operations). The figure shows a 2-deep instruction buffer FIFO (first-in, first-out), and the concept can easily be extended to other configurations.

of a *parallel bit* (used in the TI C6x family) to identify whether the next operation is in parallel with the current one. Figure 3.6 shows an example of distributed-overhead encoding.

Template-based Encoding

Template-based encoding has been used in some architectures as a fixed-overhead encoding that does not use an entire syllable of overhead per instruction. In a template-based scheme, a number of bits per instruction (or group of operations) designates the types of operations in the instruction and the boundaries between parallelizable operations. Typically, the template encoding is not complete (that is, there are more possible combinations than can be expressed by the template bits), and thus only certain combinations of operation types or parallelizable boundaries can be expressed. Template-based encoding makes for relatively low overhead, does not require expensive decoding, and does not penalize short instructions. However, the limited set of legal template values necessitates additional compiler support, and some nop instructions may still need to be encoded when the available templates do not match the generated code. Finally, templates for groups of operations can be chained to construct wider instructions. IPF is the most

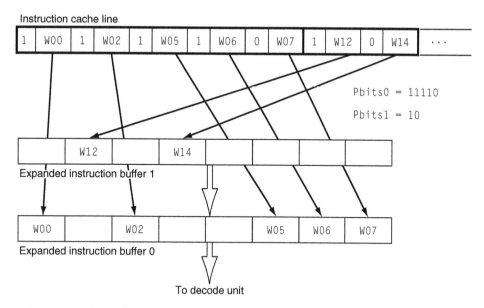

FIGURE 3.6   Example of distributed encoding. This diagram shows an example of variable-size, variable-overhead distributed VLIW format (similar to the scheme the TI C6x adopts). Here, we use *p-bits* (parallel bits) to identify what operations are executed in parallel (*stop bits* are negated *p-bits*). The decoding logic needs to scan the *p-bits* to find the end of each instruction.

prominent current example of a template-based VLIW encoding. Figure 3.7 illustrates template-based encoding.

3.5.3 Dispatching and Opcode Subspaces

Dispatching is the action of identifying the correspondence between operations and functional units, and routing the corresponding bits to them. Typically considered an implementation aspect, dispatching also affects VLIW instruction encoding. In the "*n:n*" naive encoding, the mapping from syllables to functional units was determined entirely positionally. After we have compressed out nops, this correspondence is lost. Some architectures reuse encodings per functional unit (i.e., a particular syllable indicates a different operation to the integer adder than to the load/store unit), and thus additional encoding bits must be dedicated to show what goes where. To specify this, the choice is to use one or a combination of *template bits* (using a fixed number of bits per VLIW instruction), *unit identifiers in the operations* (using a fixed number of bits per operation), or *positional encoding* (based on syllable ordering within the instruction). There are additional microarchitectural issues of aligning instructions and dispatching them to the appropriate functional unit (these issues are covered in the next chapter).

Clusters add another layer of encoding hierarchy between instructions and operations. On a multicluster machine, operations will need to be routed to clusters and functional units within the clusters. This is an encoding and dispatching problem

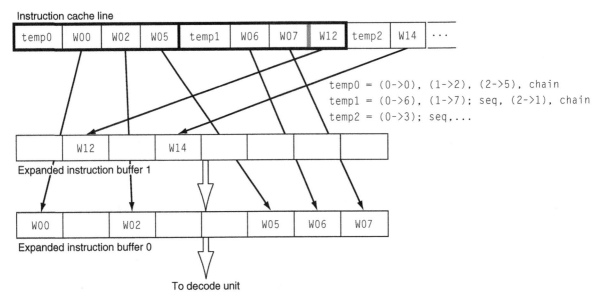

FIGURE 3.7 **Example of template-based VLIW encoding.** In this example of template-based encoding (similar to IPF) templates encode combinations of three operations, can specify sequential or parallel execution, and can be chained with following groups. Template encoding is similar to mask encoding. Here, unlike Figures 3.5 and 3.6, we need three separate templates to encode the sample combination. The description shows the semantics of the template entries, wherein "*chain*" indicates a chaining with the next group and "*seq.*" indicates a sequential point.

analogous to the problems of matching operations to functional units (many encodings just add another layer to the encoding hierarchy between the instruction and operation level). However, clustering can be encoded many different ways with different scopes: in longer or shorter register specifiers, in additional per-operation flags, or in cluster-level flags within an instruction. For example, the TI C6x architecture uses an encoding bit per operation to select clusters, whereas the HP/ST Lx (ST200) architecture uses *cluster-start* bits that work similarly to *instruction-start* bits.

Dispatching and clustering also offer opportunities for partitioning the opcode space. In a 32-bit RISC operation, operation codes can be precious resources, as there may be only a 5- or 6-bit opcode field in the encoding. ISA designers can shift some of this encoding burden into the dispatch or cluster encoding by treating different functional unit types or clusters as different encoding subspaces. That is, an opcode that means one thing for one functional unit or cluster might mean an entirely different thing on another functional unit or cluster. This technique, used by many architectures, might be called "opcode subspaces."

VLIW architectures allow some forms of encoding flexibility that is not available to other architectural styles. The most prominent example is long immediate values. A long immediate is exactly that: dedicating one or more encoding syllables to an immediate operand value by using special template or operation boundary values to indicate the presence of the long immediate (this breaks the nice 1:1 correspondence between

---

Pitfall: Effective Instruction Size

Many manufacturers claim compact code size as a benefit of their ISA or architectural style. RISC encodings are considered "less dense" than comparable CISC encodings, and experience with server machines does indeed suggest that x86 programs are smaller and require less instruction memory bandwidth than the same programs compiled for RISC-based servers. This means that both statically and dynamically the average x86 instruction, of variable size but made up of 8-bit syllables, is smaller than 32 bits.

In response to a need for more compact instruction sets, some RISC architectures (notably ARM and MIPS) have introduced alternate instruction sets (called Thumb and MIPS16, respectively). Such compressed RISC instruction sets use 16-bit syllables and instructions, but do so at the cost of omitting some opcodes and even some register specifiers. Transitions between 16-bit and 32-bit code are performed by special *mode-switch* instructions. Functionality available only in 32-bit mode can therefore be expensive to access.

However, small syllable size is no guarantee of small code size. The Agere/Motorola StarCore architecture has a 16-bit syllable size, but its average dynamically weighted instruction length tends to be closer to 32 bits than the 16 bits the syllable size would suggest, because important features are encoded as "prefix" syllables that modify the meaning of what follows, and such prefixes are surprisingly common.

For embedded processing, beware manufacturers' claims of "compact" code size. Check their numbers.

---

syllables and operations). Long immediates complicate decoding hardware but simplify the compiler and operating system support required to build large immediate values.

3.6 Encoding and Instruction-set Extensions

Over their lifetimes, successful ISAs grow and change. This section briefly discusses how extensions affect encoding instructions. Chapter 6 covers the much larger topic of how to use scalability and extensibility in the design process.

Many architectures leave room to grow in their encoding spaces by reserving values for future definition. In fixed-length instruction sets (e.g., RISC), this is commonly implemented by reserving opcodes or sub-opcodes, which can be assigned to operations in a later version of the architecture. In variable-length instruction sets (e.g., CISC), expansion is in principle even easier, because a single reserved opcode can be defined to indicate that an entirely new encoding for the rest of the instruction follows. Variable-length instruction sets also use prefixes to extend the instruction set, whereby a previously unused prefix value changes the interpretation of the rest of the instruction. All types of instruction sets can be extended using *mode bits*, whereby administrative instructions tell the processor to switch to a different decoder.

ISA extensions make a break with previous implementations. A processor without the new instructions might be able to emulate them more slowly in software, but typically code that uses ISA extensions causes illegal instruction exceptions on processors lacking the necessary hardware. In general-purpose computing, this complicates the software task, as multiple versions of the code (some taking advantage of the extensions, some built to run on hardware lacking the extensions) must be distributed. This issue is much less important to embedded designers, who exercise greater control over which versions of hardware and software are used together.

Of the CISC-style instruction set architectures, x86 has had one of the most varied histories, morphing in different generations from a 16-bit to a 32-bit architecture (and possibly even to a 64-bit architecture with the latest Opteron processors from AMD) and adding new operation types and register banks. Changes to the x86 ISA have come through all of the encoding tricks listed previously: mode bits, reserved opcodes, and special prefix syllables. Detractors of the x86 architecture observe that the architecture carries its history into every implementation (it is still possible, for example, to use a modern Pentium in the old 8086 20-bit addressing mode). The burden of supporting backward compatibility does not appear to be hurting x86 performance.[9]

RISC architectures also gather extensions and modes over time. Both MIPS and ARM support a compressed instruction-set variant (see the sidebar "Pitfall: Effective Instruction Size") with 16-bit instruction words. The MIPS architecture also began its life with endianness selection at boot time, and it gained another mode when the floating-point register file effectively doubled in size. RISC designers also tend to leave room to grow in their encoding spaces (each of the multimedia instruction set extensions was placed within the existing encoding space of the original RISC ISA).

The smallest type of instruction-set extension is a new operation that operates on an existing data type. Extensions give a small degree of customizability that can pay large dividends for specific applications. Such extensions also make for entertaining gossip. For example, the primary use of "population count" operations (which count the number of 1-bits in a register) is in cryptography applications. Other operation-based extensions have included prefetch support, endianness byte swaps, conditional moves, conditional selection, and bit extraction/insertion for protocol processing. Start-ups such as Tensilica dedicate encoding space to user-defined opcodes that use the standard general-purpose register file but may be handled by special functional units.

Other common types of ISA extensions add support for new data types. Floating-point coprocessors are just one of many such examples in the general-purpose world. More recently, multimedia extensions, micro-SIMD extensions, and DSP-related extensions have been added to a variety of processors. Data types that require special registers (e.g., extra-precision accumulators for fixed-point arithmetic, or double-precision floating-point results for multiplies and divides) sometimes also require new encodings,

---

9. However, Bob Colwell, architect of the Pentium Pro through Pentium 4 implementations, claims that he could have gotten 30% more performance if he did not have to support backward compatibility.

although the special registers are equally often implied by the exotic opcodes for the new data type.

ISA extensions apply to all architectures, but VLIW architectures have particular advantages in *scalability* and *customizability*, which we will revisit throughout this book, particularly in Chapter 10.

3.7 Further Reading

An important reference for the subject of instruction-set design is the Hennessy–Patterson [2003] book on computer architecture. Much less popular these days, but an interesting taxonomical journey through ISAs, is Blauuw and Brooks' book on computer architecture [1997].

Although successful ISAs have a long history of extensions and versions, this history can be difficult to find, as manufacturers would prefer that developers use the most recent version of the architecture. Nonetheless, even current ISA manuals can give some idea of how ISAs are extended, because they typically cover a couple of versions of each architecture: the old one and the new one. An instructive way to learn about instruction-set architectures is to download, read, and compare and contrast ISA manuals for widely used processors. For example, MIPS, Alpha, and PowerPC for RISC architectures; the IPF architecture for an example of complex encoding; x86 for the "canonical" CISC instruction set; the TI C54 for DSP; and ARM for embedded.

More details on the information theory aspects of encoding can be found in any good information theory book, such as the book by Cover and Thomas [1991].

Much early work on dataflow machines was performed by Jack Dennis's group at MIT, and is described by Dennis and Misunas [1974]. Interest in this subject quickly spread to Manchester, England; Japan; and the University of California at Irvine and later MIT (via Arvind). A good reference for Arvind's group's work was written by Arvind, Kathail, and Pingali [1980].

For broader architecture issues, in addition to Hennessy and Patterson, a good collection of computer architecture papers was collected and annotated by Hill, Jouppi, and Sohi [1999]. A classic paper that talks about weakness and power in computer design is Lampson's *Hints for Computer System Design* [1983].

3.8 Exercises

1. The TI C6x DSP processor architecture is an *equals* machine that exposes the latency of memory operations to the compiler (for example, five cycles for the TI C62xx). Comment on the implications of this architectural choice with respect to register pressure, register allocation algorithm, and interrupt responsiveness.

2. Find two commercially available processor architectures such that one hides and the other exposes the latency of the same nonmemory operation to the compiler.

3. The IPF architecture dedicates 5 template bits for every 128-bit bundle (of three operations). The template field specifies two properties: stops within the current bundle and the mapping of instruction slots to execution types. Using the architecture reference manual, determine the number of possible combinations of the three operations (and their stop bits) in a bundle, and what percentage of them is allowed by the 5-bit template.

4. Using VEX on a benchmark of choice, compute how many horizontal nop operations are removed through the use of the stop bit with respect to a naive VLIW encoding that contains all nops as explicit operations. What if you used a run-length encoding method that compresses sequences of nops in a single operation? Repeat the experiment by varying the width of the target VEX machine.

5. Look up the encoding manual for a RISC instruction set of your choice (e.g., ARM, PowerPC, or MIPS). Pick two ALU operations. Write a C function that given the two operations returns *true* if and only if the second operation depends on the first. Make sure to handle opcode decoding, operand decoding, identification of immediates, and predication (if applicable). Draw a block diagram logical circuit equivalent to the C function (this would be part of the superscalar issue logic).

6. Using the same information of the previous exercise, identify opportunities for instruction-set extension (or scaling) in that ISA. Are there any parts of the encoding space that are especially "precious," such as immediate modes (PowerPC), memory encodings, and so on?

7. In the text (Section 3.2) we say it is difficult to imagine a VLIW system that violates the following characterization: "compiling to target a specific implementation is required for correctness." Write a short essay on whether the IPF architecture is a VLIW according to this definition.

8. In Figure 3.5 it says, "...and at the same time to precompute the address of the next PC, so that we can keep filling the pipeline." What is the ambiguity about what the next PC is? Can you describe the computation that must be done?

9. Using the VEX compiler and the provided assembler parser "template," generate the assembler for a program of your choice. Estimate the code density for a variety of different horizontal nop schemes: explicit nop, mask-based encoding (make a reasonable assumption about mask size), template-based encoding (define your own templates), and stop-bit encoding.

10. Using the VEX compiler and the provided assembler parser "template," generate the assembler for a program of your choice. Collect statistics when instructing the compiler to generate multiple nops (*xnops*) or expanded nops.

Assuming different costs of an *xnop* operation, what is the break-even point for which using *xnop* is not beneficial?

11. Write a C program that exercises a "population count" function (count the number of 1s or 0s in a register). Implement an efficient version of the function in C. Using the VEX compiler and the "custom instruction" facility of VEX, implement the same function as an assembly language intrinsic. Measure the performance difference of the two implementations.

12. Repeat the previous exercise for the "find leading 1" (or "find leading 0") operation.

13. Using the VEX compiler and simulator, compile and simulate a benchmark of your choice and run it on representative inputs. Collect the static IPC information for each function (using the *pcntl* utility) and the dynamic IPC information (from the simulator output). Compare and contrast the two sets of data. Why are they different?

14. Characterize programs that could run on the Intel Xscale processor but could not run on an ARM7TDMI processor core. Describe the reason for the incompatibility. Give some examples. Are the two processors binary compatible? Are they compatible in one direction but not the other?

15. What is ARM-Thumb? Is it object-code compatible with ARM? Can they be mixed in the same program, and if so at what granularity and under what conditions? Why would anybody want to do such a thing?

16. Compare and contrast MIPS-16, ARM-Thumb, and/or other compressed ISA-visible instruction-set variants of existing commercial microprocessors.

17. Design a compressed VEX instruction set that would still be useful. Using the VEX tools and a static program analysis, compute what compression ratio would be achievable with the proposed compressed scheme. Draw a block diagram that describes the impact on the fetch mechanism.

4

Architectural Structures in ISA Design

Architecture is the art of how to waste space.

— Philip Johnson, *American architect*, b. 1906

This chapter forms a bridge between the ISA-wide architectural issues of the previous chapter and the ISA-invisible microarchitectural techniques discussed in the next chapter. The following sections discuss the most distinguishing topics in the design of a VLIW ISA, and in particular they discuss many of the common hardware *structures* (and the operations that drive them) within the ISA. Far from exhaustively covering all areas, we emphasize those areas most relevant to embedded architectures.

We begin in Section 4.1 with the datapath, the heart of any processor core. Datapath design includes the types of execution units, the widths of the data lines, and the common arithmetic and logic operations performed by the core. The next section covers registers and clusters. Clusters are intimately related to the datapath, but can be considered the next level of design "above" the datapath level (all machines have datapaths with associated registers, but only some machines need to have clustered designs).

The two following sections discuss seemingly straightforward topics: the memory architecture and the branch architecture. Memory architecture includes considerations of addressing modes, access size, alignment issues, and the effect (and visibility) of caches and the memory hierarchy. Branch architecture includes deconstructing branches into their fundamental components, handling multiway branches, handling branches in clustered architectures, and handling branches in loop-dominated code.

The next section discusses speculation and predication, high-performance techniques that might be seen as questionable in the embedded domain. Both involve performing work that might not turn out to be used by the processor, which might

A VEX Primer

The remainder of this chapter includes several illustrative examples with code snippets written in VEX ("*VLIW Example*") assembly. Appendix A gives a more complete discussion of the VEX architecture, but we provide a quick overview here to make it easy for the reader to understand this chapter. VEX *instructions* (what gets issued in a cycle) consist of *operations* (units of execution). A VEX operation is described through its *opcode*, followed by a list of destination and source *operands*. On clustered VEX variants, the opcode may be preceded by a *cluster* specifier that identifies the executing cluster (the cluster specifier and register number are separated by a dot). In VEX assembly, instructions are separated by a double semicolon, and there is one operation per line. For example, the following sequence shows two instructions: the first with two operations, the second with three operations.

```
add $r13 = $r3, $r0 # i0, op 0
sub $r16 = $r6, 3 # i0, op 1
;; ## end of 1st instruction

shl $r13 = $r13, 3 # i1, op 0
shr $r15 = $r15, 9 # i1, op 1
ldw.d $r14 = 0[$r4] # i1, op 2
;; ## end of 2nd instruction
```

VEX opcodes are mnemonics that represent the corresponding operations (e.g., *add* is an addition, *sub* is a subtraction, *shl/shr* are left/right shifts, *ldw* is a memory load, and *stw* is a memory store). VEX registers start with a "$" followed by the register bank specifier, the (optional) cluster identifier, and the register number. For example, *$r0.3* identifies general register "*$r*" number 3 in cluster 0 (often abbreviated as *$r3*), whereas *$b1.4* identifies branch register "*$b*" number 4 in cluster 1. VEX supports three types of register banks, general registers ("*$r*"), branch registers ("*$b*"), and link registers ("*$l*"). Immediates and constants are written without any additional prefix. Memory operands follow the notation "*offset[base]*" with a constant offset and a register base (e.g., *ldw $r3 = 4[$r5]*).

After the opcode, the "=" sign divides the list of output destinations (left of the "=") from the list of input sources (right of the "=").

VEX exposes latencies, and we use the "*xnop <num>*" pseudo-operation to represent empty cycles. Depending on the microarchitecture, this can be turned into explicit nop instructions or might be directly supported by hardware. The *xnop* pseudo-operation does not require a ";;" instruction delimiter.

waste transistors, power, or space. However, history teaches us that today's embedded processor was yesterday's high-performance general-purpose processor, and thus we can expect speculation and predication to make their way into embedded processing as well.

The last section of this chapter describes system operations. System operations are all of the complicated maintenance- and security-related work required for building a real system, but these are typically only briefly mentioned except in hardware reference manuals.

4.1 The Datapath

We define the datapath of a VLIW architecture (see Figure 4.1) as the collection of its execution units, which perform data transformation. A compiler breaks down the computation of a program into basic operations it then maps to the corresponding computational units. In the following paragraphs, we characterize computational operations and the datapath across their many dimensions, such as operand locations, widths, and operation repertoire. We also touch on special-purpose operations, and we discuss how immediate operands (constants) are managed and used.

4.1.1 Location of Operands and Results

Traditional CISC and DSP instruction sets favor operations that read and write their results directly to and from memory (*memory-to-memory*). Sometimes (in *stack machines)* the processor stack holds operands and results. VLIW architectures, like many RISC processors, rely on large register files and simpler instruction semantics. As a consequence, a VLIW instruction set is largely limited to *register-to-register* operations that read and write values to and from individual registers.

DSPs commonly use special-purpose registers with dedicated connections, called *accumulators.* An *accumulator* is a target register of an ALU that can be used to facilitate reduction operations, such as the dot product. Accumulators also have power advantages, as they reduce accesses to the central register file in inner loops.

Clean VLIW architectures eschew these idiosyncratic types of storage, because they force the compiler to make binding choices and optimizations too early. Ideally, a compiler would decouple the problems of scheduling and register allocation (as we discuss in the chapters about compilation). The presence of special-purpose registers with limited connectivity forces some register allocation choices to be made during scheduling, or vice versa. The VLIW design philosophy aims to enable the compiler to optimize the program, and special locations complicate this task.

4.1.2 Datapath Width

By *datapath width* we mean the bit width of the basic architecture containers (registers) that manipulate *integer, long,* and *pointer* data types in C. Once the size of the containers is fixed, the rest of the datapath and the execution units follow. Traditional CISC and RISC instruction sets adopt one or two datapath widths (typically, a narrower integer datapath and an optional wider floating-point datapath). DSP architectures tend to include a more liberal variety of widths to accommodate different precision requirements. For example, it is not uncommon to find 40-bit or 56-bit accumulators and functional units in DSPs dedicated to audio processing (often, the 40-bit or 56-bit

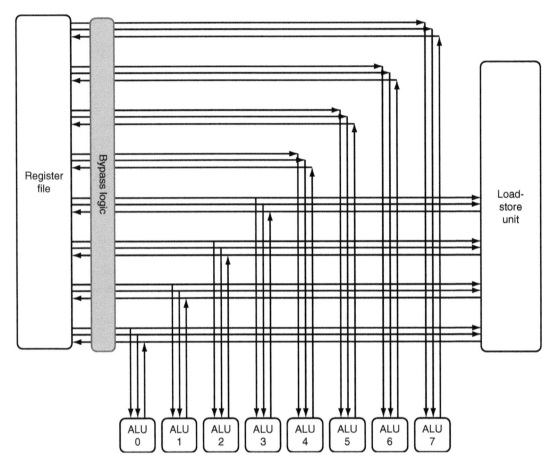

FIGURE 4.1 **Logical VLIW datapath.** This figure shows the basic connections of an eight-unit VLIW datapath (single cluster), where eight ALUs are connected to a single multiported register file. The datapath is organized in *lanes* (one per unit) that roughly correspond to issue slots in the VLIW instruction. Each unit uses a dedicated lane and a dedicated set of ports in the register files. All units are connected through a bypassing network that reduces the visible operation latency. In this example, we show four ports to a multiported memory unit that can only be accessed through some of the issue slots. Many details of a real datapath are omitted (such as pipeline staging registers, control paths, and so on), and the schematic is not representative of the physical layout, but we can certainly see the congestion of wires in the center of the datapath that ultimately limits the scalability of a fully connected machine.

accumulators can only be accessed through narrower buses). In this respect, VLIW architectures are much closer to the RISC mentality, and are partial to a few generic widths at which the compiler can comfortably map computation.

In the context of embedded CPUs, it is important to understand the relationship between datapath width and bandwidth to memory (note that clock rate and bus protocol overhead also have first-order impact on memory bandwidth). Some embedded architectures might require wider paths to memory than what is offered by the natural datapath width. For example, architectures targeting intensive media processing favor memory accesses that are wider than the standard 32-bit integer access. In a scalar 32-bit machine, the only way to widen the access to memory is to introduce wider containers (for example, 64-bit registers) and corresponding memory operations. This implies adding an extra datapath (register, wires, units) in addition to the standard 32-bit datapath. In a wide-issue VLIW machine, we have a cleaner alternative in coalescing adjacent parallel issue slots to virtually widen the datapath. This requires only small amounts of extra hardware. One might call this technique "superword parallelism" because it assembles larger operational units out of the standard-width units of the machine. For example, in an 8-wide 32-bit VLIW what we really have are eight independent 32-bit datapaths. In this configuration nothing prevents us from treating the machine as four 64-bit datapaths, two 128-bit datapaths, one 256-bit datapath, or any intermediate combination (see Figure 4.2). In other words, we can easily implement wider accesses to memory (as well as wider functional units) without overhead (except the encoding of new operations and the possible inter-unit connections). In this configuration, absent wider hardware containers expressing a 64-bit operation require explicitly naming multiple registers. In VEX, a 64-bit load/store pair might look like the following:

```
## This implements:
##      long long *p, *q;
##      q[1] = p[0];
## (p in $r1, q in $r2)
## Where "ldd" is a 64b load and "std" a 64b store
##
      ldd $r3, $r4 = 0[$r1] ## 2 reg outputs
      xnop 2 ## assuming 3-cycle load
;;
      std 8[$r2] = $r3, $r4 ## 2 reg inputs
;;
```

4.1.3 Operation Repertoire

Choosing the operation repertoire of an ISA is complicated by the fact that there are many ways to implement the same functionality. Each of the alternatives presents a different tradeoff among efficiency, performance, complexity, design, and silicon cost. As the philosophy behind RISC design teaches us, the choice of which operation to implement in hardware (and which we should leave to the compiler) ought to be driven by a balanced decision process that takes into consideration application analysis and execution frequency of each operation, compiler technology, implementation complexity, and progress of hardware technology over the estimated life of the architecture. Other considerations — such as design style or code size, not to mention the personal preferences of the principal architects — also play an important role that should

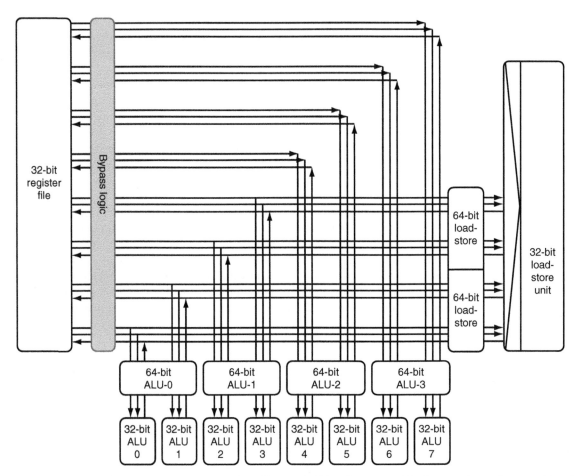

FIGURE 4.2 **Datapath widths in a VLIW architecture.** This diagram shows the versatility of a VLIW datapath, wherein starting from the base VLIW structure of Figure 4.1 it is possible to simultaneously implement multiple widths with minimal additional hardware complexity. In the example, we show how an 8-wide 32-bit VLIW datapath can be configured to appear as a 4-wide 64-bit VLIW datapath. Note how 32-bit operands in adjacent functional units can be grouped and operated upon as 64-bit quantities (this also allows the creation of large constants). In a similar way, VLIWs can also be configured to support operations with more than two input operands or a single output operand.

not be underestimated. In the embedded world, the characteristics of the application domain are also one of the most important decision criteria.

In some cases, choices are rather straightforward. Figuring out whether an application needs hardware support for floating-point operations can be as simple as a "visual inspection" of the application domain. In other cases, this is not always an easy accomplishment. Deciding whether an application needs a generic *bit-extract* operation or whether it can use a combination of shifts and logical operations is a very

Pitfall: Relying on Execution Frequency for ISA Design

Early RISC papers (ca. 1983) said exactly that execution frequency should be the major driving force behind the choice of an instruction set. Although in principle this is true, we have all learned a lot since then. This part of RISC philosophy was responsible for branch delay slots, for example, a choice that would have made it through the filter above but is in retrospect a bad idea. One should be very careful about making architectural choices based on microarchitectural expedients, because microarchitectures can change very rapidly with process or packaging technology, whereas (successful) architectures are forever. There is far more to product success than cranking applications and execution frequency through a spreadsheet.

(Contributed by Bob Colwell)

difficult decision. To make these choices, an architect would have to collect static and dynamic profiling information, evaluate the implementation complexity and the impacts on cycle speed and pipeline depth, experiment with both options implemented in a compiler, estimate the impact on code size and performance, and extrapolate all of the previous for varying ILP and likely improvements of the circuit technology.

Many of the operations discussed in this section allow architects to make a trade-off between hardware and software complexity, decomposing larger operations into smaller components that can be implemented more easily in the microarchitecture. This is similar to the division between "assembly" and "machine" language in some RISC architectures, wherein semantically useful assembly operations are translated by the assembler into a small, fixed number of machine operations. Because of this hardware/software tradeoff, many of the parts of this section include code samples with code sequences that have equivalent effect.

Simple Integer and Compare Operations

These are the basic units of the execution of any program, and must be coded and executed efficiently. For example, VEX defines an extended set of operations that includes addition, subtraction, left and right shifts (with signed/unsigned variants where needed), a full set of compare operations, and bitwise operations (binary AND, OR, and XOR). Most architectures include these with little variation. Some of the minor choices here involve the legal combinations of register and immediates, as well as the handling of various corner cases, such as flags.

Carry, Overflow, and Other Flags

The handling of flags merits special mention. Operations in CISC architectures implicitly set arithmetic flags (carry, overflow, zero, negative, and sometimes more) based on the result of any computation. The problem with operations that implicitly set status flags is that they also implicitly enforce sequential execution, because reordering instructions will change the value of the status register. The compiler must model the extra flag results, increasing the complexity of the dependence analysis and limiting the valid set of code motions. When issuing parallel operations in a VLIW instruction, an additional complexity comes from the fact that multiple operations may attempt to write the same set of flags, causing an ambiguity in the execution behavior.

A simpler approach, adopted by more modern ISAs, requires all results of any operation to be explicitly named so that the compiler does not get confused about what can be reordered and what cannot. For example, only one of the simple integer operations in VEX explicitly reads and sets flags (*addcg*, "add with carry and generate carry"), whereas no other operations produce flags. In addition, the approach of having a single location for flags (normally the *program status word*), is a poor match with VLIW, in that it inhibits parallel execution. A better approach stores flags in architecturally visible containers. For example, VEX stores the carry generated by *addcg* in *branch registers* (a set of single-bit registers).

Common Bitwise Utilities

These include the operations the compiler uses to extract and deposit bit fields, and to sign-extend or zero-extend values when implementing conversions. Strictly speaking, none of these operations is necessary, because they can be synthesized from shift and logical operations, but they are useful and easy enough to implement. A minimal set (for example, what is implemented in VEX) includes sign and zero extensions for 8-bit and 16-bit quantities (used to manipulate *char* and *short* data types in C). A more extensive set could include generic *extract* and *deposit* operations to manipulate arbitrarily sized bit fields.

Integer Multiplication

Most embedded processors require an efficient set of multiplication operations. Unfortunately, multipliers are large and slow, and thus it is not uncommon to break down a general 32-bit multiplication into simpler components. For example, VEX supports a set of 16 x 32 multiplication operations. To implement a 32-bit multiplication, the compiler emits the following sequence:

```
## A 32-bit integer multiplication, such as:
##      int a, b, c;
##      c = a * b;
##
## Can be broken down as:
##      int low = ((short)a) * b;
##      int high = (((short) (a >> 16)) * b) << 16;
##      c = low + high;
##
## In VEX (with 2 multipliers), this becomes:
## (a in $r1, b in $r2 and c in $r3)
```

```
##
      mpylu $r4 = $r1, $r2 ## mpy low
      mpyhs $r5 = $r1, $r2 ## mpy high and shl by 16
      xnop 1 ## assuming a 2-cyle mul
;;
      add $r3 = $r4, $r5 ## add the two parts
;;
```

The compiler is able to detect simpler cases (short multiplications) and emit the correspondingly simpler sequences. Even though the latency of a 32×32 multiplication is longer, a VLIW datapath with two 16×32 multipliers still supports a throughput of one long multiplication per cycle, as the following VEX example shows:

```
## Three 32-bit integer multiplications, such as:
##      int a0,b0,c0, a1,b1,c1, a2,b2,c2;
##      c0 = a0 * b0; c1 = a1 * b1; c2 = a2 * b2
## (a0 in $r1, b0 in $r2 and c0 in $r3)
## (a1 in $r11, b1 in $r12 and c1 in $r13)
## (a2 in $r21, b2 in $r22 and c2 in $r23)
##
      mpylu $r4 = $r1, $r2
      mpyhs $r5 = $r1, $r2
;;
      mpylu $r14 = $r11, $r12
      mpyhs $r15 = $r11, $r12
;;
      mpylu $r24 = $r21, $r22
      mpyhs $r25 = $r21, $r22
      add $r3 = $r4, $r5     ## First result
;;
      add $r13 = $r14, $r15 ## Second result
;;
      add $r23 = $r24, $r25 ## Third result
;;
```

Fixed-point Multiplication

In the embedded domain, the traditional C semantics for multiplication that preserve the *least significant* bits are not sufficient to represent other important data types, such as fixed-point, that require preserving the *most significant* bits.[1] As a consequence, most embedded ISAs include some form of support for these types of multiplications. Supporting *short* fixed-point multiplications is reasonably straightforward, and

---

1. This is sometimes referred to as *fractional arithmetic*, in that it represents values in the range $[-1.0, 1.0)$, with the convention that the decimal point is *fixed* to the left of the most-significant bit (the sign bit) of the registers.

it requires only a few more operations, such as the VEX *mpyll* (multiply low 16 with low 16), *mpylh* (multiply low 16 with high 16), and *mpyhl* (multiply high 16 with low 16). These operations can be easily expressed in C, as the VEX example below shows:

```
## A 16-bit fixed-point multiplication preserves the
## most significant bits of the result. In C, this is
## expressed as:
##      short a, b, c;
##      c = (a * b) >> 15;
## For example, with this notation, 0.5 is represented
## (in 16 bits) as 0x4000 (that is, 2^(-1)), and if we
## multiply 0.5 * 0.5, we get the value 0x2000 (0.25).
## In VEX, using the mpyll operation, this becomes
## (with a in $r1, b in $r2, c in $r3):

   mpyll $r3 = $r1, $r2
   xnop 1 ## assuming a 2-cycle mul
;;
   shr $r3 = $r3, 15
;;
```

Supporting higher-precision fixed-point multiplications that preserve the most significant bits of a 32×32 multiplication is more expensive and requires changing the multiplier architecture (basically, it requires a full 32-bit multiplier array). A further complication comes from the fact that we cannot easily describe this behavior in plain C, and efficient implementation requires the use of *assembler intrinsics*, whereby assembly code operations are exposed as special C function calls.

```
## A 32-bit fixed-point multiplication (z = x*y)
## requires breaking the operation into 16-bit
## components, absent a container that is larger than
## 32 bits. This can be graphically represented as
## follows:
##      [xhi        xlo] *
##      [yhi        ylo] =
## ----------------------------------
## (            (xlo * ylo)   +
## ((ylo * xhi)      +
##      (yhi * xlo)) << 16 ) +
## ((yhi * xhi) << 32)    ) >> 31
##
## This becomes (in C)
## unsigned xlo = x&0xffff; unsigned ylo = y & 0xffff
## int xhi = x >> 16; int yhi = y >> 16;
## z = ( (xlo * ylo) >> 31 ) +
##      ( ((xhi * ylo) + (xlo * yhi)) >> 15 ) +
```

```
##      ( (xhi * yhi) << 1 )
## And, in a VEX model with two 2-cycle multiplers
## (with x in $r1, y in $r2, z in $r3):

        mpylhu $r8 = $r1, $r2
        mpylhu $r7 = $r2, $r1
;; #1
        mpyllu $r4 = $r1, $r2
        mpyhh $r5 = $r1, $r2
;; #2
        add $r8 = $r8, $r7
;; #3
        shru $r4 = $r4, 31
        shru $r8 = $r8, 15
        shl $r5 = $r5, 1
;; #4
        add $r4 = $r4, $r5
;; #5
        add $r3 = $r4, $r8
;; #6
```

When a floating-point unit is available, it is common to extend it to support integer multiplication and division. However, general-purpose processors that use this strategy do not excel in performance on integer-multiplication-intensive code. The reason is that the communication between integer and floating-point registers can be expensive. The HP PA-RISC 1.0 architecture is an extreme example, wherein integer and floating-point units communicate only through memory, and thus an integer multiplication may require up to two pairs of load/store operations for the operands, the multiplication, and another pair of store/load operations for the result.

Integer Division

When no floating-point unit is available, integer division is rarely supported as a native multicycle operation, and the hardware implements only some basic support for a *nonrestoring division step*. For example, the VEX *divs* instruction implements the following:

```
/*
** Inputs are s1, s2 (32-bit) and cin (1-bit)
** Outputs are out (32-bit), and cout(1-bit)
*/
if (s1 > 0) {
    cout = 0; out = ((s1 << 1) + cin) + s2;
} else {
    cout = 1; out = ((s1 << 1) + cin) - s2;
}
```

The *divs* operation is the basic component for an integer division, which in VEX could be implemented (in 35 cycles) as follows:

```
## Non-restoring 32-bit division (c = a/b)
## with a in $r1, b in $r2 and c in $r3
## (assumes a > 0 and b > 0)

    mtb $b1 = 0 ## Initialize carry
;;
    addcg $r14, $b0 = $r2, $r2, $b1
;;
    divs $r14, $b0 = $r0, $r1, $b0    ## Step 1
    addcg $r16, $b1 = $r14, $r14, $b1
    mov $r20 = 14 ### set up to loop 14 times
;; ## ---------------------------------------------
Ldivloop: ## Steps 2-29
    cmpgt $b2 = $r20, $r0
    divs $r14, $b1 = $r14, $r1, $b1   ## Quotient
    addcg $r17, $b0 = $r16, $r16, $b0 ## Remainder
;;
    divs $r14, $b0 = $r14, $r1, $b0   ## Quotient
    addcg $r16, $b1 = $r17, $r17, $b1 ## Remainder
    add $r20 = $r20, -1
    br $b2, Ldivloop
;; ## ---------------------------------------------
    divs $r14, $b1 = $r14, $r1, $b1    ## Step 30
    addcg $r17, $b0 = $r16, $r16, $b0
;;
    addcg $r17, $b1 = $r17, $r17, $b1
    cmpge $r14 = $r14, $r0
;;
    orc $r16 = $r17, 0 ## Negate remainder
;;
    shladd $r3 = $r16, $r14    ## Restoring step
;;
```

Using a similar concept, the compiler could optimize shorter divisions, or divisions by constants, and generate shorter sequences. However, division performance is rarely critical, and thus many systems favor code size, choosing to implement division (and remainder) through function *intrinsics*. Intrinsics are part of the system library and are called or inserted (as inline functions) when the compiler needs to emit an integer division/remainder operation.

Floating-point Operations

An extensive discussion of floating-point formats and operations is beyond the scope of this book (and is extensively covered elsewhere). Full IEEE compliance and double precision are rarely required in embedded applications. What is more common is the use of single-precision (*float*) operations, and even for those it is rarely required to be able to support the full set of IEEE rounding modes and exceptions. Even single-precision floating point is limited to a very well-defined set of applications, to the point that it is common to have variations of processors that include or exclude hardware floating point depending on the target market (for example, TI DSPs and IBM PowerPC microcontrollers).

For the majority of embedded applications that do not require hardware floating point, it is common practice to give priority to code size considerations, and use a shared *floating-point emulation library*, which the compiler can invoke through function calls when it is necessary to perform floating-point computations. Given the complexity of supporting IEEE rounding modes, overflow, underflow, and the propagation of *NaN* (*not-a-number*) values, emulating a typical fully IEEE-compliant single-precision addition could require hundreds of operations. Even if a VLIW can exploit some ILP, this solution is only viable when floating-point computation is not in the critical path of the performance of any target application.

Saturated Arithmetic

The standard C semantics imply a *wraparound* behavior for integer data types. For example, if we add 1 to the largest unsigned 32-bit integer value (0xffffffff), we obtain 0. In certain embedded domains (everything that manipulates audio and video), overflows are not acceptable. In order to deal with this problem, these domains commonly implement their algorithms using a different form of arithmetic, called *saturated arithmetic*, in which values that overflow are clipped to the maximum (for positive numbers) or minimum (for negative numbers) of the acceptable range. For example, an addition between two 24-bit saturated values could be implemented as follows in C:

```
/* A 24-bit saturated addition, such as:
 *     int a, b, c;
 *     c = saturated_add_24(a,b);
 *
 * Can be broken down as:
 */
    int c = a + b;
    if (c > 0x007fffff) c = 0x007fffff;
    if (c < 0xff800000) c = 0xff800000;
```

Strictly speaking, hardware support is not required for saturation. An ISA that supports *min* and *max* operations (such as VEX) can efficiently implement saturation in a few cycles, as the following example shows:

```
## int a,b,c;
## c = saturated_add_24(a,b)
## (a in $r1, b in $r2 and c in $r3)
```

```
##
    add $r3 = $r1, $r2
;;
    min $r3 = $r3, 0x007fffff
;;
    max $r3 = $r3, 0xff800000
;;
```

Even though the latency is longer (three cycles) than we can obtain with hardware support (one cycle), a 4-wide VLIW datapath can achieve a throughput of one saturated addition per cycle, as the following VEX example shows:

```
## Four 24-bit sat. adds on a 4-wide VLIW in 4 cycles
## with inputs in $r1-$r4, $r11-$r14,
## and outputs in $r21-$r24
##
    mov $r30, 0x007ffffff # load long immediates
    mov $r31, 0xff8000000 # not to waste issue slots
;; #1
    add $r21 = $r1, $r11
    add $r22 = $r2, $r12
    add $r23 = $r3, $r13
    add $r24 = $r4, $r14
;; #2
    min $r21 = $r21, $r30
    min $r22 = $r22, $r30
    min $r23 = $r23, $r30
    min $r24 = $r24, $r30
;; #3
    max $r21 = $r21, $r31
    max $r22 = $r22, $r31
    max $r23 = $r23, $r31
    max $r24 = $r24, $r31
;; #4
```

The same VLIW datapath supporting saturated operations can perform up to four saturated additions per cycle, and thus executing the saturation in software reaches only 25% of the efficiency of a fully customized solution. This is because the clipping performed with *min* and *max* operations does not come for free, and ILP can only partially make up for the inefficiency derived from longer latencies (three operations), code size (two operations more than necessary), and increased competition for the issue slots of the machine.

Despite the reduced efficiency, a software implementation can still be the most cost-effective solution for applications that use saturation occasionally. If saturation is used pervasively, implementing a set of saturated operations in hardware is likely to be cost effective. For example, many DSP architectures adopt this strategy, to the point of exposing the saturated types at the language level. Although this might sound like a convenient

---

Flame: MAC or Non-MAC?

Multiply-accumulate (MAC) operations have been the cornerstones of DSP processors since they first appeared on the market. Indeed, for a sequential engine, having hardware support for MACs makes a lot of sense.

Unfortunately, MAC operations tend to be awkward to implement in an orthogonal ISA, as they require three input operands. Even if we could design a simple encoding with a read-written operand (after all, they are largely used to implement *a += b*c* operations), MACs still require three read ports and one write port in the register file. Oversizing the datapath just for a MAC is expensive and not necessarily the best engineering tradeoff.

Fortunately, once we start adding ILP to the mix, the balance changes. For example, a 4-wide VLIW processor that supports two multiplications and two additions per cycle can sustain a throughput that is equivalent to two multiply-accumulate operations per cycle. The advantage of the VLIW approach is that it is more general and flexible. The disadvantage is that it takes two operations in place of one, and is then less code-efficient.

Until recently, the mere suggestion of using a processor for a DSP application without a MAC was considered heresy. When TI, the leading DSP manufacturer, introduced the C6 architecture *without a MAC*, developers were very skeptical for a long time, until the benefits of a cleaner VLIW architecture and compiler became evident.

---

enhancement to the language (after all, inlined operators such as "+" or "−" are simply a syntactic convenience), it can be misleading for programmers. For example, in wraparound mode, additions preserve their arithmetic properties, such as *commutativity* and *associativity*. In saturated mode they do not [for example, $(x+y)+z \neq x+(y+z)$]. Algorithms thus should be written carefully, to avoid intermediate saturations.

4.1.4 Micro-SIMD Operations

Over the course of their life, many architecture families routinely announce instruction-set extensions to address new market needs or to reflect advances in VLSI technology that enable more functionality to be crammed in the same clock cycle. One has to be careful to evaluate the effectiveness of these special-purpose operations, especially because of the marketing hype that touts them as the latest and greatest advance in processor design. In many cases (e.g., most of the micro-SIMD extensions) these new instructions simply add hardware support for operations that would otherwise be slower if implemented from orthogonal ISA operations. In other cases (e.g., random number generation, or security features) the new instructions are not synthesizable from other existing instructions.

Even operations that add no new functionality to the ISA can be very valuable by providing major improvements in performance (and code size) for a specific set of applications. Examples are legion: ARM's Piccolo for DSP, ARM Jazelle for Java, the various multimedia instruction-set extensions for general-purpose processors (MMX, SSE, and SSE2 for the x86 line, Altivec for PowerPC) (see Table 4.1 for details).

Manufacturer	Architecture	Extension Name	Year of Intro.
HP	PA-RISC	MAX	1995
Sun	SPARC	VIS	1995
Digital	Alpha	MVI	1996
Intel	x86	MMX	1997
Intel	x86	SSE	1999
SGI	MIPS	MDMX	1998
Motorola/IBM	PowerPC	AltiVec	1998
AMD	x86	3DNow!	1998

TABLE 4.1 Micro-SIMD and application-specific extensions to general-purpose architectures (courtesy of *http://www.eecg.toronto.edu/~corinna/vector/svx/index.html*).

Micro-SIMD operations (sometimes called *short-vector* operations) are operations that manipulate *sub-words*. A *sub-word* is a smaller unit of data (typically 8 bits or 16 bits) contained within a larger container (32 bits or 64 bits), which corresponds to the natural register size of an architecture. Micro-SIMD operations come from the observation that several media-processing applications (audio, video, and imaging) operate on small-precision quantities. Implementing algorithms that manipulate short data on a standard 32-bit datapath "wastes" hardware resources (registers and units), which we can attempt to utilize for microparallelism. With small modifications of the functional units, we can implement sub-word parallelism simply by partitioning the hardware and avoiding the propagation of signals across the partitions (such as the carry chain in adder circuitry). Because the same operation applies to all sub-words within the container, this is a form of SIMD.

Micro-SIMD and VLIW are not incompatible techniques, and the two approaches can be naturally integrated. VLIW is a more general approach and does not require manual intervention to the code to exploit ILP. Micro-SIMD is a lower-level optimization within each functional unit (and multiple micro-SIMD units can be active in the same cycle), but it requires some code restructuring, or hints to the compiler, to be effective.

The simplest form of micro-SIMD occurs when simple loops that operate on small quantities can be trivially parallelized, and when the compiler can infer (or be told about) the alignment of arrays and structures. The following code shows a simple micro-SIMD vector add transformation, in which the transformed version takes approximately one-fourth of the execution cycles of the original version.

```
// original version (vector add)

char a[], b[], c[];
```

```
for(i = 0; i < N; ++i)
  c[i] = a[i] + b[i];

// with 32-bit micro-SIMD operations, this becomes:

int *ap = (int *)a;
int *bp = (int *)b;
int *cp = (int *)c;
for(i = 0; i < N/4; i++)
  cp[i] = PADD4(pa[i], pb[i]);

// under the assumption that a[], b[], c[] are
// word-aligned, and that PADD4() is a 4-way parallel
// micro-SIMD operation that executes four
// parallel additions for each byte of the inputs
// registers
```

However, the situation is rarely this simple, and in practice many factors contribute to complicate the picture and diminish the advantages of micro-SIMD.

Alignment Issues

Structures that contain sub-word elements rarely align cleanly to word boundaries. Language standards only enforce natural alignment to the largest element size (so, for example, an array of bytes has no alignment restrictions). Even if we can circumvent this problem by forcing alignment or using *union* workarounds, it is common for programs to operate on random subsections of an array by passing a pointer to the middle of the array. In this case, the only options are either to use code versioning (by keeping both versions of the loop code and switching on an initial alignment test) or to write unoptimized pre-loops and post-loops until we reach the right alignment condition. Both solutions add inefficiency to the overall execution and complicate the compiler strategy.

Precision Issues

Even when we manipulate byte-sized quantities (as in the case of most pixel-based images, for example), the precision requirements of the majority of manipulation algorithms require keeping a few extra bits around (9, 12, and 16 are common choices) for the intermediate stages of an algorithm. This has a few implications. First, we need special operations to expand data into larger containers, so that we can still maintain the reduction of memory operations while we meet the precision requirements. Worse, this forces us up to the next practical size of sub-word. For example, most byte-oriented algorithms require 16-bit containers. This has the disadvantage of reducing the potential parallelism by a factor of two up front. For this reason, micro-SIMD is often implemented in the double-precision (64-bit) floating-point datapath, so that we can at least achieve parallelism across four 16-bit operations. Implementing the same on a 32-bit datapath limits the parallelism to 2 x 16-bit operations, and by the time we factor in all other inefficiencies it severely diminishes the payoff.

Dealing with Control Flow

One major disadvantage of micro-SIMD (or any other SIMD technique) is that micro-predication is the only way to deal with control flow. If the original code contained branches (such as an if-then-else statement), the micro-SIMD code must mimic this branching behavior. Most micro-SIMD instruction-set extensions include at least a mechanism for partial predication, which allows selecting individual sub-words from two input words based on multiple condition bits. Additionally, the extension must have a "parallel comparison" operator that sets up the conditional execution.

```
// simple conditional vector add/sub

char a[], b[], c[];
for(i = 0; i < N; ++i)
  if (a[i] > x)
      c[i] = a[i] + b[i];
  else
      c[i] = a[i] - b[i];

// with 32-bit micro-SIMD, this becomes:

int *ap = (int *)a;
int *bp = (int *)b;
int *cp = (int *)c;
for(i = 0; i < N; i += 4) {
  int pcond = PCMPGT4(ap[i],x);
  int tadd = PADD4(pa[i],pb[i]);
  int tsub = PSUB4(pa[i],pb[i]);
  cp[i] = PSELECT(pcond,tadd,tsub);
}
// where PSUB4 is a parallel substraction, PCMPGT4
// is a parallel compare (greater than) generating
// four 1's or 0's into pcond, and PSELECT is a select
// operation that picks each individual bytes
// of tadd or tsub based on the bytes of pcond.
// Note that PSELECT is a 3-operand operation, and
// as such, suffers the same datapath complexity
// of a MAC operation. In practice, it could be
// implemented with a pair of "packed conditional
// moves" or through a special bank of packed
// predicates
```

Pack, Unpack, and Mix

Some programs require rearranging the sub-words within a container to deal with the different sub-word layouts. From time to time, the ordering of the sub-words within a word (for example, coming from loading a word from memory) does not line up with the parallelism in the code. This happens frequently when dealing with various types of 2D matrices. The only solution is to rearrange the sub-words within the containers through a set of permutation or copying operations (for example, the *MIX* operation in the HP PA-RISC MAX-2 extension).

Reductions

One last issue is *reduction* operations, which are used when the separate sub-words of a micro-SIMD word must be combined at the end of a computation. This also typically requires a separate type of operation.

```
// simple reduction

char sum = 0;
char a[];
for(i = 0; i < N; ++i)
    sum += a[i];

// in a 32b micro-SIMD, it could be transformed to:

int psum = 0;
int *ap = (int *)a;
for(i = 0; i < N; i += 4)
    psum = PADD4(psum, ap[i]);

sum = (char) PREDUCE(psum);

// the intermediate variable psum in reality contains
// four intermediate sums (one in each byte), that
// are combined at the end of the loop by the PREDUCE
// operation, which adds the four sub-elements of a
// register, to produce the final result
```

Under the right conditions, micro-SIMD can achieve impressive results with a minimal overhead in terms of hardware complexity. However, micro-SIMD is far from being a cure for all diseases. The complexity of implementing a *complete* set of micro-SIMD extensions is much higher (and requires several more operations) than it may appear at first glance. The benefits of 16-bit extensions (necessary for precision) on a 32-bit machine are questionable. The ability of compilers to automatically extract micro-SIMD without hints (and in particular, without pointer alignment information) is still unproven, and manual code restructuring is still necessary to be able to exploit micro-SIMD parallelism.

4.1.5 Constants

Datapaths must also provide support for *immediate operands* (sometimes called *literals*), which are compile-time or load-time *constants*. Immediates are sometimes awkward to handle, because they can occur in the instruction stream, but the values from the instruction stream must be moved into the datapath to be used by the execution units.

Most scalar machines have at least two sizes of immediates: a *short immediate* size (which fits in the encoding of a single operation) and a *long immediate* size (up to the datapath width), which requires special handling. Among the various mechanisms, two of the most popular are:

- *Partial immediate load* (e.g., *load-low* and *load-high*), whereby long immediates are loaded to a register in two sequential steps. Architectures that use this technique include MIPS, PowerPC, HP PA-RISC, and SPARC.

- *Memory-allocated immediates*, whereby the compiler allocates the long immediate in memory and emits an instruction that loads the immediate. The immediate will be loaded using a load instruction, but the immediate value might come from either code or data (global) memory. Such strategies can require a mixture of support from OS, compiler, and hardware to ensure that the proper data segment is available and addressable by the program. Variants of this method are used by the ARM and Alpha architectures.

A VLIW datapath has an intrinsic advantage with respect to scalar machines: it is wide enough to cover the largest immediate that needs to be manipulated by the architecture. In this respect, dealing with long immediates involves using bits from an adjacent issue slot and ensuring that they are interpreted correctly.

Branch offsets warrant special mention. The largest size of a branch offset identifies the area of code that is reachable from each program location, without additional complication. For local branches, this limits the size of the largest procedure. For global branches (in a statically linked model), it identifies the section sizes that can be reached without extra trampoline stubs (see the exercises and Chapter 9, for more about trampoline stubs). While code reachability may be a concern for large server applications in 64-bit address spaces, most 32-bit embedded architectures include a branch offset immediate that is large enough to cover local branches.

4.2   Registers and Clusters

A *register* is basically any architecturally visible container that is not memory. The collection of registers represents the state of the processor core. Registers are organized in homogeneous sets, called *register files*. In VLIWs, functional units are connected only to register files and not directly to other functional units. When this is the case, we say that the architecture does not expose bypassing. Although most implementations use bypassing, it is not wired into the instruction set, and thus the only visible effect of bypassing is the reduction of the producer-consumer latency for dependent operations.

In addition to the standard properties of register files (addressability, nonvolatility, speed, and small size), VLIW architecture follows two major design tenets. First, all registers are individually addressable,[2] and the hardware provides a mechanism to access any register and copy its content elsewhere. Second, operations never write registers implicitly; all destinations must be explicit.[3]

Simple VLIW architectures support *direct* addressing of registers (i.e., through their specifiers in the register files), wherein the identifier of the register being addressed is fixed at compile-time. More complex architectures (such as IPF) also include *indexed* register addressing, in which the content of another register specifies which of a set of registers should be accessed.

This subsection has four major parts. The first, on clustering, describes the relationship between register files and groups of functional units on wide-issue machines. The second part describes cases in which specialized or heterogeneous register files are beneficial. However, the third part warns against using specialized address register files. The last part describes indexed register files in more detail.

4.2.1 Clustering

One of the most challenging aspects of ILP machines is how to keep execution units busy. For example, a fully connected VLIW with eight execution units (two inputs and one output each) must read 16 values and write eight values every cycle when it is operating at its performance peak (which is the best case for performance but the worst case for register file accesses). The traditional solution to the problem has been to design ever-larger multiported register files, but that solution quickly reaches its scalability limits. As we describe in the next chapter (on microarchitecture), the area of a register file grows with the square of the number of ports. Each port requires new routing in the X and Y direction, and the design is limited by routing and not by transistor density. Unfortunately, wires and wire capacitance do not scale well with reduction in VLSI geometry. In addition, the read access time of a register file grows approximately linearly with the number of ports, and in many cases this has a negative impact on the overall cycle time. Finally, register files are tightly coupled with the forwarding logic (also known as the *bypassing network*), which is again largely wire-dominated (and unfortunately grows with the product of the number of read ports and write ports).

A solution to register file bottleneck is to *partition the register file*. If we break the register file into smaller units (see Figures 4.3 and 4.4) so that each unit is connected to only a subset of the execution units, we can put an upper bound on the full connectivity, and at the same time adapt the design to technology improvements. Partitioning the register file and functional units in this manner is called *clustering*. Each pairing of

---

2. Although "addressable" is often used to describe memory, we use it in the context of register files with the meaning of "program-accessible."

3. For example, operations that implicitly set condition codes should be avoided, as discussed in Section 4.1.3. Explicitly setting conditions is fine.

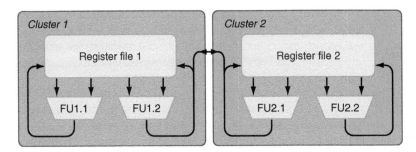

FIGURE 4.3 **Conceptual model of a partitioned register file.** Each register file is connected to multiple execution units (labeled "FU," from "functional unit"). Today's technology can easily support several units per register file.

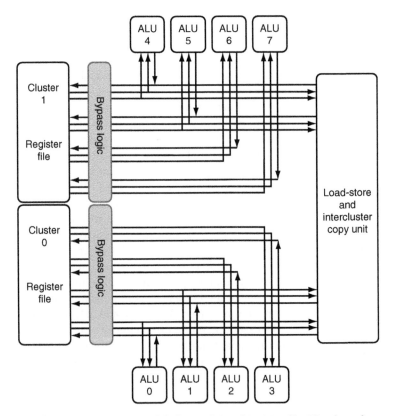

FIGURE 4.4 **Datapath model of a partitioned register file.** The chart shows an 8-wide VLIW datapath partitioned as two clusters. If we compare this with Figure 4.1, we can see both the reduction of the number of ports in the register file (from 24 to 12) and the reduction of wires and multiplexing in the bypass logic.

a register file and its directly connected functional units is called a *cluster* (the price of clustering comes from intercluster communication).

Note that an ideal VLIW machine would be unified, and clustering is solely due to implementation limitations. From this point of view, clustering is a "necessary evil" that ideally should be hidden in the microarchitecture. However, a completely invisible solution is complex, and it turns out that the compiler can often do a good job of working around it. Consequently, there are two basic approaches to the implementation of clustering, depending on whether we decide to expose clustering to the ISA or not.

Architecturally Invisible Clustering

When clustering is *architecturally invisible*, the partitioned register files appear as one large register file to the compiler, and the hardware is responsible for copying between register files. In this case, detecting when copies are needed can be complex. This approach goes against the VLIW philosophy of exposing the features the software can optimize. It is also not architecturally scalable, because it still requires enough bits in the instruction encoding to address all registers in all register files. Finally, because hardware-issued copy operations may stall the machine, the compiler opportunities to optimize the code are limited. Architecturally invisible clustering is actually a *microarchitectural* technique, in that it is effectively invisible to the ISA. Invisible clustering appears in some superscalar architectures (for example, in the Alpha 21264 processor).

Architecturally Visible Clustering

If we decide to expose clustering at the architecture level, the ISA must include some way of specifying how operations within an instruction are assigned to each cluster. As mentioned in Chapter 3, this encoding problem is related to the problem of dispatching operations to correct functional units and the problem of encoding instruction length. Handling operands in an architecture with exposed clusters raises the choice between an *implicit-copy* or *explicit-copy* mechanism. Regardless of the mechanism adopted, visible clustering implies the presence of an *explicit-copy* operation (in which, by *copying* we mean the operation of duplicating the value of a register directly into another register — in a different cluster — without going through memory).

- *Implicit copy* means that operations may read operands (or write results) in non-local register files. From the compiler point of view, this implies a less flexible scheduling mode, in that the time and resources to execute the copy have to be appended for any nonlocal operation. In its simplest form, an implicit copy architecture is not scalable, as it still requires addressing bits for all registers in all clusters. Some architectures (e.g., TI C6x) allow extended register specifiers only for certain operands of certain operations, but this approach complicates decoding and imposes further constraints that must be modeled by the compiler.

- *Explicit copy* means that only a special operation (*copy*) can access a remote register. From the compiler point of view, this yields a more flexible scheduling

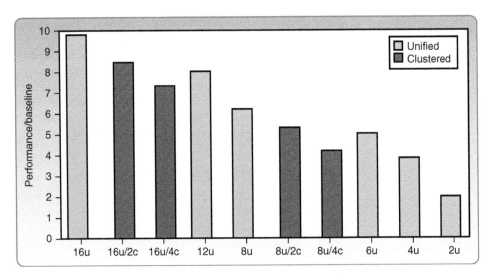

FIGURE 4.5   **Effects of clustering on performance.** The chart shows the result of a set of experiments using the Multiflow VLIW compiler on a collection of media-oriented integer benchmarks. The x axis lists a few combinations of units and clustering (for example, "16u/2c" stands for "16 units, 2 clusters"). The y axis shows execution cycles relative to a baseline (a 1-unit/1-cluster configuration).

model, in that it separates normal operations from copy operations. This model is architecturally scalable, because encoding only needs to account for local registers, and the cluster specification identifies the register partitioning. However, copy operations compete for resources and may increase issue pressure, code size, and instruction cache footprint.

Although clustering helps overcome implementation constraints, it is certainly not free in terms of performance. Regardless of the clustering style, the compiler has to partition the computation, and the copy operations (implicit or explicit) may add to the critical path. Two of the authors' research shows that, as a rule of thumb, dividing the datapath into two clusters costs 15 to 20% in extra cycles, whereas dividing the datapath into four clusters costs 25 to 30%. Figure 4.5 shows an example of the performance degradation for a few configurations of units and clusters, using state-of-the-art clustering algorithms (Section 8.2.6 describes compiler methods that support clustering). Note that the performance evaluation metrics of Figure 4.5 are cycle based and expressed versus a 1-unit/1-cluster baseline. However, when factoring in other technological issues, particularly cycle time, conclusions may be different. As we mentioned previously, clustering is likely to be a "necessary evil" if we want fast clock rates when we scale ILP and registers. In other words, Figure 4.5 tells us that a clustered configuration becomes the better choice if we can get a 15 to 20% clock speed increase by partitioning the register file and bypass logic into two disjoint clusters.

4.2.2 Heterogeneous Register Files

Other forms of register file partitioning are driven by data type, and have smaller effects on performance than clustering because of the natural division between data types. For example, partitioning *integer* and *floating-point* registers is a common technique motivated by the observation that we rarely mix integer and floating-point computation within the same piece of code. Even though this is a form of clustering, the compiler's job is much easier in this case (the register file choice is obvious from the language data type and the executed operations). In the same category, we can also group all other types of register file partitioning where different register files are designed to contain data types with distinctively different characteristics. For example, *predicate register banks* (for ISAs with full predication support), *branch register banks* (for ISAs with split branch architectures), and register banks for sub-word parallel data types appear in many architectures.

When designing partitioned register files, keep *reachability* in mind. A well-behaved ISA should always define a simple method to copy values to and from any architecturally visible container. The reason for this comes from the way in which compilers allocate values, and from the need to spill and restore those values under certain conditions (for example, around function calls). If a simple method to access any value in any location exists, optimizations that move operations around have a good degree of freedom. If values can "get stuck" in some container that is difficult (or impossible) to reach, the compiler is forced into a much more conservative strategy. Although this may sound like an obvious concept, history is filled with examples of designs in which this rule was violated in subtle ways,[4] causing extreme complications in the compiler and consequently the generation of conservative, inefficient code sequences.

4.2.3 Address and Data Registers

The VLIW design philosophy suggests register files designed for general-purpose use. This means that the compiler should be free to allocate values regardless of their intended use, but simply based on the interconnection pattern with the functional units. This is in contrast with some DSP architectures, which distinguish between *address registers* (used to access memory) and *data registers* (used to manipulate data). Separate "address" registers are common to many DSPs, and occurred commonly in general-purpose processor designs before the RISC revolution. Although the RISC philosophy merged "address" and "data" registers into a large general-purpose register file, DSP designers found that they required different handling. For example, many DSPs operate on fixed-point or floating-point data values, implying bit widths and transformations that are not especially useful as addresses. At the same time, most address computations can

---

4. One "classic" example is the push-pipe design of the floating-point unit in the Intel 860 processor, wherein the result of the multiplier has to be taken away (with a special operation) as soon as it is generated, and before the next result coming down the multiplier pipeline overwrites it.

be easily mapped to integer registers and operations. When additional special addressing operations are needed (such as bit-reversed addressing for Fast Fourier Transform [FFT] or circular addressing for buffers), these are unlikely to be useful for data operations. In the DSP case, separate address and data register files are actually an example of heterogeneous register files. For non-DSP applications, however, we see few reasons for separate address and data registers.

At first glance, it may appear odd that we advocate separate floating-point and integer register sets, separate clusters, and even separate predicate register sets but discourage the distinction between address and data registers. Our reasons have to do with functionality. Floating point is indeed a separate data type that requires different functional units (a floating-point adder and an integer adder have nothing in common), as well as different datapath widths (e.g., 64 bits for double precision). Predicate bits also participate only in "special" operations (comparisons, predicates, selects, and branches), requiring only a few single-bit containers. On the other hand, address and data registers are very similar: they almost always have the same data width, and they require a similar set of manipulation operators (integer arithmetic, comparisons, shifts, masks, extracts, deposits, and bitwise logic).

In machines with both integer data types and addresses, the *address/data* partitioning forces the compiler to make early arbitrary choices, and introduces redundant movements whenever a value is used in a way that is not entirely consistent with its assumed type. Although this problem can be kept under control for array-oriented languages like FORTRAN, the situation gets much worse for C or C++, where pointer manipulation and multiple indirections are ubiquitous.

Note that in Section 5.1.3 we discuss some of the potential microarchitecture benefits of separate address and data registers. In general, the choice is never a black-and-white issue, but is a tradeoff taking into account the architecture, microarchitecture, and compiler consequences.

4.2.4 Special Register File Features

A number of VLIW architectures, both historical and modern, provide special ways to access their register files. We discuss two such techniques: *indexing* for procedure nesting and *rotation* for efficient looping.

Indexed Register Files

Indexed register files add *base* + *offset* to the standard direct addressing of register files. This is usually done only for a section of the register file, and can be exploited to limit the overhead of stack management for procedure calls and returns. In other words, we can see an indexed register file as a small compiler-managed cache of the machine stack. Along the same line, we can also view indexed register files as a generalization of *register windows*, which appear in a few RISC architectures (most notably in Sun SPARC processors). For example, the IPF architecture includes the notion of *register stack*, wherein the compiler can explicitly allocate (with an *alloc* instruction) a variable-sized section of the register file. At procedure call, the base of the indexed register file advances, making sure that the outgoing parameters line up with the incoming parameters. At procedure return, the base returns to the caller's value. This avoids spills and restores around procedure calls for a few nesting levels.

Rotating Register Files

Rotating register files are indexed register files, for which it is possible to define a regular policy to update the *base* of the indexed area so that it cycles across a finite number of registers. Rotation is a form of dynamic register renaming that is particularly useful in modulo scheduling (a form of *software pipelining* described in Chapter 8). With hardware support for rotation, the compiler can produce a smaller version of the loop body and let the hardware deal with the issue of avoiding overlaps in register lifetimes that belong to different iterations. Register rotation is implemented in IPF.

Indexed and rotating register files have implementation costs, as the base register must be read and added to the offset to compute the correct register to access. This adder is relatively small (register specifiers do not occupy many bits), but it could be on the critical path for an implementation with a large register file. Having the extra registers for indexing or rotation adds to chip area, pipeline stages, and design complexity. These features slow down the register file, and slow down many of the paths going in and out of the register file whose routing gets longer. These costs can be significant, especially in applications in which the rotating support and the extra registers remain idle for long periods of time, suggesting that a smaller bank with traditional spill/restore (to cache) strategy might be an effective alternative.

4.3 Memory Architecture

VLIW reuses most RISC memory-addressing concepts. The same considerations that led to the adoption of *load/store* architectures in RISC machines apply to VLIWs. It is better to limit memory accesses to basic read and write operations, and let the compiler arrange the rest of the work as regards how to use them.[5] Architectures that allow memory operands create barriers to ILP, because the latency of memory operations and possible data dependences through memory limit the opportunities to execute operations in parallel. Splitting operations with memory operands into two or more separate operations can make it possible to execute other useful work while we wait for the longer latency memory operation to complete.

In architectures for which *load* and *store* are the only operations that access memory, the choice shifts to deciding addressing modes, access sizes, and alignment, which we cover in this section.

---

5. Both RISC and VLIW architectures are called "*load/store*" architectures because memory is accessed strictly through explicit *load* or *store* operations, whereas functional units operate only on values in registers.

Our emphasis in this chapter remains on *architecturally exposed* aspects of the memory system. Section 5.5 discusses implementation-specific aspects of the memory system, and Chapter 6 describes how memories integrate into an SoC.

4.3.1 Addressing Modes

Memory access is often on the critical path of an implementation, and when that happens supporting address computations on the memory access path is likely to require an increase in the number of pipeline stages for a memory access (or reduce the cycle frequency). Note that removing addressing modes that require address computations does not guarantee a faster processor. For example, the designers of the IPF architecture decided to remove all addressing modes to keep memory accesses off the critical path, but they still ended up with an implementation whose speed lagged behind the more complex (but more mature) x86 family.

However, most memory accesses in a program execution naturally map to a *base + offset* form, because accesses to aggregates (structures or unions) and arrays or pointers to aggregates involve a constant offset. In the embedded domain, code size considerations bias the choice toward supporting at least a *base + offset* (with constant offset) mode. Memory accesses amount to about 30% of static instructions, and thus expanding the *base + offset* computation into two operations would cause 30% code expansion, which is generally unacceptable. Many CISC architectures offer *base + offset* addressing modes in which the offset can be as wide as the datapath width—up to 32 bits.

Once we opt for a *base + offset* addressing mode, it is convenient also to plan for a *short offset* format, whereby we can use a short field in the instruction without code size penalty. RISC architectures often implement short offset formats, using encoding bits within the relatively large 32-bit size of the ISA.

As we explained in Section 4.1.5, VLIW architectures can extend constants simply by drawing extra bits from a neighboring *extension syllable* in the same instruction without additional cycle penalty, and thus supporting memory operations with long offset comes nearly "for free," costing in code size but requiring no extra architecture or microarchitecture support.

Depending on the availability of encoding space, it is sometimes convenient to support *post-increment* addressing modes, whereby the address register is automatically incremented (or decremented) by a short constant provided in the memory operation itself. Note that *post-increment* mode is preferable to *pre-increment* mode, in that it does not impact the critical path of the memory access and can be performed in parallel to the access itself. The argument against pre- and post-increment operations is that that they have two results, which can complicate the datapath and the exception hardware.

In most architectures, the memory unit also has some datapath-like functionality that computes memory addresses from register values and immediates. Many older (i.e., CISC) machines expose this functionality in the form of "*load-effective address*" instructions. Most modern implementations have a dedicated adder or address unit that is separate from the primary ALU. Such separation allows the address computation to be moved earlier in the pipeline, closer to (or sometimes in parallel with) register fetch and instruction decoding.

4.3.2 Access Sizes

Early RISC machines (and many cacheless microcontrollers) supported memory accesses only with sizes that matched the *natural* width of the external memory (e.g., only *word* accesses for 32-bit machines). In this case, the compiler had to emit extra code to insert the proper sign/zero extensions when the programmer wanted to manipulate sub-word quantities.

More modern architectures (and architectures that worry about code size) include support for sub-word memory accesses, to read and write all integer data types (*int*, *short*, *unsigned short*, *char*, *unsigned char*) without additional extract and deposit operations. This again may have consequences on the memory load access time, in that it requires a dedicated multiplexer after the memory access itself. When architectures support sub-word accesses they tend to limit them to be *naturally aligned*, as we describe in the following section.

Occasionally, architectures require accesses to memory that are wider than the basic datapath (and container) width. A typical example is a 64-bit access in a 32-bit machine. Scalar machines have limited choices in this respect: either add a wider set of containers (commonly done, for example, for double-precision floating-point registers) or resort to more awkward modes (such as writing pairs of registers). Wide-issue architectures, as we described in Section 4.1, have the additional option of issuing two independent memory accesses, or of coalescing two issue slots and writing two independent registers.

Correctly making this tradeoff depends on application and cost considerations. Supporting a 64-bit access is less expensive in implementation, but it requires pervasive changes in the application code to be able to exploit it efficiently. On the other hand, a dual-ported memory is completely transparent to the application, but requires almost twice the area of a single-ported memory.

4.3.3 Alignment Issues

Physical memory (whether it is cache, local, or external memory) is organized so that accesses are quantized to a multiple of a base width. Typically, memory is byte addressable, but is physically organized in 4-byte words. This configuration causes accesses to be restricted to *natural alignment* (i.e., 0 modulo 2 for *short*, 0 modulo 4 for *int*).

Ideally, application writers could ignore alignment issues. For example, it happens quite often that a byte pointer is passed to a function that would like to access that array one word (4 bytes) at a time. In this case, the programmer would rather rely on the machine to "do the right thing" without having to worry about checking alignment and writing multiple versions of the code.

Because of the way in which physical memory and buses are organized, misaligned accesses need be handled as a special case. In many cases, a misaligned access causes the processor to issue an exception (*bus error*). Misalignment exceptions are difficult to recover from: most recoverable exceptions assume that a handler (either hardware or software) can adjust the state of the machine so that the faulting operation can be restarted and executed correctly (for example, as with a page fault). With wide-issue machines, these handlers are complicated, in that it is not possible to isolate the faulting access and execute it without the other operations that were issued together.

One possible workaround (with a significant performance penalty) requires the handler to *emulate* the faulting instruction (in case of a VLIW, this includes the other "innocent" operations that happen to be issued at the same cycle), and then restart the processor from the instruction that follows. This is a rather complex solution, and many architectures simply choose to treat misaligned accesses as a *nonrecoverable* exception, which signals the error condition to the OS. Typically, the OS then terminates the application.

There are a quite a few application domains for which efficient support for misaligned accesses is important, such as algorithms that perform correlation, many video algorithms, and applications that use micro-SIMD operations. See "Exercises" for more details.

4.3.4 Caches and Local Memories

Strictly speaking, caches are a microarchitectural technique, and thus belong in the next chapter rather than this one. However, many architectures expose the cache through special operations, and many embedded architectures also provide special-purpose local (fast and small) memories that can be used for time-critical storage.

Memory architecture is becoming one of the major distinguishing factors between embedded systems and their general-purpose counterparts, largely because of energy consumption considerations, and the need to take advantage of specific data-access styles (e.g., streaming) common to embedded applications.

Prefetching

A prefetch operation is a hint to the memory system that a particular location is likely to be used soon. From an architectural standpoint, a hint is equivalent to a nop, in that no implementation is required to do anything about it. However, aggressive implementations will use prefetch hints, and aggressive compilers will generate them. Implementations that prefetch perform loads early, so that values move into the memory hierarchy. The hope is that the prefetched values will be used by subsequent memory operations, and that the latency to respond to those operations will thereby be reduced. Like any speculation, the guesses can be wrong, in which case the system will have wasted the prefetch bandwidth and might incur additional latency in handling normal requests. Section 5.5.5 describes how memory hierarchies implement prefetches, and Section 8.4.3 describes compiler techniques for generating prefetch operations. Prefetching is really a specific form of memory speculation, which we cover in more detail in Section 4.5.

Some RISC architectures added prefetch operations after their first generation, and opted to implement prefetch operations by reusing memory load operations to the

Pitfall: Relying on Users for Coherency

When building complex heterogeneous memory hierarchies for an embedded system, one normally faces two basic choices. Local memories exposed to the instruction can (1) be mapped to separate parts of the same address space and accessed by the same operations, and (2) be mapped to separate address spaces and accessed through distinct operations. In case 1, users have to decide a different allocation strategy (by providing hints during declarations or specialized *malloc* functions). In case 2, special operations (such as the load-X and load-Y for XY memories in DSPs) are required.

A common pitfall is to combine systems that use local memory in separate address spaces — case 2 — with a data cache. In that case, we are effectively asking the users (programmers) to be responsible for the coherency between the private memories and main memory (including all cache flushes). Every time we pass a pointer around the code, we have to remember where it came from and what is the right way to access the memory to which it points. Even though extensions of the language type systems and compiler checks can go a long way, subtle errors and hard-to-find bugs lurk at every corner.

A much safer strategy (alas, more costly) is certainly case 1, where — by using a single address space — we can have a hardware safety mechanism that enforces coherency by always snooping the accesses to the local memories and reconciling the cases when we have previously accessed the same data through a cache operation. In this case, at the expense of some hardware complexity, we can still provide hints to the compiler to direct critical accesses to the local memory. However, unlike case 2, these hints don't have to be obeyed, and a programmer's mistake is only going to affect performance, but not correctness of the execution of the program.

constant-zero register. Such operations are architectural nops, but they are not typically generated by the compiler (which usually encode nops as ALU operations to the constant-zero register). Turning these into prefetch operations scavenged a register value from the encoding space and reused many existing control paths.

A more recent variant of prefetch operations falls under the term *replacement policy hints*. Such hints allow memory operations (either prefetches or actual loads and stores) to specify either the expected type of locality (spatial or temporal) or the explicit place in the implementation's cache hierarchy to which to prefetch data. IPF includes such hints (implementation compliance is straightforward, but compiler techniques and tools that use these hints are still under development).

An alternative approach to deal with streaming accesses to regular data structure is the use of separate *stream buffers*, which could be seen as a separate data cache (in parallel to the L1 cache) used only to store data that exploits spatial locality and not temporal locality. If the stream buffers are coherent with the data cache (the recommended approach; see the sidebar "Relying on Users for Coherency"), the programming model for their use could simply be an ISA extension to be able to specify which accesses are streaming. For example, we could attach hint bits to prefetch operations to direct the data back into the stream buffer.

Local Memories and Lockable Caches

Many embedded systems break with the traditional "monolithic" memory hierarchy and instead define local "fast" memories that are on-chip, or they allow programs to "lock" cache lines under program control. These mechanisms seem inelegant compared to the general-purpose alternative, but they provide two benefits. First, they provide deterministic control over memory latencies, which is important to many applications with real-time requirements. Second, they can be space efficient compared to the alternatives. In particular, local, fast memories do not follow the same cache inclusion properties required through most multilevel memory systems, and thus data is resident in only one place in the machine rather than replicated inclusively through each level of the memory hierarchy.

4.3.5 Exotic Addressing Modes for Embedded Processing

Some embedded processors, and DSPs in particular, support relatively exotic ways of accessing memories. Some of the memory access mechanisms are straightforward, such as uncached memory accesses or accesses to fast on-chip memory. The more algorithmically specialized modes include XY memories, Harvard architecture tricks, bit-reversed addressing, and circular addressing. XY memory instructions tell the processor to execute a loop of code over a stream of data values from the normal data memory, while combining (typically, through a convolution operation) that stream with a second stream of data values that comes from a second memory bus. In some DSPs with Harvard architectures, the second memory bus is the instruction bus, and the DSP executes instructions from a small loop buffer, while the instruction bus provides the second data stream. This allows designers to reuse the instruction bus as an additional data bus, while complicating programming or compilation (because coefficients must now live in program memory). Bit-reversed and circular addressing modes speed up some of the typical memory accesses in Fast Fourier Transform [FFT] and Viterbi encoders/decoders, respectively. Circular addressing modes are also useful for filtering operations, which are what DSPs traditionally do efficiently, as they enable the processor to avoid physically shifting the input data.

4.4 Branch Architecture

Branches include all of the architectural techniques that support changes of control flow in program execution. In this book, we use the following terminology:

- *Conditional branches* are changes of control flow based on a condition. If the condition is false, execution continues on the fall-through path.

- *Unconditional jumps* (sometimes called *gotos*) always cause the program to change control flow to the new program location.

- *Function calls* (sometimes called *branch-and-link*) are unconditional jumps that also save the location of the instruction following the call (the *return address*).

- *Indirect jumps* unconditionally cause the program to jump to a variable address (typically the address is stored in a register). Note that *function returns* are just a form of unconditional indirect jump that returns to the location saved by a preceding function call.

The importance of branches for performance comes from the fact that *branches break the execution pipeline*. The initial stages of an execution pipeline (front end) are used to fetch, decode, issue, and prepare the operations for execution, and must proceed ahead of a branch on the most likely path. When a branch mispredicts, the speculative work done on the mispredicted path is wasted, and we say that "the pipeline is broken." Depending on the pipeline depth and on the branch style, the penalty of breaking the pipeline can be severe. If we pair this penalty with the average frequency of a branch every five to seven instructions in general-purpose code, we can see how the branch architecture may amount to a large component of the performance of an architecture. For example, Figure 4.6 shows a seven-stage pipeline that exhibits a five-cycle branch misprediction penalty. The misprediction penalty is what the hardware has to pay when a branch is mispredicted. This happens when the program takes a path different from the path that the compiler predicted ahead of time (for machines with static branch prediction), or the path that the hardware predicted while the program is running (for machines with dynamic branch prediction).

The traditional monolithic compare-and-branch operation needs to wait until the compare finishes (most likely after the execution stage) before it can resolve the branch address. The misprediction penalty gets worse with longer pipelines, in that it depends on the distance between the fetch and the execution stages.

Execution pipelines are properly the province of microarchitecture, but we discuss them here rather than in the next chapter because the interaction between branches and the pipeline is so central to modern processor performance. This is an example of

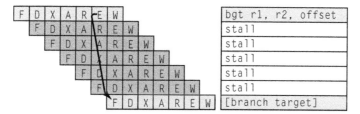

FIGURE 4.6 Example of a mispredicted branch. The example shows a seven-stage pipeline (Fetch, Decode, eXpand, Align, Read, Execute, Write), and the effect of a monolithic compare-and-branch instruction on it (that is, five cycles of misprediction penalty). Note that the grayed-out instructions are actual instructions from the mispredicted path (for simplicity, the non-taken path) that normally proceed through the machine pipeline until the branch instruction realizes the pipeline has been fetching from the wrong place. At that time, in the picture, the end of the "E" stage, it flushes the pipeline by squashing the pending instructions (for example, by preventing operations from writing back values), and starts a new fetch. As a consequence, the "wrong" instruction does no useful work, as if the machine had stalled for five cycles.

a microarchitectural feature that rises to having systemic complications: branch-related architectural features require new operations at the ISA level, new implementation techniques, and new levels of compiler support.

Traditionally, architectures have attacked the problem of branches in two ways: predicting branches and removing them. *Predicting branches* attempts to steer instruction fetch, decode, and execution along the most probably followed path. Branch prediction techniques and speculative execution follow this approach. *Removing branches* attempts to execute down both paths. Predication follows this approach.

In the following sections, we only cover the areas of branches that are more relevant for VLIW architectures, such as exposing part of the branch latency to the compiler, and dealing with multiway and multicluster branches. Section 4.5 deals with speculation and predication in more detail.

4.4.1 Unbundling Branches

Mispredicted branches cause a potentially large number of wasted cycles, proportional to the pipeline depth. In terms of power, the waste is even bigger, in that the number of mispredicted operations can be as high as the pipeline depth times the issue width of the machine.

Superscalar machines attack the problem by speculatively executing on the predicted path, but what about VLIW? One possible workaround to reduce the branch penalty is to break the branch into its basic components (this is sometimes referred to as *unbundling branches*). (See Figure 4.7.) Branches can be broken into three separate pieces[6]:

1. *Where*: prepare the target instruction streams to fetch

2. *Whether*: select the instruction stream that will be taken

3. *When*: execute the instruction stream that was selected

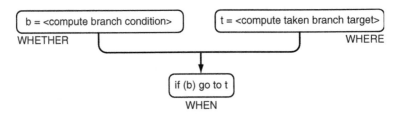

FIGURE 4.7 **Unbundling branches.** We can think of a change in control flow as consisting of three atomic actions: *compare* ("whether"), *prepare-to-branch* ("where"), and the *branch* ("when") itself. With proper architectural support, these three phases can be implemented as separate operations and scheduled independently, to reduce the misprediction penalty.

---

6. This terminology is due to the IMPACT group at UIUC.

These three parts are unified in *compare-and-branch* instructions, but they can be divided to form two-step or three-step branch structures. Breaking a branch operation has the advantages of exposing the intermediate latencies to the compiler, increasing the flexibility, and allowing the individual operations to be moved independently. On the other hand, it also increases code size, issue pressure, and cache footprint.

Two-step Branching

Separating the comparison from the branch instruction (which handles both where and when) gives a two-step branch architecture. This allows the compiler to attempt to fill the delay between the compare and the branch with useful operations. With a set of *branch-condition* registers, legal code sequences can prepare more than one branch at a time, and the compare operations can be moved anywhere by the compiler. Branching (the "when" point) still requires an address computation in addition to the conditional decision ("whether"). However, the address computation could be done speculatively as soon as the branch target offset is decoded. Many RISC architectures separate comparison operations from branch operations, storing comparison results in general-purpose registers.

Three-step Branching

By placing the target address and the comparison result in a composite *branch-target* register, an architecture can also decouple the address computation from the branch. The correct next target is selected at the branch point ("when"). With multiple composite branch-target registers, the system can prepare multiple comparisons and addresses at the same time. Compare and offset computations can be moved anywhere by the compiler, in any order. However, now there are three operations per branch, increasing code size.

Figure 4.8 shows an example of the pipeline implications of a two-step and a three-step branch structure. These diagrams make some arbitrary assumptions about the logic complexity that fits in a single cycle. Although the absolute numbers can certainly be different for other pipeline organizations, it is certainly true that the workload to execute at the branch (the "when") step diminishes with progressively unbundled branches.

The embedded domain poses an interesting issue about how aggressively to pursue the path of decomposing complex instructions, because of code size considerations. For example, a two-step branch architecture doubles the operations per branch. With a typical static frequency of one branch every seven operations we can estimate a code growth of 14%, which might be acceptable given the potential performance benefits. With a three-branch structure, the code growth increases to 28%, which is more difficult to justify. Whereas two-step branch architectures are not uncommon for embedded CPUs, we are aware of only one embedded architecture with a three-step branch, the Hitachi SuperH SH5 processor.

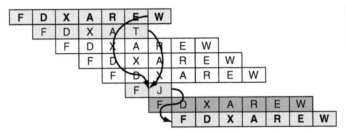

FIGURE 4.8 **Example of two-step and three-step branches.** The two diagrams show the same configuration of Figure 4.6, except that we decide to expose the intermediate branch steps to the ISA. In the two-step case, we break the branch into *compare-branch*, in the three-step case into *compare-prepare-branch* (the "prb" instruction, prepare-to-branch, prepares the target address). The arrows show the pipeline dependences that turn into latencies that are visible by the compiler. Unlike the unbundled case, here the compiler can try to be smart and fill the latency with useful operations.

4.4.2 Multiway Branches

VLIW architectures allow multiple operations per cycle, and thus can we have multiple branches per cycle? The answer is yes, although this necessitates certain precautions.

Multiple branches per cycle are called *multiway branches*. One can think of them as one branch with multiple outcomes. Amdahl's law justifies multiway branches: with increasing ILP, sooner or later branches become a bottleneck. General-purpose programs encounter a branch every five to seven operations. With predication and if-conversion, some of these branches can be removed and turned into straight-line code, whereby the machine effectively follows both paths of the branch. For example, removing 20 to 30% of the branches increases the branch distance to 8 to 10 operations, allowing ILP of 8 to 10 operations with a single branch unit. Reaching higher ILP requires multiway branches.

The problem with multiway branches comes from the requirement to preserve the original sequential program semantics. If two of the conditions in a multiway branch are true, the branches must be prioritized so that the hardware knows which one to take.

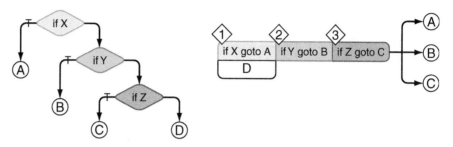

FIGURE 4.9 **Example of a multiway branch.** The problem occurs, for example, if both conditions X and Y are true. According to the sequential program semantics, we need to jump to A and not to B. For the hardware to be able to disambiguate, the compiler emits a priority encoding for each comparison operation (shown in the small diamonds above the operations), so that X is considered before Y.

Figure 4.9 shows an example of this problem. To solve this, the compiler must guarantee that all conditions in a multiway branch are mutually exclusive (which is almost impossible), or the architecture must be able to specify a priority encoding (which could be as simple as sequential ordering if the encoding allows it) of the branch operations.

4.4.3 Multicluster Branches

In a clustered architecture, any cluster must be able to compute a branch condition in order to minimize data motion between clusters. In contrast, the computation of the destination address frequently consists of adding a constant to the current program counter and does not require data from arbitrary clusters. The problem is: how should branch conditions and branch targets be efficiently managed (computed and communicated) across multiple clusters? VLIW architectures have approached the problem with different techniques.

The Multiflow TRACE architecture allowed multiple branches per cycle but required each cluster to have its own branch unit using local conditions and targets, as well as a global controller to select the final next PC. The major disadvantage of this approach is the communication through the global controller to perform a branch, which affects both speed and cost. Another minor disadvantage is that it is not possible to use data in one cluster to trigger a branch in another cluster without using intercluster copy operations.

The TI C6x architecture allows one branch per cluster and only single-way branches that can be executed on any cluster. This has the same disadvantages of the Multiflow TRACE (i.e., long connection paths, and the need to move branch targets to a "global controller").

A third solution consists of keeping the PC address computation and multiplexing local to a single cluster, and communicating branch conditions from any cluster to the branching cluster. This enables the microarchitecture to optimize the address

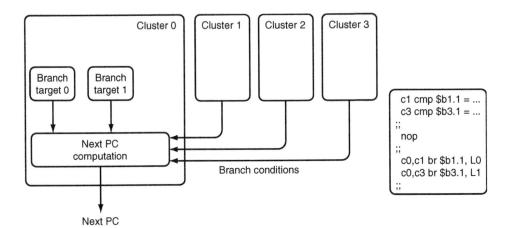

FIGURE 4.10 **Multicluster branches.** In the diagram, we show a clustered architecture with four clusters that can execute a two-way branch per cycle. The example shows how to execute a two-way branch using compare conditions from clusters 1 and 3 and two instruction slots in cluster 0 for the branch targets. The notation *c0,c1 br $b1.1, L0* indicates that we issue two operations: one in cluster 0 to produce the branch target (and start the address computation) and one in cluster 1 to send the condition register (in this case, *$b1.1* and *$b3.1*) to the branching cluster. Some delay (in the example, one extra cycle) may be necessary between the producer of the compare conditions and the branch.

computation for speed, by avoiding long and slow global communication delays for the PC targets. The cost of this approach comes from the need to issue a "shadow" branch instruction in both the condition-generating cluster and the branching cluster. This approach can be easily extended to support multiway branches, by exploiting the multiple-issue capability of the branching cluster. For example, if cluster 0 (the branching cluster) allows four operations to issue per cycle, we can support up to a four-way branch per cycle. Other clusters can participate to the branch conditions by sending the appropriate condition bits to the branching cluster. Figure 4.10 shows a block diagram of this multiway multicluster branching structure.

4.4.4 Branches and Loops

Many DSPs also include special hardware and instructions that support *zero-overhead looping*. Instances of DSP loop control vary, but they normally consist of a pair of *loop-start* and *loop-end* instructions that mark the code constituting the loop, followed by another instruction that tells the processor to execute out of the loop buffer. Like many DSP features, such loop support takes an implementation feature (in this case, a small, straight-line code buffer) and exposes it in the ISA. Many general-purpose machines have similar features (such as IPF's *loop count* registers and *branch top* operations, or PowerPC's *link and count* registers) that accomplish similar goals without mandating a particular implementation and with better compilability characteristics.

4.5 Speculation and Predication

Researchers have attacked the branch problem in two different directions: ignore branches and move operations above them, or remove branches and convert them into other forms of dependences. These two complementary techniques are *speculation* and *predication*.

In the following, we discuss *software speculation*, in which the compiler speculatively moves code above branches, and the hardware simply executes it, with the necessary support for exception recovery. Software speculation is a fundamental component of any VLIW compiler. The other form of speculation, *hardware speculation*, implies that the hardware transparently fetches, issues, and executes operations ahead of branches. Hardware speculation is a fundamental component of superscalar microarchitectures, but it is less relevant for VLIWs. As such, we consider it beyond the scope of this book, and we suggest that interested readers consult the extensive available literature on superscalar microarchitectures.

Under the term *predication* we collect all architectural techniques that deal with the problem of how to *remove* branches. In practice, not all branches create barriers to compilers. For example, global scheduling techniques (such as *trace scheduling*) know very well how to deal with predictable branches, without any need for architectural support. The speculation techniques presented in the next section enable compilers to effectively move operations above predictable branches. Unfortunately, speculation is not always beneficial for unpredictable branches, which limit instruction-level parallelism.

4.5.1 Speculation

Many programs contain operations that are probably safe to execute in parallel, but unfortunately cannot be proven safe at compile-time ("statically"). Examples of this include instructions following predicted branches and loads following probably-independent stores.

- *Conservative techniques* (both hardware and software) that rearrange code will always serialize operations unless legality of a reordering can be proven.

- *Speculative techniques* (both hardware and software) allow instructions to be executed ahead of time based on probabilistic assumptions, and provide mechanisms for fixing program semantics if the assumptions are wrong.

Speculation brings many benefits but also limitations. Speculation breaks data and control flow dependences, reduces the critical path of computation, increases ILP, can help tolerate latencies, and helps issue long-latency instructions earlier. On the other hand, speculation increases register pressure, may increase the critical path of other parts of code, and adds complexity to the exception-handling mechanism. Two major questions arise when dealing with speculation. First, how can we be confident we are making the "right guess"? Second, what do we do with the exceptions generated by a speculated operation? We can distinguish two basic types of speculation: *control* and *data*.

- **Control speculation** is executing an instruction before knowing that its execution is required or needed. Control speculation techniques must ensure that other parts of the program are unaffected by the early execution. Moving an instruction above a branch is an example of control speculation. As we said before, control speculation is a fundamental technique for ILP machines, as it removes control dependences and potentially increases ILP. Control speculation is a big win when branches are predicted correctly, but can potentially waste computation and resources when branches are mispredicted.

- **Data speculation** is executing an instruction before knowing it can be executed correctly. Moving a load and its uses above a store that might write the same location is an example of data speculation. Similar considerations apply concerning critical path reduction. Again, in case a memory conflict exists, hardware and software must ensure correct program semantics by reexecuting the speculated load and its uses. This can be expensive in complexity, performance, and power. Data speculation is much less important than control speculation, and is by no means a substitute for it.

Control Speculation

From the compiler point of view, control speculation means optimizing and scheduling operations along the predicted control path, ignoring the original position of branches with respect to the operations under optimization. In Chapter 8 we extensively discuss some of the most frequently used approaches, such as *trace, superblock* and *hyperblock* scheduling. A common characteristic of all the approaches is that control speculation requires the generation of *compensation code* to properly preserve live values. What more deeply affects architecture and microarchitecture is dealing with the complication of *correctly reporting exception conditions*. There are two basic strategies employed to constrain control speculation: (1) *avoid exceptions*; that is, do not speculate any instruction that can cause an exception and (2) *resolve exceptions*; that is, speculate instructions that can cause exceptions, relying on a combination of hardware and software to resolve the errors.

Besides speculating instructions that are always safe (such as integer arithmetic operations), we can use "safety analysis" to identify safe memory references (for example, all memory references inserted by the compiler), add guards (although this is expensive), or search for guards (such as looking at previous branches that may already guard the exception). If we decide we need to deal with unsafe speculation, there are two basic choices for handling the exceptions generated by mispredicted operations.

Nonrecovery Speculation Model. This model uses the concept of *silent instructions* when speculating an operation. Silent instructions, first introduced by Multiflow, are versions of normal instructions that ignore nonrecoverable exceptions. Silent memory read operations are sometimes called *dismissable loads*. For example, if a segmentation fault condition occurs during the execution of a silent memory load instruction, the instruction is canceled before it reaches the memory system and an arbitrary garbage value is returned. The nonrecovery speculation model guarantees that correct programs run correctly, although the exception behavior of the program can change. *Recoverable* exceptions (e.g., page faults) must be handled to completion, in that they affect the values produced by the speculative operation. This can be expensive when speculation is unsuccessful and should raise the threshold required to speculate an instruction.

There are a few other implications of using "silent" instructions. Upon incorrect speculation, the garbage value of a silent instruction is not used, and the possible exception condition is correctly ignored (the silent instruction should not have been executed in the first place). Upon correct speculation, an exception condition might be ignored (incorrectly), and the invalid result (i.e., "*garbage*" *value*) generated may be used by a subsequent instruction without warning.

The nonrecovery speculation model is not acceptable if exceptions must be reported accurately (i.e., in original program order). For example, certain operating systems use exceptions to implement extended functionalities. In other domains, such as embedded, this model is much more useful, in that exceptions are only used to signal errors.

In terms of architectural support, the nonrecovery model is rather simple: operations that can generate exceptions require one opcode bit to identify the *silent* ("dismissable") version. The hardware protection mechanism uses that bit to mask the exceptions that could be generated by the operation.

Recovery Speculation Model. Also called *sentinel scheduling*, recovery speculation is a model that supports full recovery from speculative exceptions. The basic idea behind it is to delay speculative exceptions by splitting each speculated instruction into two parts: the *nonexcepting* part, which performs the actual operation, and the *sentinel* part (check) that flags an exception if necessary. The nonexcepting part can be safely executed speculatively, whereas the sentinel part must stay in the "home" basic block (where the speculated operation originally was). Note that the compiler can eliminate the sentinel under certain conditions.

In terms of architectural support, the recovery model requires additional opcode bits to identify the speculative instructions, and registers must be augmented with additional tag bits to preserve information about the validity of their content. When an exception occurs, we need to save information about the exception in additional bits associated with the result of the speculated operation, to be able to delay it in the general case. For example, we can label the result of a speculated operation whose exception we want to delay with a *NaT* (*not-a-thing*) qualifier, so that the hardware can trigger the proper recovery code when it hits the sentinel. Note that these extra bits must be preserved across context switches, spills, and restores, and that all computational units need to be augmented with extra logic so that the *NaT* bits are correctly propagated and do not get "laundered" by successive transformations. Instead of garbage, we can use the normal register bits to store other useful information, such as the program counter of the excepting operation. Handling *NaT* bits is a rather complex task because all functional units in the datapath need to ensure that speculative exceptions get correctly propagated

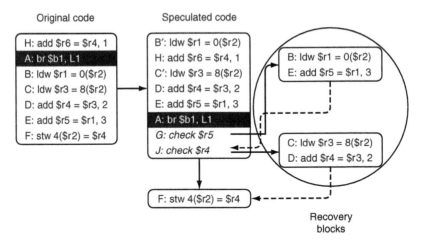

FIGURE 4.11 **Example of recovery speculation.** An example of the sentinel scheduling transformation. In the code on the left, we show a fragment of original pseudocode. The code in the middle box shows the same fragment, with operations B, C, D, and E speculatively moved above branch A. The scheduler breaks operations B and C in two parts: the nonexcepting part (B' and C') and the check part (G and J). If an exception occurs at B' or C', the target registers (either r1 or r3) get a NaT tag and save the excepting PC in the register bits. The hardware propagates the NaT tag, and thus in the example the compiler inserts check operations for both r4 and r5 into the code. When we execute the sentinel, depending on the value of the excepting PC, we can either proceed (no exception occurred) or jump to one of two possible recovery blocks (shown on the right). The purpose of the recovery blocks is to reexecute the excepting operation (thus producing a real exception), as well as all the other operations that depend on the misspeculated value. In the example, we show that is necessary to recompute the values of r5 and r4, in that they are necessary for the rest of the computation (such as operation F).

forward until an operation is known to have been on the true (not speculative) path of execution. Figure 4.11 shows an example of what a "recovery" speculation model requires from the point of view of the scheduling algorithm and the basic architectural support.

All architectures that support IEEE floating point also support a limited form of recovery speculation for floating-point operations by using *NaN* (*not-a-number*) special values. However, this only covers a restricted set of exceptions, and presents problems because the program could "launder" a value coming from an exception—for example, by executing a floating-to-integer conversion (in this case, there is no integer representation for *NaN*, and thus the *NaN* is lost and the user might never see that a serious exception had occurred). The *NaT* model overcomes this limitation and uses the extra register bit so that the correct flags can always be preserved regardless of the register value. This comes at a rather large cost of one extra bit per register (~1.6% for a 64-bit register file).

Unlike nonrecovery speculation, the full-recovery model allows expensive recoverable exceptions (e.g., a page fault) to be delayed until they are certain to execute. In nonrecovery speculation, silent operations are forced to complete the code necessary to recover a recoverable exception, which can have rather damaging effects on performance. With full-recovery support, we can simply mark that an exception occurred and then let the recovery code (only invoked when the operation is not speculative anymore) deal with the exception handler. This advantage is significant in a server environment, in which, for example, virtual memory faults trigger expensive routines to load pages from secondary storage. In embedded environments, virtual memory is usually adopted to implement protection and translation, and thus there is less obvious benefit from a full-recovery model. At the time we write this book, we are not aware of any embedded CPU with a full-recovery speculation model.

Data Speculation

The basic idea behind data speculation can be summarized as: *do run-time memory disambiguation*. When it is impossible to know that two memory accesses do not collide (address the same location), it may still be beneficial to schedule code using the assumption that the accesses do not indeed collide. For example, Figure 4.12 shows how to make it safe to schedule a memory load ahead of a memory store, and then check if the load and store addresses did not overlap. With this transformation we could hide the latency of the load operation by starting early. Unfortunately, executing the necessary checks (in software) to fix misspeculations is expensive, and that is where architectural support comes to the rescue.

Hardware support for data speculation involves a mechanism that "remembers" the locations of speculated memory loads. The compiler then inserts "check" instructions (much in the spirit of *sentinels* for control speculation) that test whether intervening memory loads overwrote one of the speculated locations. If the check fails, the *check* operations jump to a block of recovery code.

Checks for aliasing violations are more subtle than they appear at first glance, in that they must account for "false sharing" issues derived from accesses with different sizes. For example, to speculate the load from address q above the store to address p in the following code

```
*((int*)p) = x;
y = *((char*)q);
```

FIGURE 4.12 Run-time memory disambiguation in software.

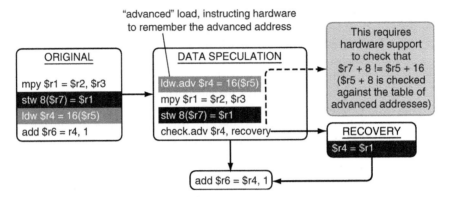

FIGURE 4.13 Example of data speculation with architectural support. To avoid software checks of speculation assumptions, an architectural mechanism must verify that no violation occurred. In the diagram, the compiler speculates the memory read operation, and adds both the check operation and the block of recovery code. The speculated load operation records its address to an associative table (called the ALAT in IPF implementations). Any successive store operation (before the check) looks up its address in the ALAT and records a conflict if it arises. Finally, the check operation tests for the presence of a conflict, in which case it jumps to the recovery code. The recovery code reassigns the correct value to the outcome of the speculated load and reexecutes any dependent computation.

it is not sufficient to check for inequality (p != q), because of the mismatch of the access sizes. The correct check is whether p != (q & ~3).

The IPF (the only architecture we are aware of that supports data speculation) implements this mechanism through the *Advanced Load Table* (ALAT), whereby speculative memory operations record their respective addresses. The ALAT implements a cache-style lookup table for speculated locations, and branching "check" operations can access it to determine whether an intervening store operation violated the speculative assumptions. Figure 4.13 shows an example of the typical sequence of operations required in recovering from a mispredicted data speculation operation.

Although hiding the latency of memory operations is important, the ALAT table comes at a cost in terms of area, power, and complexity, which is comparable to an extra TLB. For many cost-aware and power-aware embedded architectures this premium is likely to be prohibitive for many more generations.

4.5.2 Predication

Predication is a set of architectural and compilation techniques that *convert control dependences to data dependences.* It is a very important technology, in that it gives the compiler an alternative to branches. Predication (also called *conditional execution* or *guarded execution*) always involves some form of conditional execution of instructions based on a Boolean guard or *predicate*. For the sake of discussion, consider the following VEX code.

```
### C code:
### if (x > 0)
###     c = a * b; // 2 cycle latency
### p[0] = c;
###
### VEX code (x=$r5, a=$r1, b=$r2, c=$r3, p=$r10)

    cmpgt $b1 = $r5, 0
;;
    br $b1, L1
;;
    mpy $r3 = $r1, $r2;;
    xnop 1 ### (assuming a 2-cycle mpy latency)
;;
L1:
    stw 0[$r10] = $r3
;;
```

There are two ways to use predication to remove the branch from this code.

Full Predication

Full predication conditionally executes all individual operations in both paths based on a condition derived from the branch.[7] Full predication requires adding an extra Boolean operand to all instructions. It also requires a set of predicate-defining instructions, and a separate bank of 1-bit predicate registers. For example, the multiplication (*mpy*) operation predicated by operand *p1* might look like this:

```
### Here we extend VEX to support full predication
### The notation "($p) op" means "if (p) op;"
###
    cmpgt $p1 = $r5, 0
;;
    ($p1) mpy $r3 = $r1, $r2
    xnop 1 ### (assuming a 2-cycle mpy latency)
;;
    stw 0[$r10] = $r3
;;
### if p1 is TRUE, the mpy executes normally
### if p1 is FALSE, the mpy is treated as a nop
```

---

7. Examples of fully predicated architectures include the Cydra-5, IPF, TI C6x, and StarCore.

Partial Predication

Partial predication unconditionally executes all individual operations in both paths, and then selects the final values of variables based on a condition derived from the branch.[8] Partial predication requires a few new operations (in the form of *conditional move* or *select*). This is a more limited approach that does not require extensions to operand format.

```
## Here we use the VEX "slct" operation
##
     mpy $r4 = $r1, $r2
;;
     cmpgt $b1 = $r5, 0
;;
     slct $r3 = $b1, $r4, $r3
;;
     stw 0[$r10] = $r3
;;
## the add always executes (speculatively)
## if b1 is TRUE, $r3 gets the new value ($r4)
## if b1 is FALSE, $r3 keeps the old value

## And this is the equivalent code with a "cmov"
##
     mpy $r4 = $r1, $r2
;;
     cmpgt $b1 = $r5, 0
;;
     cmov $r3 = $b1, $r4
;;
     stw 0[$r10] = $r3
;;
```

For full predication, there are many ways to define and combine predicates. For example, in the TI C6x architecture, operations determine whether they execute on a true or on a false predicate by means of an additional bit in the encoding. The cost of this extra encoding bit is equivalent to doubling the size of the predicate set. A reasonable alternative allows operations to execute only on a true predicate, but adds predicate-generating operations that generate both the *true* and the *false* version of a predicate. This method is used by IPF. This approach has a few additional advantages: in many cases only one predicate is needed, and it is possible to define "complex" compare operations that perform Boolean *and* and *or* operations on multiple predicates, to efficiently handle the various combinations of nested control flow.

---

8. Examples of partially predicated architectures include Multiflow TRACE, SPARC, Alpha, MIPS, Pentium III, and Lx.

For partial predication, similar considerations apply, and it is useful to include a set of Boolean (logical) operations in the architecture, so that it is easy to compute the predicates used to select values coming from nested control flow.

Full predication and speculation can be combined so that they cooperate to increase ILP. Strictly speaking, predication does not reduce the critical path, as we can see from the previous full predication example, in which the *mpy* operation depends on the *cmpgt* operation because of predicate *p1*. To overcome this, we can use speculation to *promote* predicated operations (so that they can float freely above the predicate definition) and predicate only the data assignments just before their use. This can shorten the critical path because longer-latency predicated operations can issue earlier. The following code shows a simple predicate promotion.

```
## Here we "promote" the predicated operation
## to remove a data dependence. The predicated
## operation becomes speculative, and we can
## schedule it before the predicate definition
##
    mpy $r4 = $r1, $r2 ## promoted
;;
    cmpgt $p1 = $r5, 0
;;
    ($p1) mov $r3 = $r4
;;
    stw 0[$r10] = $r3
;;
```

As we promote more and more predicated operations to speculative, the difference between full predication and partial predication disappears. We can also see this from the similarity of this simple predicate code example to the partial predicated code with a conditional move.

Cost and Benefits of Predication

Although predication lets the compiler better use ILP resources, this is not an unconditional benefit. This ILP is artificial, in that only one of the execution paths produces useful results, but they all appear as one combined path by virtue of predication.

Predication greatly improves code with difficult-to-predict branches, removing misprediction penalties (which can be severe for deep-pipeline microprocessors). Data-driven, branch-intensive codes (such as those for sorting, data mining, data compression, and databases) are those for which predication is likely to be more beneficial. From the compiler point of view, predication widens the scope of compiler optimization by creating larger "basic blocks" and enabling advanced loop optimizations. Predication is also the only solid technique that enables a compiler to software pipeline loops with control flow.

For programs dominated by loops, predication has been proven in product compilers to improve IPC performance because it enables better software pipelining. Starting in the mid 1990s, several studies have been conducted to evaluate the benefits of predication, and predication in combination with speculation. Academic studies on hypothetical machines presented promising results that inspired the design of real machines with full predication support (such as Intel's IPF). More recent studies evaluating measured benefits on a real machine have, however, shown benefits that were much smaller than anticipated.

Predication is not a magic bullet for branches. For example, a predicated block includes cycles for all scheduled operations, and thus shorter paths may take longer and be penalized. Predication is most effective when paths are balanced or when the longest path is the most frequently executed, but making this determination at compile-time is difficult, even in the presence of profiling information. Considering the cost of predicating a block, it is difficult to decide what to predicate and what not to, and heuristics are weak.

In addition, full predication complicates the hardware, the ISA, and the compiler. Unlike speculation, which favors deeper pipelines and faster clocks, predication adds levels of logic to critical paths and potentially degrades clock speed. Predicate operands use precious encoding bits in all instructions, and bypassing operations with predicate operands considerably complicates the forwarding logic. Predication's benefits for acyclic or "control-oriented" code have been the subject of lively academic and commercial debate, and the jury is still out on whether the benefits of predication justify the massive hardware cost to support full predication.

The argument between *full predication* and *partial predication* is even more subtle. Full predication is more expressive and allows the compiler to predicate blocks that contain any combination of operations. Partial predication requires aggressive speculation and embeds some intrinsic limitations (for example, it cannot predicate blocks containing *call* operations). In terms of implementation complexity, full predication has much higher demands on the instruction encodings and the microarchitecture, as described previously, whereas partial predication with *select* operations is a good match for most microarchitectures and datapaths and has no impact on complexity, area, or speed.

Predication in the Embedded Domain

In the embedded domain, it is difficult to justify the code size penalty of a large set of predicate registers. Full predication implies a "*pay up front*" philosophy, in which the cost of the predicate machinery needs to be paid regardless of how often it is used. For example, adding 6 predicate bits to address 64 predicates helped push the IPF encoding to 42 bits per operation—an approach that would be prohibitively expensive for an embedded processor. DSP architectures that support full predication (such as the TI C6x family) constrain predicates to a reduced set (three registers designated as predicates in cluster A, and three in cluster B),[9] with severe limitations to the compiler usage.

---

9. The C62x and C67x have five predicates. The C64x has six predicates.

Considering that every if-then-else consumes two predicates, six predicates can safely cover only two levels of control-flow nesting.

On the other hand, partial predication follows a "*pay-per-use*" philosophy, increasing code size (and latency) only with *select* operations (every live value with multiple definitions requires an additional *select* operation for each pair of definitions). We believe that this incremental approach, together with the implementation simplicity, makes partial predication particularly appealing for embedded processors.

4.6 System Operations

Under the term *system operations* we group all functions that control and observe the system around the processor, such as dealing with I/O and peripherals. All architectures require such operations.

Few system operations affect performance, and thus simplicity is the driving force.[10] One of the most efficient approaches is to deal with system functions through a set of *control registers* that are memory mapped to a reserved, noncached, nontranslated (physically addressed) memory page (for example, page 0). In this way, we can access control registers through simple load and store operations. This also enables different implementations to implement different sets of control registers, without any visible impact to the ISA. This feature is particularly appealing for *families* of microprocessors that include several variations of the base architecture, as it is common for embedded cores. Similar considerations apply to I/O and peripherals, which can be memory mapped similarly.

The combination of memory-mapped peripherals and memory speculation needs, however, to be handled with care. We cannot guarantee that read accesses to memory-mapped peripherals never cause irreversible side effects (such as incrementing a counter). Unfortunately, a speculative load gone astray can hit any location in the address space. As a consequence, systems must protect memory-mapped I/O pages against any speculative access, and ensure that an application accessing I/O uses only nonspeculative operations. This safety mechanism is normally implemented as part of the protection unit, or the MMU.

Without getting into much detail, there are several classes of system operations we can implement through the *control register* mechanism.

- *Synchronization support*, including mechanisms to implement cache flushing, cache invalidation, semaphores, and atomicity

- *Interrupt support*, including mechanisms to identify the interrupt source, set and examine priorities, and set interrupt masks

- *Protection and virtual memory support* in the systems that support virtual memory, including ways to access the protection and translation registers, handle the TLB to load and flush pages, and so on

---

10. One key exception is TLB miss handlers, which are critical to the performance of many modern machines. TLBs are hardware support for virtual memory, which used to be rare in embedded machines but is rapidly becoming more common due to the rise of Linux and PocketPC.

- *Debug support*, including ways for a debugger to break the execution streams (often simply implemented through an illegal instruction) and to set hardware breakpoint registers

- *Analysis and profiling support*, including performance counters (hit-miss counters, stall counters, and so on), profile functions (such as a *trap-on-taken branch* mode), or PC queues that let you analyze the history of program execution at an interrupt handler

These special operations are rarely compiled as part of application code. Instead, they are written by operating system and compiler developers, in hand-coded assembly. Special operation support has so far not migrated into optimizing compilers, as the types of operations performed cannot naturally be represented linguistically (even in systems-oriented languages such as C), and the semantics of the special operations prohibit most optimizations.

4.7 Further Reading

This chapter takes for granted some knowledge of computer arithmetic, as when we describe VEX implementations of multiplication, division, and so on. For a good detailed description of the various algorithms, we refer you to extant literature on the subject, such as Goldberg [1990], Waser and Flynn [1982], and Cavanagh [1984].

You might have noted the strange way in which we draw datapaths (e.g., Figure 4.1). The vast majority of architecture books show pipeline diagrams to represent datapaths. In our case, we prefer to show a diagram driven by the interconnection buses between register files and units (which are indeed what dominates area in modern designs). For example, this is more common in architecture manuals for VLIW processors, such as the HP/ST Lx (ST200).

Sections 4.1.3, 4.1.4, and 4.1.5 provide many hands-on examples of the "lore" of how various operations are used in practice. Unfortunately, this lore is often missing from ISA manuals, which describe the manipulations performed by an operation without describing its intended use in applications. Often this information can only be discovered by reading source code examples, looking at assembly language compiler output, or by reading application notes from the manufacturer. Most processor manufacturers include "Application Notes" among the web pages that support their processors. These notes are typically a grab bag of varying degrees of interest and application, but they can be worth skimming for techniques that get the best performance out of a processor. On Micro-SIMD, see Intel's "white paper on MMX". To learn in greater depth about floating-point theory, Kahan [2004], Kahan [1983], and Cody et al. [1985] are the serious sources.

The original idea of clustered VLIWs (i.e., partitioned register) files dates back to Fisher [1983]. A more recent work that describes more details on clustering VLIW with an emphasis on embedded is the HP Technical Report HPL-98-84 [Faraboschi et al., 1998] (this also describes the experiment from which Figure 4.4 is derived). As we described, clustering is not unique to VLIWs. For example, a good description of clustering in the superscalar domain is the Farkas et al. [1997b] paper.

Rotating register files were first popularized [Charlesworth, 1981] by FPS, and then appeared in the Cydra-5 [Dehnert et al., 1989] and more recently in the IPF family.

There is far too much material available on cache memories to be able to present a comprehensive literature. However, to learn more about the history of caches, the Goodman [1983] paper is the place to start. Other good references are the Smith [1982] survey and the Przybylski [1990] book.

For examples of exotic addressing modes related to embedded processing, any "traditional" DSP instruction manual and application notes would give a good idea of what they are and what they are used for. The idea of unbundling branches was first introduced by Schorr [1971], and was popularized by the EPIC team (see, for example, the HPL-1999-111 Technical Report [Schlansker and Rau 2000]). The idea of multiway (*n*-way) branches appeared in Fisher [1980].

The concept of negating the execution of the next instruction, as well as limited forms of guarded execution (based on flags), dates back to the 1970s (or even before). The Cydra-5 architecture also includes architectural support for full predication. To understand predication in the modern sense (including both full and partial predication), we recommend the paper by Mahlke et al. [1995].

The concept of software speculation was introduced in the early trace scheduling papers [Fisher, 1979, 1981]. The Mahlke et al. [1993] paper on speculation with sentinel scheduling describes both compiler and architecture features that address the challenge of efficiently handling exceptions for speculative instructions.

4.8 Exercises

1. Write the C code that implements the multiplication of two 24-bit fractional values to produce a 48-bit fractional value, assuming 32-bit registers. Use it to implement an FIR filter, and measure the performance in VEX.

2. What special operations (intrinsics) can we add to speed up the code from the previous exercise? Define the operations, write the sample algorithm, and test them with the VEX "assembler intrinsics" functionality.

3. Write the C code that implements a saturated add of two 8-bit integer values to produce an 8-bit integer value, assuming 32-bit registers. Write a filter that changes the brightness of a 2D image using this code. Test it on an image of your choice, using VEX. Measure the resulting performance.

4. Write a C implementation of an unsigned integer division routine without using the C division operator. Compare the performance with the version provided in the text. Do the same for signed division.

5. In what cases can a compiler replace a multiplication by a constant with a sequence of shift-and-addition operations? In what cases can a compiler

replace a division by a constant with a sequence of shift-and-subtraction operations?

6. Write the simplified form of an algorithm to find the remainder after division by a constant, where the constant is a power of 2. Do both the signed and unsigned cases.

7. Show that saturated addition is not associative. In other words, show that the order in which one performs saturated addition of three numbers produces different results.

8. Describe how to use indexed register files to hide or remove the cost of register spills and reloads around function calls, prologues, and epilogues. (Hint: assume an *allocate* operation like that in the IPF architecture that reserves or frees a section of the register file.) Why does this technique work for a limited level of function call nesting? Can you suggest a way to remove this limitation?

9. In a clustered VLIW, we have the choice of providing implicit or explicit copy operations, for which in the implicit case operands must include encoding bits for the full register space specifier, and in the explicit case we only need a cluster bit in the encoding, at the possible expense of requiring extra copy operations to move values between clusters. For a 4-wide VLIW architecture with 32 registers per cluster, draw a figure showing the number of bits in an instruction associated with the register specifiers in the two cases. Compute how many (%) intercluster copy operations can be issued before the explicit-copy mechanism becomes less efficient than the implicit copy.

10. Write a short essay about the relevance of rotating register files to modulo scheduling. Hint: consider rotating predicates as well as rotating general-purpose registers.

11. Pick five computer architectures. Describe how each of them supports constructing constants at the natural word size of the architecture.

12. Trampoline stubs are a way to support branches with spans larger than what is representable by the immediate field in a branch instruction. For example, an architecture with a 32-bit address space and 32-bit operation encoding might reserve only 16 bits for branch offset information. Describe the steps the linker has to perform to identify where trampoline stubs are needed and to insert them to ensure correct program operation. In VEX, write an example of trampoline code.

13. Survey the set of architectures that provide efficient support for misaligned memory accesses (hint: x86, MIPS). What motivations might the architects have had for including such support?

14.   Write an optimized *memcpy* operation (see the standard C library definition) that efficiently handles misaligned source and target addresses. Write a performance test set that covers the various cases (aligned and misaligned source and target, short and long vectors) and compare the performance versus the built-in *memcpy* routine of the VEX system.

15.   Using whatever resources seem appropriate, make a list of applications that benefit from efficient support for misaligned memory access. Hint: where must data be packed in ways that do not match power-of-2 boundaries?

16.   Compare the low-overhead loop support of the TI C54x DSP family with the counted branch support of the IPF architecture. Describe how to extend these structures to support nested loops. Why is support for nested loops more important to DSPs?

17.   Modify the following code fragment so that the VEX compiler succeeds in if-converting it. Compare the performance of the original and the if-converted code. How would the assembly code and performance change with a fully predicated architecture?

```
void foo(int *p)
{
    int i;
    for(i = 0; i < 1000; i++){
        if(p[i] > 0x80)
            p[i] = 0x80;
    }
}
```

18.   How should a misaligned speculative access be handled in a nonrecovery (silent load) speculation model? Consider the two cases: (1) the architecture provides support for misaligned data access and (2) the architecture does not. In the second case, what if there is support for software exception recovery of a misaligned access?

19.   Full and partial predication can be seen as different ways of using code space to support if-conversion. In the full predication case, every operation must include some number of bits to encode predicate registers. In the partial predication case, extra operations must be added only to those parts of the code in which predication is applied. Pick a benchmark program (for example, *gzip*). Under VEX, compile it with if-conversion enabled and disabled (see Appendix A for details on VEX compiler switches). Compare the resulting code sizes and performance. Compute the overhead (if any) of if-conversion. Discuss how this would compare to the code size that would be achieved by a fully predicated version of VEX.

5

Microarchitecture Design

I first observed the "doubling of transistor density on a manufactured die every year" in 1965, just four years after the first planar integrated circuit was discovered. The press called this "Moore's Law" and the name has stuck. To be honest, I did not expect this law to still be true some 30 years later, but I am now confident that it will be true for another 20 years. By the year 2012, Intel should have the ability to integrate 1 billion transistors onto a production die that will be operating at 10 GHz.

— Gordon Moore, *Chairman emeritus of Intel*, 1992

By now readers should be familiar with the distinction between architecture and implementation. The members of an ISA family are related by sharing instruction encoding, compilers, and aspects of implementations. This chapter focuses on microarchitecture, or implementations of architecture. We have already discussed a number of implementations and architectural families in the preceding chapters.

The x86 architecture has a long history of generations that over many years of changes in process technology and advances in computer architecture have evolved from the very first 8086 to today's Pentium 4 and Athlon.[1] Today's ARM family includes myriad variants, and modern DSP families include processors built over a variety of clock rates and silicon processes. All members of an architectural family have a degree of code compatibility with one another. They also vary widely in terms of price, performance, and functionality, and it is these variations we discuss here.

One can view an ISA as a *specification*: it determines what any instance of that ISA must do, and it provides a model any programmer can use on any implementation of the architecture. However, ISAs are also intentionally *under*specified, either implicitly

---

1. In an earlier draft of the book we called the Pentium 4 a "variant" of the 8086 because the two ultimately run the same instruction set. However, Bob Colwell reminded us that this would be "*kind of like saying the space shuttle is only a variant of the Wright brothers' flier.*" We agree.

(by not addressing a particular aspect of behavior) or explicitly (by stating that behavior in a particular case is implementation dependent). Underspecification is a deliberate choice. It leaves some decisions open in order to afford implementers room to try various techniques. It also gives the architecture room to change and grow as technology changes. In a fuzzy way, architecture is about *what to do*, and microarchitecture is about *how to do it*.

In considering the boundary between architecture and microarchitecture, it helps to consider the related boundary between the *architectural state* and the *physical state* of the implementation. Architectural state is the state of the abstract machine common across all implementations of the ISA. Physical state is the state of the particular implementation currently under consideration. Physical state includes architectural state, and the additional physical information has to do with the design choices made by implementers. In principle, there ought to be a clear mapping at all times from the physical state to the architectural state—a way of relating the state of the implementation to the idealized ISA model it is simulating. However, it turns out to be surprisingly difficult to produce such a clean mapping at all times. For example, pipelining is one of the best-known and most well-documented microarchitectural techniques. However, relating the state of a pipelined implementation back to the architectural specification is complicated by the depth of the pipeline and the degree of speculative execution taking place in that pipeline. In Section 6.3 we discuss the relationship between simulators and actual machines, which is similar in complexity to the relationship between architectures and implementations.

Although invisible to most programmers, the split between ISA and microarchitecture is increasingly visible to those who build compilers. Many modern architectures (most notably Intel's x86) have both generic (architecture-wide) and implementation-specific optimization guides. To get the best performance out of a particular implementation, the compiler (or hand coder) needs to know the structure of that implementation. These implementation-specific guides often yield the best clues as to how designers have chosen to build a particular implementation. Of course, implementation-specific optimizations are at best a wash and at worst bad for the next implementation to come along. In some cases, however, some optimizations do survive across multiple generations, because it is not uncommon for one generation's peculiarities to find their way into the next.

The relationship between ISA and microarchitecture has pluses and minuses for designers. ISAs give compatibility and reusability across implementations and compilers, but compatibility has its price. Even in relatively "clean" architectures, implementers must spend some silicon on architectural compatibility. The original architecture may have been designed with an entirely different set of technological assumptions from that of the current implementation, and managing this mismatch becomes increasingly complicated over the life of the architecture.

Microarchitecture spans the range from the architectural model to the physical level: transistors and wires on the chip. Microarchitecture designers have two major problems: building *structure* into their designs and adapting to the constraints of the underlying technology. These two themes run throughout this chapter. Structure relates to the large-scale problems of pipeline design: what parts are needed, how to connect them, and how to balance the pieces. Structural details include the datapath width and pipeline depth, the degree of clustering and corresponding shape of the register files and functional units, the form of the bypass/forwarding network, and the integration of exceptions into the design.

In the past decade, technological constraints in microarchitecture have changed from transistor-bound to wire-bound. Whereas historically microarchitectural techniques were primarily limited by the number of transistors on chip, today designs are limited by wiring and interconnection congestion. In general, structures requiring global interconnection or many wires, such as register files and bypass/forwarding networks, are expensive in today's silicon processes. This is a new regime for designers and design tools, and we are still adapting to it.

The nature of the CAD design methodology exacerbates wire-bound problems in current microarchitectures. Each new process generation reduces the size of transistors, which reduces the net contribution of transistors to cycle time. However, many embedded systems cannot afford full-custom designs, which means that designers must rely on automated synthesis tools. Microarchitectural objects with many wires and connections cause congestion in the design, and automated tools perform worst when they must deal with this type of congestion.

The tradeoff between full-custom and synthesized designs in microarchitecture parallels the tradeoff between hand-coded assembly and compiled code at the software level. Just as "portable" C code can easily be moved to a different platform, a well-qualified standard-cell (i.e., synthesizable) design will be quickly portable to a new process. C code will run immediately (and possibly well, depending on the compilation technology), but will not run as fast as hand-tuned code. Similarly, well-qualified standard cells mean a conservative design, which will improve production yields but will worsen the clock cycle time and frequency of the resulting parts. In both cases, more automation (either the optimizing compiler or the synthesis tools) speeds up development time, reducing time-to-market and NRE costs. In both cases, hand tuning increases costs and time for improvements in some dimension of performance. Finally, it is also true that humans are not getting smarter at hand coding, whereas compilers (both software and hardware) are steadily improving, and thus the gap is closing. Large investments into hand coding anything will become rare.

Our analogy is not perfect. The exotic design styles associated with the full-custom approach affect yield and the portability of the design to different technologies. And although there is a definite preference in embedded designs for standard cells, the most regular structures (e.g., register files and memories) tend to be rebuilt full-custom for each design port. The reason for this is simple: the regularity of register files and memories makes full-custom design of their underlying cells relatively simple, but their large area and impact on cycle time makes them immediate targets for optimization. Predefined versions of these structures can be fast, but tend to waste space.

This chapter begins with a section on register file design, which seems appropriate, as the register file holds the architectural state. We continue to pipelining in Section 5.2. Section 5.3 describes how VLIW machines fetch, decode, and sequence instructions.

The next four sections return to topics introduced in the previous chapter, on architectural structures in ISA design. Section 5.4 discusses the datapath and the implementation of bypassing, Section 5.5 describes the memory architecture, Section 5.6 describes the control unit, and Section 5.7 talks about control registers, the items manipulated by special operations. We conclude the chapter with a discussion of power-related issues.

5.1 Register File Design

We begin with register file design because many aspects of register file design are determined by the cells and lines of the register file itself. Even though the register file is connected to other parts of the chip, these intrinsic aspects of the design can be considered without worrying about interactions with other parts of the chip. Register files are dense, in both transistors and wires, with a regularly repeating structure.

Despite the vast advances in process technology, register file design remains important in embedded systems. Along with the bypass network, to which we turn in Section 5.4, the register file is one of the datapath limiters of the ILP of a fully connected cluster.

5.1.1 Register File Structure

In this section, we review the basic structure of a multiported register file design, and we provide some better justification for some of the choices (such as clustering) we presented in the architecture chapter.

Register files are *addressable*, in that each read or write port can specify an independent register to read or write during the current cycle. Accesses to the register file are *word parallel*, in that processors access registers in their natural size; typically 8, 16, or 32 bits. Each bit of a register is represented by a *bit cell*, which is the fundamental building block of the overall register file. There are two levels of organization to the register file: how the bit cells are grouped and how things work within each bit cell.

To build up a register file, bit cells are grouped to form individual registers, and the registers are grouped to form the overall register file. Register files are normally organized as two-dimensional grids of wires, wherein (for example) control paths run horizontally and data paths run vertically. Consider a canonical RISC register file, with 32 registers, each of 32-bit word size. Suppose the register file supports only a single access (read or write) at a time. In this case, the vertical datapaths correspond to the bit positions within the word, whereas the horizontal control paths select a single register out of the file. Asserting one of the 32 control lines causes each of the bit cells in that row to place data on its corresponding data line, allowing the 32-bit value of the register to be read from the datapaths.

In register files with multiple ports, there are correspondingly many additional control and data lines, since the control lines must be asserted separately and the data lines must be implemented separately for independent access to the bit cells (and by

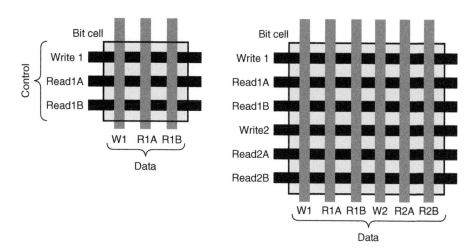

FIGURE 5.1 **Organization of a multiported register file.** Each picture depicts only a single bit cell in the array that constitutes the register file. In the picture, control lines run horizontally and data lines run vertically. As you can see from the ratio between a 2R/1W register file (left) and a 4R/2W register file (right), size grows with the square of the number of ports. What is even worse is that what determines size here are wires and not transistors. Finally, a bigger register file is a slower register file, which might limit the clock cycle of the entire core.

extension, the registers) to take place. Figure 5.1 depicts the control and data lines that cross a single bit cell within a register file. Each intersection between a control line and its corresponding data line contains gates that connect the data line to the value of the bit cell when the control line is asserted, reading from or writing to the bit cell as appropriate.

One can see from Figure 5.1 that the linear size of the bit cell scales directly with the number of ports, because that many lines (either control or data) must be able to connect to the value stored in the bit cell. Thus, the area of a register file grows with the square of the number of ports (each port requires new routing in the X and Y direction). Register file designs are limited by routing and not by transistor density. In addition, the read access time of a register file grows approximately linearly with the number of ports. As the number of ports increases, the internal bit cell loading becomes larger, the larger area of register file causes longer wire delays, and longer wires and larger cells yield to more power-hungry circuitry.

Register files are usually tightly coupled with the bypassing circuitry that implements pipeline forwarding paths. Bypassing logic is largely wire dominated, and unfortunately grows with the product of the number of read ports and write ports. We will return to bypass logic in Section 5.4.2.

5.1.2 Register Files, Technology, and Clustering

For any given generation of VLSI technology, there is always a "sweet spot" in terms of the number of register file ports that can be implemented without creating critical paths in access to the register file. In other words, when designing a register file it is not necessary to *minimize* the number of ports. For example, in a typical 0.18μ process, we can easily build around 12 ports (8 read + 4 write), and possibly 15 to 20 ports with some small speed compromise. Such a design would support five to seven execution units with simultaneous operand access. Beyond the sweet spot, additional ports exact higher marginal costs (cycle time, power consumption, design complexity), whereas below the sweet spot one is not using all that the technology has to offer.

However, applications can have more available ILP than the technological sweet spot supports. To go beyond the limits imposed by register file width, one must move to a clustered design. Each cluster has its own register file, bypass networks, and functional units, and the width of the cluster's datapath will be optimized to match the underlying VLSI technology. Clustering keeps the size of the register file down. For example, splitting a large register file into two clusters results in two small register files, each roughly one-quarter the size of the original file. However, the clustered design allows the core to achieve more ILP at the cost of cluster management overhead at the ISA, microarchitecture (intercluster connection), and compiler levels.

The ISA chapter described the various cluster designs: ISA-visible, ISA-invisible, compiler-controlled cluster placement, hardware-controlled cluster placement, and explicit intercluster moves versus "wide" register specifiers and implicit copies. Of these possibilities, only the ISA-invisible hardware-controlled possibilities are purely microarchitectural approaches.

Although reducing register pressure within a cluster, architecturally visible clustering adds a register pressure overhead for remote register access or explicit move instructions. The buses between clusters that implement implicit or explicit copies are expensive resources, and they require read and write ports on either side. This imposes a microarchitectural "tax" on register file size even within a cluster, and the scarcity of the resource requires that the compiler use such moves carefully.

5.1.3 Separate Address and Data Register Files

Microarchitecturally, separate address and data registers have benefits whose costs are only apparent in other areas, such as architecture (instruction encoding) and compilation (premature placement decision). In Section 4.2.3 we argued against separate address and data registers from an architecture viewpoint, and showed that this tradeoff needs to be carefully evaluated on a case-by-case basis.

Most VLIW designs follow the philosophy of combining integer computation and addressing operations into a single general-purpose space. From a microarchitectural standpoint, the transistor drought that motivated separate address registers and address-generation units (AGUs) is over, and few new architectures maintain the address/data separation. However, smaller address and data clusters require smaller bypass networks, which can lead to easier routing and shorter wires — key to modern microarchitectural concerns.

Separating address and data registers adds complexity, but saves hardware. The area of a register file grows with the square of the number of ports. Address register files are

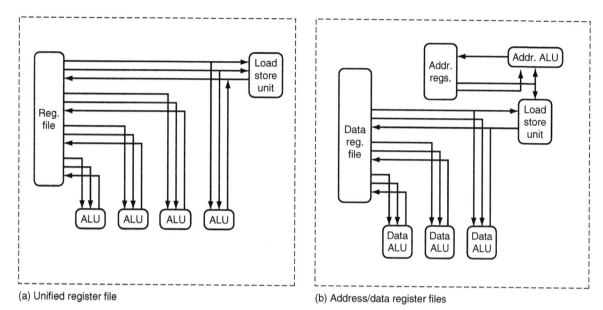

(a) Unified register file

(b) Address/data register files

FIGURE 5.2 **Address and data registers.** This figure shows two examples of a 4-wide (VEX- like) VLIW architecture: one with a unified register file (a) and the other with a partitioned address/data register file (b). We can see that (a) is a cleaner and simpler datapath organization, although it requires an 8R/4W register file. In (b) we can reduce register file size, since we need only a 6R/3W data register file and a (probably smaller) 2R/1W address register file. However, the structure is more complex, and we still need to provide paths (not shown) to enable data movement between data and address registers (this could be done by reusing some ALU datapath). Finally, it is evident how (b) forces the compiler to make early choices for allocation of values and computation to either the data or the address datapath.

likely to require fewer ports than data register files. Thus, if we divide a unified register file and assign part of it to a separate set of *address registers* with fewer ports we save silicon area. In addition, for a smaller register set (such as address registers) it is easier to build more complex mechanisms, such as post-increments, rotations, and special address arithmetic units. Figure 5.2 shows two possible VLIW organizations that use unified or separate data/address register files. Similarly, DSPs benefit from separating the AGU from the main ALU (which, as we said before, might handle fixed-point data rather than integers).

Without discussing the specifics of a target technology it is difficult to quantify the hardware savings of a separate set of *address* registers. As we discussed, the drawbacks of such designs are many, and the technology trends point to a future in which these types of choices will have small effect on cost, especially given the "sweet spot" in multiported register file designs. For these reasons, we acknowledge the choices of many previous-generation DSP architectures, but we omit further details of machines with separate *address* registers.

5.1.4 Special Registers and Register File Features

Many architectures provide special registers for control purposes. We discussed predicate registers and their precursors, control flags, in the ISA chapter. Other architectures include explicit branch registers that give hints to the implementation that a particular branch target is likely to be used soon. Microarchitecturally, predicate and control registers tend to be small compared to word-sized registers. All of their implementation complexity comes from correctly setting and reading them, from properly handling them in the bypass network, and from applying their effects to instructions. Branch registers tend to be closely coupled to the mechanisms in the fetch unit, making their implementation especially complex.

Some architectures add a level of indirection between register specifiers and physical register location. In particular, architectures with register windows, interrupt registers, and rotating registers require additional logic before the select lines of the register file. A register window architecture can be implemented using a larger register file in which the register-selection bits come from the current window register concatenated with the basic register specifier. Interrupt registers must be substituted for their corresponding normal registers when in an interrupt mode, which is effectively using the interrupt level as part of the register specifier. Last, in architectures with rotating registers (e.g., IPF), the rotation register must be *added* to the normal register specifier (and possibly requiring a modulo wraparound as well) to map between the register specifier and the actual physical register location. All of this logic occurs before the control lines of the register file, but it may affect the cycle time of the design or make the pipeline longer.

In the case of the register stack of the IPF architecture, a combination of compilation, run-time, architecture, and microarchitecture techniques must conspire for correct operation to occur.[2] The microarchitectural engine of the register stack must steal load/store slots from the memory unit to transparently spill or load register values into their stack locations. Further, the register stack must stall procedure calls if it ever falls behind the architectural expectations on spilling/reloading. These control lines may be long and difficult to route, but the majority of the implementation complexity is in well-defined orchestration of the various cooperating components.

5.2 Pipeline Design

This section discusses wider design questions associated with pipelined implementations. A number of pipeline-related questions are deferred to Section 5.4, on datapath design.

Many architecture textbooks cover the fundamentals of pipelined design, and we will not repeat what has been covered elsewhere. For example, the pipelining

---

2. IPF is not unique in this respect. Every computer is — in some respects — a house of cards in the sense that compiler, architecture, and microarchitecture have to work together to guarantee that programs execute correctly.

discussion by Patterson and Hennessy [1997] begins with a combinatorial, single-cycle-per-instruction machine and then gradually refines the design into the standard MIPS/RISC five-stage pipeline. However, tradeoffs in microarchitecture have changed somewhat since the RISC five-stage pipeline. Transistor count limitations convinced designers to reuse the ALU for address computations (and generated the famous load-delay slot architecture). Today, transistors are plentiful but wires are expensive, and pipelining in ILP-oriented machines adds the dimension of issue width to the mix.

Although pipelined wide-issue machines have more complex datapaths than their single-issue brethren, we can still talk about major sections of the pipeline. There remain three major sections of the pipeline: the "front end," which fetches, decodes, and issues instructions/operations; the execution section (or "datapath"), in which operations are performed; and the "back end" (or commit section) which handles commitment and retirement of operations. In modern designs, such as the Pentium III, each of these is a disjoint, separately stallable or even out-of-order pipeline segment (so that the architecture does not have to stall everywhere if only one of the segments stalls).

The datapath scales with both issue width and pipeline depth, whereas the front end and back end scale directly with issue width and only indirectly with pipeline depth. Unfortunately, each dimension of scaling tends to add new requirements for wide-scale communication, which adds to the number of wires required by a design. Not everything can be pipelined (for example, memory accesses). Logic that cannot be pipelined must be spread across multiple clock cycles or it will place a lower bound on the length of a single clock cycle, decreasing the clock frequency of the design.

In addition to pipeline design complexities introduced by issue width and pipeline depth, the exception model adds a level of complexity to the pipeline. Exceptions, like their more common conditional-branch relatives, disrupt the pipeline of the machine. We return to exception handling in more detail in Section 5.6.

Pipelining involves making engineering tradeoffs. One could in principle design a single-cycle machine (and Patterson and Hennessy [1997] in fact start with such an example), rendering a relatively simple design (everything is combinatorial) but a rotten cycle time. Each additional pipeline stage has a marginal benefit in terms of spreading out the work of the machine in smaller steps that might allow a lower cycle time, and a marginal cost in terms of added design complexity and global overheads. Front-end stages (before execution) and execution pipeline stages add to the branch penalties experienced by a machine. Execution and commit pipeline stages increase the visible latency of operations and may complicate exception handling.

5.2.1 Balancing a Pipeline

One of the key issues in pipeline design is achieving a *balanced* design. In an ideal microarchitectural design, the critical path through every pipeline stage would have equal latency, so that no pipeline stage has "slack time" or wastes time during a clock cycle. In practice, this is difficult to achieve because designers are simultaneously altering different parts of the design, making such global balance a moving target. Designers must divide the work of processing each instruction and its component

Can You Do This in One Cycle?

During the lifetime of a design, designers continually ask themselves how much work fits into a single machine cycle. Designs typically begin with a "cycle target," which is a guess at what the natural cycle time of the design should be. From the cycle target, one can attempt to divide a pipelined operation into "reasonable" chunks of work. However, stages of a pipeline only come into balance as the design matures. Early in the design, the pipe stages are out of balance. During the second- or third-generation redesign, designers move functionality across stage boundaries in response to various design issues. After three generations of products based on the same microarchitecture, pipelines tend to be reasonably balanced.

operations into pipeline stages. This section discusses many of the considerations involved.

Pipeline balance involves factors from both neighbors of microarchitecture: bottom-up issues from circuit design and top-down issues primarily caused by architectural concerns. Circuit technology, global clock distribution and skew, and testability are bottom-up concerns. Microspeculation (described below), operation latency, and branch and exception penalties carry architectural decisions into the microarchitectural level.

Circuit technology drives the bottom line of microarchitectural design. One heuristic for balancing the stages of the pipeline is to specify a number of gates per pipeline stage (or equivalently, specifying the number of levels of logic). Assuming that wire delay is low and the delay through a gate is fixed, this provides a ballpark estimate for how fast a design will run in a given technology.

These circuit-level computations can be refined to an arbitrary degree, modeling the degree of load on gates that have wide fan-out or long wires, modeling wire delay, and even modeling impedance effects between parallel wires. With more detailed models (driven by increasingly detailed versions of the design and CAD tools), designers can find *critical paths* in the design. At any given point in the design of a pipeline, the critical path is the sequence of wires and gates that requires the longest latency for correct operation. The critical path thus determines the shortest cycle time at which a design can safely operate. Much of the microarchitectural task involves avoiding (through careful design), finding (through accurate simulation), and removing (through iterative redesign) a design's critical paths. Figure 5.3 illustrates the tradeoffs between microarchitectural decisions that affect pipeline design.

Designing and distributing an accurate global clock signal is a particularly difficult aspect of modern designs (reducing clock skew is an entire subfield in its own right). Many modern designs are lucky to lose only 10% of the cycle budget to problems deriving from clocking.

Another global goal with microarchitectural effects is *design for testability.* In an ideal world, simulations would represent perfectly accurate models of the hardware under design. In reality, the chip that comes back from the foundry will probably behave slightly differently than the best simulations predict. When such differences occur, it is useful to have mechanisms for inspecting the internal (not just architectural) state of the chip. One simple way to do this is to implement *scan paths*, which effectively connect all of the state of the chip (registers, latches, flip-flops, or whatever design idiom of choice you have) into a giant shift register. Scan paths allow implementers to read out and examine the entire state of the chip, and they allow implementers to plug in a new state for debugging purposes. The scan paths need not function at operational speeds, but they do add cost in terms of control wires and transistors associated with implementing the scan.

One of the most simple microarchitectural tricks is *microspeculation*. As distinguished from architectural speculation, microspeculative techniques are invisible at the ISA level but might manifest themselves in terms of reduced cycle times or pipeline latencies. Because transistors are cheap, it can be worthwhile to compute multiple possible results in parallel with the signal that selects them, and then choose the desired result. As an example, a pipeline might always assemble the value of an immediate operand, even before the decoding has taken place to determine whether the immediate operand will be used. Assembling the immediate operand has no side effects, and is thus architecturally "safe." Performing the assembly in parallel with decoding makes the operand available earlier in the pipeline, which might allow some operations to have shorter latencies or remove work from a later, overpacked, pipeline stage. Overall, microspeculation trades power and chip area (transistors) for shorter latencies and/or better cycle times.

VLIW machines expose operational latencies. Compiler writers think of these latencies as "determined by the hardware," and parameterize them as inputs to their compilers. However, at the microarchitectural level designers must provide circuit- and transistor-level implementations of each operation in the architecture. Operations can easily be grouped into "families" that can share hardware. For example, the simple MIPS pipeline divides operations among the shifter, ALU, and memory unit. Modern general-purpose and embedded designs will often have other functional units to handle floating-point (with separate pipelines for adds, multiplies, and divides), streaming-SIMD, and other types of data. Within a family, designers have a number of implementation choices, which translate into various operation latencies, area, and power requirements. At the time of the initial RISC designs (circa 1980), the latency to access a register file, an ALU, and an on-chip memory were roughly proportional. As of this writing, these values have changed. Designs tend to target cycle times about equal to the latency of register file access, whereas ALUs take less than a cycle time and most cache accesses are spread over multiple, pipelined cycles.

Branch penalties are a key issue in pipeline design. Most pipelined designs implement branch speculation, in which the system guesses the direction of a conditional branch before the condition is resolved, and then continues executing down the guessed path. If the guess is correct, the system behaves as if the branch were like any other low-latency operation. On an incorrect guess, however, the system must back out of the work done on the incorrect path and then resume execution on the correct path. The number of cycles lost to an incorrect prediction is called the *branch mispredict penalty*, and the

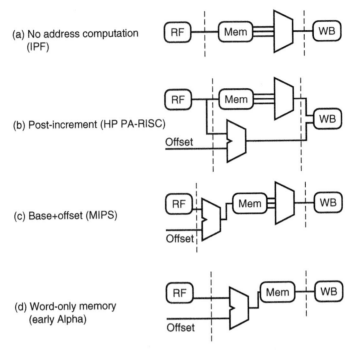

(a) No address computation (IPF)

(b) Post-increment (HP PA-RISC)

Offset

(c) Base+offset (MIPS)

Offset

(d) Word-only memory (early Alpha)

Offset

FIGURE 5.3 **Examples of architectural choices, possible microarchitecture implementations, and their effects on the organization of a memory load pipeline.** In all cases but (a) the adder is used for computing a base+offset address. The multiplexer selects among sub-word values when the memory returns an entire word result. The dotted lines indicate a possible cycle subdivision of the pipeline, and they show how various partitioning choices might affect the amount of work we have to do in each stage (for example, cases (c) and (d) require an address computation in sequence with the memory access). In reality, the available choices are more numerous, as we can play with subsections of the address (for example, when we access a cache array) and we can choose to move some of the final byte-selection logic to the write-back stage (by penalizing the visible latency of sub-word accesses).

techniques used for guessing branch conditions are called *branch prediction*. Branch prediction can be *static* or *dynamic*, depending on whether the prediction is performed as a function of the branch instruction itself (static) or as a function of the instruction, the processor state, and other history information (dynamic).

The branch misprediction penalty of a combined compare-and-branch instruction is usually proportional to the number of pipeline stages between the first pipeline fetch stage and the execution unit, at which branch conditions are resolved. We say "usually" because a number of architectural and microarchitectural techniques (e.g., predication, decoupled fetch/execute units, layered branch prediction schemes, predecoding, and trace caching) complicate the actual computation of the penalty. Together with the accuracy of the dynamic branch predictor and the frequency of branches in code, many machine cycles can be lost to mispredictions. Fortunately, dynamic branch prediction techniques made large strides in the 1990s. These advances allowed deeply pipelined designs, such as the Pentium Pro (typical penalty of 11 to 14 cycles) to be viable.

5.3 VLIW Fetch, Sequencing, and Decoding

The front end of every ILP-oriented microarchitecture transforms the stream of instructions from instruction memory into operations, including both control and data, at the appropriate execution pipelines. This transformation has many subproblems. Assuming a standard instruction cache that feeds the front end, the front end must *fetch* instructions from the instruction cache into a VLIW instruction buffer, which may include *aligning* the instruction from its original memory position to match the layout of the instruction buffer. Depending on the instruction and operation encoding, the front end may have to *segment* the instruction into separate operations. Then it at least partially *decodes* each operation, which provides information about register and functional unit requirements. After decoding, the front end *disperses* operations to the appropriate functional units. We described these issues from the instruction encoding point of view in Section 3.5. For example, Figure 5.4 shows a typical structure of the operations that need to be performed when fetching a long instruction.

5.3.1 Instruction Fetch

Assuming a first-level instruction cache exists, designers must provide sufficient bandwidth between instruction cache and front-end structures. These take the form of large,

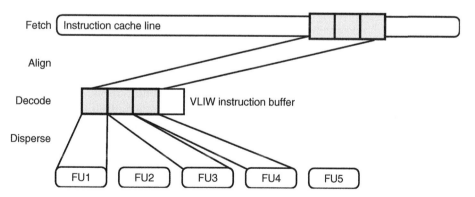

FIGURE 5.4 Fetching VLIW instructions. Extracting long instructions from the cache and preparing them to issue to the appropriate functional units is a challenging task for the front end of the execution pipeline. Starting from the cache lines, a first phase (alignment) shifts the fetch packet to a known position. Then a second phase (dispersal) routes the operations to the slots that correspond to the controlled functional units. To achieve high pipeline clock rate, it is common to introduce one or two extra pipeline stages to account for the additional shifting and routing required. Functional units may also have their own queues for operations.

regular buses, and because of the constraints deriving from the congestion of wiring inter-connect designers prefer that such buses run for short distances. Fortunately, the front end is the only client of the instruction cache, and thus this bus is point-to-point (and good layout will place the instruction cache near the entrance to the front end). As of this writing, typical instruction cache-line sizes are 32 or 64 bytes, which corresponds to 8 or 16 RISC-style 32-bit operations. This is usually wider than the issue width of many ILP machines, meaning that a bus that can deliver a line per cycle provides sufficient instruction fetch bandwidth. (We defer discussion of instruction memory, and memory in general, to Section 5.5.)

5.3.2 Alignment and Instruction Length

Recall from Chapter 4 the distinctions between instructions, operations, syllables, and bundles. A VLIW operation corresponds to a single operation for a single functional unit, regardless of the latency the operation requires for completion. A VLIW instruction con-sists of a set of VLIW operations (an instruction might have variable or fixed length, depending on the encoding scheme for the ISA). A bundle is a fetch- and decoding-oriented unit, which might include multiple, single, or partial instructions and single or multiple operations but aligns cleanly with cache-line boundaries.

The fundamental issue in the alignment step is determining instruction boundaries; that is, where each VLIW instruction begins and ends. Once the instruction bound-aries have been found, the alignment unit uses a large shifter or multiplexer to select a contiguous subsequence of the instruction cache line (or in some implementations, lines) and place it (them) in the instruction buffer. (Chapter 4 describes a number of possible encodings for VLIW instruction boundaries.) All of these encoding styles (fixed instruction width, instruction stop or start bits, and templates) lend themselves to rapid determination of alignment, although the microarchitectural implementation requires an extra decoder to detect the nearest instruction boundary to the beginning of the current instruction.

Many ISAs use bundles to ameliorate implementation difficulties with cache-line boundaries. In the CISC-style x86 architecture, instructions are of variable length and can span cache-line boundaries. This complicates the design of the fetch unit: Pen-tium and Pentium Pro/II/III micropipelines kept dual instruction-cache buffers so that instructions could be assembled if they crossed cache-line boundaries. Many VLIW and superscalar implementations avoid this problem by prohibiting parallel issue groups from spanning cache-line boundaries. This simplifies the fetch hardware at the possi-ble expense of wasted issue slots. The IPF splits the difference: 128-bit bundles are always aligned with cache-line boundaries, but the template encodings of parallel issue groups in IPF instructions can span multiple bundles, and therefore multiple cache lines.

In variable-length VLIW encodings the alignment hardware must perform expansion of vertical nops (horizontal nops are the province of decoding and dispersal, discussed in Section 5.3.3). Implementing vertical nop expansion is relatively simple, requiring

Classic VLIW Flame: Superscalar Hardware Must Search for Instruction Boundaries

The alignment issue couples with other decoding issues in a superscalar architecture, because the determination of the beginning and end of a sequence of parallelizable operations happens dynamically. This is in addition to the task of *decoding* the operations, which — regardless of the architectural style — consists of looking at some bits and computing the next program counter. A VLIW architecture simultaneously decodes all operations constituting an instruction, and then the instruction can be directly issued. Likewise, a superscalar architecture decodes multiple parallel operations simultaneously. However, because the architecture leaves no room for instruction-boundary bits, the front end of a superscalar machine must find or recall *parallel* instruction boundaries whenever an instruction is executed. These instruction boundaries are determined by the dependences between operations, which in turn must be decoded before dependences can be found. Some superscalar implementations perform this independence decoding at cache fetch time or in a trace cache, partially hiding some of these latencies from the front end of the pipeline, but the complexity remains.

only a sequencing unit and control signals that indicate nops to the next stage of the pipeline.

Instruction-length information interacts with architectural scalability. In a VLIW with a stop-bit encoding system, code compiled for a machine of a particular width *requires* a machine of at least that width to execute correctly. EPIC architectures (i.e., IPF) attempt to preserve some degree of scalability in implementation width. In the EPIC encoding scheme, compilers may specify wide parallel operations within an instruction, but they also must emit code that allows correct operation if only certain subsets of a wide parallel instruction are executed in parallel. The allowed subsets follow a sequential constraint; that is, any wide parallel issue group must also yield the same results if it is executed piecewise at bundle-wide granularities. This architectural flexibility in EPIC architectures allows some degree of issue-width flexibility (code compiled for a wide-issue machine will still be executable on a narrower machine). The cost of this flexibility is reduced scheduling freedom within a "parallel" instruction, which has to preserve sequential semantics.

As in any pipelined machine implementation, a VLIW machine must keep track of the pipelined notion of the current program counter. It is relatively easy to assign a PC (program counter) value to an instruction: it is simply the instruction memory address at which the instruction begins. Similarly, each operation can be assigned the address at which its encoding begins, and these addresses can be kept throughout the execution pipeline for precise accounting in case of exceptions. Updating the PC, which depends on instruction alignment, requires an adder that follows the output of the instruction boundary decoder.

5.3.3 Decoding and Dispersal

With the instruction aligned in the instruction buffer, the remaining tasks of the front end are to partially decode the operations in the instruction and disperse those instructions to the clusters and functional units that will execute them. *Clustering* issues manifest themselves at the encoding level and in register specifiers. At the encoding level, grouping operations that belong to the same microarchitectural cluster is similar to grouping operations into an instruction. As we discussed in the ISA section, techniques similar to instruction-boundary encoding are used for cluster-boundary encoding. Such techniques use start bits, stop bits, and templates. Clustering can complicate register specifiers if the ISA allows operations to specify operands that come from remote clusters, rather than using explicit cross-cluster move instructions. Such longer register specifiers may require decoding of instruction opcodes to detect the remote register specifier which also implies reserving and operating cross-cluster buses.

Clustering also affects the design of the instruction cache. Early VLIW designs (such as the Multiflow TRACE) used a physically distributed I-cache in which individual I-cache "slices" were dedicated to each cluster. Although this was a good design decision for LSI/board designs, VLSI considerations and the density/speed characteristics of monolithic memory designs today favor the adoption of a centralized I-cache structure. In the future, localization consideration might swing the pendulum the other way, and thus it is important to understand the various design options and always see them in the context of the hardware technology tradeoffs available to designers.

Within a VLIW instruction, the RISC-like encoding of operations makes decoding or partial decoding relatively simple. Opcode bits for operations may be entirely independent (as with RISC encoding), or they may depend for some information on the higher-level information about instruction, cluster, and template encoding. In this latter case, the higher-level information supplies additional information about functional unit or cluster type that restricts the opcode information to a subspace.

Once decoding is complete, dispersal can be microarchitecturally expensive. Because clusters and functional units are geographically separated entities, the connections between the dispersal unit and its clients are long wires, which operate slowly because of the diminishing drive capabilities of shrinking transistors in today's technology. There is little to be done about this, and many microarchitectures allocate one or more cycles for wire propagation delay at the dispersal stage. Depending on the encoding strategy and implementation choice, there may be separate dispersal steps for clusters and for functional units within clusters.

Different dispersal strategies also interact with microarchitectural and ISA constraints. Many VLIW architectures require decoding down to a level that specifies an opcode space (such as ALU and memory), and then disperse to the matching cluster and functional unit. Such a dispersal strategy requires multiplexers that select operations from the instruction buffer to route to the target cluster and functional unit, and the cross-connection of multiplexers to the VLIW instruction buffer can be large in terms of wires and gates. The TI C6x ISA and microarchitecture follow this strategy, with four different flavors of functional unit in each of two clusters. The M unit performs multiplications, whereas the L, S, and D units can each perform ALU operations, with additional shift and branch capability in the S unit and memory accesses in the D unit.

The HP/ST Lx (ST200) microarchitecture uses a nearly universal functional-unit strategy to simplify operation dispersal within a cluster. Lx specifies a uniform data type within a cluster and its associated register file. Within the functional units of a cluster, virtually all pipelines are designed as "universal" functional units, without specialization to operation type. If all functional units within a cluster are universal, we can eliminate the multiplexers in the dispersal stage and directly wire the instruction buffer to its target functional unit. This dispersal strategy requires compiler support for cases in which the functional units are not completely universal. For example, if the load/store unit occupies a particular slot in the datapath, the compiler must ensure that memory operations occur only in the corresponding operation slot within an instruction. Given that wires are expensive in terms of area relative to the cost of transistors, the Lx arrangement removes multiplexers at the expense of more complicated (i.e., universal) functional units (see Figure 5.5).

Long immediate instructions complicate the dispersal stage. A long immediate value must be sent to the desired datapath section. This requires multiplexing the instruction *value* into a bus normally used by a register value. Depending on how long immediates are encoded by the ISA, long immediates may also have to be transferred between "lanes" in the machine, just as operations must be dispatched to matching functional units. This adds to the complexity of the multiplexer, or in the case of an Lx-style architecture may limit the placement of long immediates within an instruction. In some cases, the decode stage may be able to avoid a register fetch operation (hence, save power) if it can determine that a long immediate will be used before the register fetch stage of the pipeline.

5.3.4 Decoding and ISA Extensions

ISA extensions exact various microarchitectural costs, depending on how they are built. The least cost comes from reclaiming unused values in the encoding space, either for opcodes (adding new operations to an existing functional unit) or register specifiers (widening a register file). Such changes include new logic and new wiring, but they will not necessarily require global redesigns or affect the cycle time of the design. Extensions based on a mode bit do require global control, but most of the complexity will likely occur in the control circuitry that smoothly changes modes while operations are still in the pipelines of the machine. CISC-style extensions involving new syllables or prefix values are the most expensive for decoding, as they increase the height of dependent values that must be analyzed to interpret an instruction, possibly affecting cycle time or increasing the number of decoding stages.

5.4 The Datapath

By "datapath" processor microarchitects mean the middle part of the pipeline, at which functional units actually process data. Strictly speaking, the term *datapath* comes from

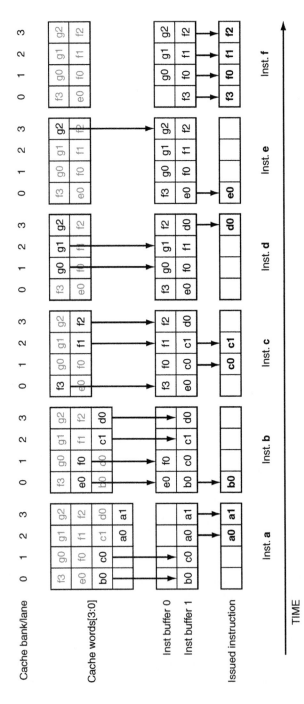

FIGURE 5.5 **The decoding scheme of the HP/ST Lx (ST200).** The ST200 uses symmetry and uncommitted issue slots to reduce the complexity of dispersing the operations to individual functional units. The chart shows the progress of six VLIW instructions (*a*, *b*, *c*, *d*, *e*, *f*) through the fetch/issue unit of a 4-wide datapath. The cache-line structure is shown horizontally (slots are numbered 0 to 3) and the progress through the instruction buffer vertically (the double buffer for instruction composition is shown beneath the cache). The individual operations of an instruction are not dispersed but remain in the "slot" where their alignment in the cache happens to be. For example, initially the instruction buffer contains instruction *a* (on slots 2 and 3), *b* (on slot 0), and *c* (whose first operation *c0* is on slot 1). As *a* issues, the instruction buffer frees up slots 2 and 3, which are then occupied by the second *c* operation (*c1*) and *d0*. As the pipeline proceeds, operations issue to the execution unit and free up slots in the instruction buffer, which are occupied by the operations that are in the corresponding cache location. In this way, the hardware dynamically assigns execution units based on the position of the slot (for example, {*a0*, *a1*} executes on slots {2, 3}, whereas {*c0*, *c1*} executes on slots {1, 2}). This is only possible if the individual execution units are universal (i.e., can execute the entire operation repertoire) or if the code is scheduled with certain symmetry constraints.

a description of a regular two-dimensional structure of wires and logic defined by the width of data being processed and the amount of logic that modifies that data, wherein data runs along one dimension and control lines along the other dimension. Although other parts of the machine (such as instruction fetch) may contain simple datapaths, for simplicity we refer to the *execution* stage of the pipeline and exclude the front end (where instructions are fetched, decoded, and dispatched) and the back end (where operations retire). What is left remains a large structure, with its own control and data communication issues. It is one of the ironies of modern machine design that today's functional units make up a miniscule fraction of the die size. The rest of the design relates to storage, caching, and control.

This section starts by discussing the functional units themselves, which are relatively straightforward, largely combinatorial (except for pipelining), pieces of logic. We then continue by discussing bypassing and forwarding logic, which are of course central to basic pipelining and become more complex and expensive when both pipelining and wide issue are used. The next subsection discusses exposed operation latencies and the control logic one might or might not deploy to manage those latencies. The last subsection describes the effect of predication and select operations on the pipeline(s) of a machine.

5.4.1 Execution Units

Modern machines include a variety of types of functional units, although the ALU remains the basis of many operations. Entire volumes have been devoted to the efficient design of various types of functional units. We avoid such detail here, summarizing and providing relevant tidbits instead.

Functional units are indeed *functional* in the sense that their output is a well-defined function of their inputs. They do not include state of their own (although some may lump the memory unit in with other functional units, it really is its own entity with its own section later in this chapter). However, functional units are not necessarily *combinatorial* because of pipelining concerns. Depending on the number of levels of logic required to implement a particular function, designers may choose to split the levels across multiple clock cycles, and therefore multiple pipeline stages. Such *pipelined functional units* remain functional (they still compute the same logical function), but the corresponding results may not be available until several clock cycles after the inputs have been presented. This pipelining is the reason for exposed latencies in many ILP-oriented machines.

Depending on implementation cost and operation frequency, designers may restrict the number, flexibility, or pipelinability of some functional units. As we described in the section on dispatch and dispersal, some functional units may be too expensive to replicate symmetrically, leading to various microarchitectural, ISA, and compiler complications. Other functional units may be too large or may serve too infrequent operations to warrant complete pipelining. For example, floating-point dividers are large units for relatively infrequent operations, and are rarely fully pipelined. There is also middle ground between a fully pipelined functional unit (which has a latency of n cycles but can accept new inputs and produces a pipelined output every cycle) and an unpipelined functional unit (which has a latency of n cycles and remains busy, unable to accept new input, until the first operation completes). Such a *partially pipelined* functional unit might reuse some but not all pipeline stages, economizing on hardware while allowing new operations to be launched somewhere between every cycle and every n cycle. Finally, a special type of functional unit is the *memory unit*, which despite not being "functional" in a strict sense implements complex operations such as address computations and pipelined accesses to the memory hierarchy.

In the early days of integrated circuit design, an ALU was an expensive piece of logic because it required a large fraction of the transistors that could be integrated in a single piece of silicon. Because ALUs were expensive, it made sense to add control logic to reuse the ALU as much as possible. Today, an ALU is cheap (i.e., the fraction of a chip area occupied by an ALU practically disappears), and thus having many replicated functional units has become affordable. At current and foreseeable transistor densities, most of the cost of an integrated circuit is in the wiring required to move data around, and the area occupied by simple functional units (such as an ALU or comparator) is more or less irrelevant.

There is a variety of ALU designs, and much of the optimization in them concerns handling carries for arithmetic additions and subtractions. From the simple but slow "ripple-carry" adder to variants called "carry look-ahead," "carry save," "carry select," and "Ling adders," designers made a variety of tradeoffs among transistor count, design area, and implementation speed in ALUs. There are important circuit-level design issues in building efficient and correct adders, but for the most part one can think of ALU construction as being solved at a different design level. No modern machine uses an ALU design with longer than a single clock cycle latency. For area estimates, the size of an ALU scales linearly with the bit width of its operands.

Hardware shifters come in a variety of shapes and sizes. Many ISAs include "inexpensive" small-value shift operations as part of other operations. Such shifts have the effect of scaling a result by a small power of 2. Implementation of such small shifts requires a multiplexer, and this additional level of logic in the ALU may or may not affect the overall critical path.

The most general of shifters is the *barrel shifter*, which can shift or rotate an arbitrary word by an arbitrary number of bit positions. Barrel shifters are implemented in layers of multiplexers, with each layer implementing a shift by a different power-of-2 amount. For example, in a 32-bit barrel shifter there would be five layers of multipliers. The first layer would shift values by 0 or 1 bit positions, the second layer would shift values by 0 or 2 bit positions, and so forth, up to the last layer that shifts by 0 or 16 bit positions. By routing the bits of the shift amount to the control lines of the different layers, arbitrary shifts can be assembled. Depending on the number of layers of logic, barrel shifters are implemented in one or two machine cycles. Their area is somewhere between linear and quadratic in the bit width of the shifted operand. There are only logarithmically many levels of multiplexers, but wiring constraints make the actual scaling factor more complicated than O($n \log n$).

A wide variety of multiplier designs exist and there are clever techniques that change the representation of the numbers being multiplied from binary to a form that allows more rapid or compact computation. However, all multipliers retain the fundamental operation of computing and summing partial products to produce the product. The sums of partial product limit the cycle time or the minimum number of pipeline stages to compute a product, and these sums also affect the area required. One useful rule of thumb is that a multiplier requires space proportional to n times the size of an ALU, where n is the bit width of the smaller multiplicand. For example, a 16×32 multiply will require roughly as much area as 16 ALUs in the same technology. Another way of saying this is that the size of a multiplier is proportional to the product of the size of its inputs.

Dividers tend to be even larger structures than multipliers, as the approximation steps (essentially a binary search for the correct quotient) each resemble a multiplier. In an effort to save transistor space, many architectures provide only a "divide step" operation that must be iterated in order to produce all of the bits of a quotient.

Micro-SIMD operations can often be supported by modifying an existing ALU design. That is, these operations tend to partition a single register value into subdomains that are operated upon independently. These subdivisions essentially "cut" the carry chains of a traditional adder, but are otherwise similar to the full-width variant of the same operation (see Figure 5.6). Early micro-SIMD designs reused ALUs this way with minimal cycle time effects. More modern micro-SIMD designs sometimes place the SIMD operations in different clusters of the machine, which allows designers to build dedicated functional units.

Last, the quirky nature of the embedded design space sometimes necessitates similarly quirky functional units. Many DSPs support fixed-point saturated arithmetic operations, which require an additional switching step after the ALU that replaces an overflowed value with the maximum representable value. Other applications implement specific bit manipulations (for example, population count in cryptography) or specific graphics primitives (which might already be covered in part by the micro-SIMD operations).

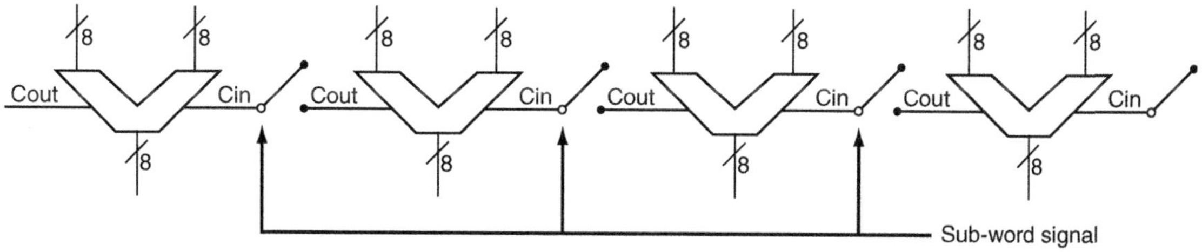

FIGURE 5.6 Simplified illustration of the microarchitecture behind a micro-SIMD operation. By "cutting" the carry chain of a 32-bit adder with switches, one can build a set of four 8-bit adders with low cost and effect on cycle time. However, not all micro-SIMD operations are as simple to implement as this micro-SIMD addition, and actual 32-bit adders tend to have additional complexities designed to reduce the cycle time by more rapidly calculating carries.

5.4.2 Bypassing and Forwarding Logic

In the standard RISC pipeline, the bypass network allows results that have been produced but not yet written back to the register file to be used immediately by dependent operations. In one sense, the network "bypasses" the register file, which gives us the name "bypass network." In another sense, one functional unit "forwards" its results to the next (dependent) functional unit, which gives us the name "forwarding network." The two terms are interchangeable. Regardless of what you call it, though, the bypass network becomes more complicated in machines with both deep pipelines and wide-issue logic.

Figure 5.7 illustrates how the bypass network scales with increasing pipeline depth and operation issue. In general, if there are p pipeline stages between a result becoming available and its being written back to the register file, and if there are w different functional unit pipelines, then there are $w*p$ possible sources for a bypassed input to an operation. However, these sources might be needed at each of the various functional units, and each functional unit might have multiple inputs that need to be bypassed, giving another factor of w and an additional factor (say 2 to represent the typical number of inputs to a functional unit) for an overall value of $2w^2p$ bypass connections. For a 32-bit architecture with $w = 4$ execution units, and $p = 2$ pipeline stages, each with two inputs, you have 2048 wires.

Beyond the simple latency of pipelined functional units, the exception model can also complicate the bypass network. To support precise exceptions, many VLIW architectures require that the earliest commit stage be later than the latest exception-throwing

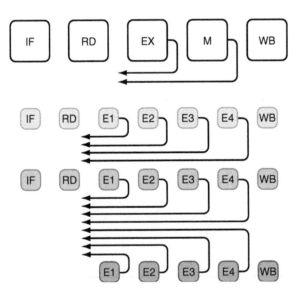

FIGURE 5.7 **Bypass paths, in the traditional five-stage RISC pipeline, in a more deeply pipelined machine, and in a two-issue deeply pipelined machine.** The number of bypass wires grows as the product of p (the pipeline depth) and w (the issue width). Each input function unit may require its own copy of a bypassed result, adding more wires to the design.

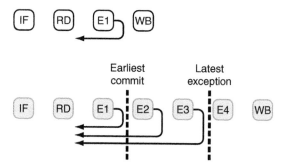

FIGURE 5.8 Bypass and exceptions. Even the pipeline of a simple single-cycle operation may affect the bypassing network when we take exceptions into account. The figure at the top represents a "naive" pipeline of a one-cycle operation. The figure at the bottom shows the same pipeline if we consider it as part of a VLIW architecture that can issue operations of length up to four cycles, whose latest exception point is after stage 3. In this case, we need to artificially delay the results of the operation after E1, so that we can still kill (quash) the operation all the way to E3 if needed before it commits to write the results. However, to preserve the single-cycle architectural delay (for example, to the compiler) we need to model each individual delay stage as another data source for the forwarding logic, and in doing so we have to increase the size of the bypassing network.

stage. However, the latest excepting stage for a long pipeline may be much later than the point at which a short pipeline produces complete results (we see this even in the five-stage RISC pipeline, in which the results of the EX stage are not immediately written back to the register file). This model allows flushing the pipeline (abort in flight) at an exception, and restarting execution after a software recovery. For instance, MMU exceptions and virtual memory can be fully supported. To achieve this, it is necessary to save a small amount of control and to make sure that no side effect is committed in any pipeline stage before a stage that can generate exceptions. A unit that would commit too early is forced to delay the commit point until the designated stage. If necessary for performance, the architecturally visible latency can be shortened via additional bypassing logic from the intermediate stages. In this respect, the difference between the earliest commit and the latest exception stages causes extra complexity in the bypassing circuitry, in the sense that each stage that is artificially delayed behaves like an additional producer for the bypassing logic (see Figure 5.8).

Bypass networks also lead to strange layout effects. Register files and functional units tend to be regular, organized structures. The bypass network needs to connect everything together. When combined with synthesis tools, the usual result is a heterogeneous mixture of regular objects connected by a cloud of synthesized bypass wires.[3]

---

3. This would be different if we considered what a datapath-specific layout and synthesis tool would produce. However, datapath synthesis tools are still not mature enough to be widely used in the industry, and thus we prefer reporting what a standard CAD tool could achieve, with all its limitations.

The wires in this cloud are found by heuristic search methods common to synthesis tools, which accounts for their irregularity. However, these clouds also unfortunately tend to be the critical paths in the design, limiting the cycle time of the entire system. It is particularly unsatisfying to designers that these clouds are under control of synthesis tools, which are notorious for making large-scale structural changes (with matching changes to critical path and cycle time) as a result of small design changes.

Some researchers have investigated partial bypass networks. In such an incomplete network, either the control logic must delay issuing operations until a valid bypass can be used or the compiler must model another level of resource constraint. Clustering reduces bypassing complexity, but trades it off for additional complexity in orchestrating intercluster communication and placing operations in clusters during scheduling.

5.4.3 Exposing Latencies

Nontrivial pipelined machines have varying functional unit latencies. In a VLIW, the compiler is responsible for scheduling operations so that no operation will be issued before all of its input operands are available. Ideally, a VLIW compiler can find other work for the processor to perform while a functional unit performs a long-latency operation, but this is not always the case, and the compiler must emit some sort of nop to fill the space. We have already discussed a number of ways to implement nops, including encoding techniques that compress nops out of instructions and vertical nops that expand to many cycles of delay.

By contrast, a superscalar implementation relies on its decoding hardware to find dependences between operations, and it uses some sort of *scoreboarding* mechanism to delay dependent instructions. One can imagine a variety of scoreboard implementations, but all of them track the inputs to an operation, releasing that operation only when that operation's inputs become ready. Scoreboards exploit dynamic variability of the latency between producers and consumers of a value. This means that if an input arrives earlier than expected the machine can issue the dependent instructions that much earlier. However, one can imagine that sophisticated scoreboard implementations might require long control lines, if not especially complex logic. Out-of-order dynamic schedulers, on the other hand, implement a form of distributed "micro-dataflow," in which there is no centralized scoreboard, and in which the individual operations launched by the front end must find their own way to the commit stage.

The simplest form of scoreboarding involves adding one extra bit to the register file that indicates whether the corresponding value is valid or not (where "not valid" implies "waiting to be written"). In a 32-bit architecture, this translates to about 3% of the register file size. Additionally, scoreboarding also requires the logic to set and reset the valid bits, which is usually tied to the pipeline control circuitry, the latency of the functional units, and the exception recovery mechanism.

VLIW machines must also handle dynamically variable latencies, and the various approaches to variable latencies have architectural and microarchitectural implications that interact with how exceptions are handled. First, we need to distinguish between *expected* and *worst-case* behavior. In the strictest sense, it is *unsafe* for a VLIW machine

Pitfall: Scheduling for the Worst-Case Latency

As we mention in the text, architecture, microarchitecture, and compiler should conspire so that operations expose their expected latency and not their worst-case latency. For example, in the Multiflow TRACE, a memory access would normally take seven cycles. In case of an ECC (error correction codes) error, it took three extra cycles to process and repair the error. In other words, memory latency was either seven cycles (error-free mode) or 10 cycles (ECC error). If the architects had routinely run all accesses through the ECC hardware, it would have made them all uniformly 10 cycles, and the architects would never have had to worry about handling ECCs. However, that would have been a tragic, unforgivable waste of performance, burdening all accesses for the sins of a small minority. Instead, they decided to have the ECC hardware stall the entire machine for three cycles until the error was fixed, but only when an error occurred. Stalling the entire machine was expensive, yes, but considering that ECC errors almost never happened the net effect was in the noise. Increasing every access from seven to 10 cycles would not have been in the noise.

(Contributed by Bob Colwell)

to schedule for anything other than the worst-case latency for all operations. However, making such an assumption means that one must ignore the potential (and frequent) benefits due to caches in memory operations, or the benefits if other functional units finish their work early. Scheduling all memory accesses as if they required a main memory access is clearly silly. We want to schedule for the expected case; that is, for cache hits, which we expect to be the common case.

Fixing this problem (call it the "overdue operation" problem) requires that we fall back on hardware, and adopt some (but not all) of the approach taken by superscalar designers. The compiler schedules for the expected memory latency, wherein the expected latency is part of the contract between implementation hardware and compiler software. In the (uncommon) case in which an operation will exceed its contracted latency it is up to the hardware to *stall* the machine for some number of cycles until the operation's result is ready, at which point the machine can resume as if the overdue operation had taken its normal latency. Such a stall mechanism looks similar to the scoreboarding technique used in superscalar designs. The difference is one of granularity and implementation complexity. The VLIW implementation will stall *the entire machine* in the (hopefully unlikely) event of an overdue operation. A scoreboarding superscalar needs to keep track of *each operation*, preventing it from issuing until its input operands are ready.

Now, assuming that we have handled the overdue operation case, what happens if an operation completes *early*? We divide VLIWs into two categories, depending on whether operations are allowed to commit results before their expected latency. Machines that allow operations to complete early are termed *less-than-or-equal* (LEQ) machines, whereas machines that require all operations to commit their effects at the same time as their expected latency are termed *equals* (EQ) machines.

In an **LEQ** machine, the pipeline implements a *variable commit point*, whereby the destination registers can be written at any point during the operation latency. In this case, the compiler must assume that the previous value of the register is overwritten at the earliest time the operation could complete, and—in practice—must prevent other operations from reading the content of the destination register(s) during the operation latency.

In an **EQ** machine, the pipeline implements a *fixed commit* point, whereby the destination(s) of an operation are not touched by that operation during the operation's latency, but only at the end. This means that the compiler can rely on the previous content of the register to still be available during the operation execution. For example, in this case destination registers can be reused as temporaries during the operation latency window, assuming one has a compiler that can safely identify these situations. The TI C6x family of DSPs are EQ machines, and their compilers do exactly this.

EQ machines with aggressive compilers may have better register usage, but there is a tradeoff in handling exceptions. If an exception occurs while a long-latency operation is in flight, what will the resulting state of the machine be? Should the hardware abort the long-latency operation? Will the operations that use target registers as temporaries commit or not? We suspect that a complex combination of architectural support and compiler conventions and limitations might allow precise interrupt handling on EQ machines, but this is open research. In practice, EQ machines (including C6x) disable interrupts when long-latency operations are in flight. This is further complicated by software pipelining, where for some loop kernels long-latency operations are *always* in flight. The designers of the C6x decided that making interrupts unserviceable for the duration of a software-pipelined loop was acceptable; it is up to users and the compiler to ensure that these loops exit frequently enough to allow adequate interrupt service.

5.4.4 Predication and Selects

Architectures with support for predication require some changes to the datapath. Fully predicated architectures typically have a separate predicate register file, necessitating a bypass network for predicate values in addition to the bypass network for regular data values. Happily, predicates tend to be relatively small (single bits in most representations, although one could imagine hardware with "don't-care" values), and thus the predicate bypass network although requiring wire connectivity is not as large as the data bypass network.

Full predication interacts with data bypassing, but on the control side rather than the data-forwarding side. In a nonpredicated machine, the control network must find valid bypasses (wherein the destination of an earlier instruction is a source of a later instruction) and select the most recent of the valid bypasses (so as to get the most recently generated value for an architectural register, rather than an old value that was overwritten). In a predicated machine, the forwarding instruction must also have a true predicate. Depending on where predicates are generated in the pipeline, this path can add wiring

Pitfall: Seemingly Excellent Microarchitecture Ideas Can Have Bad Effects

Hardware designers sometimes make subtle changes to an ISA that seem harmless but have a high price in compiler engineering cost or effectiveness, especially in an instruction-level parallel system. A classic example is what compiler writers call "hot spots," which have appeared in several architectures, especially early DSPs offering ILP (such as those from Floating-Point Systems). A hot spot is a register with ephemeral data, which could disappear without being explicitly overwritten (for example, after some set number of cycles, typically one, or as a silent side effect of some operation). Hot spots require the scheduler to schedule all readers of an operation before the data disappears. As far as the scheduler is concerned, this produces one big operation with intermediate writing of data, and that type of operation runs afoul of all the compiler technology that has been developed to extract and exploit ILP.

This same phenomenon (the far-reaching effects of small, visible microarchitecture artifacts) can be found in decisions involving nonorthogonal latencies, hidden register mappings, and elsewhere. A dramatic example of this occurred during the development of the Multiflow TRACE, the first high-ILP general-purpose computer. A microarchitecture decision caused the TRACE /200 and /300 ISAs to have what the developers referred to as a "split brain." Because of it, each of the two ALUs in a single cluster had access to only half the registers, counter to the intended ISA. The compiler writers later described the situation.

> Due to limits on the size of our gate arrays, no integer ALUs shared a register file. This fact, coupled with the low latency of integer operations, makes it difficult for the instruction scheduler to exploit parallelism in integer code. The cost of moving data between register files often offsets the gains of parallelism. [Lowney et al., 1993]

"Limits on the size of our gate arrays" is a charitable description. The reality is that the hardware designers were on a tight schedule, since startups are constantly under the gun. The night the register gate array was to ship, the automated routing just wouldn't fit within the gate-array specifications. Rather than slip the schedule, the microarchitects did what they felt was right. They knew it would potentially have some performance effect, but they had to do *something*, and this seemed as good a choice as any. Although their intentions were good, the effect on the performance of the Multiflow compiler — a compiler that has since been used by much of the high-performance computer industry — was terrible. There was undoubtedly a better choice, had the entire system been considered. And when the hardware designers designed their next ALU, they were glad to be able to fix this:

> For instance, the integer register files are now 64 deep, are shared directly by two integer ALUs, and no longer exhibit the "split brain" effect (the ALUs can access any of the 64 registers and can target any of them in any beat, unlike the /500's predecessors.) [Colwell et al., 1990]

The lesson, of course, is that compiler writers, OS designers, and systems people of all stripes need to be a first-class part of all aspects of the architectural decision-making process. That this was not always the case even at a company as "compiler-first" as Multiflow is a telling story.

complexity and wire delay to the overall design. The control for the bypass network may end up being the wiring critical path.

Partially predicated architectures (which rely on conditional move and select operations) look more like unpredicated architectures, as they reuse the existing register files and predication is represented by separate operations rather than guard tests performed on every operation. (See Section 5.6 for more discussion of the complexities of conditional move/select operations.)

5.5　Memory Architecture

In a block diagram of the layout of a microprocessor, memory sometimes looks like "any other" functional unit. However, memory is not functional; it contains state, which complicates its correct implementation, how the operating system manages it, and how the ISA presents it to the programmer.

One level below microarchitecture, silicon process determines much about the types of memory available on-chip; the size, shape, and cost of the memory cells (and therefore the same characteristics for the memory banks they constitute); and the speed of the connection network used to access memory. As of this writing, many systems combine processing logic, static RAM (SRAM), and cache memories on the same chip and therefore use the same silicon process. On-chip memory most often takes up the large majority of the silicon area and much more space than the CPU itself. Hence, it has a bigger impact on chip area and cost than many of the other parts of the system.

Many embedded systems also include flash memory on chip, whereas ROM is increasingly rare in chip designs today because flash is cheap enough and efficient enough, and because flash is reprogrammable. In reality, a lot of flash memory is actually used as a ROM (factory programmed and never touched again). On the other hand, it is much more rare to see dynamic RAM (DRAM) on-chip, because there are larger differences between processes designed for processors and SRAM and processes designed for DRAM. The major advantage of using DRAM is density, as DRAMs are intrinsically much denser than SRAM, and you can put more storage in the same die area. Unfortunately, this comes at the cost of more complexity in the silicon process, as well as refresh circuitry and slower performance.

The gap between on-chip DRAM and SRAM is the subject of active research and a lot of work has been done to narrow that gap. The fabrication processes of high-density DRAMs require exotic structures and are diverging from logic-based silicon processes. At the same time, SRAM depends on balanced devices for stability, and in deep submicron technologies discreteness of doping and other effects are causing the transistors to be much more variable, greatly reducing the noise margin of SRAMs. As of this writing, it is not clear what technology will become dominant.

5.5.1　Local Memory and Caches

Our readers should already be familiar with the basics of memory hierarchies: a system of memories that combine small, fast, expensive levels with large, slow, cheaper levels to provide the illusion of a large, fast, affordable memory system. We note that most introductory discussions of memory hierarchies consider each cache level in isolation, with a "client" that summarizes the processor and all cache levels above it and a "backing store" that represents lower cache levels and main memory below it. Our discussion will focus on embedded-specific issues and on issues in integrating the levels of the memory hierarchy.

The heart of a multilevel memory system is the cache controller, and its complexity is a function of the number and configuration of caches (cache latency, refill policy, set associativity), the operations between caches (coherency rules), and the connection to the memory bus of the next hierarchy level (multiple outstanding references, signaling of the memory bus protocol). Even embedded cores often include separate first-level instruction and data caches, and some designs also include an integrated second-level cache. Cache-line size and number, associativity, writability (instruction caches are rarely directly writable), writeback/write-through policy, and support for writing part of a cache line vary per design (these topics are well discussed in introductory texts). However, some features of individual caches in the hierarchy are rarely described at the introductory level but are nonetheless frequently implemented in real systems.

- *Writeback queues* adjust for the difference in performance between higher and lower memory levels. Instead of stalling a write when the lower memory level is busy, the buffer allows the system to store the write and perform it in the background. The writeback queue then becomes a sort of cache itself, which must also be searched to service misses. Note that writeback queues handle a *latency* problem (allowing the processor to continue operating). However, the underlying memory system must still have adequate *bandwidth* to handle the sustained rate of memory writes.

- *Critical-word-first operation* answers a memory request with the first word needed, rather than the first word in the cache line (depending on line size, the actual requested word might be many words, and therefore many bus cycles, into the cache line). This optimization improves latency, requires the same bandwidth (since the entire cache line must end up in the higher level), and increases complexity.

- *Support for multiple outstanding misses* is somewhat self-explanatory: the system continues processing memory requests, even when other memory requests have missed. Multiple outstanding misses are only useful in out-of-order superscalar designs.

- *Stall-on-use support.* As mentioned in Section 5.4.3, hardware and software must agree about the expected (versus the worst-case) latencies of operations when scheduling. When the latency differs from expected, we can either stall the machine as soon as we detect that we cannot meet the architectural latency or delay until the result of the memory operation is accessed. The latter is often called *stall-on-use*, which requires hardware support in the execution pipeline to identify when a memory operand is ready. Stall-on-use can be advantageous when the compiler schedules memory operations with slack as late as possible, in this way hiding more latency cycles with other useful operations.

Controllers can be thought of as finite-state automata (each design feature or complication in the memory system adds another dimension of complexity to the controller automaton). Beyond the usual parameters of individual cache design, a number of other factors complicate real-world implementations.

- *Prefetching* is a form of speculation sometimes implemented by the memory controller. The general idea is to move data into the memory hierarchy before it is demand-fetched by an executing program. Prefetch operations spend power and may have opportunity costs versus other operations in the system, but they have the potential to reduce program latency. Prefetch can be controlled by either hardware or software (ISA-exposed) mechanisms.

- *Arbitration* occurs anywhere multiple clients access the same resource. Examples include L1 instruction and data caches competing for the L2 interface, and a processor core competing with DMA (direct memory access) peripherals for access to main memory. In many cases, it is not obvious that one arbitration choice or another will improve overall performance. It is also difficult to design an arbitration system that is in some sense "fair." Arbitration decisions may also interact with correctness constraints imposed by the memory model.

- *Split transactions* divide memory hierarchy operations into two phases — a "request" phase and a "reply" phase — allowing other operations to use the bus during the latency of the memory operation. Split transactions improve the usable bandwidth (efficiency) of the bus while complicating all of the controllers connected to the bus.

- *Interactions with SoC buses* and *memory-mapped peripherals* also complicate the design of the memory controller. SoC buses have a larger variety of transactions and protocol modes than those in the memory system. (Chapter 6 describes SoC buses in greater detail.) Memory-mapped devices expose their control and data registers as memory locations, but this means that access to these registers should not be cached by the regular memory hierarchy. Incorrectly interfacing to an SoC bus or incorrectly handling a memory-mapped device will affect correctness in addition to the performance of the resulting system. Unfortunately, such problems are especially difficult to find because they fall between the boundaries of design domains, and therefore also of verification domains. One final complication is that these areas are only truly exercised when the processor is running in its target system, and thus often the only recourse is to fix the bug in follow-up designs.

Building a cache controller is a rather complex task and it is difficult to cover all corner cases with simulation because bugs may come from interactions that happen rarely and over long-running programs. Thus, there has been much effort in developing techniques to formally verify the correctness of cache controller designs. Much of the research literature on such verification actually concerns itself with supporting multiprocessor systems (e.g., work was done on the COMA [cache-only memory architecture]-style KSR (Kendall Square research) machines and on the SGI Origin directory-based SMPs. As with any verification methodology, much of the merit depends on the accuracy of the specification and the usability of the verification tools. Unfortunately, the heterogeneous and specially tuned nature of embedded memory systems is an even more complicated space than that of directory-based shared-memory multiprocessors. As we describe in more detail in Section 6.6, the resulting verification process is thus largely ad hoc.

5.5.2 Byte Manipulation

In handling the bytes that make up a word, two microarchitectural issues come up. The first (for lack of a better term, called "byte swizzling") deals with moving sub-word quantities into the proper positions. The second, endianness, extends up to the architectural and SoC levels. The two are related.

Any architecture that supports sub-word memory operations (e.g., "load byte" or "store half-word") requires microarchitectural support to adapt between the width of the operation and the word width of the memory unit. On the load side, such operations are implemented by loading the entire word containing the smaller piece of memory, and then using a multiplexer to put the correct half-word or byte into the correct part of the register. This multiplexer adds a small latency to loads that can be shifted among pipeline stages, but this must occur between the arrival of the response from memory and the writeback stage. The multiplexer must also be placed before the bypass network.

Issues on the store side are similar, although in addition to multiplexing there is the control issue of reading the entire affected cache line, modifying the relevant piece, and then writing back the entire line. This issue is discussed in most introductory texts about caching (the byte-swizzling issue only further refines the granularity of operations).

Endianness is a seemingly simple problem with nasty administrative implications throughout the architecture, microarchitecture, and software. Simply stated, endianness is the convention for byte ordering within a word. In a little-endian machine, the least significant byte of a word occupies the lowest memory address of the word, whereas the opposite is true for a big-endian machine.

Many general-purpose architectures mandate a particular machine-wide endianness. In contrast, many embedded designs mix and match parts from a variety of manufacturers, mixing endianness in the process. Although conceptually simple, managing the various endianness "domains" within an SoC can be administratively complicated.

Supporting multiple endiannesses within a processor core is relatively simple: it requires only a byte-swapping device at the memory interface and a way of marking memory areas as reverse-endian. This can be handled either as a separate set of operations (load-reversed/store-reversed) or by attributes assigned to memory regions by the memory management unit. Alternatively, one can add an endianness-swap instruction, placing endian management under programmer or compiler control.

5.5.3 Addressing, Protection, and Virtual Memory

Embedded processor cores span the entire spectrum of virtual memory options, from no support whatsoever (i.e., the processor addresses physical memory directly) to a full general-purpose MMU (memory management unit) — with virtual-to-physical mapping, protection, and other attributes for various memory regions; a TLB (translation look-aside buffer) in the memory pipeline; and exception paths for TLB misses and page faults. In the area of possible implementations, there are three major issues: virtual address management, protection, and memory region semantics.

The primary goal of virtual memory is to allow compilers and programmers to ignore the size and configuration of physical storage in the machine (memory and cache sizes). Systems with virtual memory insert a mapping layer between the addresses used in the program (*virtual addresses*) and the addresses used to access physical memory (*physical addresses*). This mapping, or indirection, provides a number of benefits, such as removing fragmentation problems in physical memory, enabling different processes to have separate address spaces, and enabling swapping main memory to a secondary storage device.

In practice today, virtual memory is managed at a *page* level of granularity, wherein each page is of known size, is always a power of 2 in bytes, and is on the order of 4 KB. The mapping from virtual to physical page numbers is recorded in a *page table* (which, ironically, is kept somewhere in physical memory), and the commonly used page table translations are held by a cache of mappings called the translation look-aside buffer, or TLB.

In processors with page tables and TLBs, the page table entries provide a natural place for storing protection information. For each page, the system keeps flags stating whether the page is readable, writable, executable, and so forth. The pipeline then verifies that the current access matches the protection settings. In some cases, micro-architectural techniques can allow memory access to occur simultaneously with the protection check.

Some embedded operating systems, most famously PocketPC, require virtual memory support. In the particular case of PocketPC, some of the processor's main memory is used as secondary storage and the virtual memory support and protections help to enforce the distinction and to prevent programs from accidentally overwriting the (memory-based) file system. Virtual memory support also makes it easier to support multiple processes under PocketPC. Embedded Linux also favors processors that include virtual memory support, although limited Linux ports to simple microcontrollers exist (e.g., the *uClinux* project). These use dynamic loading and relocation-on-the-fly to enable multiple processes, but do not support the full set of protections and separation modes that virtual memory with a separate address space for each process guarantees.

For processors without TLBs and virtual memory support, protection remains relevant but is implemented using *segments* rather than pages. In a segmented design, a small number (typically four to eight) of regions of memory share protection attributes, and the regions are delimited by starting or ending addresses, or equivalently by a starting address and a segment size. Such a segment-based protection system provides reasonable expressive power at a relatively small implementation cost.

Memory system *semantics* sometimes require support in the virtual memory or protection hardware. When using memory-mapped I/O devices, it is typical to disable caching for the region in which device registers are mapped (reading a cached value of a device register is probably not the desired behavior). There are similar issues with speculative memory access (to which we return in Section 5.5.5), for which prefetching or caching activities would similarly not be desirable.

ILP architectures that support multiple simultaneous memory accesses per cycle need to be prepared to handle multiple exceptions generated in a single execution cycle. This usually implies imposing certain ordering to the memory ports and dealing with the complexity of multiple recoveries.

5.5.4 Memories in Multiprocessor Systems

In multiprocessor systems, caches must often be shared among processor cores. Maintaining consistency among values in caches and memories for various processors could fill a book in its own right (and has, as is evident in the Bibliography). An ideal shared-memory system would work like a theoretical PRAM (parallel RAM), in which a write by one processor is immediately visible to be read by all other processors. The reality involves much more implementation detail, as few systems can amass the memory bandwidth or hide the latency of propagation delay to approximate a PRAM. Instead, designers provide rules about how and when memory operations on one processor become visible to other processors in the system. By relaxing these rules from the PRAM model, designers gain the flexibility to build efficient implementations. Under such relaxed models, it is possible for a write on one processor to be hidden from another (the second processor might be able to read a "stale" copy of the data even after the first processor has completed its write). The question is the circumstances under which such behavior is permissible.

Because all modern memory systems use caches, this topic is generally called *cache coherence*. There are two parts to any cache coherence protocol: how things are viewed locally by each processor and how things can be evaluated globally, as seen by some model of "the system as a whole."

For an individual processor within a multiprocessor, the notion of how memory operates can become complicated. One can view a single processor core as performing a sequential stream of operations (out-of-order superscalar cores perform operations in a different order from that specified by the original program, but the reorderings they perform do not affect the important parts of this discussion). Memory operations can occur entirely on-chip, as long as the required memory lines are currently resident on the processor cache (private local memories, supported by many embedded processors, also work entirely locally). Complications arise at the processor's interface to the outside world; in particular, in fetching the results of reads that miss in the on-chip cache, and in informing other processors when writes have occurred to the on-chip cache. Out of the many different dimensions of cache design, the *writeback* versus *write-through* variant has the most relevance here. Write-through caches expose all write operations to the bus shared among processors, whereas writeback caches will not do so until they are forced to perform writebacks. Regardless of how this implementation decision goes, most ISAs include *memory barrier* instructions that tell the on-chip memory system to synchronously write back all dirty cache lines. After such a memory barrier instruction completes, the processor knows that its changes are now visible for other processors to read. Depending on the ISA, there may also be a variety of *synchronization* instructions, whose explicit purpose is to allow different processors that share memory to coordinate operations.

At the system level, multiprocessors fall into two major categories: "snooping" systems and directory-based shared memory systems. For small-scale multiprocessors (i.e., four or fewer processors), a "snooping" bus approach is common. In such systems, all processors share a common bus, upon which all write traffic is made visible, with the addition of a few extra signals to support coherency protocols (such as MESI [modified, exclusive, shared, invalid], pronounced "messy"). By continuously observing the traffic on the common bus, each processor (or more specifically, the memory controller hardware on the processor core) can update or invalidate cache lines to reflect the operations performed by other processors. Snoopy buses provide closely coupled fine-grain multiprocessing because processors see updates from other processors as fast as the speed of the bus permits. Their biggest limitation is that they do not scale well beyond a small number of processors, as the common bus becomes a bottleneck.

Higher levels of multiprocessing (i.e., where more than four processors share a memory system) are currently rather rare in embedded systems. This is not to say that there are not plenty of embedded systems that incorporate more than four processors. Rather, such systems tend to be built as hierarchies of processors, in which each processor shares memory with a small number of peers but has a lower-bandwidth connection to a supervisory processor. For example, many network switches are built around a "backplane" populated by circuit boards. The switch as a whole tends to have a single high-level control board (possibly with many processors). This board communicates through the backplane with the many regular boards, each of which in turn may have "daughter cards" with additional processing power. Building such a system with a single shared memory bus would be expensive and impractical. Instead, memory sharing occurs among processors that share a card.

In the general-purpose world, many-node multiprocessors use "directory-based" coherence techniques to allow processor nodes to see memory traffic that relates only to pages or cache lines on which they are working. In most directory-based systems, every page has an owning node at which its "directory" lives. Each directory entry keeps information about the current location and status of that page.

Regardless of the coherency schema (snooping or directory-based), pages can be in one of the MESI states, which correspond to modified, exclusive, shared, or invalid. MESI is a subset of the more general protocol MOESI, where "O" stands for "owned" (the owned state is so rare, however, that most systems only implement MESI). Extensions and improvements to the basic MESI protocol abound. To access a page, a processor may have to communicate with its directory, which may in turn communicate with other users of the page, but there is no intrinsic requirement for broadcast communication in a directory-based design. General-purpose directory-based multiprocessors use descriptive acronyms such as NUMA (non-uniform memory access) and COMA (cache-only memory architecture). We are aware of no embedded system currently using such schemes.

5.5.5 Memory Speculation

As with many high-cost operations, one can speculate with memory, trading off effort (memory bandwidth, power dissipation) in the hope of improving performance. Memory speculation involves performing memory reads early, in the hope that by fetching values to the correct level of the memory hierarchy the values will be available more quickly (ideally immediately) when needed.

Prefetching is by far the most prevalent form of memory speculation. Microarchitectural implementations of prefetching can be complicated. At each cache level of the memory hierarchy, one can choose to prefetch into the cache or into a separate "prefetch buffer" that resides at the same level of hierarchy as the cache. Prefetching into the cache is complicated by contention. First, how does one "schedule" the prefetch access so as not to conflict with outstanding memory accesses (expected latency for a prefetch might differ from that for a load). Second, a value prefetched into a cache might displace useful data. Prefetching into a dedicated buffer requires more complex control logic to maintain consistency between the cache and its prefetch buffer, but it at least has the benefit that no cached data is displaced by prefetched values. On a prefetch "hit," the prefetch value may also be moved from the prefetch buffer into the corresponding cache level. One can also build a prefetch buffer without a corresponding cache. For example, some systems have a second level (L2) prefetch buffer without choosing to implement an L2 cache.

Prefetch can be controlled either through hardware or software means. In their most simple form, software prefetch instructions look like normal loads but serve as hints to the memory unit in which a particular address is likely to be used in the future. More sophisticated software prefetching mechanisms allocate additional encoding bits to specify *where* in the memory hierarchy the prefetch value should move. For example, one might prefetch a value into the first- or second-level cache, or into the matching prefetch buffers. Software prefetch schemes can be sophisticated, requiring likewise sophisticated compiler support.

Hardware prefetch controllers are invisible at the ISA level; that is, they are purely a microarchitectural feature. The most simple hardware prefetch mechanism fetches the next memory line after one that has been demand-fetched. More sophisticated predictors analyze the strides of memory accesses (not surprisingly they are called stride predictors).

The IPF architecture commercially introduced two more forms of memory speculation. In *dismissable load* speculation, some load instructions can be marked as nonexcepting, whereby exceptions are suppressed but stored where they can be detected by later check instructions. In *load/store address speculation*, load instructions are moved before potentially conflicting store instructions, and a special hardware table records and tracks address conflicts. Ideally, such conflicts are rare, and thus the speculative access retrieves valid data. For cases in which the speculative load and the store instruction *do* overlap, the system (compiler, operating system, and so on) must provide

---

Flame: Should the PC Be a Register?

In some architectures (most popularly, ARM) the program counter appears as a register in the register file. Proponents of such architectures claim that this makes the PC look like any other register. Thus, jumps become moves to the PC register, whereas saving a return address requires only reading that register.

We think that treating the PC as a register is a bad idea. Implementing this is a microarchitectural nightmare, as the PC is *not* housed in the register file, and it autoincrements on most (but not all) instructions. Calls and returns do indeed need to save and restore the PC, but these operations are handled by special operations on most architectures. The only other time the PC is read or written is for context switches, which already involve privileged instructions. Finally, making the PC a normal register is a vulnerability that can expose serious security issues. Letting users make arbitrary changes to the PC could potentially open up security holes through which malicious users can subvert the security policy imposed by the OS.

---

a means of redoing the load instruction with the proper value. Both of these speculation techniques are relatives of the IPF support for nonexcepting instructions, whereby the ISA allows speculation but provides hardware support for checking the validity of the speculation that took place.

5.6   The Control Unit

The control unit, simply stated, is about what executes next. Within normal user-mode operation, the familiar procedure calls, returns, jumps, and conditional branches determine execution. More recent architectures use predicate values and predicated execution to attempt to remove branch penalties from the execution stream. One of the most difficult topics in microarchitecture is handling interrupts and exceptions. The *control unit* (which is more likely to have a highly distributed implementation) must combine the aforementioned architectural features into a smooth, single sequence of actions. Control units also include *interrupt controllers*, which arbitrate among various possible asynchronous sources of interrupts.

5.6.1 Branch Architecture

Branch delays in pipelined processors were a major bottleneck for general purpose computing in the 1990s. Today's deeply pipelined general purpose designs depend on a number of aggressive branch-prediction and branch-target-buffering strategies to achieve performance on branch-intensive integer code. By contrast, branch delays matter in only a subset of embedded applications. For example, many embedded applications, especially those in signal processing, are dominated by loops. Counted loops are entirely predictable with a small amount of hardware support.

Any pipelined design must correctly handle changes in control flow; the expense and sophistication comes from attempting to do this while minimizing *branch penalties*, the extra execution cycles required for correctness. (Section 4.4 described a number of architectural techniques for reducing or avoiding these penalties.) Fortunately, the varieties of control flow changes are well known, as are many techniques that reduce branch penalties. For any type of jump (i.e., any instruction that breaks from sequential instruction fetch), *branch target buffers* record and predict target addresses. The second time the control unit sees a branch, it will have a good guess as to the likely target of that branch. Procedure returns can be accurately predicted if hardware keeps a *return address stack* and the ISA marks call instructions distinctly from other jumps. Predictions for the direction of conditional branches can be provided by *branch history tables*, which can be built in a variety of sophisticated ways to capture correlations among branches. Many of these aggressive techniques require power and space, which can be at a premium in embedded processors (deploying them requires a cost/benefit analysis).

Some architectures have distinct counting and link registers in the encoding of their ISAs (the IBM Power and PowerPC architectures are the most popular architectures with this feature). Separate control-related architectures can be placed in their own chip or off the chip, allowing control functions to be somewhat decoupled from the execution units. In early Power architecture designs, the instruction fetch, integer execution, and floating-point execution units occupied separate chips of a multichip module (MCM). Today, a Power processor core easily fits onto a single chip, but the modularity arising from the design of the ISA in a different era still confers benefits in wire-dominated design processes.

As mentioned in the ISA chapter, many DSP architectures have explicit looping support, wherein special instructions mark the beginning and end of a likely loop. Microarchitecturally, such features are implemented with an L0 loop buffer, into which the marked instructions are loaded. Operating out of the loop buffer helps with overall power consumption, in that instructions do not come from the cache and hence the instruction cache is not accessed and can be powered down for the duration of the loop.

5.6.2 Predication and Selects

Predicated and partially predicated (conditional move and select) execution were discussed in the section on bypassing. Moving to a fully predicated architecture complicates the control side of the bypass network and may change the critical path of the design.

Functional units that support predication require additional control inputs, but because of the simplicity of the predicate input, the functional unit itself is not necessarily more complicated than an unpredicated unit. Operations with false predicates must be transformed by the architecture into nops. Depending on the implementation timing, predicated-false operations can give some small opportunities for power savings.

Microarchitectural support for partial predication seems small in impact, but there is one subtlety to supporting conditional move operations. A conditional move needs access to the predicate, the old value of the target, and the source (the possible new

---

Terminology: Exceptions, Interrupts, Traps, Breakpoints, and Faults

There are many different terms for breaks in the normal flow of the instruction stream, and no common rules for using them. We use the term *exception* both as an umbrella term for all such breaks and as a specific term for the synchronous case, in which an exception arises as a result of an operation's execution. Synchronous exceptions include page faults, TLB misses, decompression faults, and divide-by-zero exceptions. We use the term *interrupt* for asynchronous exceptions, which primarily result from I/O or other external events. We try to avoid the terms *trap* and *fault*, except for *page faults*, which are the common terms in VM discussions. *Trap* is sometimes a synonym for an intentional exception (for example, to invoke code with a higher privilege level, in a library or in the operating system). A *breakpoint* is normally a trap inserted by the debugger to interrupt the execution of a program under debug.

This is one of the few cases in which we break with Hennessey and Patterson's [2003] terminology: they use *exception* generally, qualifying it to restrict its meaning.

---

value of the target), which adds up to three input operands. Regardless of the width of the predicate (most likely, 1 bit), this implies three operand specifiers, which use precious instruction encoding bits. Because most RISC-style operations use only two input operands, conditional moves can complicate register file and datapath design.

5.6.3 Interrupts and Exceptions

Handling interrupts and exceptions in a pipelined machine is something of an arcane art. Few designers have to solve the microarchitectural problems that arise here, and little is published in the literature.

As we define exceptions and interrupts in this book, exceptions arise synchronously as a result of executing a particular operation, whereas interrupts occur asynchronously due to external sources. Exceptions require careful handling of the multiple operations within an instruction (e.g., which commit and which do not). In VLIW architectures, interrupts can in principle happen "between" the parallel ISA-exposed operations that constitute an instruction.[4] We also use *exception* as an umbrella term (see the sidebar "Terminology" above).

At a minimum, the response to any interrupt or exception requires the fetch unit to stop fetching instructions from the current PC location and redirect input to an interrupt handler routine. To begin executing the interrupt handler routine, some combination of

---

4. This is not true for architectures in which the ILP is not ISA-exposed, such as, for example, x86 instructions. The microarchitecture of the Pentium II (and successors) goes out of its way to ensure that the streams of micro-operations being retired to architectural state are only interruptible at instruction boundaries, and never between operations.

Pros and Cons of Interrupt-Specific Registers

Interrupt-specific registers, or any other registers multiplexed into and out of the register set (depending on the processor mode), still require space in the register file and width in the multiplexers. However, they are not generally accessible to user programs, which limits their utility. Such registers (or alternate register contexts) might make sense in a register-starved architecture, but they seem to have little place in register-rich RISC and VLIW instruction-set encodings wherein you normally try not to hide power.

On the other hand, in embedded architecture that has to support hard real-time requirements, having special register sets to aid interrupt handling can be beneficial. In such real-time systems, being able to switch threads on real-time inputs can be far more important than the performance on any given thread.

hardware, software, and coding conventions must move the processor into a minimally safe state. Such a state consists of a place to store values in memory (typically a stack, which might be specific to the interrupt handler routine, part of the kernel stack, or part of the user stack, depending on the OS, hardware, and conventions) and some number of "safe" registers that can be overwritten without irretrievably losing information about the interrupted work.

Interrupt-safe registers can be provided in a number of ways. In register-rich architectures, run-time conventions may specify some of the registers to be permanently reserved for interrupt service routines, and normal programs are thus not allowed to depend on such registers behaving correctly. Assuming that there is an interrupt stack area already set up, either hardware or software can "push" register values onto the stack to free them for use in the handler routine. Some architectures (notably ARM) also provide interrupt-specific overlay registers, whereby some subset of the normal user-level registers is "swapped out" and replaced by interrupt-specific registers. (We discuss interrupt handlers and returning safely from them in much more detail in Chapter 9.)

Interrupts are normally organized into levels of priority that match the time criticality with which the input must be serviced. The architecture of the interrupt-servicing infrastructure needs to deal with higher-bandwidth devices (such as network interfaces and disk drives) and lower-bandwidth devices (such as keyboards or mice). These two categories of devices require a tighter real-time response, however, because of interactivity. Although we might argue that it is more critical to serve a keyboard character input, the response times are much slower than those required by high-bandwidth peripherals, which can be supported by properly sizing the FIFO buffers used to queue the requests.

Priorities exist to prevent the system from missing an interrupt and thereby dropping useful data on the floor. The interrupt controller allows the processor to specify an interrupt "masking level" below which low-priority interrupts will not be delivered. This prevents a high-priority interrupt handler from being interrupted by a lower-priority interrupt. The typical interface from the controller to the processor involves a single interrupt control line (the controller signals that some valid interrupt has taken place). The processor can then examine the controller's state to determine the type of interrupt and the appropriate way to handle it.

5.6.4 Exceptions and Pipelining

How the pipeline handles in-flight operations when an exception occurs varies widely. In a pipelined processor core, exceptions can be raised by various pipeline stages. For example, a floating-point divide operation would be able to raise a divide-by-zero exception early in the pipeline, whereas other floating-point exceptions (such as *inexact result* or *underflow*) might require more computation (and thus more pipeline stages) before they could be raised.

Drain and Flush Pipeline Models

For every operation in the execution pipeline we can define an *exception point* as the latest pipeline stage at which an exception can be generated, and a *commit point* as the earliest pipeline stage at which the operation can make changes to the architecture state that cannot be undone. Every time an operation passes its exception point, it is guaranteed to commit. Even though an operation that has passed its exception point is guaranteed not to except, it does not deliver its results until the commit point. If an exception occurs in a later (or concurrent) operation, the long-latency operation will still be "in flight," and still scheduled to affect architectural state in its commit (write) stage. Within limits, implementers can trade off complexity in various parts of the system by moving the commit point in the pipeline. The exception mechanism has two choices: it can let the operation complete (pipeline drain) or it can quash the in-flight operation (pipeline flush).

In the *drain* model (see Figure 5.9), the exception mechanism waits for the in-flight operations to complete. This potentially complicates resumption after the exception has been handled, as the long-latency operation has already occurred out of order, rather than occurring at the originally specified point in the schedule. Overall, a *drain* model makes it difficult to define a "precise" exception state. Even though the operations immediately around the excepting instruction are committed or aborted in some sense "precisely," the long-latency operations that preceded the exception will muddy things up. If we allow operations to change architectural state out of order, software must ensure that the destination of any operation is not reused while the operation is in flight (i.e., it must observe an LEQ model). A drain model requires the handler to implement a recovery fragment that contains only those operations that have not yet completed (for example, the long-latency operation that was in flight and committed should not be reexecuted). This technique is sometimes called *partial reexecution,* and its complexity should not be underestimated. (See Section 9.1 for further discussion of these issues).

In the *flush* model (see Figure 5.10), the exception mechanism quashes (aborts) all in-flight operations after an exception. The flush model preserves *in-order* instruction

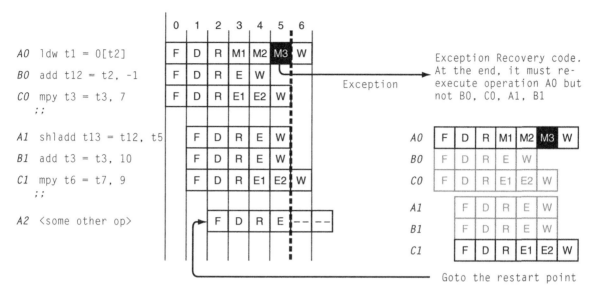

FIGURE 5.9 The *drain* exception model. The assumption is that operations in the pipeline that can complete terminate their execution and commit their results (operations are called "self-draining"). The exception recovery mechanism has to "remember" which other operations in flight have reached the commit stage (the bold dotted line) and not reexecute them. In the case in which a single instruction contains operations with different latencies, some of them may have terminated, and thus the instruction needs to be partially reexecuted. In the example, an exception occurs at cycle 5 (M3 stage of operation A0) when operations B0,C0,A1,B1 have already committed. Thus, once the recovery code has serviced the exception, it copies instruction 0, turns B0,C0,A1,B1 into nops, appends a branch back to A2, and reexecutes only A0 (the excepting operation) and C1 (not committed).

commit semantics, making it appear that all operations in instructions preceding the exception/interrupt commit and that no operations in the excepting instruction or subsequent instructions commit. In this case (assuming that the exception point occurs before any commit point) it is easy to determine a clean restart point in the instruction stream, which is the instruction that contained the excepting operation(s). Although flushing the pipeline penalizes long-latency operations that have to be restarted, it makes for a much simpler model.

Early Commit

Systems that perform *early commit* have an intuitive appeal: operations reach the commit point regardless of what happens to other operations that are still in the pipeline or are issued in the same cycle. This simplifies the control logic of the pipeline, and not much bookkeeping must be done by hardware to support exception handling. The biggest problem with early commit has to do with the combination of short-latency and long-latency operations, which may lead to imprecise exceptions.

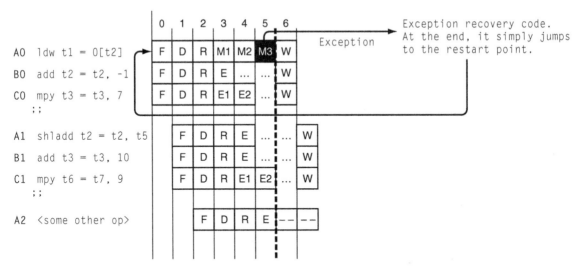

FIGURE 5.10   **The *flush* exception model with delayed commit.** The model is based on two assumptions: all operations in flight when an exception occurs are quashed (i.e., "flushed") and no operation can commit before any other operation can cause an exception. The second assumption implies that shorter operations delay their commit point after the latest exception point. In the example, the latest exception point is M3, and thus operations of latency 1 (such as B0) need two stages of delayed commit and operations of latency 2 (such as C0 or C1) need one stage. In this way, all operations proceed as if in a fixed-length pipeline (of depth 7 in the example). As we described earlier, by providing extra bypassing paths delayed commits have no architectural effect on latency. The first assumption greatly simplifies restarting the code after the exception is serviced (the restart point is exactly the instruction containing the operation A0 that caused the exception).

Delayed Commit

The other end of the exception spectrum is *delayed commit*, in which the commit point for all instructions occurs late in the pipeline and it is guaranteed to be after any exception point. Implementations with delayed commit must maintain more speculative state. Short-latency operations have to artificially delay their commit point so that it happens after the exception point (we showed a variant of this in Section 5.4.2 and in Figure 5.8). Because we do not want to lengthen the visible operation latencies, this also implies that the forwarding logic becomes more complicated. On the other hand, delayed commit simplifies the software support for exception handling by providing a much cleaner, in-order view of excepting instructions.

Detecting exceptions early simplifies the delayed commit hardware, given that results need to be propagated (and bypassed) for every stage between the earliest commit point and the latest exception point. However, this may require additional hardware in another area, to determine whether an operation will except before that exception would normally have been calculated. This can be done in parallel with the actual computation associated with the operation (e.g., it might be possible via clever examination of exponents to determine that a floating-point operation will underflow, which is a process that can be completed much more quickly than performing the entire calculation).

In architectures with EQ-machine semantics, memory operations in software-pipelined loops make it impossible for the processor core to service interrupts during the loop. Short of expensive interrupt-suspend and interrupt-resume operations (which would be capable of saving not just the PC and architectural registers but the state of in-flight operations), there does not seem to be a good microarchitectural solution to this problem.

5.7 Control Registers

Within a processor core, there are some control values that are similar to the control registers of memory-mapped devices. These are exposed as special-purpose or special-function registers. The ISA may expose these registers through special operations that read and write control registers, or it might rely on memory mapping.

Control registers serve a variety of purposes necessary to maintaining the processor core but are not so frequently modified that they deserve an architectural fast path. Examples of control register values include the location of the page table in a virtual-memory-based system, the segment description registers for a segmented memory-protection system, the address of the interrupt service routine or interrupt service table, miscellaneous access to the MMU, and instrumentation functions such as performance counters.

5.8 Power Considerations

One of the defining characteristics of many embedded systems, specifically in the consumer domain, is their requirement to operate with a limited power or energy budget. The typical equation for the switching power consumption of a CMOS circuit is linear with frequency f_s and complexity (the gate loads C_i and the number of active *gates*), and quadratic with voltage V_{dd}. Usually, lowering the frequency also allows lowering the voltage, yielding a net energy benefit.

$$E = \frac{V_{dd}^2}{2} \sum_i^{gates} f_s \cdot C_i \approx k \cdot f_s \cdot V_{dd}^2$$

Reducing voltage and frequency without disrupting the normal operation of a processor is a delicate operation, and only recent processors have started adopting this technique pervasively. Changing frequency and voltage does not happen instantaneously. The time constants that govern the analog circuitry driving the PLL (*phase-locked loop*, for clock control) and the DVC (digital voltage controller) easily reach the microsecond scale, which is several hundreds of processor cycles even in the embedded domain.

As a consequence, the granularity of frequency-voltage control is well above the ISA level, and many argue that it should be the OS's responsibility. Indeed, the OS has probably good supervision of the process deadlines, and can consequently optimize the available *slack* by slowing down or accelerating processes so that they finish *just-in-time* and not much ahead of time. This is sometimes referred to as "*slack control*" at the OS level, at which the energy-optimal point is reached when processes terminate as close as possible to their execution deadline (assuming a deadline exists).

To enable OS handling of power, what needs to be exposed at the ISA level is simply a set of control operations (that are mapped to control registers, as described in Section 5.7) to implement *idle, sleep,* and *low-power* modes.

- *Idle mode* is a state in which the processor runs at a much reduced frequency in an idle loop but still preserves the internal state. This still requires powering the processor core, and — although switching power can be lowered to almost zero — leakage power is still consumed. A simple interrupt can awaken the processor from idle mode.

- *Sleep mode* is a state in which the processor power is shut off, and the processor can only be awakened by an external source. This also requires a method to save and restore the entire state of the processor to some external nonvolatile state, so that it is possible to implement an *instant-on* functionality when the processor exits sleep mode.

- *Low-power modes* are a discrete set of states in which the processor executes at a reduced frequency and voltage (or with certain units switched off). As we discussed, the OS can use these modes to control the available slack.

From these high-level considerations, we can argue that little control for power is left at the ISA level, the architecture being squeezed in between the OS-VLSI sandwich. Although this is likely to remain true for a few generations, as we move into nanometer scale geometries and subunit voltages we are rapidly approaching the limits of power reductions from voltage scaling from silicon. At that point, architecture-level techniques may become more important. In the following, we review some of the most promising research trends for ISA-level power control.

5.8.1 Energy Efficiency and ILP

Because of their simultaneous use of parallel execution units, VLIWs can be misperceived to be inefficient with power. On the contrary, this section shows that using ILP to achieve performance for a given task favors energy efficiency, which is better than unconditionally playing the high-frequency game. From the basic equation that determines power consumption (shown previously), we can improve our efficiency in performing a job if we do the same job at a slower frequency and lower voltage. Thus, if we have an ILP architecture, an application that exploits ILP, and a lower clock frequency, we ought to come out ahead. On the other hand, adding ILP to an architecture complicates the datapath, and increases the power budget dedicated to it (more transistors switch at the same time). Thus, what is the net effect of the two contrasting trends?

The answer is not simple, and depends on VLSI technology, design style, and various implementation constraints. However, to give an idea of the issues we present a simple case study and let readers extrapolate from that. We can start by taking a look at where the power budget goes in a scalar CPU. For example, the chart in Figure 5.11 shows the breakdown of power dissipation for an Intel StrongARM processor running the Dhrystone benchmark (which only stresses CPU execution because code and data fit in the caches and virtual memory is rarely exercised). If we focus on the execution datapath, we can see that the *integer unit* (EBOX) uses 8% of the power, the *decode and issue* (IBOX) 18%, and *memories* more than 55%.

Let's then evaluate a hypothetical VLIW implementation of the same StrongARM ISA. On first approximation, we are likely to see a sharp increase of EBOX power, due to the extra execution units; a smaller increase in clock distribution tree (CLOCK) and IBOX power, due to more registers and gates; and a marginal increase in the ICACHE power, because of wider lines and extra routing. Based on these considerations, suppose that on a 4-wide VLIW StrongARM EBOX grows by 4x, CLOCK and IBOX by 2x, and ICACHE by 1.3x, adding up to a total power growth of about 60%. Note that for more complex workloads that also stress the memory subsystem the relative weight of the datapath will be smaller, and the power growth of the hypothetical VLIW will be smaller as well.

If we need to run a job that has to meet a real-time deadline, we have basically two choices: (1) increase clock speed, and (2) increase ILP at the same frequency and voltage. Let's say that we can hit our deadline with a scalar machine (M1) running at 500 MHz and a voltage of 1.8 V, or with a 4-wide VLIW (M2) running at 250 MHz and 1.3 V. Because the performance is the same by hypothesis, we need to sustain an average IPC of 2.0 in the VLIW configuration. Finally, plug in the power numbers we estimated in

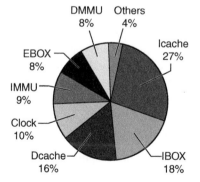

FIGURE 5.11 Power dissipation in a StrongARM (from Montanaro et al., [1996]). EBOX (execution unit) is the integer unit, and IBOX (instruction unit) is the decode and issue unit. IMMU (instruction memory management unit)/DMMU (data memory management unit) are separate memory management units for instruction and data. Note that memories add up to more than 55% of the total power. Data was collected on an evaluation board running Dhrystone 2.1, with the bus running at 1/3 of the CPU frequency (160 MHz). After warm-up, Dhrystone fits in the caches — there is basically no pin activity. This is the worst-case scenario for CPU power because the absence of cache misses always forces the processor to run at the faster core frequency.

the previous paragraph and assume that M2 consumes 1.6x the power of M1 (at the same frequency). The energy ratio of the two configurations is

$$\frac{E_1}{E_2} \approx \frac{t \cdot k_1 \cdot f_1 \cdot V_1^2}{t \cdot k_2 \cdot f_2 \cdot V_2^2} = \frac{k_1 \cdot 500 \cdot (1.8)^2}{1.6 \cdot k_1 \cdot 250 \cdot (1.3)^2} \approx 2.4,$$

where t is the time to run the job, k_1 and k_2 are the power scale factors for M1, and M2 ($k_2 = 1.6\ k_1$); f_1, f_2, V_1, V_2 frequency and voltage of M1 and M2. In this hypothetical example, the slower VLIW configuration requires less than half ($\sim$40%) of the energy of the faster scalar machine. Of course, this simple example is far from being a proof, but it clearly highlights the technology trends and tradeoffs that allow ILP to be used to improve energy efficiency.

Although this example demonstrates dynamic voltage scaling (DVS) in a 1.8V-processor (roughly corresponding to a 0.18µm process technology), DVS is a viable technique also for improving energy efficiency for deep submicron circuitry. Although maximum V_{dd} decreases in deep sub-micron processes (thus reducing the potential of DVS), this is alleviated by a smaller threshold voltage, V_t.

These considerations are based on the assumption that we can operate a "perfect" voltage scaling and change the frequency accordingly. In reality, the relationship between voltage and frequency is not linear, and can be approximated with

$$f = k \cdot \frac{(V - V_t)^\alpha}{V},$$

where V_t is the threshold voltage and α is a factor that depends on technology-specific parameters and is normally about 1.5 to 2.0. This means that, as we reduce the voltage V, lower threshold voltages (V_t) limit the useful frequency range of the perfect voltage scaling. Circuit considerations can also limit the practical implementation of DVS. Typically, processors target a semifixed range of supply voltage (about 10% voltage variations). The fact that processors with DVS must operate over wider voltage ranges impacts both design and verification, and special design techniques may be required to avoid having to verify the processor at every frequency/voltage combination.

System-level Power Considerations

In the previous sections, we concentrated on the power aspects of the *CPU+cache* sub-system. However, when looking at the power footprint of an embedded design one should not limit the analysis and optimization to CPUs and caches. In many domains, the majority of power is spent elsewhere, with CPUs and caches representing a relatively small fraction of the overall system power.

Treating the complex aspects of system design for power and energy optimization is well beyond the scope of this book. However, in order to present an example of the system tradeoffs, in Figure 5.12 we show the breakdown of system energy for a handheld device based on a StrongARM processor. The chart shows that the CPU power (grouped under

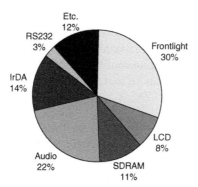

FIGURE 5.12 **Power usage in an HP IPAQ handheld device.** The device includes a StrongARM (SA-1110 at 206 MHz) processor. As we can see from the chart, audio and screen represent more than half the power in the system, and the CPU (bundled in the "etc." slice) only about 10%. From Cho [2000].

the "*etc.*" slice) only contributes to approximately 10% of the system power, whereas the majority of the energy goes to audio, screen, and memory (approximately 60%).

An important consideration that arises from this data is that many of the architecture and microarchitecture tweaks for power could in many embedded designs be swamped by other factors at the system level. If we believe that a CPU contribution to overall system power is in the range of 10 to 20%, it is probably much more critical to ensure that the OS can control system-level power than to save small fractions of power by shutting down individual ALUs in the processor. This said, the overall considerations and tradeoffs among ILP, clock speed, and power still remain valid and maintain their importance for energy-efficient designs.

5.9 Further Reading

To learn more about microarchitecture design, a good place to start is the standard reference by Hennessy and Patterson [2003]. Older references can be misleading because of changes in implementation technology, but can still supply valuable perspective. These include the seminal work of Tomasulo [1967], as well as the Flynn [1995] computer architecture book, and the Johnson [1992] superscalar book.

There is a lot of good material available about commercial microarchitectures. We recommend Gwennap [1995] for a good overview of the Pentium Pro microarchitecture and Gwennap [1996] for the DEC Alpha 21264. Other good readings include Colwell and Steck [1995] for the Pentium Pro implementation, and Hinton et al. [2001] for the Pentium 4.

Most of the advanced readings on microarchitecture topics we recommend come from the superscalar world, and cover topics such as memory prefetching, branch prediction, and value prediction. The paper by Yeh and Patt [1991] provides good background material on the topic of branch prediction and Young, Gloy, and Smith [1995] give a comparative evaluation of several branch predictors. Palacharla, Jouppi, and Smith [1993] expand on the theme of superscalar ILP. Gallagher et al. [1994] and Mahlke et al. [1994] describe the basics of data speculation and sentinel scheduling for safe control speculation. Lipasti and Chen [1996] and Sazeides and Smith [1997] describe two approaches to value prediction. Rotenberg et al. [1996] is a good place to start for insight into trace caches.

On prefetching and bypassing (software and hardware), Jouppi's [1990] paper and the follow-up work by Farkas, Chow, Jouppi, and Vranesic [1997] introduce the concepts of prefetch buffers and victim caches. Gupta et al. [1991] show the benefits of prefetching for latency reduction. Fu, Patel, and Jannsen [1992] introduce stride-directed prefetching, while Tullsen and Eggers [1993] describe the limitations of prefetching benefits. Chen and Baer [1994] give a good overview of hardware versus software prefetching techniques. Mowry's thesis [1994] is a good introduction to the area of software-driven prefetching.

On the subject of register file design, we suggest the paper by Farkas et al. [1995] for superscalar considerations, the paper by Jolly [1991], and the paper by Podlesny et al. [1997] for VLSI implementation notes. Fernandes, Llosa, and Topham [1997] investigate novel register file microarchitectures with support for software pipelining and Zyubian and Kogge [1998] describe the effect of multiported register files on power.

On instruction fetch, decoding, and issue for VLIW, we recommend the work by Conte et al. [1996] for an overview on instruction fetching for VLIWs with compressed code—extended, along with further work on code compression, by Larin and Conte [1999]—and Banerjia's [1998] paper on the subject of fetching for clustered VLIWs.

The work by Chang et al. [1991] provides a good overview on the evolution of basic VLIW concepts towards EPIC. The HPL Playdoh architecture is a conceptual example that sums up many of these ideas and is described by Kathail, Schlansker, and Rau [1994]. Finally, Rau [1993] discusses in detail the necessary extensions that make VLIW compatible with dynamic scheduling.

For exception recovery through checkpoints, we recommend the work of Hwu and Patt [1987]. For precise interrupts and their effect on processor pipelining, we recommend the paper by Smith and Pleszkun [1988]. And, for VLIW-specific interrupt discussions, we recommend the work of Ozer et al. [1998].

The Microprocessor Report [May 1996] issue provides a good overview of DRAM in microprocessors and DRAM versus SRAM technology trends, while Bhavnagarwala [2001] discusses more recent developments in the memory technology process itself.

On power considerations and frequency-voltage scaling, we recommend the Transmeta white papers by Klaiber [2000] and Fleischmann [2001]. The Transmeta Crusoe and Efficeon processors include many power management techniques that have been amply explored in academic literature. We recommend the papers by Flautner and Mudge [2002]; Fan, Ellis, and Lebeck [2002]; Pering and Brodersen [1998]; Pillai and Shin [2001]; Semeraro, Magklis et al. [2002]; and Ranghunathan, Jha, and Dey [1998].

Another aspect of power-related research deals with measurement and analysis of power, as well as energy consumption at the processor, system, and application levels.

The paper by Montanaro, Witek et al. [1996] contains an excellent overview of the power analysis that led to the design of the first StrongARM. A good set of system-level experiments on an iPaq handheld are in the report by Cho [2001]. The work by Brooks, Tiwari, and Martonosi [2000] introduces a widely used tool [Wattch] for architectural-level power analysis. Other recommended readings include the papers of Albonesi [1998]; Flinn and Satyanarayanan [1999]; Li and John [2003]; and Zeng, Fan, Ellis, Lehbeck, and Vahdat [2002].

5.10 Exercises

1. Using the web, quantify the incremental effect of adding ports to a register file in a particular technology (e.g., 0.18μ). Describe the effects of adding read ports versus write ports. Describe speed, area, and power effects. Find the "sweet spot" of register ports for banks of 16, 32, and 64 (32-bit) registers. Repeat the experiments for 64-bit registers.

2. Repeat the measurements of the previous exercise for a clustered architecture in which the register file is partitioned in two or four.

3. Take two program kernels written in C: one pointer-oriented (e.g., *quick-sort*) and one DSP-oriented (e.g., an FIR filter). Compile them with the VEX compiler and obtain the assembly language code. By hand, examine the assembly language code, and partition the registers into address and data registers. Count the number of times you have conflicting assignments (i.e., you would have to move data across the banks). Is there a significant difference between the two kernels?

4. Draw the block diagram corresponding to the part of the pipeline implementing register accesses for the following register bank organizations: (1) direct-access register file, (2) windowed register file with fixed window size, (3) rotating register file, and (4) rotating register file with register base index for the rotating section (hint: this roughly corresponds to MIPS, SPARC, Cydra, and IPF organizations).

5. Using the VEX compiler, compile a set of publicly available benchmark programs. Using the assembly language parser that comes with VEX, analyze the distribution of the operations per instruction, and define a set of templates that captures the patterns of operations. How many templates do you need to catch all combinations? If you can only afford 16 templates, which would you pick, and how many extra instructions do you need to be able to encode the benchmarks?

6. Draw the block diagram of the bypassing network (including the multiplexers and comparators) for a 4-wide symmetrical VLIW architecture (such as the VEX default). Repeat the same exercise for a fully predicated version of the same architecture.

7. Using the VEX compiler, compile a set of publicly available benchmark programs and run a simulation on significant inputs. Using the VEX simulation API, collect and save the data memory access traces. Design and simulate a simple hardware prefetching mechanism (stride based) that preloads data on the L1 cache. Collect statistics on successful prefetches, false positives (prefetches never used), and false negatives (predictable locations that are accessed but not prefetched).

8. Repeat the previous exercise, but model a separate coherent prefetch buffer instead of prefetching to L1. Model various sizes, associativity properties, and refill times for the prefetch buffer.

9. Using the VEX compiler, compile a set of publicly available benchmark programs and run a simulation on significant inputs. Using the VEX simulation API, collect and save the instruction memory cache miss-access trace. Postprocess the instruction trace to find the top 10 instructions (program locations) that account for the majority of memory traffic (misses). Examine the assembly code to determine whether a prefetch instruction would be beneficial.

10. Consider three of the widely used families of embedded processors (e.g., MIPS, PowerPC, and ARM). Describe, compare, and contrast the schemes they adopt for predicting branches.

11. Consider three of the widely used families of embedded processors (e.g., MIPS, PowerPC, and ARM). Describe, compare, and contrast the schemes they adopt for implementing virtual memory, and specifically the organization, sizes, and functionality of the TLBs.

12. General-purpose processors (e.g., x86 family) have followed a path toward faster frequency and deeper execution pipelines. On the contrary, embedded processors prefer moderate frequencies and shallower pipelines. Discuss the implications of these choices with respect to power, levels of gate delays per pipeline stages, design complexity, design styles (full-custom versus synthesized), and scaling properties.

13. When fetching instructions of variable width that might straddle across cache lines, we may be forced to pay some stall cycles every time instructions straddle. Draw a block diagram of a microarchitecture mechanism that would ameliorate this problem. (Hint: distinguish the two cases of normal sequential execution, and when the first instruction after a branch straddles across cache lines.) If your mechanism does not involve double buffering in some form, consider filing a patent.

14. Describe the interaction of bypassing with indexed and rotating register files. Draw a block diagram of the bypassing network (multiplexers and comparators) for each of the two cases.

15.   Consider a 16×32-bit integer multiplication array and the VEX repertoire of multiply operations (*mpyl, mpyh, mpyll, mpylh, mpyhh*). Draw the block diagram of the multiplier, and specifically describe the selection logic that determines the output value for the various operations.

16.   Using shift and mask VEX operations, implement the endian-byte-swap function.

17.   Using the VEX compiler, compile a set of publicly available benchmark programs and run a simulation on significant inputs. Using the VEX simulation API, collect and save the data memory access traces. Count the number of speculative memory accesses and how many of them are actually used. Assign an energy value to each memory access and compute the energy cost of speculation. Turn speculation off and rerun the experiment. Considering that the execution time is likely to be longer, which configuration reduces energy consumption?

6

System Design and Simulation

Any intelligent fool can make things bigger, more complex, and more violent. It takes a touch of genius—and a lot of courage—to move in the opposite direction.

—Ernst F. Schumacher, *German economist*, 1911–1977

This chapter covers a variety of topics that involve the integration of multiple components, one of which is usually a processor. This material is important to an understanding of embedded processing, but we do not believe we can treat it in the same depth as the topics in the other chapters of the book. Our primary design focus is on *processor cores*, and we feel this is difficult enough within our goals for the book. Here, we provide readers with a feeling for the higher-level issues and provide them with pointers to appropriately detailed sources.

This chapter is organized in two parts. The first part describes the integration of components into SoC and how processor cores fit into them. The second part deals with the simulation and verification of such single-chip systems, and in particular with the simulation and verification of cores at the instruction-set level.

6.1 System-on-a-Chip (SoC)

As we noted in the introduction to the book, economic factors in VLSI design have driven integration to levels at which designs that previously took entire boards and multiple chips now fit into a single die, usually called a *system-on-a-chip* (SoC).

SoC has contradictory implications. On the one hand it provides ample cost-reduction opportunities, and on the other it implies a higher degree of specialization that reduces the aggregate volume of each individual component. In other words, the combination of two general-purpose components is less general than either component by itself. Consequently, as we integrate more components the resulting piece of silicon becomes more specialized and its potential volume (related to the applicability to various products) decreases. The increase in complexity and design costs also implies that designers must find new ways to reuse work across designs, and fosters a culture of design reuse and plug-and-play components.

One must also consider the wildly nonlinear nature of volume silicon production, which pushes against specialization. If a VLSI component ships with enough volume, its price per part will drop very quickly. Thus, a design that may appear to be too complex or expensive might indeed be the best option if its aggregated volume (on all products using it) will drive the price below the price the volumes of individual parts would cause.

Another major social implication of the shift to SoC is the increased importance and difficulty of ensuring system correctness. This includes specification, simulation, validation, verification, and testing. We dedicate Sections 6.3 through 6.6 to a better explanation of this set of problems and some of the most widely adopted solutions.

6.1.1 IP Blocks and Design Reuse

The great promise of SoC design reuse is to make hardware components as interchangeable as nuts and bolts in the manufacturing of physical goods. Semiconductor companies and design houses cannot design complete SoCs from scratch for every new product. This leads to the central concept of *reuse* of SoC components, often called intellectual property blocks (or *IP blocks*). With the term *reuse* (borrowed from the software engineering domain), the SoC community indicates the capability to employ the description of hardware blocks in various designs with minimal or no changes. IP blocks can be anything from analog periphery, bus controllers, and bridges to complete microprocessor cores. Semiconductor companies talk a lot about reuse, but so far they are still struggling with an efficient way of putting it into practice. Licensing IP from third parties also raises legal and compatibility issues, adding more challenges to IP reuse.

The major problem with IP reuse has to do with the lack of standard interfaces, system simulation methodology, and common verification strategy. Todd and McNelly [2001] Cadence Inc., distinguish four levels of reuse, as shown in Figure 6.1.

- *Personal reuse* is traditional in disciplined ASIC design teams. In this method parts of a design are reused for successive generations. It has the advantage of not requiring any special infrastructure, but it does not scale to larger teams or different designs, and it usually implies a reuse of the design team.

- *Source reuse* provides an existing RTL (register transfer level), or netlist, description to bootstrap a new design. Its effectiveness depends on the quality of the code, the documentation, the test suite, and the availability of the original designer. Unfortunately, the time to understand, evaluate, and verify what is available often takes as long as rewriting the source from the specification. Lack of good documentation is usually one of the big hurdles to source reuse.

- *Core reuse* implies a portfolio of well-defined blocks, either hard or soft, with careful characterization of timing, functionality, and verification strategy.

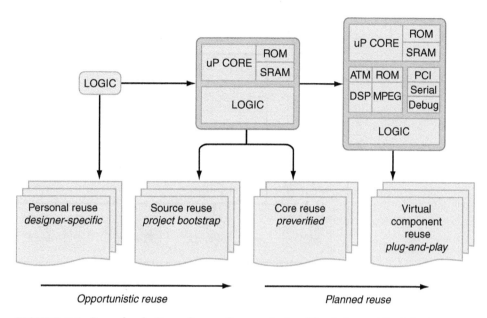

FIGURE 6.1   Reuse levels. Depending on the complexity of the design and the infrastructure to support it, we distinguish between *opportunistic* reuse (when the decision to reuse a block happens after the block is created) and *planned* reuse (when the decision to create an IP block is before the beginning of the design activities). The profitability of each model depends on team organization, design density, and typical design turnaround time.

Soft cores are available as either RTL or technology-independent netlists. Hard cores have already been placed and routed for a specific VLSI process. Most IP is offered today in either soft or hard core form. Using cores greatly improves productivity, but still poses significant challenges in system verification, implementation of changes, adaptation of the core to different buses or signaling conventions, implementation of new process technology, and coordination with multiple silicon manufacturers.

- *Virtual component reuse* is what guarantees a complete separation of authoring and integration roles. A virtual component is a fully characterized, verified, modeled block. This implies adopting a strict interface specification, a rigorous documentation discipline, and a clean system partitioning. Initially, this works against time-to-market and performance, and a few generations are necessary to reach maturity in the process.

A Concrete SoC Example

SoCs normally integrate blocks that originate from several vendors. For example, the *Cirrus Logic* Maverick EP9312 (see Figure 6.2) audio processor is an SoC that integrates an ARM920T processor together with all functionalities to enable digital music

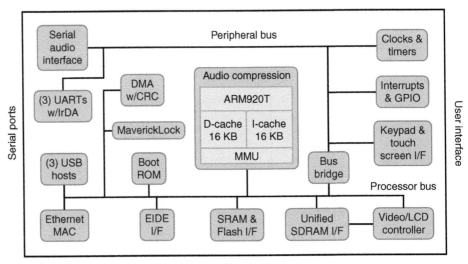

FIGURE 6.2 **Example of a commercial SoC.** The diagram shows the Cirrus Logic EP9312 chip. This includes all components of a typical SoC: a 32-bit RISC core (the ARM920T), standard peripherals (audio, UARTs, USB, Ethernet), memory interfaces (SRAM, Flash, SDRAM), video and input-device interfaces, proprietary IP blocks (the MaverickLock security component), and an interconnection bus.

jukebox-recorders (playing and recording) applications. The rest of the SoC components include signal processing capability, communications, storage, and user interface. In this particular example, the chip includes blocks for standard interfaces, as well as proprietary blocks for more market-specific functions. The latter set of blocks includes a programmable math coprocessor for integer and floating-point audio filtering and the *MaverickLock* component to address security concerns for digital rights management.

SoCs are complex integrated circuits. For example, the EP9312[1] includes 5.7M transistors in a 0.25-micron CMOS technology, delivering high speed (the processor runs at 200 MHz) and low power (~1.5 W) compared to a general-purpose processor.

A typical application for the EP9312 is the *home jukebox*, for which multiple streams of compressed audio data need to be created, manipulated, and decompressed throughout the home for a variety of digital music players (e.g., a portable personal player, an entertainment center, a car stereo).

---

1. Data from "Introducing Maverick EP9312" by Jeff Klaas, presented at the Embedded Processor Forum, San Jose, CA, June 2000.

Virtual Components and the VSIA Alliance

Several industry-wide initiatives have emerged in the last decade to address the issue of design reuse and virtual components. The most visible is the *Virtual Socket Interface Alliance* (VSIA, see *http://www.vsia.org*), a consortium of the major SoC players that sets guidelines, documentation standards, design methodology, and interface specifications for SoC designs. VSIA was formed in 1996 with the goal of establishing a unifying vision for the system-chip industry and the technical standards required to enable mixing and matching IP blocks from multiple authors. VSIA is an open organization with more than 200 members (in 2000); it does not develop products or business strategy.

The central concept of VSIA is the *virtual component* (VC), a fully characterized IP block that fits into *virtual sockets* at both the *functional* (interface protocol, transaction types, and so on) and *physical* level (clock tree, power structure, test signals).

Virtual components are connected to a hierarchy of *on-chip buses* (OCBs) through *bus wrappers*, which enable VCs to implement standardized transactions compatible with other VCs and OCBs. The *transaction layer* of the VSIA specification deals with point-to-point transfers between VCs and OCBs.

Note that the OCB structure is hierarchical in nature. Tradeoffs in SoC design are significantly different from those in traditional board (PCB) designs. The relatively low cost of OCBs makes it more convenient to design multiple bus systems based on bandwidth and latency considerations. A typical complex SoC usually involves two to three levels of buses (processor bus, system bus, and peripheral bus), as depicted in Figure 6.3.

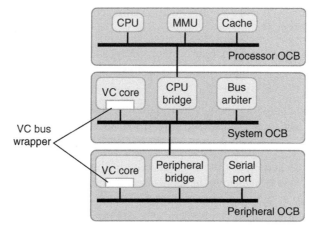

FIGURE 6.3   Example of OCB hierarchy. Using a hierarchy of buses is common in SoC design. For example, the processor OCB is likely to be a faster bus supporting complex transactions (such as pipelined and split transactions). System and peripheral buses usually run at slower clock speeds and support simpler transaction models (such as in-order request/acknowledge).

6.1.2 Design Flows

Every modern hardware design environment includes an EDA (*electronic design automation*) toolchain that enables one to specify hardware blocks and signals, instantiate them, and connect them. This method of designing hardware is very similar to the way in which software development toolchains allow designers to specify variables and functions that manipulate them. Whereas in the past this was accomplished through structural schematic design, today this is commonly accomplished using RTL representations that use *hardware description languages* (HDLs) such as Verilog or VHDL. Just as traditional software refers to library code (or objects) with well-defined interfaces, hardware design languages allow designers to connect an externally specified block, and often the same language can be used to define and connect blocks.

As we saw in the previous sections, we can distinguish between authors (creators) and integrators of IP blocks for SoC designs. Given the complexity of the information flow that has to be exchanged in the world of SoC, rigorous and well-documented design flows are the key to successful projects and efficient reuse. For example, Figure 6.4 shows the typical division of responsibilities and design flow between creators and integrators of SoC IP blocks.

We can classify the phases of an SoC design in two major design flows: *creation* and *verification*.

Creation Flow

This is what is traditionally known as the *design* phase, and involves front-end and back-end phases. Depending on the characteristics of an IP block (for example, whether it is a hard or soft macro), IP creators and integrators divide the corresponding responsibilities in a variety of ways. Hard macros (delivered as a fully verified hardware block) rarely require back-end activities, while soft macros (delivered as an RTL description) demand a full pass of place-and-route tools with a specific technology mapping.

- *Front-end activities* include system specification, RTL design, synthesis, functional simulation, and timing analysis. This amounts to roughly 20 to 30% of the design effort.

- *Back-end activities* include floorplanning, placement, routing, design for testability (e.g., scan-chain insertion), full-custom block generation (such as RAMs), and — for system integrators — chip integration, pad design, and packaging.

In addition to getting the design right, one of the most challenging aspects of the IP creation process is managing the large amount of information each of the phases generates. Behavioral and functional models, RTL description, netlists, interconnect models, power estimates, and test vectors are some of the several formats designers have to deal with. Each of these descriptions represents a different abstraction level of the design, with different details, timing assumptions, and observability constraints. For example, a behavioral model of a processor is usually functionally complete and faithful to the architecturally visible state changes of the machine (i.e., registers and memory).

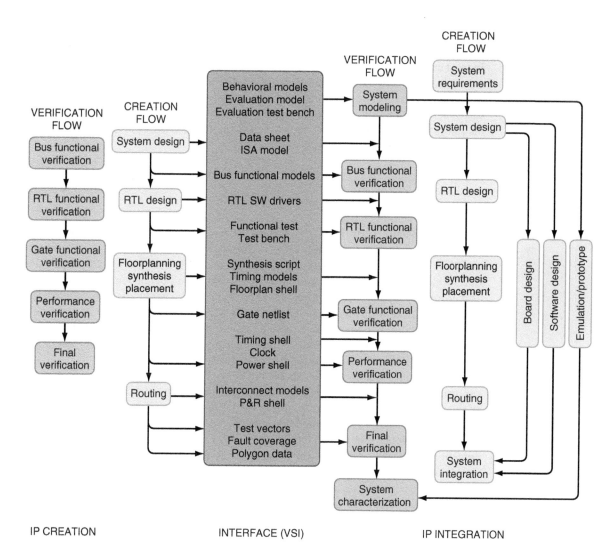

FIGURE 6.4 Design flows in SoC design. Creators and integrators of SoC components use a standardized design flow (such as the one proposed by VSIA) to interface with each other and ensure design reuse. The two major flows are *creation* and *verification*, which usually happen on both sides of the VSI interface. IP creators have to produce a preverified description and IP integrators have to glue the system together and reverify the overall functionality. In addition, system integrators are normally responsible for board and software design, as well as the production of test chips or hardware emulators. Design discipline and strict interfaces are what makes this approach feasible. Different semiconductor vendors propose variations of this approach that use some proprietary components, tools, or descriptions.

However, it usually does not model the details of the microarchitecture (such as microarchitected pipeline registers), even if it can provide very accurate *cycle-budget* estimates. In most cases, different tools deal with the different abstraction levels, and they all have a reason to exist to the extent that they target a differentiated performance/accuracy trade-off point. For example, behavioral processor models achieve simulation performance in the range of 10^6 to 10^7 operations per second, whereas cycle-accurate (or RTL) models rarely exceed 10^4 to 10^5. Sections 6.3 through 6.5 deal with the issue of simulation models in more detail.

Verification Flow

Verification parallels creation in the sense that a good methodology implies a verification step for each change of abstraction level in the design flow. Like design, verification is a multilevel activity, and ideally each level should be able to cross-verify with the abstraction level above it, so that we can minimize the likelihood of specification mismatches and errors. Verification of complex blocks (such as CPU cores) may involve a lockstep simulation of multiple models that cross-verify equality of state changes at every common observability boundary. For example, we can run a functional model together with an RTL model and compare the state of the registers at every commit phase, so that it is easy to spot differences and narrow down the faulty parts of the design.

At the highest abstraction levels the challenge is to make sure that we are correctly capturing the design specification in our model. Here is where formal verification (such as theorem provers) helps and structured modeling languages—such as UML (unified modeling language)—have gained acceptance. Verification of bus protocols is a good example of a domain in which formal verification can be very effective for items (e.g., detecting live-lock conditions) that would be very difficult to catch with traditional simulated test vectors.

As the design phases get closer to silicon, so do the verification tasks, and they extend to other domains beyond functionality, such as timing, clocking, and power dissipation. Synthesis tools usually provide good static timing analysis estimates based on critical path extraction. Similarly, the same synthesis tools also incorporate power estimation modules and *design assistants* for efficient clock-tree generation. Once the design moves over from the world of netlists to that of silicon geometries, LVS (layout-versus-schematic) tools help reextract the resulting circuit (which can be checked for equivalence), and capacitance extraction tools precisely compute the wiring loads that can be fed back (*back-annotated*) to the RTL or netlist description.

The verification process of an SoC is very complex and time consuming, and it adds a big burden on the computation and storage infrastructure of design houses. Even the most powerful workstations take several days for some of the most time-consuming tasks (place-and-route and simulation), and each snapshot of the design database swallows several gigabytes of storage. As we mentioned previously, verification easily exceeds 60% of the effort required for the completion of an SoC project.

6.1.3 SoC Buses

The first difficulty in understanding the concepts behind an *SoC bus* is that it is not a "bus" in the traditional sense of a shared set of interconnecting wires. The second difficulty is that — despite the efforts of VSIA — there is no established standard across the major semiconductor companies. The bad news is that one reason for the lack of standards is the absence of motivation to have them from the major semiconductor companies. This is because proprietary portfolios of IP blocks and buses help them retain their customer bases. The good news is that most SoC buses follow similar driving principles, which we will attempt to summarize in the following paragraphs.

SoC buses are specifications of communications standards for designing integrated systems consisting of multiple heterogeneous IP blocks. SoC buses rarely come with an implementation. Instead, they define signals, transactions, timings, and test methodology for the "legal" combinations of how blocks can be interfaced with each other. The implementation of an SoC bus standard is far from trivial, in that the supported transaction models imply arbitration, synchronization, pipelining, split transactions, retransmissions, and so on. Some buses (such as *IBM CoreConnect*) also embody *automatic data-generator* modes, which can be used to produce regular streams of data, and can be programmed through a simple set of arithmetic operators.

SoC buses do not mandate an interconnection topology; rather, they define various classes of interconnection "building blocks" that can be assembled to design a complete system. Each "building block" carries different cost/performance/complexity tradeoffs and usually comes with a suggested application. The topology of an SoC bus system is typically multilevel, in which a high-performance bus connects microcontrollers, fast memory, and DMA engine, and a low-performance bus is used for slower peripherals (such as UARTs, timers, or network adaptors).

From an implementation point of view, SoC buses are not made of shared wires driven by tri-state buffers. Tri-state design is generally not recommended in SoC design, because of the bad implications for timing analysis, verification, and manufacturing testing (they tend to break the typical *stuck-at* fault model used in automatic test pattern generation). SoC buses involve point-to-point connections and large multiplexers that route signal sources to multiple destinations.

As we can see in Figure 6.5, a typical microprocessor-based SoC consists of a high-performance *backbone* bus (the *advanced high-performance bus*, or AHB, in the AMBA standard; the *processor local bus*, or PLB, in CoreConnect) that is able to sustain the high bandwidth and complex transactions required for an efficient use of the CPU, its local memory and caches, and the primary direct memory access (DMA) devices. In addition, the high-performance bus typically connects to a *bridge* component that ties it to a slower peripheral subsystem (the *advanced peripheral bus*, or APB, in AMBA; the *on-chip peripheral bus*, or OPB, in CoreConnect). Different features and tradeoffs characterize the two bus structures. Whereas the high-performance bus emphasizes speed and pipelining, simplicity and flexibility have a higher priority for peripheral buses.

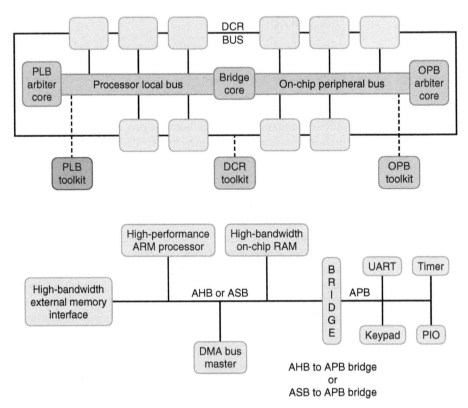

FIGURE 6.5 Example of SoC bus topologies. The top figure shows the IBM CoreConnect bus topology, and the bottom figure the ARM AMBA bus topology. Despite several differences, the similarity is obvious: both approaches propose a multilevel bus configuration with a faster and more complex processor bus (PLB or AHB/ASB) and a slower, simpler peripheral bus (OPB or APB). Other buses (such as the STMicroelectronics STbus) follow similar guidelines.

Data Widths

Bus standards rarely imply a fixed data width, as advances in VLSI technology (number of stacked metal layers for interconnects) make the use of wider paths progressively more economical and buses are designed to be largely technology-independent. For example, AMBA allows data transfers from 8-bit wide to 1024-bit wide (with most systems in the 32 to 256 range). Given that the specifications of the transactions should be independent of the width, this complicates the design of the bus components, which must perform byte-lane selections to extract the correct portion of data. On the other hand, this enables designers to mix and match widths of buses and components. For example, it is possible to implement a narrow component on a wider bus simply by providing an additional level of logic at the input and the output of the component so that only the right part of the bus is read (or driven) based on the transaction address. Likewise, a wider component

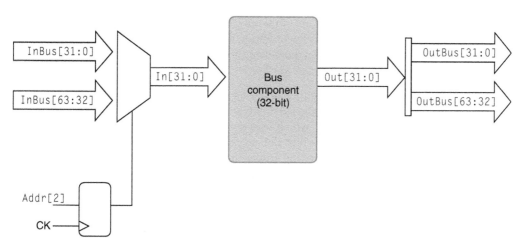

FIGURE 6.6 **Interfacing components of different widths.** The figure shows how to mix and match bus widths and components widths. In the diagram, a wider bus (64-bit) is connected to a narrower component (32-bit) through multiplexing (input) and data replication (output). The 32-bit component uses the third address bit (*Addr[2]*) to select the two halves of the input bus and multiplex them to the internal 32-bit bus (*In[31:0]*). The output can simply be replicated on the wider bus, and bus controls used to signal the rest of the system. The logic to widen and narrow the datapaths is local to the component, so that the rest of the system can be completely unaware of the mismatch. This is a key concept for encapsulation of components to achieve reuse.

can be easily interfaced to a narrow bus through sequential multiplexing of individual parts of the input or output values. Figure 6.6 shows an example of matching different widths.

Bus specifications are not simple, and components rarely implement the full feature set. In the following sections, we examine some of the key concepts that are common in many SoC bus specifications. Far from being complete, this set is supposed to be an introduction for readers who want to gain some familiarity with SoC buses. For a complete description of bus functionalities, readers should consult the proprietary bus documentation, such as the AMBA specifications or the CoreConnect manuals.

Masters, Slaves, and Arbiters

A typical SoC bus connects three types of components: *masters, slaves,* and *arbiters.*

- *Bus masters* are components that can initiate transfer operations by generating address and control information. Only one master at a time can have access to the bus. Modern SoC buses support multiple masters, wherein a unique identifier characterizes each master.

- *Bus slaves* are components that service bus master requests by providing (or reading) the data in the specified address range. Slaves are normally mapped to a certain address range the SoC designers assign during system specification.

Slaves acknowledge masters of the success, failure, or delayed completion of the transfer. Note that advanced transaction modes (such as split transactions, discussed below) require a more complex signaling protocol between masters and slaves.

- *Bus arbiters* ensure that only one master at a time has control of the bus (usually, each bus has a single arbiter). Arbiters normally implement a request/grant interface for bus masters, which uses a priority scheme to decide which master has the right to access the bus. Some systems (such as AMBA) distinguish the addressing functionality of the arbiter in a separate *bus decoder* used to decode the address of each transfer and provide an enable signal to each individual component (master or slave).

Even a single-core design can include multiple bus masters that require arbitration. For example, CPUs with a separate level-1 instruction and data cache may decide to issue separate bus requests for instruction and data cache refills. Depending on the core architecture, this could be arbitrated internally, so that the core acts as a single bus master. Alternatively, separate caches could be designed to appear as separate bus masters, so that the system can support more complex transactions and interface to a wider variety of components.

Complex SoC designs that adopt a hierarchical bus structure employ *bridge* components to connect the individual bus subsystems. A *bridge* component usually acts as a slave in the higher-performance bus (such as an AHB for AMBA) and at the same time is the master in the peripheral bus (such as the APB for AMBA). The purpose of a bridge component is to separate the two subsystems and to provide synchronization for the requests that cross the boundary (the two subsystems often have separate clock domains).

Bus Transactions

In the SoC domain, a transaction is an atomic transfer of data that happens between a master and a slave. In some cases, a transaction can be broadcast to multiple slaves, or can omit the data (*address-only* transactions, used to send commands to components). A bus transaction typically involves a *request phase* (send address and controls), a *transfer phase* (data is sent around), and an *acknowledge phase* (transaction terminates). Depending on the complexity of the bus protocol and the type of components, transactions can be pipelined. For example, the request phase of a new transaction can overlap the transfer phase of a previous transaction (issued by another master). On first approximation, we can identify three types of transactions: *simple*, *burst*, and *split*.

Simple Transactions. A simple transfer reads or writes an individual piece of data in a single transaction. Typically, simple transfers match the natural width of the slave component (for example, a 32-bit word access to a 32-bit-wide memory component), and require a single request-acknowledge bus transaction. A typical *read* sequence is:

1. The master issues a request (address and controls).

2. The slave samples the request and transmits the data.

3. The master receives the data and the transfer completes.

Note that the slave can insert *wait cycles* in the transaction sequence if the request cannot be serviced within one clock cycle.

Burst Transactions. Burst transfers are used to move blocks of data that are spatially related and are addressable through a regular pattern (in the simplest case, a contiguous block of data sequentially addressed). Burst transfers improve the throughput utilization of the bus, but still require the master to retain control of the bus for the entire duration of the transfer. Burst transfers are particularly effective for slave components whose random-access performance is much slower than sequential-access performance. A typical example is DRAM memory, wherein a random access can take as much as 10x longer than a sequential access. For example, a read burst access sequence is:

1. The master issues a burst request (address, burst length, and controls).

2. The slave samples the request and starts transmitting the data.

3. The master receives the data.

4. Master and slave increment the address and repeat steps 2 and 3 until they reach the burst length.

5. The transfer completes.

Typically, SoC buses support a few burst lengths (4 to 16 is a common range) and various burst modes (such as simple increment, stride increment, or wraparound), and impose alignment restrictions to the initial burst address. In microprocessor based SoCs, burst accesses are commonly used to refill the outermost level of cache lines from DRAM memory.

Split Transactions. Split transfers are used to improve the overall utilization of the bus by separating the operation of the master from the operation of the slave servicing the request. Unlike burst transfers, the bus is freed in the time between the master request and when the slave is able to respond with the data. Split transfers are effective when the slave knows that the request takes a large amount of time to be serviced. However, they significantly increase the complexity of the transaction: the slave must signal the arbiter that the master requesting the transfer should only be signaled when the slave is ready to complete the request. In order to disambiguate concurrent split transactions, they have to be tagged with the master identifier, so that the arbiter can signal the requesting master when the servicing slave issues the proper number. Split transactions effectively make slaves as complex as masters, in that they too now must arbitrate for bus access.

For example, the basic stages of a *read* split transaction include:

1. The master issues a request (address, controls, and identifier).

2. The slave records the master identifier and returns a split response.

3. The arbiter stalls the outstanding transaction at the requesting master and grants bus access to others.

4. The slave (when ready) signals the master identifier to the arbiter.

5. The arbiter grants the requesting slave access to the bus.

6. The slave drives the requested data to master and relinquishes the bus.

7. The master receives the data and the transfer completes.

Note that this mechanism assumes one outstanding transaction per bus master. Bus masters that have the capability to support multiple outstanding transactions appear as multiple individual masters (with their own identifiers) as far as the bus is concerned. It is also important to observe that an indiscriminate use of split transactions could cause bus deadlocks. For example, if different masters attempt to access the same slave with incompatible split transactions, the slave may never be able to service them.[2]

Finally, we should mention that one commonly used form of split transactions is *pipelined transactions*, whereby a master can generate addresses ahead of data from the previous transaction (in a pipeline *read*). In pipelined transactions, data returns strictly in-order back to the master, as if the bus were physically pipelined. As for any other form of pipelining, pipelined transactions do not affect the bus latency but are very effective in increasing the bus throughput.

Test Modes

A very interesting feature of the AMBA bus is the support for testing of the SoC. As we outlined in the previous sections, verification is by far the most complex and expensive task of an SoC design. Components connected through an SoC bus would naturally not be observable in isolation unless the bus included specific support for this.

The idea behind the AMBA test philosophy is to allow individual components in the system to be tested in isolation, without interacting with other components. For this, the bus needs to expose inputs and outputs of each component to the outside world. AMBA standardizes this operation through a *test interface controller* (TIC) bus master component that converts external test vectors to internal bus transfers. The TIC uses a very simple handshake mechanism and a 32-bit interface to transfer the test vectors. The interface can be implemented as a separate bi-directional port, or can be overloaded with other SoC ports during test mode.

---

2. Details on deadlock detection and avoidance are beyond the scope of this book. Both the *AMBA specification* and the *Core Connect PLB manual* describe strategies for avoiding bus deadlocks.

Flame: Once You Have Designed the Processor, You Are Done

When approaching the embedded domain from the world of general-purpose computer architecture, the temptation to exaggerate the processor-centric view of the system is strong. In the general-purpose world, the design of the processor is an activity that can often be undertaken independently of the rest of the system, which is usually seen as a commodity, and is often considered the most difficult and important milestone.

In the majority of embedded systems — even those dominated by a few processors — the idea that "once you've designed the processor, you're done" needs to be adjusted. The programmable component of an embedded system is indeed important, and one should not underestimate the difficulty of building the processor and the circuitry around it (such as caches, coherency mechanisms, and multiprocessor support).

However, not less important or difficult is the design of the rest of the system, the way in which the processors interact with it, and the decisions that govern the partitioning between hardware and software.

A complex system-on-a-chip today often includes multiple processors, each with its own caches and memory hierarchy, DSPs and nonprogrammable accelerators, interfaces to devices, and a very irregular structure of memory blocks and random logic. The design and integration of the processor core is just one of several complex activities necessary to completion of the SoC (the most time consuming of all being the final system verification).

A common mistake is to confuse the importance of a processor with the effort necessary to design it. The RTL of a simple VLIW processor might require two or three engineers and six to nine months. Completing the design, system integration, and verification of an SoC using that processor can take up to an order of magnitude bigger effort. In summary, a better description would be: *once you've designed the processor, you've barely started*.

6.2 Processor Cores and SoC

Processor cores in an SoC are not "just another IP block." Their complexity, speed requirements, and programmability make them very different from the other system components. Complex cores are often offered as preverified placed-and-routed *hard macros*, simply because running them through the back-end tools for every SoC would add too much burden on the CAD tools and cause serious performance degradation or area bloat. In addition, it is common for embedded cores to include full-custom components, such as register files and sometimes entire datapaths.

In a single-core system, the processor core is typically the only SoC bus master, and is responsible for controlling most of the bus transactions. Given their complexity, writing a bus wrapper for a processor core is far from a trivial task. As a consequence, the choice of the processor core normally mandates the bus standard: including an ARM forces an AMBA-based SoC, using a PowerPC forces a CoreConnect SoC, and so on.

Typically, a "core" IP block contains the core itself, plus level-1 caches, the memory controller, a debug support unit, a bus interface, and the basic interrupt controller. These are the components more closely tied to the core itself, and whose functionality is likely to be encapsulated within a monolithic IP block. Everything else is likely to be an external IP-block that can be configured separately. For this reason, most cores come with a fixed-size cache, and vendors offer separate combinations for the most common cache sizes.

The fact that a core is a programmable component also presents new challenges when we view it as an IP block, because of the requirements of software debugging environments. One might say that including a processor core whose state cannot be accessed externally is verification suicide. As a consequence, all cores include a debug support unit that implements (at a minimum) a set of *peek* and *poke* commands to enable the external world to examine and change the internal processor state (we cover this in more detail in Section 6.6).

The rest of this section deals with some of the typical uses of processor cores. Section 6.2.1 discusses the combination of processor cores with nonprogrammable accelerators, and Section 6.2.2 briefly covers some of the aspects of multiprocessing in SoC designs.

6.2.1 Nonprogrammable Accelerators

The choice between the use of programmable and nonprogrammable hardware is never an easy one (see Figure 6.7). In general, nonprogrammable hardware gives the best *bang for the buck*: it only uses hardware to implement what directly contributes to the application core functionality, and in doing so optimizes cost, speed, and power dissipation. However, designing a nonprogrammable piece of hardware is time consuming, error prone, and usually very expensive. When processor cores are easily available, fast enough, and cost effective, the temptation to just migrate the entire application to software and pay the fetch-decode-execute penalty is certainly very strong.

Many applications get by with a single programmable microcontroller or DSP core. However, when it comes to leading-edge appliances programmable cores are often not fast enough to address the required performance. Even if they were, their power consumption and design/production cost would likely exceed the budget. Under these assumptions, it is common practice among SoC architects to mix programmable cores with custom signal-processing pipelines (sometimes called *hardware accelerators* or *hardware assist blocks*).

For example, by assigning the final components of the imaging pipeline of a color printer to a block of custom hardware the system processor core can easily handle the rest of the application. Similar considerations apply to the telecommunication components—e.g., GSM, CDMA—of a cellular phone, or the initial CCD acquisition and demosaicing of a digital still camera.

Looking at these examples, it is important to observe that in many cases hardware accelerators deal with computation at the *periphery* of the application; that is, at the

Relevance to performance and specialization

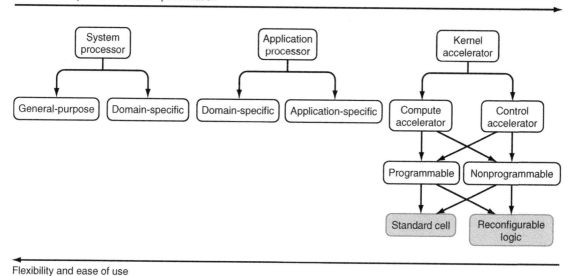

Flexibility and ease of use

FIGURE 6.7 Classification of programmable and nonprogrammable processing. The chart shows a variety of computing styles and where they are usually applied in an embedded system. Specialization grows from left to right and flexibility from right to left. We can break an embedded system into system processing, application processing, and kernel acceleration. Depending on the desired cost/performance, we can apply various degrees of customization to each level: general-purpose, domain-specific or application-specific processors to the high-level components, and programmable or nonprogrammable acceleration to compute-intensive kernels. In reality, a combination of these techniques is commonly found in many of today's embedded systems.

source (input devices) or at the sink (output devices) of the computing pipeline. This is not a coincidence: using hardware assist at the periphery of an application minimizes the disruption to the development of the application software. Although examples of hardware acceleration that sits at the *core* of the application exist (e.g., motion estimation in an MPEG encoder), these are less common. These also require more complex interfaces between the core and the accelerator, and a more awkward structure of the application software. In addition, history shows that hardware acceleration of core functionality is often the first candidate for getting absorbed by software, as soon as the speed of the processor core becomes adequate for the required performance. Another reason for the accelerator to be at the periphery is due to the fact that hardware accelerators are particularly efficient when dealing with *streaming* data, for which the cost of bringing the data to the core (and traverse the memory subsystem) can be prohibitive.

Using custom datapaths is most effective when the cost pressure is extremely high, functionality is fixed, algorithms are well established, and the probability of leveraging the design across future generations is high. In rapidly evolving markets, for which these conditions may not apply, the convenience of hardware assist is more questionable.

Sometimes, however, it is possible to build flexibility into the nonprogrammable accelerator to account for some of the easily foreseeable changes.

Correctly picking which algorithms are important, and of those which standards have reached sufficient maturity to justify hardwiring them in a product, remains one of the biggest challenges. Even seemingly stable standards evolve very quickly (Bluetooth version 1.0 was quickly obsoleted by version 1.1 just a few months after its introduction, and similar stories can be told about audio/video encoding standards and 3D graphics primitives.)[3]

From the point of view of the overall application design, deciding what to do in hardware and what to do in software is a very complex problem, for which no automated solution exists today. Many research groups have attacked the area of *hardware/software partitioning and co-design* in the last two decades. Despite their efforts, this remains an open research topic.

Reconfigurable Logic

In some cases (for example, those in which the expected product volume does not justify the design and NRE costs of a custom SoC), other technologies come to the rescue, such as FPGAs (*field-programmable gate arrays*) and PLDs (*programmable logic devices*). The cost of some NRE components (such as mask sets) are growing in inverse proportion with VLSI feature sizes, and these are becoming fundamental limiters on the economic viability of a specific design at a given part volume. This means that the break-even volume point for the use of alternative technology (such as reconfigurable logic) is growing, and fewer designs can envision volumes that justify a full VLSI investment.

FPGAs and PLDs (often grouped under the common term *reconfigurable logic*) enable designers to achieve performance similar to custom hardware assist blocks on standard off-the-shelf components. Reconfigurable logic trades *higher part cost* (and often speed, but not always) with *lower design costs* and *quicker time-to-market*. In this respect, it is a good match with low-volume products.

More recently, designers have started using FPGAs and PLDs to implement *dynamically reconfigurable computing engines*, whereby mutually exclusive tasks are loaded and executed on demand on the hardware substrate. Although this improves the cost effectiveness of the reconfigurable solution, it is only applicable to domains in which the application can easily be partitioned into a set of well-defined tasks that run on a fixed, deterministic time schedule. Programmable logic also makes the design turnaround time much shorter. Developers can simply download a new configuration to the device and it is ready to run in seconds. This is in contrast to the multi-million-dollar effort to respin a traditional ASIC.

To address these types of applications, thanks to increases in circuit density a promising technique that recently emerged is the idea of *system-on-a-programmable-chip* (SoPC). SoPCs (see Figure 6.8) combine a large block of reconfigurable logic with

---

3. For example, this is a major reason Intel never included 3D graphics support in its processors.

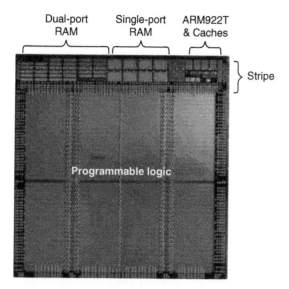

FIGURE 6.8 **Example of an SoPC.** A picture of the Altera Excalibur EPXA10 chip, which combines a 200-MHz ARM922T core with a large block (up to 1M gates) of programmable logic, memory (up to 256 KB single-port and 128 KB dual-port SRAM), and standard interfaces (UART, DRAM controller, timer, debug support, and so on).

a standard nonreconfigurable processor core and a set of standard peripherals and memory controllers. This combines the best of both worlds: the processor core and the standard peripherals can be implemented as a hard macro, with state-of-the-art ASIC design techniques, and the reconfigurable logic can be easily programmed to implement proprietary IP blocks that exceed the capacity of the programmable core. The idea behind SoPC is ultimately to provide a *one-size-fits-all* component that efficiently supports software through a legacy core, and at the same time that provides an easy path to a limited degree of hardware flexibility without incurring the cost of a full-blown ASIC design.

Most major FPGA/PLD vendors are now offering SoPCs that include popular processor cores. For example, Altera offers ARM-based components in the *Excalibur* line and Xilinx offers PPC-based chips in their *Virtex-II-Pro* family (up to four cores per FPGA).

Finally, although programmable logic devices are best suited for low-volume products, they are also sometimes used for the initial production ramp-up of high-volume devices. Given the continuously increasing time-to-market pressure of new products and the shrinking lifetime of product generations, even the relatively short four to six weeks for mask fabrication, initial testing, and volume production bootstrap of an ASIC could be in the critical path. In this case, it is not an uncommon practice in the industry to start shipping initial versions of a product with a higher-cost FPGA device and then to replace the component (and sometimes the board) with the ASIC version when that becomes available. This explains the increase in the offering of programs and services (such as Altera's *HardCopy*) that enable quick migration from an FPGA database to a library of ASIC standard cells.

6.2.2 Multiprocessing on a Chip

Many readers who are familiar with general-purpose computing associate multiprocessing only with high-end servers, database engines, or workstations for scientific workloads and heavy-duty tasks, such as 3D graphic rendering or weather forecasting. In reality, multiprocessing in the embedded domain is also very common, although it often takes very different forms.

The most successful form of multiprocessing in general-purpose computing is *symmetric multiprocessing* (SMP), in which the operating system transparently handles multiple identical processors connected through some form of shared memory. In SMP, tasks are scheduled and allocated to the individual processor automatically by the OS, which is often also responsible for migrating processes across processors to balance the overall load of the machine and optimize the throughput.

In the embedded domain, the most widely adopted form of multiprocessing is *heterogeneous*, wherein potentially different processors are in the same system but each can be seen as a standalone subsystem (with private memory) that is largely unaware of the presence of the other programmable components. In other words, different operating systems (or microkernels) control the individual processors, each of which runs a predefined, statically allocated set of tasks. Communication between processors happens through well-defined regions of shared memory and explicitly handled synchronization mechanisms, similar to the way in which we deal with other DMA engines. In these configurations, it is common to designate one processor to be the *master* processor of the system. The master usually controls the activation of tasks on the other processors (*slaves*) by explicitly sending the appropriate control commands to the microkernels running on the slaves.

Another common form of embedded multiprocessing exploits the inherent *data parallelism* in the application. If we can write the application in an SPMD fashion, we can use multiple identical processors with private data memories to independently process individual data regions. We can find instances of this in many DSP applications that manipulate 2D images (e.g., in medical imaging) or other regular data streams (e.g., telecommunications, audio, and video). This approach is not new, and examples date back to as early as the mid 1970s. These were continued throughout the 1980s including the "extreme" development of processors that were explicitly designed to be arranged in parallel (such as Inmos's *Transputers*), and struggled for a long time before being ultimately abandoned.

Symmetric Multiprocessing

Until recently, SMP hardware was expensive and usually built around customized platforms, which made it prohibitively expensive for everything but high-end workstations and servers. Now, SMP boards are becoming more common, and some silicon manufacturers are starting to announce SMP chips (such as dual-MIPS and dual-PPC components). In this scenario, the embedded domain is also riding the wave of commoditization of SMP, and embedded SMP systems are becoming economically more viable.

Software development still remains a challenge, given the immature level of SMP support of embedded OSs and compilation toolchains, and it is usually up to the designers to check the safety of the concurrency model and the proper allocation of shared resources.

From a pure cost perspective, embedded SMP is still not very competitive and its adoption is limited to the small high-performance, high-cost market segment, whereas other solutions (such as heterogeneous multiprocessing, covered next) are more effective in cost-conscious, high-volume consumer products.

Heterogeneous Multiprocessing

Also known as *asymmetric multiprocessing*, heterogeneous multiprocessing is the most common form of multiprocessing in embedded SoCs today. The first question that comes to mind is: given that general purpose processors are available, why should one use different types of processors for a single task? The reasons come once again from cost, power, and customization considerations. Using different processors for different tasks enables system designers to choose the most cost-effective alternative for each application stage. For example, DSPs and general-purpose processors have distinctively different feature sets that make them best suited for very different types of workloads. In an application that includes both a DSP and a general-purpose computation component, partitioning the two tasks and using a heterogeneous system is much more cost-effective than trying to force-feed the entire application to a traditional general-purpose SMP (too expensive) or to a bank of DSPs (too rigid).

Unfortunately, heterogeneous multiprocessing does not come for free. The biggest barrier comes from the absence of an intuitive programming model. Tasks have to be explicitly partitioned for the individual processors, interprocess communication and synchronization has to be manually handled, compilation tools and binaries are different, and debugging is awkward (see Section 6.6.1 for more on debugging issues).

Despite the intrinsic difficulties in the programming model, several industry trends are pushing strongly in the direction of heterogeneous multiprocessing. Many vendors and industry-wide initiatives are advocating a few *microcontroller + DSP* combinations that target some of the most promising market areas. For example, both the *Intel PCA* and the *Texas Instruments OMAP* product lines belong to this class of new SoC platforms. One of the major driving forces behind the adoption of these architecture styles comes from the contrasting requirements of having to deal with legacy code in the presence of fast-changing feature sets. Whereas legacy applications and operating systems take a long time to migrate to new architectures, new products continuously push the envelope with more requirements and a faster adoption rate. Combining a legacy core (such as ARM) with a performance-oriented programmable accelerator (such as many modern DSP engines) promises to provide the flexibility to cope with both sets of requirements.

Example: A Multicore Platform for Mobile Multimedia

The world of *mobile multimedia* provides us with an interesting example of a successful heterogeneous SoC multiprocessing platform. The third generation (3G) of wireless technologies will soon offer enough bandwidth for cellular communication devices to enable a new set of multimedia services, including video messaging, video conferencing, speech recognition, and e-commerce applications. In this scenario, hardware platforms have to offer both speed and flexibility, given that they will have to support a large variety of evolving standards and applications. At the same time, the cost pressure for terminal appliances (phones and PDAs) and their strict power requirements demand a highly integrated solution.

Texas Instruments's OMAP platform (see Figure 6.9) addresses many of these requirements. For example, the OMAP1510 device is a dual-core SoC that includes a 200-MHz, C55x DSP core (400 MIPS peak performance), and a 175-MHz ARM9 processor core (210 MIPS peak performance). Together with the two cores, the component also integrates several banks of local memory (a 192-KB frame buffer for video, more than 64 KB of data memory and 12 KB of I-cache for the DSP, and 16 KB of I-cache and 8 KB of D-cache for the ARM) and various other standard I/O peripherals.

The combination of a DSP and general-purpose core is a good compromise for performance, cost, and power consumption. The ARM handles control and system code well (operating system, user interface, interrupt handlers, and so on). The DSP is a much better match for real-time baseband signal processing and multimedia manipulation (such as video). Trying to run the entire application on a faster RISC processor would have severe consequences on the power consumption and code size requirements of the system. Running OS and system code is simply beyond the capabilities of a C55x DSP.

From an application development viewpoint, a dual-core heterogeneous platform poses a series of significant challenges. First, as we mentioned, firmware designers have to statically decide what to run on the DSP and what to run on the ARM. Once they have done that, to simplify the development, the compilation toolchain has to abstract the architecture of the DSP accelerator and present it through a user-friendly API so that the master application can be written independently of the DSP. This DSP API (called a *DSP bridge* in the TI environment) provides mechanisms to initiate and control tasks on the DSP, move data to and from the DSP, and exchange messages. In this way, functions implemented on the DSP are accessible to the system programmer through a simplified form of *remote procedure call* interface, which look like standard C functions.

On the DSP side, DSP programmers typically implement individual functions through a separate compilation toolchain. It is also common for the system manufacturer to provide a set of canned DSP libraries that implements the most common functions (filters, transforms, codecs, and so on) so that the lack of user friendliness in the DSP is only minimally exposed to the application programmers.

An application example of OMAP is the implementation of a 3G video-conferencing standard in a mobile terminal. Video conferencing includes a media codec (to compress the transmitted speech and audio and video streams and to decompress the received streams) and several signaling protocols (media transport to sequence the packets over

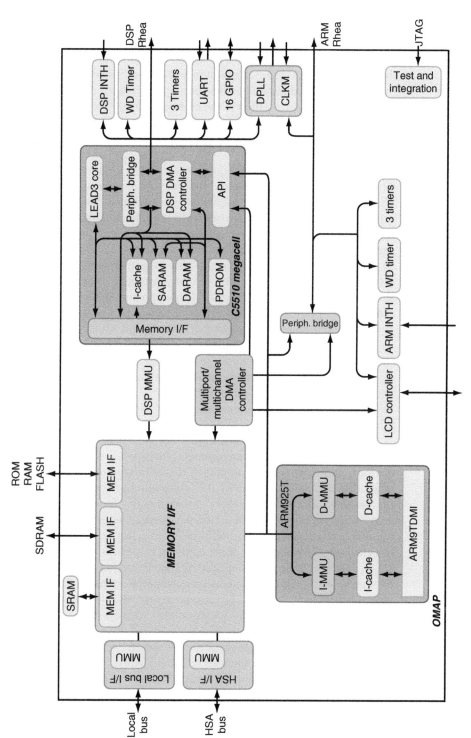

FIGURE 6.9 **The TI OMAP hardware architecture.** The diagram shows an example (the TI OMAP) of a dual microcontroller-DSP heterogeneous multiprocessor architecture on a chip. This includes an ARM9TDMI 32-bit RISC core and a TI TMS320C5510 DSP engine, together with memory and standard peripherals. Although OMAP was mainly designed for wireless multimedia applications (wherein the telecommunication component runs on the DSP and the rest of the application runs on the ARM), it is easy to generalize the concept to other areas that have a mix of signal-processing and general-purpose (or legacy OS) requirements.

the channel, a control protocol to handle the call, and a session protocol to describe the content). In this case, compression and decompression are implemented in the DSP (using some of the dedicated codec-specific instructions of the C55x), whereas the ARM runs the protocols in addition to the system code and user interfaces.

6.3 Overview of Simulation

Any processor design project requires a simulator, for a number of reasons. Simulators allow hardware and software teams to work with a degree of independence, overlapping tasks that would otherwise be sequentially constrained. Simulators assist in architecture exploration, allowing designs to be roughly compared without committing to full implementations. They allow components to be tested for correct operation before all other parts of the system are available (functional or unit testing). They also allow pieces of a larger system to be put together and tested together, either to debug component interactions when only a subset of the system is available or to provide a controlled testing environment even if all pieces are available (integration testing). In addition, simulators can be used to validate or diagnose performance at a variety of design stages.

Simulators come in a variety of shapes and sizes, covering different parts of a system. The bulk of this chapter focuses on simulating processor cores. However, simulations of larger aggregations—including chips, boards, or entire products—are of course possible. Such larger-scale simulations often involve connecting or interfacing smaller simulators that efficiently model the relevant properties of the components. Such integration can be a very complex task (it is unfortunately beyond the scope of this book).

A variety of simulation techniques are known today, spanning a spectrum from software-oriented to hardware-oriented. *Interpreted* simulation is the most flexible, obvious, and slow software approach (in an interpreter, both the target program and target data are treated as data by the interpreting program). *Compiled* simulation uses the resources of the host processor more directly, translating the target program into a host program. Compiled simulation yields much better performance while still retaining much of the flexibility of software approaches. *Dynamic* binary translation uses translation techniques at run-time, applying a "pay-as-you-go" strategy to the (presumably expensive) translation step. Binary translation (both static and dynamic) has been applied to recent and historical mainstream processor technologies (at least one start-up company has begun applying dynamic binary translation to embedded processors). More hardware-oriented approaches are associated with hardware design languages (HDLs). A *logical* hardware simulation includes the parallelism and interfaces of different hardware blocks in a design without precisely specifying their implementation, whereas a *gate-level* hardware simulation uses the actual hardware specifications to perform a very accurate but very slow simulation. Last, *in-circuit emulation* requires a relative of the chip being designed to already exist, and then uses a mixture of hardware execution and software emulation to simulate the device being developed. In-circuit emulators can run at or near the speed of the eventual product. Each simulation technique comes with its own set of tradeoffs.

Controversy: "Cycle-Accurate" Simulation

Many simulators are labeled "cycle-accurate," but few live up to the term. In fact, "cycle-accurate" has become so diluted it is sometimes used to refer to simulators that attempt to report cycle counts, regardless of the level of accuracy. Even hardware design simulators diverge from the actual implementation because they abstract away the behavior of system components such as peripherals. Software-based simulators often simplify away details of simulation timing in order to run efficiently.

How accurate must a simulator be? It depends on the goal of the simulator. Functional simulators don't need to accurately model performance; they just check whether a program or system produces the intended results. Performance simulators have more exact requirements, but lower accuracy might be acceptable when comparing possible designs or to development-marketing estimates of performance. Very few studies are performed on the accuracy of simulators. Unfortunately, measuring the accuracy of a simulation is at best considered an academic discipline and at worst never performed because the arrival of hardware makes designers believe that the simulator is no longer needed.

Sometimes it is also possible to get very useful information out of tools — other than simulators — custom built by the designers to analyze traces or very specific behavior. These can identify very important areas in which simulation may be lying to the users, or help increase the confidence when the simulator finds the same results.

Making a simulator pay off requires extensive work in *verification*. That is, a simulator is only as good as its representation of what it simulates. By their nature, simulators make simplifying assumptions about the software, hardware, and environment they simulate, and these simplifying assumptions can be trivial or crucial. Validation and verification techniques (which are, alas, poorly codified and mostly experiential) are the most easily overlooked part of simulation.

The quality of a simulator is often judged by its *speed* and *accuracy*. Whereas speed is not difficult to quantify, accuracy is a much more controversial metric, as it is closely related to the abstraction level of the simulation model and its observability granularity. For example, it is possible that a functional simulator (written in C) and an RTL-level simulator (written in Verilog) report the same number of cycles. That does not mean that they have the same accuracy, as the observability granularity of the RTL model is likely to be much finer than the functional model. Conversely, it is also true that if we are just interested in measuring overall performance, a functional level model is probably all we need, and we do not need to pay the 10 to 100x performance overhead of a cycle-accurate simulation. In general, choosing the right simulation and modeling techniques is not easy, and even the most experienced designers often find themselves making the wrong decisions.

6.3.1 Using Simulators

Aside from the obvious purpose of helping to design the hardware, another important reason for simulators is *decoupling* the hardware and software design processes. There is a long latency from the beginning of a hardware project to the arrival of the first prototype hardware. During this time, the software team needs a platform on which to develop and test their code. Of course, someone has to build and maintain the simulator for this to happen. However, having a simulator allows the software team to try out its toolchain (compilers and the like) and the code the toolchain generates. For new architectures (for which the toolchain may not yet exist), the simulator gives designers a degree of confidence that their tools will work at all, before the actual hardware is even available.

Decoupling, of course, does not mean that the hardware and software teams work independently. At the same time the software team is building its tools, the hardware team will be looking for confirmation that its ideas are implementable and useful. The simulator forms an interface between the hardware and software teams; allowing both to validate ideas they are trying out. Simulators can be valuable design and development tools, exposing inadequacies and design flaws long before they are committed to hardware or buried deeply in the structure of a software program. More strongly, this interface allows *co-design* ideas to flow between the hardware and software teams. Any well-designed modern processor requires active collaboration between hardware and software teams. Before hardware becomes available, the simulator is the place where "the rubber meets the road" and the coupling of hardware and software is tested.

In the early phases of a project, simulators are useful tools for *architecture exploration* and *performance validation*. They also happen to be much more convenient than the traditional choice of building hardware development boards. Design choices affect how the eventual product will run. Using a simulator can show what benefits, costs, and unforeseen effects a choice will have. The accuracy and expense of these

---

Controversy: How Many Simulators?

Today, most systems are developed using two simulators: architectural level and "cycle-accurate." We think this is the right approach, because of the various needs of developers in the various stages of development before the final hardware is available. The architectural simulator is most important early in development, when design studies are being conducted and when various features must be evaluated (at least coarsely). The more accurate simulator is important later, for exploring performance aspects of the design and for validating or even debugging early hardware. Projects that try to build a single all-singing/all-dancing simulator end up with one piece of code that does neither job well (too slow for architectural exploration; not enough detail for "cycle-accurate" simulation). Note that neither of these can replace the HDL simulator, necessary for hardware design and verification. Indeed, functional simulators usually work together with HDL tools as part of the overall verification strategy.

exploratory efforts depends on the accuracy of the simulator being used. High-level simulators will provide preliminary results with very little effort, whereas detailed simulators can provide very accurate results but may require large modification effort to explore a particular idea. This means that high-level simulators can eliminate certain choices without resorting to a full-blown hardware or software implementation. If a simulator, making simplifying assumptions, cannot deliver the desired performance, it is unlikely an implementation that sweats all of the details will magically resolve the problems encountered by the simulator. Note that the converse is not true: if the simulator delivers the desired performance, an actual implementation is not guaranteed to deliver the performance found in simulation. Chapter 10 explores automated systems for architectural exploration and the human intuition that drives such searches.

Simulators are also used to test or validate components during design. In *functional testing*, also called *unit testing*, a single component is tested in isolation. The idea is to check that its behavior matches its specification. In *integration testing*, two or more components that have been functionally tested are connected and tested as a larger system. Integration testing exposes failures that result from the interaction of multiple components. Functional testing perforce must precede integration testing. It does little good to verify a system if the components are not known to behave correctly.

Simulators help in both types of testing. Simulators can substitute for parts of the system that are unavailable or not under test, providing a "correct" implementation and focusing the testing on the particular device. Simulators are also (presumably) entirely controllable, and thus can be initialized to particular states in order to exercise particular behavior in the device under test. Last, simulators are by their nature "instrumented," and thus can record and display the reactions of the component being tested.

The rest of the chapter deals with simulation in more depth. Initially, we concentrate on processor simulation. Section 6.4 discusses the various techniques (interpreted, compiled, trace-driven) relevant to the simulation of programs running on processor cores. Section 6.5 deals with several aspects of system simulation, which is the problem of simulating an entire SoC. Section 6.6 discusses some of the uses of simulation in the verification of complex SoCs.

6.4 Simulating a VLIW Architecture

Simulation involves two machines: host processor and target processor. The *host* processor performs the simulation, and is typically a state-of-the-art PC or workstation. The *target* processor is the one being simulated, and can be whatever you want. As we will see, similarity between host and target processor enables efficient simulation, in both hardware and software.

Simulators can work at a variety of levels. Much of this chapter discusses *instruction-level simulation*, in which the focus of the simulation is correctly modeling the semantics and execution of instructions in the target machine. The next level of depth is *cycle-level simulation*, in which more effort is placed in modeling the clock of the machine and the state preserved from one clock cycle to the next. The most detailed level of simulation we discuss is *gate-level simulation*, in which signal propagation and timing of logic gates and

```
typedef struct {                          for(;;){
    unsigned int opcode;                      unsigned long instr;
    unsigned int rs1, rs2, rd;                DECODED_INSTR decoded;
    ...
} DECODED_INSTR;                              instr = fetch(progmem, &pc);

/* note: gprs[0] always == 0 */              decoded = decode(instr);
unsigned int gprs[32];
double fprs[32];                              switch(decoded->opcode){
unsigned int pc;                             case ADD:
unsigned int flags;                              gprs[rd] =
unsigned long progmem[...];                          gprs[rs1] + gprs[rs2];
unsigned char datamem[...];                      pc += 1;
                                                 break;
/* initialize architectural state */
progmem = ...                                case BRANCH:
datamen = ...                                    ...
                                             }
                                         }
```

FIGURE 6.10 Outline of the main loop of an interpreted simulator.

wires are the fundamental focus. One can even go further, to physical simulations, but such work is beyond the province of architecture and more the work of device physicists. Note that the level of detail of a simulator is not directly related to accuracy (a functional simulator could be very accurate in terms of overall cycle budget, power consumption, and so on). For example, it could be very precise in computing the total number of cycles without being able to produce a detailed accounting of where each cycle was spent.

The rest of this section is organized by *simulation technique*, which tends to be related to but is not exactly determined by simulation level. The first three techniques we discuss—interpretation, compiled simulation, and dynamic binary translation— most easily lend themselves to instruction-level simulation and can (with some effort) support cycle-level simulation. The fourth, HDL simulation, spans the range between cycle- and gate-level simulations. For each simulation technique, we describe how it works, how fast it works, and how easy it is to build and debug. We also discuss how accurately each type of simulation models the performance of the target machine.

6.4.1 Interpretation

As stated previously, interpreted simulation is the most flexible, straightforward, and slow simulation technique. When simulating, the host processor runs a program, the *interpreter*, with a simple main loop that mimics the execution of each target instruction at a time. This main loop is depicted in Figure 6.10. Interpreted simulation executes a loop iteration per target instruction, rather like microcoded implementations execute a microcode sequence per target instruction. The interpreter keeps data structures that represent the target's architectural state: registers and memory. In an interpreted simulator, both the code and data of the target processor are treated as data by the host processor. For each instruction, the interpreter reads the instruction from simulated program memory, decodes the instruction, and then executes the semantics that correspond to that instruction.

Interpreted simulators typically show slowdowns of 1000:1 or worse; that is, they execute thousands of host cycles per target instruction. This slowdown varies with the complexity of the target's instruction set. Instruction sets with regular encodings and simple semantics (e.g., RISC instruction sets) require fewer host instructions than more complex architectures. Interpreters are slow because every target instruction corresponds to a loop iteration on the host processor. Every target instruction traverses a *path* through the interpreter loop. The path changes with each iteration (instruction), and the average path loop will be long because each class of instruction in the ISA requires its own set of code in the loop. Furthermore, general-purpose host processors are not typically designed for the bit-oriented manipulations required to fetch and decode instructions.

Interpreters are easy to build, easy to debug, and easy to instrument. Everything is visible in the main loop of the interpreter program. Every piece of architectural state is available as a piece of interpreter program state. Explicit debugging and control facilities can be built into the interpreter program, or a host debugger program can manipulate the interpreter like any other debugged program. The easiest way to support debugging with an interpreted simulator is for the interpreter to support the same debugger interface as the target processor (e.g., the debugging interrupt or a PTRACE interface). Then the cross-platform debugger (running on the host, but connected to the "target") can be connected to the interpreter.

Interpreted simulation is most commonly used for instruction-level simulation on machines with sequential execution semantics. The sequential semantics naturally match the structure of the main interpreter loop, at which each instruction completes before the next one begins. Accurately simulating machines with exposed pipelines such as VLIWs require more complicated accounting, as the effects of long-latency operations must be recorded and applied at the proper time. This accounting is somewhat awkward because it applies across instructions (and thus across loop iterations), and thus the accounting routine must be "polled" at every instruction and must keep its own state separate from the architectural state.

Before continuing, we note that this description of interpreters is a sort of straw man; that is, there are many techniques for building efficient interpreters. Many of these techniques resemble those from compiled simulation, and thus we will return to efficient interpreters after discussing compiled simulation.

6.4.2 Compiled Simulation

General-purpose machines are not good at the bit manipulations associated with fetching, aligning, and decoding arbitrary instruction sets. However, they are very good at performing these same things for *their own* instruction sets. The basic idea behind compiled simulation is to translate from the binary code of the target machine to the binary code of the host machine. The translated program runs directly on the host machine, uses the fetch and decode units of the host machine, and avoids the usual interpretive overhead.

FIGURE 6.11 **How compiled simulation works.** This workflow diagram shows an embedded toolchain producing a "target program," which is translated by the compiled simulator to the "C program," which is compiled by the host's native C compiler into the "host program." We then run the host program on the actual data for the simulation.

For example, the compilers for general-purpose machines are good at translating from high-level programming languages (such as C) into general-purpose instruction sets. Thus, if we translate the target program into a C program we can use the host's C compiler to translate the C program into the ISA of the host processor. We then run the resulting program natively on the host processor. The compiled simulator of the VEX toolchain uses the two-step process of translating from target assembly code to C and then compiling C to host native code.

Compiled simulation (see Figure 6.11) gets its name from the fact that the simulator itself produces executable code that runs on the host machine, and it derives the same performance benefits over normal (interpreted) simulation that compilation derives over the interpretation of high-level languages.

The key to compiled simulation is the translation step from the target machine language back into C. Each target instruction will translate into some number of C language statements. The question is, how many? By carefully choosing how we translate architectural state back into C, we can simultaneously reduce the number of C statements and improve the likelihood that the host's C compiler will produce an efficient translation. For example, consider the following simple C code (add elements of an array).

```
int sumarray (int array[], int n)
{
    int i, t = 0;
    for (i = 0; i < n; ++i) {
        t += array[i];
    }
    return t;
}
```

This compiles into the following set of VEX instructions (7 instructions and 12 operations, individually labeled). Note that the compiler also needs to emit additional annotations for the VEX compiled simulator (VEX-CS), to instruct it about the calling convention (the .entry and .return directives in the example).

```
.entry caller, sp=$r0.1, r1=$r0.63, asize=0,
arg($r0.3:u32,$r0.4:s32)
sumarray::
        c0      sub $r0.4 = $r0.0, $r0.4 ## (1)
;;
        c0      mov $r0.2 = $r0.4 ## (2)
        c0      mov $r0.5 = $r0.0 ## (3)
```

```
        ;;
        L0?3:
                c0    cmplt $b0.0 = $r0.2, $r0.0 ## (4)
                c0    ldw.d $r0.4 = 0[$r0.3] ## (5)
                c0    add $r0.2 = $r0.2, 1 ## (6)
                c0    add $r0.3 = $r0.3, 4 ## (7)
        ;;
        ;;
                c0    brf $b0.0, L1?3 ## (8)
        ;;
                c0    add $r0.5 = $r0.4, $r0.5 ## (9)
                c0    goto L0?3 ## (10)
        ;;
        L1?3:
        .return ret($r0.3:s32)
                c0    return $r0.63 ## (11)
                c0    mov $r0.3 = $r0.5 ## (12)
        ;;
```

VEX-CS then converts the VEX assembly program to C, which is eventually compiled with the host C compiler and linked with the rest of the modules, libraries, and simulation helper routines. The following code is what VEX-CS produces.

```
int sumarray(unsigned int arg0, unsigned int arg1)
{
    unsigned int t_client_rpc = reg_r0_63;
    int t_labelnum;
    sim_check_stack(reg_r0_1, 0);
    reg_r0_3 = arg0;
    reg_r0_4 = arg1;
    reg_r0_63 = (103 << 5);

    reg_r0_4 = (0) -(reg_r0_4); /*(1)*/
    reg_r0_2 = reg_r0_4; /*(2)*/
    reg_r0_5 = 0; /*(3)*/
  l_L0X3:;
    reg_b0_0 = ((int) (reg_r0_2) < (int) (0)); /*(4)*/
    reg_r0_4 = ((int) (*((int *) reg_r0_3)))); /*(5)*/
    reg_r0_2 = (reg_r0_2) + ((unsigned int) 1); /*(6)*/
    reg_r0_3 = (reg_r0_3) + ((unsigned int) 4); /*(7)*/

    if (!reg_b0_0) goto l_L1X3; /*(8)*/
    reg_r0_5 = (reg_r0_4) + (reg_r0_5); /*(9)*/
    goto l_L0X3; /*(10)*/
```

```
l_L1X3:;
  reg_r0_3 = reg_r0_5; /*(12)*/
  t_labelnum = reg_r0_63; goto labelfinder; /*(11)*/

  reg_r0_63 = t_client_rpc;
  return reg_r0_3;
labelfinder:
  switch (t_labelnum >> 5) {
    case 103: reg_r0_63 = t_client_rpc; return reg_r0_3;
    default: sim_bad_label(t_labelnum);
  }
}
```

As we can see, this simple example shows almost a 1:1 correspondence between VEX operations and simple C statements. In addition to the operation code (easily identifiable by the same labels used in the VEX listing), compiled simulation also requires some initialization and helper code in each function. The initialization code checks (or initializes) the routine stack (sim_check_stack()) and sets up the return address pointer. The helper code (labelfinder) is responsible for implementing the table of indirect jumps, including the function *return*. Note that the example does not show any instrumentation code that gathers statistics (such as cycle count).

The rest of this section describes each piece of a compiled simulation in turn, starting with straightforward translations such as memory and registers and then moving to more complex issues of control flow and exception handling.

Memory

We start with *memory*. In a compiled simulation, the program memory from the target will be translated into a host program. However, it may still be necessary to keep the original target program around as data, especially if the toolchain generates programs that mix code and data, or worse yet treat code as data. The copy of the original program memory allows the original values to be read as data, even if the original program is not executed directly on the host. Compiled simulation techniques do not work on *self-modifying code*, as there is no support for handling instructions generated at run-time. However, more sophisticated dynamic binary translation systems can handle self-modifying code, because they are capable of detecting when the program jumps to untranslated code and have facilities for translating the new instructions.

For data memory, portions of host data memory can be mapped and used directly, similar to the way they were set up in our interpreter example. Depending on the memory configuration of the target processor, different pieces of memory may have to be set up to mimic ROM or Flash memory tables, initialized data memory, and the target processor stack. These tasks would be the job of the operating system's *loader* on the target processor (under a compiled simulator they happen during initialization of the translated program). During initialization (before the compiled simulation code begins to run), it is easy to read files in from disk that contain the desired values. Note that the compiled simulator stack and the target program stack both exist. The former is set up by the *host* machine loader, whereas the latter is set up by the initialization routines.

In the example above, we map the simulated address space into the host address space. Whenever this is possible, it increases performance, as it allows us to translate simulated memory accesses directly to host memory accesses without additional address computation. If this is not possible (for example, because we want to track simulated addresses precisely), we need to separate the two address spaces and then add one level of translation (in the simplest case, a linear offset computation).

Registers

Registers are perhaps the least intuitive aspect of compiled simulation. In an interpreter, the registers of a general-purpose machine are typically represented as an array, indexed by their register number. This makes for simple access once a register specifier is decoded. In a compiled simulator, representing the target registers with an array is usually a mistake. The reason is register allocation by the host's compiler. If it is possible, we want the host compiler to represent target registers using host registers. However, many register allocators work only on *scalar* (nonarray) variables. Thus, representing the target registers as an array will prevent them from being translated into host registers. Instead, it makes sense to give explicit scalar variable names to each register (e.g., gpr0, gpr1, and so on). Then the host's C compiler will assign the most frequently used "target registers" to host registers, yielding an efficient program.

A second register-related subtlety involves aggregate registers, which can be addressed at different granularities in the target ISA. For example, the pieces of the condition code register of many architectures are often handled this way, either addressed individually (e.g., branch based on a single condition code) or collectively (e.g., save or restore the entire flags register). A compiled simulator must choose whether to store the entire aggregate in a single C variable or to break it into multiple variables. The choice really depends on the common ways in which the aggregate is used. If the flags register is saved and restored rarely but the individual condition codes are used frequently it is better to have separate variables for each piece of the aggregate, whereby only the rare save/restore operations require multiple C statements. In this example, even though a single bit would suffice we dedicate an entire 32-bit integer for each branch register (such as $b0.1, which becomes `int reg_b0_1`).

Control Flow

The *program counter* also requires careful treatment in a compiled simulation. Straight-line code is simply translated. A sequence of target instructions maps to a corresponding sequence of C statements. Branches and function calls, however, are more complex. Because the compiled simulator has access only to the target machine code, higher-level control structures such as conditionals, loops, function calls, and returns are only implicitly represented. It might be possible to run a control-flow analysis to regenerate this information, but such an analysis might be expensive, and it might fail because compiler optimizations produced code with complex control flow. Fortunately, such an analysis is not necessary because C itself is permissive, and we are translating into a format a compiler, not a human, will read. Most control flow within a function can be represented using C *goto* statements and conditionals. This will lead to a translated program that is unreadable by humans but is entirely analyzable by the host's C compiler. We will return to computed *goto*s (or *switch* statements) in a moment.

Function calls might also be handled using *goto* statements, but this is undesirable for a number of reasons. First, this technique translates the entire program into one giant function, which might stress compiler resources. Second, it obscures the functions and the calling stack of the original program, hiding information useful to debugging the simulated program. Third, it is relatively easy to get the toolchain to generate debugging information that indicates function names and entry points. This information can be used by the compiled simulator to partition the target program into functions. Last, the host machine already has mechanisms that efficiently support function calls (e.g., a calling convention and instructions that support it, a stack, and hardware such as branch target buffers and return address stacks that make calls and returns efficient). For these reasons, we *do* recommend analyzing (or having the toolchain record) the functional structure of the target program and mapping it back into C functions. Note that the calling conventions of the host and target may differ. It may be easier to use the host calling convention or the (simulated) target calling convention in different circumstances.

Mapping the simulated calling convention to the host calling convention has the advantage that one may mix native and simulated code. For example, it enables having simulated code call host libraries. This is particularly useful when a simulated implementation of the library does not exist (either because it is not yet written or because we are in the process of developing the library). The application could use the GUI of the host (such as X windows) or the host networking layer from within the simulated environment. Without this functionality, we would need to implement the entire system in our own simulated world. The VEX system adopts exactly this strategy, as in the following simple call

```
int foo(int a, int b)
{
    return bar(b,a);
}
```

This call gets compiled as:

```
.entry caller sp=$r0.1, rl=$r0.63, asize=-32
            arg($r0.3:s32,$r0.4:s32)
foo::
   c0    add $r0.1 = $r0.1, (-0x20)
   c0    mov $r0.3 = $r0.4
   c0    mov $r0.2 = $r0.3
;;
```

```
.call bar, caller, arg($r0.3:s32,$r0.4:s32), ret($r0.3:s32)
  c0    call $r0.63 = bar
  c0    stw 0x10[$r0.1] = $r0.63
  c0    mov $r0.4 = $r0.2
;;
  c0    ldw $r0.63 = 0x10[$r0.1] ## restore ## t3
;;
;;
;;
.return ret($r0.3:s32)
  c0    add $r0.1 = $r0.1, (0x20)
  c0    return $r0.63
;;
```

Note that the compiler emits additional directives for the compiled simulator (.entry, .call, .return) to pass information about the calling convention, which is otherwise implicit in the register assignments. For example, when VEX-CS encounters a .call directive, it knows what registers are being passed, and it can then use the host C calling convention (so that the program also works when the callee is a host function). Similarly, at function entry it can copy the host-generated arguments into the VEX-designated register variables, so that the case of a host-function calling into simulated code is also covered. VEX-CS translates the previous example into the following routine.

```
unsigned int foo(unsigned int arg0, unsigned int arg1)
{
  reg_r0_3 = arg0;
  reg_r0_4 = arg1;
  reg_r0_63 = (103 << 5);

  { int t__i32_0 = reg_r0_3;
    reg_r0_1 = (reg_r0_1) + ((unsigned int) -32);
    reg_r0_3 = reg_r0_4;
    reg_r0_2 = t__i32_0; }

  (*((int *) (((reg_r0_1 + 16)))) = (reg_r0_63);
  reg_r0_4 = reg_r0_2;
  reg_r0_63 = (103 << 5);

  reg_r0_3 =
   (*((unsigned int (*) (unsigned int, unsigned int)) bar))
      (reg_r0_3, reg_r0_4);

l_1r_1::;
  reg_r0_63 = ((int) ((*((int *) (((reg_r0_1 + 16))))))));
```

```
reg_r0_1 = (reg_r0_1) + 32;
t_labelnum = reg_r0_63;
goto labelfinder;
reg_r0_63 = t_client_rpc;
return reg_r0_3;
labelfind7er:
switch (t_labelnum >> 5) {
  case 103: reg_r0_63 = t_client_rpc; return reg_r0_3;
  default: sim_bad_label(t_labelnum);
}
}
```

The last control-related issue we discuss is *computed gotos*, whereby the target program jumps to the address stored in a register. *Return* instructions from function calls are a special case of computed *goto* we have addressed previously. The other types of computed *gotos* typically arise from C *switch* statements or from function variables in the original program. Note that the term *computed goto* is something of a misnomer: the target address is not calculated by arithmetic operations; it is usually looked up from a table of values (in the case of a *switch* statement) or is one of a few possible valid function targets (in the case of a function variable). In both cases, it suffices for the compiled simulator to keep a *translation table* that maps from addresses in the original (target) assembly code to their corresponding locations in the compiled (host) C code. When a jump through a register occurs in the target program, the compiled simulator examines the jump operation to extract the target address, translates the target address, and jumps or calls to the appropriate point in the compiled program. A sophisticated compiled simulator might also try to reverse-engineer a C *switch* statement. This might be particularly easy if the embedded toolchain uses a particular style or emits special debugging information about *switch* statements.

Exceptions

Just as compiled simulators reuse host instructions to emulate target instructions, they can also use host exceptions to emulate target exceptions. We might also need to *suppress* host processor exceptions that would not occur on the target processor, and we might need to *simulate* exceptions that would occur on the target processor but are not raised on the host processor. In principle, there are just four cases: neither processor excepts, just the target excepts, just the host excepts, or both except. In practice, there are not exactly four cases, as the causes of various exceptions and the behavior in handling an exception will vary from host to target machine. The compiled simulator and its run-time support must ensure that normal and exceptional behavior on the target are simulated correctly as normal or exceptional behavior on the host. The case in which neither host nor target excepts is just normal processing using compiled simulation.

If the target processor raises an exception, the host processor must explicitly check for the circumstances that would cause the exception. For example, if the host did not raise division-by-zero exceptions while the target did, the translation of a target division instruction must include code that raises a *target-level* exception if the divisor is zero. A target-level exception might be handled by directly calling the exception-handling code in the compiled simulator. It may not be necessary (depending on various aspects of privileges and protection) to raise a corresponding host processor exception.

If only the host processor raises an exception, the interrupt-handling code in the host processor must be patched to suppress the exception. Many operating systems provide system calls that allow user programs to install exception handlers. The UNIX signal(2) system call, for example, allows users to specify on a per-exception basis to either suppress the exception, terminate the program, or invoke a user-defined callback function. The case in which both host and target processor raise the exception is similar, as a target exception should not cause the simulator to exit.

A particularly interesting problem is how to deal with speculative memory operations in compiled simulation. For example, VEX supports speculative loads that silently ignore exceptions, and VEX-CS maps the VEX address space into the host address space. This can cause problems if we do not have a way to communicate to the host that the memory operation is indeed speculative. VEX-CS deals with this issue by guarding speculative memory operations and ensuring that possible exceptions deriving from the execution are discarded. Depending on the host architecture and OS support, this operation can be rather time consuming.

Analysis of Compiled Simulation

Compiled simulators range from about one to 100 host instructions per target instruction. This wide variation depends on the differences between the host and target instruction sets. If the host and target architectures are similar, a target instruction will translate into only a few host instructions. If they differ greatly, multiple host instructions (or even loops of host instructions) per target instruction may be required. Mismatches in the exception-handling models also penalize the compiled simulator approach. Operating systems typically require hundreds of host cycles before returning control to the user trap handler or user program.

Compared to interpreters, compiled simulators eliminate a level of interpretation (the decoding loop that is the main loop of an interpreter). The host processor directly executes the compiled simulation program, removing the loop control and indirection associated with the interpreted loop. Another benefit is that the instruction footprint of the compiled simulated program uses the instruction resources of the host machine directly, whereas interpreters tend to be very small programs that do not take advantage of the caching and prefetching capabilities of modern instruction fetch systems. Eliminating this level of indirection is the largest factor contributing to the efficiency of compiled simulation over interpretation (it can account for a 5 to 20x speedup in simulation time).

Debugging is more complex on a compiled simulator. As with interpreters, there are two levels of debugging: debugging the target program and debugging the compiled simulation process itself. We can get some help from the C preprocessor: using preprocessor directives, we can alter the debugging information in the translated program, so that file and line references from the target program are mapped to their corresponding lines in the compiled simulation program. Program variables from the target may be missing or unnamed by the time they are translated back into C. This depends on the quality of the debugging information emitted by the toolchain and whether it is preserved by the compiled simulation process.

Debugging the compiled simulation process itself involves verification. Part of this can be very simple, as a suite of regression tests can isolate each instruction category and verify that the simulation continues to produce the expected results after the compiled simulator has been altered. However, it is difficult to come up with an exhaustive suite of regression tests *ab initio*. It often takes an actual benchmark program running on real data to expose cases that were not considered when the compiled simulator was built. Debugging the combination of compiled simulator and toolchain can be involved and complex. We don't have much advice to offer here.

Performance Measurement and Compiled Simulation

What we have described so far about compiled simulation applies largely to instruction-level simulations. For more detailed simulations, compiled simulation still retains much of its appeal. Compiled simulation works particularly well on targets with few or no dynamic implementation techniques, because the performance accounting code that is awkwardly located in an interpreter can be distributed and optimized across the translated code. For a statically scheduled architecture, the toolchain knows and can emit (annotate its output with) the expected number of cycles a block of instructions will take to complete. The compiled simulator can use this information while translating instructions into additional C code that updates performance measurement variables. Depending on the nature of the variable being measured, the C code might do as little as increment a variable (e.g., a cycle counter) to as much as invoke a general routine (e.g., to fire the cache simulator). The point is that the measurement code becomes part of the translated code, and thus it is subject to all of the same optimizations performed by the host's C compiler on the main translated program.

6.4.3 Dynamic Binary Translation

Before proceeding, we revisit the topic of efficient interpreters. Our earlier description of interpreters is something of a straw man. One can build better interpreters by blending aspects of the interpreted and compiled simulation approaches. Efficient interpreters typically have two pieces: a front end that translates from target code to an interpreter-specific intermediate representation (IR) and a back end that executes (or interprets) the IR. The IR is designed to strike a balance between ease of translation in the front end and ease of execution in the back end. One might view compiled simulation as an efficient interpretive approach in which the IR is the machine language of the host machine and the back end is the hardware of the host machine.

Examples of IR-based approaches abound. The most popular IRs are the Java Virtual Machine (JVM) bytecodes and Microsoft's .NET Intermediate Language (MSIL). Both interpreted and compiled execution environments exist for these platforms, with the compilation techniques gradually displacing the interpreted ones. Our biases for embedded simulation are toward compiled techniques (even the best interpreters still retain a level of indirection that hurts performance).

As we described previously, simple interpreters begin executing immediately but run slowly. Compiled approaches will run efficiently, but they require additional up-front time to compile or translate the target program. To try to get the best of both worlds, one can use dynamic (run-time) techniques to hide, delay, or amortize the costs associated with translation and compilation. These techniques use the same techniques as those used in compiled simulation, but they apply them using two optimizations, *lazy evaluation* and *caching*.

Laziness means not doing work until it is absolutely needed. In the case of dynamic translation, this work is the translation step, which might be expensive to perform over the entire program, especially if (as is common for many programs) only a fraction of the program is executed on each program run. Rather than translating the entire program, a dynamic binary translation system (see Figure 6.12) translates only a chunk of the program at a time. The size of the chunk varies, but it usually corresponds to a simply defined program unit (such as a procedure), a basic block, a trace of blocks, or a small group of blocks. Chunking allows the pay-as-you-go approach: the translator is only applied to chunks that are going to be executed.

After translation, the translated code is jumped to and executed. Eventually, the translated program will exit the current chunk. The translation system knows where the program should go next. It will either be a previously translated chunk or it will be code that has never been executed. By saving away the translated chunks in a cache, the dynamic translation system can make the former case very fast. It can direct the program to enter the already-translated code, and in most cases it can patch the exited chunk to directly call the next chunk. During the course of program execution, the cache will grow in size as more pieces of the program are translated, but this also means that

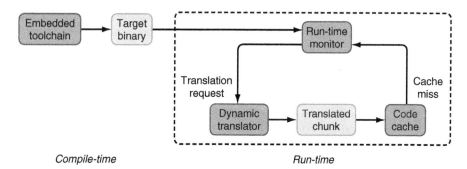

Compile-time   Run-time

FIGURE 6.12 Diagram of a dynamic binary translation system. Starting from an interpreted simulator, we can directly translate the most frequently executed fragments of simulated code into native code of the simulation host. Then, based on profile information, we can cache these fragments in a private *code cache* so that successive execution of the same fragments runs directly in the cache. This approach combines the advantages of an interpreter with the performance of compiled simulation.

more of the translated program can execute without needing to invoke the translator. For various reasons, it may be useful or necessary to occasionally remove chunks from the cache. A chunk that is removed becomes equivalent to code that has never been executed.

Dynamic translation systems are in many ways the best of both worlds: they can be as efficient in execution as compiled simulators but like interpreters have much lower up-front costs. Their major drawback is engineering. Building a dynamic translation system requires complex run-time and operating support, and is a significant software project in its own right. Recent simulation systems (such as *MaxCore* from AXYS, recently acquired by ARM) have started to use dynamic caching approaches to improve simulation speed. Beware, though, that these commercial products (often labeled "JIT-based simulators") could be misunderstood as dynamic binary translators, but in reality they adopt less aggressive techniques. In such simulators, no translation to native code takes place. Instead, the simulator keeps a cache of decoded target instruction information, avoiding the fetch and decoding steps but never actually translating into native code.

6.4.4 Trace-driven Simulation

One last basic set of techniques that has been used for simulation is through the use of *traces*.[4] A simulation trace is a *postmortem* dump of simulation information collected during a sample run of an existing system (or simulator). The idea behind trace-driven simulation is that we can use traces to replay the execution of the experiment with different assumptions about the system under simulation.

There are several advantages to trace-driven simulation. First, a trace-driven simulator does not have to precisely model the entire system. It can approximate some of the aspects it is not interested in measuring. This is because, unlike other simulators, a trace simulator fundamentally just collects statistics and does not have any effect on the execution itself (it already happened). In addition, the collection of traces is usually a simple operation, and it is easy to instrument existing simulators (or existing systems) to emit the information necessary to create meaningful traces. Finally, trace simulation is fast, and it is also possible to simulate multiple configurations with a single pass through a trace simply by maintaining an array of counters that gather the desired statistics.

On the other hand, trace-driven simulation has severe limitations that seriously constrain its applicability and accuracy. Traces are based on a previous execution of an existing system, and as such are tied to the configuration of the system used for the trace collection. If the system under simulation is very similar, chances are that the accuracy will be acceptable. For example, modeling variation in cache sizes (within reasonable limits) is an acceptable use of trace simulation. System variations that change basic assumptions are likely to produce very inaccurate results. For example, attempting to

---

4. The term *trace* means many different things. In this section only it refers to a log of program actions produced by a simulation. In the rest of the book, a trace is a linear (path-shaped) region for instruction scheduling.

model speculation from traces can be a prohibitive task, given that a trace only records the true execution path, and it is impossible to recover the complete control flow of the program to model misspeculated paths.

Despite its limitations, trace simulation is commonly used in many areas of processor and system simulation. Simulation of decoupled and (on first approximation) additive components to performance is generally acceptable. As we mentioned, cache simulation is a good example of an area in which traces can be very effective.

6.5 System Simulation

Complex multicore SoCs pose new challenges to the simulation environment and tools. In printed-circuit-board (PCB) designs, simulating the entire system is not a common activity, partly due to the fact that individual components are already verified, chip-to-chip interfaces are standard, and the cost of producing a test PCB is minimal. In SoC design, creating a fast and accurate virtual prototype of the design is fundamental. As we saw, interfaces offer many degrees of freedom, and the components themselves are often not verified in isolation. This means that we must use a virtual prototype to functionally verify the entire system. In addition, we can use the same virtual prototype to develop, test, and integrate the embedded software written for the SoC core(s).

What further complicates the simulation infrastructure is the fact that the models for the individual IP blocks of an SoC are usually available at different levels of abstraction. For example, it is common to use a high-level model of the processor cores — often the most complex part of the SoC — together with an RTL (presynthesis) or gate-level (postsynthesis) model of glue logic and other nonprogrammable blocks. Different parts of the design may have different clock regimes, which adds another level of complexity. This heterogeneous collection of models needs to be connected through a common simulation engine, which has to match the various abstraction levels. This is normally referred to as *co-simulation*.

RTL and gate models are usually described with *cycle-accurate* models, wherein the simulation state matches the state of the actual hardware at every clock cycle and it is possible to individually observe each state element of the model (i.e., registers).

On the other hand (as we saw in Sections 6.3 and 6.4), standalone models of processing cores usually reason in terms of instructions, without worrying about the cycle-by-cycle behavior within the boundary of each instruction. Integrating such a model within a system simulation environment is a tricky problem, and usually results in significant loss of accuracy as well as additional complexity, even for models that are very accurate in terms of cycle budget reporting (i.e., the total number of executed cycles).

What is more appealing from a perspective of system simulation is a so-called *cycle-callable* model, wherein the system simulator can invoke the instruction-set simulator of the core to execute up to a certain number of cycles (not instructions). This requires the core simulator to perform additional internal bookkeeping, but greatly simplifies the integration in a system simulator. Unfortunately, compiled simulation is largely incompatible with a cycle-callable model because the cycle accounting is only performed retroactively and it may be impossible for the simulator to correctly identify a consistent machine state at a given cycle.

In the rest of the section, we cover some of the aspects of system simulation: dealing with concurrent activities in a compiled simulator, simulating hardware descriptions, and accelerating simulation.

6.5.1 I/O and Concurrent Activities

Embedded systems typically perform I/O through DMA or memory-mapped I/O registers. DMA is a typical example of an *asynchronous concurrent activity* that happens while the processing core is executing instructions outside the processor's control. This type of event is complicated and is difficult to simulate with a compiled simulator, as the DMA engine operates separately and in parallel with the processor core. The closest way for a compiled simulation to simulate a DMA engine that transfers a chunk of data per cycle would be to use a co-routine approach in which every translated instruction contains a call to the DMA co-routine, which then returns control to the original compiled simulation routine. Unfortunately, this is not very efficient on modern processors. If the accuracy of the system or simulation permits, it can be much more efficient to "fudge" the timing of DMA operations in the compiled simulator and omit cycle-by-cycle DMA operations. For example, a simplification might make DMA operations appear to happen instantaneously when they are triggered. Depending on the way in which the processor core consumes the data, such a simplification may not at all affect the relevant timings.

Some ISAs include separate I/O instructions that access a different memory space from the main memory. Other approaches to memory-mapped I/O place I/O and memory in disjoint parts of the same address space. The first case is easy to handle in compiled simulation, as the I/O instructions are distinguished by their opcodes. The latter case requires slightly more sophistication. Memory-mapped I/O registers are typically placed at fixed memory locations during a program run. If the translator can statically determine which loads and stores access memory-mapped registers, it can use a different translation for the specific behavior of those locations. Another possibility requires operating system support and uses the memory protection hardware of the host processor. By protecting the pages on which memory-mapped I/O occurs, the simulator can force an exception on an access to I/O memory, which can then be handled differently from normal memory accesses in the exception handler. If the amount of I/O is small, the exception handler overhead can be amortized over the run-time of the simulation. Without some sort of address discrimination, all memory accesses in the compiled simulation slow down, as every translation requires a check to distinguish memory from I/O.

6.5.2 Hardware Simulation

Most of the simulation techniques we have described pertain to simulating instructions executing on a core without reference to the underlying hardware implementation. Those familiar with HDLs will recognize such simulations as *behavioral* simulation. In contrast, HDLs also allow one to specify precisely how the hardware will be physically organized and connected.

Controversy: In-house or Outsourced Simulators?

Many semiconductor (or IP) companies proposing new programmable components (processors or accelerators) are continually faced with the question of developing their own simulator versus adopting a commercially available platform and adding the support for the new processor to it.

Undoubtedly, the temptation to develop one's own simulator is strong. With one's own simulator, several experiments can be run quickly, we can avoid the learning curve of a new toolset, and we can build in-house expertise for simulation technology, which is often key to a successful design. In addition, the development of a functional instruction-level simulator is not a very time-consuming task (a few engineering months).

In the initial "architecture exploration" phase of a design this is clearly the right decision, given that a low degree of accuracy, moderate interoperability, and very limited support is required.

However, the situation changes drastically when the first products including the processor appear. The processor simulator needs to be used for a variety of tasks (verification, co-design, performance assessments, firmware development), by a variety of users (hardware developers, system architects, operating system integrators, the firmware team), and across companies. In addition, the simulator needs to be able to interact with a very diverse set of tools, including debuggers, device drivers, hardware simulators, hardware emulators, compilers, and software development platforms. Each of these comes from different vendors, requires accesses to different abstraction levels and often compatibility with several alternative tools.

At this stage, the availability of the processor model for a commercial toolset is very appealing. Commercial toolsets come (at a price) with customer support, industry-wide acceptance, and "wrappers" for a variety of other interacting tools. In a word, they leverage widespread adoption.

We believe that the situation for simulation tools for processor cores resembles that of CAD tools in the 1990s. It used to be that every semiconductor company had its own layout and simulation tools, and now they have virtually disappeared and have been replaced by a few tools that have been consolidated by very few players (most notably Cadence, Mentor Graphics, and Synopsys). We think that simulators for processor cores are now starting to follow a similar consolidation path, with the appearance of several offerings that combine good performance, seamless integration, and industry-standard toolsets.

In summary, building your own simulator initially is a good idea, as long as you don't get too attached to it and are willing to jump on a commercial offering when the time is right.

HDL simulation works at a variety of levels, depending on the detail with which components have been specified at the current stage of design. HDLs typically present a "block-and-wire" view of hardware, in which components are connected by wires (signals output by one component are input into the connected component). The inside of the block might be described functionally (that is, by a sequential piece of code that mimics the desired hardware but looks more like an imperative programming language such as C or Pascal), or it might be described in terms of finer-grain blocks, all the way down to the individual gate level. Test inputs can be attached by using special blocks that generate wire values based on files on the simulating machine (outputs can similarly be recorded by other types of special blocks).

HDL simulation performance varies from slow to excruciatingly slow, depending on the level of detail in the design being simulated. Because they simulate hardware components, they are another level of abstraction below ISA interpretation. And because hardware components operate independently and in parallel, the simulation may have to visit and simulate each component at each time step of the simulation (there are event-driven simulation design techniques that can help this to some extent, but the scale of the problem remains). HDL simulations require tens of thousands to millions of host cycles per target cycle.

On the other hand, HDL simulation is the only simulation that uses the same design information that will produce the eventual processor. Therefore, running test programs on an HDL helps immensely in validating designs. It is just too expensive to use for all levels of testing, and it is far too slow for use in software-related tasks, such as verifying the correctness of emitted code.

Discrete Event Simulation

Hardware simulation above transistor level is a form of *discrete event simulation* (DES), wherein the state of the system is representable through discrete-value variables whose values change over time. In its simplest form, the variables are the binary values (0 and 1) of the interconnection wire signals. Modern simulators adopt more than two values (e.g., X for unknown, Z for high impedance, H for weak high, L for weak low, and so on) but rely on the same principles.

There are two basic techniques we can adopt for DES: at each point in time, we can loop over each "component" of the system and record its change (*state-driven simulation*) or we can loop over each "transition" of the values and propagate them across the system (*event-driven simulation*). As a historical reference, the YSE (Yorktown Simulation Engine, a special-purpose, highly parallel programmable machine for the gate-level simulation of logic built in the 1980s) could be considered the "grandfather" of state-driven simulation engines.

Intuitively, if the average ratio between the number of transitions and the number of components (*activity level*) is low, the performance of an event-driven simulator should be better. Indeed, activity levels for real-world circuits are very low, with typical values about or below 0.1% (an activity level above 1% is considered high). This explains why the large majority of commercial HDL simulators use some form of event-driven simulation. Handling the propagation of events is not free, and it requires the simulation to maintain a dependence list between components, as well as a timestamping mechanism (normally called *time-wheel*), which is intrinsically sequential in its simple implementation.

Given the large impact on productivity of simulation system performance, a large body of research has attacked the problem of *parallel and distributed simulation* in the last 20 years. Techniques for *parallel DES* (PDES) exploit parallelism by distributing the processes and the event queue over different processors with one of two strategies.

1. *Centralized time* (*synchronous* or *conservative*) algorithms execute events in parallel only if they have the same timestamp. Parallel executions must resynchronize before any event with a greater timestamp can be processed. This limits parallelism to noncausal changes and requires the generation of *null* events to signal when time can be safely advanced.

2. *Distributed time* (*asynchronous* or *optimistic*) algorithms execute events in parallel regardless of their timestamps. Parallel executions can proceed with their own local time, but they must guarantee the correctness of the simulation results. This is normally accomplished through a checkpoint-based rollback mechanism (*time warp)* to recover from out-of-order event evaluations. When the system detects a timestamp violation, it *rolls back* to a previously saved state and reexecutes events in the right order.

Although optimistic techniques theoretically outperform conservative approaches, a major drawback of using time warp is the need to keep a very long history of the states of each process. The only way around this is by performing global checkpointing and garbage collection at regular intervals, which adds significant overhead to the simulation, thus reducing its advantage over the conservative approach.

6.5.3 Accelerating Simulation

As we discussed, the largest fraction of time in the development of an SoC product comes from verification and debugging of the hardware component. Consequently, one of the areas in which companies invest to reduce their time-to-market for new SoC-based products is acceleration of simulation.

For complex SoC designs, the fastest software simulators running on the fastest available workstation only reach a few thousands of cycles per second of simulation for a gate-level description of the component. At these speeds, the idea of co-simulating the software running on the core (or multiple cores) is prohibitive. It can take days to get through a handful of instructions that would not even cover the processor boot sequence. In other cases, it may be necessary to interface the simulator with the real world to use inputs from sensors in real time, in which case there are strict lower bounds to simulation performance to be useful at all.

Under these assumptions, the use of *hardware accelerators for simulation* may become cost effective. In the following two sections we briefly cover two of the most common approaches.

In-Circuit Emulation

One simulation option for microprocessor cores requires that the chip being designed already have an existing related chip and system. With an *in-circuit emulator* (ICE), the related chip stands in for the chip being designed, with an additional hardware harness that allows access to the pins between the chip and its system. The harness allows a separate control workstation to observe and manipulate all signals between the chip and the system. For example, the harness might allow the workstation to reset, probe, or single-step the chip, and it would allow the workstation to examine and change memory while the chip is paused.

In-circuit emulators are typically used for debugging hardware, providing a very fine degree of control over execution of the chip and the system. However, they can also be used to some extent for simulation. They can be extremely fast (as fast as the related chip, depending on the mismatches between the relative and the chip being designed), possibly allowing simulation at real or near real time. In-circuit emulation is commonly used to simulate the software running on a standard core when binary-compatible versions exist and are easily available.

Another very common use of emulation boards is in the development of system software. For example, most DSP vendors routinely ship hardware evaluation boards that allow direct control over the processor through the software environment through the use of dedicated interfaces. This is particularly useful for debugging applications in a real-time environment that cannot easily be replicated by a simulator. Hardware emulators also allow for the insertion of hardware breakpoints (and sometimes hardware-based data breakpoints), as well as step and run commands paired with a variety of tracing options.

Hardware Accelerators for Simulation

Hardware accelerators (such as the Mentor Graphics *Celaro* product line, *Aptix* boards, or *IKOS* systems) are special-purpose machines designed solely to accelerate gate-level simulation. These are high-end products (with list prices in the $1 to $5M range) that create a virtual model of the system (usually described as a gate-level netlist) and map it into a set of hardware components, typically implemented as a rack of reconfigurable logic boards. These approaches reach speeds in the million-cycle-per-second range, and allow the system to operate for seconds of *real* time to verify its correct behavior. Many of these systems also include interfaces so that in-circuit emulation boards for standard cores may be plugged in. Thus, developers can simultaneously debug the firmware running on the core, while the rest of the system is emulated by the accelerator (see Figure 6.13).

6.6   Validation and Verification

What makes a simulation good? We have described various goals of simulation, and we have outlined a number of techniques that trade off flexibility for efficiency in simulation design. However, we have so far avoided discussing simulation accuracy. Obviously, a simulator must be accurate to be useful, but accurate in which ways? Validation and verification techniques track how closely one design matches another.

According to IEEE's *Standard Glossary of Software Engineering Terminology*, *verification* is the process of evaluating a system or component to determine whether it

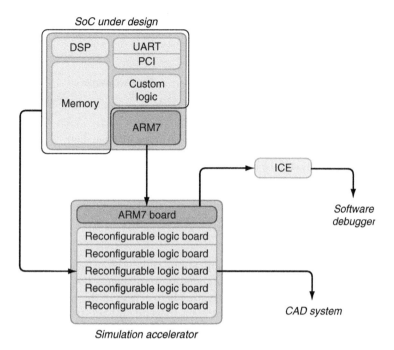

SoC under design

Simulation accelerator

FIGURE 6.13 Hardware accelerators for simulation. Complex SoC designs require the co-simulation of complex logic circuitry together with the firmware running on an embedded core. This often requires the use of hardware accelerators to reduce the time impact of verification and debugging. For standard cores, hardware accelerators also come with in-circuit emulation (ICE) capabilities, so that it is possible to run a software debugger together with the circuit simulator.

satisfies the conditions imposed before the design phase ("Did we build the system right?"). *Validation* is the process of evaluating a system or component to determine whether it satisfies specified requirements ("Did we build the right system?"). In the following, we largely deal with *verification*, which is where simulation helps the most, although the ideas behind many of the techniques we present could also be applied to system validation after the system has been built.

Verification parallels creation in the sense that a good methodology implies a verification step for each change of abstraction level in the design flow. Like design, verification is a multilevel activity, and ideally each level should be able to cross-verify with the abstraction level above it, to minimize specification mismatches and errors. Verification of complex blocks such as CPU cores may involve a lockstep simulation of multiple models that cross-verify equality of state changes at every common observability boundary. For example, we can run a functional model together with an RTL model and compare the state of the registers at every commit phase, so that it is easy to spot differences and narrow down the faulty parts of the design.

Let's (briefly) formalize what we mean by a "lockstep simulation that has been cross-verified." Suppose we have two simulations at different levels of detail. Call the less

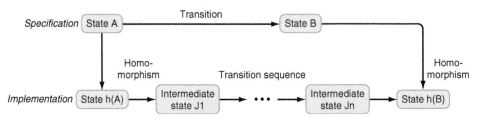

FIGURE 6.14   **The simulation homomorphism diagram.** Both "Specification" and "Implementation" are finite state machines, with well-defined states and transitions. Usually, the specification is the less detailed simulation, whereas the implementation is more detailed. To prove that an implementation is a valid implementation of the specification, one must show a mapping, h(), that takes states in the specification to states in the implementation such that every valid reachable transition in the specification corresponds to a valid (possibly empty) sequence of transitions in the implementation.

detailed simulation the "specification" and the more detailed simulation the "implementation." Formally, the implementation implements the specification if every reachable state in the specification corresponds to a state in the implementation, such that every transition in the specification maps to some number (possibly zero) of transitions in the implementation. The correspondence from specification states to implementation states is a mathematical homomorphism. This term captures precisely the notion of correspondence (of both states and transitions) that we want. Informally, we are simply saying that every valid execution sequence in the specification maps to a corresponding execution sequence in the implementation. Figure 6.14 illustrates the homomorphism relationship.

There are a few subtleties worth noting in our formal definition. The first is that we discuss only *reachable* states in the specification (and because of the homomorphism, in the implementation). It is possible for a model to have unreachable states, but we do not care about them because they will never be executed. The second subtlety is the "some number" of transitions in the implementation. If one specification transition mapped to exactly one implementation transition, we would have an isomorphism rather than a homomorphism, and there would be no room for the implementation to differ from the specification. By allowing a variable number of implementation transitions, we allow designers to apply different implementation techniques. More concretely, a "simple" operation in the specification (e.g., a store instruction) might actually be implemented by a more complex sequence of operations in the implementation. Last, "some number" leaves open the possibility that the implementation *does nothing* when mirroring the effects of a specification transition. For example, a speculative or prefetch instruction might be implemented as a *nop* in some implementations. This last case can be rare, but it must be included to allow flexibility.

6.6.1 Co-simulation

As we mentioned in Section 6.5, getting multiple simulators to cooperate and agree is one of the key challenges in SoC simulation. From the point of view of verification, a good

Flame: Who Sells What in the CAD Market?

There are relatively few product and company names in this section of the book. Those that do appear might be out of date by the time you see this, because CAD companies are continually buying, selling, and merging with each other. We don't have any control over this, but it does mean that it is difficult to guess which companies, products, and names are likely to be around in the future. Please see the book web site for our best guess at the current state of affairs.

co-simulation methodology is one of the key factors for the overall verification strategy. Verification of a core-based SoC implies co-verification of the embedded firmware and the logic blocks. This mandates fast firmware simulation (with interactions at the bus level) and RTL (or gate-level) simulation of individual IP blocks.

The problem is tough, in that the observability boundaries of the different subsystems are difficult to match while preserving acceptable simulation speeds. Most major CAD players have tools that target this domain (e.g., *CoWare*, *COSSAP*, *SystemC*, and so on). On paper, these enable the mixing of RTL simulation with functional (or *cycle-callable*) models of the processing core.

6.6.2 Simulation, Verification, and Test

The verification of a complex SoC is one of the the most critical activities for success, and it is what usually differentiates a good system-design methodology. Despite the massive verification efforts, more than 50% of today's SoC designs require at least a silicon respin, and about 75% of these respins still exhibit functional errors. Considering the cost of a silicon respin (above $1M), this means that there is a lot of room for improvement of verification tools and strategies.

Verification relies heavily on the availability of several simulation tools that target the different abstraction levels in the system description. Verification spans the software/hardware boundary, and requires the bridging of tools that belong to separate worlds. These tools include compilers, functional simulators, and RTL simulators. Cross-validation of various simulators at different abstraction levels relies on the concept of a "*golden model*," which is a fully verified model of the system under design. For example, the design of an SoC core usually starts from a high-level (functional) model, typically written in C or C++, that developers can use to start writing applications and tools until some form of hardware is available. As the design of the RTL implementation of the core progresses, the functional model is used to verify the correctness of RTL design. An efficient way of doing this is by running the two simulations side by side and checking equivalence of the architecturally visible state at every common observable boundary. Note that different abstraction levels imply different observability constraints. For example, a functional description is usually tied to the commit stage of an instruction (that is, when registers or memory are written), whereas an RTL description could observe transient values that traverse the processor pipeline stages. Matching these two simulations involves running the two simulators in parallel and comparing the values of the registers after each instruction commits. Cross-validation of multiple models at different levels is a time-consuming and quite complex task, and thus it is also important to minimize the number of models. Although even cross-validation leaves room for errors, it is an invaluable help to quickly and precisely identify trouble spots in the RTL design.

Formal Verification

Other techniques, generally grouped under the umbrella of "formal verification," complement simulation. Formal verification does not replace or remove the need for simulation, which is indeed a necessary step in any hardware design. The major advantage of formal verification techniques is that they do not depend on a specific set of input *stimuli*, and as such are very good at catching corner cases that would be difficult to exercise. The major disadvantage is that they require a formulation step that may introduce mismatches with the system under design. In addition, their combinatorial nature stretches the computing requirements when applied to large and complex systems.

One of the areas in which formal verification has become a standard in chip design is *equivalence checking*, which includes the set of tools whose goal is to verify that two representations of the design (such as RTL and gate-level) indeed implement the same behavior. This is extremely useful in detecting synthesis problems, or errors in one of the many transformation phases that take place between a validated RTL design and the final layout. *Logical equivalence checkers* ensure that the RTL and the gate (or transistor) designs are logically equivalent (that is, they implement the same Boolean function). *Functional equivalence checkers* also attempt to eliminate structural and semantic inconsistencies in the RTL reference design (such as unconnected inputs or mismatches in bus widths).

Design for Testability

Whereas verification techniques aim at increasing the confidence that what we are building really is what we want to build, the goal of *design for testability* (DFT) methods is to improve our chances of finding defective parts after manufacturing.

The cost of testing is an important component in the overall cost of a chip, and is usually proportional to the time it takes to generate a set of test vectors that guarantees an acceptable fault coverage. Hence, making an SoC more easily testable decreases the cost of testing it. In addition to ad hoc techniques, two major approaches are commonly used in complex chip design: scan-chain insertion and built-in self-test circuitry.

Scan-chain insertion is a technique that connects all flip-flops of an integrated circuit in a "virtual" shift register that can be scanned in and out of the component through some dedicated pins. In this way, we can scan in and out all flip-flop values before and after each test vector and thus achieve full observability and controllability of the entire state of the chip. Implementing full scan is expensive, in that every flip-flop must include additional circuitry to implement the scan chain. However, it greatly simplifies the problem, in that we only need to test the combinatorial logic functions of the circuit and can successfully apply *automatic test pattern generation* (ATPG) tools to the problem.

Boundary-scan insertion techniques address the issue of checking for the correct connection of a chip on a board, which is becoming very important as modern packaging (such as *ball-grid arrays*) reduces the physical access to the components of a board. Like the other scan-chain techniques, boundary scan connects all pins of a chip in a shift register that can be shifted in and out during the test phase. IEEE 1149.1 (JTAG) is the most widely adopted standard for handling boundary scans.

Finally, *built-in self-test* (BIST) circuitry is used to test regular full-custom layout structures, such as memory blocks and register files. The concept behind BIST is that it is sometimes simpler to provide an on-circuit exerciser than to make the block observable from the outside. For example, the BIST component of a block of embedded memory usually includes a pseudorandom number generator, an address generator, and a signature checker to verify memory read and write operations. For some types of embedded memories in an SoC, we can also use the attached processor core to perform the memory testing.

Debugging Support for SoC

Traditional software debugging systems quickly hit their limit when faced with the new challenges of multicore SoC designs. The basic problem a debugger faces in this environment is the difficulty in accessing interprocessor communication channels from the outside world. When the design includes heterogeneous cores with different instruction sets (such as a combination RISC + DSP), the debug environment has to be extended to cope with the fact that two programs (most likely compiled with different toolsets) are running simultaneously on the two processors.

In practice, the only viable approach so far is to consider only one programmable part of the design at a time, and assume that the rest of the design is stable and correct. Modeling the complex interactions between the DSP algorithms (usually running under tight real-time constraints) and the microprocessor core is beyond the capabilities of today's debugging systems. For example, we can think of debugging the DSP code (usually smaller) in isolation, or on a simulator, and then attack the problem of debugging the microcontroller firmware under the assumption that the DSP behaves correctly. This strategy only partially relieves the debugger of the need to be aware of the rest of the system (the DSP still needs to be initialized, controlled, and paused whenever necessary).

From the point of view of hardware requirements, the first mandatory step is to enable communication and control to individual cores through a common interface. In addition, it is good practice to ensure that components can be tested *in isolation*; that is, independently from the rest of the system. Independence of the individual components is particularly critical in master/slave configurations, in which the slave still needs to have enough hooks to be able to run regardless of the master's state.

Normally, the same JTAG interface used for boundary scan can also be used to provide basic debugger functionality to an external cross-debugger (running on a workstation host but controlling an embedded target). To do this, each SoC core must include a debugging module that connects to the JTAG interface and enables basic observation tasks (*peek* and *poke* memory and registers), and also gives access to the core debugging functionality (such as hardware breakpoints or watches). Sometimes we can also use the JTAG interface to simulate parts of the system that are not available in the embedded target. Common examples of this include the file system, terminals, and displays. In some cases, we may also need to simulate more complex components (e.g., an antenna) in order to debug other parts of the system.

Finally, one of the most complex interactions designers have to deal with is between the debugger and the real-time operating system. If we take a deeper look at how a debugger works, we can see that some of its functionality (e.g., taking control of interrupts) overlaps and interferes with the operating system. Ideally, the debugger would like to gain control of the low-level software interfaces of the system, but this could be problematic in the presence of real-time constraints and multiple cores. For this reason, most debugging platforms are closely tied to a specific combination of processor, DSP, and operating system.

6.7   Further Reading

The area of system-level embedded design includes a wide variety of disciplines, so it is not easy to come up with a comprehensive list of reading material that can be considered representative of the domain. But we can point interested readers at a lot of useful literature on some of the topics of greatest interest.

On the subject of design reuse in SoC designs and the entire SoC "revolution," we suggest the book by Chang, Cooke, Hunt, Martin, McNelly, and Todd [1999] and its follow-up by Martin and Chang [2003]. A Cadence, Inc. whitepaper by Todd and McNelly [2001] provides some lighter reading on the same subject, and we also recommend the article by Cordan [2001] and the Virtual Component Interface Standard by VSI [2000] to readers interested in more detail on VSI standards (see also *http://www.vsi.org*). Finally, the book by Wolfe [2002] and the SystemC book by Müller, Rosenstiel, and Ruf [2003] provide excellent coverage of design methodologies and system-level programming languages.

The best approach to the understanding of SoC buses is, in our opinion, reading the technical documentation of some of the most widely adopted standards. For example, the IBM CoreConnect Bus Architecture can be found at *http://www.chips. ibm.com/products/coreconnect* and the paper by Aldworth [1999] contains a good overview of the AMBA bus. For a comparison of a handful of SoC buses, we also recommend the paper by Ryu, Shin, and Mooney [2001]. For more advanced topics, such as user-configurable logic in SoC buses, we recommend Winegarden's [2000] paper.

As we have mentioned, some of the hardest problems in SoC design come from the difficulty of testing them. Some references on design-for-testability for SoC designs include the papers by Aerts and Mariniseen [1998]; Jas and Touba [1998]; and Jas, Pouya, and Touba [2000]. For a general reference on validation and verification techniques, we also recommend the IEEE Glossary of Software Engineering Terminology by IEEE [1990] as well as the description of the validation/verification techniques used by NASA in the paper by Rosenberg [2001]. Finally, the book by Rashinkar, Paterson, and Singh [2000] contains a good overview of many of the SoC verification techniques.

Modern SoC designs include multiple processing cores. On multicore chips, we recommend the paper by Cesario, Baghdadi et al. [2002] on component-based SoC design, and the paper by Walls and Williams [2002] on multicore debugging. Concerning industrial examples of RISC + DSP multicore designs, the paper by Chaouni, Cyr, Giacalone et al. [2000] introduces the TI OMAP (ARM+TMS320C54 DSP) architecture. Abundant information on the Intel PCA (Xscale + MSA DSP) family can be found at the PCA (Intel Personal Internet Client Architecture) developers' web site at *http://www.intel.com/pca.*

On programmable/nonprogrammable accelerators and customized architecture (which we also cover in Chapter 10), the custom-fit processors paper by Fisher, Faraboschi, and Desoli [1996] is a good place to start, together with the follow-up paper by Faraboschi, Brown, Fisher, Desoli, and Homewood [2000] showing the application of the earlier research ideas to a real-world VLIW processor core. The work by Schreiber, Aditya, Rau, Kathail et al. [2000] is an excellent example of high-level synthesis techniques for nonprogrammable customized accelerators.

The combination of processors and reconfigurable logic has been an active subject of research since the early 1990s. Some of the early projects discussing a joint CPU and FPGA system targeting a single computational task are the PRISM and GARP projects at UCB, described in the papers by Athanas and Silverman [1993] and Hauser and Wawrzynek [1997], respectively. Other recommended readings on the subject of mixed microprocessors and hardware-programmable functional units include the paper by Razdan and Smith [1994] on PRISC, Wittig and Chow [1996], the PhD thesis of DeHon [1996], and the book by Brown, Francis, Rose et al. [1992].

Simulation of embedded systems and processors is another area where the massive amount of literature makes it very difficult to distill a short list of recommended readings. A very useful web site that includes a large body of information on simulation for computer architecture is *http://www.xsim.com.* A slightly dated, but excellent, collection of papers is in the book "Fast Simulation of Computer Architectures" by Conte and Gimare [1995]. However, in order to really understand the fundamentals of simulation, our recommendation is to start from the foundations of discrete-event simulation, for which the seminal works of Chandy and Misra [1979], Jefferson and Sowizral [1982], Jefferson [1985], and Fujimoto [1990] are the places to start. A very educational early example of simulation acceleration is the YSE (Yorktown Simulation Engine), covered in the paper by Pfister [1982], and we also recommend the paper by May [1987]. A description of more "modern" commercial simulators (such as Virutech Simics) can be found in the papers by Magnusson [1997] and Magnusson, Christensson et al. [2002]. One of the most commonly used toolsets for academic simulation is SimpleScalar, described in the paper by Burger and Austin [1997] and for which ample documentation can be found at *http://www.simplescalar.com.*

Trace collection and trace-driven simulation have been widely used for as long as people have studied computer architecture. The paper by Sites and Agarwal [1998] is a good introduction to the concept of traces for the cache analysis, and the work by

Smith [1991] extends it to instruction tracing (via the *pixie* tool set). A tool similar to *pixie* that was widely adopted by the research community is ATOM, described in the work by Srivastava and Eustace [1994]. Validation of trace-driven simulation is the subject of the work by Goldsmith and Hennessy [1993], and more advanced techniques for program tracing are covered in the work of Larus [1993].

The acceleration of simulation has also been a continuous thread in the research community. Examples of using the technique of compiled simulation can be found in the papers by Zivojinovic et al. [1995]; Maurer and Wang [1990]; Reshadi, Misra, and Dutt [2003]; and Nohl, Braun, et al. [2002]. The idea of using dynamic translation, caching, and optimization to accelerate simulation is covered in Bala, Duesterwald, and Banerjia [2000]; Wang [2002]; and Almasi [2001].

6.8 Exercises

1. Draw a diagram of how to connect a narrower SoC bus (32-bit) to a wider component (64-bit). Describe the steps that happen during a simple read and write transaction.

2. Can an SoC bus support pipelined transactions that originate from the same master? If it can, under which conditions? If it cannot, find a sequence of transactions that causes the system to behave incorrectly.

3. Starting from a set of collected instruction and data memory traces of a VEX execution of a benchmark (see Appendix A for instructions), write a cache-miss trace simulator that models an SoC configuration in which instruction and data caches act as separate bus masters for the SoC bus. Compute bus utilization and performance degradation for typical memory parameters. Compare the effectiveness of single burst-and-split transactions. Evaluate the effectiveness of various arbitration policies (higher I-cache priority, higher D-cache priority, first-come-first-served).

4. Write a specification for an SoC that includes an ARM7TDMI processor core, 8 MB of SRAM, a DMA controller, and a UART. Specify both a processor bus that supports split transactions and a peripheral bus. Describe the set of transactions supported by each bus.

5. Compare and contrast the state of the art in verification for hardware and software components. In which ways are software methods more advanced (e.g., type systems)? In which ways are hardware methods more advanced?

6. Using whatever resources seem appropriate, find two IP providers that offer comparable components (e.g., a PCI bridge or a UART, or an IEEE 1394-FireWire bridge). Compare and contrast the offerings in terms of their functionality, their interfaces to the rest of the SoC, the technologies in which

they can be implemented without major redesign, and the level of support provided by the vendor.

7. Describe how split transactions on IBM CoreConnect differ in structure, timing, and capability from the split transactions supported by AMBA.

8. Using whatever resources seem appropriate, collect technical material on both the Intel PCA and the TI OMAP platforms. Compile a competitive analysis table that compares the characteristics of the general-purpose cores, the DSP cores, the hardware acceleration capabilities (if any), the estimated prices (if available), the target application markets, and the programming models.

9. Add statistics-gathering code to the VEX-CS code of Section 6.4.2 to count cycles, operations, instructions, and taken and not-taken branches. Under which assumptions is the cycle count different from the instruction count?

10. The VEX-CS code of Section 6.4.2 shows a call to sim_check_stack() in the initialization part of the translated code, which is part of the VEX-CS stack-handling mechanism. Describe the rest of the stack-handling mechanism a compiled simulator needs to implement for the most common functions. What additional steps are required in the *main()* (primary entry point) of a VEX program?

11. The VEX-CS code of Section 6.4.2 makes the assumption that simulated memory coincides with host memory. Rewrite the code example assuming that simulated memory is mapped into a separate array. Under this assumption, is it still possible to call host functions from a piece of simulated VEX code? What are the restrictions on the type of arguments that can be passed?

12. Write a probe routine that checks the validity of a memory location for a read access (hint: consider user-installed trap handlers and the *setjmp/longjmp* low-level interface). How would you use this in implementing a compiled simulator that supports speculative data accesses?

13. Using the VEX system, compile an integer matrix multiplication routine and run it for various matrix sizes (e.g., 10 x 10, 50 x 50, 100 x 100). Compute the performance of the VEX-CS simulator (in millions of VEX operations per second) and compare the cases in which (1) no instrumentation is present, (2) we count cycles only [−mas_tb], (3) we collect full cache statistics [−mas_t]. For case 1, using the cycle speed of your host machine, roughly how many host cycles are necessary to simulate a VEX operation? For case 3, is there a correlation between simulator performance and data cache misses of the simulated system? Explain your answer.

14. Using the VEX system and the VEX simulator API, write a plug-in that replaces the built-in cache simulator with your own two-level cache simulator. Choose an application of interest and compare the performance of various cache configurations by varying size and associativity of L1 and L2 caches.

15. Using the VEX system, write your own simulation code to model a very simple memory-mapped graphical display driver that supports plotting of dots to the host screen. Test the system by writing VEX code that draws a square, a triangle, and a circle. (Hint: you need to use the simulator API to check memory accesses that detect whether VEX is attempting to write in the memory-mapped device space.)

7

Embedded Compiling and Toolchains

A worker may be the hammer's master, but the hammer still prevails. A tool knows exactly how it is meant to be handled, while the user of the tool can only have an approximate idea.

— Milan Kundera, *Czech writer*, 1929–

This chapter is about the embedded toolchain, specifically the parts that concern the production and testing of code. In an ILP system, any discussion of code construction must necessarily focus on compilation, in that compiling for ILP is very difficult and many of the necessary technologies are still the subjects of intense research. The most advanced specifics of compiling for ILP are presented in Chapter 8.

Advanced ILP compiling is just one part of a development system. After a short discussion of our views on compilers in this environment, this chapter begins with an overview of an embedded cross-development toolchain, including supporting tools such as profilers, linkers, postlink optimizers, and simulators. Then we describe the parts of an ILP-optimizing compiler. Understanding what the toolchain can and cannot do is necessary in order to set realistic expectations and goals about what part of the system will be responsible for each aspect of power, performance, and cost in the end product. We then cover the critical and often-overlooked topic of code layout. Compiling for DSPs and embedded-specific compiler optimizations is the subject of the last two sections of this chapter.

7.1 What Is Important in an ILP Compiler?

Most computer science compiler courses march through a standard curriculum, based on the canonical "Dragon Book" [Aho, Sethi, and Ullman, 1986], which describes the huge improvements in *front-end* compilation that took place during the 1970s. Such courses typically begin with lexical analysis, graduate to parsing and the marvelous variants of LALR(1), continue with type checking and expression trees, and then make short shrift (the last assignment, if any) of code generation and optimization. In short, such courses document solved problems (granted, they were elegantly and beautifully solved). Front-end experts do not even call themselves compiler researchers anymore; they have moved on to become language designers and type theorists.

From our point of view, the syllabus should be reversed. Code generation and optimization are for us the interesting parts of the compiler, where active research still takes place. Techniques such as these are crucial to exploiting ILP, and they are documented in only a few places. In fact, we take this view so seriously that when we teach compiler courses we give students the entire compiler up to the back end. Once they implement their own back ends, we work our way toward the front, letting them implement modules to replace those we have withdrawn. That way, if we run out of time we know that the students will have had experience with the novel parts of the compiler, rather than the parts that implement what is already well understood. We are encouraged that new back-end-oriented compiler textbooks are currently under development.

The compiler, by which we mean the back end of the compiler, is possibly the largest investment of engineering effort in a VLIW system. In ILP systems, the compiler has primary responsibility for finding and organizing parallelism, and parallelism is the key to performance, price/performance, power, and cost. Finding the right tradeoffs among these is an art, and the algorithms for analysis and transformation of programs are complicated and difficult to implement correctly. The typical investment for a compiler back end before maturity is measured in man-decades, and it is common to find compiler platforms with man-century investments. The lifetime of a good compiler platform is typically in the 10-year (and above) range.

Good compilers are "built to last," like a bridge. Solid engineering infrastructure is paramount to the success of the compiler. Front ends may be solved problems, but all language-specific processors must target a common intermediate representation. Intermediate representations (IRs) form an academic and engineering battleground. An IR fundamentally limits the lifetime of a compiler in the same way addressing bits limit the lifetime of an ISA: at some point the entire structure must be abandoned. Every compiler also targets a machine or class of machines. However, there are tradeoffs here, too. A compiler specifically tuned for a single machine can be difficult to adapt even to related machines, whereas a one-design-fits-all compiler (e.g., *gcc*) cannot possibly optimize well for all platforms. Finally, compilers are large programs. Over their lifetime, they become inflexible and difficult to modify, and they accumulate warts and scars that are frustrating to work around. Almost every component will be rewritten from scratch over the lifetime of the compiler, and more than just components may have to be replaced to accommodate new features.

People tend to underestimate the complexity of building a *robust* and *aggressive* ILP compiler. It is easy to find compilers that have one of these two properties but very difficult to find something that has both. Compiler speed and host requirements (largely memory) cannot be ignored. Many of the existing VLIW embedded tools (including those offered with the most popular DSPs) have very high requirements, often unacceptable.

Controversy: Start with an Existing ILP-Oriented Compiler?

When it launches, any ILP architecture project must decide between using (typically buying) an existing compiler or rolling its own. The temptation to do the latter is strong. Existing compilers always have drawbacks, whereas the homegrown compiler will be designed with the project's goals and needs in mind. We hope that our discussion (in this sidebar and in the main text) of the cost of building and maintaining compilers will make you think twice about this.

There are many types of risk in embedded development: hardware development risk, software development risk, and time-to-market risk. Hardware risk involves getting the chips right: Do they function correctly, and at the right speed? Hardware designers build debugging revisions into the schedule. (We have already discussed software development risks.) Another consideration is customer perceptions of software stability. If your product's success depends on your customers using your development tools, the customers must believe that the tools are stable and effective. Time-to-market risk involves more than keeping to schedules; it incorporates the lost sales and weaker relative performance from delays in shipping products. A few months can make a huge difference in the microprocessor business, and consumer electronics are similarly cutthroat. Last, solving open research problems is *not* the job of a development group. It seems unwise to add research risk to all of the above.

Compiler technology lags behind hardware. The unfortunate truth is that the compilers for a particular chip are best just before the chip is retired. For example, Microsoft's optimizing compilers produce excellent code for the previous-generation x86 microarchitectures (which includes Pentium Pro, II, and III chips; Pentium Xeons; and Celerons), but support for the new microarchitecture of the Pentium 4 is weaker.

When using a superscalar design, there is a temptation to ignore the compiler effort. Early versions of superscalar designs rely on hardware for speed gains and may already have an installed base that generates sales. Superscalar compilers contribute more later in the life cycle of the product. This may contribute to the short shrift that compilation has historically received from the superscalar community. By contrast, VLIWs cannot rely on backward compatibility for sales. VLIW performance depends from day one on harmonious collaboration among hardware, process, and compilers. VLIW compilers cannot be ignored during the design stage.

From the viewpoint of developers, one has to remember that it takes a while to mature a compiler and toolchain. Consequently, we need to make sure that, by the time a new architecture enters the market, its tools are perceived to be risk-free by the developers' community. This requirement becomes stronger as embedded systems are increasingly programmed in high-level languages. The "legacy" problem is not at the binary compatibility level. It shifts up to the tool level. This is usually underestimated.

Controversy: "Compiling" for a DSP

Although compiling for modern general-purpose architectures is difficult, compiling for most DSPs is even more difficult. DSP instruction sets have evolved over time, but they have many nonstandard features compared to general-purpose machines. These features are intended for specific applications and can be used by hand coders to extract performance. However, such features have seldom been designed with compilation in mind. No algorithms exist to generate such code automatically, and the features rarely match anything that is efficiently described in a high-level language. Further, even if algorithms did exist they would be difficult to integrate into existing compiler infrastructure. Furthermore, such code-generation techniques are not currently seen as research. It is difficult to publish papers at mainstream compiler conferences about code-generation techniques for DSPs.

DSPs, although superficially similar to general-purpose processors, often lack many of the features that allow a compiler to improve performance on general-purpose machines. Register sets are small, registers often have dedicated uses, and the transfer network between registers may be incomplete or require using functional units. All of these complicate register allocation. DSP instruction sets seldom allow for ILP. Those instructions that specify parallelism, such as multiply-accumulates, typically encode for only a limited subset of possible sources and destinations. Such limited parallelism possibilities hamstring the instruction scheduler.

The net result is that DSP compilers often generate correct but terrible code. This is very similar to the situation in the 1970's ILP community described in Chapter 2: hand coders can often produce much better code than compilers. However, the ILP community has developed many new compilation techniques during the intervening three decades.

Finally, it is common to find robust scalar compilers (even the open-source *gcc* is a good example), but adding the structure necessary to expose high ILP is very difficult, and often impossible. There are two good principles that summarize this situation, neither of which is well understood in the business planning of many processor/compiler roadmaps.

1. Don't build an architecture based on a compiler technology/optimization that doesn't exist yet.

2. The compiling technology you have on the day you start to design the ISA is the compiling technology you will have for the first several years of shipping the product.

7.2 Embedded Cross-Development Toolchains

This section describes the various tools that constitute an embedded cross-development toolchain. By *embedded* we mean a toolchain that targets an embedded device. *Cross-development* indicates that the system on which development occurs is different from the target embedded device. Cross-development allows developers to use familiar operating systems, user interfaces, and storage. Many embedded devices are not designed for compilation (after all, they are specialized). Even if capable of compilation, they are unlikely to have interfaces that lend themselves to design.

Toolchains (see Figure 7.1) come in two major styles: *toolkits* and *integrated development environments* (IDEs). These two styles roughly correspond to the workstation and PC marketplaces from which they originated. Workstations are often based on the UNIX operating system, where the infrastructure encourages multiple small tools with orthogonal capabilities. In UNIX-style toolkits, each tool is learnable and usable independently. Users must also master a shell that allows tools to be chained, combined, or composed. IDEs are more familiar to personal computer users. As their name implies, IDEs are giant applications wherein all tools live under a single graphical user interface (GUI). As in Windows applications, all tools are available by browsing menus or finding the correct path of button clicks through hierarchical dialog boxes.

Whether one prefers a toolkit or IDE-based approach is largely a matter of religion, with a few important caveats. IDEs tend to have easier learning curves because of their friendly GUI-based interfaces. Toolkits are sometimes preferred by experts because they allow scripting, which allows higher levels of automation. Toolkits also allow external or homegrown tools to be integrated more readily. IDEs are much more difficult to expand, but IDEs for popular environments sometimes have capabilities that would be difficult to contemplate in a toolkit. This is because of the level of investment that can be put into them by their developers. For example, the Microsoft Visual C++ IDE tightly integrates its editor with the compiler's front end, giving it access to information that could be difficult to extract from the compiler for use in a homegrown tool.

The rest of this section explores common pieces of an embedded toolchain, briefly describing each.

7.2.1 Compiler

The compiler translates from *high-level* (i.e., not assembly) languages into binary code and data. The current high-level language of choice for embedded development is C, but C++ and Java are also mentioned by developers (see Chapter 10). All such high-level languages have notions of named code (functions) and data (variables). These must be translated by the compiler into the specifics of operating system calling and layout conventions and correct executable binary code. In addition to correct translations, compilers also perform optimizations, which are key to performance in any ILP-oriented machine. For example, few (if any) high-level programming languages have explicit notations for machine registers, parallelizable operations, and caching locality of code or data. Optimizing compilers must find equivalent correct code sequences that exploit these features of the underlying machine.

Compilers also play a role in analyzing applications and the space of possible hardware designs for an embedded application. By varying machine descriptions, compilers can search a space of machines with different functional units, latencies, pipeline designs, and costs to find the best one for an application or set of applications. Chapter 10

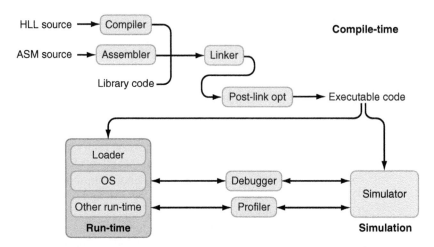

FIGURE 7.1   **Toolchain workflow.** This diagram illustrates how various pieces of the embedded toolchain relate to one another. Rectangular boxes show tools described in this chapter. Unlabeled items indicate source or binary code.

has more detail about using compilers and simulators in architecture evaluation. The compiler is the core of any ILP-oriented toolchain, and compiler structure concerns most of the rest of this chapter.

7.2.2 Assembler

For the hero programmers who eschew automation, the assembler is the tool of choice. The assembler translates human-readable assembler mnemonics and numbers into binary code. Assemblers provide very limited automation for programmers, largely by calculating addresses of symbols and data or including enough information for the linker to perform such calculations later. Assemblers are necessary for writing low-level routines that directly control the hardware, as no compiler generates the exotic opcodes needed. Such low-level routines are typically part of porting the operating system to a new platform, and include tasks such as setting the interrupt priority level, handling traps and exceptions, and returning from interrupts or switching contexts. Application code rarely requires such exotic instructions.

In embedded applications, and especially for DSPs, hand-coded assembly is sometimes used to expose performance or reduce code size. In some cases, compilers are not available and assembly is the only option for programming a machine. Manual coding leads to high development costs (the embedded market structure has tolerated this balance for a long time). Building the assembler itself is not typically expensive, although some assemblers (notably TI's *horizontal assembler*) are complicated by grammars that are syntactic rather than lexical.

Many of today's embedded processors have RISC or VLIW instruction sets, allowing (perhaps even requiring) compilers to be used to build efficient programs from high-level

Controversy: Smart Assemblers

Beginning in the 1980s, the definition of "assembly language" shifted. RISC designers, notably those in the MIPS camp, broke the isomorphism between assembly and machine languages by having the assembler perform some program transformations. The simplest of these mapped *pseudo-operations* in assembly language to legal machine language. Examples of such pseudo-operations include *nop* and *move* operations, which were synthesized from standard arithmetic and logical operations. More complex assembler optimizations included filling branch delay slots, filling load delay slots, and unrolling loops.

Some DSP architectures include smart assemblers, called *assembly optimizers* (AOs), as part of their toolchain. For such assemblers, the input language is termed *linear assembly*, whereby the AO performs aggressive optimizations, sometimes including scheduling and register allocation. In other words, the assembler embeds features of the optimizing compiler. Often, the compiler itself emits linear assembly and invokes the AO to complete code generation.

We view smart assemblers and AOs skeptically. The mapping from assembly to machine language performed by RISC assemblers appears largely harmless but can be insidiously costly and dangerous. Assembler programmers no longer code to "the raw machine"; instead, they must view their assembly code as something that will be transformed by the assembler. This means that programmers must anticipate the effects of the assembler's optimizations or disable those optimizations. Either case is more work. Worse still, the assembler optimizations must be as correct as those performed by a compiler, complicating assembler construction. A recent assembler for the Intel IXP architecture failed to model a register dependence on a rare instruction (the IXP architecture sometimes relies on registers encoded in the previous instruction because of lack of space in the current instruction). The optimized, assembled code failed because the assembler reordered the dependent instruction to fill a delay slot. The bug was found through single-stepping through the code. Such errors decrease programmer confidence in supposedly "safe" parts of the toolchain.

If the compiler invokes the AO to complete code generation, the linear assembly is unlikely to capture all of the information available to the compiler. Such information includes profiles, analysis of variable lifetimes and scopes, and type information. This is necessary for ILP-oriented optimizations. Redoing the analysis work is costly, and information such as profiling is simply lost.

Beefing up the assembly-language layer is a bad linguistic idea. Linear assembly is a new language that is too low level to be expressive (no types, no descriptive control flow) yet too removed from the hardware to give exact control (scheduler reorders operations; register allocator places variables). This seems the worst of both worlds to us. For systems with existing optimizing compilers, much of the functionality of AOs could be achieved through language-level *intrinsics* that extend the set of operations available to the programmer (some C compilers also support assembly coding through "*asm*" directives). We can think of three motivations for using AOs: when no compiler is available, to support legacy assembly code, and to allow manual tweaking of compiler-optimized code. The second seems of little value when a high-level language compiler is available. The latter indicates that the compiler still has room for improvement. As occurred in systems for horizontal microcode (see the Introduction), we expect that over time AOs will disappear and their functionality will be absorbed into compilers.

language code. These increasingly normalized embedded architectures allow larger fractions of application code to be written in high-level languages, increasing programmer productivity and application maintainability. The situation is analogous to the 1950s and 1960s in mainstream computing, during which language designers proved that high-level languages were usable for all but the lowest-level programming tasks. As compilers for embedded targets mature (or conversely, as the targets become easier for compilation), we expect the same trends to affect the embedded market. In a decade, it is unlikely that many embedded system designers will use assemblers, except possibly through sophisticated interfaces or as part of more far-reaching tools.

7.2.3 Libraries

Libraries provide ready-made code for projects, supplementing the development performed using compilers or assemblers. They are useful for implementing standards-related code and for reusing code within one development organization. Libraries commonly add networking support — TCP/IP, UDP, and various routing protocols — floating-point emulation or functionality (how many programmer-centuries were spent on DAXPY?[1]), and media formats such as JPEG, MPEG, and MP3. Libraries also encourage use of new architectural extensions and can encapsulate performance-oriented code that exploits a particular machine at its peak.

Exploiting new architectural extensions and achieving peak performance are dual goals of some libraries. For example, Intel and HP give away libraries for MPEG decoding using their micro-SIMD graphics-related extensions — MMX and MAX, respectively. Similarly, libraries for the early VLIW supercomputers included FIR filters and convolutions as self-contained pieces of code. Such libraries allow the use of new instructions before the compiler is available, without forcing application programmers to resort to assembly code. Such libraries can be difficult to build, but their development cost can be amortized over many users in different companies and organizations. Hardware vendors find them especially compelling because they increase the overall usefulness of their product.

Libraries are distributed in a variety of forms and with a variety of licensing agreements. Binary and source-code distributions are the most common. Binary distributions protect the library-writer's intellectual property but prevent users from fixing bugs or adding functionality to the library. Code shipped to end users is typically in binary form (what use have they for source code?), but development shops prefer source-code versions of libraries. In rare cases, libraries are shipped in "obfuscated"-source form. Obfuscated sources have been processed by a program rewriter that removes comments, modifies variable names, and reformats the text. The resulting mess can still be compiled but is difficult to reuse. If the obfuscated code is written in a language

---

1. DAXPY is the name of a subroutine (part of the BLAS [Basic Linear Algebra] library) that computes a linear combination of vectors $y = \alpha \cdot x + y$.

Flame: The Popularity of Libraries Is Inversely Proportional to the Compilability of the Architecture

The less general the architecture, the more libraries become necessary. A good compiler should be able to get most of the performance on a compiler-friendly architecture if the code is well written (see Chapter 10 for discussions of well-written code). More specific architectures have less compiler support, and thus vendors fall back on libraries in order to live up to performance claims.

Optimized libraries also constrain programmers to develop in a mode that is more appropriate for the machine. Many numerically oriented high-performance computers come with numerical libraries, such as BLAS (a delightful-sounding acronym for basic linear algebra subprograms), which codify a standard interface to vector and matrix operations. Signal-processing DSPs hand the programmer these and, given the difficulty of hand-generating different assembly-level routines and the near impossibility of compiling different high-level language routines, the programmer must learn to live with what's there. Vector supercomputers are a big step up in generality, and there the programmer can write new routines the compiler can do well with, as long as they don't have such a complex flow of control that it is difficult or impossible to map the computation into the structure of the vector hardware. Compilers for vector computers can usually do an excellent job on routines such as the BLAS, which map well. CPUs that gain their performance via ILP and sophisticated compiling rather than hardware structures permit the developer a far greater range of high-performance computation. Although their manufacturers offer numeric libraries for convenience, most programmers eschew their use and instead write their own routines. This permits the compiler to perform optimizations based on the specifics of the user's code and significantly lessen the reliance of those architectures on the existence of sophisticated libraries.

---

such as C, distributors of the library receive binary-like intellectual property protection without the porting headaches of binary distribution. Marshall Kirk McKusick has commented:

The way it was characterized politically, you had copyright, which is what the big companies use to lock everything up; you had copyleft, which is free software's way of making sure they can't lock it up; and then Berkeley had what we called "copycenter," which is "take it down to the copy center and make as many copies as you want."

— Marshall Kirk McKusick, *inventor of FFS and Berkeley UNIX guru,* 1999

Licenses for third-party libraries vary greatly in structure. Many libraries are available under open-source licenses such as GPL (the GNU Public License). Although free software has no up-front acquisition costs, other lifetime software costs (porting, maintenance, system integration) should not be underestimated. Some companies (e.g., RedHat's Cygnus Solutions group) make revenue from open-source code by providing (and charging for) technical support and bug fixes. Commercial users also must beware the fine print in free software licenses. Some constraints may make business use of the free software impossible. Other licensing agreements are more standard, with fixed and recurring fee structures and various limitations on redistribution.

7.2.4 Linker

The linker builds a coherent program from components produced by compilers, assemblers, and other binary-production tools. Compilers and assemblers produce object code; libraries come as source code (which can then be compiled to object code) or as archive files. Building this larger aggregation involves resolving cross-references, computing offsets, and verifying that all external references have been resolved. Some linkers also perform simple types of interprocedural optimizations, including calling convention optimizations, global variable placement, and branch distance/opcode substitutions.

Linkage comes in two forms: static and dynamic. Static linking takes place entirely before the program runs. All program pieces need to be present for static linking (missing pieces — unresolved external references — are reported as errors). Dynamic linking can be viewed as lazy evaluation of linking, in which resolution of some cross-references is delayed until run-time. Dynamic linking requires a mixture of compile-time and run-time support and collaboration between the linker (compile-time) and the loader (run-time). (See below for more about loaders.) The dynamic linker checks that unresolved external references satisfy type specifications, but instead of inserting jumps or data access instructions with addresses it inserts "stubs" into the program. Stubs are small pieces of code that tell the loader to locate, read, and execute/operate on a named piece of memory. Stubs can also fail to find a cross-reference, in which case a run-time exception will be generated that halts the dynamically linked program. Static and dynamic linking make a classic "compile-time versus run-time" tradeoff. Static linking usually takes more compile time because many resolved references are never used. Dynamic linking is faster to compile but slower at run-time, and run-time exceptions may not show up in testing. Embedded systems rarely deploy dynamically linked code because of the potential for catastrophic problems. However, dynamic linking speeds up development by reducing programmer waiting time in the edit-compile-debug loop.

Implementing a linker involves surprising subtleties. Most programs include provision for global and initialized data (operating systems and architectures have varying conventions for how these are accessed). For example, data might be addressed absolutely in physical memory (x86), or it might be indirectly accessed through a global pointer (MIPS/Ultrix), or it might be doubly indirect through a table of contents with pointers to the actual data (Power/AIX). In the middle case, limitations of the processor's instruction encoding may prevent global and initialized data from exceeding a certain size. Linker builders must choose whether to raise an error, fix things quietly, or require users to specify special linkage options. Similar issues occur for calling conventions and dynamic-linkage stubs. The linker may have to be aware of all of these and rearrange arguments and stack locations.

Linker users also occasionally run into subtle problems. When multiple archives/ libraries are used, symbol names may overlap. Which version of *malloc*() or *printf*() gets called by the user program is determined by a combination of operating system conventions and linker decisions. For static linking, an ordering of libraries is interpreted out of the environment and command-line arguments. In some dynamic linkage conventions (e.g., True64UNIX), library routines from one archive will call routines from higher-priority archives rather than their own group of routines. Static linkers are usually careful to include the minimum set of routines necessary to satisfy linkage requirements, so that unused archive routines do not contribute to the resulting object code. However, the unit of inclusion is often an entire object file or archive file, and thus this "smart" inclusion may not provide as small a program as desired.

7.2.5 Post-link Optimizer

Post-link optimizers at first seem redundant: Why not make the compiler perform all of the optimizations? The difference is in scope. Most compilers work on a single source-code file (or even a single procedure) at a time. For a compiler to perform interprocedural optimizations or whole-program optimizations, it must be able to examine *all* source for the program simultaneously (at high optimization levels, several production compilers do exactly this, using a special file format and requiring a lot of memory). This is not always possible, especially in a system for which some coding must be performed in assembly or libraries from third-party vendors as part of the system. By its nature, a post-link optimizer sees the entire program.

Post-link optimizations include many of the optimizations we attributed previously to linkers. They include code and data layout (especially important on machines with direct-mapped caches), code and data compression, call distance optimization, calling convention optimization, and C++ template optimization (crucial for code size). Profile-based optimizations may also be conveniently implemented at the post-link stage. Doing so simplifies or removes some of the accounting headaches normally associated with managing profiles.

Constructing a post-link optimizer can be a surprisingly development-effective way to produce efficient or compact object code. The linker's output object file format is necessarily the input IR. The post-link optimizer can assume that it has all program pieces, and thus can perform whole-program analysis that is much more effective than conservative piece-wise analysis. All external references have been resolved, and profile data may be available to guide the optimizations. Note that a post-link optimizer does not replace all compiler optimizations. Some compiler-derived linguistic information (e.g., types, aliasing) is unavailable, and thus most optimizations rely on features that can be inferred just from the machine code. Post-link optimizations have become increasingly important as embedded firmware moves to a modularized development style.

7.2.6 Run-time Program Loader

The program loader is part of the operating system. It prepares programs for execution. Preparation includes relocation, decompression, and moving the program from

Controversy: How Many Intermediate Representations?

Every significant compiler project we have known has started life with the laudable goal of using a single intermediate representation (IR). IRs are languages used to express the state of the program being compiled between phases, so that the state can be passed from one phase to another or to represent the state of the program while a phase operates on it. The problem with having a single IR is that different jobs done by different phases of the compiler require information in different forms. Typically, phases earlier in the compiler want to see something closer in form to the original data structures as existed in the source program. For example, a high-level optimizer would prefer to see an array index computation with the index expression separate from the underlying array. A phase of the machine-specific optimization might prefer a lower-level representation, with the index expression translated into separate ALU operations and a base+offset mode memory operation. Phases later in the compiler typically make better use of lower-level representations, where redundancies can be more apparent and the mapping into machine structures is more natural. Picking these levels is an art because, for example, going too low with the low-level language could make the job of the scheduler very difficult. The motivation for a single IR is largely an engineering one. Not only would a reduced number of IRs be inherently easier to deal with, but the IRs become important aspects of the entire compiling system, with many tools written to manipulate them, display them, and so on.

Although having a single IR is awkward, especially for high-performance compilers, some compromise is necessary, otherwise every phase, and possibly every adjacent pair of phases, would require its own language. The usual compromise is two IRs: one closer to the source and one closer to the ISA. This appears to work well most of the time, and compilers often have a high-level IR and a low-level one. Sometimes a compiler will be built with what is purported to be one IR, but really is two glued together, in the sense that both levels are evident in the language and most tools have to deal with two very different types of objects. This adds complexity, and rarely buys much in engineering savings, though it can give something of the benefit of many (not just two) levels.

It is worth noting that this discussion does not concern languages that are involved in the lexical analyzer and parsing process. That level of a compiler has become so packaged that, although there often is an intermediate language built into the process, the compiler developer does not have to worry about issues of language levels, tools, and so on. One just takes what comes with the package. It would be nice to imagine that the same thing could be true for the other intermediate representation(s), but the goal of using an IR for more than one compiler, never mind an IR that is prepackaged, is also elusive. As we have pointed out, a modern high-performance compiler is an engineering monster. The freedom to define data structures in which the compiler stores its representations is regarded as a necessary freedom by most compiler writers. A valuable addition to the compiler tool set would be an extensible language geared toward being a compiler IR, with a complete set of tools, visualizers, and so on that are extensible as the language is extended. Despite some attempts to do this, none has gained sufficiently wide acceptance, undoubtedly due to the difficulty of the problem.

secondary storage to memory. If a system includes virtual memory and an MMU, the loader may also prepare the MMU and set up paging support for the program. During the run of the program, the loader may also resolve references to dynamically linked code and perform some call optimizations (e.g., to remove calls to stub routines and replace them with direct calls to resolved dynamic links).

Many of the purposes of a program loader in a general-purpose machine are less important in embedded applications. Few embedded devices store programs in secondary storage. Instead, programs are often resident in ROM or flash memory. Memory management is also rare in the embedded domain, and thus setting up page tables and TLB miss handlers is also rare. Dynamically linked or loaded code is also currently rare in embedded systems, as few devices have facilities for downloading new code. However, as embedded devices gain in power and capabilities, many of these formerly general-purpose-related issues will find their way into embedded devices, and loaders will have to handle them.

Code and data decompression are more common in embedded designs than in general-purpose designs (saving memory space reduces device unit costs). In many software-based compression schemes, the program loader handles decompression. This can happen all at once, before the program executes, or it can happen on demand, with the program and hardware generating decompression faults that are analogous to the page faults in general-purpose systems.

Relocation is the most common loader task. It involves fixing up absolute and relative references to various parts of the program. This is largely an accounting task, but it is surprisingly difficult to get right.

7.2.7 Simulator

After the compiler, the simulator is the next most important piece of the toolchain. The simulator's job is to replicate the *target* machine and environment on a *host* processor (typically a PC or workstation). Simulators make a variety of tradeoffs between fidelity and simulation performance. They are used to estimate the performance of various possible designs, to validate the current design, and to develop software and hardware in parallel. There are a number of approaches to simulation (e.g., interpreted, compiled, through hardware description languages). These approaches were described in detail in Chapter 6.

Writing interpreted or compiled processor simulators can be surprisingly simple, in large part because the environment is entirely that of the host processor. Host processors are typically well-documented workstations or PCs running well-known operating systems, and thus development on them is familiar. The largest difficulty is correctly modeling the idiosyncrasies of the target machine. The farther apart the target and host machine, the more accurate the simulation must be, and the more difficult ensuring fidelity becomes. Chapter 6 also talks about various ways to validate a simulator, and the various ways in which a simulator can be "correct."

With the advent of SoC designs in recent years, simulation has become even more complex, as any simulator must be a "system simulation." This means modeling not just the processor core(s) but peripherals, buses, memory, and other pieces of the SoC. These pieces are often designed or modeled with many different tools, requiring disparate pieces to be integrated into the system simulation. Performing this integration while maintaining performance and accuracy can be very complex.

7.2.8 Debuggers and Monitor ROMs

Debuggers allow developers to examine and modify the state of a simulated or actual system. They can be the only way to track down some types of bugs. Most often, debuggers are used to examine corpses (core images) of crashed programs, which often suffice to find the error in the original program.

Functionality varies widely among debuggers, from very low-level consoles that support only hexadecimal displays of data to source-level debuggers that can handle optimized code and are part of integrated development environments. Many debuggers will show local variables (those on the stack frame). Some will show the names of fields in heap-allocated records (this requires type information to be recorded by the compiler and passed through the linker and loader). Some debuggers even include facilities for examining chains of dynamically allocated objects, perturbing the stack, or tracking memory leaks.

Debugging approaches vary widely, but most match the style of simulation or actual system being debugged. All debuggers require conventions for passing information about the original program. This information is usually added to the program's symbol table. Interpreted debuggers are usually integrated with the interpreter to access and display program state. This is also true for dynamically translated simulators (where the debugger must be integrated with the dynamic translation system). Debuggers for compiled simulations often use the host machine's normal debugger but specially process the debugging information of the compiled simulator to make its state appear like that of the simulated machine.

Debugging a target machine from a host machine is called *cross-debugging*, in analogy to cross-development. Cross-debugging is performed using code in each machine, a data connection between the two pieces, and a protocol between the two pieces. The piece that runs in the target machine is called the *stub* or *monitor*; the piece on the host machine is often just the standard host debugger. The data link protocol can have varying degrees of sophistication, allowing state (registers, memory) to be read and set and allowing change of control in the processor (single-step, run, debugger interrupt). The protocol also typically allows the target processor to tell the host debugger that some exceptional condition has occurred. Cross-debugging data links are very often simply serial interfaces or can be tunneled through a dedicated ethernet debugging port.

Monitors are complicated by interfaces to the lowest levels of hardware on the machine. They need to be able to intercept some of the interrupts encountered by the machine before they reach the operating system. This requires cooperating with the operating system to modify the trap table. They also require privileged access not just to the state of the machine but to control mechanisms. The debugger must be able to return from interrupts, to change the program counter, and to single-step the program, all of which interact with the operating system. Some cores provide hardware support for breakpoints and watchpoints (data locations that stop the program when they are accessed). Using this support is the monitor's job.

Differences between host and target machine complicate cross-debugging. Host and target can never be assumed to have the same "natural" word sizes and endianness, and thus code that translates to some protocol-specified order is required in both halves. The speed of the link between host and target can also affect debugging, limiting how quickly new versions of a program can be downloaded or test data can be uploaded or downloaded.

In cross-developed embedded systems, the target's debugging system is actually much more important than in traditional desktop environments. Once the code is loaded on the target, it is the only way to observe behavior and track bugs. The target debugging system usually works in cooperation with the architectural support for debugging (data/address debug registers) and board-level support (JTAG). For example, when code is in ROM the only way to set a breakpoint is through architectural support accessed by the debug interfaces. Target debugging systems can be quite complex, but they can be a critical component in the success of a platform.

Debugging is complicated by optimized code and by read-only code. The former is an open research problem that, sadly, too few researchers are attracted to. Program transformations such as instruction scheduling make it difficult to linearly relate operations in the object code back to lines of the source program. Most compilers offer a tradeoff between optimization and debugging, whereby the highest level of one prohibits some features in the other. Debugging read-only code (i.e., ROM or Flash programs) often requires hardware support, as instructions cannot be replaced by the monitor to form breakpoints.

Using debuggers is an underemphasized skill of at least the same complexity as program development. The worst trap is using the debugger as a crutch instead of thinking analytically about the ways a program could have failed. Debugging methodologies are covered in other books. See Kernighan and Pike [1999], Bentley [1999], and McConnell [2004] for good advice about debugging methodologies.

7.2.9 Automated Test Systems

Computers are the ultimate in automated tools, yet few undergraduate courses discuss automated means of exploring problem spaces or validating programs. We will have more to say about the former in Chapter 10. One method for the latter is *regression testing*, a proven method for ensuring that software continues to perform its desired functions as it evolves.

Most of the work in automated test systems involves building scripts. Building robust scripts that report errors is very similar to writing robust programs. Some tools (e.g., UNIX-style make) can be very useful in building testing systems, but they do not always include all of the desired features. Finding a good system can save a lot of work. Finding good test problems for searching a problem space or finding tricky examples for a regression system are also a lot of work. One of the best methodologies for finding such examples comes from McConnell's *Code Complete* [2004]. Whenever a programmer fixes a bug, he installs a regression test that verifies that future changes do not undo the effects of his fix. In SoC designs, automated test systems can be the only way to make sure that the combination of core and custom IP blocks works.

7.2.10 Profiling Tools

Profiles are statistics about where a program spends its resources, and profiling tools are invaluable to both manual- and compiler-driven optimizations. Most often profiles are simply time or frequency counts of where a program spends its time, measured per procedure, per basic block, or per instruction. More elaborate statistics are also sometimes collected, including path frequencies, load/store collision profiles, memory access footprints (for prefetching), and other information collected using performance-related hardware counters.

Profiles can be used in both simulated and real environments. The main point is to provide feedback about program execution that can be used to analyze or optimize a program (see Figure 7.2 for a typical use of profile information in a compiler). Different profiling methodologies trade efficiency (slowdown of the profiled program) for accuracy. However, recent low-overhead profiling systems are also surprisingly accurate.

One of the most difficult issues with using profiles is maintaining the correspondence between profile data and program code. Optimizing compilers rearrange the program, complicating these bookkeeping steps. Profiling must be implemented in some stage of the compiler (or the post-link optimizer). Optimizations further down the compilation pipeline require that intermediate stages preserve and propagate profile statistics.

The majority of compiler-related profiling research deals with automated use of profiles in compilers (we focus on this topic in much more detail later in this chapter). However, one should never underestimate the value of profiles to developers. Bentley (1999) spends a large percentage of his book on tips for analyzing programs and tuning their performance. Our Chapter 10 also discusses this topic.

7.2.11 Binary Utilities

A number of smaller utilities round out the pieces of a development toolchain. These include various disassemblers, string searching and matching tools, and resource builders, such as bitmap, font, and image editors.

7.3 Structure of an ILP Compiler

Modern compilers span a large gap between source language and object code. For engineering and practicality reasons, the translation is typically not direct; the distance between the syntax and type constraints of a programming language and the registers, functional units, and instruction encoding of a target machine is too great. Most compilers rely on a number of intermediate representations (IRs) and perform the translation in

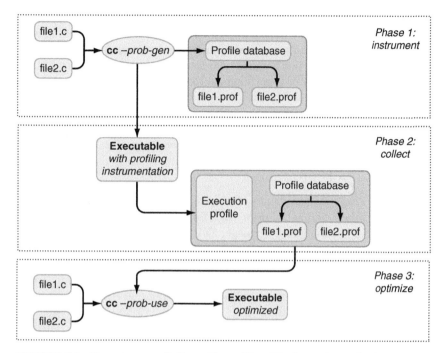

FIGURE 7.2 **Two-step compilation with profiling.** The figure shows the three components of a two-step compilation technique: *instrument*, *collect*, and *optimize*. In the instrumentation phase the compiler adds profile-gathering code to the compiled program and stores additional information into a separate profile database (such as the correspondence of branches to source lines). In the collection phase, the instrumented executable is exercised with a training set and, at the end of the execution, dumps the execution profile containing execution statistics tagged with enough information to be able to relate it back to the original profile database. In the optimization phase, the compiler uses the profile database and training execution statistics to guide heuristics (such as the selection of regions). The major complexity of this procedure lies in the added burden of having to separately maintain, validate, and regenerate the profile database, which needs to be kept in sync with changes to individual compilation units.

multiple stages. The typical division of labor includes at least two intermediate representations and three stages: a language-specific front end, a common machine-independent optimizer (sometimes called the middle end), and a machine-specific back end.

Each major part of the compiler comprises smaller pieces called *phases*. A phase typically implements a single optimization or transformation. This division of labor allows multiple developers to work on different parts of the compiler simultaneously. The IRs between two given phases are usually tailored to the data structures used internally in each phase. For example, within front ends usually the program is represented using a tree or directed graph-like structure, whereas machine-independent optimizers use a single assignment form that is not very different from a directed graph. Not surprisingly, IRs between those phases often have a graph-like flavor. Back ends and low-level optimization phases usually work on code that is closer to the machine representation (their distance from the internal representation of a middle end often makes finding a suitable IR between those phases problematic). In our experience, compiler developers most often find it convenient to use an IR between the middle end and back end that is closer to, or even identical to, the internal representation of the back end, and ask the middle end to emit that structure. It is irresistible, but invariably unsuccessful, to attempt to design a single IR that works for all of the compiler or, quixotically, for all compilers (see the sidebar "Controversy: How Many Intermediate Representations?"). See Figure 7.3 to get an idea of the workings of an ILP-oriented compiler.

7.3.1 Front End

Production compilers often have multiple front ends, each corresponding to a particular programming language. Each front end must handle the specifics of parsing and typing its programming language. This complexity varies greatly across languages. Different languages also have different semantics associated with their code. It is the job of the front end to capture this information (e.g., alias information in FORTRAN programs) and encode it so that later optimizations will be able to use it. Front ends also incorporate language-specific optimizations (for example, virtual function call elimination in object-oriented languages).

Internally, a front end often uses a tree- or DAG-oriented program representation. This naturally matches the parsing structure of all modern programming languages. A variety of tools exists to automate building front ends. These include lexical analyzers (UNIX's *lex*), parser generators (UNIX's *yacc* and GNU's *bison*), tools for generating finite-state automata, and macro processing packages (Ritchie's *m4* language may be the best example, but the C preprocessor is most familiar).

7.3.2 Machine-independent Optimizer

The machine-independent optimizer performs "high-level" optimizations that are both language and machine independent. These include various loop-level transformations, constant propagation, dead code elimination, and partial redundancy elimination (PRE).

Unfortunately, many of these optimizations are only superficially machine independent. Loop-level transformations often target pipeline latencies or cache arrangements in the target machine. PRE can remove or reduce computations but may also increase the lifetimes of variables, thereby increasing register pressure. The optimizations are only machine independent in the sense that they can be performed without knowledge of the target machine. Performing them *beneficially* does require target knowledge, blurring the line between the middle and back ends.

Many of the "machine-independent" optimizations are useful throughout the optimization phases of the compiler. For example, many optimizations generate dead code as a side effect. Being able to rerun the dead code elimination pass after such optimizations in theory simplifies the construction and maintenance of the compiler. Actual practice is complicated by the variation in intermediate representations. A utility that works in one phase of the compiler may not work at a later phase without significant reengineering.

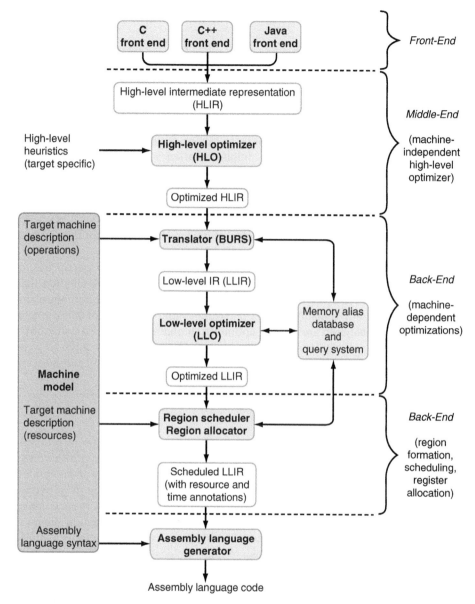

FIGURE 7.3 Phases of an ILP compiler. The figure shows the typical "plumbing diagram" for an ILP-oriented compiler. One (or more) front ends usually generate a first intermediate representation (in the form of abstract syntax trees or similar), which is immediately converted to a machine-independent representation (HLIR, usually tree- or stack-based) used by the high-level optimizer (inlining, loop transformations). The back end of the compiler normally moves to a lower-level machine-dependent IR through a rewriting phase that takes into account the peculiarities of the target processor. The LLIR is used for most of the low-level transformation as well as the region formation and loop strategy. Finally, the scheduling phase simply annotates the LLIR with resource usage (registers, units) and cycle assignments, before emitting the target assembly language code.

In his book, *Advanced Compiler Design and Implementation*, Muchnick [1997] recommends building constant propagation and dead code elimination as reusable utilities of this sort.

7.3.3 Back End: Machine-specific Optimizations

The back end houses machine-specific optimizations (the optimizations that know exactly which target implementation will run the resulting code). Most ILP-oriented optimizations are in the back end, although profiling may take place earlier. These optimizations can require heroic programming efforts, but they also pay off handsomely in performance and code size. Machine-specific back ends are what distinguish vendor-supplied compilers from generic compilers such as *gcc*. Vendors have economic incentives to build high-performance back ends (duplicating or exceeding these efforts happens rarely in generic compilers).

The back end gradually "lowers" the program from the machine-independent intermediate representation to a machine-specific representation that corresponds directly to machine code. Each back-end phase makes assumptions about its input and output representations. This makes changing the order of phases complicated. Interactions between and among optimization phases are difficult to quantify. The "phase-ordering problem" remains open research. The current state of the art in phase ordering is based on trial and error and limited software engineering experience, and we describe it in the next chapter.

7.4 Code Layout

Instruction scheduling, register allocation, and clustering primarily address the datapath of the machine: registers, functional units, and control hardware. A number of other techniques aim to improve the performance of the memory system (although what is good for the memory system is also typically good for the pipelines). These include code layout, code compression, prefetching, and load/store speculation.

Code layout techniques seek to reduce instruction memory traffic. Memory systems include caches, and caches improve performance by exploiting locality; thus, code layout techniques seek to improve locality. Current practice uses greedy methods that place related pieces of code together, either at the basic block level within a procedure or in ordering procedures within a program's executable image. Profile edge weights determine when two pieces are related. More sophisticated techniques separate hot and cold pieces of procedures, exiling the cold pieces and clumping hot parts of procedures together. Still more sophisticated techniques model the details of the cache hierarchy and line size, attempting to minimize conflict misses based on trace-driven analysis and simulation.

7.4.1 Code Layout Techniques

One significant source of performance inefficiency in modern computer architectures comes from the instruction cache. In the embedded domain in particular, large first-level caches and high levels of set associativity are often not economical. Often, embedded processors adopt rather simple instruction cache structures, such as direct-mapped caches. Simpler caches are even more strongly preferred in the case of wide-issue machines (such as VLIWs), in that the instruction cache fetch path is usually among the most critical drivers of the overall processor clock cycle. Combined with the limited budget for first-level instruction caches, the trend toward even larger programs significantly increases the pressure on the instruction cache. As for any cache structure, we can identify three sources of cache misses in instruction caches.

- *Capacity misses* come from a program whose dynamic footprint is larger than the available cache size. There is not much we can do about capacity misses beyond reducing code size.

- *Conflict misses* come from the limited associativity of the cache, and are caused by separate instructions that compete for the same line in the instruction cache. Conflict misses depend on the layout of the program, and various techniques have been proposed to attack the problem.

- *Compulsory misses* (also called "cold" misses) come from the initial loading of cache blocks. The first access to a block (for example, at program load or after a context switch) is not in the cache, and thus the cache needs a compulsory miss to load it, regardless of the cache size or associativity.

The set of techniques that addresses the reduction of instruction-cache conflict misses falls under the category of *code placement techniques.* The proposed approaches attempt to lay out code in such a way that code blocks estimated to be competing for the same cache lines are moved apart in main memory. Code placement is not a new research field. In the 1960s and 1970s programs were extensively manipulated to improve virtual memory paging, and in the 1980s and 1990s researchers started to apply similar techniques to attack instruction cache issues.

Different approaches have involved experimentation with various code block shapes and sizes, ranging from loops, to functions, to entire compilation units. The choice of a specific code block depends on the tool organization and the type of relocation information available when the code layout phase runs. Typically, the most effective time to re-layout the code is during (or after) linking, in that the full information about the binary is available (except dynamically linked libraries).

Ideally, one would like to have the smallest code block available for relocation, because this would allow fine-grained decisions. However, that is often in contrast with the way the compilation toolchain works. Changing the layout of a program implies relocating code blocks. This is only possible to the extent that all tools upstream preserve the relocation information emitted by the compiler. For example, it is typical to keep around *external* relocation information — necessary for the linker to create a fully bound binary — so that the natural code block size would be a compilation unit. Unfortunately, compilation units (i.e., entire files) tend to be too coarse-grained to be effective.

Another common choice is to deal with *functions*, which is possible if we convince the assembler to keep function boundary information around in addition to the associated relocation information. Usually, assemblers resolve symbols that point to objects whose scope is internal to the compilation unit (such as static data and code). To be able to move functions around, the relocation information has to be preserved in the object file. Modern object file formats (such as ELF) are compatible with this functionality, and this is not an unusual extension in embedded compilation toolchains.

Decreasing the granularity of code blocks below functions could be a challenge. For example, the resolution of local branches within a function is often the responsibility of the compiler, and delaying the final binding for these could raise complex issues, such as code reachability. A few of the approaches we present below show some benefits in dealing with loops or basic blocks, but they break the problem by forcing the compiler to lay out small code blocks, and defer to the linker the layout of functions.

The other dimension in which different approaches diverge is the technique used to choose and prioritize code blocks. Most of the known algorithms use a combination of *program structure* and *profile information*. The use of program structure (the *call graph* in particular) is based on the observation that functions that call each other tend to be in the cache at the same time. The use of profile information attempts to reduce the overlap of most-frequently executed functions or code blocks.

Most of the presented techniques apply to direct-mapped caches. Gloy and Smith [1999] showed that an algorithm that works for a direct-mapped cache also applies to set-associative caches. Intuitively, this can be explained with the observation that a conflict miss in a direct-mapped cache is caused by two addresses mapping to the same cache line. In a two-way set-associative cache we need three addresses mapping to the same cache line before a conflict arises. Any technique that reduces these types of mapping conflicts will reduce the probability of a cache miss regardless of the set associativity. This effect is going to be less noticeable on a set-associative structure, but it is possible to limit the study to the simpler direct-mapped case.

The following subsections present some of the most relevant techniques that deal with code layout. Of the many published algorithms, we present a few examples that use distinctly different concepts (see also "Further Reading").

DAG-based Placement

One of the early techniques for program layout optimization (published by McFarling in 1989) constructs a DAG (dependence acyclic graph) consisting of loops, functions, and basic blocks as nodes. Based on profile information, it prunes nodes that are never executed from the DAG. It then partitions the DAG into subtrees, so that each of them fits in the cache. Finally, the algorithm places each subtree starting from the root of the DAG, and ensures that each successor is placed next to the root node. This continues until we reach the cache size. The technique primarily concentrates on loops. Its major drawback consists of only using profile information to prune the graph, without really affecting cache placement. (See also Figure 7.4.)

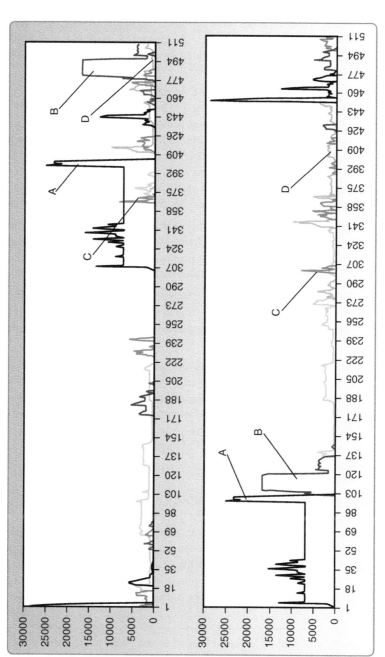

FIGURE 7.4 **Effects of code placement techniques.** This example shows what happens before and after a code layout optimization phase. In the charts you can see the execution profile of a sample program (MPEG2 decoding) mapped to a 512-line direct-mapped instruction cache. For example, this could be a 32-KB cache with 32 B per line. The x axis represents the cache lines; the y axis represents the number of times an instruction in that line is executed. The top chart shows the execution of a nonoptimized placement. You can see that potential miss sources come from procedure A conflicting with the group of procedures C, and procedure B conflicting with the group D. The profile-driven optimized placement shown at the bottom minimizes the overlap of the most important procedures (A and B, for example) by making sure they are assigned an address that maps to a cache location that cannot possibly conflict with other important procedures. In this example, the reduction of cache misses is about 50%.

The "Pettis-Hansen" Technique

In 1990, Pettis and Hansen published a code layout method that set the standard for all subsequent work. Their method combines profile information with program structure. Procedure positioning, basic block positioning, and procedure splitting are implemented guided by profile data through a *weighted call graph* (WCG). Procedure positioning is implemented in the linker; basic block positioning and procedure splitting are implemented in the compiler.

- *Procedure Positioning*: Based on profile data, the Pettis-Hansen technique first builds an undirected weighted call graph of procedures. Then, going from the heaviest edge to lightest edge, it merges function nodes and coalesces edges. This iterates until a single function node remains (this last node represents a priority order of functions). The linker then takes the ordered list of procedures and lays them out in sequence. In this way, functions that are close to each other in the call graph do not conflict in the cache, and among all call graphs priority is given to the most frequently executed functions according to the profile.

- *Basic Block Positioning*: The control graph contains profile information for each control flow edge. Starting from this annotated graph, the algorithm groups basic blocks into chains based on profile data. Basic blocks in a chain are then placed sequentially, and a later phase reestablishes the links between the basic blocks.

- *Procedure Splitting*: Finally, this technique splits used and unused blocks and places them in different regions of the overall address map. In this way, we place the used and unused portions in such a way that they end up in different cache "pages."

The Pettis-Hansen technique has one major drawback: cache parameters (size, line size, and so on) and function sizes are not considered. This is reasonable in a general-purpose workstation domain, in which the same code is likely to be deployed in machines with different cache configurations. However, in embedded domains we usually know much more about the parameters of the system on which the code will be executed, and we should be able to take advantage of them.

Procedure Inlining

The approach taken by the IMPACT compiler uses another technique based on the weighted call graph that adds the concept of *inlining* a function where it is important for cache behavior. Thus, function calls with a high execution frequency are replaced by the code of the function itself, ensuring adjacency in cache mapping. The algorithm is also extended to code blocks within functions by grouping basic blocks in *traces* based on the profile information and placing traces in a sequential order to increase spatial locality.[2] Again, this method does not consider cache parameters.

---

2. Note that a similar approach is used in any *trace scheduling*-based compiler, by virtue of the fact that the basic program unit is indeed a trace.

Cache Line Coloring

An improvement to Pettis-Hansen (based on a coloring technique) maps functions in the call graph to cache lines assuming each cache line is a color. Based on the program call graph, a parent function gets a color different from its descendants, as an attempt to prevent cache conflicts when the functions call each other.

The algorithm classifies functions and edges in the call graph as *popular* and *unpopular*. Popularity is based on how frequently a function or an edge is visited, and edges are sorted on descending popularity. Finally, the algorithm assigns colors to the functions and lays them out, starting from the highest weighted edge.

In this case, cache function sizes are considered when mapping cache lines. However, the algorithm does not use that information during the layout phase.

Temporal-order Placement

An approach that diverges from most of the others considers the *temporal* order of procedures as an important component of the behavior of program execution. Based on their previous work on path profiling, Gloy and Smith [1999] observed that a significant source of conflict misses comes from the nonuniform interleaving of function calls during program execution. To overcome this, the approach first collects (during the profile phase) the temporal information in a *temporal relationship graph* (TRG), and then uses it in a greedy pass similar to Pettis-Hansen to merge the graph of code blocks. Unlike Pettis-Hansen, the priority function is not based purely on distance in the call graph, but it also accounts for the temporal ordering of functions. This approach also considers the cache size and organization by finding the *best offset* of the initial location of each procedure within the cache mapping, and defers to a later stage the precise placement in main memory. The technique also does not assume a uniform function profile, but it assigns profile information at a finer granularity to individual function *chunks*. This enables a finer-granularity placement decision, whether we allow functions to be split or not. For example, in loop-dominated code this approach enables prologues and epilogues of functions to overlap, while ensuring that important loops do not overlap.

As with other memory-system optimizations, hardware alternatives may also be worth examining. Historically, many of the code and data layout techniques have attempted to reduce conflict misses, whereas current silicon processes and circuit disciplines allow associative caches and four-way set associativity has been long known to be sufficient for almost all general-purpose applications. Hardware/software tradeoffs of this sort are extremely important in designing systems that offer speculation, prefetching, or predication applied to memory operations. Depending on cost and time-to-market constraints, either approach might be better for a particular project.

7.5 Embedded-Specific Tradeoffs for Compilers

In principle, there is no reason the design of an embedded compiler should be significantly different from a general-purpose compiler. Historically, however, embedded compilers lagged the state of the art of general-purpose compilers for a variety of reasons.

In the past, target processors for embedded compilers implemented rather idiosyncratic instruction sets that were not amenable to high-level optimizations and aggressive code-generation techniques. This was particularly true in the 8-bit and 16-bit microcontroller area, as well as some of the dedicated DSPs.

Applications were simple enough that manual assembly-level programming was still effective, and hardcore firmware engineers would regard high-level languages with suspicion.

System resources were scarce, and needed to be heavily optimized. It is usually true that a good assembly-language programmer intimately familiar with a target architecture can do a better job of manually squeezing the last ounce of performance and code size for a small application. For example, if your target were an 8-bit microcontroller with 8 KB of on-chip memory that cannot be exceeded, a compiler's limitations would become quickly evident.

In summary, compilers did not seem to add a lot of value, because *designers used to compare compiler-generated code against manually optimized assembly code.* Even for low-level languages such as C, compilers cannot compete with heavily optimized manual code because humans can still perform optimizations the compiler cannot prove to be safe, and because of some intrinsic overhead a compiler introduces.

As we saw in the previous chapters, the embedded environment has changed dramatically in the last decade. Application complexity has increased by orders of magnitude, more processor targets have adopted orthogonal RISC-style instruction sets, and productivity and time-to-market factors have become much more important than saving a handful of program memory bytes. Nobody today would consider manually writing assembly language code for products such as printers (more than a million lines of C/C++ code) or even cellular phones (approaching half a million lines of code). Assembly language programming still survives in kernel code for DSPs, although language support for nonstandard operators and data sizes is slowly eroding that segment as well.

For all of these reasons, modern embedded compilers are not simpler than general-purpose compilers. Indeed, they are often more complex, as we will see in the rest of this section.

7.5.1 Space, Time, and Energy Tradeoffs

Traditional compilers have one and only one goal foremost in mind: to accelerate applications. In other words, most of the effort in a traditional compiler goes toward optimizing a one-dimensional cost function represented by the number of cycles necessary to execute a program. In the embedded world, other performance dimensions are as important as execution speed.

- *Code size* is important for both cost and overall system performance. Static code size (the overall dimension of the program) is often directly proportional to cost in terms of program ROM size. Dynamic code size (application footprint) has direct repercussions on instruction cache effectiveness and can seriously impact performance, particularly for systems with a simple memory hierarchy (such as a single level-1 cache).

- *Energy* is important in mobile systems, as it directly translates into the battery life of a product. Note that we talk about the overall energy requirements more than power consumption. The energy a program uses is the integral of its instantaneous power consumption over time, and thus a program that takes less time tends to be more energy efficient than one that takes longer, all other parameters being constant. Energy is also important in a thermal sense, especially when the speed of high-end processors is thermally constrained. In this case, the fact that the processor can run no faster than what would produce the highest power level extends the run time of a program. This extension may decrease the processor's energy efficiency.

Although it is true that many "traditional" compiler optimizations equally benefit speed, code, and energy, these are sometimes contrasting goals that require the compiler to choose among strategies. Most of the so-called "*scalar optimizations*" are clearly worthwhile. For example, removing memory operations (using register promotion, load/store elimination, register memory detection) certainly benefits speed, reduces code, and reduces power consumption. The same is true for transformations such as dead code removal, common subexpression elimination, strength reduction, copy propagation, and constant folding.

However, things get messier with ILP-oriented optimizations. In the following, we list some of the most visible examples that benefit speed but may hurt code size and power consumption.

Loop unrolling creates multiple versions of the body of an inner loop to increase the chances of exposing useful ILP, and hence it always negatively impacts code size. However, when the 90/10 rule applies (10% of the code size contributes to 90% of performance), unrolling is generally acceptable. For example, if we unroll all innermost loops eight times but they only add up to 10% of the original static code size, the overall code expansion is just a factor of 1.7. In addition, if the dynamic footprint of the unrolled loops still fits in the first-level instruction cache, unrolling is clearly worthwhile. Finally, unrolling reduces loop overhead as well as execution time, and thus it arguably has a positive effect on overall energy efficiency.

Tail duplication is another transformation used to remove complex control flow (join points) from code to facilitate other compiler tasks. Similar considerations as for loop unrolling apply: tail duplication increases code size, but it is likely to be limited to important inner loops, and as such only affects a small fraction of the overall application program.

Procedure inlining and cloning are used to widen the scope of optimizations even more. If inlining is done indiscriminately, the code growth penalty can be severe. Most compilers include the concept of an *inlining budget*, whereby users can specify (through a command line switch or a *pragma* annotation) a code size growth threshold the compiler cannot exceed when inlining functions. Given a limited budget, better compilers have an opportunity to use it more profitably if they can better estimate the dynamic path profile across the call graph of the program. Profile information is invaluable in making these types of decisions, focusing attention on important functions. Finally, although counterintuitive, inlining can be beneficial to code size. Calling conventions require compilers to generate additional instructions around function calls, entries, and returns in order to store parameters and result values in designated locations (registers or memory) and to manage the stack frame. This overhead can be significant for short procedures, and inlining removes it completely.

Speculation is one of the techniques compilers apply to reduce the critical path of a code region, by attempting to execute some instructions earlier than their original source order position. When a compiler moves an operation above a branch, it becomes *speculative*: the compiler will not necessarily use its results. Speculation is largely invariant with respect to code size,[3] but it may negatively impact energy efficiency. In thermodynamic terms, incorrectly speculated operations waste work. For example, if we move a memory operation above a branch that goes in the predicted direction 70% of the time, 30% of the speculative memory accesses will be wasted. From the pure speed perspective, this is generally a win. From the point of view of energy efficiency, this causes an energy reduction due to shorter execution time, but it also causes an energy increase due to the execution of the redundant memory operations. Consequently, the overall effect could go either way. Making these tradeoffs is extremely difficult, and compilers often resort to simple-minded heuristics based on weak and approximate assumptions.

As we first described in Section 4.5.2, *predication* converts control flow dependences to dataflow dependences by guarding instructions with *predicate* registers. Although predication does not normally impact code size, it negatively affects energy efficiency. The visible effect of predicated operation with a false predicate is a nop. However, that operation has to be issued, fetched, and decoded; its operand has to be read; and sometimes (depending on where the microarchitecture decides to quash it in the pipeline) the operation has to be executed. Unlike speculation, whereby the wasted work depends on the probability of correct speculation, for predicated operations with complementary predicates we always waste some energy. Considering that predication is most effective in innermost loops, the power implications could be severe, although we are not aware of any quantitative study.

Global code motion is a generalization of speculation, in which compilers move code (including branches) not just above branches but above join points. In its most general form (such as *trace scheduling*), global code motion generates extra *compensation code* to maintain the semantics of the original program. Compensation instructions are extra copies and increase code size. Previous research shows that in some pathological cases compensation code can grow exponentially, but effective compiler heuristics exist that limit the growth without affecting the performance benefits of global code motion.

As we can see from this short overview, finding the right balance is a daunting task, and most of today's compilers do not follow a "scientific" approach in this respect.

---

3. Strictly speaking, if speculation requires code that repairs the program state after misspeculations it could increase code size, but only marginally, and only for certain speculation models.

Tradeoffs among speed, code size, and energy efficiency require a global view of the execution of a program (something compilers are notoriously poor at). The problem is that a compiler has a limited view of the execution of a program, usually because compilation units (i.e., individual source files) are small and independently compiled. Profile information can help significantly but requires new extensions to capture parameters that correlate well with code size and energy efficiency. Whole-program optimization potentially enables the compiler to understand program behavior, but it is often impractical due to excessive compilation time, the effect of applications that grow faster than compilers can handle, and a more pervasive use of late-binding techniques (such as dynamically loaded libraries).

The usual approach compilers take is to simply expose a large set of options that selectively modulate (enable, disable, or control the aggressiveness of) individual optimization phases. Although this is routinely done today, it shows the inadequacy of compilers to deal with these types of "global" optimization issues. In other words, exposing low-level compiler options shifts the burden of optimizing the cost function to application developers.

This practice forces application developers to answer certain questions. How do we know if we want to turn on or off an optimization? What is a good granularity for an optimization: a file, a function, a loop, or something else? Typically, developers enforce various compiler policies in the build environment itself (through complex *makefiles*), which is awkward and prone to inconsistency. Even worse, to do a good job at this task application developers are forced to understand compiler internals well beyond the depth at which they would like to. In our experience, this is often the source of endless frustration among software engineers ("Why is this stupid compiler not behaving as I told it to?") and can have a very negative impact on overall productivity.

Ideally, an embedded compiler should only expose some linear combination of the optimization dimensions to application developers, such as:

$$K_1\{speed\} + K_2\{code\_size\} + K_3\{energy\_efficiency\}.$$

Using this model, K_1, K_2, and K_3 are the "knobs" in the hands of a software engineer used to indicate the relative importance of each of the individual factors. Then, individual compiler phases and optimization algorithms should autonomously decide how to tweak the internal parameters to optimize the desired objective functions. Unfortunately, this is not the case in today's state-of-the-art compilers, and this is clearly an obscure area that remains in the research domain.

7.5.2 Power-specific Optimizations

It is tempting to suppose that only hardware dissipates power, not software. However, that would be analogous to postulating that only automobiles burn gasoline, not people.

— Mark Johnson and Kaushik Roy, *Professors of Electrical Engineering at Purdue University*

Most of the improvements that have been made or studied in the realm of power management come from process technology and hardware design techniques. Reduction of transistor features, lower supply voltages, clock gating, frequency, and voltage scaling are some of the relevant approaches.

The research area of software design for low power is relatively young. Only between 1994 and 1995 did microprocessor power models become accurate enough to justify a more scientific approach to the problem. Since then, researchers have investigated various aspects of software's impact on power, ranging from the reorganization of applications to operating systems and compilers.

The advantages of writing power-aware software are the same that drive the success of software in the first place. Software can perform tuning at a much higher level of granularity than circuit techniques, can adapt to applications and workloads, can use smarter techniques, and (most important) can be changed until very late in the development process of a product.

Fundamentals of Power Dissipation

To explore the role of software in active power management it is necessary to understand first the physics of energy dissipation. As described in Section 5.8, there are two main sources of power consumption in CMOS circuits.

Switching. Unlike TTL or ECL, CMOS transistors drain only minimal current (leakage current) when they are open or closed. Instead, they consume current while switching. The power dissipated in a CMOS circuit depends on the voltage swing, the load capacitance driven by each net in the circuit, the operating frequency, and the switching activity (the fraction of wires that actually toggle) according to the equation

$$P = A \cdot V_{dd}^2 \cdot \sum_{i}^{nets} f_s \cdot C_i,$$

where V_{dd} is the supply voltage, f_s is the switching frequency (also called *toggle rate*), C_i is the load capacitance on net i in the device, and A is the fraction of nets in the circuit that actually switch. Important facts to learn from this equation are: power dissipation depends *linearly on frequency* and *quadratically on voltage*. As nothing can be done in software about capacitive load, software techniques that reduce switching power address both frequency and voltage, although at different levels of granularity.

Leakage. The current that flows through a CMOS gate when it is not switching is called leakage. Leakage used to be small in absolute value (about 1% of the total dissipation up to 0.25μ process technology), but it is now growing to much higher levels for deep submicron geometries (30% of the overall power budget due to leakage is not uncommon for 90nm and below). In other words, leakage is becoming a major part of the power dissipation of modern VLSI circuits. Leakage is also important because it affects the *standby* operation of a device. To reduce leakage dissipation, software techniques can selectively turn off parts of the device. However, the hardware itself is quite effective at turning off blocks that are not used, and thus it is unclear what value software adds.

We can categorize software techniques that address power by the granularity at which they operate. In the following we present a short overview of some of the operating-system-level approaches, largely focusing on compiler tactics because these relate more closely to VLIW architectures.

One of the most effective power-reduction strategies uses voltage-frequency scaling. By reducing the operating frequency of a processor, it is usually possible to also lower its supply voltage (Section 5.8.1 includes a more detailed discussion on power and ILP). This produces a cubic reduction of the energy consumption. However, the program execution time increases as well, due to the slower frequency. Assume that we decrease the voltage from V_1 to V_2 and the frequency from f_1 to f_2. This increases the run time from t_1 to t_2, which we can roughly approximate as $t_1(f_1/f_2)$. Then, the energy savings become

$$\frac{E_1}{E_2} = \frac{\int_{t=0}^{t_1}(k \cdot f_1 \cdot V_1^2)dt}{\int_{t=0}^{t_2}(k \cdot f_2 \cdot V_2^2)dt} \approx \frac{t_1 \cdot f_1 \cdot V_1^2}{t_2 \cdot f_2 \cdot V_2^2} \approx \frac{t_1 \cdot f_1 \cdot V_1^2}{t_1 \cdot \frac{f_1}{f_2} \cdot f_2 \cdot V_2^2} = \left(\frac{V_1}{V_2}\right)^2$$

Thus, energy savings are null if we cannot reduce the voltage. Unfortunately, as VLSI technology shrinks, the voltage reduction we can apply also diminishes significantly. For example, at 0.35μ feature size, typical operating voltage is 3.5V. If we can reduce it to 1.5V, we get an impressive power reduction (a factor of about 5.4). However, at 0.10μ the typical operating voltage is 1.0V and we cannot reduce voltage below 0.8V (it approaches the threshold voltage for silicon). Thus, the power reduction is limited to a factor of about 1.5. In a few more process generations, frequency-voltage scaling will run out of benefits (unless some new technology breakthrough happens). At that time, software-driven power techniques will become more important.

Power-aware Software Techniques

Frequency-voltage scaling is usually controlled by the operating system. The OS can see the granularity of the running processes (or threads) in the machine, and thus can play with the *slack* of a process deadline to make it run longer at lower voltages without significant performance degradation. In other words, the previous equation tells us that it is more energy efficient to have a process finish exactly at the desired deadline (at lower frequency-voltage) than to run it as fast as possible and have it sit idle the rest of the time.

At the compiler level, the most promising areas involve optimization techniques that address memory accesses, switching activity reduction, and instruction selection. Before we cover each of these in detail, it is worth observing that most compiler optimizations that reduce the number of executed instructions or program run time have a positive effect on overall energy efficiency, due to the linear dependency of energy on time. Some exceptions include speculation and predication, as we discussed in the previous sections. Given that these techniques are covered elsewhere in the book, this section deals with power-specific optimizations that would not be used in a compiler for performance optimization.

Controversy: Are There any Compiler Optimizations That Really Save Power?

As the power-saving features of embedded processors become more important, many advocate research in the area of power-aware compilers. Although some of the techniques certainly have some merit, we remain skeptical of the overall effectiveness of a compiler-driven power strategy. The reason is that a compiler normally operates at the wrong level of abstraction and with too narrow a scope to be able to make good power decisions. The most effective power optimizations come from either below or above the compiler level. In other words, even with an application developer that is trying to maximize battery life and is willing to play all the cards the cost of adding compiler heuristics to optimize power might outweigh the advantages.

Circuit techniques, transistor technology, and microarchitecture design are the major drivers for low-power implementations. By definition, all of these layers are invisible to a compiler, which operates at the architecture level.

At the application level, the key is to dedicate the *right amount of computing power* to get the job done *just in time*. This means playing with the slack of job completion times versus real-time deadlines, as well as with voltage-frequency control knobs. All of these activities naturally map to an abstraction level that is typical of operating systems (or upper middleware layers, such as *thread* packages), whereby we can reason around a time granularity of milliseconds.

Compilers tend to have a very limited visibility (if any at all) into the absolute timing effect of a localized piece of code, and only through statistical profiling can they usually make any heuristic decisions. Power decisions often come from dynamic phase changes or events with a much coarser time scale (for example, the events that trigger a processor going in or out of *sleep* or *hibernation* modes).

Finally, many of the proposed techniques for saving power tend to overlap with similar techniques for improving performance (for example, we can save power by preferring register accesses to memory accesses, but this is far from a new problem). In addition, because of the off-line nature of a static compiler many of the compiler decisions are made based on aggregate statistics and characterizations that may be extremely misleading in capturing power effects.

We think a static compiler is the wrong place to make fine-grain power decisions. Dedicating the effort to implementing the right architecture hooks for power (which can be exploited at the OS level or above) would be a much better investment. The situation might change when considering dynamic compilers (which continuously transform code at run-time, such as *Transmeta's code morphing system*), in which case the amount (and timing) of available information might allow code transformations to save significant power.

Reducing Switching Activity. The idea is to change the priority function of the instruction scheduler to minimize control path switching between successive instructions. A table can hold the power characterization corresponding to the switching activity observed by executing pairs of successive instructions. The compiler can then use this table to sort the data-ready queue of operations to be scheduled. After scheduling an operation, the algorithm recomputes the new priorities for all other data-ready operations. Experimental evaluations show a reduction of 20 to 30% of the switching activity in the control path.

Power-aware Instruction Selection. This approach influences the instruction selection phase with actual measurements of the power footprint of instructions. One can measure the current in general-purpose and DSP processors, and use these measurements to drive the cost function of the rewriting rules in the instruction selection phase of the compiler. Research experiments also extend to pairs of commonly used instructions, and to the choice of register-oriented instructions versus memory-oriented operations. They show energy reductions up to 40%. In general, these sets of techniques are rather straightforward to implement, as long as a characterization of energy consumption for each operation (or combination of operations) is available. This is because the instruction selection module already contains the notion of a cost-driven selection algorithm, and the question becomes what weight to associate to the power component versus what weights to associate to other factors (such as code size or speed). Intuitively, processors with heterogeneous instruction sets (such as traditional DSPs) are likely to benefit more from these techniques, although we are not aware of any study in this specific area. One variation of the instruction selection technique consists of controlling optimization heuristics based on power considerations. For example, certain classes of strength reduction transformations (such as replacing multiplies with add-and-shift sequences) are beneficial to power.

Scheduling for Minimal Dissipation. Another aspect of software optimization deals with the reduction of power peaks ("spikes") during program execution. Although this does not address energy requirements, it is important to reduce the maximum current requirement of the power supply, which can itself impact battery life (for reasons beyond the scope of this book). Some of the proposed algorithms modify the cycle-by-cycle list scheduler for a VLIW target. The compiler can keep track of the accumulated dissipation "footprint" of each functional unit for the scheduled instructions. When the schedule reaches a predetermined dissipation budget, the scheduler advances to the next cycle. This approach achieves significant power savings without noticeable performance degradation.

Memory Access Optimizations. Recently, a few techniques have emerged to optimize the memory access patterns for power consumption. In general, these approaches advocate the use of local storage (registers or scratch-pad memory) to reduce the number of accesses to local memory. Beyond register allocation, it is worth mentioning some of the most interesting techniques. The use of *register pipelining* aims at reducing memory operations by temporarily moving array elements into registers and shows energy reduction up to 25%, depending on assumptions about the memory architecture. The use of *scratch-pad* local memories to store temporary values is another technique that attempts to avoid access into the memory hierarchy. Minimizing the access width of memory operations might have a beneficial impact on power for architectures that directly implement short/byte memory accesses.

Data Remapping. A promising technique called *data remapping* uses a compile-time data reorganization of the application's data in memory, so that memory elements that are accessed near each other temporally are near each other in memory. In contrast to loop skewing and other locality-improving techniques, data remapping works on very dynamic pointer-intensive code, and uses a profiling-based method to work on programs with irregular memory access patterns. Unlike other recently considered methods, data remapping does everything at compile-time and is completely automated. By improving the locality of this type of data, a lot of needless fetching can be avoided. This appears to bring significant benefit in performance and cache size, could be used for design exploration, and could significantly improve power consumption. Indeed, using a realistic modeling technique, memory-system power (a significant part of overall power) was reduced an average of 40% on a wide range of benchmarks.

7.6 DSP-Specific Compiler Optimizations

To a man with a hammer, everything looks like a nail.

— Mark Twain

As discussed previously, DSP architectures tend to be specialized for a narrow domain of applications in an attempt to minimize cost and power dissipation. Although it is true that specialization usually helps reduce hardware costs and power, this often comes at the expense of programmability and flexibility. At one end of the spectrum, ASICs (hardwired logic blocks for one specific function) and ASIPs (application-specific instruction-set processors) are implementation styles that favor hardware cost reductions. At the other end of the spectrum, general-purpose microcontrollers (such as 32-bit embedded RISCs) accept some inherent inefficiency to achieve better programmability and to be more compiler friendly. DSPs sit in the middle. Traditional DSP engines (such as the Texas Instruments TMS320C54x family) resemble ASIPs and include very specialized computing resources, as well as rather severe restrictions in their usage. As DSP applications become more complex, DSPs gradually mutate in the direction of general-purpose processors. A clear example of this trend is in the Texas Instruments TMS320C6x (C6x) family, which implements a fairly clean and orthogonal clustered VLIW instruction set that represents a good target for the most advanced techniques of ILP compilers. Figure 7.5 shows a block diagram of the datapaths of the two TI DSPs that highlights the evolution trajectory.

In this section, we take a step back and briefly analyze some of the compilation techniques that proliferated in the 1990s to explicitly target more traditional DSP hardware. As a disclaimer, we need to say that we consider these techniques a good example of excellent science applied to a problem whose relevance is likely to diminish as

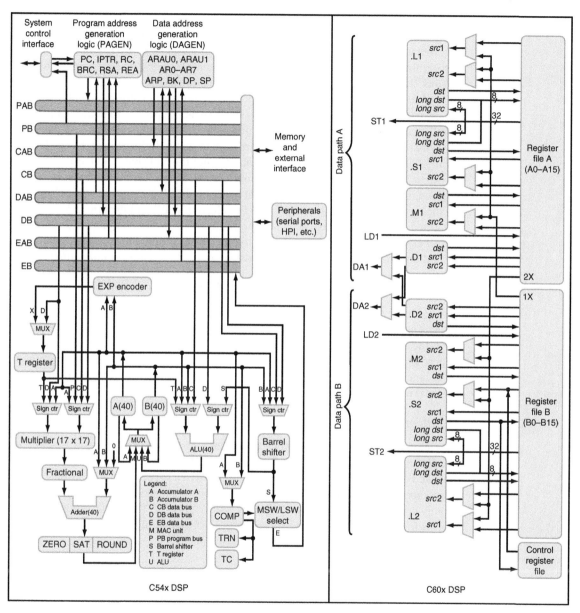

FIGURE 7.5 **Structure of the TI C54x and C60x DSPs.** The C54x family is a good example of "traditional" DSP data-paths: a few heterogeneous registers, with specialized functionality and connectivity constraints; dedicated paths to and from memory; a Harvard architecture (separate code/data memory paths); and separate address-generation unit. The C60x is a good example of what DSPs are evolving into: clean VLIW architecture, orthogonal datapaths, homogeneous register files with many registers, well-connected functional units, and no specialized paths to memory. Redrawn from: Texas Instruments, TMS320C54X, TMS320LC54X, TMS320VC54X fixed-point digital signal processors, Literature Number SPRS039C, February 1996 (Revised December 1999).

technology progresses. Most of the considerations that drove DSP hardware minimization guidelines are losing much of their appeal with the advent of deep submicron VLSI technology. Just to give an example, in a 0.13 μ process, an entire four-issue VLIW processor (integer datapath) — with four ALUs, two multipliers, 64 fully connected 32-bit registers, 32 KB of data cache, and 32 KB of instruction cache — fits in less than 5mm^2 of silicon.[4] At this density, a VLSI designer's priority shifts from minimizing the number of transistors to improving testability and reuse, increasing speed, and better managing the overall complexity of the design. The hardware limitations of traditional DSP designs are driven by the goal of truly *minimizing* hardware costs (including the cost of code size in on-chip ROM). In practice, true minimization is not the real goal. There is a cost threshold below which we are not willing to compromise other desirable properties (such as programmability). Our feeling is that most traditional DSP designs are well below such a threshold, and a slightly more expensive but cleaner VLIW architecture is a much more desirable target from the compiler viewpoint. In this respect, compiler techniques that address DSP-specific limitations caused by the lack of proper hardware support are less relevant once we move to more regular instruction sets and microarchitectures.

7.6.1 Compiler-visible Features of DSPs

DSPs are more than "processors with multiply-accumulate (MAC)." Although it is true that the performance of MAC-intensive code is still what people use to benchmark DSPs, the differences compared to a general-purpose (or VLIW) processor go much deeper. At a very coarse-grain level, we can distinguish four areas that are unique to DSPs: heterogeneous registers, complex addressing modes, very limited connectivity, and local memories.

Heterogeneous Registers

DSPs are famous for their abundance of special registers, with dedicated functionality at the inputs and outputs of computational units. Wide registers at the output of multipliers and accumulators at the output of adders are two very common examples. Special address registers for accessing memory and special data registers for storing data to/from memory are also present in the majority of traditional DSPs. These features are historical artifacts from the days when multiported register files had high costs.

Addressing Modes

Because many DSP programs traverse data in a linear way, DSP architectures have traditionally adopted indirect addressing modes through specialized registers, with auto-increment and auto-decrement capabilities. In order to diminish code size pressure and hardware, the increment range is typically small (in some cases just +1 and −1), and only a few registers can be used as memory address registers. More complex DSPs also

---

4. This example is derived from technology projections of the specification of the ST200 embedded VLIW core, a member of the HP/ST Lx family of cores, published in *Microprocessor Forum 2000*.

include application-specific addressing modes, specified as qualifiers of memory operations and auto-increments. These more complex addressing modes include *bit-reversed addressing* (useful for FFT-like butterfly operations) and *circular addressing* (useful in accessing circular buffers and filter masks). The main motivation for auto-increment memory accesses is to reduce code size by saving the cost of an extra operation for address computation.

Limited Connectivity

Perhaps the most severe obstacle to compiler optimizations is that DSP registers are only partially connected to functional units. Although this is true also for clustered VLIW architectures, the difference is that a clustered VLIW still assumes the individual units within a cluster to be fully interconnected with the cluster *register files*. Hence, a compiler can deal with clustering through a separate assignment phase, as we discuss in Section 8.2.6. DSP registers are usually tied to a specific subset of units, and data transfers are controlled by special operations. Yet again, this philosophy enables a more size-conscious encoding, in that only certain operations can access certain registers.

Local Memories

Traditional DSPs do not use cache memories but prefer on-chip storage under direct compiler control. Although this is very effective when the compiler perfectly understands the program, DSPs must often rely on user *directives* to allocate data objects. A common approach driven by a large fraction of dual-array DSP algorithms is the so-called *X-Y memory* organization in which the processor can access two separate memory regions through separate operations and datapaths (see Figure 7.6). Note that this has a 1:1

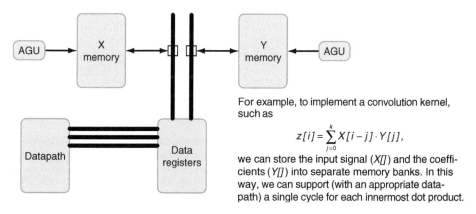

For example, to implement a convolution kernel, such as

$$z[i] = \sum_{j=0}^{k} X[i-j] \cdot Y[j],$$

we can store the input signal ($X[]$) and the coefficients ($Y[]$) into separate memory banks. In this way, we can support (with an appropriate datapath) a single cycle for each innermost dot product.

FIGURE 7.6 **X-Y memories.** Many DSPs support partitioned memory banks (traditionally called X-Y memory) along with parallel load/store instructions to each bank, to support the necessary bandwidth to feed the parallel functional units without sacrificing hardware complexity of code density. To effectively utilize the parallel load/store instructions, compilers must partition memory-allocated values (both scalars and arrays) and assign them to the X or Y bank. For example, the Motorola 56k, the Analog Devices ADSP-210x series, and the ARC family fall into this category.

correspondence with some of the proposed DSP-specific language extensions discussed in Section 10.1.6.

Harvard Architecture

Given that DSPs do not normally include cache memories, they often require separate physical memory buses to enable simultaneous memory accesses. This is usually referred to as *Harvard architecture*, a contrast to the (initial definition of the) von Neumann architecture (which interleaved program and data memory accesses to the same bus). However, whereas "traditional Harvard" architectures (see Figure 7.7) use separate buses for instruction and data accesses, in the DSP world the "program" bus can also be used to fetch data operands.[5]

Finally, we need to point out that this is far from being an exhaustive list of DSP-specific features. Other important characteristics include:

- *Low-overhead looping* constructs to directly support a few levels of counted loop nests with a single operation

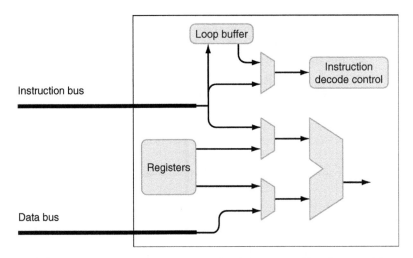

FIGURE 7.7 Harvard architecture in DSPs. Like many DSP architectural features, memory organization reuses implementation hardware in an effort to conserve transistors and wires. Many DSPs are built around a "Harvard architecture," in this case meaning that there are separate buses for instruction and data memory. The "loop buffer" allows the DSP to execute instructions without accessing memory. This frees the instruction bus to supply additional operands to the functional units of the machine. These operands are read from instruction memory. For example, the filter coefficients of an FIR or IIR filter might be stored in program memory and convolved with input data.

---

5. For example, this variation of the basic Harvard architecture to include a small program cache is what triggered Analog Devices' SHARC (*Super Harvard ARChitecture*) trademark.

- *Control of arithmetic modes*, such as the possibility of switching between *saturated* and *wraparound* overflow modes

- *High-precision accumulators* that store more than the standard-machine word length (a typical size is 40 bits, suitable for audio-manipulation algorithms)

As some of these features start appearing in general-purpose processors,[6] the more general compiler techniques described in the rest of the book are usually appropriate for generating efficient code for them. For this reason we do not extensively discuss them here, but encourage the readers to consider the applicability of the known compiler techniques previously discussed.

7.6.2 Instruction Selection and Scheduling

One of the major obstacles to optimizing compilers for traditional scalar DSP targets comes from the necessity of tightly coupling *instruction selection* and *register allocation*. The fact that often only a few registers (sometimes as few as one) can be used to address memory further complicates the picture. Compilers targeting more orthogonal instruction sets deal with the problem by decoupling the two phases, since the choice of an operation usually does not constrain register usage (true in modern RISC and CISC processors alike).

For traditional DSP targets with parallel execution units, the same problem percolates to the scheduling phase and in the exploitation of ILP. Often we can issue parallel operations only if the operands are in the "proper" locations (registers or memory) and if we are using the right "combinations" of operations. Once again, this complicates compiler algorithms, and often yields problems that cannot be efficiently solved in polynomial time. Indeed, several DSP compilation approaches propose using nondeterministic iterative methods (such as genetic algorithms or simulated annealing).

Consider a simple example of a multiplication feeding the result to an addition. In the C54x datapath, we can see that we already have a few choices: the result of the multiplication could be kept in one of the accumulators, it could be transferred to one of the address or data registers (through specialized instructions), or it could be saved to memory and restored from memory as a memory or address register. Unfortunately, these are the types of choices that are difficult to make during instruction selection, and ideally a compiler would like to delay the binding of containers (register or memory) for the program values at a later stage (such as register allocation). In contrast, for the TI C60x datapath we can see that there are really only two choices (cluster A or cluster B) in terms of allocation of computation to functional units, and that we can safely delay register assignments to a later stage. This is an example of what we call a *compiler-friendly* datapath.

Compilers typically use a form of *tree pattern matching* to implement the instruction selection phase (such as the IBURG method). This approach uses dataflow trees to represent the intermediate representation syntax trees, wherein nodes correspond to operands

---

6. Two examples: the Intel IPF family includes a low-overhead looping instruction used in software-pipelined loops; many media-oriented micro-SIMD extensions include saturated arithmetic modes.

(variables or immediates) and operations and edges correspond to data dependences. The matcher algorithm uses a set of patterns characterized by a cost, and finds the optimal covering of the dataflow tree based on the aggregate cost function. Tools such as IBURG are generator-generators that produce the C implementation of the matcher starting from a grammar description of the patterns and their cost. A typical IBURG description consists of a set of rules that matches input expression trees with target operations while assigning them a cost. For example, the following rule set describes three simple VEX operations (*add, mpy,* and *sh1add*).

```
terminals: {*, +}
non-terminals: {reg}
rules:
    reg: +(reg, reg)       = "add"    (1);
    reg: *(reg, reg)       = "mpy"    (2);
    reg: +(*(reg, 2),reg) = "sh1add" (1);
```

The IBURG algorithms will generate a pattern-matching code (see Figure 7.8) so that all rules are attempted with the goal of finding the lowest cost configuration. Thus, in the above example, when presented with an input tree containing the expression $\{a * 2 + b\}$, IBURG will use the *sh1add* rule (with cost of 1) instead of a combination of the *add* and *mpy* rules (with a combined cost of 3).

The presence of heterogeneous register sets adds a further complication: the patterns to match now become dependent on the specific register allocation chosen for the operations. This suggests that register allocation should be performed together with instruction selection, which is what many DSP compilation techniques propose. For example, one approach involves extending the pattern matcher to also consider the costs of moving the results into any other reachable location in the datapath.

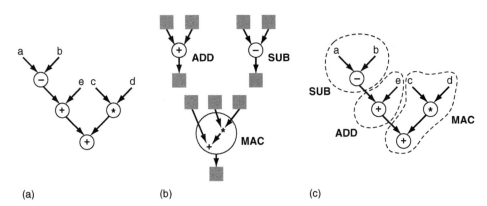

(a)   (b)   (c)

FIGURE 7.8 **Example of tree pattern-matching for instruction selection.** Figure *a* shows a snapshot of the dataflow graph, representing a simple combination of arithmetic operations. Figure *b* shows the patterns that represent the available instructions in our target architecture. Figure *c* shows the optimal coverage of *a* using *b*.

Finally, other approaches depart more radically from the IBURG-style pattern matcher and add nondeterministic iterative components such as simulated annealing or genetic algorithms.

7.6.3 Address Computation and Offset Assignment

DSPs have few registers, and thus memory addressing is necessary to store temporary data in expressions — in a similar way to early CISC machines. As we discussed, DSPs usually include support for auto-increment and auto-decrement in parallel with memory operations, and only a limited number of address registers can access memory. Unfortunately, many DSPs do not have base-plus-offset memory addressing, and thus it is necessary to perform address arithmetic to access stack-allocated variables.

DSP compilers typically include a peephole pass to optimize auto-increment operations, as well as some heuristics to place variables in local storage (i.e., the stack) so that the opportunities to use the auto-increment operations increase for a given access sequence. The problem of assigning locations to variables is often referred to as the *offset assignment problem*. In the case in which there is only one address register, the problem is called *simple offset assignment* (SOA). Starting from the operations on a dataflow graph, the SOA problem (see Figure 7.9) consists of determining the best order in which to access the variables (*access sequence*), and the location of the variables in memory (i.e., their offset in the local stack). Starting from the access sequence, we can construct an *access graph* weighted with a cost derived from the fact that the access to two variables is adjacent in the given access sequence. The best solution is the one that maximizes the weight, in that it is the one that better uses the auto-increment modes. The problem is NP-complete and can be generalized to the case of multiple address registers.

7.6.4 Local Memories

As we mentioned in the previous section, several DSPs include two separate memory banks (usually called X and Y), which are accessible in parallel. This raises the problem of partitioning the program variables between X and Y in such a way that potential parallelism is maximized. Naive compilers use only one of the two banks, or leave the partitioning decision to the programmer by means of C language extensions.

More aggressive compilers use a variety of heuristics, ranging from simple round-robin assignment (alternate assignment to X-Y banks based on access order in the sequential intermediate code) to assignments based on variable interference graphs.

Variable partitioning is a very difficult task. It is intrinsically a global operation, and decisions made during scheduling need to be propagated to the compilation for the rest of the program. The lack of precise memory alias information may force very conservative decisions (assume overlap) for nonscalar accesses, or accesses through pointers. Additionally, X-Y assignments should ideally balance the bank accesses and allocations across the entire program, but the compiler can make only local decisions. Finally, reconciliation between contrasting requirements (two regions requesting different bank assignments) may involve reallocations or issuing copy operations to position the values where required.

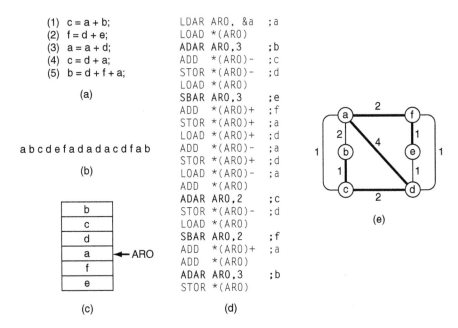

```
(1)  c = a + b;              LDAR ARO, &a    ;a
(2)  f = d + e;              LOAD *(ARO)
(3)  a = a + d;              ADAR ARO,3      ;b
(4)  c = d + a;              ADD  *(ARO)-    ;c
(5)  b = d + f + a;          STOR *(ARO)-    ;d
                             LOAD *(ARO)
        (a)                  SBAR ARO,3      ;e
                             ADD  *(ARO)+    ;f
                             STOR *(ARO)+    ;a
                             LOAD *(ARO)+    ;d
  a b c d e f a d a d a c d f a b   ADD  *(ARO)-    ;a
                             STOR *(ARO)+    ;d
        (b)                  LOAD *(ARO)-    ;a
                             ADD  *(ARO)
                             ADAR ARO,2      ;c
                             STOR *(ARO)-    ;d
                             LOAD *(ARO)
                             SBAR ARO,2      ;f
                             ADD  *(ARO)+    ;a
                             ADD  *(ARO)
                             ADAR ARO,3      ;b
                             STOR *(ARO)
```

Memory layout (c):

| b |
| c |
| d |
| a | ← ARO |
| f |
| e |

(c)   (d)

FIGURE 7.9 **Example of simple offset assignment (SOA) problem.** Figure (a) is the original sequence of operations, and figure (b) one of the possible access sequences to evaluate the expression. Figure (c) shows the result of the memory offset assignment, and figure (e) the access graph for the sequence with the weighted edges. Figure (d) represents the resulting sequence of operations (in TMS320C25 assembler) for the expression, where ADAR is *add address register*, SBAR is *subtract address register*, LDAR is *load address register*, and LOAD/STORE are the memory operations (possibly with auto-increment and auto-decrement modifiers). Note that we omit the *accumulator* operand, used as the result of ADD/LOAD operations, as well as the second operand of ADD/STORE operations.

Several of the advanced partitioning techniques use the concept of an *interference graph* (computed from the data dependence graph), whereby nodes represent variables and edges represent potential parallel accesses to them. Finding a good partitioning implies maximizing the sum of edge weights between the X and Y subsets of the graph (this is the NP-complete *max-cut* problem). Heuristics and linear programming approaches have been proposed to solve this problem, but it is important to remember that the interference graph only maximizes the *possibility* of exposing parallel memory operations, whereas the final determination can only be resolved during scheduling. From this observation, we may argue that a simpler preassignment technique might represent a good tradeoff.

7.6.5 Register Assignment Techniques

Registers in a DSP processor are assumed to be *scarce resources* that must be carefully optimized. This is another cause of problems for DSP compilers. A VLIW compiler (as well as the corresponding VLIW architecture philosophy) takes the opposite approach: it makes the assumption that registers are not the limiting resources. In general, designing a compiler based on the assumption that there are never going to be enough registers is a guarantee of major headaches. Traditional coloring-based register allocation techniques for modern RISC-like processors rely on the assumption that spilling and restoring are "exceptional" events, and that in general there are enough registers to cover most of the cases.

Traditional coloring-based register allocation techniques are not adequate for machines with heterogeneous register sets that have scarce resources and poor interconnections. Much research has been done on this problem, and many of the complications arise from the tight coupling of scheduling, instruction selection, and register assignment.

Compilers targeting machines with homogeneous register sets normally decouple the register allocation issue by implementing it in a separate phase (see Section 8.3.1). The scheduler only needs to estimate the register pressure, in that the only effect of register allocation is the insertion of spill/restore code. Likewise, for a clustered architecture (separate homogeneous register files) it is common to preassign operations to clusters, so that the register allocation task is again simplified.

In the DSP — or ASIP — domain, register assignments may have very deep consequences on the scheduling, as well as on the available parallelism. For example, a common DSP feature enables parallel register assignments, as long as certain registers are used for certain operations. Other DSP features allow only certain registers to be used by auto-increment (or auto-decrement) operations, and rearranging the code to take advantage of auto-increments might reduce the number of register assignments. Finally, given the limitations of paths to memory it is sometimes necessary to take into account register assignment even during traditional "scalar" optimization phases, such as common-subexpression elimination.

These considerations tie the register assignment phase to the other compiler phases (first and foremost, the scheduling phase), and it is common for the DSP and ASIP domains to attempt to solve the problem in one phase by applying integer linear programming techniques that account for all constraints simultaneously. Given the time complexity of these techniques (they can take minutes for medium-size regions), their applicability is limited to cases in which the program is small or for which a very long compile time is affordable.

7.6.6 Retargetable DSP and ASIP Compilers

Retargetable compilers are compilers that can generate code for a variety of target processors, usually starting from a description of the machine resources. (We cover retargetability in more detail in Chapter 10.) In this section we describe some of the different techniques that apply to the area of retargetability for DSPs and ASIPs. Under the term *ASIP* we include (usually small) processors dedicated to one specific application, and whose instruction set is highly specialized for that purpose. ASIPs have been commonly adopted in areas with extremely high cost pressure that cannot tolerate the complexity (power, code size, and so on) of a more general-purpose processor, as they normally contain just enough resources to "get the job done." ASIPs are normally used in systems in which the application tends to be fixed (or nearly fixed) from the beginning. They are often deployed in combination with *nonprogrammable* parts that implement the most performance-intensive components of the application. An ASIP-based product usually requires both a retargetable compiler, to be able to adjust the resources of the programmable parts, and a *hardware/software partitioning* strategy to decide what needs to be implemented in nonprogrammable logic. Figure 7.10 shows the role of a retargetable compiler in a co-design environment.

Unlike the more regular VLIW engines, customizable DSPs and ASIPs support drastic changes in instruction and memory types, sizes and partitions, bit-widths of address

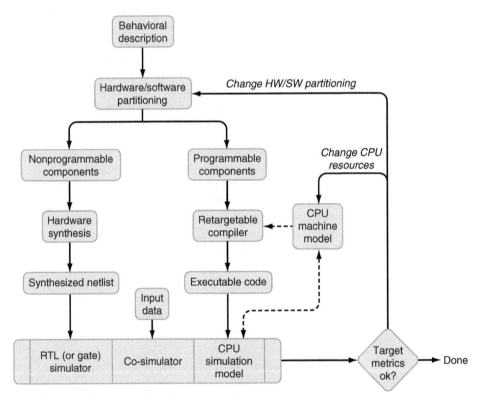

FIGURE 7.10   Hardware/software co-design and retargetable compilers. The chart shows the basic steps of a hardware/software co-design loop using a custom ASIP for the programmable components. The process involves a double-nested decision loop, whereby the outermost choices involve deciding the nonprogrammable parts and the innermost loop tunes the computing resources of the programmable processor. A *retargetable* compiler (as well as simulator) is fundamental to be able to quickly evaluate several design alternatives without having to rewrite compiler optimization phases.

and data, specialized registers with dedicated connections, specialized loop units, and so on. This makes the task of retargeting in the ASIP space extremely difficult, and shifts the emphasis heavily in the direction of instruction selection, register allocation, and scheduling. In contrast, the job of retargetable compilers that target a more regular architecture space (such as VEX) is much easier in the instruction selection phase. This also makes it possible to dedicate much more effort to ILP-enhancing optimizations such as region scheduling.[7]

When instruction selection becomes the most important phase, phase ordering among code selection, scheduling, and register allocation play very important roles in the overall quality. In this case — and for small-enough program regions — it is conceivable to apply *integer linear programming techniques* to solve the combined problem, so that we can account for all machine constraints and optimize an objective function that combines the various target metrics. There have been several approaches to the problem of retargetable compilers, which we can roughly divide into two camps.

- One camp is compilers that target "regular" architectures. Such compilers include the VEX compiler (and its predecessor Multiflow), HP Labs' Elcor, Impact from UIUC (and the Trimaran platform), the GNU C compiler (*gcc*) and derivatives, and Stanford's SUIF. All of these compilers make some assumptions on the regularity of the target architecture space, and as such are probably better described as "parameterizable" compilers. Here the emphasis is on robustness, a large set of ILP-enhancing optimizations, region scheduling, and a limited retargeting range.

- The other camp is compilers that target "irregular" architectures (ASIPs and DSPs). These include CHESS from IMEC, AVIV from MIT, Express from UC Irvine, and Lance from Dortmund University. These compilers are largely a derivation of high-level synthesis and co-design efforts, and have traditionally focused on optimizations dedicated to the irregular features of target machines, with some compromises for more advanced region transformations, loop restructuring, and ILP enhancements.

We believe that, as DSPs becomes more regular, the distinctions between the DSP and ASIP approaches will gradually decrease and ultimately disappear. Many of the considerations that drove ASIP-specific techniques are becoming less important with the diminishing cost of hardware and the widespread diffusion of "clean" architectures in the embedded domain. We think that the capability to integrate a retargetable compiler in the rest of the compilation toolchain — as well as the capability to leverage the target description for simulation, verification, and design — will be the differentiating factors of a successful retargetable platform. Chapter 10 covers some of these considerations in further detail.

---

7. In this sense, the VEX compiler can also be called "*parametrizable*," in that the variations in the architecture target can largely be expressed through a set of tables. This would not be possible for an ASIP, wherein the variability also includes structural elements and usually requires more complex description languages.

7.7 Further Reading

We are not aware of books that cover embedded toolchains in detail, but given how open-source software (particularly Linux) has gained a lot of mindshare and design wins in the embedded development community we recommend reading the documentation that comes with the GNU *gcc* compiler, the GNU *gdb* debugger, and the GNU *binutils* binary utility distribution (all available from the GCC web site, the ucLinux web site, the ucDot web site, and the embedded Linux web site).

The intermediate representation (IR) is the spine of every compiler, and thus traditional compiler books are good references for some of the guidelines to follow in the area of IR design. In addition to the "Dragon Book" by Aho, Sethi, and Ullmann [1986], we also recommend the books by Appel [1998], Morgan [1998], Muchnick [1997], and Allen and Kennedy [2002].

For a good start on tree matching we recommend the paper by Aho et al. [1989]. Additionally, the seminal work by Fraser et al. [1992a] on Iburg is mandatory reading for anyone interested in the foundations of instruction selection in modern compilers.

The textbooks by Leupers [1997] and Leupers and Marwedel [2001] provide a good coverage of compilation topics relevant to retargetable compiling for DSPs and ASIPs. The works by Liao et al. [1995a and b] also present some embedded-specific code optimization techniques. An example of a theoretical approach addressing the memory assignment problem for X-Y memory is the paper by Wess and Gotschlich [1997].

In Section 7.6 we mention a variety of retargetable compilers available in the research domain. For Trimaran, Mescal, Lance, SUIF, Machine SUIF, IMPACT, Zephyr, and GCC we recommend exploring their web sites and the associated documentation. The paper by Laneer et al. [1995] is a good introduction to CHESS (which has since been commercialized by Target Compiler Technology). The work by Hanono and Devadas [1998] discusses the techniques used in the MIT AVIV compiler.

Code Layout

One of the earliest techniques for program layout optimization was published by McFarling [1989]. An independent technique based on weighted call graphs (and successively implemented in the IMPACT compiler) was proposed by Hwu and Chang [1989]. The work by Pettis and Hansen [1990] at HP is what gave name to one of the most widely used techniques. Hashemi et al. [1997] proposed an improvement to Pettis-Hansen based on a coloring technique. Finally, the approach by Gloy and Smith [1999] diverges from most of the other approaches in considering the temporal order of procedures.

Power-aware Software Techniques

Several researchers have attacked the problem of reducing power through software optimizations. For example, Su et al. [1994] propose a technique (called *cold scheduling*) that applies Gray code addressing to the list-scheduling phase of an optimizing compiler. Tiwari et al. [1994a and b] propose a technique for power-aware instruction scheduling based on real measurements. Toburen et al. [1998] attack the area of power dissipation, and attempt to minimize "power spikes." Steinke et al. [2001] propose the use of *register pipelining* to reduce power by reducing memory addresses. Panda et al. [1999] favor the use of *scratch-pad* memory for the same purpose. Rabbah, Palem et al. [2003] propose the technique of data remapping. Kandemir et al. [2000] describe some of the effects of compiler optimizations on power. Macii et al. [1998] and Lee et al. [1995] provide (respectively) a CAD- and DSP-oriented perspective on power analysis and scheduling techniques. In the area of architectural support, Asanovic [2000] and Hajj et al. [1998] propose different approaches to expose some of the features that would let software better control power aspects. Finally, measurement and simulation are another important aspect of power optimization techniques. Brooks et al. [2000] propose the use of Wattch, a framework for power analysis and optimization. For a discussion of how to design embedded software for low power we suggest the paper by Roy and Johnson [1996]. For more details on transistor-level power analysis, a good overview can be found in the work of Chou and Roy [1996].

7.8 Exercises

1. Build an assembler for an ERISC (one add, load, store, branch instructions only) machine. Then add delay-slot filling.

2. Build a compiled simulator for the ERISC machine.

3. Consider one of the applications of Chapter 11. Try various code layouts by manually changing the order of routines within a compilation unit. Use the VEX cache simulator to see how things turn out. Note: changing the link order would normally have similar effects, but it does not for the VEX toolchain because of the dynamic linking behavior of the compiled simulator. Explain what happens.

4. Make up a simple VEX loop example (e.g., DAXPY) and software-pipeline versus loop-unroll-then-region-schedule by hand. Compare the results. Try it with a machine with predicates and rotating registers.

5. To do their job, debuggers require information about the program being debugged (for example, where the procedures are located, how structures are defined, and so on). Look up how this information is represented in two of the most commonly used debugging formats, STABS and DWARF.

6. Using the VEX toolchain, compile and simulate a simple program ("hello world"), collect static compilation statistics, and collect dynamic execution statistics.

7. Write VEX sequential assembly code (one operation per instruction), using the following standard function template, to implement the following set of functions: saturated 16-bit addition, $32 \times 32 \rightarrow 64$-bit integer multiplication, string comparison, and memory copy.

```
##
## This is the "standard function template" for a function f1()
## with the following signature
##
##        int f1 (int a, int b, int c);
##
## That the framesize (ASIZE) needs to be set by the user; it can be 0
## if the function does not require local stack space
##
.rta 2                  ## Set the ABI convention
.section .text          ## Start a text section
.proc                   ## Start a new procedure
##
##  Add more arguments to the .entry directory if needed
.entry caller, sp=$r0.1, rl=$10.0, asize=0, arg($r0.3:s32,$r0.4:s32,$r0.5:s32)
f1::            ## procedure entry point
        c0    add $r0.1 = $r0.1, ASIZE ## push frame
;;

        ##
        ## Here is the function body, using ARG1 in $r0.3,
        ## ARG2 in $r0.4, ..., ARG8 in $r0.10, and the
        ## stack pointer in $r0.1
        ##
        ## Return values (up to 8) must be assigned to
        ## $r0.3, $r0.4, ..., $r0.10
        ##
## Add more return values if needed
.return ret($r0.3:s32)
        c0    return $r0.1 = $r0.1, ASIZE, $10.0 ## pop frame and return
;;
.endp        ## End procedure
```

8. Repeat the previous exercise, and manually schedule the operations for
    a standard 4-wide VEX architecture to minimize cycle time. Construct
    a measuring framework and related data sets and measure the achieved
    performance improvement.

9. Optimize the VEX assembler implementation of the memory copy function
    (hint: exploit data alignment). Measure the throughput, in bytes per second,
    of the various implementations. Compare your VEX implementation with
    the performance you get on your desktop computer of the *memcpy()* library
    routine.

10. You are about to do a new academic architecture research project, and you need a compiler. Consider the following alternatives: *lcc*, *gcc*, pro64, SUIF, TI C6x compiler, Itanium compilers, the VEX compiler, Trimaran, and IMPACT. Rate each compiler in all of the following aspects: (1) legal availability and licensing restrictions, (2) support for region scheduling, (3) support for soft- ware pipelining, (4) degree of retargetability, and (5) robustness, given the benchmarks you want to run for your research. Your project is so successful you decided (totally ignoring all historical precedence) to start a company based on commercializing the architecture. What would change in your decision-making process?

8

Compiling for VLIWs and ILP

To find a form that accommodates the mess, that is the task of the artist now.

— Samuel Beckett, *Irish dramatist and novelist*, 1906–1989

This chapter focuses on the optimizations, or code transformations, critical to compiling for ILP architectures. The style of this chapter is closest to that of textbooks on optimization and compilation. However, our treatment of these topics stops short of the pseudocode, data structures, and algorithmic description that are the bread and butter of such works. Our goal is to give a sense for the major issues associated with back-end compilation rather than to describe all aspects of the algorithms. We recommend that readers follow the links in the "Further Reading" section for more detailed and precise algorithmic descriptions.

Much of the material in this chapter is common across all ILP-oriented architectures, including both VLIWs and superscalars. Any ILP architecture tries to maximize performance (and sometimes performance/price) by increasing the number of instructions per cycle that are processed. This chapter describes the compiler techniques that expose and enhance ILP in object code, so that an ILP-oriented implementation can exploit that ILP.

It is only recently that the topics discussed in this chapter have become relevant for embedded processors. As these techniques were pioneered and developed in the general-purpose world, most of this discussion is framed in that language. Where embedded issues are relevant to the techniques we present, we describe how they are relevant. The compilers and toolchains used for embedded processors are often the same or very similar to those used for their general-purpose counterparts. The previous chapter singled out a number of embedded- and DSP-specific optimizations. This chapter collects much material that is common across all types of ILP-oriented processors, for both general-purpose and embedded applications.

This chapter begins with profiling, collecting the statistics that drive many of the most important ILP optimizations, and many aspects of processor design. Even though many embedded applications can be considered "loop-oriented," profiling can still indicate the hottest parts of the program and the related "trip count" information that many loop-oriented code transformations can use. Section 8.2 covers various aspects of instruction scheduling, including an overview of the many types of schedulers, region formation, acyclic schedule compaction, resource management, cyclic scheduling, and scheduling for clustered architectures. We continue with a section on register allocation, a topic that interacts closely with scheduling. Section 8.4 discusses a variety of mechanisms for speculation, and the somewhat orthogonal technique of predication. Both of these techniques are used sparingly in embedded applications because of the power and complexity costs associated with their implementations. We end with Section 8.5, a discussion of instruction selection, which is especially important to processors (such as DSPs) with idiosyncratic instructions sets.

8.1 Profiling

Profiles are statistics about how a program spends its time and resources. Many crucial ILP optimizations — including instruction scheduling, clustering, and code layout — require good profile information. This subsection starts by describing the types of profile data, continues by summarizing the methods for collecting the profiles, goes on to describe heuristic techniques that avoid profiling, discusses the bookkeeping subtleties in using profiles, and then concludes with a discussion of how profiles apply to embedded systems.

8.1.1 Types of Profiles

Perhaps the earliest collected profile type was the *call graph,* such as that returned by the UNIX *gprof* utility. In a call graph, each procedure of the program is represented by a node, and edges between nodes indicate that one procedure calls another procedure. The profile shows how many times each procedure was called, or (in more detailed versions) how many times each caller procedure invoked a callee. Some utilities also include the percentage of time the program spends in each procedure, which is very useful (both humans and compilers can use such a profile to determine where optimization can be applied most profitably). Unfortunately, that is the limit of call graph profiles: they indicate which procedures might benefit from optimization, but they do not help one decide what to do to those procedures. The top half of Figure 8.1 shows a call graph profile.

For the next level of detail, and the profiles typically used in optimizing compilers, systems construct *control flow graph profiles*. In a control flow graph (CFG), each *basic block* of the program is represented by a node, and edges between nodes indicate that one basic block can execute after another basic block. A basic block is a sequence of

---

Controversy: Why Don't Developers Use Profiling Tools?

Profiling is a major piece of high-performance compiling technology, yet few application developers are willing to use it. This fact has been a major disappointment for compiler developers, and has been the subject of much discussion.

There is no consensus on what the critical issues are that discourage developers from profiling, but there is no shortage of reasons that seem to contribute to it. The reasons fall into two categories: engineering effort and trust. On the engineering effort front, profiling requires a separate compiling pass that even if it is engineered well by the tool producer significantly lengthens compile time when it is used. Also, as profiling is performed, a database must be kept around to gather the profiles, and the developer must deal with a persistent additional piece of data. The developer must decide when the data is getting stale, and clear out this database, as well as consider when the code has changed too much for the database to be relevant. Is the data really representative? Should it change as the understanding of the application and its uses change? These latter two considerations are also matters of trust in the process: Does the developer trust that the data chosen is really "representative" of what users will run? What will be the effects of telling the compiler that the data is realistic but then data of a totally different nature is actually run? Will the program be pessimized instead of optimized?

The larger aspect of trust concerns the question of aggressive optimization. Usually, compiler vendors do not want to give their customers a wide array of knobs to turn in controlling the compiler. Thus, the more common choice presented is a simple choice of degree of optimization, using command-line switches to specify which collection of optimizations to invoke. A common scheme is to use $-O1$ for the least level of optimization and $-O2$, $-O3$, and $-O4$ for the most aggressive optimization. Because compilers typically use profiling to perform the most aggressive optimizations, profiling is usually only invoked when the application developer specifies the highest level of optimization on the command line. Unfortunately, developers do not trust that level, since in many compilers it performs some optimizations that are so aggressive they can be unsafe or can expose program bugs that have gone unnoticed at lower optimization levels. For example, high-optimization levels may make code motions or remove memory locations that might cause an exception of some sort, when the code would not have excepted without the optimization. Because the developer does not use the highest level of optimization, profiling is not invoked.

---

instructions that are always executed together. There may or may not be a branch operation at the end of a basic block, but any branch into a basic block must (by definition) branch to the first instruction in the block. Prior to 1994, virtually all back-end profiling work concentrated on *points* in the CFG (either nodes or edges in the graph). A node or edge profile would then tell how many times a particular basic block was executed, or how many times control flowed from one basic block to one of its immediate neighbors, respectively. The bottom half of Figure 8.1 depicts a CFG edge profile.

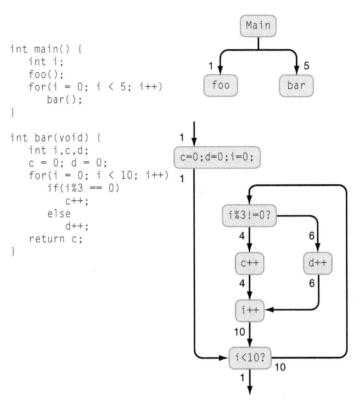

```
int main() {
    int i;
    foo();
    for(i = 0; i < 5; i++)
        bar();
}

int bar(void) {
    int i,c,d;
    c = 0; d = 0;
    for(i = 0; i < 10; i++)
        if(i%3 == 0)
            c++;
        else
            d++;
    return c;
}
```

FIGURE 8.1 Illustration of the call graph of a simple program and the control flow graph of a simple procedure.

In the last decade, researchers have also started collecting *path profiles*,[1] which measure the number of times a path, or sequence of contiguous blocks in the CFG, is executed. Path profiles have been built in a variety of forms: forward paths, "general" but bounded-length, and whole-program. Each type of profile has a graph-theoretic definition (comparing the merits and costs of each type has occupied many researchers). The major differences have to do with trading off the resolution or context associated with each data point with the efficiency of collecting the profile. Each level of additional information allows distinguishing different aspects of program behavior. Advocates of each level have produced optimizations that benefit from this information (e.g., various path optimizations). Optimizations that use path profiles or path-like optimizations have

---

1. Proponents of path profiles call the prior work on call graphs and control flow graphs "point profiles," in that the earlier techniques collected statistics about points in those graphs, whereas path-based techniques collect statistics about paths in graphs.

appeared in dynamic optimization systems and in research compilers, but we are not aware of any path optimizations that have been built into production compilers.

8.1.2 Profile Collection

Profiles can be collected in a number of ways. The oldest technique is *instrumentation*, whereby extra code is inserted into the program text to count the frequency of a particular event. Instrumentation can be performed either by the compiler or by a post-compilation tool. More recently, hardware manufacturers have added special registers that record statistics on a variety of processor-related events. These registers have been used to perform profiling, and processor manufacturers often supply tools to access the performance counters. Hardware techniques can have very low overheads, but they do not usually report exhaustive statistics, as instrumentation does. Some researchers have built statistical-sampling profilers, wherein an interrupt occasionally examines the machine state. Statistical profiles are noisier than exhaustive profiles but can be collected with extremely low run-time overhead.

Because instrumentation usually measures exhaustively, there has been work on the efficiency of profiling as well. Edge-profiling techniques need not sample every edge in the CFG. It suffices to sample enough edges to break all cycles in the undirected CFG, then the weights of the remaining edges can be calculated. Path profiles can similarly be collected efficiently, either by efficiently enumerating path identifiers or by lazily enumerating the set of paths encountered during runtime.

8.1.3 Synthetic Profiles (Heuristics in Lieu of Profiles)

Historically there were arguments about whether profiles were legal to use, practical to collect, or part of proper benchmarking methodology. Synthetic profile techniques attempt to assign weights to each part of the program based solely on the structure of the source program (running the program is not required). The danger of these methods is that you do not get to see how the program behaves with real data. You may not be able to tell what is common code and what is exceptional code, and you may then spend valuable optimization time and program space on the uncommon case. However, the benefit is that you might not have to collect statistics on actual running programs, which can be a daunting operational task. None of the synthetic profile techniques does as well as actual profiling, and no path-based heuristic techniques have been published. However, the techniques remain interesting as a way of avoiding building and installing a profiling pass.

Because profiling has been deployed in dynamic optimization, compilation, and translation systems, the arguments against profiling have faded into the past. Training data sets are now part of standard benchmark suites such as SPEC. Further, in the emerging embedded space devices are built for a single purpose, and both the common code and sample data sets fall readily to hand. For purposes of discussion, we will refer to both the heuristic and profile-based approaches as producing profiles. Think of the heuristic techniques as producing synthetic profiles.

8.1.4 Profile Bookkeeping and Methodology

If the profiling pass and the instruction scheduling pass are not adjacent in the compiler's design, there are bookkeeping issues to manage whenever an intervening pass transforms the program. Further, profiles only measure the parts of the program that were visible before the profiling pass. Changes to the CFG made after instrumentation was inserted will not be visible to the profiling code. Region formation itself can transform the program in ways that change the applicability of profile information. For these reasons, most textbooks advocate profiling as close to the point at which profile information is used as possible. Regardless, bookkeeping issues still must be faced.

Most bookkeeping involves applying what we call the *axiom of profile uniformity*:

When one copies a chunk of a program, one should equally divide the profile frequency of the original chunk among the copies.

In the case of point profiles, there is probably nothing else to be done. The independent nature of profile measurements means that no other information remains to disambiguate copies. However, recent work on path profiling suggests that profile uniformity is a poor assumption to make. Rather, there are correlations among branches in a program; or more succinctly, programs follow paths. Path profiles are not immune to such problems (e.g., one might duplicate an entire path, in which case the profile would not be able to disambiguate between the two copies), but because they capture more dynamic context, they are more resilient to program transformations.

Although not strictly a bookkeeping issue, we note here that cross-validation is crucial to properly studying profile-based optimizations. It is bad methodology to train (profile) and test (evaluate) on the same input, because a real-world application will probably face a variety of inputs. Training and testing on the same input is called *resubstitution* in the learning theory community. It provides a useful upper bound but not a practical performance value. Part of the early debate about using profiles concerned variability across training data sets. This issue is fundamental to profile-driven optimizations, but there is broad consensus that good training data sets can be found and usefully applied for optimization.

Many of the synthetic profile approaches described previously also use a training corpus to derive branch biases or to train the neural network. Such training corpora are similar to training data sets. Results using them without cross-validation should be considered warily.

8.1.5 Profiles and Embedded Applications

Are profiles useful for embedded applications? Many embedded programs, especially those that are oriented toward signal processing, would appear to be loop dominated. That is, they do not have complicated control flow, and the few loops that execute frequently can be easily identified from the source code. In such cases, we still believe that profiles are useful, although they may play more of a diagnostic role during the analysis and design phase than a crucial role in compiler-based optimizations. Many software engineering studies have shown that programmers are notoriously bad at guessing where their code spends time. Profiles of actual operating code remove all guesswork and replace them with hard statistics. Profiles can also tell how much emphasis to place in different areas, and are still useful in determining *trip counts* for loops. Many loop-oriented optimizations do a better job with exact or reliable trip count information (for example, unrolling or peeling loops in exactly the way the application typically operates).

Other aspects of embedded applications make profiling much easier than it is for general-purpose applications. Test inputs fall readily to hand with embedded applications. Some standards (notably those in cellular telephony) even specify test data sets.

From this point on, we assume that the compiler has access to some sort of profile information, whether observed or synthesized. We now examine optimizations that use profile information, starting with the central ILP optimization, instruction scheduling.

8.2 Scheduling

Instruction scheduling is the most fundamental ILP-oriented phase.[2] Other phases indirectly affect or enable parallelization at the operation level, but the scheduler is directly responsible for identifying and grouping operations that can be executed in parallel. This section describes various aspects of instruction scheduling. We begin by summarizing the major categories of scheduling techniques. Then we describe the two major pieces of any scheduler: region formation and schedule compaction. Next, we treat modeling and managing machine resources during scheduling. Section 8.2.5 describes scheduling loops, and Section 8.2.6 discusses clustering and the additional complications it adds to the scheduling problem.

The largest taxonomical split in schedulers is that between *cyclic* and *acyclic* schedulers. Cyclic schedulers operate on loops in the program, whereas acyclic schedulers consider loop-free regions (which are themselves often inside loops or entire loop bodies, minus the back edge). Most cyclic schedulers work only on simple loops (loops having no internal control flow), but some more sophisticated cyclic techniques also handle internal control flow and nested loops. Acyclic schedulers do not deal directly with loops, but use a variety of preprocessing steps to enhance ILP opportunities across loop branches.

Schedulers of all types benefit from hardware support. In acyclic scheduling, it can be beneficial to move an operation above a preceding branch instruction. This type of code motion can cause unintended side effects such as overwriting a value or throwing an unnecessary exception. A number of hardware techniques — including more physical or architectural registers, explicit or implicit support for renaming, and a variety of exception-suppression or -delay methods — can increase the choices available to the

---

2. Terminological note: we use the term *instruction scheduling* because that is what is used throughout research and development literature. Using the standard terminology of the book, this is really grouping operations into instructions, which might be more correctly called "instruction formation" or "instruction compaction."

scheduler (see Figure 8.2). Similarly, a number of cyclic scheduling algorithms benefit from predicates and predicated execution (conditional execution of instructions based on special register values), from a form of register renaming called "register rotation," and from special control instructions that combine with the predicates and rotating registers. All of these techniques have hardware implementation costs and require software support to exploit.

Noncontroversy: Which Is Better, Cyclic or Acyclic Scheduling?

During the 1980s, industrial and academic debates raged over whether acyclic schedulers could handle loops and how cyclic schedulers might be generalized to handle complex control flow and loop nests. The camps might be labeled "Multiflow" and "Cydrome," for the pioneering VLIW start-ups that promoted acyclic and cyclic scheduling, respectively.

The Cydrome camp advocated architectures with predicated execution and rotating registers. Hardware with these features was able to handle complex control flow within loops and to suppress the prologue and epilogue compensation code that increases code size in many cyclic scheduling techniques. The Multiflow camp eschewed such hardware support, believing that wider machines, aggressive instruction fetch mechanisms, and aggressive loop unrolling could capture all of the cyclic benefits while performing especially well on acyclic regions.

Current practice embraces both approaches, and product compilers include both cyclic and acyclic schedulers. Compiler development and application market realities dictate that one technique or the other may be favored, but the two techniques are viewed as complementary rather than competitive. It is especially interesting to note that the second-generation Multiflow and Cydrome products (neither saw the light of day before the companies closed) embraced features from the opposing camp.

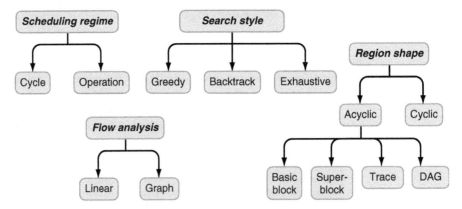

FIGURE 8.2 A set of decision trees characterizing compaction techniques.

8.2.1 Acyclic Region Types and Shapes

Most of the alternative methods of acyclic scheduling differ in the shape of the regions they form. Indeed, the algorithms are usually named after the region shape. This subsection enumerates the most commonly implemented regions.

Basic Blocks

Basic blocks are a "degenerate" form of region. Scheduling by picking basic blocks is not what we mean by region scheduling; a region usually comprises multiple basic blocks. However, region-scheduling algorithms have to work even when their region selection procedures pick a single basic block (for example, when there is an unscheduled basic block with no unscheduled contiguous blocks). We mention basic blocks here because despite the generally held belief that region scheduling is necessary for good performance its engineering is seen as so daunting that many compilers implement only basic block (local) scheduling, leaving a region-scheduling implementation for the indefinite future.

Traces

Traces were the first proposed region, and with their variants are probably the most commonly implemented. Traces are linear paths through the code, but a trace can have multiple entrances and exits. A trace consists of the operations from a list $B_0, B_1, \ldots, B_n$ of basic blocks with the following properties.

1. Each basic block is a predecessor of the next on the list (i.e., for each $k = 0, \ldots, n-1, B_k$ falls through or branches to B_{k+1}).

2. For any i and k there is no path $B_i \rightarrow B_k \rightarrow B_i$ except for those that go through B_0 (i.e., the code is cycle free, except that the entire region can be part of some encompassing loop).

    Note, as Figure 8.3 shows, that this definition does not prohibit forward branches within the region, or flow that leaves the region and comes back into the region at a later point. Indeed, the lack of these restrictions has been controversial in the research community because it makes trace-scheduling compilers considerably more complex than many researchers feel they need to be for the added benefit (if any). Adding those restrictions, sometimes with code duplication to mitigate their impact, is the principle behind several of the later region-scheduling techniques discussed in the following.

Superblocks

Superblocks are traces with the added restriction that there may not be any branches into the region except to the first block (see Figure 8.4). In other words, superblocks are single-entry, multiple-exit traces. Thus, a superblock consists of the operations from a list $B_0, B_1, \ldots, B_n$ of basic blocks with the same properties as a trace.

1. Each basic block is a predecessor of the next on the list (i.e., for each $k = 0, \ldots, n-1, B_k$ falls through or branches to B_{k+1}).

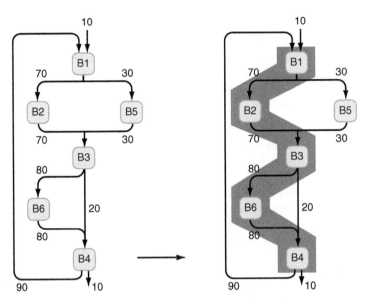

FIGURE 8.3 Example of building a typical region. In this case, the shaded region is a linear, multiple-entry, multiple-exit region. This is also called a "trace," used in trace scheduling. The blocks represent program basic blocks (maximal straightline code fragments), and the edges represent the program *control flow*.

2. For any i and k there is no path $B_i \rightarrow B_k \rightarrow B_i$ except for those that go through B_0 (i.e., the code is cycle free, except that the entire region can be part of some encompassing loop).

   The additional property is as follows.

3. There may be no branches into a block in the region, except to B_0. These outlawed branches are referred to in the superblock literature as *side entrances*.

The restriction against side entrances is made to eliminate the very difficult engineering surrounding compensation code in trace scheduling. Stopping trace formation at every side entrance is at first glance very severe, but superblock formation involves a region-enlarging technique called *tail duplication*, which allows superblocks to avoid ending the moment a side entrance is encountered (see Figure 8.4). Superblocks are built by first selecting a trace. Then, when a side entrance is encountered a copy is made of the rest of the trace. The side entrance then branches to this copy, and the new code finally branches to the end of the region, thus eliminating the side entrance. This process is continued as more blocks are added to the region and more side entrances are encountered. Tail duplication, in essence, adds the compensation code mandated by an entrance to the region *before* the region is scheduled.

As discussed later, all of the region-scheduling techniques rely on region-enlarging techniques to increase the amount of ILP the compiler can exploit. To a much greater extent, superblock scheduling relies on tail duplication as an essential feature.

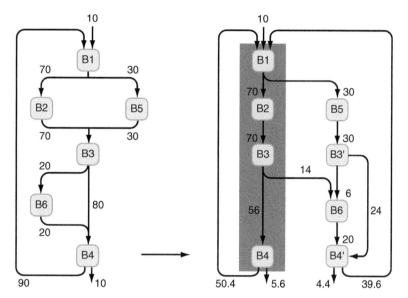

FIGURE 8.4 Superblock formation through tail duplication. To eliminate side entrances, a *superblock* duplicates the "tail" portion of a trace. Once we identify the trace, we can simply replicate all basic blocks from the first side exit to the bottom of the trace and redirect all side entrances to the duplicated basic blocks (making sure we copy each basic block at most once). While doing that, we also need to adjust the profile information to ensure that we preserve the right edge probabilities (shown as percent values next to the edges in the figure). In the example, we identify blocks B1, B2, B3, and B4 as part of the trace selection, and duplicate basic blocks B3 and B4 to generate the superblock. In general, this method of tail duplication guarantees that the maximum code expansion is smaller than 2.

Hyperblocks

Hyperblocks are single-entry, multiple-exit regions with internal control flow (see Figure 8.5). They can be seen as variants of superblocks that employ predication to fold multiple control paths into a single superblock.

Treegions

Treegions are regions containing a tree of basic blocks within the control flow of the program. That is, a treegion consists of the operations from a list $B_0, B_1, \ldots, B_n$ of basic blocks with the property that each basic block B_j except for B_0 has exactly one predecessor. That predecessor, B_i, is on the list, where $i < j$. This implies that any path through the treegion will yield a superblock; that is, a trace with no side entrances.

Like superblocks, treegions have no side entrances. Therefore, treegion compilers also use tail duplication and other enlarging techniques. Sometimes regions in which there is only a single flow of control that stays within the region are referred to as "linear regions." In that sense, traces and superblocks are linear regions, whereas treegions are "nonlinear regions."

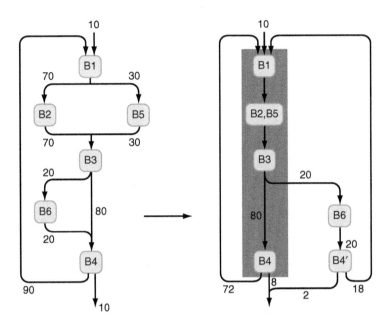

FIGURE 8.5   Hyperblock formation. Using the same procedure of Figure 8.4, hyperblock formation additionally if-converts basic blocks B2 and B5, thus removing some control flow complexity. The if-conversion step has the advantage of creating a hyperblock with a higher execution probability (as we can see from the probability labels), as well as removing a side exit and its scheduling constraints.

There are several other regions that have been suggested, and some that have been implemented. We do not cover them in detail for various reasons: some because they have only been suggested and leave many of the required implementation details to the reader; others because they are scheduling frameworks that have similar goals but are difficult to describe as scheduling algorithms.

One such method is *Trace-2*. Trace-2 is a nonlinear region with a single entrance (like treegions) but without the restriction on side entrances (see Figure 8.6). Its implementation was so difficult that its proposer gave up in disgust, and knows of no one who has attempted to implement it and succeeded.

The description of Trace-2 is one of those that leaves many details to the implementer. It is worth noting that the author concluded that a good implementation would require a very thorough use of program dependence graphs. Table 8.1 summarizes the various region-scheduling regions examined thus far.

Percolation Scheduling

Percolation scheduling is an algorithm for which many rules of code motion are applied to regions that resemble traces. It can also be seen as one of the earliest versions of *DAG*

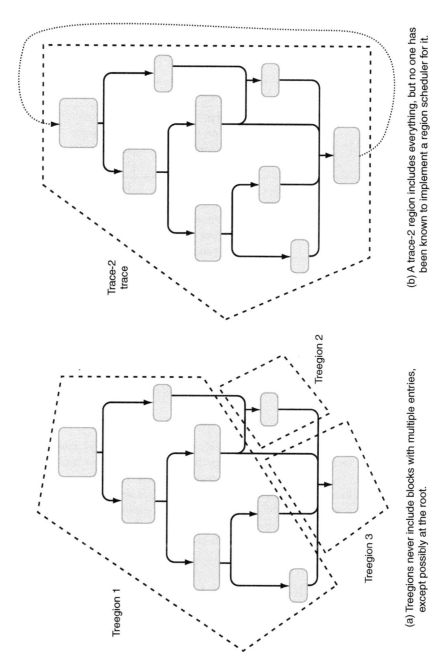

(b) A trace-2 region includes everything, but no one has been known to implement a region scheduler for it.

Trace-2 trace

(a) Treegions never include blocks with multiple entries, except possibly at the root.

Treegion 1

Treegion 2

Treegion 3

FIGURE 8.6   Treegions and trace-2 regions.

	Trace	Superblocks	Hyperblocks	Treegions	Trace-2
Year proposed	1979	1988	1992	1997	1993
Policy at splits	One way, usually most likely	One way, usually most likely	Predicate when possible	Both ways	Both ways
Policy at joins	Continue	Stop	Stop	Stop	Continue
Policy at back edges	Unrolled loops regarded as essential feature	Stop, but apply region enlargement techniques	Stop, but apply region enlargement techniques	Stop, but apply region enlargement techniques	Stop
Proposed measures to increase region size	Loop unrolling	Tail duplication, peeling, unrolling, and target expansion	Predication for rejoins, tail duplication for unpredicated splits, peeling, unrolling, and target expansion	Tail duplication, peeling, unrolling, and target expansion	Bigger regions probably not as desirable
Implementation status	Research and product compilers	Research and product compilers	Research and product compilers	Research and product compilers	Never implemented

TABLE 8.1 A summary of some proposed region-scheduling regions.

(*directed acyclic graph*) *scheduling*, which is the most general of acyclic scheduling techniques in that any edge in the CFG that is not a back edge can be included in a DAG.

In a cyclic scheduler, region shape is often quite limited, either to a single innermost loop or to an inner loop that has very simple control flow. These structural requirements mean that a cyclic scheduler can be applied in only a few places, albeit possibly the hot loops of many programs. Profiles will of course show when the cyclic scheduler will actually be beneficial (and conversely, cyclically scheduling a loop with a low trip count can be disastrous).

8.2.2 Region Formation

The previous section introduced a number of region shapes used in instruction scheduling. Once one has decided on a region shape, two questions present themselves: how does one divide a program into regions of a particular shape, and having chosen those regions, how does one build schedules for them? We call the former problem *region formation* and the latter problem *schedule construction*. They are the topics of this subsection and the next subsection, respectively. In a sense, the division of instruction scheduling into these two areas indicates the difficulty of the problem or the weakness of the known solutions. One would like to "just schedule" an entire program, but the technology and algorithms do not allow such a direct approach. Instead, schedule construction solves the scheduling problem for those limited cases we do understand, in which the region has a particular shape. Region formation then must divide the general control flow of the program into manageable, well-defined pieces for the schedule constructor to consume.

The combined effects of region formation and schedule construction are critical to performance. Well-selected regions will cover the CFG of the program in a way that keeps the program executing along the expected paths in the scheduled code. Poorly selected regions penalize performance because the schedule constructor will add instructions from infrequently executed parts of the program to the critical execution path. Perhaps stating the obvious, the goal of region formation is to select regions that will allow the schedule constructor to produce schedules that will run well. For this reason, it is important to keep in mind what the schedule constructor will do. The schedule constructor examines only one region at a time, and thus the goal of region construction is to find frequently executed basic blocks *that execute together* and group them into the same region. If two chunks of the program that execute together are placed in separate regions, very little benefit will be extracted by instruction scheduling. Designers of region formation passes face three main questions. Which program chunks are frequently executed? How can we tell that two chunks execute together? How does region shape interact with the first two questions? The traditional answer to the first two questions is to use profiles, as described in the previous section, to estimate how frequently each part of the program is executed.

Once one has a usable set of profile statistics, the question remains how to use them to form useful regions. Region formation often means more than just *selecting* good regions from the existing CFG; it also includes *duplicating* portions of the CFG to improve the quality of the region. Duplication increases the size of the final program, and thus many different algorithms and heuristics have been applied that make a variety of tradeoffs. We call these techniques, collectively, *region enlargement*. Region formation must also produce valid regions the schedule constructor can use. This may entail additional bookkeeping or program transformations. The selection and enlargement pieces of region formation can be applied in a variety of orders, and these phase orders produce an additional set of engineering constraints and tradeoffs.

This subsection treats the issues roughly in what might be termed "compiler-engineering order." We assume that the compiler begins with CFG edge profiles. We first describe region selection without regard to enlarging techniques. Then we elaborate on enlargement and duplication techniques. This subsection closes with a discussion of phase-ordering issues that relate to region formation.

Region Selection

The most popular algorithm for region selection is *trace growing* using the *mutual most likely heuristic*. As described before, a trace is a path through the program CFG (it is legal

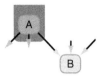

FIGURE 8.7   An illustration of the mutual-most-likely heuristic for picking traces. Suppose that block A is the last block of the current trace, and block B is one of A's successors. If B is A's most likely successor, and A is B's most likely predecessor, then A and B are considered mutually most likely, and the heuristic extends the trace to include block B. Then the process repeats with B's successors, until no mutually-most-likely successor can be found, a cycle would be formed in the trace, or another heuristic (perhaps limiting the number of operations or blocks in a trace) terminates formation. Mutual-most-likely also works to grow traces backward, using predecessors instead of successors, *mutatis mutandis.*

for a trace to have many side entrances and exits). The mutual most likely heuristic works as its name implies. At any moment, a trace has a first block and a last block selected so far. The mutual most likely heuristic can be used to extend either end of the trace. Consider the last block, *A*, of the trace. Use profile edge statistics to find its most likely successor block, *B*. Next, consider *B*'s predecessors. If *A* is *B*'s most likely predecessor, then *A* and *B* are "mutually most likely," and the heuristic adds *B* to the trace, making it the new end of the trace. The trace can be grown either forward or backward in the CFG. Trace growing stops whenever no mutually most likely block can be found to extend the trace, the heuristic picks a back edge (which by definition cannot become part of an acyclic trace), or the mutually most likely block is already part of a different trace. The process iterates by finding the highest-frequency unselected block in the program and using that as a seed for the trace. The process ends when all blocks have been assigned to traces. Some traces may consist of only their seed block. Figure 8.7 illustrates how the mutual-most-likely heuristic works.

One unsatisfying aspect of trace formation using point profiles is the cumulative effect of conditional probability. In point profiles, the probability of each branch is measured independently. Whenever the trace crosses a split or join in the CFG, the probability of traversing the entire trace changes. With point profiles, we must assume that this probability is independent for each branch, and thus the probability of remaining on the trace falls away rapidly. For example, a trace that crosses ten splits, each with a 90% probability of staying on the trace, appears to have only a 35% probability of running from start to end. Researchers have addressed this problem in three ways: building differently shaped regions, using predication hardware to remove branches, and getting better statistics.

Forming nonlinear regions appears to simplify the region selection process, in that the region selector can choose both sides of a difficult split or join. However, nonpath-shaped regions require more complicated schedule construction passes or more complicated hardware, or both. Complexity is not avoided; it is just handled elsewhere.

Predicated execution allows a different approach to difficult (forward) branches: go both ways. Predication necessarily complicates the hardware, the ISA, and the compiler.

Hyperblock formation, the most recently documented approach to using predication, still uses the mutual-most-likely trace formation mechanism as a basis. It then adds blocks to the region based on a heuristic that considers block size and execution frequency. Predication is a very powerful tool for removing unpredictable branches and exploiting otherwise-unused machine resources, but it can also negatively affect performance. The time to execute a predicated block includes the cycles for all scheduled operations, and thus shorter paths may take longer under predication. Predication is most effective when paths are balanced or when the longest path is the most frequently executed.

Young and Smith explored getting better statistics in a series of papers. Their initial work used global, bounded-length path profiles to improve static branch prediction. Their technique, *static correlated branch prediction* (SCBP), collected statistics on how the path by which a branch was reached affected its direction. By analyzing this information globally, they produced a transformed CFG with extra copies of blocks, but in which the extra copies were statically more predictable. Unfortunately, although SCBP was intended to help back-end tasks such as scheduling, its transformation of the CFG led to complex graphs in which the branches were individually predictable but in which linear execution traces were difficult to find. In later work that directly addressed instruction scheduling, Young and Smith used path profiles to drive the region formation stages of a superblock scheduler. The later work, on path-based instruction scheduling, used a very simple technique to select superblocks: treat the current trace as a path and consider its execution frequency, then consider the execution frequency that results from extending the trace to any of the possible successor blocks. Because the general path profiles include this frequency information, there is no need to invoke profile uniformity. Correlations are preserved through the region formation process.

Enlargement Techniques

Region selection alone does not usually expose enough ILP for the schedule constructor to keep a typical wide-issue machine occupied. To further increase ILP, systems use *region enlargement* techniques. These techniques increase the size of the program but can improve the performance of the scheduled code. Using them involves a space/time tradeoff. Many of these techniques exploit the fact that programs iterate (by making extra copies of highly iterated code, more ILP can be found). Such loop-based techniques draw criticism from advocates of other approaches, such as cyclic scheduling and loop-level parallel processing, because the benefits of the loop-based enlargement techniques might be found using other techniques. We are aware of no study that has quantified this tradeoff.

The oldest and simplest region enlargement technique is *loop unrolling* (see Figure 8.8). To unroll a loop, make multiple copies of the original loop body, rerouting loop back edges from one copy to the header of the next copy. For the last copy, reroute the loop back edges to the header of the first copy. One is said to "unroll n times" when one ends up with n copies of the loop body after unrolling. Loop unrolling typically takes place before region selection, so that portions of the larger unrolled loop body are available to the region selector. When renaming, copy propagation (including

```
Original loop          Unrolled by 4          Pre-cond by 4          Post-cond by 4

L: if-- goto E     L: if-- goto E          if-- goto L     L: if-- goto X
   body               body                 body               body
   goto L             if-- goto E          if-- goto L        body
E:                    body                 body               body
                      if-- goto E          if-- goto L        body
                      body                 body               goto L
                      if-- goto E       L: if-- goto E     X: if-- goto E
                      body                 body               body
                      goto L               body               if-- goto E
                   E:                      body               body
                                           body               if-- goto E
                                           goto L             body
                                        E:                 E:
```

FIGURE 8.8 **Simplified illustration of variants of loop unrolling.** The first column, "Original loop," illustrates the original loop, where the *if* and *goto* statements indicate the loop condition and repeat branches, and *body* represents the part of the loop without loop-related control flow. In the most general case (e.g., a *while* loop), unrolling must replicate both the body and the loop condition test with each copy, since the compiler cannot determine how many iterations of the loop will take place. This general case is represented by the second column, labeled "Unrolled by 4." For counted loops (i.e., a *for* loop), a compiler can unroll loops in a way that removes loop condition tests from the body of the unrolled loop. The "Pre-condition by 4" and "Post-condition by 4" columns illustrate these cases. Unlike these examples, production compilers rarely keep unconditional branches at the bottom of the loop body. If the expected number of iterations is greater than one, it makes more sense to "reroll" the loop so that the loop condition occurs at the bottom of the loop, and a separate conditional branch tests for entry into the loop at the top. This removes one unconditional branch from each dynamic iteration of the loop.

simple arithmetic operations) and induction variable simplification are judiciously performed (see Figure 8.9) so that parallelism across iterations (if present) can be exposed. In this way, the scheduler can overlap operations belonging to different iterations in the unrolled loop body. Loop unrolling has no awareness of region shape, and thus duplicates entire loop bodies without regard to control flow within the loop. Engineers of trace schedulers do not consider this a problem, as the hot trace through the unrolled code will still be found and the side blocks do not overly burden the schedule constructor. Loop unrolling (used in many industrial compilers) is often rather effective because a small amount of unrolling is sufficient to fill the resources of the target machine.

The engineers of superblock schedulers take a different approach, forming superblocks before they perform enlarging transformations. They describe three techniques: *superblock loop unrolling*, *superblock loop peeling*, and *superblock target expansion*. Superblock loop unrolling resembles basic loop unrolling. After superblock formation (but before schedule construction), the most likely exit from some superblocks may jump to the beginning of the same superblock. Such superblocks are called *superblock loops*. Unrolling them involves making additional copies of the basic blocks in the superblock and connecting them in a manner similar to the connection in loop unrolling. Superblock loop peeling is similar, but is applied in cases where the profile

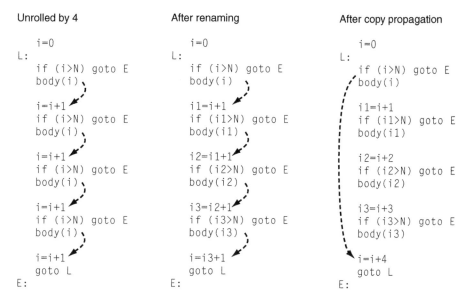

FIGURE 8.9 **Typical induction variable manipulations for loops.** Simply unrolling loops does not normally expose ILP, because (as we can see in the left picture) each copy of the loop body still keeps a dependence with the other copies above and below, enforced by the induction variable update ($i = i + 1$ in the example). To break these dependences, compilers normally operate two simple transformations: *renaming* (middle picture) and *copy propagation* (rightmost picture). After renaming, each of the unrolled loop bodies depends on a separate variable ($i1$, $i2$, and $i3$) derived from the induction variable. However, as we see from the arrows, the dependence still remains, and to remove it requires propagation of copies (including simple arithmetic operations). The copy-propagation phase understands that the sequence of operations {$i1 = i + 1; \ldots;$ $i2 = i1 + 1$} could be transformed into {$i1 = i + 1; \ldots; i2 = i + 2;$}. After copy propagation, we obtain the pseudocode of the rightmost figure, which shows how the inter-iteration dependences have been removed, and now (if no other dependences exist) the schedules can potentially parallelize the four unrolled bodies.

suggests a small number of iterations for the superblock loop. In such cases, the expected number of iterations is copied, but the last copy is connected to the exit block from the loop and a special extra copy is made to handle extra iterations not forecast by the profile. Superblock target expansion is similar to the mutual-most-likely heuristic for growing traces downward: if superblock A ends in a likely branch to superblock B, then the content of superblock B is appended to superblock A to make it bigger. Figure 8.10 illustrates these three transformations.

Young and Smith's path-based approach to superblock selection also lends itself to superblock enlargement. The same algorithm performs both jobs: grow downward only, and choose the most likely successor block. A number of thresholds stop growing traces: low likelihood in the successor block, low overall likelihood of reaching the end of the trace, and sufficient number of instructions in the trace. General path profiles provide exact execution frequencies for paths within the bound of the profiling

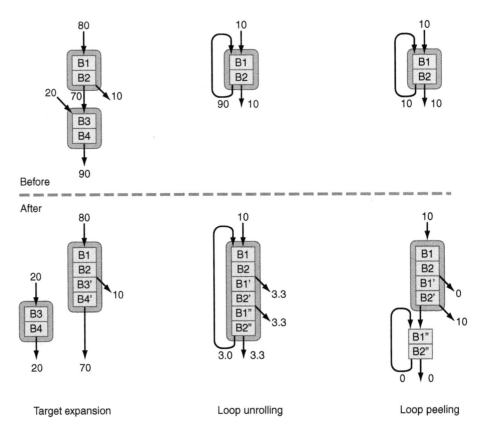

Before

After

Target expansion   Loop unrolling   Loop peeling

FIGURE 8.10 **Superblock-enlarging optimizations.** The figure shows three transformations commonly applied to enlarge superblocks: target expansion, loop unrolling, and loop peeling. In the loop peeling case, the profile weights after transformation reflect the assumption that the loop peeling optimization has correctly guessed the number of iterations typical of the loop. Other assignments are also possible.

history depth. Young and Smith found modest performance improvements from using path profiles.

Phase-ordering Considerations

Even within region formation passes, there are phase-ordering considerations. The designers of the Multiflow compiler chose to place enlargement (loop unrolling) before trace selection. The superblock-based techniques chose and formed superblocks before enlarging them. Neither is clearly preferable, and they are determined by the engineering constraints of the chosen approach.

Other transformations also have phase-ordering interactions with region formation. Other ILP-enhancing optimizations, such as dependence height reduction, should be run before region formation. Hyperblock-related techniques have an entire suite of

---

Flame: "Code Explosion" and ILP-oriented Optimizations

Many region-scheduling transformations increase the size of the object code. Compensation code and region enlargement techniques can be potentially large multipliers on code size. The early innovators of ILP-oriented techniques worried that such code expansion would add so much code that performance might suffer, swamping any ILP benefits through (for example) cache misses. They dramatized their concern by coining the term *code explosion* to describe this effect. Although compensation code has a smaller effect, inlining and loop unrolling were dangerous in this respect.

However, applying the good system principle of doing things only where they do the most good came to the rescue. *Judicious* application of ILP optimizations can reap most of the ILP benefits while incurring small code-expansion-related costs. Profiles can guide where ILP optimizations can be applied most profitably, and numerous profiling studies and the weight of experience shows that programs spend most of their time in a small fraction of the code. Even in the absence of profiles, compilers can be engineered to limit the overall amount of code expansion, or to keep the size of the object code within a certain budget. This is a classic cost/benefit tradeoff, and is one of many such tradeoffs made in building a production-quality compiler.

One might argue that code explosion is even more of an issue for embedded applications, wherein size and cost are at a premium. However, this argument is really in favor of economy or parsimony, rather than against using code-expanding optimizations at all.

---

transformations, including if-conversion and reverse if-conversion, which we discuss in Section 8.4.2.

8.2.3 Schedule Construction

The previous subsection described techniques for selecting and enlarging individual compilation regions. This subsection discusses assigning operations in the selected region to units on the target machine and time slots in the schedule. A *schedule* is thus the set of annotations that indicate unit assignment and cycle time of the operations in a region. A *schedule constructor* (or *scheduler*) is the phase that produces such a schedule. Like region formation, schedule construction techniques vary depending on the shape of the region being scheduled (different types of regions require different transformations).

The goal of any scheduling algorithm is to minimize an objective cost function while maintaining the semantics of the program and obeying the resource limitations of the target hardware. In most cases, the objective function is the *estimated completion time* of the region, although it is also possible to find domains that demand more complex objective functions. For example, a scheduler for an embedded target may add *code size* or *energy efficiency* to the objective cost function. This section concerns itself with schedule construction while maintaining the semantics of the program.

Pitfall: The Hard Part of Compiling Is Instruction Selection or Scheduling

Anyone educated in computer science, upon hearing for the first time about VLIW architectures, comes to the (correct) conclusion that compiling for them is a formidable process. However, they usually arrive at this conclusion for the wrong reasons. Most people assume that the process of arranging the operations into instructions is very difficult. Although that can be tricky, and a lot of technology has been thrown at this problem, it is not considerably out of the normal range of difficulty for compiler tasks, and simply represents yet another thing a compiler has to do. Similarly, people expect that instruction selection, covered in Section 8.5, is particularly difficult here. It is not. Although there are some new nuances, instruction selection for a VLIW largely resembles instruction selection for any compiler for a high-performance architecture, and complexity is more a function of how idiosyncratic the ISA is than anything else. In that good VLIW design should be very orthogonal and not very idiosyncratic (or else it is difficult to expose parallelism), instruction selection should not be particularly difficult.

So what is difficult about compiling for VLIWs? It is the region selection and manipulation of the regions, rather than the actual selection of operations in the ISA and their assignment to units, cycles, and registers. This only gets difficult when it is decided that the region in question will include several basic blocks or will be a software pipelined loop, and the decision to do so is usually motivated by the degree of instruction-level parallelism that must be exposed. For the degree of parallelism to be high, many branches must be included in the region, and then the complexity is great.

This misconception is what is behind another widely held misconception we have mentioned before: VLIWs are significantly more difficult to compile for than superscalars. Superscalar control hardware cannot realistically be expected to move operations past hundreds of others in order to exploit parallelism at run-time. Instead, a compiler has to expose the parallelism (to itself) and then leave operations that could be executed in parallel near each other so that their independence can be rediscovered by the control hardware. This involves precisely the same effort whether for a VLIW or a superscalar. Thus, the major difficulty is more a function of the ILP to be exposed than of what style the architecture is. VLIWs are more difficult to compile for simply because they offer more ILP. The added work for a VLIW is only in scheduling the exposed instructions, which is not nearly as difficult as finding them. This, then, is the source of the fallacy we described in Chapter 2, "Fallacy: VLIWs Require 'Heroic Compilers' To Do What Superscalars Do in the Hardware."

Depending on the ISA and microarchitecture of the target machine, different schedules may maintain or violate the semantics of the original program. Different machines can have different amounts of hardware support or checking to support ILP. We now consider some alternatives.

Visible versus hidden latencies. Basic operations vary widely in complexity. Some execute in multiple cycles and produce their results some cycles after their issue time (e.g., divides typically require multiple cycles). When the ISA exposes visible nonunit latencies to the compiler (most VLIW machines fall into this category), an erroneous latency assumption in the scheduler may change the semantics of the program. Alternatively, the microarchitecture can independently check latency assumptions (through some form of scoreboarding technique, commonly used in superscalars) and correct violations through stalls or dynamic rescheduling. In this case, the compiler can assume average or worst-case latencies without additional work to maintain program correctness.

Explicitly parallel versus superscalar. Machines that include instruction-level parallelism may choose to expose it in the ISA (VLIW) or to hide it with sequential instruction semantics and let the hardware rediscover it at run-time (superscalar). In the former case, the compiler must monitor machine resources to avoid generating illegal code. In the latter case, the compiler may estimate resource usage for performance reasons, but it need not monitor them for legality. However, the compiler may still need to follow certain encoding rules to ensure that the underlying implementation is able to find the parallelism the compiler has discovered. For example, all Alpha implementations can issue multiple instructions per cycle, but early implementations required instructions to come from the same cache line for them to be able to issue in parallel.

Recently introduced EPIC architectures blend the explicitly parallel and superscalar approaches. Such ISAs closely resemble VLIWs, but they also allow limited sequential execution within a parallel execution unit (called an issue group) to accommodate the resource limits of various implementations. This blended approach allows binary compatibility over a set of implementations, but still allows much of the ILP extraction to be performed by software.

This subsection begins by describing how schedulers analyze programs. Armed with the analysis techniques, we then describe a number of approaches to compaction, or actual schedule construction, under "Compaction Techniques." Maintaining program semantics (or correctness) is treated under "Compensation Code." We return to search methods under "Another View of Scheduling Problems."

Analyzing Programs for Schedule Construction

Dependences (sometimes also called *dependencies*) are sequential constraints that derive from the semantics of the program under compilation. Dependences prohibit some reorderings of the program. Program dependences are either *data* dependences or *control* dependences. The data flow of the program imposes *data dependences*, and similarly the control flow of the program imposes *control dependences*.

Data dependences come in three types: *read-after-write* dependences, *write-after-read* dependences, and *write-after-write* dependences. The first type, read-after-write dependences (also called *RAW, flow,* or *true*), occur when one operation uses the result of another (reordering would break this flow of data in the program). Write-after-read dependences (also called *WAR* or *anti* dependences) occur when one operation overwrites a value after it has been used by another operation (reordering would overwrite the correct value before it is used). Third, write-after-write dependences (also called *WAW* or *output* dependences) occur when two operations write to the same location (reordering the operations will cause the wrong value to be the final value). The latter two types

```
x = *ap;
if (x > 0)
    t = *bp + 1;
else
    t = x - 1;
*zp = t
```

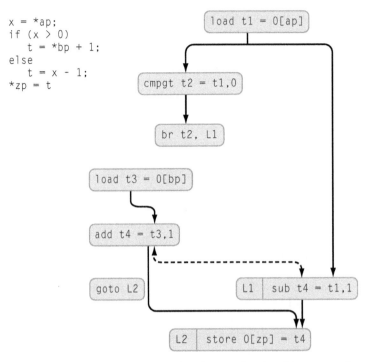

FIGURE 8.11   **Example of data dependences, showing the source code on the left and the dependences among the resulting assembly operations on the right.** Solid arcs are flow dependences. Dashed arcs are output dependences. Note that the *goto L2* operation has no data dependences, but is included to show all operations. Also note that the output dependence between the *add* and *sub* operations interacts in a complicated manner with control flow. Neither the *add* nor the *sub* operation can be moved down into the store block without changing program semantics.

of dependences, WAR and WAW, are also called *false* dependences because they can be removed by renaming (adding extra temporary variables to the program). Figure 8.11 shows an example of data dependences expressed as arcs between operations.

Control dependences represent constraints imposed by the control flow of the program. Note that control dependence and control flow are not the same. Formally, block B is control dependent on block A if all paths from the start of the program to B pass through A and some path from A to the exit of the program omits B. In other words, the result of the control decision made in A directly affects whether or not B is executed.

Although control dependences do not constrain the scheduling of instructions within basic blocks, they do constrain the process of scheduling instructions within more complex region types (with multiple entrances or exits). Control dependences may prevent certain operations from executing before an entrance (*join*) to a block, or after an exit (*split*). Once the program reaches the scheduler, the compiler usually represents

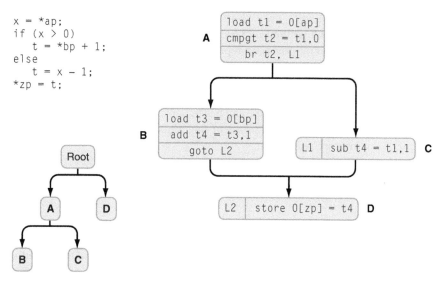

```
x = *ap;
if (x > 0)
    t = *bp + 1;
else
    t = x - 1;
*zp = t;
```

FIGURE 8.12 **Example of control flow (right) and control dependence (lower left) among basic blocks.** In the control flow graph, the edge from block A to block B means that program execution can flow from A to B. The control-dependence tree shows that B and C are control dependent on node A, but that nodes A and D are control independent. See the exercises for more information about these topics.

the control dependences as arcs connecting control-dependent pieces. For example, Figure 8.12 shows the control dependences among basic blocks in a simple program.

As described previously, both data and control dependences are constraints between instructions in a region being scheduled that make some reorderings illegal. In practice, we often think of the constraints as being between sections of code, as shown in Figure 8.11. These constraints induce a partial ordering on the pieces (whether the pieces are instructions or larger regions), and any partial ordering can be represented as a DAG. Such graphs of dependences are used frequently in scheduling analysis passes. Variants (depending on how the graphs are built) are known simply as the DAG, as the *data dependence graph* (DDG), or as the *program dependence graph* (PDG), which typically also encodes the control dependences. All such variants are graphs in which nodes represent operations and arcs are the data-dependence (and sometimes control-dependence) constraints among them. Building the variants typically requires quadratic time complexity in the number of operations.

The DDG represents the constraints the scheduler must obey to maintain program semantics. However, it also includes information that allows the scheduler to evaluate the relative order and importance of operations. After building a DDG, we can label operations with some interesting properties. Two obvious ones are *depth* (the length of the longest path from any root of the DDG) and *height* (the length of the longest path to any leaf of the DDG). Operations for which *depth* equals *max_height − height* are on the critical path of the region. For noncritical operations, the range [*depth*,

($max\_height - height$)] are the time slots in the schedule at which the operation can be placed without increasing the schedule length.

The intermediate representation adopted by the upstream phases of the compiler may choose various methods to represent dependences, such as virtual register names, arcs of an SSA (static single assignment) web, and various methods for annotating memory references. The case of memory references is particularly interesting. Unlike other types, the scheduler often has to make conservative assumptions for memory references. *Alias analysis* is the set of techniques that help the scheduler *disambiguate* among memory references.

After regions have been formed, classical optimizations (e.g., constant propagation and partial redundancy elimination) can often serve to remove operations and their corresponding data dependences.

Compaction Techniques

This subsection briefly reviews some of the most widely used scheduling techniques for ILP targets. Research and production compilers in the last 20 years adopted many different approaches, making exhaustive description impossible. Instead, we enumerate techniques that are components of almost all approaches to compaction.

We classify compaction techniques according to different features, such as cycle versus operation scheduling, linear versus graph-based analysis, acyclic versus cyclic regions (previously introduced), and greedy versus backtracking search. Figure 8.2 shows a set of decision trees characterizing compaction techniques. We largely focus on *greedy* scheduling techniques for acyclic regions, although the last part of this subsection discusses more exhaustive approaches.

Cycle Versus Operation Scheduling. As discussed previously, the goal of the scheduler is to allocate operations to cycle slots while minimizing an objective function. The two parts of this allocation, operations and time slots, suggest two approaches to overall scheduler strategy: *operation-based* and *cycle-based* scheduling.

Operation scheduling repeatedly selects an operation in the region and allocates it in the "best" cycle that dependences and target resources allow. Operation scheduling techniques vary based on the selection method, which can be guided by a number of heuristics or priority schemes.

Cycle scheduling repeatedly fills a cycle (usually corresponding to an issue group) with operations selected from the region, proceeding to the next cycle only after exhausting the operations available in the current cycle or when some heuristic decides we should advance to the next cycle.

Operation scheduling is theoretically more powerful than cycle-based scheduling because it can take into account the effects of resource usage in long-latency operations. For unit-latency machines, in which operations are always scheduled in the earliest possible cycle, *operation* and *cycle* scheduling are equivalent.

Operation scheduling is much more complicated to engineer than cycle scheduling. It is especially difficult in complex regions that extend beyond basic blocks, and there are always worries about producing deadlocked schedules that must be backed out of.[3] We are not aware of any production compilers that use operation scheduling.

Linear Techniques. The simplest schedulers use linear techniques. When compile time is of utmost importance, linear methods have the major advantage of having $O(n)$ complexity for a region composed of n operations. Techniques that use data-dependence graphs have at least $O(n^2)$ complexity. However, for practical region sizes and machine speeds, differences are often not significant enough to justify the performance loss of an inferior technique. For this reason, graph-based techniques have almost universally replaced linear techniques in modern compilers.

Most of the linear techniques use either or both:

- *As-soon-as-possible* (ASAP) scheduling is the technique whereby we place operations in the earliest possible cycle that resource and data constraints allow through a single top-down linear scan of the region. Note that a graph is not necessary to enforce data dependences. A simple time-annotated table of produced values suffices.

- *As-late-as-possible* (ALAP) scheduling is the technique whereby we place operations in the latest possible cycle that resource and data constraints allow through a single bottom-up linear scan of the region.

For example, critical-path (CP) scheduling uses an ASAP pass followed by an ALAP pass to identify operations in the critical path of the computation (those that have the same cycle assignment in both schedules). Remaining noncritical operations are allocated in a third linear pass.

Even though linear techniques have long been abandoned in static compilers, they have enjoyed recent resurgence in systems in which a scheduling-like pass happens at run-time, such as dynamic optimization systems.

Graph-based Techniques (List Scheduling). The major limitation of linear techniques is their inability to make decisions based on global properties of the operations in considered regions. Such global properties are incorporated in the DDG described above. Most of the scheduling algorithms that operate on DDGs fall into the category of *list scheduling*. List scheduling techniques work by repeatedly assigning a cycle to an operation without backtracking (greedy algorithms), and efficient implementations have $O(n\,log(n))$ computational complexity (in addition to the DDG creation, which has $O(n^2)$ complexity).

List scheduling repeatedly selects an operation from a *data-ready queue* (DRQ) of operations ready to be scheduled (see Figure 8.13). An operation is *ready* when all of its DDG predecessors have been scheduled. Once scheduled, the operation is removed from the DRQ and its successors that have become ready are inserted. This iterates until

---

3. The deadlocking issue, and the terminology and framework of cycle versus operation scheduling for ILP, were first worked out by John Ruttenberg at Yale University in 1980–81 (in unpublished work).

```
// initialization phase
for (each root r in the program DAG, sorted by priority) {
    enqueue(r) // init DRQ with root nodes in priority order
}
// list-scheduling phase
while (DRQ is non-empty) {
    h = dequeue() // pick highest-priority node from the queue
    schedule(h)
    for (each DAG successor s of h) {
        if (all predecessors of s have been scheduled) {
            enqueue(s) // s is now ready, so enqueue it in the
                       // queue position corresponding to its
                       // priority
        }
    }
}
```

FIGURE 8.13 **Pseudocode for manipulation of the data-ready queue (DRQ) in a list-scheduling algorithm.** The algorithm keeps scheduling ready operations until no operations are left. Each scheduled operation might "activate" one of its successors, and thus the entire program DAG will eventually be visited. Note that the algorithm remains the same, regardless of whether cycle or operation scheduling is performed. Initial "root" nodes are nodes in the DAG that can be started from the beginning (i.e., they have no predecessors). The functions commonly used to prioritize ready nodes in the queue include node height (distance from the end of the DAG), node depth (distance from the beginning of the DAG), and a combination of both height and depth.

all operations in the regions are scheduled. The performance of list scheduling is highly dependent on the order used to select the scheduling candidates from the DRQ, and — in case of cycle-based scheduling — on the scheduler's greediness.

We can tackle the first problem (DRQ order) by assigning a priority function to each operation in the DDG. Ideally, the *height* of the operation is what should drive the priority function (at any point during scheduling, operations with the greatest height are the most critical). However, depending on other scheduling considerations, compilers have also used the *depth*, a combination of the two, or a depth-first topological sorting of operations within a connected component of a region. In general, all of these choices are based on heuristics, and have to strike a balance among schedule quality, implementation complexity, and compile-time performance.

The second problem (greed control) is more complex, in that cycle-based schedulers often tend to be too greedy. Excessively greedy scheduling may impact performance in two ways:

- Operations we schedule too early and that occupy resources for multiple cycles may prevent more critical operations that become ready later to be scheduled due to resource constraints.

- Operations we schedule too early may unnecessarily increase register pressure and force spills that could be avoided if we had decided to delay their schedule.

Unfortunately, most workarounds for this problem rely on heuristics that rarely apply outside the domain in which they were introduced.

Compensation Code

Under the term *compensation code* we cover the set of techniques necessary to restore the correct flow of data and control because of a global scheduling phase or a global code motion across basic blocks. Depending on the shape of the region the compiler adopts, the complexity of the task of generating compensation code varies from trivial to extremely complex. Superblock techniques generate compensation code as part of the tail duplication process, as we described in the previous sections. Scheduling techniques that primarily deal with basic blocks and move operations around them generate compensation code as part of the code motion itself. Trace scheduling (as well as other techniques that allow multiple-entry regions) involves a more complex bookkeeping process, in that the compiler is allowed to move operations above join points, as well as move branches (split points) above operations that were below them in the original program sequence.

A complete discussion of all the intricacies of compensation code is well beyond the scope of this book. However, compilers base many of the compensation techniques on a variation of a few simple concepts (illustrated in the following). When the compiler schedules a region, and is allowed to move operations freely with respect to entries and exits, we can identify four basic scenarios (illustrated in Figure 8.14).

No Compensation (Figure 8.14a). This happens when the code motions do not change the relative order of operations with respect to joins and splits. This also covers the case in which we move operations above a split point, in which case they become *speculative,* as we discussed previously. The generation of compensation code for speculative code motions depends on the recovery model for exceptions. In the case of *nonrecovery speculation* (also called *silent speculation* or *dismissable speculation*), no compensation code is necessary. In the case of *recovery speculation*, the compiler has to emit a recovery block to guarantee the timely delivery of exceptions for correctly speculated operations.

Join Compensation (Figure 8.14b). This happens when an operation B moves above a join point A. In this case, we need to drop a copy of operation B (called B′) in the join path. A successive phase of the region selector picks operation B′ as part of a new region and schedules it accordingly. Note that if operation B is only *partially moved* above the join point A (this can happen for multicycle operations in explicitly scheduled machines) we only need to partially copy B to the join path. In addition, in this case (called *partial schedule*) the partial copy must be constrained to be scheduled exactly before the join point.

Split Compensation (Figure 8.14c). This happens when a split operation B (i.e., a branch) moves above a previous operation A. In this case, the compiler produces a copy of A (called A′) in the split path. The same scheduling considerations from the join case apply to the split case: A′ is successively picked as part of another region unless it is a partial copy, in which case it is constrained to happen right after the split.

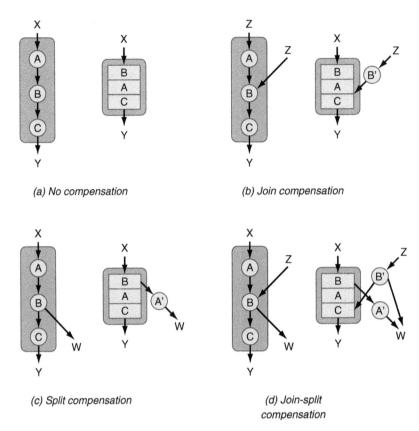

(a) No compensation   *(b) Join compensation*

(c) Split compensation   *(d) Join-split compensation*

FIGURE 8.14 **The four basic scenarios for compensation code.** In each panel, the picture on the left represents the original control flow graph, with the selected region to be compacted. The picture on the right represents the compacted schedule (with B moved above A) and the compensation code added to the resulting flow graph to restore correctness.

Join-Split Compensation (Figure 8.14d). Cases that are more complicated appear when we allow splits to move above joins (presented in the figure), or splits above splits. For example, if we move a split B above a preceding join A, in addition to having to copy A to A′ we need to create a copy of the branch B′ to target the split destination, to guarantee the correct execution of the Z–B–W path.

In general, the rule to keep in mind when thinking about compensation code is to make sure we preserve all paths from the original sequence in the transformed control flow after scheduling. Obviously, the order of operations may be different, but we nonetheless need to execute all operations from the original control flow. For example, the copy B′ in Figure 8.14b restores the Z–B′–C–Y path, and the copy A′ shown in Figure 8.14c restores the X–B–A′–W path. If certain conditions apply, it is possible to optimize (that is, inhibit) the generation of compensation copies. For example, in Figure 8.14c we do not need to copy A′ to the split path if A has no side effects and the values produced by A are not live at the exit point W.

Another View of Scheduling Problems

Scheduling problems are not unique to compilers. In fact, the entire field of operational research (OR) is dedicated to solving scheduling problems. From an OR viewpoint, region compaction is very similar to many *job-shop scheduling problems* (JSPs) from the manufacturing realm. In JSP, a finite set of machines process a finite set of jobs. Each job includes a fixed order of operations, each of which occupies a specific machine for a specified duration. Each machine can process at most one job at a time and, once a job initiates on a given machine, it must complete uninterrupted. The objective of the JSP is to find an assignment of operations to time slots on the machines that minimizes the completion time of the jobs. Deterministic representation and techniques that apply to JSP problems include:

- Mixed integer linear programming (MIP). MIP represents the problem as a linear program with a set of linear constraints and a single linear objective function, but with the additional restriction that some of the decision variables are integers. The simplex method is one of the best-known algorithms for MIP problems.

- Branch-and-bound techniques dynamically explore a tree representing the solution space of all feasible sequences. Bounding techniques prune the search space. Tight bounds improve the efficiency with which the algorithm converges to a good solution.

- Iterative improvement methods, starting from an initial legal solution, optimize a cost function by exploring neighboring solutions. These are analogous to techniques used to solve max-flow/min-cut problems in other domains.

- Approximation methods, bottleneck-based heuristics, constraint satisfaction AI techniques, neural networks, adaptive searches, hybrid approaches, and iterative improvement are other techniques that have been proposed.

Nondeterministic iterative methods include techniques such as:

- Simulated annealing (SA), a random-oriented search technique introduced as an analogy from the physics of the annealing process of a hot metal until it reaches its minimum energy state.

- Genetic algorithms (GAs), based on an abstract model of natural evolution, wherein the quality of individuals improves to the highest level compatible with the environment (constraints of the problem).

- Tabu search (TS), based on intelligent problem solving.

Why have compiler writers not extensively used these techniques? In general, OR techniques seek optimal or near-optimal solutions and are designed to solve small numbers of large-scale problems. On the other hand, a compiler can often compromise optimality for the sake of compile speed, and it needs to solve a very large number of comparatively small problems. We omit more details of OR techniques; they are readily available in the related literature.

8.2.4 Resource Management During Scheduling

During schedule construction, the constructor must be aware of a number of constraints on the schedule. The previous subsection described management of the data dependence graph during scheduling and different possible orders and techniques for scheduling the DDG. Resource management is the other major concern during scheduling. Although dependences and operational latencies may allow an instruction to be scheduled in a particular cycle, the target machine may not have enough of the appropriate functional units, issue slots, or other pieces of hardware to launch or execute the instruction in the desired place. These constraints on scheduling are called *resource hazards*, and a separate module of the schedule constructor typically models all of them. This module maintains its own state in response to scheduling actions, and answers queries about whether a given instruction can be scheduled in a particular place given the already-scheduled instructions.

Early approaches accounted for resources in the underlying machine using reservation tables. A second approach used finite-state automata to model resource constraints, allowing an instruction to be scheduled in a slot if a transition existed in the resource automaton. The last decade has seen innovation in both approaches. Applying automaton theory to FSA models, researchers have factored resource automata into simpler components, have used reverse automata to support reverse scheduling, and have used nondeterminism to model functional units with overlapping capabilities. Responding to these innovations in automata-based resource modeling, reservation-vector proponents have built reduced reservation vector schemes that approach the abilities and efficiencies of the new FSA techniques.

Resource Vectors

The basic resource vector approach involves simple accounting. A *reservation table* is a matrix with a row for each cycle of a schedule and a column for each resource in the machine. When an instruction is scheduled, the system records the resources it uses in the appropriate table entries. Reservation tables allow easy scheduling of instructions (unscheduling can be supported by keeping a pointer from each resource to the instruction that uses it). They can easily be extended to include counted resources, whereby an instruction uses one resource from a hardware-managed pool of identical resources. They are less good at managing instructions that can be handled by multiple functional units (e.g., an integer add might be processed by either the ALU or the AGU). In their simplest implementation they require space proportional to the length of the schedule times the number of resources in the machine. Determining whether an instruction can be scheduled requires examining all of the resources used by the "template" of the instruction, which although linear in complexity could be a large constant factor on the

	Integer ALU	FP ALU	Memory	Branch
Cycle 0	▓		▓	
Cycle 1	▓	▓		
Cycle 2	▓			
Cycle 3			▓	▓

FIGURE 8.15 A simple resource reservation table. Shaded boxes indicate that the resource is busy for the cycle.

computation time of this process. Figure 8.15 illustrates a simple resource reservation table.

More recent work has reduced the size, and therefore improved the efficiency, of resource vector techniques. The key observation is that many explicitly modeled resources are in fact schedule-equivalent. For example, in the canonical in-order RISC five-stage pipeline any instruction that uses the decode phase in a cycle will certainly use the execute phase in the next cycle. These stages do not require separate vector entries (they will always be allocated together). Researchers have demonstrated techniques to synthesize a minimal set of resources that are equivalent to but less numerous than the actual machine resources. Such reduced reservation vector models are much better users of space and time than the original vectors.

Finite-state Automata

Finite-state automata have intuitive appeal for resource modeling. The boolean decision "Is this sequence of instructions a resource-legal schedule?" is similar to the boolean decision "Does this finite-state automaton (FSA) accept this string?" A schedule is a sequence of instructions; a string is a sequence of characters from an alphabet. One can view the set of resource-valid schedules as a language over the alphabet of instructions. It turns out that these languages are simple enough to model using finite-state automata. Early models built FSAs directly from reservation vectors. Later, more refined models simplified the resulting FSAs by modeling *conflicts* between pairs of instructions. Finite-state automata do not support backtracking, unscheduling, or cyclic scheduling well. However, they could answer queries about forward cycle scheduling (less so, operation scheduling) very quickly.

A number of research studies during the 1990s greatly improved the efficiency and scope of FSA-based approaches. These advances used well-known theoretical properties of finite-state machines: breaking them into "factor" automata, reversing automata, and using nondeterminism. We focus on the work of Bala and Rubin, the primary innovators in the FSA space.

Factor automata reduce the number of FSA states (and therefore the size to store them) by observing that the different functional areas of modern machines tend to operate independently. For example, many processors have separate integer and floating-point sides (they share issue and load/store hardware but not much else). These independent pieces can then be modeled by separate (factored) automata. The cross-product of the

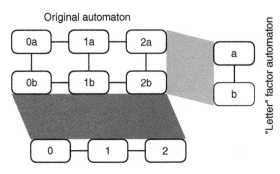

FIGURE 8.16 **Simple automaton representing a two-resource machine, with its corresponding factor automata.** The original automaton represents two resources. The *letter* resource is either busy or free. The *number* resource has two units of resources available. The original automaton has six states, representing all possible cases of resource utilization. The two factor automata have two and three states, respectively, and their cross-product is equivalent to the original automaton.

factors produces an automaton equivalent to the original, but the state of both factors can be represented more compactly than the state of the larger (product) automaton. These interact only in issue resources; otherwise, they run independently. Bala and Rubin [1995] report that factoring reduced an automaton for the Alpha 21064 of 13,524 states to two automata of 237 and 232 states. Figure 8.16 shows the intuition behind factor automata, although the reality is much more complex.

Resource modeling across control-flow merges (joins or splits) has long been a thorny engineering problem. One must model the state that results from either path. Resource vector approaches can logically *OR* the vectors of the parent blocks, but not until Bala and Rubin proposed join tables did the FSA approaches have a complementary technique. A join table maps from the cross-product of states to a single state, allowing two FSA states to be mapped to a single state that represents both sets of resources being used.

Adding instructions to an already-scheduled block of code has also posed engineering problems in the past. The forward automaton allows its users to verify that a sequence of instructions holds no structural hazards, but it only allows new instructions to be appended to the sequence. Insertion requires a linear rescan to verify that the new instruction did not conflict with any later instructions. Reverse automata[4] provide a partial answer to this problem, by allowing the system to model the resource constraints of those future instructions. A scheduler that maintains both forward and reverse automaton states can verify that there are no structural hazards for a single inserted instruction.

---

4. The reverse automaton can be thought of as an automaton that accepts the reverse of the language of the original automaton. Thus, if the original automaton accepts resource-valid schedules of instructions the reverse automaton accepts backward resource-valid schedules of instructions, which is exactly what is desired to represent future resource constraints.

However, inserting additional instructions still requires linear rescanning to recompute the forward and reverse automaton states affected by the first inserted instruction.

What about nondeterminism? Bala and Rubin's later work uses nondeterminism to model flexible pipeline resources that can execute a variety of instruction classes. Suppose a machine has two functional units, FU1 and FU2, and three instruction classes (A, B, and C). FU1 can execute instructions of types A and B, and FU2 can execute instructions of type B and C. In a deterministic automaton or a reservation vector model, scheduling a type B instruction requires it to be assigned to either FU1 or FU2. This excludes the future possibility of issuing an instruction of type A or C, respectively. With nondeterminism, the FSA can model simply issuing the type B instruction without committing it to FU1 or FU2. Then a later type A or type C instruction can still be scheduled, in effect lazily choosing the unit on which the type B instruction executes.

8.2.5 Loop Scheduling

Many programs spend most of their time in loops. Therefore, a good loop-scheduling strategy is a fundamental component of an optimizing compiler. The simplest approach to loop scheduling, *loop unrolling*, was mentioned in Section 8.2.2 (on region enlargement). Loop unrolling does not actually allow acyclic schedulers to handle loops; rather, it enlarges the acyclic part of a loop to allow the acyclic scheduler room to work. More sophisticated techniques directly address scheduling loops and their back edges.

Software pipelining is the class of global cyclic scheduling algorithms that exploits interiteration ILP while handling the back-edge barrier (see Figure 8.17 for a conceptual illustration). Within software pipelining algorithms, *modulo scheduling* is a framework that produces a *kernel* of code that sustainably overlaps multiple iterations of a loop. The kernel is built so that neither data dependence nor resource usage conflicts arise. Correctly entering and exiting the kernel code is handled by special code sequences called *prologues* and *epilogues*, respectively. They prepare the state of the machine to execute the kernel and correctly finish executing the kernel and recording its results. Prologue and epilogue code is analogous to compensation code generated by acyclic schedulers. That is, it is necessary to maintain correctness but causes code expansion. Hardware techniques can reduce or remove the need for prologues and epilogues.

Modulo scheduling efficiently explores the space of possible kernel schedules to find the shortest legal one. The length of the kernel, which is the constant interval between the start of successive kernel iterations, is called the *initiation interval* (II). The resources required by the operations in a loop and the interiteration data dependences in a loop place lower bounds on the II. These are called the *resource-constrained minimum II* (ResMII) and the *recurrence-constrained minimum II* (RecMII), respectively. To enforce II-derived resource constraints, the modulo scheduler uses a *modulo reservation table* (MRT) for machine resources that checks for conflicts not just in the current cycle but in all schedule cycles that differ from the current cycle by II cycles. The scheduler begins searching schedules at the lowest II, and heuristics guide whether to continue searching, to backtrack, or to abandon the current II for the next higher one. In practice, iterative modulo scheduling generates near-optimal schedules (optimality in about 96%

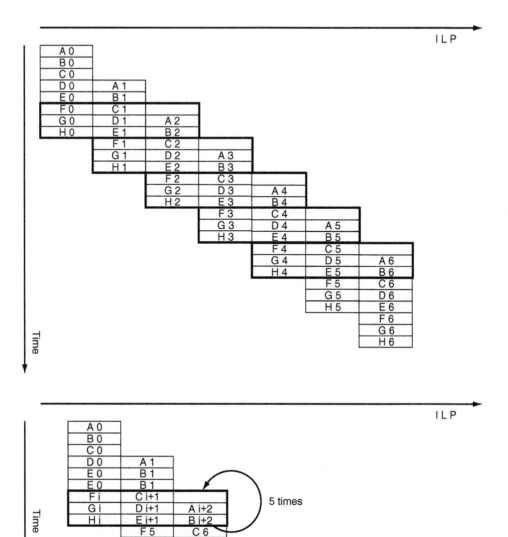

FIGURE 8.17 Conceptual illustration of software pipelining. The figure shows the similarity of software pipelining to hardware pipelining techniques. In a software pipelined loop, multiple iterations are executed at the same time, but each iteration is executing operations from a different part of the original loop. The goal of modulo scheduling is to find the *kernel*, which overlaps operations from different iterations of the loop into a compact but equivalent schedule. The top part of the figure shows a seven-iteration loop with eight operations (A through H) in the loop body, which overlaps every three iterations so that we can exploit three units in most of the cycles. We can notice that a regular "kernel" of three iterations repeats five times once the schedule "warms up." Software pipelining exploits this regularity, and as we can see in the bottom part of the figure "collapses" the loop iterations by repeating a small kernel (three cycles in the example) that contains operations that belong to different iterations.

of observed loops). In addition, its compile-time performance is good, and it is often much more efficient than any other cyclic or acyclic scheduler based on loop unrolling.

On the downside, modulo scheduling is most effective on well-structured single loops. Nested loops can be handled by recursively invoking the modulo scheduler, but outer loops must then include the prologue and epilogue code of the inner loop. Loops with exits can be handled, but at the expense of a much greater complexity. Control flow in the loop body (e.g., even a single *if-then-else*) can be handled only through predication, even if the paths are unbalanced and the advantage of if-conversion is dubious.[5]

Several approaches have been proposed to generate a software pipeline. In the following section, we describe the basics of *modulo scheduling*, the technique that by far dominates any alternative in research as well as production compilers.

Modulo Scheduling

At the conceptual level, modulo scheduling operates on a fully unrolled loop body, attempting to generate a schedule assignment under the constraint that *the assignments for all copies of the same operation in different iterations are identical*. A side effect of this model is that the scheduling interval between the start of two successive iterations is a constant number of cycles (the aforementioned initiation interval). Additionally, if we look at the overall unrolled schedule we can see that a group of *II* cycles is repetitive, with the exception of the warm-up (*prologue*) and cool-down (*epilogue*) phases. This is what is normally called the *kernel*. We can now collapse all identical kernels to one, and what is left is the combination of prologue, kernel, and epilogue, which synthesize the execution of the entire loop (see Figure 8.18).

At the algorithmic level, we do not need to fully unroll a loop but can simply create a schedule for a single iteration by imposing enough scheduling rules so that we are sure the same *kernel* schedule can be repeated at regular intervals of II cycles without violating resource constraints or data dependences (both intra- and interiteration). Note that in comparison to an acyclic scheduler the constraints that govern modulo scheduling add the complication of interiteration dependences. This occurs when the current iteration of a loop uses values calculated during the previous iteration, either passed through induction variables or through memory. For example, in the following loop

```
for (i = 0; i < 100; ++i)
    a[i + 3] = a[i] * x + 7;
```

we can find two interiteration dependences: one between iterations *i* and *i* + *1* through the induction variable *i* and one between iterations *i* and *i* + 3 because of the memory dependence through array a[ ].

Generating code for a loop body within a modulo-scheduling framework is very different from scheduling acyclic regions. One important observation about the scheduling

---

5. To be fair to modulo scheduling techniques, no acyclic scheduling technique handles loops of any type, let alone loop nests. The closest acyclic techniques get is to unroll or peel inner loops and then repeat the unrolling or peeling for nested loops. Scheduling loops well is difficult.

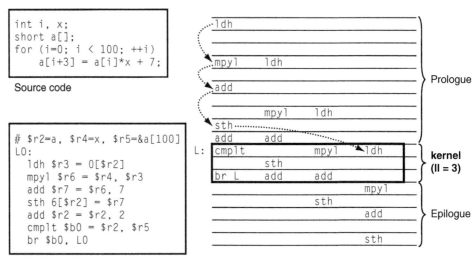

```
int i, x;
short a[];
for (i=0; i < 100; ++i)
    a[i+3] = a[i]*x + 7;
```
Source code

```
# $r2=a, $r4=x, $r5=&a[100]
L0:
    ldh $r3 = 0[$r2]
    mpyl $r6 = $r4, $r3
    add $r7 = $r6, 7
    sth 6[$r2] = $r7
    add $r2 = $r2, 2
    cmplt $b0 = $r2, $r5
    br $b0, L0
```
Sequential VEX code

FIGURE 8.18 Conceptual model of modulo scheduling. Generation of prologue, kernel, and epilogue starting from a simple sequence of VEX code. In the example, II = 3, which is the minimum allowed by resource constraints and data dependences (represented by the dotted lines, see Figure 8.19 for details on the *minII* computation). The target machine is the default VEX architecture (4-wide, one cluster, load latency of 3 cycles, multiply latency of 2 cycles, compare latency of 2 cycles).

procedure we just described is that the loop performance only depends (for long-enough trip counts) on the II. The schedule length of the single iteration (called *stage count*) is largely irrelevant. This means that the heuristics of a modulo scheduler do not have the goal of minimizing the stage count of individual iterations, but rather of arranging operations so that they can be repeated at the smallest possible II distance. In other words, modulo scheduling trades the *latency* of a single iteration to get a better *throughput* of the overall loop execution. This is distinctively different from the unrolling strategy, which minimizes the schedule latency for the straight-line code obtained by concatenating the unrolled iterations.

In reality, the stage count is also important because it relates to the duration of the prologue and epilogue of the loop. Before reaching the kernel steady state, a loop requires a number of {stage_count − 1} cycles to fill the software pipeline. Likewise, it requires the same number of cycles to drain the pipeline at the end of the loop (epilogue). In addition to increasing loop code size, given that the schedule is partially empty during the execution of prologue and epilogue, this could affect the overall performance when the loop trip count is close in size to the stage count.

The Modulo Reservation Table (MRT). Producing a legal schedule for a software pipeline (from a resource point of view) requires finding an assignment that guarantees absence of resource conflicts when we repeat the schedule over multiple II intervals.

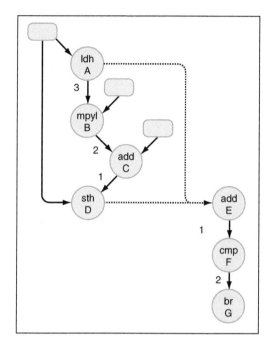

	cycle				
0	0	ldh(A)			
1	1				
2	2				
0	3	mpyl(B)	ldh(A)		
1	4				
2	5	add(C)			
0	6		mpyl(B)	ldh(A)	
1	7	sth(D)			
2	8	add(E)	add(C)		
0	**9**	**cmp(F)**		**mpyl(B)**	**ldh(A)**
1	**10**		**sth(D)**		
2	**11**	**br(G)**	**add(E)**	**add(C)**	
0	12				mpyl(B)
1	13			sth(D)	
2	14				add(C)
0	15				
1	16				sth(D)

	ALU				MUL		MEM	BR
0	F(9)	---	---	---	B(3)	---	A(0)	---
1	---	---	---	---	---	---	D(7)	---
2	C(5)	E(8)	---	---	---	---	---	G(11)

FIGURE 8.19 **The modulo reservation table.** Using the loop of Figure 8.18 and a default (4-wide) VEX target, the picture shows the allocation of operations on the MRT. The diagram on the left represents the dependence graph of a single iteration (with nodes labeled A through G and arcs annotated with the operation latency), whereas the table on the top right is the cycle-by-cycle schedule of each of the operations. The table on the bottom right is the MRT, which contains the corresponding modulo resource usage of the schedule above. For example, operation D (the *sth*) scheduled at cycle 7 uses resources in the MRT at cycle 1 (*7 mod 3 = 1*). Note that D could have been scheduled in cycle 6 (MRT cycle 0), but we had to delay it to cycle 7 to be able to avoid the module resource conflicts with the *ldh* operation (A) already scheduled at cycle 0 (MRT cycle 0 as well). Finally, note that the loop-back branch operation (G) has to be scheduled with the additional constraint of occupying the last slot in the MRT, so that code for the kernel generates the correct execution.

In practice, we can enforce this by ensuring that the same resources are not reused more than once in the same cycle, or in following cycles that — modulo the II—collide with it. This particular way of tracking resources (*modulo constraint*) is usually enforced through the use of a *modulo reservation table* (MRT), which records (and checks) resource usage for cycle c at the slot corresponding to $\{c \bmod II\}$. As we can see from the example shown in Figure 8.19, the MRT is the "modulo" equivalent of the resource table normally used in acyclic schedulers to enforce the constraints imposed by the target machine (see more details in Section 8.2.4)

Searching for the II. The modulo scheduling procedure we have described thus far relies on a candidate II we need to choose before attempting to create a legal schedule. Usually, the driver for a modulo scheduler implements a search procedure in which we attempt to find a legal schedule for all IIs within a range computed through the analysis of loop body, machine resources, operation latency, and data dependence graph.

```
// basic scheme of iterative modulo scheduling
minII = compute_minII();
maxII = compute_maxII();
found = false;
II = minII;
while (!found && II < maxII) {
    found = try_to_modulo_schedule(II, budget);
    II = II + 1;
}
if (!found)
    trouble(); /* wrong maxII */
```

The computation of *maxII* is trivial, as we can simply pick the sum of all latencies of the operations in the loop body (this is the boundary case converting the modulo scheduling problem into a linear scheduling problem, which is always solvable). The computation of *minII* is much more complex, for two reasons: we need to obey interiteration dependences and we need to keep the run-time performance of the modulo scheduler within reasonable bounds.

Once we narrow down a reasonable II range, we still need to assign a *budget* to the algorithm that attempts to find a legal schedule. The budget is typically related to the amount of compilation time we are willing to dedicate to the modulo scheduling phase (see the section "Iterative Modulo Scheduling" later in the chapter).

The computation of *minII* involves two components: the minimum II that derives from resource constraints (*resII*), and the minimum II that derives from dependence (recurrence) constraints (*recII*). The computation of *recII* must take into account both the intraiteration and the interiteration dependences among loop operations. Recurrence cycles are what drives the computation of *recII*, in that we cannot possibly generate a legal schedule with a II smaller than the delay of the longest recurrence cycle. Once we know *resII* and *recII*, we can compute *minII* as $minII = max(resII, recII)$. Setting a reasonable value of *resII* is straightforward, as we can simply map every operation in the loop body to the target resources — ignoring dependences — and report the resulting number of cycles. More accurate *resII* calculation might take into account latencies, interiteration dependences, and combinations of operations. Figure 8.19 shows an example of how to compute *resII, recII,* and *minII* on a simple loop.

Scheduling Heuristics. For a candidate II and stage count budget, the goal of the scheduler is to find a legal cycle and resource assignment. To this end, we can usually apply a modified version of *list scheduling* in which resource checking for each assignment happens through the MRT. For the heuristics used to decide the ordering of operations, height-based priority strategies of acyclic scheduling tend to work well for a modulo scheduler. The scheduling *budget* does not usually interfere with the list-scheduling phase, but it impacts the number of different list-scheduling attempts the driver is allowed to try with different stage counts (this is often described as the *backtracking budget*).

Prologues and Epilogues. The scheduler is also responsible for generating the special prologue and epilogue code, which consists of a partial copy of the kernel wherein selected operations have been removed. The situation is more complex in the presence of multiple-exit loops, which in general require multiple epilogues. In practice, multiple epilogues are almost always a necessity. A software pipeline with a single epilogue can only execute a certain number of iterations n where

```
n = k * II + stage_count - 1.
```

For a more general case (or unknown trip count) we need multiple epilogues, some of which may be collapsed under certain conditions. A detailed description of multiple epilogues is beyond the scope of this book and can be found in the relevant literature.

Given that prologues and epilogues are proper subsets of the kernel code in which certain operations have been disabled, we can think of reusing the kernel code with a set of predicates that progressively shifts enable conditions (for the prologue) or disable conditions (for the epilogue). If we assume a fully predicated architecture, this can be implemented by adding a rotating function to the predicate bank and preassigning a set of II predicates with the proper number of true and false values.[6] Figure 8.20 shows an example of kernel-only loop scheduling.

Modulo Variable Expansion. Although the MRT takes care of ensuring that resources are not oversubscribed for a given II, it does not address the issue of guaranteeing that a legal register allocation exists for the same II. The register allocation problem arises when the lifetime of a value used within an iteration exceeds the II length. In that case, a simple register allocation policy will not work, since the definition of that specific value of the following iterations is going to overwrite the previous one before the last use of the current iteration has had a chance to consume it. Fortunately, the solution is not difficult (see Figure 8.21). By unrolling the scheduled loop body we artificially extend the II without performance degradation, while maintaining constant lifetime lengths of the troubled values. In other words, we can always find an unrolling factor that causes the new II to be larger than the longest lifetime. This operation is called *modulo variable expansion*, and we can prove that if v is the length of the longest lifetime we must unroll at least by a factor of $k = \left\lceil \frac{v}{II} \right\rceil$ to ensure that we can find a legal register allocation.

Modulo variable expansion does not come for free. It increases the length of the kernel code (and consequently the length of prologues and epilogues), complicates the exit strategy (multiple exit points), and adds to register pressure (distinct registers for each of the overlapping values). In other words, it reduces many of the advantages of modulo scheduling over a simpler unrolling-based loop strategy. To avoid some of these issues, it is possible to use hardware support so that registers are dynamically renamed in different iterations even if they use the same logical identifier. This is one of the uses of *rotating registers,* whereby the instantiation of a physical register comes from the combination of a logical identifier and a register base incremented at every iteration. In this way, a reference to register r at iteration i points to a different storage location

---

6. This is what the IPF architecture implements, as does the TI C6x at a smaller scale.

0	p0 ? cmp			p2 ? mpyl	p3 ? ldh
1		p1 ? sth			
2	p0 ? brt	p1 ? add	p2 ? add		

Kernel-only code. The operations are guarded by predicates *p0*, *p1*, *p2*, and *p3*.

The *brt* branches to the top and rotates the predicate by shifting *p1 = p0*, *p2 = p1*, *p3 = p2*, and *p0 = p3*.

Stage	Predicates	cyc					
Prologue stage 1	p0=0 p1=0 p2=0 p3=1	0		p3 ? ldh			
		1					
		2					
Prologue stage 2	p0=0 p1=0 p2=1 p3=1	0		p2 ? mpyl	p3 ? ldh.d		
		1					
		2		p2 ? add			
Prologue stage 3	p0=0 p1=1 p2=1 p3=1	0				p2 ? mpyl	p3 ? ldh
		1		p1 ? sth			
		2		p1 ? add	p2 ? add		
Kernel	p0=1 p1=1 p2=1 p3=1	0	p0 ? cmp			p2 ? mpyl	p3 ? ldh
		1		p1 ? sth			
		2	p0 ? brt	p1 ? add	p2 ? add		
Epilogue stage 1	p0=1 p1=1 p2=1 p3=0	0			p0 ? cmp		p2 ? mpyl
		1				p1 ? sth	
		2				p1 ? add	p2 ? add
Epilogue stage 2	p0=1 p1=1 p2=0 p3=0	0					
		1				p0 ? cmp	p1 ? sth
		2					p1 ? add

Execution of the kernel-only code. As we fill the predicates with 1s, the operations of the prologue start executing. As we fill the predicates with 0s, the operations of the epilogue complete. The steady state corresponds to all predicates being set to 1. The loopback jump (*brt*) includes special semantics to rotate the predicates for the prologue and triggers the execution of the epilogue (start filling 0s) when the loop terminates.

FIGURE 8.20 **Example of kernel-only code.** Using the loop of Figure 8.18, and a predicated extension of VEX, the figure shows the use of rotating predicates to remove prologue and epilogue.

than the same reference to *r* at iteration *i + 1*. By using the appropriate set of rotation commands and register references, it is then possible to use this mechanism to avoid modulo variable expansion and reduce the software pipeline to kernel-only code.

Iterative Modulo Scheduling. Most of the proposed modulo scheduling approaches are variations of the basic *iterative modulo scheduling* algorithm, which increments the candidate II until the scheduler finds a solution. However, even if a schedule exists for a given II we may not be able to find it because of the complexity of the MRT. To improve the probability of finding a schedule, we can allow a controlled form of backtracking (unscheduling and rescheduling of instructions) based on a scheduling *budget* that throttles the number of scheduling attempts per instruction, as well as the stage count of each scheduling attempt. In addition, a scheduler also has to deal with the register requirements at a given II, in that different allocation policies have different effects on the variable lifetimes that might change the modulo variable expansion requirements. If the register requirements exceed the available machine registers, we can either increase the II or attempt to introduce spill code.

Advanced Modulo Scheduling Techniques. As we described in the previous paragraphs, software pipelining involves several heuristics to be effective: predication, choice of a good *minII*, scheduling budget for every attempt, node ordering, register allocation,

0	0	ldh r1 = 0[r20]			
1	1				
2	2				
0	3		ldh r1 = 0[r20]		
1	4	mpy r2 = r1,r22			
2	5				
0	6	add r3 = r2,7		ldh r1 = 0[r20]	
1	7		mpy r2 = r1,r22		
2	8	sth 6[r20] = r3			
0	9	add r20 = r20,2	add r3 = r2,7		ldh r1 = 0[r20]
1	10	cmp b0 = r20,r21		mpy r2 = r1,r22	
2	11		sth 6[r20] = r3		
0	**12**		**add r20 = r20,2**	**add r3 = r2,7**	**ldh r1 = 0[r20]**
1	**13**		**cmp b0 = r20,r21**		**mpy r2 = r1,r22**
2	**14**	**br b0**		**sth 6[r20] = r3**	
0	15				add r3 = r2,7
1	16				mpy r2 = r1,r22
2	17				sth 6[r20] = r3
0	18				add r3 = r2,7
1	19				
2	20				sth 6[r20] = r3

Register *r1* needs to hold the same variable in two different iterations, but the lifetimes overlap.

$$Unroll = \left\lceil \frac{MaxLifetime}{II} \right\rceil = \left\lceil \frac{4}{3} \right\rceil = 2$$

0	0	ldh r1 = 0[r20]				
1	1					
2	2					
3	3		ldh r11 = 0[r20]			
4	4	mpy r2 = r1,r22				
5	5					
0	6	add r3 = r2,7		ldh r1 = 0[r20]		
1	7		mpy r2 = r11,r22			
2	8	sth 6[r20] = r3				
3	9	add r20 = r20,2	add r3 = r2,7		ldh r11 = 0[r20]	
4	10	cmp b0 = r20,r21		mpy r2 = r1,r22		
5	11		sth 6[r20] = r3			
0	**12**		**add r20 = r20,2**	**add r3 = r2,7**	**ldh r1 = 0[r20]**	
1	**13**		**cmp b0 = r20,r21**		**mpy r2 = r11,r22**	
2	**14**	br b0		**sth 6[r20] = r3**		
3	**15**			**add r20 = r20,2**	**add r3 = r2,7**	**ldh r11 = 0[r20]**
4	**16**			cmp b0 = r20,r21		**mpy r2 = r1,r22**
5	**17**		**br b0**		**sth 6[r20] = r3**	
	18				add r3 = r2,7	
	19					mpy r2 = r11,r22
	20				sth 6[r20] = r3	
	21					add r3 = r2,7
	22					
	23					sth 6[r20] = r3

FIGURE 8.21 **Modulo variable expansion.** When II = 3, if the ldh operation of Figure 8.18 has a latency of four cycles (instead of three, as we assumed so far) the standard scheduling technique causes the lifetime of the *ldh* destination (*r1*) to overlap with the same value of the following iteration (top of the picture). To solve this problem, we can unroll the loop kernel twice (bottom of the picture) and use two registers (*r1* and *r11*) so that the two lifetimes now do not overlap. This achieves the same loop throughput (two iterations every six cycles) at the expense of larger code size and more register pressure. The schedule shown assumes that we can remove the intermediate loop exit (the grayed-out *cmp* and *br* operations in the first and third iteration). If we cannot do that, we need to introduce multiple exits and multiple epilogues.

and so on. Recently, many techniques have been proposed to improve the heuristics of the base modulo scheduling technique. *Hypernode reduction modulo scheduling* (HRMS) is a heuristics-based strategy whose goal is to shorten loop-variant lifetimes while keeping II constant. The ordering phase of HRMS generates a good ordering of the nodes, so that nodes are scheduled as soon (as late) as possible based on their predecessors (successors). *Swing modulo scheduling* is a version of HRMS that improves it by also taking into account the criticality (i.e., the absence of scheduling slack) of a node. The ordering strategy takes into account recurrence cycles and the lifetimes caused by a schedule assignment. To reduce the variable lifetimes, it keeps operations as close as possible to both its successors and predecessors. In that scheduling constraints usually add up as the schedule progresses, it offsets the difficulty of finding an allocation by prioritizing the most critical operations. In this way, the operations that are scheduled last have more slack, hence increasing their probability of finding a free slot.

8.2.6 Clustering

ILP architectures have high register demands. Each parallel execution unit typically consumes two operands, and produces a third. This requires a large, multiported register file and a complex bypassing network to support even narrow-issue machines. *Clustering* provides a natural solution to these problems. A clustered architecture divides a multiple-issue machine into separate pieces (obviously called *clusters*), each consisting of a register bank and one or more functional units. Functional units can efficiently access local registers in their associated bank. Depending on the architecture, remote registers may be directly addressable (*implicit move*) or reachable only using intercluster (*explicit*) move instructions. Regardless of how remote access is specified, it is typically slower than local access and is often subject to resource limitations. Figure 8.22a shows a 4-issue ILP datapath with an 8-read, 4-write central register. Figure 8.22b shows the related clustered 4-issue ILP datapath, with two clusters of two function units and one register bank each. Figure 8.22b also shows the communication link between the clusters.

Clustering complicates compilation. As long as the clusters are architecturally visible, the compiler must place operations to minimize intercluster moves and unbalanced use of the clusters. This is a new compiler responsibility, as the decision about *where* to execute an operation was traditionally either empty (e.g., for a scalar machine) or handled transparently by the hardware (e.g., for a completely connected superscalar machine). The difficulty of the compiler problem depends on the way the ISA specifies communication among clusters. When the hardware transparently supports fetching remote operands (possibly with a dynamic penalty), the compiler's task is to minimize the number of dynamic stalls. In this case, compiler choices can degrade performance, but correct code will always be generated. When connectivity is architecturally exposed (either by explicit intercluster moves or by limited ways to specify remote registers), the compiler must issue move operations (either implicit or explicit) to copy data to appropriate locations. In this case, compiler choices affect correctness as well as performance.

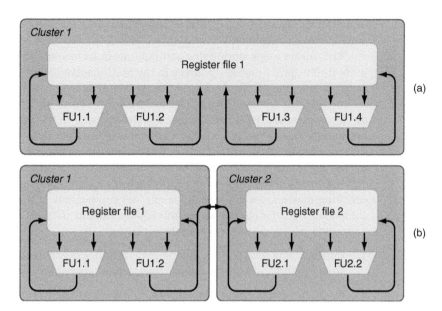

FIGURE 8.22 Clustered VLIW architectures. To keep execution units busy, we need multiple ports to the register file (a). However, register file ports are expensive (the area grows with the square of ports) and do not scale with technology, in that they largely depend on wire capacitance. That is why clustered organizations (b) with limited connectivity are more appealing from an implementation perspective. This puts more pressure on the compiler algorithms that assign operations to clusters in the scheduling phase.

Although some recent approaches (such as the *unified assign-and-schedule* technique) advocate a unified clustering and scheduling step, most compilers implement clustering before scheduling. The clustering phase preassigns operations to clusters, and then the scheduling phase assigns operations to functional units within clusters. As examples, we outline two preassignment techniques: *bottom-up-greedy* (BUG) and *partial-component clustering* (PCC).

BUG was originally designed for the Bulldog compiler at Yale in the mid 1980s. BUG has two phases. BUG first traverses the DAG from exit nodes (leaves) to entry nodes (roots), estimating the likely set of functional units to be assigned to a node based on the location of previously assigned operands and destinations. When it reaches the roots, BUG works its way back to the leaves, selecting the final assignment for the nodes along the way. To reach a final assignment, BUG estimates the cycle in which a functional unit can compute the operation based on resource constraints, the location of the operands, and the machine connectivity. Once cycle estimates for all feasible units for a node are available, BUG selects the unit producing the smallest output delay for each node.

In the second phase, BUG assigns initial and final locations to the variables that are live-in and live-out of the DDG. This phase is quite delicate, in that it affects the adjoining regions of code, and particular care must be taken to avoid redundant duplication of locations for critical values (such as induction variables in loops) without sacrificing parallelism opportunities.

BUG makes a few simplifying assumptions in its operating mode. First, functional units are the only limiting resources in the machine (conflicts over register-bank ports or buses are ignored). Second, resource costs and delays for scheduling explicit copy instructions are ignored. Third, register pressure is ignored. Under register pressure, the topology of the DDG can change significantly due to the presence of spill/restore operations. This is one of the major limitations of the algorithm.

Scheduling a DDG of 1,000 operations for a machine with four symmetrical clusters implies 4^{1000} clustering combinations. As an alternative to BUG, consider reducing the dimensionality of the problem and applying some form of componentization. To do this, construct *macronodes* for partially connected components of the original DAG. These components can then be treated as indivisible units and assigned to a single cluster. PCC adopts this philosophy. It works in three phases.

1. *Partial component growth*, wherein the compiler assembles groups of operations from the DDG into "components" (macronodes) based on connectivity criteria

2. *Initial assignment*, wherein we perform a greedy BUG-style pass to produce a reasonable cluster assignment for the components

3. *Iterative improvement*, wherein pairs of cluster assignments for components are swapped repeatedly until we meet a termination criterion

Various experiments suggest this rule of thumb: Breaking the CPU into two clusters costs about 15 to 20% lost cycles, whereas breaking the CPU into four clusters costs about 25 to 30%. Whether these results approach theoretical limits is an open issue for research. Direct computation of optimal clustering remains infeasible.

8.3 Register Allocation

All modern machines have much more memory than register space. However, values kept in registers can be manipulated more quickly than values stored in memory. This forces the compiler to trade off the relatively few, fast register locations with the plentiful, slower memory locations for values. *Register allocation* is the task of assigning values in the program to register and/or memory locations. Like many optimization problems, register allocation is NP-hard.

The register allocation program is old and well known. The standard heuristic involves *coloring* of an *interference graph*, which shows which values are active in the program ("live") simultaneously. Each node in the graph is a value (nodes joined by edges are simultaneously live and thus cannot be assigned to the same register). There is a significant body of literature on register allocation, and detailed explanations of graph coloring can be found in most compiler textbooks.

In the last decade, there has also been renewed interest in nonstandard register allocation techniques; notably those that are faster or better than the graph-coloring approach. As their name implies, *linear-scan* allocators attempt to allocate registers in time proportional to the number of instructions being allocated (constructing the interference graph typically takes quadratic time in the number of instructions). Linear-scan allocators are especially of interest in the just-in-time compiler, dynamic translation, and dynamic optimization communities because they allow quicker compilation time at the (possible) cost of slower run time.

At the other end of the compile-/run-time tradeoff, optimal register allocation techniques use a variety of solvers to attempt to find the best possible register allocation for a program. Such techniques have become feasible recently because machine speeds have increased continually, whereas procedure sizes have not grown nearly as quickly. It is especially interesting to note that optimal register allocation for *irregular* architectures (e.g., those with idiosyncratic instruction encodings and/or limited functional units and register usability) appears to be more computationally tractable than such compilation for more regular (e.g., RISC-like) architectures.

8.3.1 Phase-ordering Issues

Compiler writers inevitably face the choice of what order in which to perform various required tasks. Typically, actions taken in one phase influence the effectiveness of the following phases, and the quality of the result can be dramatically different (depending upon in what order the phases were carried out). This dilemma is often difficult to resolve, and the problem facing the compiler architect is called the phase-ordering problem (see Figure 8.23). Two important unresolved ordering controversies involve the scheduling phase: Should it be done before, after, or even simultaneously with register allocation and cluster assignment?

Register Allocation and Scheduling

Register allocation and scheduling have conflicting goals. A register allocator tries to minimize spill and restore operations, creating sequential constraints (for register reuse) between operations the scheduler could otherwise place in parallel. A scheduler tries to fill all parallel units in the target machine and may extend variable lifetimes by speculative code motion. Both of these goals increase register pressure. Register allocation and scheduling must coexist in the compiler, but how to order them is not apparent *a priori*. Some of the alternatives are discussed below.

Instruction Scheduling Followed by Register Allocation. This choice favors exploiting ILP over efficient register utilization. It assumes enough registers are available to match the schedule. It encounters problems when the scheduler increases register pressure beyond the available registers. This can happen on wide-issue machines in regions with considerable amounts of ILP (e.g., scientific code or multimedia applications). Note that the register allocator must insert spill and restore code in the already-scheduled code, which can be a difficult task on statically scheduled targets. This technique is common in product compilers for modern RISC processors.

Scheduling Followed by Register Allocation Followed by Post-scheduling. This variation of the previous technique adds a *post-scheduling* pass after register allocation.

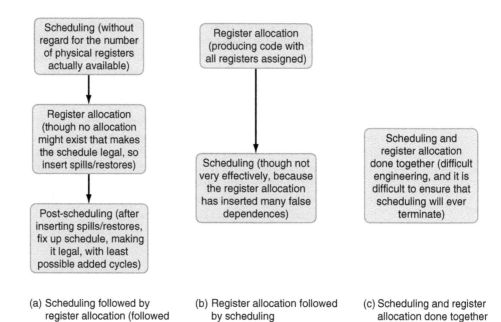

(a) Scheduling followed by register allocation (followed by a postpass)

(b) Register allocation followed by scheduling

(c) Scheduling and register allocation done together

FIGURE 8.23 **Phase ordering.** The decision of what *phase-ordering* register allocation and scheduling should have in a compiler for an ILP CPU is a tricky one, especially for a VLIW. All of the methods shown here have been implemented with varying results. Choice (a) is the most popular, though newer techniques that resemble choice (c) may be better over time. Choice (b) is natural and easy, but very limiting.

The post-scheduler rearranges the code after spill code has been placed and register assignments are final. To guarantee convergence, the post-scheduling phase cannot increase the number of required registers. This approach makes a good engineering/performance tradeoff and is common in industrial compilers.

Register Allocation Followed by Instruction Scheduling. This technique prioritizes register use over exploiting ILP. This technique works well for target machines with few available registers (such as x86 architectures). However, the register allocator introduces additional dependences every time it reuses a register. This leads to very inefficient schedules.

Combined Register Allocation and Instruction Scheduling. This technique attempts to build a single pass that trades off spill costs against lost ILP. Although potentially very powerful, this approach involves the most engineering complexity. Because register resources may never be freed, a straightforward list-scheduling algorithm may not converge, and additional measures are necessary to ensure that scheduling terminates. The DAG changes dynamically with the addition of spill and restore operations. These changes affect operation heights, operation depths, and the critical path of the region, possibly invalidating previously made choices. The integrated scheduler-allocator must handle values that pass through but are not used in the region. A mechanism called "delayed binding" (to defer the choice of a location of a value until needed) addresses this problem, but further complicates the scheduler.

Finally, it is worth mentioning *cooperative approaches* in which the scheduler monitors the register resources of the target and estimates register pressure in its heuristics. A postpass register allocator adds spill and restore code when needed. This approach is particularly promising because the scheduler remains simple but the system can still avoid pathological register pressure cases.

8.4 Speculation and Predication

Most scheduling decisions obey the constraints found in the DAG. However, some of the most powerful scheduling techniques aim to relax or remove dependences. Two fundamental techniques, predication and speculation, are employed by schedulers (or in the preceding phases) to transform or remove control dependences. These two techniques are often presented as alternatives to each other. They are not quite that. Although sometimes one could use either technique (but not both) effectively on a given operation, by and large they are independent techniques. Usually, one is much more appropriate than the other. Speculation is used to move operations up past a branch that is highly weighted in one direction. Predication is used to collapse short sequences of alternative operations after a branch that is nearly equally likely in each direction. Predication can also play an important role in software pipelining, as described in Section 8.2.5.

8.4.1 Control and Data Speculation

During instruction scheduling, some code motions may be *unsafe* because the instructions being moved may generate exceptions, and thus relocating the instruction will change the exception behavior of the program. Mechanisms for load/store speculation allow the hardware and software to collaborate to maintain safety while still performing the code motion of an excepting load or store. The mechanisms involve delaying exceptions from the point at which they are generated (where the instruction was moved to) until the point in the original program at which the exception would have been raised (where the instruction was moved from). We described the hardware support for such mechanisms in Section 4.5.1.

From the compiler perspective, it is complicated to support nonexcepting loads because of the need to generate recovery code. If multiple instructions are speculated in this manner, the shape and size of recovery code can be substantial. Techniques are appearing in the research literature that make recovery code size manageable, but it is not entirely a solved problem. In addition, code size expands when nonexcepting loads are used because the check instruction and any recovery code are extra. Nonexcepting load speculation also affects register allocation and usage because the live range of the destination register becomes longer.

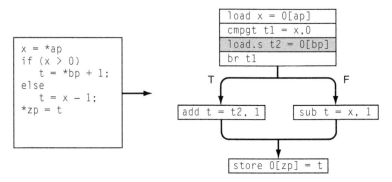

FIGURE 8.24 **Example of speculative code motion.** Compare this with Figure 8.12. The *load* operation becomes speculative (marked *load.s*) once we move it above a branch.

Speculative code motion (or *code hoisting* and sometimes *code sinking*) moves operations above control-dominating branches (or below joins for sinking). Note that this transformation does not always preserve the original program semantics, and in particular it may change the exception behavior of the program. A compiler may only introduce speculative operations when certain conditions are satisfied, depending on the degree of ISA support for the execution of speculative memory operations and in general on the exception model imposed by the run-time system. Note that unlike predication speculation actually *removes* control dependences, thus potentially reducing the critical path of execution. Figure 8.24 illustrates speculative code motion (compare it with Figure 8.12). The load operation becomes speculative (marked *load.s*), once we move it above a branch. As another example, a *trace scheduler* may be able to move operations either above splits or below joins, knowing that a successive *bookkeeping* phase will generate compensation code to reestablish the correct program semantics.

8.4.2 Predicated Execution

Predication was described in detail in Section 4.5.2. This is a technique whereby with hardware support the behavior of an operation changes according to the value of a previously computed bit. Predication is used to convert multiple regions of a control-flow graph into a single region consisting of *predicated* (*conditional*) code. Predication has the effect of transforming control dependences into data dependences, but doing so requires extensive compiler support. In the case of *full predication*, instructions take additional operands that determine at run-time whether they should be executed or ignored (treated as nops). These additional operands are called *predicate operands* or *guards*. In the case of *partial predication*, special operations (such as *conditional move* or *select*) achieve similar results. Figure 8.25 shows the same code used in Figure 8.12 after predication. The case of full predication is particularly relevant to region compaction, in that it can affect how the scheduler chooses units and allocates registers. Partial predication — for example, using *selects* — is a more natural fit to the scheduling phase and we will not treat it separately.

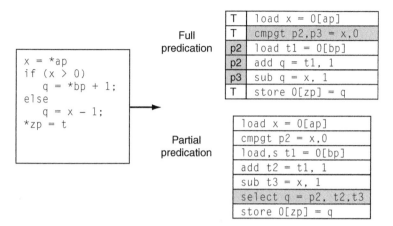

FIGURE 8.25 Example of fully and partially predicated code. In the full-prediction case, the *cmpgt* operation produces the true (p2) and false (p3) predicates at the same time. A predicates T means "always executed." In the partial-prediction case, we use a *select* operation to implement the "$a = b\,?\,c:d$" function. Note that partial prediction usually requires speculation to be effective (the load operation becomes a speculative *load,s* operation).

A number of compiler techniques have been developed to support predication. They include if-conversion, logical reduction of predicates, reverse if-conversion, and hyperblock-based scheduling. *Modulo scheduling*, arguably the most important of predicated-oriented scheduling techniques, was treated earlier in this chapter.

If-conversion is the main transformation from unpredicated to predicated code, or equivalently it is one of the few techniques that translates control dependence into data dependence. If-conversion converts an acyclic subset of a CFG from an unpredicated intermediate representation into straight-line code in a predicated version of that intermediate representation. The predicated IR is supplemented with guard or predicate values that precede the operations of the IR. If-conversion is actually relatively simple: for each block, synthesize a predicate variable that is true if and only if that block will be executed. Then, rewrite each operation in the CFG to be predicated based on the corresponding predicate variable. At a high level, this corresponds to transforming the conditions of *if* statements into predicate definitions, although this transformation is complicated by subsequent branches and merging control flow paths.

Building a single predicate per basic block in an if-converted region can be expensive in terms of predicates, and thus many if-conversion techniques also attempt to minimize the number of predicate values generated during if-conversion. This sort of predicate minimization can also be performed separately from if-conversion (for example, when code that is if-converted and then further transformed ends up with a poor set of predicates). Optimizations that perform this *logical reduction of predicates* can have other benefits, including reducing the dependence heights of computations.

Reverse if-conversion is somewhat self-descriptive, removing the predicates from code and returning it to an unpredicated representation. It can sometimes be

Controversy: Is Full Predication Support Worthwhile?

Fully predicated ISAs seem costly compared to their unpredicated counterparts at each of the architecture, microarchitecture, and software levels. Predicate register specifiers require encoding space within virtually all operations and instructions. Witness the IPF's adoption of a 128-bit three-operation encoding "bundle." Predication requires a new predicate register file that may add new wiring constraints to the design. Control logic is complicated by the predicate values, as is pipeline bypassing. An entire new suite of compiler optimizations must be built and tuned to support emitting predicated code. The benefit of predication is being able to remove branches from the instruction stream, increasing ILP. These benefits appear most dramatic in conjunction with modulo scheduling, but are they worthwhile overall?

Partial predication provides a relatively low-cost middle ground between full predication and unpredicated architectures. Adding *conditional move* and *select* operators to an otherwise unpredicated architecture can be done with relatively little architectural (ISA and encoding) or microarchitectural impact. Such operations look largely like other ALU operations, although the select operator looks like a three-input ALU operation. Compiler support for partial predication can be built incrementally or aggressively. At the simple end of the spectrum, peephole-style optimizations can identify opportunities for conditional moves and select operations. At the aggressive end of the spectrum, one can build an entire predicated compilation infrastructure, produce fully predicated code, and then map the fully predicated code back into an equivalent set of partially predicated operations.

Unfortunately, the tradeoff question remains open. Studies of partial predication have shown the expected result that partial predication produces faster code than the equivalent unpredicated architecture. Partial predication also removes almost as many branches from the instruction stream as full predication. However, no one currently knows whether a combination of partial predication and aggressive speculation can provide equivalent performance results to a fully predicated system.

worthwhile to if-convert, optimize, and then reverse if-convert code with complex control flow. The resulting code will be logically equivalent to the original program but will end up with different control structure — possibly a more efficient one. Reverse if-conversion also helps when the compiler runs out of predicate registers or resources. By selectively reverse if-converting, a legal program for the predicated architecture can still be produced.

The *hyperblock* is one of the few approaches that provides a unified framework for both speculation and predication. We described hyperblock formation in Section 8.2.2. One can think of a hyperblock as being like a superblock (having only a single entrance), but where the region formation heuristic also has the option of pursuing *both* halves of a forward branch when profiles do not indicate a strongly preferred successor. After choosing a hyperblock region, if-conversion transforms all basic blocks within the hyperblock to be control equivalent. This gives the schedule constructor much more freedom to schedule, as many sequential or speculative constraints that would otherwise have blocked scheduling moves are removed and a larger set of candidate operations are available.

Support for predicated execution exists in surprising places in embedded processors, although not nearly to the extent it has been embraced by the fully predicated IPF architecture. The ARM instruction set includes a 4-bit set of condition code predicates in every operation. ARM instructions can be viewed as *always* being predicated, but the predicate register set is the usual set of condition code flags instead of an index into a more general predicate register. This allows for interesting instruction selection strategies for short *if-then* and *if-then-else* statements, in which predicates rather than branch instructions are used. ARM compilers typically use peephole optimization techniques to identify and transform such code sequences.

The TI C6x architecture supports full prediction for a very small predicate space. Five of the general-purpose registers in the machine can be specified as condition registers (this requires three encoding bits per operation, with the remaining three values unconditional or reserved), and a separate bit indicates the sense of the condition to apply. Compilers for the TI architecture exploit this predication feature, although the limited number of predicate registers also limits the loop nest depth to which it applies.

8.4.3 Prefetching

Memory prefetching is a form of speculation that can be performed entirely by hardware, invisible to the program except insofar as it affects (and hopefully improves) performance. Compiler-supported prefetching has been shown to be better than pure hardware prefetching in a number of cases.

For the compiler to assist in prefetching, the ISA must include a prefetch instruction that allows the compiler to pass hints to the hardware. Because a prefetch instruction is only a performance hint, many ISAs have used memory-related nops to encode prefetches. For example, in HP PA-RISC a load to the constant-zero register (r31) has no effect on the architectural state but is treated as a prefetch hint by the implementation. Other architectures may have explicit prefetch encodings. The IPF architecture and the Intel SSE instructions include prefetch instructions that specify not just a target address but the level of the memory hierarchy at which a prefetch should occur.

Automatic insertion of prefetch instructions requires the compiler to understand the structure of inner loops. The analysis for prefetching strongly resembles standard induction-variable analysis techniques used in most loop transformations. Induction-variable analysis discovers the stride of a sequence of memory accesses across loop iterations we can use to determine the prefetch distance.

Ideally, one would like to insert exactly as many prefetch instructions as are required to exactly prefetch the data that will be used by the program. Reality is unfortunately inexact. Unneeded prefetches waste program space, memory bandwidth, and cache locations, whereas prefetches that do not get placed extend the running time of the program.

Production compiler designers report being able to get both reasonable sensitivity and specificity in their prefetch placement decisions.

Prefetching compiler passes have relatively simple phase interactions with other phases. Prefetch operations take up operation slots and may therefore affect schedule length, but they do not interact with register allocation.

8.4.4 Data Layout Methods

Data layout methods also seek to increase locality. Simply grouping commonly accessed fields so they fit in a single cache line has been shown to improve performance. More sophisticated data layout optimizations target the prefetch hardware of the processor, organizing data so that it is likely to be prefetched just before it is needed.

8.4.5 Static and Hybrid Branch Prediction

In addition to the profile-driven optimizations described previously profiles can be used more or less directly in *static branch prediction*. Some architectures (e.g., HP PA-RISC and PowerPC among RISC architectures) dedicate instruction encodings to specify the preferred direction for a conditional branch instruction. Profiles can be used to set these bits, and implementations can then use them to direct the fetch pipeline at run-time.

More sophisticated branch prediction techniques combine static and dynamic methods. Some researchers have proposed encodings that tell the hardware to select statically or dynamically among various predictors. Such *hybrid* prediction schemes, although not widely commercially deployed, allow the compiler to fix a static prediction or to choose at compile time which of a set of dynamic predictors might be the best at predicting a branch. For example, the IPF architecture includes four branch encoding hints: *static taken*, *static not-taken*, *dynamic taken*, and *dynamic not-taken*.

8.5 Instruction Selection

Most of the previous sections of this chapter assumed that the compiler was manipulating an Intermediate Representation that was relatively close to the target machine code (operations with opcodes and addressing modes rather than a syntactic representation of the parse tree of the source program). *Instruction selection* bridges this gap, translating from a tree-structured linguistically-oriented IR to an operation- and machine-oriented IR. Instruction selection is especially important on machines with complex instruction sets, complex addressing modes, or complex instructions (many DSPs come to mind).

Instruction selection is also unfortunately known as *code generation*, although this latter term is also synonymous with the process performed by the entire back end of the compiler, or the code generator. This terminological confusion probably dates back to the early days of compilation, when instruction selection actually was the last phase of the compiler before outputting machine code. As should be clear from the other sections of this chapter, today's compilers perform many more transformations and optimizations after instruction selection has completed.

Today, instruction selection can be accomplished efficiently through cost-based pattern-matching rewriting systems, such as BURS (bottom-up rewriting systems). Such systems model each operation in an ISA as a tree, with operands (such as registers and constants) as leaves and operators (such as addition, multiplication, comparison, and memory accesses) as interior nodes of the tree. The basic problem is to "match," "cover," or "tile" the parse tree produced by the front end using a minimum-cost set of operation subtrees. The sophistication in such approaches is in how efficiently and optimally such tilings can be found, and in how much precomputation (at compiler compile-time) can be performed to simplify evaluation of specific parse trees (compile-time). BURS uses a particularly efficient technique wherein only two passes are made over the parse tree, using finite-state automata. The first pass labels each node in the parse tree; the second pass reads the labels and generates target machine operations.

Instruction selection is particularly difficult on traditional DSP architectures. As we have noted before, such architectures tend to have instructions that are idiosyncratically and nonorthogonally encoded, allowing certain combinations of operations but not others. Instruction variants were typically designed into the machine with particular code sequences in mind — a situation fine for hand coding but especially difficult for a compiler to handle. Correctly using an instruction variant requires the source code to meet just the right set of conditions, some of which may be obvious to a human but impossible for a compiler to prove.

8.6 Further Reading

In recent years, a number of excellent textbooks on back-end compilation have emerged, going far beyond what is described in the original classic "Dragon Book" of Aho, Sethi, and Ullman [Aho et al., 1986]. Steve Muchnick's *Advanced Compiler Design and Implementation* [Muchnick, 1997] has detailed algorithmic descriptions, whereas Bob Morgan's *Building an Optimizing Compiler* [Morgan, 1998] provides a look inside the production-strength GEM compilers from Digital Equipment Corporation. More recently, Cooper and Torczon's [2004] *Engineering a Compiler* is more of an omnibus compiler book (including front-end and back-end techniques, but a more generous helping of the latter). It is also worth mentioning Allen and Kennedy's *Optimizing Compilers for Modern Architectures* [Allen and Kennedy, 2002], which covers compiler optimizations for high-performance parallel architectures. Although it is not by itself a textbook, the final journal paper about the Multiflow compiler [Lowney et al., 1993] describes the research and development behind a production compiler that defined ILP for over a decade.

Profiling and Instrumentation

One of the earliest references to profiling described the *gprof* profiler [Graham et al., 1982]. The Multiflow paper describes its profiling engine, the IFPROBBER. Ball and Larus wrote the definitive paper on edge profiling [Ball and Larus, 1994]. They had earlier observed that edge profiling can sample a subset of edges in the CFG but still reconstruct all edge weights [Ball and Larus, 1992]. Their technique samples enough edges to break all cycles in the undirected version of the CFG. The first appearance of path profiles, and an optimization using path profiling, was proposed by Young and Smith [Young and Smith, 1994]. Ball and Larus proposed their efficient path-profiling technique two years later [Ball and Larus, 1996]. Young's thesis describes an efficient method for collecting general path profiles [Young, 1997]. Larus [1999] extended path profiling into an efficient trace compression mechanism.

The Multiflow compiler experimented with loop-nest heuristics for synthetic profiles. Wu and Larus [1994] used Dempster-Shaffer theory to combine various heuristics under a weighting strategy. Calder et al. [1997] used a neural network and a training corpus of C programs to build synthetic profiles.

Low-overhead profiling techniques and dynamic optimization systems took off in the second half of the 1990s. DCPI (later CCPI) [Anderson et al., 1997] exhibited a low-overhead profiling system, whereas Dynamo [Bala et al., 2000] and Morph [Zhang et al., 1997] were some of the first projects to combine low-overhead profiling with dynamic optimization. Intel's VTune tool exposed the hardware counters of Pentium processors to developers.

Interestingly, dynamic binary *translation* goes back somewhat further, to Digital's FX!32 project. Virtual machine emulation goes back even further, to IBM's work in the 1970s on VM/370. Later dynamic translation projects include IBM's Daisy [Ebcioglu and Altman, 1997] and the commercial efforts by Transmeta. Much less has been published about profile accounting or bookkeeping. The topic may be too difficult or unglamorous. See the Multiflow paper for the closest to a good description we know of. Some later work was done on reusing profiles from older versions of a program, and on profiles based on optimized program code [Albert, 1999]. Fisher and Freudenberger's [1992] study remains the definitive work on the relationship between training runs and target data.

Scheduling

Traces and trace scheduling were the first region-scheduling technique proposed. They were introduced by Fisher [Fisher, 1979 and 1981], and described more carefully in Ellis's thesis [1985]. Superblocks were introduced by Chang et al. [Chang, 1991a and b], with hyperblocks following a year later [Mahlke et al., 1992]. Treegions were proposed by Havanki [1997]. The most readable exposition of Treegions was written by Zhou, Jennings, and Conte [2001]. Recent work by Zhou and Conte [2002] has made treegions more effective, gaining most of the advantage of the technique with little code growth.

Nonlinear region approaches include percolation scheduling [Aiken and Nicolau, 1988] and DAG-based scheduling [Moon and Ebcioglu, 1997]. Trace-2 is described by Fisher [1993].

Some optimizations improve the quality of any schedule that can be built. Schlansker et al. [1994] proposed *dependence-height reducing optimizations*, which rearrange the DDG to make it wider and less tall before the scheduler runs. Chekuri et al. [1996] survey heuristics used to prioritize operations in a scheduler constructor.

The earliest reference to resource reservation tables is attributed to Davidson (1975). Müller proposed FSA-based approaches [1993], and Proebstring and Fraser refined them a year later [1994]. Bala and Rubin introduced a host of new FSA-based techniques in their sequence of papers [1995]. Eichenberger and Davidson [1996] responded with their efficient resource table technique soon after. The *gcc* project has recently added support for FSA-based resource modeling.

Software Pipelining

In Chapter 2 we covered in depth the history of the development of software pipelining and modulo scheduling techniques. Here, we describe some of the more recent and advanced techniques. The work of Eichenberg and Davidson, [1995] is a good place to start to understand the register requirements of a modulo schedule. The work done at Universitat Politècnica de Catalunya [Llosa et al., 1995, 1996, 1998] gives interesting variations of the basic iterative modulo scheduling technique introduced in [Rau, 1994]. Finally, an interesting analysis in [Llosa and Freudenberger, 2002] shows the application of modulo scheduling to VLIW embedded processors without specific hardware support for loops.

Clustered VLIWs

The work at Multiflow [Colwell et al., 1987] and the BUG (bottom-up greedy) clustering algorithm derived from Ellis's thesis [Ellis, 1985] paved the way for much of the activity around clustered VLIW architectures (with partitioned register files) from the mid 1990s to today. Capitanio et al. [1994], present a more theoretical approach to register partitioning for partitioned register files. The papers from Farkas, Jouppi Chow, and Vranesic [Farkas et al., 1995, 1997a, 1997b] show how clustering concepts can also benefit dynamically scheduled superscalars. More recent work on clustering extended the concepts of partitioned register files to the embedded domain [Faraboschi et al., 1998] and related compiler clustering techniques [Desoli, 1998]. A slightly different and more theoretical perspective on clustering for ASIPs and DSPs can also be found in work by Leupers [2000], Lapinskii et al. [2002], and Terechko et al. [2003].

Several research groups have also proposed comprehensive approaches to the problem of combined scheduling and register allocation, with a particular emphasis on clustered VLIW. Among these it is worth mentioning the UAS (unified assign-and-schedule) approach [Ozer et al., 1998a and b], as well as the CARS framework [Kailas et al., 2001].

Finally, it is important to point out several interesting techniques that address the problem of partitioning code for clustered VLIWs when dealing with cyclic schedules (software pipelining), such as the work presented by Fernandes et al. [1997 and 1998], Zalamea et al. [2001], and Sanchez and Gonzalez [2000].

Register Allocation

The original formulation of register allocation as a graph-coloring problem is due to Chaiten [1982]. Preston Briggs' thesis was well regarded as representing the state of the art in its time [Briggs, 1992]. Goodwin and Wilken produced the first register alloca-tor to use a linear programming approach [Goodwin and Wilken, 1996]. Appel and George [2001] translated this approach to the irregular registers of the x86 architec-ture. Moving in the opposite direction, Traub et al. investigated linear-scan register allocators in dynamic optimization systems [Traub et al., 1998].

Integrated and cooperative register allocation and scheduling is well described in Ellis' thesis [Ellis, 1985], as well as in the Multiflow papers [Lowney et al., 1993]. Others who attacked similar problems in the RISC domain included Bradlee [1991a and b], Pinter [1993], and Motwani et al. [1995].

Prefetching, Speculation, and Predication

Software-directed prefetching first appeared in hardware and software works by Mowry and Gupta [1991], and Klaiber and Levy [1991]. Mowry continued work in this vein with his students. A production compiler implementation of prefetching is described by Santhanam et al. [1997]. More work by Mowry at Stanford [Mowry and Gupta, 1991; Mowry, 1992, 1994] is among the most referenced for prefetching (as well as the followup work with Luk [Luk and Mowry, 1996, 1998] at CMU. One of the initial formulations of the *if-conversion* problem dates back to the early 1980s [Allen et al., 1983]. What brought the concept of full predication to maturity, together with its applications to compiler region selection mechanisms, is the work by the Impact group at UIUC, which also formulated most of the theory behind *sentinel scheduling* and its interaction with predication [Chang et al., 1991a and b; Mahlke et al., 1992, 1993; Hwu et al., 1993]. The most commonly cited study comparing full predication and partial predication is due to Mahlke et al. [1995]. More recent work on predication involves techniques to reduce control recurrences [Schlansker et al., 1994] to "undo" if-conversion through specu-lation where not profitable (the so-called "reverse if-conversion" presented by Warter et al. [1993]). A more formalized set of analysis techniques for predicated code was done by Johnson and Schlansker [1996]. Most of these early papers presented evalu-ations of full predication on conceptual architectures that were not implemented but simulated, such as the very interesting analysis [August et al., 1998] that shows the combined benefits of speculation and predication. More recent work, such as the study by Choi et al. [2001] on a first-generation Intel IPF processor (Itanium), showed more realistic (and somewhat disappointing) results for the benefits of predication on branches, in which short pipeline and small branch penalties of the Itanium implementation make it much more difficult for predication to shine.

Instruction Selection

Instruction selection is today considered a mature topic. Fraser, Hanson, and Proebsting's article [Fraser et al., 1992a] describes Iburg, a system from 1992, and Iburg's predecessors, including Twig [Aho et al., 1989], BEG [Emmelman et al., 1989], and Burg [Fraser et al., 1992b].

8.7 Exercises

1. The nonlinear scheduling techniques presented in Section 8.2.1 are not the only ones that have been suggested in the literature. Compare and contrast trace scheduling and superblock scheduling with *selective scheduling* [Moon, Ebcioglu, and Agrawala], *Wavefront Scheduling* [Bharadwaj, Menezes, and McKinsey], and *all-path scheduling* [Chen and Smith].

2. Preconditioning is a technique used to eliminate copies of the loop-terminating branch from the body of an unrolled loop. Construct a simple for loop in C which operates on an array element in each iteration. Then rewrite the code to use preconditioning. Hint: the unrolled loop body should have only one exit branch.

3. Induction variable (IV) simplification is a technique used to eliminate the dependence between loop iterations of an unrolled loop caused by updating the induction variables (e.g., $i = i + 1$). Rewrite the for loop from the previous exercise so that the iterations could be executed in parallel. Hint: you do not have to use only one IV.

4. Consider the control flow graph in Figure 8.12. Find all control-dependent pairs of blocks. Explain why block D is not control dependent on block A.

5. As part of exploring the space of possible schedules, most modulo scheduling algorithms backtrack (undo previous decisions). In contrast, few list schedulers backtrack. Give an example of a cycle-scheduling algorithm that could benefit from the ability to backtrack. Why would an operation-scheduling algorithm not suffer from this problem? Hint: mix critical operations with short latency and noncritical operations with long latency.

6. Top-down (as early as possible) scheduling and bottom-up (as late as possible) scheduling have a different effect on split compensation. Explain why this is so. Write an example that illustrates your answer.

7. In Section 8.3.1 we present scheduling and register allocation as an example of a phase-ordering problem. Another such problem is the interaction of clustering and scheduling. Describe the difficulties and advantages of performing clustering before scheduling versus clustering during scheduling.

8. Assume you have the following program, and a 2-issue machine with two registers and unit-latency operations.

```
t1 = p[0];
t2 = t1 * 3;
q[0] = t2;
t1 = p[1];
t2 = t1 * 3;
q[1] = t2;
```

Perform register allocation (minimizing the number of used registers) before scheduling, and scheduling (assuming infinite registers) before register allocation. Which strategy produces the shortest schedule? Describe the problems encountered in using each method.

9.   Repeat the previous exercise with the following program (hint: you may need to spill and restore temporaries). Assume that some mechanism exists for spilling and restoring without the use of additional registers (use *spill* <t> and <t> = *restore* to indicate these operations).

```
t1 = p[0];
t2 = t1 * 3;
q[0] = t2;
t1 = p[1];
t2 = t1 * 3;
q[1] = t2;
t1 = p[2];
t2 = t1 * 3;
q[2] = t2;
```

10.   Suppose you have an architecture (such as the IPF) that only offers indirect (no base + offset) addressing modes to access memory. How would you implement spilling and restoring in such an architecture? (Hint: if you need to spill, it means you are out of registers.)

11.   Compare data speculation and prefetching. Consider the analysis required for each technique, the effect of architectural state and hardware support, and the differences in code transformations.

12.   Consider the following VEX loop:

```
LOOP:
    A) $r5 = ldw 0[$r2]
    B) $r6 = ldw 0[$r3]
    C) add $r7 = r5 + $r6
    D) stw 0[$r4] = $r7
    E) add $r2 = $r2, 4
    F) add $r3 = $r3, 4
    G) add $r4 = $r4, 4
    H) add $r1 = $r1, 1
    I) cmplt $b0 = $r1, 100
    J) br $b0, LOOP
```

Draw the data dependence graph, with data flow (solid lines), and anti and output dependence arcs (dotted lines) for a single iteration, ignoring memory dependences.

13. Consider the loop of the previous exercise and a target VLIW machine with two integer ALU/compare units (latency of one cycle), one branch unit, (latency of one cycle), and two memory units (latency of two cycles). Produce a (good) legal schedule for the unrolled iterations.

14. Consider the loop and the machine target of the previous exercise. Unroll the loop twice, rename the variables, and propagate copies (hint: remember to also propagate simple arithmetic expressions, to simplify the induction variable computation). Make sure to write your assumptions (if any) for each transformation. Write the resulting serial unrolled code and produce a legal schedule for the unrolled iterations.

15. Consider the loop of the previous exercise. Apply modulo scheduling for the same machine target and generate the optimal kernel (minimum II). Compare the performance of the modulo scheduled code and the unrolled code.

16. Devise and evaluate alternatives to the mutual-most-likely heuristic for trace selection (hint: the Multiflow compiler paper [Lowney et al., 1993] describes a number of such alternatives based on point profile information). Can you find better alternatives? Can you find better alternatives using path profiles?

17. Choose two acyclic scheduling-region shapes (e.g., trace and superblock) and compare and contrast the effects the region shapes have on the engineering of a compiler and the quality of the resulting code. This exercise can take a number of forms. As an essay, it is suitable for a homework assignment. As a technical evaluation, it is publishable research, because no widely accepted comparison has been made across acyclic scheduling techniques.

9

The Run-time System

If everything seems under control, you're just not going fast enough.

— Mario Andretti, *Italian-American auto racer, 1940–*

Even in the embedded world, where devices usually run few programs, it is rare for an application to take complete control of the processor. There are too many low-level details for this to be an effective approach. Many techniques are common across wide varieties of architectures, processor implementations, and (especially) devices. Collecting these features into common utilities with common interfaces introduces a layer of abstraction but also greatly simplifies application development.

Traditionally, most run-time problems have been the province of the *operating system*. However, the correspondence between embedded and mainstream operating systems is quite rough. Common mainstream operating system features such as virtual memory and file system support are not always needed by embedded applications. Conversely, few mainstream operating systems support real-time processing or code compression. Some embedded systems have their own proprietary code that handles operating system-like tasks. These are called *microkernels* or *monitors*, depending on their degree of complexity. We lump all of these types of support into the *run-time system*, and discuss aspects of them in this chapter.

This chapter covers a selection of topics that relate to embedded run-time support. We begin with support for multiple contexts, which is necessary even in uniprocessor systems because of the realities of I/O processing and program errors. Section 9.2 continues with the *application binary interface* (ABI), which is a contract between compile-time software and run-time software in a manner similar to the way the ISA is a contract between compile-time software and run-time hardware. Section 9.3 covers software code compression, whose hardware aspects are discussed elsewhere in this book. Section 9.4 describes and surveys the current set of commercially available embedded operating systems. The last section is more speculative. Section 9.5 briefly covers multithreading and multiprocessing, which are migrating into embedded systems.

There are a number of traditional operating system issues we omit. These include the bootstrap process, how to write device drivers (for various flavors of devices, including network adapters, displays, and storage devices), programming memory management units and handling translation look-aside buffer (TLB) misses, scheduling (of processes), supporting virtual memory, and performing I/O. We refer readers to the standard operating system textbooks and to the web resources on porting open-source operating systems for details on these topics.

9.1 Exceptions, Interrupts, and Traps

Even uniprocessors must juggle multiple tasks simultaneously. It is common to overlap communication and computation. A computer would not be very useful without some way to communicate with the outside world. Many computers perform multiple application activities simultaneously. The operating system and the scheduler "time-share" the single computation core to give the appearance of responsively handling all of the activities. Last, there are cases in which an application fails or requires support from the operating system. In each of these cases, the system must be able to suspend the current activity, respond to the new situation, and possibly return to the suspended activity. The mechanisms for performing these suspensions and resumptions go by a variety of names, including exceptions, interrupts, traps, faults, and context switches. We discussed the hardware mechanisms that support exceptions in Chapter 5. We now turn to how the run-time system uses these mechanisms.

9.1.1 Exception Handling

Regardless of the causes of exceptions, they are all handled in a similar manner. First, sufficient processor state must be saved so that the code that is the victim of the exception can be resumed later. At the very least, this includes a subset of the architectural state (e.g., the condition codes, the program counter, and part of the register file) so that a basic exception-handling routine can begin execution safely. The saved state can be complicated by the way in which the hardware handles exceptions. In particular, implementations with "imprecise" exception models (as described in Chapter 3) may also require large amounts of *implementation* state to be saved. Embedded processors may also increase the amount of state that must be saved, because of special-purpose registers or other information that is part of the architectural state. In general, there is a very small amount of state that must be saved by hardware (at least the address of the excepting instruction) in order to put the machine into a known state.

After the hardware has saved the necessary state to resume after the exception, the hardware begins executing an *exception-handling routine* (see Figure 9.1). All architectures include methods that specify how to invoke this routine as part of the processor's architectural state. The address of the routine might reside in a special register or be required to exist at a particular location in physical memory (often on the first or last page of memory). Depending on the sophistication of the architecture, there might be

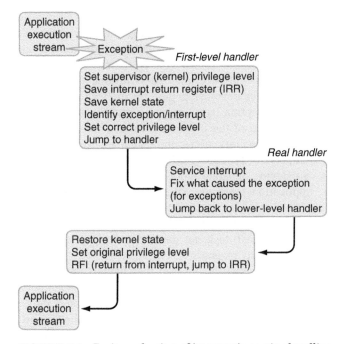

FIGURE 9.1   **Basic mechanism of interrupt/exception handling.**

only a single exception-handling routine or there might be a table of pointers to routines, wherein the choice of table entry depends on the cause of the exception (i.e., one table entry for divide-by-zero exceptions, another for disk I/O, and so on). In table-driven interrupt controllers, the hardware is sometimes said to *vector* to the correct exception-handling routine. Functionally, the difference between a single-entry and a table-driven architecture is small, as the single-entry routine will be implemented as software that reads special-purpose registers, determines the type of interrupt, and vectors through a software-specified exception-handling table. However, the difference between single-entry and table-driven architectures can be important for performance. If a particular type of exception is relatively frequent (e.g., TLB miss handlers in RISC processors), the cycles spent in a software dispatch routine may affect overall processor performance.

Next, the exception-handling routine performs the appropriate response to the exception. Of course, this varies widely. An I/O interrupt handler might read or write data from or to memory-mapped or ported I/O registers, or it might invoke or disable the next DMA transaction. A division-by-zero exception handler might abort the user program, invoke a user-specified callback routine, or suppress the exception and modify the destination of the excepting operation to a special value. A decompression fault handler would invoke the decompression routine on the desired page, either performing the work directly or by setting flags that caused a different routine to perform the decompression later. The point is that the exception-handling behavior is specified by software in the run-time system.

After the exception has been handled, the processor must perform the next task. If the exception is not one that terminates the program, the run-time system usually resumes execution where it left off. This task is usually performed by special architectural instructions with names such as "Return from Interrupt" or "Return from Exception." If the excepting program cannot be resumed, the run-time (i.e., the scheduler in the operating system) must select the next task to perform and switch to that task.

To facilitate exception handling and switching tasks, a number of special instructions are usually part of the ISA (but restricted from general program use). Even on machines without memory protection, such instructions typically run in a "privileged" or "supervisor" mode that is accessible only by the operating system or its run-time equivalent. Separate modes allow some degree of security and belief that "normal" application programs will not subvert processor-wide functions. We have already described the special instructions for returning from exceptions. There are also typically special instructions for setting exception-handling tables, for switching to a normal (not exceptional) task, for modifying the processor's mode, and for accessing various supervisor-only registers.

As we have discussed before—in the chapters on ISA (Chapter 4), implementation (Chapter 5), and compilation (Chapters 7 and 8)—supporting precise exceptions on VLIW machines is difficult. With multiple-issue and multicycle operation latencies, many operations can be in flight at the moment the exception is raised, and some operations launched at the same time or even after the excepting operation may have committed. Supporting precise exceptions requires that all operations from instructions before the excepting operation commit, whereas all operations in the excepting instruction and all instructions after the excepting instruction abort. The accounting required to perform precise exceptions in hardware can be complex, and thus implementers sometimes consider alternatives that shift the complexity to other parts of the system.

Unfortunately, the easiest way out for hardware designers moves the work into the hands of software designers. In systems that deliver imprecise exceptions, the set of operations that completes when an exception occurs is not cleanly defined. Addressing this in software can require heroic measures between the compiler and the run-time system. The compiler has to emit code in such a way that imprecise exceptions can be recovered from (that is, enough information is available so that the required operations can be reexecuted), and the run-time system must find a way to simulate the operation of the machine up to some known safe point. Such complicated recovery strategies are beyond the scope of this book (see the "Further Reading" section for more about how they are implemented).

9.2 Application Binary Interface Considerations

In the previous section we showed how most exceptions happen "invisibly" to the excepting code. Externally generated exceptions (interrupts) are serviced and the interrupted code is resumed. Internally generated exceptions that are not fatal are serviced, the problem that caused the exception is fixed, and the interrupted code is

Controversy: Are Precise Interrupts Necessary for Embedded Processors?

The short answer is yes, we absolutely think so. Precise exceptions are necessary to guarantee a clean programming model in any architecture, and to enable it to evolve beyond an attached processor.

The main justification for imprecise exceptions is reduced hardware cost. Many DSPs and some embedded VLIWs today do not support precise exceptions, and have unprotected pipelines that prevent interrupts from being serviced during an "unprotected" state (which in some cases, such as the TI C6x, extends for entire loops). This has several bad side effects: it is difficult to debug, difficult to deal with system software, difficult to deal with real time (if we have to turn off interrupts), and incompatible with virtual memory. By this point, our readers know well that hardware cost is just one component of total system cost, and that total system cost is the one that matters.

It is not that difficult to support precise exceptions once the architecture adopts a clean execution model. This is unfortunately an easily overlooked area in many architectures, particularly in those that derive from traditional DSP philosophy.

Precise exceptions are considered necessary to implement Virtual Memory and IEEE floating point on general-purpose processors. As these features begin to appear in embedded devices they bring their requirements with them. As the complexity of embedded systems increases, it is our belief that "natural selection" will ensure that only architectures with a clean exception model will have a relevant role in the embedded domain.

resumed. Making this work seamlessly requires cooperation between interrupting and interrupted code. This section describes the ABI, wherein application code and the processor run-time explicitly and visibly connect.

The ABI is a contract between compile-time software and run-time software, analogous to the way the ISA is a contract between compile-time software and run-time hardware. The ABI is the set of conventions that allows the application and run-time systems to coexist. Part of the ABI expresses the needs of the application to the run-time, such as conventions for accessing shared data and invoking external code. Part of the ABI constrains application code so that the run-time can safely cooperate with it (for example, ensuring the safety of registers during calls or under exceptions). However, unlike the ISA—which focuses very much at the instruction and operation level— the ABI includes items of larger program scope (such as functions, compilation units, linkage units, libraries, and whole programs).

Although we treat the ABI as part of the run-time system, it also affects all stages of the development toolchain, especially compilation and linking. We have already described the various parts of the development toolchain, and thus we will first describe the *loader*, the run-time component most closely related to ABI issues. Then we will describe a number of cross-cutting issues and their effects on each piece of the toolchain and the run-time system. These issues include data layout, accessing globals, and calling conventions. The last part of this section describes advanced ABI topics such as variable-argument functions, dynamic stack allocation, garbage collection, and linguistic exception support.

9.2.1 Loading Programs

Traditionally, the *loader* is a part of the operating system or run-time that transforms a program stored on secondary storage into a program executing in main memory. In embedded systems there may be no secondary storage, but issues regarding correctly initializing the machine to a state the program expects and regarding starting execution remain unchanged. For the sake of exposition, we will act as if all embedded systems stored their programs in secondary storage. For systems in which there is no secondary storage, the program is stored in the same memory where it will be executed, and the issues faced by the loader (if there is any) may be simpler than those we describe here.

Stored programs consist of many components beyond just machine code: program data (constants, global or static variables, and tables), debugging information, compression tables, and linkage or entry point information are all parts of the program that occur in storage. Roughly analogous to these types of components, a stored program typically contains a number of *segments*, each of which represents data that will reside contiguously in memory. The names of the segments roughly describe their contents. *Program*, *text*, or *code* segments typically contain code (depending on the architecture, such segments may also contain data). The *data* segment typically holds initialized data, such as tables or string constants, whereas another data segment (called *bss*, from "block segment start" in an old IBM assembly language) holds data that is by convention initialized to zero. Other program information — such as linkage information (e.g., names and offsets of function entry points), debugging symbols (e.g., names and locations of variables), and garbage collection annotations — might be integrated into the main segments or might be placed in other segments of the file (the location varies from format to format). Figure 9.2 sketches the major portions of the ELF (executable and linkable format) file format, which is used by many UNIX-style operating systems.

Before the program runs, the loader moves the program data to an accessible place. Initialized variables may need to be copied from read-only or secondary storage to the RAM, where they will reside (the data segment might also be compressed, necessitating a decompression step). The *bss* segment must be allocated and cleared, and other areas of memory must be set up for the program stack and/or heap. In systems with dynamic memory allocation, the heap will have to be initialized, and for garbage-collected systems the collector will also have to be started.

Depending on the system, program code may or may not need to be copied before it can be executed. Some systems can execute code directly out of flash or (EP)ROM; others store code in secondary storage that does not allow direct execution, requiring copying to some type of executable memory. Decompression can also take place during the copying, and debugging information may be fed to the debugger or otherwise manipulated into a convenient format.

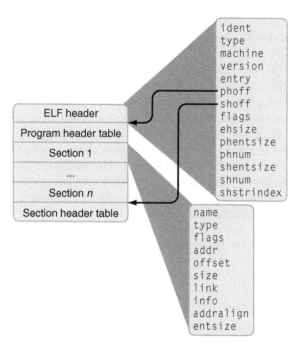

FIGURE 9.2 **A sketch of the ELF file format.** Fields within the ELF header tell the offsets and sizes of other sections of the file. Each section then describes its own size and attributes. Sections can have a variety of values for the "type" field, including symbol tables, string tables, relocation information, and dynamic linking information. (Derived from the ELF specification.)

Most importantly, a typical loader will *relocate* code and data. In relocation, the loader examines the compiled-in offsets in the program (e.g., pointers of various types) and adjusts them to point to locations at which those resources actually reside for this run of the program. This is very similar to part of the job performed at compile-time by the linker, except that the loader is the *last* such relocation that will take place. Note that embedded compilation toolchains often draw a distinction between *position-independent* code (and data) and *relocatable* code (and data). Position-independent code (PIC) normally refers to code that is independent of its load address, which means the code must use only PC-relative jumps and may not refer to global data. Position-independent code is also compiled for load-time binding, which is typical of dynamically linked libraries. We discuss the issues associated with *dynamic linking* below, when we address calling conventions. Relocatable code is in some sense a misnomer, because it *must* be relocated before it can be run. Relocatable code contains placeholders for pointers, such as object files or library code.

For many embedded systems, loaders do not relocate code, as the code gets compiled in a fixed position. When code is compiled for a relocatable — or PIC/PID (position-independent code/position-independent data) — model, an embedded loader simply initializes the global pointer to the right initial location. The full use of dynamically linked modules is less common, and limited to the most complex embedded OSs (such as PocketPC or embedded Linux).

Various other resources may need to be initialized by the loader or the operating system before the program can begin execution. Depending on the sophistication of the processor core, page tables, compression tables, and TLBs may need to be initialized, and various protection settings may have to be adjusted to match the program's requirements. Depending on the operating system or run-time, there may be a standard sequence of instructions that is always executed at the start of the program (but which is not the responsibility of the linker). The loader will copy and place this piece of code so that it will be executed at program startup (on many UNIX systems, this code sequence is an assembly code module usually named something like *crt0.o*, where *crt* stands for *C run-time*). After everything has been set up, the loader jumps to the first instruction in the program. The file format may specify the entry point of the program, or convention may specify that it is just the first instruction of the first code segment.

9.2.2 Data Layout

For different parts of a program to access the same data, they must agree on how the data is laid out in memory. This is especially important if different tools (e.g., compiler and assembler) produce code that is meant to work together. Most ABIs specify *alignment constraints* for each type of scalar variable. These constraints most frequently require that variables that take up 2^n bytes of space must be placed at memory locations whose addresses are also multiples of 2^n. Such constraints simplify code generation and can improve the speed of the resulting code. Many architectures can quickly access data that is properly aligned, whereas access to unaligned data happens much more slowly or causes an exception. Further, some architectures can only access memory at certain granularities (e.g., loads and stores may read or write only 32-bit words). For such architectures, accesses to smaller scalar variables may need to be synthesized from reads, extracts or inserts, and writes (some ABI conventions specify padding for small scalars to simplify writing them).

Unfortunately, data layout is more complicated than just knowing the address of the variable in memory. There are further permutations of the placement of bytes at and after the starting address. Even scalar variables have *endianness* concerns, which we introduced in Section 5.5.2. Endianness refers to the order in which the bytes of a multi-byte variable are stored in memory. On *big-endian* machines, the most significant byte is stored at the starting memory address (less significant bytes are placed in ascending memory locations), whereas on *little-endian* machines the least significant byte is stored at the starting memory address (more significant bytes are placed in ascending memory locations). On most general-purpose machines, the entire machine is big-endian or little-endian, and thus programmers can ignore endianness unless they have to write networking code (*network byte order*, the order typically used by networking protocols, is big-endian). Embedded systems have fewer guarantees, especially because multiple cores with different byte orders can be integrated in a single system. Some architectures allow users to specify at power-up (or boot) which endianness the processor uses. These are called *bi-endian*.

Some systems provide hardware help with endianness issues. Some embedded processors have endianness-swap instructions, which transform the bytes in a register from one format to the other. Other processors (e.g., the Intel 960 series) allow the programmer or operating system to specify different endianness for different regions of memory, using hardware in the load/store datapath to permute the bytes from their order in memory into the correct order in a register. In any case, endianness issues can bedevil debugging and development efforts on a project.

Last, structures (which are also called *aggregates*) are the most complicated part of data layout. One would like for code built by one tool to be able to share structures with code built by another tool. To do this, all tools must agree about the offset of fields from the structure's starting address. In languages such as C, a structure is more than just an ordered list of typed fields. C structures also obey a *prefix property*, whereby a structure A that has a substructure B as its first field can be passed to code that uses B (with the appropriate type casting), and that code will correctly modify the fields within B. Most ABIs specify that fields occur in memory in the order in which they are defined, and that each field be *padded* as necessary to ensure that the field meets the basic alignment constraints. For example, if a structure consisted of a 1-byte character followed by a 4-byte integer, most compilers would place the byte at offset 0, and then insert 3 bytes of padding and place the integer at offset 4. Because structures can contain other structures, layout is a recursive bottom-up process requiring that all structure definitions be available.

9.2.3 Accessing Global Data

Global data (and its equivalents, such as static data and some types of program constants) has its own set of problems; namely, how does one find it? The answer requires a combination of compile-, link-, and load-time conventions. The compiler can identify global variables from type information, and it knows the form of the typical sequence of instructions to access the global but typically does not decide where the global will reside at run-time (this is the job of later steps, such as the linker or loader). Among the linkage information in object files and linked files is *relocation information* that identifies each piece of code or data that refers to an address that is not known at compile-time. The linker combines multiple object files into a single linked file, and at the same time combines the relocation information from separately compiled object files so that references to the same globals in different object files are combined. Either the linker or loader may be able to compute or assign the final location of a global. Walking through the linked file to update accesses to match the global's location can be performed either at link or load time.

Support for global data falls into three categories: using absolute addressing, indirecting through a dedicated global register, and doubly indirecting through a table of contents.

In an *absolute addressing* scheme, each global variable is assigned an absolute address in the program's memory map. Absolute addressing for globals requires that the architecture support absolute addressing, which is common in CISC architectures but relatively rare in RISC and embedded architectures because absolute addresses require long immediate values to be embedded in the instruction stream. Either the linker or loader inserts the appropriate constants, so that instructions that access global data will use the correct location. Absolute addressing is difficult if not impossible to support in an environment with shared libraries, because each shared library will have a set of global variables that ties down part of the address space of any program that uses the library. However, no two libraries that are shared can overlap.

Schemes that use a *global register* use a single level of indirection to simplify placing and locating global variables. One of the architectural registers of the machine is dedicated to holding the *global pointer*. Then, each global variable in the program is assigned a unique offset from this global pointer. In a sense, all global variables in the program are combined into a single giant structure, which is addressed by the global pointer. The linker ensures that the offset for each global variable is consistent (and unique) in the resulting linked file. The loader places the global area, initializes it, and sets up the global pointer before the program begins execution.

Global pointers simplify using shared libraries, because each library or program with its own set of globals can have its own value for the global pointer. This slightly complicates transitions between linkage units, as the old global pointer must be saved and the correct global pointer for this unit must be loaded (finding the correct new global pointer is a complicated process, which we do not have the space to describe here). Global pointers are easiest to implement in architectures that have a *base + offset* addressing mode. It is easy to assign unique offsets to each instruction that accesses a particular global variable and then set the base register to be the global pointer. However, depending on the number of global variables in the program and the size of the architecture's offset field it may be possible to overflow the range of addresses reachable from the global pointer. Overflow has been handled in various ways, including failing to link or falling back to the table of contents approach.

The *table of contents* (ToC) scheme also uses a dedicated architectural register, but it uses double indirection instead of single indirection. Instead of pointing directly to all of the global data, the global variable points to a table of *addresses* of global data (this table is the eponymous table of contents). Accessing a global requires two memory accesses: a read that gets the address of the global and an access that actually touches the data. Whereas a global pointer scheme can run out of space if the *size* of the global area exceeds the addressable range of the machine's *base + offset* addressing mode, a ToC scheme will only run out of space if the number of distinct variable *names* exceeds the addressable range.

Like global pointer schemes, ToC schemes easily support shared libraries while incurring only a small dynamic overhead when switching between linkage units. ToC schemes appear to be inefficient because of the double memory access requirement, but a number of compiler techniques can improve the performance of ToC-based code. In particular, the pointers in the ToC are immutable data, and thus the compiler can registerize and reuse the pointers, often saving the first memory access. In addition, most ToC schemes support placing small scalar variables directly into the table of contents, making accesses to such variables just as efficient as the global pointer approach.

9.2.4 Calling Conventions

Calling conventions is the innocuous name for the surprisingly complex practices that allow one function to call another. The conventions include how registers should be used, reserved, or preserved. They specify how to make function calls, which includes finding the target of the call, setting up arguments and receiving results from calls, and generating code sequences for entering and exiting a function.

Registers

Register usage conventions specify how registers are affected by function calls and exceptions. Registers have a variety of usage conventions. *Caller-saved* registers can be overwritten by a function call, and thus the calling function must save (spill) such registers before a call and reload them after a call. However, caller-saved registers provide inexpensive temporary space. *Callee-saved* registers must be saved by a function before it can use them, and restored when the function exits. *Argument* and *return* registers are reserved for, respectively, passing values into and returning values from functions. We will have more to say about them below. Between calls, or if a function calls no other functions, the argument and return registers serve as caller-saved registers. Some registers are *reserved* by the operating system. These are typically used by exception-handling code as a "safe" place to use in bootstrapping to a stable exception state. Other registers might be reserved for use by other components. Many RISC architectures reserve an *assembler temporary* register that operates like a caller-saved register but will be overwritten (used) when translating assembly language pseudo-instructions into machine instructions. Register conventions typically follow the hardware. For example, the function call return address register must be caller saved.

Register allocations are rarely changed after the compiler generates the code, and only in exceptional cases can some other tool make changes (and these changes must follow the conventions).

Call Instructions

Calls come in a number of flavors. Within a single *compilation unit* (the span over which the compiler has complete control), the compiler is free to use whatever conventions it cares for, optimizing and rearranging code as it wishes. For example, a compiler can completely inline static functions and make them disappear. However, any calls that are externally visible must follow standard conventions, because arbitrary callers might invoke such entry points. Externally visible calls can be statically linked or dynamically linked, depending on when they are resolved. System calls allow the application to invoke the operating system or run-time to perform certain privileged tasks.

Statically linked calls are resolved by the linker. In doing its job, the linker combines all of its input files into a single output file or linkage unit. This means that all files must be available at compile-time for static linking to take place. When it links, the linker tries to adjust the object code so that calls within the output file are performed directly. This means that each statically linked function is assigned a position in the code segment, and each call site is adjusted appropriately. Typically this means using PC-relative addressing to specify call targets, although it is also possible to leave relocation information and defer the updates until a later link or load pass.

Dynamically linked calls are resolved at run-time, and involve a more complicated mechanism for *delayed binding*. Instead of combining all inputs into a single output file, the linker merely verifies that the dynamically linked calls refer to valid names in available libraries. The linker leaves relocation information about the dynamic call sites in the output file. When the loader runs, it still does not connect dynamically linked call sites to their callees. Instead, every dynamically linked caller is set to point to a run-time *stub* routine. Whenever it is invoked, the stub examines where it was called from, determines the actual target of the call, and then *patches* the original program to make the call site point at the actual target. Finally, the stub jumps to the actual target. Future executions of the call site jump through the patch without invoking the stub, and thus the stub is only executed once per call site, and only on those call sites that are executed.

There are a variety of reasons for using dynamic linking. The main benefit is the pay-as-you-go approach to resolving relocation information. Instead of always performing work to relocate every call site, dynamic linkage allows the system to perform slightly more of the work (but only for the call sites that are actually used). Some operating systems (notably PocketPC) support only dynamically linked libraries. Applications may also require dynamic linking, especially in systems that support downloadable code or field upgrades.

Shrink-wrap calls are the calls to compiler *built-in functions*. These are functions that are known to the compiler and can be called with a simplified calling convention. Examples include facilities that simulate integer division in architectures without a native divide instruction and memory-copy operations used in structure assignments.

System calls are the last type of call, whereby the user program invokes the operating system to perform some work. System calls often look very much like regular function calls, except that they use a special call instruction (trap) that changes the protection level in addition to the instruction pointer. Trap instructions are often implemented at the microarchitectural level by operations that unconditionally raise exceptions.

Call Sites

Making function calls work involves much more than the linkage conventions between call site and callee. Calling conventions also govern the set of instructions leading up to and following the actual function call instruction. Any caller-saved variables that are live across the call must be spilled before the call, and restored after it. More importantly, arguments must be set up. This is relatively straightforward for simple (scalar) variables that are passed by value (copied), but it gets very complicated very quickly when variables are passed by reference (in the programming language sense), when the address of a variable is taken, when arguments do not fit into the convention-specified argument registers, and when aggregates (structures), arrays, and variable-length argument lists (*varargs*) must be passed.

Most machines use a combination of registers and memory to pass arguments and return values across function calls. Registers are used to cover the most common cases (a few arguments). Memory is used to cover the less common cases (large arguments, *varargs*, and so on).

Under most calling conventions, scalar variables passed by value are placed in the argument register that matches the variables' place in the function's argument list (the first variable goes in the first argument register, and so forth). For architectures with multiple register banks, there may be designated argument registers in each bank and a further convention for sorting out the order in which to use the argument registers from each bank (e.g., if the first argument to a function is an integer and the second argument is a floating-point double, the second argument might be passed in either the first or second floating-point argument register). For languages that support variables that are passed by reference (wherein the callee can modify the value of the caller's variable), such as Pascal and C++, the common practice is to pass a pointer to the original variable and for the callee to modify the caller's variable by references through the pointer.

The first complicated case occurs when there are more arguments than argument registers specified by the calling convention. The arguments to a function superficially resemble the fields of an aggregate (C or C++ structure): they are a set of named variables of different types. As such, they can be laid out in memory in much the same way the corresponding structure would be laid out. Most calling conventions handle overflow arguments by specifying a region of the stack wherein additional arguments can be passed, and stating that the additional arguments are laid out like the corresponding structure. Some conventions slightly modify the structure layout rules to include more stringent alignment requirements (e.g., to 8-byte or 16-byte boundaries). In some calling conventions, stack space is allocated only for overflow arguments (minimizing use of stack space), whereas in other calling conventions stack space is allocated for *all* arguments (using more space, but leaving a place at which it is safe for the callee to spill argument registers).

Passing structures is the second complicated case. The simplest solution is to pass structures by reference, because this requires only that a pointer to the structure or array be passed (in fact, the older "K&R" version of C did exactly this, as ANSI C still does for arrays). To pass a structure by value (as is possible in ANSI C), space must be allocated to allow all of the values of the fields of the structure to flow from caller to callee. In some calling conventions, the compiler uses a special region of memory to pass the structure. This special memory has its own problems because it must be managed as functions recurse or specially handled if multiple threads or processors share program memory. Other calling conventions use argument registers as if they were memory locations, copying the structure verbatim from memory into registers. Returning a structure also requires special handling. Many calling conventions require the *caller* to allocate a space for the structure to be returned, and then pass a hidden argument indicating where the callee can copy the results.

Few languages allow arrays to be passed by value. This appears to be because copying an array is linguistically and operationally rather heavyweight: the language must maintain and verify array bounds information, and the calling convention must allocate and copy a variable-length chunk of data. Programmers appear to be willing to copy arrays explicitly when necessary.

The last complicated case is calling functions with variable-length argument lists, or *varargs*. We defer treating varargs to the next subsection, on advanced ABI topics.

Function Prologues and Epilogues

Once a function is called, its *prologue* sets things up for the function body. If the function has local variables, the stack pointer will be updated to make space. Most systems use stacks that grow downward (toward low memory), but this convention is not universal. In programs written in languages with *dynamic scope*, a *frame pointer* may be set up to allow the run-time to resolve references to enclosing scopes (the frame pointers form a linked list the run-time can traverse to examine calling contexts). Callee-saved registers (including the return address register) that will be modified by the function are spilled, and local variables may be initialized. At the end of the function (before the return), the *epilogue* performs the reverse actions, restoring the machine to the state it was in before the call. The calling conventions under a particular operating system tend to be very exacting about all of these operations, in part for safety during exceptions (it would not do for an exception to overwrite user data beyond the top of the stack), and in part to allow debuggers to work (without the conventions, a debugger might not be able to decipher the state of the machine).

9.2.5 Advanced ABI Topics

More complex considerations include support for variable-length argument lists to functions, stack allocation of memory, and linguistic exceptions such as those in C++ and Java.

Variable-length Argument Lists

In C and C++, functions can be defined to have variable-length argument lists, of which *printf* is the most well-known example. Such variadic functions are known as *varargs* functions, and support for them is called "supporting varargs." *Varargs* functions always have two parts to their argument lists: a fixed part and a variable part. The fixed part works exactly like the arguments to a normal (non-*varargs*) function. The information in the fixed part typically describes the content of the variable part. We note that there are type-checking and intermediate representation issues associated with *varargs* functions but do not discuss them here.

The caller of a *varargs* function proceeds as if it were calling a fixed argument function with a fixed argument list (the variability in *varargs* functions is across call *sites*, each of which might pass different numbers and types of arguments). All C and C++ calling conventions push arguments on the stack in right-to-left order, which ensures that the fixed part of the argument list is always at a fixed offset from the stack frame of the called *varargs* function. This allows the called function to find and access fixed arguments in the normal way.

The body of a *varargs* function is implemented through a set of horrible preprocessor macros (sometimes supplemented by compiler built-ins and other code-generation features). The macros enclose the function body and parts of the loop in the function body that iterates over variable arguments. The macros also provide means of indicating the type of the next expected variable argument, and they retrieve that argument as a value. These macros are implemented using various type-cast and pointer arithmetic operations, typically in a machine-dependent way. The macros provide machine independence by hiding these operations. We called these macros "horrible" for two reasons. First, for the regular programmer they create type casting and checking loopholes that complicate programming and debugging. Second, for the compiler and header file implementer the C code used to build *varargs* macros is extremely tricky. On the compiler side, the simplest expedient is to force all of the variable part of the argument list into memory, although the interaction between arguments passed in registers and spill space for those argument registers varies from system to system.

In the embedded domain, it is important to remember that *varargs* functions have a significant execution overhead, and thus their use should be discouraged in the performance-oriented parts of applications.

Dynamic Stack Allocation

Many systems provide support for dynamically allocating memory space on the stack. The space is freed when the current function returns, providing storage with automatic scope but variable size. Functions that perform this job are often called *alloca*. However, *alloca* is neither standard nor portable. Modern compilers and ABIs implement *alloca* directly; other systems provide it as a library routine. In principle, *alloca* adds the desired amount of space to the stack pointer, and then returns a pointer to the beginning of the space that has been placed on the stack. Unfortunately, its actual implementation is not that simple, because most code expects arguments and local variables to reside at a fixed offset from the current stack pointer. In particular, the return address is often stored on the stack, and thus changing the stack pointer will cause code to return to the wrong place. The easiest solution is to dedicate another register as the *frame pointer* in functions that use *alloca* and address arguments and local variables through the frame pointer rather than the stack pointer. However, this approach may not be acceptable on some platforms.

A common programming pitfall associated with *alloca* is to put a call to *alloca* in the argument list of a call to another function. Order of evaluation then ensures that the call to *alloca* will trash the argument list of the other function as it is being built.

Garbage Collection

Garbage collection is a relatively old technique for reclaiming unreachable dynamic storage. Some garbage collectors also compact or rearrange the active dynamic storage, which can improve locality and thus data memory system performance. Historically, garbage collection was associated with dialects of Lisp and functional languages. However, recent run-times—especially those for Java and Microsoft's .NET—include garbage collection support. Both Java and .NET intend to support or colonize the embedded space, and thus we can expect garbage collection support in future embedded operating systems and run-times. However, few current embedded devices are built with garbage collection support. Although garbage collection techniques have made huge progress in terms of speed, overhead, and concurrency, making a truly deterministic-time garbage collector remains open research. Thus, garbage collection remains questionable for use in systems with hard real-time requirements.

Run-time support for garbage collection closely resembles the support for debuggers. This should not be surprising: both debuggers and garbage collectors operate concurrently with the main program, examine its state, modify its state, and alter its execution.

Linguistic Exceptions

The C++ language supports exceptions as a language feature, which is an entirely different level from the architectural exceptions we discuss frequently in this book. Linguistic exceptions allow a program that encounters an error to transfer control directly from a function to one of its ancestors in the call stack. A typical example is encountering an error in a routine that recurses deeply. In this case, one often wants to handle the error in the nonrecursive caller of the recursive function, without replicating error-handling code throughout the recursive routine. This is called "throwing" the exception (the ancestor must have noted its willingness to handle the exception by placing a "catch" phrase that encloses the statements that might throw the exception). Typically, exceptions are used to indicate an error condition wherein it is not clear that the immediate ancestor of a function is the appropriate place to handle the error. The following code shows a simple example of the use of a *try-catch* clause in C++.

```
void initelem(int ap[], int val, int elem, int size)
{
    if (elem > size) throw "Out of range";
    ap[elem] = val;
}
int main ()
{
    int array[10];
    try {
        for (int i = 0; i < 10; ++i)
            initelem(array, 0, i, 10);
    }
```

```
        catch (char * str) {
           cout << "Exception: " << str << endl;
        }
        return 0;
}
```

Implementing linguistic exceptions also requires ABI support. The appropriate catching function is typically not determinable statically, and thus the *throw* statement must search for the appropriate handler. This search can be implemented efficiently, but the semantics of the throw/catch sequence require that the throwing function and all of its ancestors up to the catching function be *unwound*. Unwinding is the process of tracing backward through the stack of activation records of a process, and while doing so releasing all of the automatically scoped variables held in each of those functions' stack frames. In C++, this includes calling all of the appropriate destructors for the objects going out of scope. Information about how to do this is typically recorded in *unwind descriptors*, which describe what parts of a function may throw exceptions, where to go if they do, and what actions to take when they do. Unwind descriptions (when available) are also very useful for debugging. Describing unwind descriptors in detail is beyond the scope of this book.

9.3 Code Compression

Code compression techniques have shown the most promise in embedded and low-cost applications, where every bit of storage counts. Unlike techniques that improve the performance of the memory system, compression may actually hurt memory system performance in the name of saving space and cost. Data compression is rampant in consumer electronics (any media device, including video, music, and portable phones), but such data compression is most often handled at the application and standards level, rather than as a compiler optimization. Compilers help most with code compression, wherein compiler and hardware must cooperate to produce compressed programs.

Compression (see Figure 9.3) can be implemented at a number of levels in the memory hierarchy. Code can be compressed in memory but decompressed before it is placed in the cache. It could also be decompressed between cache levels in a multilevel cache machine. Either software or hardware decompression mechanisms can be used. Software schemes offer more flexibility but may not be as fast at decompressing as the hardware decompressor. The software/hardware tradeoff is very similar to that between software and hardware TLB miss handlers.

Code compression schemes are complicated by entry points and branch targets. Unlike a streaming compressor, which handles all data sequentially, a program might call a function or jump to a block partway through a compressed region. Most compression schemes compromise the compression density and add notations to the compressed code to allow decompression to begin rapidly at entry points.

As always, phase interactions complicate engineering. For example, some register allocators use a round-robin policy for choosing among free registers (which could

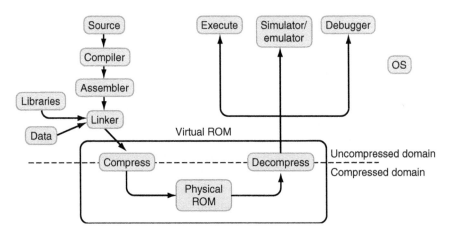

FIGURE 9.3 **A typical code compression system.** The central concept of the most effective code compression systems is a completely transparent *virtual ROM*. Even though we could achieve better compression ratios by making all tools aware of the compression phase, this would pose very significant engineering challenges. Alternatively, we can isolate compression to the very last stages of the software compilation toolchain, and decompression to the very first stages of the hardware fetch-execute pipeline. In this way, both the software tools and the hardware can be completely unaware of the existence of the compression/decompression stages. If we factor in the complexity of compilers, debuggers, operating systems, and the impact of the fetch-decode phases on cycle time, the appeal of this type of solution is obvious.

enable a scheduler to make more aggressive moves), whereas others reuse previous registers (which can yield higher compression because there are fewer, more commonly chosen, registers). Code layout optimizations attempt to improve memory system performance, but the interaction between code layout and code compression is unexplored.

9.3.1 Motivations

Several factors are increasing the typical size of code in embedded and DSP applications. Embedded applications are becoming more complex. Features such as GUIs, networking, remote administration, and Java are becoming a necessity even for simple devices. Use of high-level languages produces larger code than manual assembly language. Explicitly parallel instruction sets (VLIW/EPIC) are intrinsically less dense than CISC or DSP instruction sets. Aggressive compiler optimizations (unrolling, software pipelining, inlining, cloning, compensation code for global scheduling) adversely affect code size.

Code storage still represents a significant fraction of the cost of an embedded product, ranging from 10 to 50%, depending on the complexity of the rest of the system. ROM cost is diminishing, but is still significant, and ROM sizes are growing, forcing designers to move in power-of-2 steps, wherein for example if your application does not fit in 4 MB you have to switch to 8 MB and double your ROM cost (see, for example,

Figure 9.5). In addition to code size, instruction fetch bandwidth is still a significant part of performance, accounting for 5 to 15% of execution time for a typical 32-bit RISC embedded processor.

9.3.2 Compression and Information Theory

The binary representation of instructions has a large amount of redundancy, in the information-theoretic sense. For example, consider how many times the same opcodes and registers are reused in a program. This redundancy is usually intentional, as it simplifies the decoding hardware. However, from the point of view of code size this also means that we have a good chance of successfully applying some form of compression. The techniques for compressing programs use the same information-theory concepts that rule the compression of any other data stream.

Many different techniques have been proposed in the past, and recently — given the growing importance of embedded domains — research is going through a "renaissance," with many academic and industrial groups actively working on issues related to code compression.

In information-theory terms, we can see programs as random sources of symbols, wherein instructions (or fields of instructions) represent the symbols. To compress a program we use the fact that symbols do not have the same probability of occurring in a program. The quantitative approach that swept the architecture community in the 1980s began with instruction count studies, showing (for example) that *add* operations are much more frequent than *call* operations in virtually all programs. Whereas the advocates of the quantitative approach used it to remove infrequently used opcodes and operations from ISAs, the next logical step is to represent the *add* with fewer bits.

Under certain restrictions, optimal compression algorithms exist. For example, for infinitely long sources and symbol probabilities expressible as a power of 1/2, it can be proved that Huffman encoding is optimal and reaches the *entropy* of the source (informally, the entropy rate is the maximum possible compression rate; see the sidebar "Elements of Lossless Data Compression Theory"). Huffman encoding is a rather simple algorithm, and is one of the most frequently used within code compression systems. Figure 9.4 shows the Huffman algorithm and an example of its application.

Note that Huffman is not the only possible technique for code compression. Another interesting technique is *arithmetic encoding*, which potentially achieves better ratios when the probabilities of the symbols are not expressible in powers of 1/2. Implementation of a decompression engine based on an *arithmetic decoder* is likely to be more complex, requiring more memory and a longer decompression pipeline. However, it may be worth exploring when Huffman's results still fall short of code size requirements.

9.3.3 Architectural Compression Options

Compression can appear in a system in three places. Instructions or data can be decompressed (1) as we read them from the cache, (2) as we read them from memory on a cache miss, or (3) as we load the application in memory.

Elements of Lossless Data Compression Theory

Lossless compression is ruled by a few fundamental concepts that Claude E. Shannon formulated in his 1948 paper *"A Mathematical Theory of Communication."* Shannon proved there is a fundamental limit to lossless data compression, which he called *entropy* (usually denoted by the symbol *H*) — a term he borrowed from statistical mechanics, where it is used analogously. Computing *H* depends on the statistical nature of the information source, and although we can achieve compression ratios that approximate *H* it is mathematically impossible to do better than *H*.

Consider a stochastic source *X* (sometimes called the *ensemble* or *alphabet*) generating a random variable *x* that can assume one of *n* many possible values $A_x = \{a_1, a_2, \ldots, a_i, \ldots, a_n\}$, with probabilities $\{p_1, p_2, \ldots, p_i, \ldots, p_n\}$, where the probability of a value is $P(x = a_i) = p_i$, with

$$0 \le p_i < 1, \quad \text{and} \quad \sum_{i=1}^{n} p_i = 1.$$

We can then define the *entropy* of *X* as

$$H(X) = \sum_{i=1}^{n} p_i \cdot \log \frac{1}{p_i}.$$

The entropy measures the information content of "uncertainty" of *x*, and if the base of the logarithm is 2 it is expressed in *bits*. For example, if we consider the English alphabet (with a size *m* = 27) and an approximation of order zero, where the characters are statistically independent from each other (and have all the same probability $p_i = \frac{1}{n}$), the entropy equation becomes $H(x) = \log n$ (which adds up to ~4.75 bits). (Incidentally, it turns out that $H(x) \le \log n$ always). Also note that $H(x) \ge 0$, where the entropy is 0 if and only if one of the values has probability of 1.

The *first Shannon's theorem* (sometimes called the *Shannon lossless coding theorem*) establishes a lower-bound limit to block coding length. Block coding of order *r* is the coding we obtain if we assign a sequence of bits to a block of *r* symbols. We can show that the rate of an *r*-th order block coder is

$$R_r = \frac{1}{r} \sum_r P(B_r) \cdot L(B_r),$$

where $L(B_r)$ is the length of the code of block B_r. Then we can prove that

$$-\frac{1}{r}(p(B_r)\log p(B_r)) \le R_r \le \frac{1}{r}((-p)(B_r)\log(p(B_r) + 1))$$

and if we look at the limit

$$\lim_{r \to \infty} R_r = H.$$

In other words, Shannon's Theorem states that *the entropy of a (stationary and ergodic) source is the rate of an optimal lossless data compression code.*

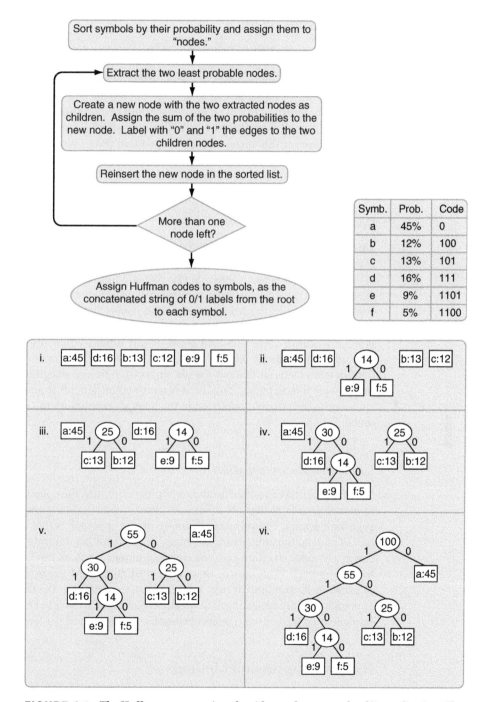

FIGURE 9.4 **The Huffman compression algorithm and an example of its application.** The figure on the left shows an application of the steps of the algorithm on top, which leads to the encoding shown in the table on the right.

Decompression on Fetch

This has the advantages of increasing cache efficiency and making the cache effectively larger, in that it holds compressed information. The disadvantage is that decompression has to happen on each cache access, and is thus on a critical timing path. This is likely to require additional pipeline stages. Because of this, decompression at this level has to be kept simple, resulting in only a modest amount of compression. For example, variable-format VLIW processors (such as the TI C6x or the HP/ST Lx (ST200) family) only remove nop operations at this level, and decompression only involves reinserting the nops in the appropriate issue slots. Other architectures, such as MIPS16 and ARM-Thumb, use microcode or instruction encodings defined with fewer bits in the instruction set.

Decompression on Refill

This has the advantage of removing the decompression circuitry from the critical timing paths. In this case, we can adopt more complex compression methods on each cache line, in that cache misses occur infrequently. Nonetheless, adding the decompression latency to each cache miss causes some performance degradation, and the method must still be kept somewhat simple. Another restriction comes from the observation that whatever compression method we use has to preserve the random-access property of the program. In other words, a cache miss can occur on any arbitrary line and thus the compression method must be able to operate on the granularity of a line (or of a small block of lines). Compression methods that require decompression from the beginning of the compressed segment are unacceptable. Finally, it is worth mentioning that another advantage of this approach is the possible reduction in the memory bandwidth in and out of the first-level cache.

Load-time Decompression

Variations of this technique decompress programs when the operating system loads them in memory, or in systems that support virtual memory on a page-by-page basis when a page fault occurs. The primary advantage of this approach is that we can compress large blocks of data, thus increasing our chances of exploiting redundancy. Here is where we can apply more standard compression techniques, such as the Lempel-Ziv dictionary-based approach. The cost of this is in additional RAM usage as well as an increase in program startup time or page fault latency. In particular, the cost of RAM makes this approach not very appealing for embedded systems. On the other hand, this is commonly implemented in modern operating systems, in the form of *compressed file systems*.

9.3.4 Compression Methods

Among the technologies that have been proposed for compressing programs we distinguish five major categories, discussed in the sections that follow.

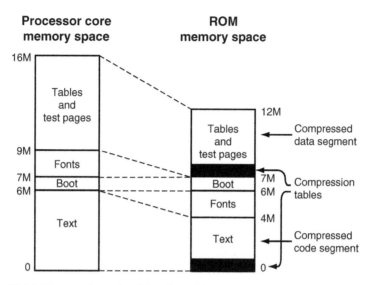

FIGURE 9.5 **Example of the effect of a compression system.** In this example, we show the breakdown of the firmware you can find in a typical high-end color printer. The figure on the left shows the memory image in the *uncompressed* space, as it is seen by the processors and the tools. The figure on the right shows the physical representation of the same space in ROM. In this example, by applying compression the designers could potentially save 4 MB of physical ROM space, with minimal software changes. Note that the compression system does not strictly apply to instructions only, but could be extended to other types of read-only data (such as fonts, test pages, or tables) in a straightforward way.

Hand-tuned ISAs

This is what has been traditionally adopted in the CISC and DSP world. Although code densities benefit from a more complex ISA, this is probably the most limiting solution. A hand-tuned ISA is difficult to compile for, in that it is usually nonorthogonal and nonflexible. In addition, the choice of the ISA strongly depends on the particular set of applications under consideration and may not extend to other applications. Finally, hand tuning usually means a more complex and rigid encoding scheme and may have negative impacts on the design of the execution pipeline of the processor.

Ad Hoc Compression Schemes

This is what is currently being designed in ARM-Thumb, MIPS16, and similar approaches, wherein fundamentally the microarchitecture specifies two different instruction lengths (32 bits and 16 bits) that are selected with a processor-wide "mode" bit. The compression is performed in software via recognition of instructions that fit into the smaller template. This technique has several advantages. Compressed instructions stay compressed in all levels of the memory hierarchy, and the level-1 instruction cache benefits from it. The expressiveness of the ISA remains intact, and the compressed instructions can be expanded to their equivalent expanded format, so that the decode unit can stay simple. On the other hand, decompression is on the critical path of the instruction cache fetch (usually one of the most critical paths in a processor). In addition, the scheme is rigid: it only limits compression to a factor of 2, and only for the instructions that fit the compressed template, thus limiting the overall maximum possible gain. Last, these schemes have compiler implications, as the compiler must be modified to emit only the shorter formats upon request.

RAM Decompression

This technique stores the program compressed in ROM and decompresses it to RAM at load time. An example of this approach can be found in LILO (the Linux boot loader), which decompresses a compressed image of the kernel during the boot process. The advantage is that compression ratios can be extremely good (up to factors of 6x sometimes). However, the price paid is the cost of the RAM space to store the expanded program. This could easily become unacceptable for embedded systems. An area that may be worth investigating is software-controlled on-demand decompression wherein only some "pages" at a time are decompressed and stored in RAM.

Dictionary-based Software Compression

This technique identifies code sequences that can be factored out into common "subroutines" and defines a very simple convention to be able to call them from anywhere in the code. In many ways it closely resembles microcode and nanocode techniques from the microprogramming era. Although it can have some potential, it is certainly very invasive and requires heavy modifications of the tools, the run-time architecture, and possibly the processor hardware to implement a fast call mechanism. For all of these reasons, this approach is probably the least appealing for an embedded system among the approaches presented here.

Cache-based Compression

In our opinion, this is the most promising set of techniques for the embedded domain. The fundamental idea is based on a few simple principles: use complex software compression and simple hardware decompression; do not change the processor ISA and do not expose compressed instructions to the compiler; find the place in the memory hierarchy at which hardware decompression is most appropriate.

The work of Wolfe and Chanin [1992] represents a milestone in these compression techniques, and establishes the foundations for many other academic activities and industrial techniques, such as the IBM *CodePack* compression technology for the PowerPC processor family.

Compression happens through a software tool that runs after linking (or is part of the linker itself), producing a compressed program that is placed into a special memory area, identified by the linker as a *compressed text* segment. The compressed text segment contains a special section with *decompression tables*.

Case Study: ARM and Thumb

Among what we defined as *ad hoc* compression schemes, the *Thumb* extension of the ARM instruction set architecture is worth examining in more detail for its growing popularity in the embedded domain. Thumb defines a set of 36 instruction formats derived from the 32-bit ARM ISA that were encoded to fit into 16 bits. This approach is particularly interesting in that it leaves the ISA expressiveness intact, and does not impose heavy constraints on the compiler.

During the execution pipeline, an ARM-Thumb processor expands the 16-bit Thumb opcodes into their 32-bit ARM equivalent instructions, which are then executed normally. If we consider the execution pipeline, the expansion of the 16-bit instructions happens *before* the decode phase, so that the ARM decoder does not need to be changed to accommodate Thumb extensions.

The two diagrams below show how the ARM7TDMI organizes the pipeline to include the Thumb decompression step, and what happens in one simple example (*add* instruction) when decompressed. Note that Thumb only enables a reduced number of registers and the same source and destination registers.

Code compiled for the Thumb instruction set (through a compiler switch) can be mixed with standard ARM code. The linker generates a special sequence to switch mode whenever a call is made from ARM to Thumb, or vice versa.

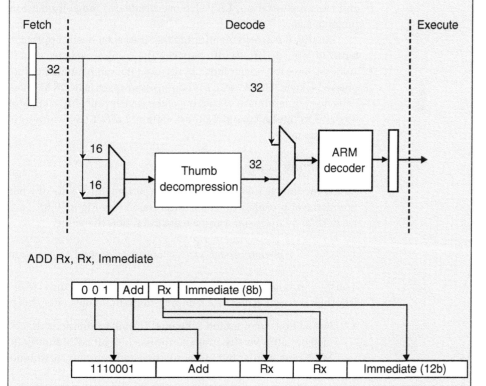

Decompression is the responsibility of a hardware block that behaves like a peripheral, is triggered by an instruction cache miss, and produces an instruction cache line given its address. The translation between compressed and uncompressed lines is held in a *line address table* (LAT) that can optionally be cached by the decompressor in a cache-line look-aside buffer (CLB).

Some parts of the program (for example, the boot code and the code to initialize the decompression hardware) have to remain uncompressed, and thus it is necessary to partition the program space into compressed and uncompressed chunks. *Compressed region mapping* is the set of techniques used to identify compressed regions. To implement the region-mapping unit we have the choice of extending an existing MMU or of implementing a private segment table in the decompression unit. Extending the MMU with a bit that specifies a compressed page is the straightforward approach (for example, implemented in the IBM *CodePack*). Alternatively, if the system does not support virtual memory or if we do not want to modify an existing MMU it is possible to implement a private *compressed segment table* in the decompression unit itself. Considering that only a few regions are going to be compressed, we only need to implement a small table. The most common method is based on a LAT that implements a mechanism similar to virtual memory translation. Note that the LAT is not free, and we have to account for its size when computing compression ratios. For this reason, LAT entries are often used to map blocks of lines instead of individual lines. Depending on cache line sizes and table organization, LAT size overheads can range from 1 to 6% of the compressed program size.

Finally, it is worth mentioning that the cache-based approach offers an advantage in terms of reduced bandwidth between the compressed space and the instruction cache, since we have to transfer fewer bytes to get the same number of instructions of an uncompressed system. However, if the compressed space is in DRAM memory with burst-access behavior, some amount of caching of the LAT is probably mandatory. Otherwise, random accesses to the LAT would almost certainly offset any bandwidth gain achieved by the compression.

Quantifying Compression Benefits

In this section we report some of the experimental results of what we consider the most promising approaches to code compression (see Figure 9.6). To avoid confusion, when we refer to *compression ratio* we always report the value:

$$(uncompressed\_size - compressed\_size) \: / \: uncompressed\_size$$

Thus, for example, if the compression method reduces the size of a program to one-third its original size it achieves a compression ratio of 66%. For this metric, higher is better.

- For ad hoc compression schemes, Thumb evaluations report compression ratios of about 30% versus an uncompressed 32-bit ARM instruction set (see Table 9.1). MIPS16, a similar but more invasive and complex technique for MIPS processors, delivers about 40% compression ratios.

Debugging Compressed Code

An interesting problem for compressed code arises with debugging. The debugger must be able to deal with compressed code, giving the impression of debugging the original application without sacrificing functionality. There are a few difficulties that arise when dealing with compressed code.

First, the debugger must initialize the decompressor system before allowing the user to interact with the code. Otherwise, some debugger commands (such as disassembling or setting breakpoints) would cause unexpected behavior.

Inserting a breakpoint is a major challenge, because compressed code is in many ways *read-only* code. If the system supports hardware breakpoints, a very limited number of breakpoints can be added through that. Alternatively, the usual method of implementing a breakpoint by replacing an instruction with a *break* (or any other trapping instruction) does not work. In general, it is not possible to change a compressed segment without redoing the entire compression, and such a task may be too heavy for a debugger.

A possible solution to this problem consists of using the translation capabilities of the LAT in combination with the compressed region mapping mechanism. When inserting a breakpoint, the debugger retrieves the LAT records containing the line, decompresses all lines pointed to by the LAT record, copies the uncompressed lines to a memory buffer, patches the uncompressed lines by inserting the breakpoints, and finally changes the LAT record to point to the new buffer, marking the entry as uncompressed. In this way, after flushing processor and LAT cache, the program can continue undisturbed and hit the newly inserted breakpoint in uncompressed code.

Inserting a breakpoint is not the only debugger issue when dealing with compressed code. Depending on the system architecture and the debugger interface (for example, whether it accesses memory directly or through a JTAG interface), even disassembling code could be a challenge. Discussing all possible scenarios is beyond the scope of this book (we leave research into common debugger functionalities as an exercise for the reader).

- For *LAT-based* compression schemes, the original work of Wolfe and Chanin [1992] shows numbers in the 30 to 50% range for the PowerPC instruction set. This is also confirmed by the evaluation of the StrongARM shown in Figure 9.6. IBM figures for the CodePack technique applied to PowerPc instructions show compression ratios between 36 and 47%.[1]

In summary, it is not easy to compute an overall figure for a technique, since this depends on many factors, including benchmarks, compiler, compilation options, and intrinsic redundancy of the target instruction set. Overall, we can say that we can expect

---

1. Note that IBM's reported numbers are higher, because they express values in a different scale (*compressed_size/uncompressed_size*).

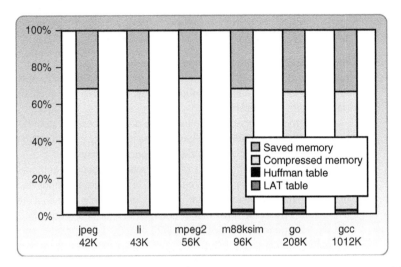

FIGURE 9.6 **Example of typical compression ratios.** The chart shows a set of SPECINT'95 benchmarks compiled for a StrongARM (SA-110) machine (with *gcc*) and compressed with a Huffman line-based technique. The *y* axis shows a breakdown of program sizes relative to the original code size. We can see that this style of compression saves about 30% of code size, resulting in compression factors of about 1.4. The chart also shows the overhead caused by the Huffman and LAT tables. These values are consistent with what is published in the literature for similar techniques.

Architecture	Eqntott	Xlisp	Espresso
ARM7 (32-bit)	16768	40768	109932
ARM7TDMI (Thumb)	10608	26388	72596
	(36%)	*(35%)*	*(34%)*

TABLE 9.1 Code compression ratios for ARM-Thumb.

about a 30% compression ratio from a simple technique such as ARM-Thumb and about a 40% compression ratio from a LAT-based technique such as IBM CodePack.

These numbers are near the first-order entropy of the programs (that is, if we do not consider intersymbol correlations). It may be possible to achieve better compression ratios if we start exploring higher-order coding techniques, and if we can get the compiler to cooperate. All of the techniques presented here are based on the self-correlation (first-order probability) of each symbol. A possibility for achieving better compression ratios is to exploit the cross-correlation between two (second-order conditional probability) or more symbols. This is related to the probability of certain combinations of opcodes (or opcode and registers/immediates) being more likely to appear than others. We are not aware of systematic studies that address these issues.

Some compiler algorithms may not be the best choice if our goal is to produce code we can better compress. For example, changing the register allocator to reuse lower-numbered registers first (instead of reusing the registers that become free) might change the distribution and achieve better compression. Explorations of combined compiler-compression approaches are rare, and we believe that they would be an important area of research in achieving the next level of code compression.

9.4 Embedded Operating Systems

A number of systems are marketed as "embedded operating systems," often with the additional adjective "real-time." Rather than presenting a description of operating systems generally (the topic of many entire textbooks in itself), this section assumes a basic knowledge of operating system concepts in pointing out contrasts between the general-purpose and embedded worlds. We begin with more or less "traditional" operating system issues, reconsidered in the light of embedded processing.

9.4.1 "Traditional" OS Issues Revisited

Many central issues for general-purpose operating systems are irrelevant or different in the embedded case. Virtual memory (VM) is perhaps the largest area of difference. In general-purpose systems, VM gives multiple processes the illusion that each has a private memory space, whereas in fact each shares a part of the physical memory of the machine. Maintaining this illusion requires hardware that translates each memory address used by a program (each *virtual* memory address) into an actual *physical* memory address in the hardware of the machine. The operating system manages the translation hardware, typically keeping *page tables* that record the virtual-to-physical mapping and updating a TLB the hardware uses to cache the most frequent translations. VM provides protection across processes, as each process is effectively confined to access only its portion of memory. More sophisticated VM-related techniques allow processes to share pieces of memory, and the technique of *swapping* allows a system with a small main memory but a large secondary storage (typically, disk) to simulate a system with a larger main memory.

VM is not always required in embedded applications for a number of reasons. Historically, the MMU hardware to support VM was considered large and expensive. However, given modern transistor budgets, this is no longer the case. In a similar historical vein, the longer circuit path through the translation unit increases pipeline depth (or cycle time and transistor count). In embedded regimes for which every transistor was counted, VM seemed a luxury. A more relevant modern concern is the complexity of the hardware and software system to support VM. Correctly designing and implementing VM software is perhaps the most complicated task in traditional operating systems. Last, there is the benefit provided by VM: many embedded devices perform a single task with a single thread of control. In such cases, VM is entirely unnecessary, as there is no need to share the physical memory among processes.

Some embedded applications and operating systems require VM support of one form or another. Applications that require VM use it to simplify freeing and reclaiming data memory, which might otherwise require expensive copying and defragmentation operations. We note, somewhat sarcastically, that PocketPC, Microsoft's entry into the embedded operating system market, not only supports but actually mandates a VM-oriented model. Our sarcasm dulls, however, when we note that embedded Linux is also driving MMU adoption. This software requirement has hardware implications: devices that run PocketPC or embedded Linux must have MMUs. Requiring VM support is much more a historical artifact of these operating systems' general-purpose ancestry than the benefit to embedded programmers it is marketed as.

Even if they do not provide VM, many embedded processors provide more limited forms of memory *protection*. For example, PalmOS relies on a particular layout of memory that places OS and protected data in one region and unprotected or application data in another region. An address comparator allows the hardware to check whether memory accesses remain in the desired region, providing coarse-grain protection without a full-blown VM implementation. There has also been both research and commercial work directed at providing *software fault isolation* (SFI) to guarantee memory protection. Instead of relying on hardware, SFI uses rewriting software that modifies the original code to dynamically verify the integrity of data accesses. Such systems of course increase the size of the resulting program, but they also remove the requirement for protection hardware.

Swapping is one of the more sophisticated uses of VM hardware. It works very much like caching: the small, fast, expensive main memory is backed up by a large, slow, cheap, secondary storage to provide the illusion of a large, fast main memory. The MMU detects *page faults*, wherein a program attempts to access a memory location that is not currently resident in main memory. On receiving a page fault exception, the operating system moves the desired page from secondary storage into main memory, and then resumes the program where it left off. Page faults, pages, main memory, and secondary storage follow analogous roles to cache misses, cache lines, the cache, and main memory in standard hardware memory-caching techniques. Very few embedded systems swap (largely because swapping trades away time to simulate space, and the current set of technologies makes space cheap, whereas time is precious).

However, swapping techniques directly relate to compression techniques in embedded processing, which we discussed in the previous section. If one thinks of a "compressed store" rather than a "backing store," all of the compression techniques of the previous section look very similar to techniques for swapping immutable data (e.g., code segments) in traditional operating systems.

The next section describes so-called "real-time" systems, and what real time means both in marketing and design terms.

9.4.2   Real-time Systems

Intuitively, a real-time system is one in which a certain set of tasks must be accomplished within fixed amounts of time. This implies that in addition to the traditional operating system task of allocating resources among competing processes a real-time operating system must also manage time, keeping track of the requirements of each real-time task and ensuring that it gets the needed resources before its deadline. Many real-time tasks have a "continuous" or "streaming" flavor to them, wherein a task must be performed repeatedly (e.g., modulating antilock brakes) or a data stream must be transformed at a certain rate (e.g., cellular telephony or digital video).

Real-time systems are typically divided into two categories. In a so-called "hard" real-time system, missing a deadline implies that the system has failed. All of the "mission-critical" systems fit into this category: avionics, automotive safety and control systems, weapons systems, and so forth. In a "soft" real-time system, a statistical guarantee (e.g., "the system meets deadlines 99.9% of the time") suffices. A soft real-time system remains usable despite the missed deadline. Soft real-time systems include most media applications, wherein some sort of streaming data must be delivered to a device and missing a deadline causes a "glitch" (fade-out or repeated video frame) rather than a system failure. It is interesting to note that the boundary between hard and soft real-time changes over time and by application (glitches in streaming video may be acceptable to desktop users, but they are not acceptable in consumer DVD players).

Designing real-time systems is complicated because designers want to be able to provide *guarantees* but many implementation techniques make the behavior of the system unpredictable. Speculative techniques are by their nature randomized: they rely on gambling that a guess is true, and they improve performance when they gamble correctly. However, this gambling does not help the *worst-case behavior*, sometimes forcing designers to aim for the worst case even when the likelihood of a sequence of worst-case events is exceedingly low. Similarly, interrupts and exceptions are a common implementation technique for systems with multiple interacting parts, but they also lead to variance in performance. One would like to be able to analyze the possible execution paths of a real-time system and determine the actual probabilities of missing a deadline on speculative hardware. Unfortunately, neither theoretical nor simulation techniques give high degrees of confidence for this type of analysis.

Real-time Scheduling

The real-time scheduling problem is usually characterized in terms of a set of recurring *tasks* that share a single processor. The job of the scheduler is to choose the task that should execute next.[2] A number of parameters describe each task. The *request period*, T, is the time between which requests for a particular task arrive. Its inverse is the rate at which the task is requested. The *duration* of a task, C, is the amount of time it takes for the processor to complete the task if it works exclusively on that task. The *deadline* is the time by which the task must be completed. In many formulations, the deadline is just the time at which the next request for the same task will occur. In other formulations it is specified separately. Most formulations also make a number of simplifying

---

2. For purposes of discussion in this section, we will use *task* to refer to a schedulable unit. Different systems will use the term *task, process*, or *thread* as the schedulable unit in different circumstances.

assumptions: for each task, C is fixed (rather than probabilistically distributed); no task depends on the execution of another task; $C < T$, and in particular no more than one instance of a task will be in the system at a time; and more generally, for all tasks i in the system,

$$\sum_i C_i/T_i < 1$$

(which just means that the system has enough throughput to serve all tasks). Many of these assumptions have been relaxed by later research.

An individual task is *schedulable* if it will not miss its deadline. A system is *schedulable* if all tasks will not miss their deadlines.

A number of scheduling algorithms can be found in the general operating system literature. These include FIFO (first-in, first-out, or sometimes equivalently "first-come, first-served"), round-robin, priority-based queuing, and multilevel queuing (which combines the previous two). None of these algorithms turns out to be usable for real-time purposes, because their intuitive descriptions and implementations do not lead to tractable timing analysis. However, the general concepts of *priority* and *preemptability* are relevant to real-time scheduling. Priority is straightforward: a ready task with higher priority should be preferred over a ready task with lower priority. Preemptability refers to the system's ability to interrupt and resume a task. In a system that supports preemptability, a high-priority task that becomes ready can displace (preempt) a low-priority task that is already running. In systems that do not support preemptability, the low-priority task must run until it blocks or completes before the scheduler can run the high-priority task.

There are two major types of preemptive real-time schedulers deployed today, both of which descend from seminal work performed by Liu and Layland [1973]. In a *static priority* or *fixed priority* scheduler, the priorities of the tasks are set before the system runs. Perhaps the most commonly deployed static scheduler is the *rate monotonic* (RM) scheduler. Liu and Layland observed that the scheduling interval of higher-rate tasks bounds the duration that should be allocated to lower-rate tasks, whereas the reverse is not true. This suggests that higher priority should be given to tasks with higher rates, which is exactly what they do (hence the name *rate monotonic*; that is, the higher the rate, the higher the priority). When combined with a set of "schedulability analysis" equations that must be satisfied (and restriction of resources used by tasks in the system), the rate monotonic scheduler can provably guarantee that no task will miss its deadline. Unfortunately, this comes at a high cost: rate monotonic schedulers can never attain full (100%) utilization because the upper bound for m tasks sharing a processor is $m(2^{1/m} - 1)$, which approaches 69% (the natural logarithm of 2) as m goes to infinity. Despite this limit in efficiency, rate monotonic schedulers are popular, in large part due to the mathematical nature of their performance bounds.

To address the utilization problems in RM, Liu and Layland [1973] also proposed a dynamic priority scheduler, which today is known as *earliest deadline first* (EDF) or sometimes as *deadline-dynamic scheduling*. In such a system, the task with the nearest deadline receives highest priority. EDF schedulers also have tractable theoretical properties and escape the utilization bound of RM schedulers (see the Bibliography for more information about these properties).

One subtlety common to both general-purpose and real-time schedulers is the problem of *priority inversion*. Priority inversion occurs in practice because the assumption of independence across tasks fails. Suppose that a low-priority task locks a shared resource and is then preempted by some other task. Suppose further that later on, before the low-priority task has resumed, a high-priority task attempts to access the same shared resource held by the low-priority task. Then the high-priority task will block, invoking the scheduler, but any medium-priority tasks will prevent the low-priority task from running and allowing the lock to be released. In the worst case, the low-priority task will not execute before the deadline of the high-priority task and the high-priority task will miss its deadline.

The solution to priority inversion is simple to describe: any process that locks a resource should *inherit* the priority of the highest-priority process that is waiting for that resource. In our example, this would (temporarily) promote the low-priority task to run at high priority. As soon as the task releases the resource, its priority would be demoted, and the scheduler would preempt the (once-again) low-priority task in favor of the high-priority task, which can now make forward progress. Although intuitively simple, priority inheritance is very difficult to implement correctly (many articles describing incorrect solutions to the problem have been published).

Priority inversion and inheritance due to locking are only the simplest version of dependence across tasks. Much of the research since the 1970s deals with scheduling systems that contain such dependences.

Many expansions and refinements on RM and EDF scheduling techniques have been explored. An interesting recent result mixes periodic real-time tasks with best-effort "sporadic" tasks, the goal being to support "non real-time" computation in the spare time available to the real-time processor. The default solution, running the sporadic tasks as a lowest-priority batch job, leads to poor response time for sporadic tasks. So-called "slack-stealing" schedulers modify EDF to examine the *slack* available to a task: the time between its completion under the current schedule and its deadline. By accounting for slack, slack-stealing schedulers can give slack time to sporadic tasks, lending better responsiveness to those tasks while still meeting the deadlines of real-time tasks.

We have mentioned before that many embedded systems employ heterogeneous multiprocessing, whereby different processor cores perform different tasks in the overall system. Heterogeneous multiprocessing is also used to divide real-time from non real-time processing, placing real-time tasks on one or more dedicated processors. This segregates non real-time tasks so that they cannot interfere with real-time tasks.

9.4.3 Multiple Flows of Control

The terms *multithreading*, *multitasking*, and *multiprocessing* have a number of overlapping meanings. The main differences refer to whether there are multiple processor cores cooperating (the *multi-* refers to hardware) and whether a single processor core supports multiple threads of control (the *multi-* refers to the threads). Multiprocessing is most often used to describe the former case, in which multiple processor cores cooperate in a single computing system. This also gives us the noun form *multiprocessor*. Multitasking is most frequently used with the second case, and indicates software that shares a single core among multiple competing tasks. In the OS community, multithreading refers to multiple "lightweight processes" or *threads*, which are in term parts of a larger "heavyweight process," sometimes simply referred to as a *process* or *task*. (The "weight" usually refers to separate memory spaces. Threads share memory within a task, but tasks or processes within a single program cannot directly access each others' memory.) Unfortunately, multithreading is also used by the hardware community to refer to a variety of means by which hardware allows multiple processes to share a single core. Such hardware multithreading has a number of variants — including "horizontal," "vertical," and "simultaneous" — although when implemented such hardware techniques appear to software as if the hardware were that of a multiprocessor. Usually, the terms are understandable from context, and thus the OS and architecture communities manage to avoid terminological collisions.

This section ignores the multiple-processor core case (to which we return in Section 9.5) and focuses on multiple software processes that share a uniprocessor. Even on a uniprocessor, the presence of multiple processes complicates all levels of the run-time system. The problem comes from *reentrancy* (also called *thread safety*, especially in the JAVA community): for any interface exposed as a utility (e.g., a system call), any or all of the processes might use that interface at the same time. For example, one process might call a routine to write a buffer to disk. While the process is waiting for its disk I/O to occur, a second process might call the very same routine to write a different buffer to a different part of the disk. If the routine is written in the standard "sequential" style of programming, it is possible that the second entrance into the routine, which happens *while the first process is still in the routine*, leads to unexpected results. In such cases, the "sequential" model of programming that is most common fails. Instead, programmers must take great pains to make their code reentrant, which means that the code must carefully protect shared data structures so that the interaction of various processes does not lead to system failures. In particular, "global" or "static" data structures will not work without significant changes to how they are accessed. Depending on the system, many parts of the OS and libraries may have to be written in a reentrant style, including (but not limited to) the memory manager, the file system, and the display manager.

Supporting multiple flows of control is by no means a uniquely embedded issue. However, even in very simple embedded systems that have only a single primary task there can still be synchronization issues. For example, the interrupt handlers through which I/O devices communicate with the processor core must be able to interoperate safely with the primary task.

Threads, Processes, and Microkernels

Embedded operating systems use a combination of the two basic forms of multiple flows of control: threads and processes. Microkernels typically add an extra level of protection to either model.

Threads. Threads are independent flows of control that share memory and global variables, and typically run at the same execution level. At every timer tick,[3] the basic processor interrupt mechanism delivers control to a centralized scheduler, which determines the order of execution of each thread. In addition to its obvious simplicity, an embedded OS based on threads has several advantages: context switches are fast, it is easy to implement preemptive policies, and supporting shared global variables is straightforward (given that all threads are compiled in the same binary as if they were a single program). The primary disadvantage is the complete lack of protection (a rogue thread can mess with other threads' state), which can have disastrous effects. VxWorks is an example of a thread-based embedded OS.

Processes. Processes are what users of a modern multitasking general-purpose computer are more familiar with. A process has a private memory space (virtual memory), set of global variables, and processor state, and relies on hardware support (the processor's memory management unit) to enforce protection. As such, a process-based model is intrinsically secure, given that each process has limited access to other processes' states (through a well-defined area of shared memory and messages). On the downside, process-based OSs require a processor with VM support, have much slower context-switch times, and preemption is not easy to implement. Process-based OSs usually also support a lightweight thread model within a process, through specific APIs (such as *pthreads*, the POSIX thread library). Lynx, PocketPC, and embedded Linux are examples of OSs that use a process model.

Microkernels. In some cases, we want to make sure that only one flow of control (the *microkernel*) has access to the highest privilege-execution levels. This is important in highly secure appliances (think of ATMs or POS registers). The microkernel itself sits at the bottom of the execution stack, and it can be compatible with both threads and processes that are implemented above it. *Mach* was the original research-built microkernel-based OS (it has had many descendants).

9.4.4 Market Considerations

A number of factors go into a successful embedded operating system. Because it is an embedded operating system, costs are paramount. There are usually costs both for development licenses and per unit shipped. There are also typically support costs or additional development costs if special features need to be added for a particular application. Processor architecture affects the market. Some embedded operating systems support a limited set of processors, and others prefer one architecture over others. Available core

---

3. Note that the OS-level timer or clock interrupt is very different from the clock rate of a chip. The former has much coarser granularity than the latter, typically milliseconds for the OS clock versus nanoseconds for the CPU clock. The former is controlled by software, whereas the latter is a function of an oscillator or phase-locked-loop (PLL) hardware driving the pins of the processor chip. The OS typically uses a hardware timer mechanism to interrupt the processor after a process has executed for a fixed amount of time.

modules can also make an embedded OS more attractive, as they allow developers to purchase rather than build code. The most commonly mentioned modules today have to do with networking, in which various optional modules support networking protocols. Last, manufacturer mandate can create an operating system for business reasons: PocketPC exists because of a conscious choice by Microsoft to enter the PDA market, whereas Symbian exists because of a conscious choice by cellular phone handset manufacturers not to use existing embedded operating systems.

Table 9.2 outlines a selection of embedded operating systems, along with the architectures they support and some guesses at their memory requirements.

Wind River System's *VxWorks* is the dominant force in the embedded, real-time operating system market. VxWorks uses a "microkernel" approach in which the kernel, or central part of the operating system, does little more than provide low-level control over thread scheduling and memory allocation. Additional functionality (for example, for networking, I/O, or file system support) is added through other modules that are not part of the kernel proper. This modular approach allows VxWorks implementations to span wide ranges of functionality. A "demonstration" board consisting of little more than a processor and a standard bus interface might run a VxWorks kernel occupying only a few hundred kilobytes of storage, whereas a sophisticated network switch might contain many processors (each running its own copy of VxWorks), with megabytes of code to support a variety of communications protocol stacks. VxWorks modules are also dynamically loadable, meaning that they can be attached to and detached from a running system without rebooting.

LinuxWorks' *LynxOS* is a real-time embedded operating system that is a relative of Linux, the popular open-source operating system. As a Linux relative, it supports many of the same programming interfaces that desktop Linux programmers are familiar with, allowing a shorter learning curve when moving from one to the other. Lynx also directly supports some versions of the Linux ABI, and thus in theory at least Linux *binaries* can run without modification on top of a LynxOS kernel.

Name	Architectures	Memory requirements
VxWorks	PowerPC, 68K, x86, ARM, MIPS, SuperH	100 KB RAM minimum, 3 MB for typical systems
Lynx	PowerPC, x86	
Symbian	ARM	8 MB RAM, 16 MB ROM (Series 60 platform)
PalmOS	68K, ARM	8 MB RAM, 8 MB ROM
Windows CE PocketPC	ARM, MIPS, PowerPC, SuperH, x86	32 MB RAM, 16 MB Flash
Embedded Linux	Many	200 KB RAM and up

TABLE 9.2 Selected embedded operating systems.

Symbian's *EPOC*[4] system differs from other embedded operating systems in that it targets a particular platform: cellular phones. Originally jointly founded by Ericsson, Nokia, Motorola, and Psion, many other cellular phone manufacturers have joined in as either partners or licensees. Symbian's marketing literature claims that cellular phones are unique devices with unique characteristics (e.g., frequent connection but occasional disconnected operation) that warrant their own specialized operating system. From a business standpoint, it seems likely that Symbian is an attempt by the cellular phone manufacturers to counter Microsoft's PocketPC (or its latest incarnation, Windows Mobile) operating system.

We list Palm Computing's *PalmOS* and Microsoft's *PocketPC* in our table as examples of PDA (personal digital assistant) operating systems. PalmOS remains the market-share leader in the market, although PocketPC machines, with their more powerful processors and stronger feature sets, have been gaining recently in market share. As an operating system, PalmOS is surprisingly limited: it supports only a single active program at a time, has very limited memory protection with no MMU support, and until recently it ran only on 68000-family devices at low clock rates (tens of megahertz). ARM implementations of PalmOS have recently arrived in the marketplace. PocketPC, by contrast, requires an MMU and runs on devices with clock rates in the hundreds of megahertz. PocketPC (originally called WindowsCE, for consumer edition) suffers to some extent from being the smaller sibling of the successful desktop operating systems, that is, some features, and especially the applications, feel like stripped-down versions of familiar desktop programs.

Embedded Linux

Many embedded developers have mounted large efforts to start using the free open-source Linux operating system in the embedded domain. Several variations of Linux are available targeting a variety of embedded platforms, ranging from simple *uClinux* for microcontrollers without virtual memory (such as the Motorola *Coldfire* family) to full-fledged Linux ports for more modern RISC processors (such as ARM, PowerPC, SuperH, and MIPS). Companies such as RedHat, MontaVista, Lineo, LinuxWorks, and VA Linux Systems all have offerings in the embedded Linux space.

During the time it took to write this book, embedded Linux has gone from virtually no products shipping to a small but significant number of shipping products. Current embedded Linux designs include storage servers and set-top boxes (we can expect a large number of new designs in the future). Why did it take so long for Linux-based products to reach the market? One of the reasons is simply the level of immaturity of embedded Linux. It takes time for an OS to mature (for example, you could purchase VxWorks in 1986), and Linux is relatively young. Despite the abundance of

---

4. EPOC is the general name of a family of operating systems for personal digital assistants (PDAs) produced first by Psion and now developed by a spin-off, Symbian. The name EPOC, claimed to stand for Electronic Piece of Cheese, is deprecated, and the name Symbian OS is preferred.

tools, you need a proven and robust integrated development environment for embedded, including cross-compilers, cross-debuggers, interfaces with hardware tools, hardware emulators, board-support packages, and other toolchain components. Although most of these tools are individually available (largely due to the massive efforts of the Free Software Foundation's *GNU Project*), integrated offerings are still in their infancy.

Embedded Linux has several real advantages, in addition to the "religious" appeal of *open-source* versus *proprietary*. There is a wealth of tools available for embedded Linux (although support is still largely freely volunteered by the open-source community), and the application base is growing at a phenomenal speed. For example, it is now possible to find a completely free implementation of an IP protocol stack for embedded Linux, which can potentially save hefty licensing fees. Most important, Linux itself is free, and as such it does not add royalty costs to your parts and does not require substantial up-front investment for the development platform.

Embedded Linux still has two severe limitations: it is not compatible with hard real time (although some proposed extensions exist) and its code size requirements are substantial. Even for a stripped-down, carefully trimmed kernel, footprints of about 200 to 400 KB for uClinux and 1 to 2 MB for VM-Linux are common. In other words, Linux is still not adequate for applications with tight cost constraints and hard real-time requirements, but is likely to become a very common choice in the higher-end segment of the embedded market.

With the exception of the areas in which legacy code and proprietary software dominate (such as Microsoft's *PocketPC* for PDAs), we are optimistic about the future of embedded Linux, and we believe that it will become an important player in the area of embedded operating systems. The formation of the Consumer Electronics Linux Forum (*http://www.celinuxform.org*) — a consortium of many companies in software, semiconductors, and consumer electronics — suggests the industrial future of embedded Linux is promising.

9.4.5 Downloadable Code and Virtual Machines

Although it may violate some definitions of *embedded systems*, many such systems now allow code to be downloaded to devices after they have been shipped. Such fixes are often called *firmware upgrades*, since embedded devices are not supposed to run software. Examples include bug fixes, new versions of code that implement standards, upgrades of existing features, and sometimes even new features. During the modem wars of the 1990s, many variations of standards were still being codified even as manufacturers were racing products to market. Rather than hardcode the draft standards into their devices many manufacturers were able to build devices that could be reconfigured by loading new code into the modem. This allowed them to ship products without worrying about obsolescence because of the standards war. An example of a new feature comes from first-generation Saturn automobiles, for which the same microprocessor controls both the automatic transmission and the antilock brake system. Saturn cars with both features received traction control for free, as the sensors of the antilock brakes and the control inputs to the engine and brakes could be combined to implement the traction control feature. Perhaps the most dramatic example of a new feature comes from the Voyager deep-space exploration spacecraft, for which image-processing algorithms that *had not been invented* when the spacecraft were first launched were downloaded to the craft to produce their famous flyby pictures of Jupiter, Saturn, and their systems of moons and rings.

Downloading code raises safety questions. How can engineers ensure that the new code will be free of bugs or unintentional side effects, in addition to the intended side effects it embodies? In the case of a closed system, the engineers themselves are the only source of code updates, and thus this is less of a concern. The same software and hardware engineering processes that ensured reliability and reduced bugs in the original product can be applied to any upgrades. The upgrades need only be distributed in binary form, and they will be applied by a controlled process that ensures that the desired bits and only the desired bits end up on the device.

In an open system, in which users can define and implement their own extensions or upgrades, the issues become much more tricky. One would like to ensure that the downloaded code does not overwrite operating system memory or the memory of other processes. Methods to ensure this type of safety take a number of forms. Hardware can check that memory accesses stay within known bounds, or virtual memory might provide access *only* to the memory owned by the downloaded code. Software methods take a variety of forms, including software fault isolation (in which dynamic check instructions are added to the untrusted code), static limitations on the control flow and instruction set of the downloaded code, and interpretation. Each technique exacts a price in terms of hardware cost or software cycles, and each may be appropriate in different circumstances. In some cases, safety may be impossible to ensure. For example, device drivers typically operate at a low level of the operating system, and they sometimes have very stringent performance requirements, making any protection mechanism too costly. Hardware mechanisms may not be supported in interrupt-service code, and no software method may have low enough overhead to check the device driver code. Interestingly, Microsoft began *certifying* device drivers in Windows XP (certification performs no run-time hardware or software checking, but it does vouch that Microsoft has tested the device driver in operating conditions).

Aside from the safety of the downloaded code, there are additional concerns whether the *mechanisms* for downloading and installing code are themselves safe. During the download process, what assurances are there that the entire download was received without tampering by third parties? Upgrading firmware involves changing bits that reside on hard disks or flash memory. While these bits are being updated, is the system always in a safe state, or can interrupting the system while the update takes place lead to a corrupted system (and therefore an unusable device)? Solutions to these operational issues can be surprisingly complicated.

In recent years, Java has been advocated repeatedly as a useful technique for running embedded code. It is important to note that embedded Java proponents are talking here about the Java Virtual Machine (JVM), a compact stack-oriented ISA, rather than the Java programming language. Further, the JVM is really being used as an ISA, which admits to many possible implementations, including interpretation and binary translation.

Sun has made a number of failed attempts to market JVM as a viable hardware ISA, with the "picoJava" processor core that directly executed JVM instructions being the most recent. Embedded Java has had much more recent success in the form of Java 2 Micro Edition (J2ME), which is a stripped-down version of workstation-class Java. J2ME excludes many megabytes of code that occur in the Standard and Enterprise editions, targeting devices that can have less than a megabyte of storage. J2ME includes a space-efficient Java virtual machine implementation, the "K" virtual machine, and it provides support for a variety of "profiles" and "configurations" that vary according to target market and hardware capability, respectively. J2ME is currently enjoying modest success as a way of building application software for mobile phones. It remains to be seen whether it will spread to other embedded devices, such as PDAs.

9.5 Multiprocessing and Multithreading

As we described in Chapter 6, most embedded multiprocessing is heterogeneous, wherein a system consists of various types of processors that cooperate. That chapter described the ways in which such cooperating processors communicate (e.g., through shared memory, buses, and interrupts). This section takes a somewhat higher-level approach, examining how multiprocessing affects the run-time (operating system) and the compiler.

This section also includes "multithreading" in its title, by which we mean hardware multithreading, where a single pipeline supports multiple contexts simultaneously. Hardware multithreading is often exposed at the ISA level in ways similar to hardware multiprocessing: the hardware appears as multiple processors, although multithreaded implementations present multiple virtual processors over shared hardware, rather than actually having separate physical processors.

From a software and run-time standpoint, there is not much to distinguish between a multithreaded and a multiprocessing system (the structure of the control and communications software remains the same). However, there can be performance differences that result from the different hardware implementations of multithreading and multiprocessing. For example, threads in a multithreaded processor share caches. Depending on the workload, this can lead to constructive (cache sharing of data or instructions) or destructive (cache thrashing) effects on performance. As another example, multithreading for Intel Pentium processors (called "hyperthreading" for marketing purposes) was built to be compatible with multiprocessor codes for the same platform, so that no code changes would be required for compatibility. Many multiprocessor systems use "spin locks" to synchronize across processors, wherein an idle processor repeatedly checks a shared memory location for the next thing to do. On a multithreaded processor, it is better to suspend an idle thread than to have it execute a spin lock, because the cycles spent spinning come at the expense of other productive threads.

9.5.1 Multiprocessing in the Embedded World

Multiprocessing is much more common in embedded applications than one might think. Even a uniprocessor system must respond to interrupts. Further, today's uniprocessors turn into tomorrow's I/O controllers, and thus, even though the code run by such secondary or tertiary processors seems simple, such processors still have their own code, storage, and flow of control. Furthermore, specialized high-end processors occur in many embedded applications. Today's cellular phones provide a very instructive example: a typical cellular phone today contains both a DSP to run the radio interface and a microprocessor to handle the user interface. Specialization so far has made it difficult to combine both functions into a single processor core, although many research projects and startups are trying. Other systems with multiple heterogeneous high-end processors include automotive and printing applications. Today's luxury automobiles contain from 50 to 100 processors each.

The examples in the previous paragraph fall into two classes, which we might distinguish as "visible" versus "invisible" multiprocessing. Handling interrupts and having a smart I/O controller are perhaps "invisible" multiprocessing, in that there is a way in which the master processor remains ignorant of the processing that is part of the implementation of its peripherals. The cellular phone example is a more visible form of multiprocessing, because neither processor can ignore the existence of the other. The general-purpose processor in the cellular phone must translate human requests into actions by the DSP (dialing, transcoding voice, evaluating signal strength), whereas the DSP must occasionally signal various events to the user interface (loss or strength of signal, fast busy tones, available carriers).

The remainder of this section focuses on visible multiprocessing. Invisible multiprocessing is well covered by traditional operating system texts.

The run-time issues in multiprocessing involve coordination of processor cores. Coordination requires communication, which is typically implemented through shared memory, interrupts, or a combination of both. We described the hardware that supports shared memory in Section 5.5.4, and gave examples of SMP and heterogeneous computing platforms in Section 6.2.2. Many embedded operating systems provide libraries that implement message passing, shared memory, remote procedure call, or some combination thereof on top of the underlying hardware. Such libraries provide only limited assistance. Coordination remains in the hands of software and application designers, and the lack of hardware support for memory coherence can greatly complicate the software task. As we noted in Chapter 6, many systems are designed with "master" and "slave" processors. The master interrupts the slave to indicate a new command to be processed. Slaves may interrupt the master to indicate a completed task or an exceptional condition.

9.5.2 Multiprocessing and VLIW

Parallelism occurs at various levels, and we would be remiss if we claimed that instruction-level parallelism, our favorite tool, were the sole means of achieving performance. The most common types of parallelism occur at the instruction level, at the loop level, and at the process level. Much of this book describes the former, and we admit that many loop-level parallelism techniques have ILP analogues, so that an architecture oriented toward loop-level parallelism (i.e., vector) can sometimes gain the same sorts of benefits as an ILP-oriented architecture through very different means. Whereas both ILP and vector techniques depend on the compiler to expose parallelism, process-level parallelism is most often found in application structure. That is, many applications are already built with parallel tasks as part of their problem structure. Such application-exposed parallelism is best exploited through multiple processes or threads. The natural way to do this with a VLIW architecture would be through multiple VLIW cores or through a threading layer built on top of the VLIW layer. Such a design suggests that VLIW and process-level parallelism are orthogonal concepts: one can exploit one, the other, or both, without much affecting the other.

Before concluding, we note that *automatic parallelization* has been a longtime goal of compiler researchers. The idea of such work is to take a sequential program and have the compiler divide that program into processes or threads that match the underlying architecture, much as an ILP compiler arranges operations into instructions or a vector compiler arranges loops into vectorizable form. Although there has been much progress in this field, it remains in the domain of research. It is not clear whether existing sequential languages provide too many barriers to parallelization or whether there are problems that fundamentally encode sequential dependences that defy parallelization attempts.

9.6   Further Reading

There are a number of well-known textbooks on operating systems. Silberschatz, Gagne, and Galvin's *Operating System Concepts* [Silberschatz, 2002], Tanenbaum's *Modern Operating Systems* [Tanenbaum, 2001], and Tanenbaum and Woodhull's *Operating Systems: Design and Implementation* [Tanenbaum and Woodhull, 1997] have each been through at least two printings. We are also partial to Stallings' *Operating Systems: Internals and Design Principles* [Stallings, 2000]. For an annotated version of the code of the one true OS, see *Lions' commentary on UNIX, sixth edition* [Lyons, 1996]. Last, the Mach operating system (described by Accetta et al. [1986]) pioneered the microkernel concept.

There is no substitute for building your own operating system from scratch, and about the only way to get this type of system-building experience today is by taking one of the few university OS classes that do this as a course project. The next best thing is to port an OS (embedded or otherwise) to a new platform. This can also be a great educational experience. Although the portable parts of the system have been abstracted away by countless other programmers, working with the remaining machine-specific pieces forces one to deal with low-level machine details in a very concrete way. Searching for "porting guide X," where X is your operating system of choice, will turn up numerous helpful web sites.

Application binary interfaces are typically documented in manuals provided by manufacturers and made available (but frequently updated) through the manufacturers' support web sites. Similarly, the ELF specification is widely available on the web.

Real-time systems have a history that goes far back in computer science. Everyone, however, cites the foundational paper by Liu and Layland [1973], which defined the terms *rate monotonic* and *earliest deadline first*. It remains readable and relevant today.

The foundational paper on information theory is due to Shannon [1948], which has also been reprinted many times since its first appearance in the *Bell Labs Technical*

Journal. Cover and Thomas' *Elements of Information Theory* [Cover and Thomas, 1991] is the standard modern textbook on the subject. For practical, efficient compression schemes, the original articles on the LZ77 [Ziv and Lempel, 1977], LZ78 [Ziv and Lempel, 1978], and LZSS [Storer and Szymanski, 1982] schemes are worth perusing.

Code compression has been explored by a number of commercial and academic efforts. Commercial instruction set extensions include ARM-Thumb [ARM, 1995] and MIPS16 (see the MIPS web site at *http://www.mips.com*). IBM's CodePack system [IBM, 1998; Kemp et al., 1998] was analyzed for overall performance by Lefurgy et al. (1997). Early research into code compression was performed by Wolfe and coauthors in the early 1990s [Wolfe and Chanin, 1992; Kozuch and Wolfe, 1994].

9.7 Exercises

1. Using VEX in its default configuration (1 cluster, 64 general registers, 8 branch registers), write the assembly code of a possible low-level exception handler, assuming that the hardware only saves the return location into a control register (called *interrupt return pointer*, or IRP). The handler needs to save the entire machine state before jumping to a user-level routine.

2. Using the VEX handler you wrote in the previous exercise, write (in C) a user-level interrupt handler triggered by SIGUSR1 that dumps all general-purpose registers of the machine to the console. Hint: you can only use low-level system calls (*write*) and you have to get the context from the low-level handler.

3. Given the following C structure, describe its layout in memory (on a 32-bit word basis) for a big-endian machine and a little-endian machine.

```
struct {
  char c;
  short s;
  int i;
  int bf:7;
};
```

4. Write a C function that returns 1 if the target machine is little endian, or 0 if the target machine is big endian. Test it on VEX and on your desktop computer.

5. What does the following code fragment output on a big-endian machine? On a little-endian machine?

```
char *s = "hello";
printf("%d\n", *((int *)s));
```

6.   Implement (in C) your own version of the dynamic stack allocation routine *alloca()*, assuming no compiler/ABI support for it. Hint: your allocated storage may live longer than the function that calls *alloca()*.

7.   Construct two functions, each taking 20 arguments: one by using *varargs*, and the other by explicitly declaring the arguments. In VEX, write an exerciser that calls both functions 1000 times, measure the number of cycles, and compare the performance of the two implementations. What is the overhead of a single *vararg* argument versus an explicitly declared argument?

8.   For a LAT-based cache compression system, compute the size overheads to store LAT entries and Huffman tables for varying line sizes (16, 32, and 64 bytes) and record sizes (1, 2, and 4 lines per LAT entry).

9.   For a LAT-based cache compression system, describe the steps a debugger has to implement to call a function in compressed code. How would you implement in the debugger a function that dumps the content of compressed memory?

10.   Compute a valid Huffman encoding for the opcodes of the following table, given the execution probability of the second column. With the computed Huffman encoding, what is the achievable compression ratio on a program that has the same distribution of opcodes?

Opcode	Probability
ADD	38%
LOAD	28%
STORE	12%
CMP	9%
BRANCH	7%
SUB	6%

11.   Compare and contrast the classical literature on paging with the corresponding code compression techniques. Describe how to handle software compression faults (hint: decompression software itself can not be compressed).

12.   Design your own 32-bit encoding for the VEX instruction set and build a simplified assembler that generates the binary representation that corresponds to your encoding. Compile and assemble a benchmark, and produce a binary. Consider the binary as a source of 32-bit symbols and compute the entropy of the source. Repeat the computation of the entropy by using the instruction subfields (operands and opcodes) of your encoding. Compute the maximum compression ratio, and the compression ratio you can get if you can only compress a 64-byte line at a time.

10

Application Design and Customization

If I knew for a certainty that a man was coming to my house with the conscious design of doing me good, I should run for my life.

— Henry David Thoreau, *American writer*, 1817–1862

One of the most important differentiators between embedded and general-purpose computing is that embedded systems typically run one single application or set of applications exclusively. This affects many aspects of computing, including code development. Although in most respects embedded application development resembles general code development, special languages can play a role when the application under development will be embedded in a product, because of different lifetime, user community, and underlying hardware considerations. Similarly, the process of making code perform well can change. Techniques that might be unacceptable in the general-purpose world can be almost essential in the embedded world, in which a product may be of no use if it cannot meet a speed or power requirement.

It may seem surprising that the subject of hardware customization belongs in this chapter. However, embedded computing is unique in that the hardware too is built to run a single application, and thus methodologies for customization become relevant. This topic is part of the larger area of hardware/software co-design. Embedded designers face issues at the hardware/software boundary that are closed to designers of general-purpose systems. Customized hardware presents an opportunity to vastly speed up individual applications. This opportunity has led to a lively research area and the foundation of more than a few startup companies.

10.1 Programming Language Choices

Language choices in the embedded domain are driven by a variety of factors, including language maturity, tool support, productivity, flexibility requirements in the application, the business model of the software development effort, and sometimes even language fashion trends. As the complexity of embedded applications grows and time-to-market shrinks, higher-level languages become more appealing. This enables better productivity, allows software reuse, and promotes more rigorous software engineering practices. With higher-level languages, the role of all compilation-related tools significantly grows and developers must rely on compilers to achieve their performance goals.

However, despite the attempts to promote many other languages, C remains the language of choice for most embedded systems. C is not perfect. It has many disadvantages (largely from the compiler point of view), but it is the natural choice for developers moving into the embedded domain, especially for its relatively short learning curve. Other languages are starting to occupy important market positions though, and in the following sections we present some of the most promising approaches.

10.1.1 Overview of Embedded Programming Languages

C remains the embedded programming language of choice, but descendants such as C++, Java, and Microsoft's C# have also been suggested as the next popular embedded language. Despite having been designed in the 1970s and popularized in the 1980s, C's mixture of structured programming, easy access to low-level hardware, and portability make it compelling for embedded designers.

C++ runs second in popularity for embedded languages, but linguistic aspects of C++ place large demands on the compiler and the target machine. In particular, support for templates and exceptions has remained expensive even on mainstream PCs and workstations, let alone embedded targets. Software engineering experts find C++ and other object-oriented languages attractive because of the potential for code reuse through inheritance. A group of companies have founded an effort to design an "embedded C++," which looks like C++ with many of the expensive features removed. A better name for the project might just be "C with Classes."

Java proponents have tried repeatedly to market the Java programming language, virtual machine, and microprocessors as appropriate to embedded applications. This has turned out to be difficult. Although Java byte codes are indeed a compact code representation, many feel that they are not well matched with embedded cores. The smallest JVMs and JITs occupy on the order of 100 KB of space, making them too expensive for some embedded applications. So far, Java native cores (e.g., *picojava*) have not caught on. Adding to these difficulties, the usual suite of Java libraries takes up megabytes of space. The latest embedded-oriented version of Java, Java 2 Micro Edition (J2ME), throws out many of the Java library routines in order to save space. J2ME is fast becoming the dominant platform for cellular phones, but it remains to be seen how far it will go in other areas of the embedded domain.

Although designed as a language for numerical analysis, Matlab has many features that enable design, algorithmic, and application exploration in numerically intensive embedded applications. Microsoft's *.NET* initiative includes many Java-like features (e.g., machine-independent code representations and many libraries) and aims to link the devices and services of the future together in one programming framework. The .NET programming language of choice is Microsoft's homegrown C# (familiarly, C# has C-like syntax and includes support for garbage collection). How .NET and C# address the embedded space also remains to be seen.

10.1.2 Traditional C and ANSI C

There are two variants of C that differ enough to have distinct nicknames, despite their syntactic similarities. *Traditional C*, sometimes called *K&R C*—from Kernighan and Ritchie, the authors of the definitive book [1978]—was the first implementation of C. ANSI/ISO C (sometimes called *C89*) is the first real C "standard" recognized by an international organization. It is defined by ANSI/ISO standard X3.159, and described by the second edition of Kernighan and Ritchie [1989]. The differences between the two are subtle but important, including type checking, prototype checking, argument conversion, type and size conversions, and structure operations. (See Figure 10.1 for a simple C example.) Unfortunately, many features in ANSI C were preserved to guarantee backward compatibility with K&R C, thus weakening the effectiveness of these improvements. There are several reasons for the popularity of C.

- The execution model of C is simple. There is a constant, known cost to each C construct, and experienced programmers know approximately what type of assembly language code the compiler will generate.

- There is a plethora of tools available from many software vendors and for most of the available architectures. Given the choice, C is the first language a processor manufacturer will support for a new processor.

- The language is stable and standardized. In particular, the transition from *traditional C* to ANSI/ISO C was a huge step forward in eliminating many of the idiosyncrasies of the early versions of C. ANSI/ISO C forces a certain discipline in programmers.

- The language can be closely tied to hardware execution. For example, it is relatively easy to control memory-mapped peripherals and control registers from C without resorting to assembly language programming.

- Expert programmers can easily use their "bag of tricks" to circumvent compiler problems and optimization issues. A good C programmer does not necessarily need to rely on compiler optimization to get performance. Even when programmers do rely on compilers for time-critical code (more common as compiler technology matures), it is relatively straightforward to rewrite the most time-critical sections.

All of these advantages become less relevant as the role of the compiler increases, due to an increase in complexity of both architectures and software. Once it is not obvious what the assembly language code is going to look like (for example, for VLIW architectures)

```c
#include <stdio.h>

typedef struct { int r, i; } cmpx;

void
fircx(const cmpx *x, const cmpx *h, cmpx *y, int N, int M)
{
    int i, j;
    cmpx *py = y + N;
    const cmpx *px = x + N;
    for (i = N; i < M; ++i, ++px, ++py) {
        int imag = 0;
        int real = 0;
        const cmpx *ph = h;
        for (j = 0, ph = h; j < N; ++j, ++ph) {
            int h0 = ph->r;
            int h1 = ph->i;
            int x0 = (px-j)->r;
            int x1 = (px-j)->i;
            real += h0 * x0 - h1 * x1;
            imag += h0 * x1 + h1 * x0;
        }
        py->r = real;
        py->i = imag;
    }
}
cmpx in[] = {
    {0,0}, {0,0}, {0,0}, {0,0}, /* padding */
    {1,0}, {2,1}, {3,0}, {4,1}, {5,0},
    {6,1}, {7,0}, {8,1}, {9,0}, {10,1}
};
cmpx cf[] = { {1,0}, {-2,0}, {3,0}, {-4,0} };

cmpx out[14];

int
main(int argc, char *argv[])
{
    int i;
    fircx(in,cf,out,4,14);
    for(i = 4; i < 14; ++i)
        printf ("(%d,%d) ",out[i].r,out[i].i);
    printf("\n");
}
```

FIGURE 10.1 **Example of a *complex FIR* in C.** As we can see from the example, C allows developers to exercise fine-grained control over the execution of the program. For example, this "optimized" version of the FIR loop explicitly controls addressing within the value (x[]) and coefficient (h[]) arrays in function *fircx*. It is possible to write this routine in a more readable way in C, but this example shows the types of source-level optimizations programmers apply when they focus on performance.

or when the sheer program size grows beyond a certain threshold, the limitations of C become more evident.

- The absence of type safety and the indiscriminate use of "dangerous" constructs (such as the abuse of pointers casts and arithmetic) is a big barrier to productivity. Debugging a pointer gone wild is very time consuming, and sometimes latent bugs appear very late in the development process.

- The absence of object-oriented concepts make reuse very difficult. It is true that software engineering is a state of mind, but the language certainly helps.

- The dynamic memory allocation model in C (*malloc*-based) is primitive. This makes identifying memory leaks a subtle process, and debugging them very difficult.

- Compilers have very limited opportunities to apply aggressive optimizations in a "vanilla" C program. The fact that a pointer can address almost any memory location kills many optimizations.

These factors have provided additional motivation for the emergence of other languages in the embedded domain. In the following, we present some of the most popular, with their strengths and weaknesses.

10.1.3 C++ and Embedded C++

From a high-level point of view, the two major advantages of C++ (see Figure 10.2) are that it forces a much stricter software engineering discipline and it can increase productivity through code reuse. C++ compilers enforce an interface-oriented abstraction through access to class members. The language includes a variety of object-oriented concepts (class encapsulation, inheritance, and templates) that can enable software reuse when applied judiciously. Finally, C++ has a dynamic memory allocation model that is compiler assisted (when using *new* and *delete* operators) and more robust than the C model.

Despite these — and many more — advantages, the adoption of C++ in the embedded domain has been much slower than expected. The learning curve to reach C++ proficiency is slow. While it is true that C++ forces better software engineering discipline, it is very easy for inexperienced C++ programmers to write very inefficient programs.

Tool support is scarce. The popularity of the GNU *gcc/g++* compilers is partially bridging this gap, but proprietary C++ compilers are still behind and do not generate very well-optimized code.

For practical purposes, the C++ standardization effort is not complete. Despite the fact that ANSI C++ is now an ANSI/ISO standard, each compiler has a slightly different interpretation of some of the most obscure corner cases. Unfortunately, these discrepancies include very pervasive features, such as *templates* and the *standard template library* (STL).

The run-time environment necessary to support all C++ features can be heavy. For example, supporting exception handling and run-time type identification (RTTI)

```
#include <iostream>
using namespace std;
class cmpx {
private:
  int r, i;
public:
  cmpx () { this->r = this->i = 0; }
  cmpx (int x, int y) { this->r = x; this->i = y; }
  cmpx operator+= (const cmpx& c) {
      this->r += c.r; this->i += c.i; return *this;
  }
  cmpx operator* (const cmpx& c) const {
      return cmpx ( this->r * c.r - this->i * c.i,
                    this->r * c.i + this->i * c.r);
  }
  friend ostream& operator<< (ostream& os, const cmpx& c) {
      os << "(" << c.r<< "," << c.i << ")"; return os;
  }
};

void
fircx(const cmpx x[], const cmpx h[], cmpx y[], int N, int M)
{
    for(int i = N; i < M; ++i) {
        cmpx t (0,0);
        for(int j = 0; j < N; ++j)
            t += h[j] * x[i-j];
        y[i] = t;
    }
}
cmpx in[] = {
    cmpx(0,0), cmpx(0,0), cmpx(0,0), cmpx(0,0),  // padding
    cmpx(1,0), cmpx(2,1), cmpx(3,0), cmpx(4,1), cmpx (5,0),
    cmpx(6,1), cmpx(7,0), cmpx(8,1), cmpx(9,0), cmpx (10,1)
};

cmpx cf[] = { cmpx(1,0), cmpx(-2,0), cmpx(3,0), cmpx (-4,0) };

cmpx out[14];

int
main(int argc, char arg[])
{
    fircx(in, cf, out, 4, 14);

    for (int i = 4; i < 14; ++i)
        cout << out[i] << " ";
    cout << endl;
}
```

FIGURE 10.2 Example of a *complex FIR* in C++. Far from using all the expressiveness of C++, here we just focus on the object-oriented concepts of *encapsulation*. For example, the operations on complex numbers can be naturally represented by a *class* object (which is now also part of the standard template library, STL). This code also uses *operator overloading* to enable developers to use the same addition ("+") and multiplication ("*") syntax for improved readability.[1] C++ programmers rely to a much larger extent on the compiler to do the right optimizations (such as *inlining*, in this particular example) so that performance is not compromised.

---

1. Operator overloading is considered harmful by a substantial set of programmers, and can be used to make code virtually incomprehensible. Use it judiciously.

may have serious run-time consequences (abusing templates may cause significant code growth). In addition to being computationally demanding, the C++ run-time environment can be deceptive to nonexpert programmers and seemingly innocuous statements may cause the compiler to generate large amounts of code.

The possibility of linking in code written in C (through the *extern "C"* scope declaration) and the presence of *casts* and *pointer arithmetic* are really Trojan horses within C++, and weaken the entire type-safe model. Sometimes, there is a great temptation to circumvent a compiler error by throwing in a *cast* operator, and inexperienced C++ developers can be very damaging to the overall software engineering structure of a project.

Embedded C++

As an attempt to make C++ more palatable to embedded developers, a language subset (called *embedded C++* or *eC++*) has been recently put forward as a proposed standard. The goal of embedded C++ is to provide embedded systems programmers with a subset of C++ that is easy for the average C programmer to understand and use. The idea is that embedded C++ is not a language, and should offer upward compatibility with the full version of C++ and retain the major advantages of C++. The embedded C++ committee established the guidelines for the subset aimed at keeping the specification simple and at the same time preserving the object-oriented features of the language. The three major guidelines for embedded C++ can be summarized as follows:

1. Control the amount of allocated memory.

2. Avoid unpredictable behavior.

3. Make the code ROM compatible.

To give the reader a better idea of the type of constraints one has to face in the development of an embedded system, we briefly present part of the embedded C++ specifications.

- *Exception handling* is not allowed. The C++ exception-handling mechanism requires compiler support, run-time support, and additional data structures. In addition, C++ requires one to invoke all destructors of the automatic objects in a *try* block when an exception is caught. This makes it practically impossible to estimate the interrupt response time, and endangers the real-time properties of the program.

- *Templates* are not allowed. This is probably the heaviest restriction from the point of view of loss of functionality. For example, not allowing templates prevents the use of the standard template library (STL). The primary reason to prevent the use of templates is the observation that an abuse of templates might cause unexpected code expansion. Other minor disadvantages include a longer compilation time, the need for link-level support, and a steep learning curve to understand how to use them efficiently.

- *Run-time type identification* (RTTI) is not allowed. RTTI causes a potentially large memory overhead to store all the information necessary to execute *dynamic_cast* operators for polymorphic classes.

- The *mutable* specifier is not allowed. This restriction allows the compiler/linker to allocate *const* objects in ROM (using *mutable* enables the compiler to change the *const* properties of class members).

- *Multiple inheritance* is not allowed. Even experienced programmers find multiple inheritance to be difficult to use. For the sake of simplicity the committee decided against this feature, although no real implementation barriers stand in its way.

- *Namespaces* and new-style casts (*const_cast*, *static_cast*, *reinterpret_cast*) are not allowed. Like multiple inheritance, there is nothing fundamentally wrong or heavy with the use of namespaces or new-style casts. This restriction is probably a simple recognition of the *de facto* situation that few embedded compilers today support these features.

Wide acceptance of embedded C++ is at risk today. Not many vendors support it, strictly speaking it is not a language specification, and compiler support for full C++ is constantly improving. As more and more compilers support ANSI/ISO C++ (and start doing a good job of optimizing it), the relevance of standardizing an embedded subset diminishes significantly.

However, we think that the work behind embedded C++ is valuable, as it identifies potential language perils that embedded developers should try to avoid. Learning the rationale behind embedded C++ is important, particularly when using a full C++ compiler (the temptation to use all available features is great, and performance is at risk). Using the Embedded C++ restrictions as development guidelines is certainly important, and it could greatly improve the chances of success of C++ in the embedded domain.

10.1.4 Matlab

Matlab (and similar systems, such as open-source *Octave*) defines a high-level integrated environment for developing scientific algorithms, applying them to discrete and continuous signals (or other various collections of data) and visualizing the results. Unlike a general-purpose programming language, *Matlab* was designed to perform numerical computation, and thus it is not easy to apply it to all possible uses. Strictly speaking, the language used to program *Matlab* includes enough control flow support (loops, conditionals, and so on) and I/O primitives to be able to run any program. However, Matlab includes several utilities for solving linear algebra problems and nonlinear equations, integrating functions, manipulating polynomials, and solving differential equations.

Users can write their own functions through the built-in language or by linking in C/C++ modules compiled to target a specific API. Matlab includes a vector-oriented language that easily manipulates vectors and matrices, as well as a set of commonly used vector/matrix operators.

The most common use of Matlab is still in the modeling phase and early development stages, for which it is often an invaluable tool for nailing down the specific algorithms and algorithm parameters for anything that involves numerical computation. For example, finding the right parameters of all types of digital filters—FIR, IIR, convolution, and so on) is the perfect task for Matlab. Some Matlab enthusiasts advocate its use well beyond modeling, and indeed some have successfully applied it in creating production software. However, vendor support is limited, only a few tools are available, debugging is weak, and—as we said—the language is not really a general-purpose tool.

Ideally, tools such as Matlab should be used more aggressively in the development of embedded software (it could help both developers and compiler writers). Matlab helps in abstracting away from the specific implementation and language idiosyncrasies and in focusing on the algorithms themselves. Matlab is also an almost-ideal compiler target (except for dynamically sized arrays), in that vectors and matrices exist as first-class citizens and memory dependences are easy to understand.

We feel that until Matlab gains wider commercial acceptance, and the tool itself matures, it will have a difficult time becoming a widely accepted language in the embedded community, despite its potential. Figure 10.3 shows an example of *Matlab* programming for a simple FIR algorithm.

```
function y = fir(x,h)

    hr = fliplr (h)
    n = size(h) (2)
    m = size(x) (2)
    for i = n : m
        y(i) = dot(hr, x(i - n + 1 : i))
    endfor

endfunction

in = [ 0 0 0 0 1+0i 2+1i 3+0i 4+1i 5+0i 6+1i 7+0i 8+1i 9+0i 10+1i ]

cf = [ 1+0i -2+0i 3+0i -4+0i ]

out = fir(in, cf)
```

FIGURE 10.3 Example of a *complex FIR* in Matlab. Unlike a general-purpose programming language such as C, C++, or Java, Matlab already contains an extensive set of primitives and libraries for manipulating vectors and matrices. In the example, the built-in *dot()* function generates a dot-product of two arrays (sum of element-by-element product) and the *fliplr()* function reverses an array. Also note the various array notations for selecting sections of the vectors, and that arrays are automatically sized. In terms of simplicity, this is obviously the best way to write code. Unfortunately, its flexibility is limited, as are its capabilities to be connected to the rest of the system code. Despite these disadvantages, high-level domain-specific programming languages have their niche and are popular among small communities of developers.

10.1.5 Embedded Java

Using Sun's terminology, Java is a simple, architecture-neutral, object-oriented, portable, distributed, interpreted, multithreaded, robust, dynamic, and secure programming language. In reality, there is much more to Java than the language itself, and the developer community commonly uses the word *Java* to refer to an entire platform consisting of the *language*, the *virtual machine*, and the collection of *library APIs*.

The execution model of the Java language (which we will not cover in any detail) is a significant departure from the more traditional C and C++. Java is designed to be compiled to an architecture-neutral intermediate representation (called *Java ByteCode*), executed by a virtual machine (the *Java Virtual Machine*, or *JVM*) running on the target system. From a high-level perspective, if developers can completely abstract their code from the features of the target machines Java achieves the ultimate *"write once, run anywhere"* dream. Note that the fact that Java was originally intended to be interpreted does not prevent one from compiling ByteCode for performance. Given the dynamic loading nature of Java, we can however distinguish between two compilation approaches. *Just-in-time* (JIT) compilers dynamically compile ByteCode methods as they are loaded or executed on the target. *Ahead-of-time* (AOT) compilers work with a more traditional paradigm and precompile ByteCode methods before they reach the execution target. A variety of Java compilers from many vendors and for many platforms is available today.

The *Java API* is a fairly extensive library of reusable components that provides a large variety of functionalities, from basic libraries such as string manipulation and I/O to advanced interfaces such as GUIs and drawing packages. Figure 10.4 shows a Java version of the simple FIR example.

The Allure of Embedded Java

The previous description might make you think that Java might be the ideal language for embedded systems. If it did, you are far from alone in your thinking. Many of Java's features make it particularly appealing for embedded environments (see Figure 10.5).

First, we need to draw a big distinction between Java ByteCode as a supported language for end users of an embedded system and Java as the development environment for embedded system firmware. There are few doubts that any interactive embedded system in the future will support Java. For example, anything with a browser is likely to include a JVM to be able to run web Java *applets*, and most new cellular phones can run downloadable Java programs. On the other hand, the use of Java to develop embedded systems is a much more interesting subject.

Many of Java's features address the concerns we expressed in the previous sections about C and C++. In a nutshell, Java preserves much of the most valuable C++ object-oriented paradigms and removes many of the C legacy features that compromise C++'s effectiveness.

- *Target independence* makes software reuse possible and allows developers to switch easily between different platforms and CPUs.

- *Automatic memory management* is programmer's heaven. There is no need to worry about forgetting to free up objects and reclaim memory, in that the system

```
import java.io.PrintStream;

class cmpx {
     private int r, i;
     public cmpx() { this.r = this.i = 0; }
     public cmpx(int x, int y) { this.r = x; this.i = y; }
     public cmpx add (cmpx c2) {
        return new cmpx(this.r + c2.r, this.i + c2.i);
     }
     public cmpx mul (cmpx c2) {
        return new cmpx (this.r * c2.r - this.i * c2.i,
                         this.r * c2.i + this.i * c2.r);
     }
     public void print() {
        System.out.print("(" + this.r + "," + this.i + ")");
     }
};

public abstract class fir_j {

     static void fircx (cmpx x[], cmpx h[], cmpx y[], int N, int M)
     {
        for(int i = N; i < M; ++i) {
           cmpx t = new cmpx(0,0);
           for(int j = 0;  j < N; ++j)
               t = t.add(h[j].mul(x[i-j]));
           y[i] = t;
        }
     }

     public static void main(String args[])
     {
        cmpx[] in = {
           new cmpx(0,0), new cmpx(0,0), new cmpx(0,0), new cmpx(0,0),
           new cmpx(1,0), new cmpx(2,1), new cmpx(3,0), new cmpx(4,1),
           new cmpx(5,0), new cmpx(6,1), new cmpx(7,0), new cmpx(8,1),
           new cmpx(9,0), new cmpx(10,1)
        };
        cmpx[] cf = {
           new cmpx(1,0), new cmpx(-2,0), new cmpx(3,0), new cmpx(-4,0)
        };
        cmpx out[] = new cmpx[14];

        fircx (in,cf,out,4,14);

        for(int i = 4; i < 14; ++i) {
           out [i].print();
           System.out.print(" ");
        }
        System.out.println("");
     }
}
```

FIGURE 10.4 Example of a *complex FIR* in Java. Much like C++, Java stresses object orientation and encapsulation in classes, as it is evident from the *cmpx* class to represent the basic functionality of *complex* manipulation. Unlike C++, Java does not have the "syntactic sugar" of operator overloading, and thus we use *mul* and *add* methods to express operations. In Java, everything is dynamic, and thus the emphasis on the compiler capabilities to achieve performance is even stronger.

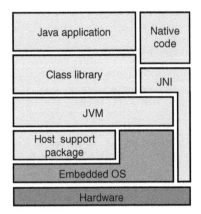

FIGURE 10.5 A typical software stack for an embedded Java application. We can distinguish three layers: application, Java infrastructure, and embedded operating system. Note that real-world Java systems usually have to compromise the architecture-neutral purity of the language by allowing native code (for example, written in C and compiled for the target) to be directly linked to a Java application. This is done through the Java-Native Interface (JNI), an API through which we can call native methods. Given the variety of embedded systems, the role of the embedded OS and the JVM porting layer is also much more invasive, as we discuss in the text.

does it for you. This is not free (as we point out later), but it certainly enhances productivity.

- *Type safety* is a huge step forward, making large classes of bugs impossible to write. Examples include overstepping array bounds (the basis of many security bugs), many pointer-related bugs, and holes created by type-casting.

- *Abolishing pointers* (which is arguably part of type safety, but deserves its own point) makes programs much safer and easier to debug, eliminates one of the most common causes of memory leaks, and eliminates null pointer crashes.

- *Single inheritance* simplifies the class hierarchy, but restricts code reuse to a single parent class. In place of multiple inheritance, Java supports *interfaces*, which allow a class to adopt consistent sets of methods in a type-checked manner.

- *Dynamic loading* of methods simplifies the entire area of firmware patching.

- *Built-in security* (in the form of ByteCode verification) allows the *sandboxing* of applications (i.e., allowing them to run in protected spaces) to make them more robust in environments that demand high safety.

Java offerings in the embedded domain have proliferated in the last few years, and several embedded developers are embracing Java with a mix of enthusiasm and concern. As we saw, there are many reasons an embedded system company should consider Java today. However, not all that glitters is gold.

Embedded Java: The Dark Side

Unfortunately, real life weakens many of Java's advantages in the embedded domain.

- *Portability*: "Write once, run anywhere" is certainly a very enticing slogan, but people often forget the implications of the "run anywhere" part. Whereas a few players dominate the desktop and server markets, the embedded world is still fragmented across a dozen different processor manufacturers with incompatible ISAs. In this context, "run anywhere" really means "port the JVM anywhere." Porting a JVM to a new platform is certainly not an undertaking people embrace lightly, and if performance matters, it will take a long time for a port to mature. When you multiply the number of embedded ISAs by the number of slightly incompatible processor variations, and by the number of embedded OSs, what you get in terms of development effort easily dwarfs the productivity advantages Java promises. Perhaps a better description would be "run once, write everywhere?"

- *System requirements*: Java is certainly not light-handed on the overall hardware and system. The interpreted nature of the language requires very fast CPUs to achieve barely tolerable performance. A typical JVM footprint easily extends into the 500KB to 1MB range; efficient implementation of many Java features requires a full-fledged OS with virtual memory support; and so on. For a large class of embedded systems, meeting these requirements is simply unthinkable.

- *Low-level programming*: Certain low-level operations, such as access to memory-mapped control registers, cannot be expressed in Java. This is a consequence of the gains in type safety and abolishing pointers (nothing comes for free). The Java Native Interfaces (JNI) allow Java code to call code written in C or assembly, providing a workaround for this case.

- *Real-time issue 1, garbage collection*: Automatic memory management does not come for free. Although desktop garbage collectors have made significant advances in the last decade (especially in the area of *concurrent* collectors, which run as separate threads), seamless concurrent garbage collection remains an open issue.

- *Real-time issue 2, thread management*: The scheduling mechanism in Java needs to be extended for Java to support acceptable thread scheduling. In particular, it needs features such as preemption, priority-based synchronization of serial resources (to handle priority inversion), handling of asynchronous events, fast asynchronous transfer of control, and safe thread termination. Recently, the *Real-Time for Java Expert Group* has come up with a set of recommendations for these (and more) extensions that would make Java more acceptable in a real-time system environment, but this has not yet been supported in the standard.

- *Licensing and market adaptation*: Finally, but not less important, are a set of business considerations around the use of embedded Java. Java was originally designed for a desktop environment, and its licensing scheme reflects that.

The combination of large up-front licensing fees, significant per-part royalties, and a lack of flexibility in choice of providers can be extremely unappealing for the embedded market.

This has led to the emergence of other players beyond Sun's Java in the embedded space. Competition is addressing some of the previously cited concerns. Paradoxically, the fragmentation of Java offerings seems to be beneficial for the overall success of embedded Java. For example, Java efforts geared toward the embedded domain are removing some of the technical barriers. JVM ports to microcontrollers exist, compact JVM-compatible platforms are lowering code requirements to the 50 to 200K range, and open-source environments are making Java environments more portable and affordable.

10.1.6 C Extensions for Digital Signal Processing

Although C found large acceptance in the microcontroller programming world, it encountered much greater resistance in the DSP world, in which many developers still write entire applications in assembly language code. The problem is that C does not have the support required to take advantage of many of the hardware structures in DSP processors, such as hardware looping, array addressing, and special operations. For these reasons, the last decade witnessed a handful of proposals to extend the standard C language to support embedded and DSP specific features.

In 1990, Waddington and Leary (from Analog Devices) proposed a new set of language extensions called *DSP/C*, loosely based on the NCEG (Numeric C Extension Group) recommendations. The proposed language is built around a fairly extensive set of new features, including matrix referencing, operator extensions, fixed-point data types, restricted pointers, variable-dimension local arrays, and math extensions. In 1998, another set of extensions was proposed by ACE (*Associated Compiler Experts*, a Dutch compiler company). These extensions were limited to fixed-point data types, memory spaces, accumulator types, and related functionalities.

So far, few of these extensions, such as *restricted pointers*, have made it into the official ISO/ANSO C standard (C99), and to date we are aware of only two production compilers (ACE CoSy and Analog Devices) that support them. In March 2004, the ISO/IEC committee standardized (TR-18037) more embedded-specific extensions. How widely they will be adopted still remains an open question. Regardless of the fate of this specific set of extensions, we present some of the features they introduce, in that they represent the typical class of problems faced by any domain-specific language support.

Restricted Pointers

The concept of *restricted pointers* first appeared as a DSP-specific C extension, and has since been included in the "official" language as part of the C99 ISO/ANSI standard. The idea behind *restricted* pointers comes from the observation that C compilers are usually helpless when they attempt to *disambiguate* pointer-based memory accesses.

Flame: Why Isn't C99 Popular?

The new International Standards Organization standard for C (ISO/IEC 9899:1999), known as C99 (and C9x before finalization), was publicly released in 1999. It offers a number of useful features, including support for complex arithmetic, type declarations that specify exact-sized or minimum-sized or "fast" representations, structure literals, variable-length arrays, and improved support for pointer alias analysis. However, adoption has been much slower than for the previous (ANSI X3.159, or C89) C standard.

So why has adoption of C99 taken so long? As of this writing, the SGI MIPSpro compiler, Sun Solaris compiler, and HP Tru64 UNIX Compaq C compiler report partial implementation of the new standard, and *gcc* appears to be the furthest along. Microsoft's web site contains no mention whatsoever of C99. Why are so few compliant compilers available? We think there are two main reasons: differences in the marketplace and the perceived benefits of compliance.

The late 1980s were the height of the workstation wars, and having an ANSI C-compliant compiler could be turned into a competitive and marketing advantage (although Sun charged extra at the time for its ANSI-compliant compiler). Every work-station vendor was building its own C compiler anyway, and thus ANSI compliance was one of a list of required features. Today, the major marketplace battle is between portable programming platforms such as Java and .NET and their corporate sponsors, Sun and Microsoft, respectively. Sun grudgingly admits that Java is not suitable as a "low-level" or "systems programming" language and provides support for "native code" (e.g., C) as a hedge. Microsoft includes C among a long list of languages supported by the .NET platform. Neither has a direct incentive to improve C.

C99 also provides a smaller benefit to compliance than ANSI C did. Before the ANSI standard, C was balkanized, with as many different implementations as there were compil-ers (although the K&R variant provided a de facto standard). Porting C programs from one system to another was fraught with peril. ANSI compliance removed these issues. It pro-vided a core, largely portable, but above all a usable version of C that was actually better for software engineering purposes than its predecessors (e.g., prototypes, and with them some forms of function type checking, made their appearance in ANSI C). With the ANSI standard in place, developers could write to the standard and believe that their programs would be widely portable. Although C99 provides features that are extremely valuable to some communities (complex arithmetic for numericists; pointer alias analysis for compiler writers), it lacks a broad compelling reason for adoption.

At the same time, pointer usage is ubiquitous, and many C front ends simply convert array accesses to the equivalent pointer-based format.

Compiler research has attacked the memory aliasing problem for the last two decades, with great improvements, but still not enough to efficiently address the needs of the most common programming practices. To be effective, memory alias analysis has to be *interprocedural*, and possibly operate on the entire program (including libraries).

This often yields unacceptable compilation times (except for very small programs), and frequently imposes a significant management overhead to ensure that interprocedural information (usually kept in auxiliary files) is up to date with respect to source files. Note that using "stale" interprocedural alias information can be the cause of very subtle bugs, and these can be a nightmare to nail down.

This discouraging scenario is what triggered the idea of *restricting* a pointer target to work around the issue of compiler maturity. The paradox is that compilers spend a lot of energy in analyzing pointer accesses, but in many cases the programmer can tell you at a first glance that certain pointers will never overlap. Consider the following C example of a simple vector add.

```
void
vadd(const int *px, const int *py, int *pz, int N)
{
    int i;
    for (i = 0; i < N; ++i)
    *pz++ = *px++ + *py++;
}
```

Unless the compiler knows about all the places vadd() is called from, C semantics tell you that there is no way to know whether pointers px, py, and pz, point to nonoverlapping memory areas.[2] For example, without additional information, the compiler cannot possibly move any read based off px or py above any preceding writes based off pz. When programmers know that vadd() can only be called with different nonoverlapping arrays, they can use the *restrict* keyword to communicate this to the compiler. The function declaration of the previous example changes as follows

```
void
vadd(const int * restrict px,
        const int * restrict py,
        int * restrict pz, int N)
```

The *restrict* keyword asserts to the compiler that the three pointers point to nonoverlapping memory regions, and it is safe to assume that accesses based on pointers pointing to *restricted* data types cannot alias. The precise definition of the *restrict* keyword, according to the C99 standard, is as follows.

> *An object that is accessed through a restrict-qualified pointer has a special association with that pointer. This association requires that all accesses to that object use, directly or indirectly, the value of that particular pointer. The intended use of the* restrict *qualifier (like the* register *storage class) is to promote optimization, and deleting all instances of the qualifier from all preprocessing translation units composing a conforming program does not change its meaning.*

---

2. The use of the *const* keyword in C is largely "syntactic sugar," because the property of being *const* can be removed through a *cast* operation. Compilers usually throw away *const* information past the front end, as it is considered unreliable.

Restricted pointers are a powerful means of helping the compiler in disambiguating memory accesses. Note that the analysis phases are still necessary, to understand the relationships among memory accesses derived from the same pointer, but this is where compiler technology is mature and very effective.

As we saw in the previous example, one of the most effective ways of applying the *restrict* keyword is in the function arguments that happen to be pointers. This is a very common case. Often programmers know the context in which they use certain functions, and it is straightforward for them to make these types of assertions.

Finally, use *restrict* carefully. If used incorrectly, it can lead to a program whose behavior is different than expected. Debugging a wrong pointer assertion can consume much time.

Fixed-point Data Types

Many embedded and DSP applications filter digitized analog signals. For all of these applications, the most common data type is the *fixed-point* data type, which is not supported in C. Although it is possible to express fixed-point algorithms in C, the lack of a native data type forces programmers to use very obfuscated idioms that throw compilers into utter confusion, and practically prevent any chance of using the hardware support the DSP engineers spent so many years to build into their processors.

To understand fixed-point data types, we can contrast them against the more familiar concept of floating point. Floating-point data types represent a subset of real values characterized by a sign, a mantissa, and an exponent, as in scientific notation. Floating-point format standards (such as the IEEE formats) define a set of characterizing parameters that specify the size of the container, the size and position of the exponent, the sign, and the mantissa. Compilers must segregate floating-point types and operators so that they can be mapped to hardware floating-point operations. Hardware support for floating point usually implements the basic operations for a limited number of formats (such as 32-bit IEEE single precision, or 64-bit IEEE double precision), wherein sizes and positions of sign, exponent, and mantissa are fixed by the standard.

Fixed-point data types are different. They are characterized by *sign* and *precision* (number of bits in the fixed-point value), but the position of the radix point is implicitly defined outside the format representation. In other words, the position of the radix point can be located anywhere before, within, or after the bits that comprise the value. Different processors implement different variations of fixed-point operations, and it is practically impossible to define a set of extensions that can cover them all. First when using fixed point we need to know the place of the radix point, and the following are a few interesting cases.

- Radix point immediately to the right of the least significant bit (LSB): this is the standard integer data type.

- Radix point is located further to the right of the LSB: this represents large and imprecise integer values and is not particularly interesting.

```
         A    B

         C    D
       ─────────────
         DA   DB

    CA   CB
    ─────────────
    CA   DA+CB  DB
```

FIGURE 10.6 **Schematic representation of a multiplication, showing partial products and the sums (without carries) of the eventual product.** A, B, C, and D represent "words" in the multiplication (they might be digits in elementary school arithmetic or sub-words in a hardware diagram). For a standard integer multiplication, the result will be R(DA+CB)+DB, where R is the number base of the computation. For a fixed-point multiplication, the desired value is often CA+(DA+CB)/R, instead.

- Radix point immediately to the left of the most significant bit (MSB): this represents values in the $[-1, 1)$ interval (signed), or in the $[0, 1)$ interval (unsigned), and is the most commonly supported format.

- Radix point somewhere between MSB and LSB: this represents values with an integral and a fractional part, and is sometimes supported.

Operations on fixed-point values must also specify what happens to the LSBs on a right shift and what happens to the MSBs on an overflow. In case of overflow, the standard integer behavior (*wraparound mode*) is usually not acceptable, and most implementations assign the maximum representable value to the result (this is *saturation mode*, using saturating arithmetic).

Fixed-point *addition* can be performed in a standard integer unit, provided the radix points of the addends are in the same position. Otherwise, the values must first be shifted to align the radix points. On the other hand, fixed-point *multiplication* returns the MSBs of the product of the multiplicands. A standard integer multiplier returns only the LSBs of the result, discarding the rest. Consequently, extra operations are necessary to support fixed-point multiplication on standard hardware. Figure 10.6 depicts the differences between standard and fixed-point multiplication.

It is straightforward for a compiler to enforce the rules to transform a data type once that data type is established and propagated through the compiler type system. This is the reason all proposals to extend C to cover fixed data types imply the creation of new basic data types. For example, DSP-C proposes the addition of two type qualifiers (_fixed and _accum) to be combined with standard C types to generate fixed-point types such as

```
signed _fixed x;   /* range is [-1.0, 1.0) */
unsigned _fixed x;  /* range is [0.0, 1.0) */
signed _accum x;   /* range is [-F, F); F is #bits */
unsigned _accum x;  /* range is [0.0, F) */
```

In general, the value of a _fixed value x, of size *n* and scale *s*, is

$$\text{signed:} \quad x = 2^{-s}\left(-2^{n-1}b_{n-1} + \sum_{i=0}^{n-2} 2^i b_i\right) \qquad \text{unsigned:} \quad x = 2^{-s}\sum_{i=0}^{n-1} 2^i b_i.$$

Similar equations can be derived for an _accum value. For example, with an extension of 8 bits, the signed _accum type can represent values in the range $[-256, 255]$. In addition, fixed types can be defined as being saturated with the _sat qualifier, such as

```
_sat signed _fixed x;
_sat unsigned _fixed x;
_sat signed _accum x;
_sat unsigned _accum x;
```

The _sat qualifier determines whether arithmetic operators within expressions have to saturate (default is wraparound). For example:

```
_sat unsigned _fixed x = 0.75;
_sat unsigned _fixed y = x + x; /* y = 1.0 */
```

Circular Arrays

The circular qualifier (circ) specifies that array subscripting or pointer addressing should perform modulo address arithmetic. This means that arithmetic on such an object cannot run out of the array's boundaries but must wrap around the beginning of the circular memory region.

Circular buffers are used in two important applications: producer-consumer communication and delay lines. In the producer-consumer case, the producer process places data into the circular buffer and the consumer process takes it out (this case also covers the use of circular buffers for temporary storage, in which case producer and consumer are not separate processes). Delay lines are a more common example in the embedded domain, and are used for a variety of filtering functions. The advantage of circular buffers is that they alleviate the need to shift the data samples in the delay line. For instance, we can write the function that produces the output of an *N*-tap FIR filter (with coefficients in coeff[...] and input data in samples[...]) through the *circ* qualifier by declaring the input buffer (and the accessing pointer) with a *circ* type, so that the compiler knows that it has to emit special wraparound code for pointer arithmetic, or use native hardware support when available.

```
circ int samples[N]; // circular buffer (delay line)
int coeffs[N];
int FIR_sample(int n)
{
    circ int *pb = samples; // circular pointer
    int i, t = 0;
```

```
      pb += n; // start from the end
      for (i = 0; i < N; ++i, --pb) { // pb wraps around
         t += *pb * coeff[i];
      }
      return t;
   }
```

Matrix Referencing and Operators

Most DSP algorithms manipulate matrices and vectors, and thus it would seem natural to have a way to express these without using the traditional sequential C semantics. DSP/C introduces a set of notations to reference arrays and operate on them. This enables compilers to apply the extensive set of matrix-oriented optimizations typical of the FORTRAN domain of numeric computation, which are usually ruled out by the more permissive semantics of C constructs.

These notations include ways to address part of a vector, or wildcards to address an entire vector, as well as operators for vector sum, vector product, dot product, and auto-correlation. The following are a few examples.

```
a[1:100:2] = 2.5 * b[1:100:2]
/* array notation [start:stop:stride] */
a[~] = 2.6 * b[~] /* array wildcard */
x = a[~] @. b[~] /* dot product */
```

Although these notations provide a compact way of expressing vector-based algorithms, we feel they may be going one step too far away from the spirit of C. As compiler technology matures, it is conceivable that compilers will be able to achieve similar levels of optimization even from standard C, or from standard C with much simpler annotations (such as *restricted pointers*). In this case, the need for such an extensive set of extensions is not clear. While we do believe that there may be niche applications for which such a language would be extremely useful, we remain skeptical about its general applicability.

10.1.7 Pragmas, Intrinsics, and Inline Assembly Language Code

Changing syntax is not the only way to extend the functionality of a language. We are aware of at least three other methods: the use of *compiler pragmas*, *compiler intrinsics*, and *inline assembly language* sections.

Compiler Pragmas and Type Annotations

Pragmas are ways to provide directives and hints to a compiler, to express properties, or to implement functionality that either contradicts or it is not available in the C language. The "canonical" way to express a compile pragma is through the *#pragma* syntax, as in the following example. Here, we override the C rules for alignment of structures.

```
#pragma(pack) /* pack the struct into 5B, not 8B */
typedef struct {char a; int b;} packed_struct;
```

Some developers object to the use of pragmas, largely because the #*pragma* syntax makes it incompatible with the C preprocessor (you cannot generate a #*pragma* from a macro) and because the semantics of a specific #*pragma* are implementation specific. Thus, two different compilers may interpret the same directive in completely different ways, leading to incompatible code. However, pragmas are very powerful and rather common in the embedded environment, in which we often need to specify "special" functions the C language does not support. An alternative to pragmas is the use of *type attributes*, advocated by the *gcc* community. The following code expresses the same packing directive of the previous example with the __*attribute()* syntax.

```
typedef struct {
    char a;
    int b __attribute__((packed));
} packed_struct;
```

Finally, we observe that the use of target annotations (whether pragmas or attributes) is always preferable to the alternative of using a global *unsafe* optimization flag. For example, we could use a global flag to override some of the language semantics, and we could tell the compiler properties such as "pointer arguments never alias." This practice is error prone and should be discouraged. Using *unsafe* flags requires developers to keep the compiler invocation in sync with the programming style of a module, and may expose bugs that are very difficult to track down and only manifest with certain combinations of *makefile* directives.

Assembler Inserts and Intrinsics

In the embedded domain, it used to be that developers had to write large portions of the application in assembly language code. With the emergence of languages such as C and advances in compiler technology, this has almost disappeared. However, developers still want to retain this functionality, and this is why most compilers support some way of inserting sections of assembly language code within a high-level language source. There are two ways in which we can instruct a compiler to directly emit an instruction.

Assembler sections are implemented through a directive that includes a totally opaque section of assembler instructions. In this case the compiler's only choice is to textually emit the characters the user inserted into the assembly language stream. The user is responsible for observing calling conventions, placing and retrieving arguments and values in the right registers, obeying scheduling and resource allocation rules, and applying the right register allocation policy. We believe that in a modern development toolchain assembler sections should (and could) be avoided at all costs. The following example shows an assembly language section of VEX instructions[3] implementing a loop with 64-bit additions.

```
typedef struct { int hi, lo; } int64;
void add64(int64 *out, int64 *a, int64 *b)
{
  __asm_section__("
      ldw $r10 = 0[$r3]
    ;;
      ldw $r11 = 4[$r3]
    ;;
      ldw $r20 = 0[$r4]
    ;;
      ldw $r21 = 4[$r4]
      mtb $b0, 0
    ;;
      addcg $r30, $b1 = $r10, $r20, $b0
    ;;
      addcg $r31, $b2 = $r11, $r21, $b1
    ;;
      stw 0[$r2] = $r30;
    ;;
      stw 4[$r2] = $r31;
    ;;
  ");
}
```

In this example, the compiler has no choice but to emit the code sequence without any modification (some compilers enable a limited form of parameter passing to *asm* sections). Latencies, machine width, and resource restrictions are all hardwired in the assembly language code, and the code is totally incompatible with any changes in the implementation of the target processor.

Compiler intrinsics implement (through the syntax of a C function call) a special functionality the compiler knows how to map into a particular sequence of assembler instructions. Unlike assembler sections, intrinsics do not specify machine-dependent features in addition to the operation itself, and thus users can ignore scheduling and register allocation issues (these are left to the compiler). The compiler can also apply some of the standard optimization passes (such as dead code removal, copy propagation, and constant propagation) if the right semantics are provided. For example, intrinsics are commonly used to invoke micro-SIMD extensions. The following code shows the same functionality of the previous example (64-bit add) written with intrinsics.

---

3. Not implemented in the VEX compiler.

```
# define __ADDCG(sum,cout, a,b,cin) { \
  struct {int t1, t2;} r; \
  r = __asm(__ADDCG __,a,b,cin); \
  sum = r.t1; cout = r.t2; \
}


void add64(int64 *out, int64 *a, int64 *b)
{
   int64 t1, t2;
   t1 = __asm(__ADDCG__,a->lo,b->lo,0);
   t2 = __asm(__ADDCG__,a->hi,b->hi,t1->hi);
   out->lo = t1->lo;
   out->hi = t2->hi;
}
```

With this method, the assembler functionality is completely isolated, and we can still use data structures, control flow, and all the other facilities of the C language. The compiler can apply standard optimizations (such as inlining), as well as scheduling and register allocation passes. Finally, the code is much easier to understand, is easier to maintain, and can be used with many different machine implementations.

10.2 Performance, Benchmarking, and Tuning

The previous section described tools that enable the programmer to override the compiler where the compiler's decisions are not acceptable for either performance or expressiveness. This is just one of the several possible adjustments that are part of a performance optimization phase, together with various forms of code restructuring and tuning of the time-consuming parts of an application. In this section we cover some of the basic aspects of performance analysis and optimization at the application level, starting from methodology aspects through the importance of profiling and down to some of the "tricks" that are most effective in improving the efficiency of ILP embedded processors. In most of the examples the proposed techniques are simply a rehash of good software engineering practices (sadly, too often ignored) or suggestions on how to overcome the limitations of programming languages (such as C) that obfuscate what is obvious to the programmer. Nonetheless, we believe this to be a very important area whose principles, if correctly understood and applied, can lead to tremendous gains in productivity and savings.

10.2.1 Importance and Methodology

It is common practice in the embedded software world to leave performance as the responsibility of the hardware (and the hardware design team). For embedded applications of growing complexity, in which software engineers are spoiled by Moore's law, the temptation to "just get a faster processor" is big. Often, performance analysis and tuning are left as the last stages of software development (just before quality control), and in many cases they get squeezed out because of delays, time-to-market pressure, and shifting milestones in the project schedule. As a consequence, the computing capability of the hardware often needs to be oversized (with inevitable higher costs), even in cases for which a simple software optimization pass could yield large factors of improvement. As you will see, we disagree strongly with the current practice. The best software teams in the industry keep performance analysis as a first-class metric during the development process.

One of the most frustrating aspects of dealing with industrial development of embedded software is that very few people quantitatively analyze where time is spent in the application under development. Instead, many programmers insist that they "just know" where their code spends its time. Continuous use of profiling tools and performance tracking is still not a widespread practice, and — as we described — only relegated to the "tuning" phase (if time allows).

The first step for a successful performance strategy requires a disciplined use of profiling, a careful development of performance inputs (which are different from defect coverage inputs), and the integration of performance tracking with the defect tracking system. Optimizing every line of code in a large application is neither practical nor effective. Profiling guides developers to the code sections that require more attention, just as profiling is what drives the compiler to selectively increase the optimization effort where needed. The guidelines presented in the sections to follow assume that developers know what program segments are more important to target metrics (e.g., speed, code size, power dissipation, or a combination of these). When profiling information (or a good back-of-the-envelope estimate) is available, what we present (which is a very reduced subset of a large portfolio of tuning techniques) demonstrates the effectiveness and importance of a performance optimization phase.

10.2.2 Tuning an Application for Performance

The most important step for performance tuning is profiling. It is also very valuable, not to mention a good engineering practice, to have an approximate idea (back-of-the-envelope) of where time is spent (based on coarse-grain considerations). Desirable information includes application-specific metrics (e.g., in a video application, quantities such as the number of pixels per frame, the number of frames per second, the amount of computation per frame) and technology-specific metrics (e.g., in a microprocessor-based system, memory bandwidth, bus bandwidth, processor speed). Matching profiles with back-of-the-envelope computation is always very important, and in many cases can be the cause of big surprises.

Profiling

Profiling can be tricky, and in some cases explicit insertion of timer calls can be necessary to gain a good picture of the execution. This happens for example when the code is threaded, includes exception handling, or has any type of control flow that escapes what can be expressed in the language (e.g., *setjmp/longjmp* constructs). Profiling is also much easier in a simulated environment, as we can instrument the simulator itself and achieve a complete overhead-free profile. In a simulated environment we can also profile instruction and data caches, which is extremely difficult on the real hardware. Profiling software running on embedded hardware is significantly more difficult than profiling a desktop computer, in that embedded targets have usually very limited observability hooks and may not include the necessary run-time support to collect and emit profile information. For example, the ability to write a file, which is taken for granted in any computer, may not be available in an embedded device that does not require file system support. In these cases, the embedded target may usually be run in *debug mode* in symbiosis with a host system that can execute the missing system calls.

Finally, profiling is only as good as the input stimuli. Ensuring that the data we use for a profiling run has the right properties is again not a trivial endeavor. As we mentioned, input data for profiling is significantly different from the test data used for verification and defect coverage. When designing a performance data set, we have to account for transient effects, such as "warming up" the caches to filter out cold starts. In addition we have to be careful to capture some of the "step" thresholds of the target architecture. For example, we want to ensure that the data set of our profile input is not reduced below the data cache size (in which case, we may be in for a big surprise when we switch to a "real" input).

Performance Tuning and Compilers

Once we are comfortable that the fraction of time spent in each module represents what we expect, we can start thinking about performance tuning. Note that some of the restructuring that is necessary to get to this stage may not be trivial. Anecdotally, one of the authors remembers an early version of code for an imaging device whereby, because of the recent adoption of C++, the very clean class hierarchy resulted in the execution of a virtual method call for every pixel in the image. Given that the function executed on the pixel was as simple as an *exclusive-or*, the C++ overhead was between two and three orders of magnitude. In this case (which was fixed in later versions, long before becoming a product), an early profiling step would have caught the problem and avoided a much heavier restructuring later. In this particular case, the problem was caused by a combination of inexperienced programmers (which represent the bulk of software developers) and of putting too much faith in the compiler's capability to remove the language overhead.

The relationship between programmers and compilers is often puzzling. On the one hand, many programmers mistrust compilers to generate correct code (many problems attributed to compilers are indeed latent user bugs) or to operate simple optimizations, such as register allocation (many programmers still use the *register* keyword, a hint that is completely ignored by modern compilers). On the other hand, the same developers trust compilers to perform optimizations that are borderline impossible. An example that comes to mind is a developer that used to write *pow(2,x)* to express power of 2 (instead of writing $1 \ll x$), hoping that the compiler would perform the simplification and ignoring the fact that *pow()* is a floating-point mathematical library call with well-defined behavior (including reporting of overflows, underflows, and other floating-point precision conditions).

In summary, *profiling early and often* and *knowing what your compilers can and cannot do* are two of the most important global suggestions every developer of embedded software should keep in mind. Several factors may negatively affect performance: poor code writing style, poor choice of the algorithm, code written to obfuscate ILP, and code that stresses the instruction/data memory hierarchy.

Tuning for performance should, however, not take priority over the other software development considerations. Pushing performance considerations to the extreme is, for example, what caused too many applications to be written in assembly languages for a specific processor, with a tremendous loss in terms of productivity and a heavy legacy burden on the entire product line. A good tradeoff to keep in mind is that any change to the code due to performance considerations should be written in such a way to be *portable across platforms and compilers*. This is almost always possible, though it requires a certain discipline and experience in spotting nonportable features. For example, excessive use of compiler-specific (or target-specific) features should be discouraged. Although this can be tolerable when the changes are language compatible (for example, intrinsic calls in C), they should be avoided when truly incompatible (for example, obscure language extensions). Additionally, maintainability is paramount. A piece of code with excellent performance but that is impossible to understand is only marginally better than the same code written in assembler. Finally, needless to say, programmers should try to *avoid assembly language* at all costs. For most modern microprocessor targets and compilation toolchains, you can express almost every behavior and get very close to maximum performance without using assembly language code.

Developing for ILP Targets

When it comes down to developing applications for ILP microprocessors, it is important to write code so that the compiler can extract the ILP. This is sometimes tricky, as it may conflict with some of the software engineering practices developers have to follow for maintainability, verification, and productivity. Striking the right balance between the two is an art, and it requires experience (and the willingness to throw away entire versions of a program) to be acquired. In general, compilers tend to prefer *simple code*; that is, code that does not use fancy pointer arithmetic, avoids complex call/dispatch constructs, has a clear structure to its memory accesses, and has a clear control flow (nested loops, with well-defined induction variables).

Writing compiler-friendly code is only effective to the extent we know the basic compiler technology. Like silicon density, memory capacity, and processor speed, developers should know the range of compiler technologies likely to be available when developing the application. Being aware of the class of optimizations a compiler tries to perform is also important, as it helps in finding the right tradeoffs between software engineering and performance considerations. For example, knowing that the compiler is good at inlining simple functions means that we can still componentize the application without losing performance. Weak inlining means that we have to plan for extensive use of preprocessor macros (with losses in clarity, type checking, and debugging interactions). If we know our compilers will deploy loop-based techniques (i.e., software pipelining) or trace-based techniques, we might make different choices in the way we write the code. Similarly, if we know our architecture is rich in registers, we are likely to write code that exposes a much larger number of scalar local variables.

A large subset of embedded applications spend their time in loops. On one extreme, DSP applications spend almost all of their time in very few, very simple, well-structured loops. More complex media-oriented domains still spend a significant amount of time in a manageable amount of loop-based code, even though the control flow can be rather complex and the structure of the loops not as simple. In general, *regular loop kernels* tend to be compiler friendly and only minimal work is necessary to get good performance. *Irregular loop kernels* often do not expose ILP (either because it is obfuscated by the programming style or simply because it is not there), and might require heavy restructuring or use of complex algorithmic techniques such as table-driven computation or memoization (caching results from prior computations).

Once we identify the important loops, a simple tuning phase is to modify the compiler region-selection heuristics, which we can do through compiler *pragmas* (for example, to identify the important loops to be unrolled) or automatic profile information. The use of pragmas requires more work on the part of the programmer, but has the advantage of being independent of a specific profile run, and does not have the obsolescence problem of profile data (which needs to be kept up to date with program changes).

In the following paragraphs, we cover some of the ILP-enhancing practices we empirically found to be important. Far from being an exhaustive list, this should give the reader a flavor of the types of transformations and considerations that need to be applied in the performance tuning phase.

Write Code for Predication. If the compiler and target support predication, we have to make sure we write the code in such a way that small *hammocks* (*if-then-else* structures in the CFG) can be predicated away. This implies, for example, avoiding the use of memory writes inside a hammock, keeping balanced paths, and paying attention to function calls that appear only in one branch and might prevent predication (in the case of a partially predicated architecture). For example, the following code shows two equivalent code sequences, for which we can more efficiently predicate the second version (even for partially predicated architectures) after we sink the memory write operations outside the *if-then-else* hammock.

```
If (x > 0) {             if (x > 0) {
    *p = 1;                  tp = 1;
    *q = 2;                  tq = 2;
} else {                 } else {
    *p = 3;        →         tp = 3;
    *q = 4;                  tq = 4;
}                        }
...                      *p = tp;
                         *p = tq;
                         ...
```

Localize Variables. Even though this might sound trivial, avoiding access to global variables in the innermost loops and functions is extremely important. When restructuring existing complex code, if we can determine that the code is free of side effects, a common transformation consists of manually hoisting the global variable in and out of local storage at the beginning and end of the function.

```
int global;                          int global;
void                                 void
foo(int *a)                          foo(int *a)
{                                    {
    int i;              ─────▶          int i;
    for(i=0;i<10;i++)                   int local = global;
        global += a[i];                 for(i=0;i<10;i++)
}                                           local += a[i];
                                        global = local;
                                     }
```

Help Memory Alias Analysis. One of the most difficult tasks for a compiler is understanding what pointers point to. If we know of properties that are obfuscated by the language semantics, it is good practice to provide hints (such as the *restrict* directive in C99) to the compiler about memory aliases that are not obvious from the code structure. The most common example is pointer parameters passed to a function. In many cases, it is obvious to the programmer that two arrays (or structures) pointed to by two separate parameters of a function refer to separate data zones. In this case, it is straightforward and highly beneficial to make sure that the compiler knows about it. These types of hints are very effective. If we had to pick only one optimization to suggest, this would be it. The following code shows a three-tap FIR filter with a *restrict* directive to the pointer parameters. In this case, we know (because it is an FIR filter) that inputs, outputs, and coefficients point to nonoverlapping memory areas. These types of annotations are much more important for ILP targets. If we compile this version of the code for a 4-wide (default) VEX target, we can see that it is 2.1 times faster than the version without the restrict (and the IPC grows from 2.0 to 3.8). If we repeat the same experiment for a scalar (1-wide) VEX target, the performance only improves by 18% (this moderate effect on a scalar machine may explain the lack of popularity of these annotations).

```
void
FIR_3(int * restrict src,
      int * restrict dst,
      int * restrict filter,
      int len)
{
    int i;
    for(i = 0; i < len - 3; ++i) {
        int j, t = 0;
        for (j = 0; j < 3; ++j)
            t += src[i + j] * filter[j];
```

```
        dst[i] = t;
    }
}
```

Eliminate Redundant Loads. Although many compilers ought to be able to do this, it is often the case that this does not happen because of alias barriers or other limitations in the analysis. If this is the case, manually loading and rotating values on temporary scalars will provide a significant performance improvement. Note that this is most effective for a target with a reasonable amount of ILP and a large set of registers. The example following shows the three-tap FIR filter rewritten so that we fully unroll the innermost loop, manually *software pipeline* the first couple of iterations, preload the coefficients into registers, and achieve a loop kernel with only one load and one store operation per iteration. Compiling for a 4-wide (default) VEX target, this version of the code is 38% faster than the unmodified version (and 2.9 times faster than the base version). In this case, the performance improvement comes from a reduced number of operations per iteration (from 21 to 16 for each output value),[4] given that the IPC decreases from 3.8 to 3.6.

```
void FIR_3(int * restrict src,
           int * restrict dst,
           int * restrict filter,
           int len)
{
int i;
int f0 = filter[0]; // Preload coefficients
int f1 = filter[1];
int f2 = filter[2];
int s0 = src[0]; // Preload inputs
int s1 = src[1];
for(i = 1; i < len - 1; ++i) {
    int s2 = src[i+1]; // 1 load/iter
    dst[i] = s0*f0 + s1*f1 + s2*f2; // 1 store/iter
    s0 = s1; // shift values
    s1 = s2;
    }
}
```

Enable Prefetching and Exploit Locality Properties. Prefetching is an important optimization that can help counteract some of the negative effects of poor cache performance. When we know that a certain algorithm exhibits a regular pattern in its access to

---

4. It is always good practice to perform a *back-of-the-envelope* sanity check: three operations per 32-bit multiplications times three multiplications (9), one load and one store (2), two moves (2), compare-increment and branch (3), for a total of 16 operations.

memory, we can trigger automatic compiler prefetching (-*prefetch* in the VEX compiler). In the FIR example, turning on automatic prefetching and the appropriate prefetching step we can cut down the miss ratio from 12 to 5% (for 32-KB data cache, 32 bytes/line, 4-way set-associative, and 100K element streams), which results in a 41% improvement of overall performance.

If the compiler and target support hints to favor spatial versus temporal locality, we can identify accesses with temporal locality (e.g., coefficients of an FIR filter) versus accesses that exhibit spatial locality only (e.g., the streaming input data of an FIR filter, which is never reused). Once we establish these properties, we can appropriately tag the data declaration (through pragmas or other annotations) so that the compiler can assign the values to the proper places in the memory hierarchy. More complex transformations to improve locality include blocking, tiling, and skewing, whose description is outside the scope of this book and can be found in the available literature.

Specialize Code. In many cases, we know that a routine, although generic in nature, is called most of the time with a certain set of fixed parameters. If the routine is important enough, it may be worth splitting it into a generic version plus a set of specialized and simplified common cases.

```
void FIR(int * restrict src,
         int * restrict dst,
         int * restrict filter,
         int len, int filtersize
) {
  if (filtersize == 3)
    FIR_3(src,dst,filter,len); // Specialized code
  else {
    int i;
    for (i = 0; i < len - filtersize; ++i)
      int j, t = 0;
      for (j = 0; j < filtersize; ++j) {
          t += src[i + j] * filter[j];
      }
      dst[i] = t;
  }
}
```

Use Look-up Tables and Memoization. A standard tradeoff application developers make is memory versus computation. For many simple input/output transformations (such as complex floating-point computation) it is possible to precompute all possible combinations and store them in a *lookup* table indexed by the input value. We can then retrieve (rather than compute) results based on the input parameter, at the cost of a single memory access, and the extra memory for the table. In some cases, to reduce the memory requirements it is possible to use multiple smaller tables and some computation to achieve the same result. The use of lookup tables is very powerful, although it can be dangerous at times (for example, when a value of the table becomes corrupted and the verification test suite does not cover that specific case).[5]

Finally, a variation on the lookup table concept is *memoization*. For complex functions that exhibit some data locality of the input parameters, and that have no side effects, we can build a cache of results hashed on the input parameters that simply returns the cached value when a hit occurs. For example, a color conversion routine might be a good target for a memoization transformation, as we can see from the following example.

```
MemoizedColorConvert(
  char r, char g, char b,           // input
  char *c, char *m, char *y, char *k  // output
) {
  typedef struct { char r,g,b, c,m,y,k; } colorcache;
  static colorcache cache[CACHESIZE];

  int index = hash (r,g,b, CACHESIZE);
  colorcache *pc = &cache[index]);

  if (pc->r == r && pc->g == g && pc->b == b) {
    *c = pc->c; *m = pc->m; *y = pc->y; *k = pc->k;
    return; // memoized branch
  }
  else {
    pc->r = r; pc->g = g; pc->b = b;
    FullColorConvert(r,g,b, c,m,y,k); // normal call
    pc->c = *c; pc->m = *m; pc->y = *y; pc->k = *k;
    return; // normal branch
  }
}
```

10.2.3 Benchmarking

Benchmarking of processors is a much more difficult problem in the embedded domain than in the workstation world. This is because in many cases it is very difficult to isolate the software of an embedded system from the system itself. Additionally, embedded software is rarely run *out-of-the-box* (that is, with only standard optimization, a common practice with general-purpose benchmarks). Typically, many optimization steps

---

5. This is the origin of the famous *floating-point division* bug in an early implementation of the Pentium processor. In this case, a logic designer tried to save a few table entries, and a formal verification specialist "proved" that the change was correct. Because of the "proof," the bug slipped past the usual design verification process.

are performed. For this reason, we believe that benchmarking results of *out-of-the-box* programs should always be taken with a big grain of salt and that ad hoc benchmarking for the application under design is always advisable. Nonetheless, several industrial and academic benchmark packages are available for the embedded domain, none of which has yet emerged as the dominant suite (as, for example, SPEC has in the general-purpose domain).

- *MediaBench* is an academic package that contains a set of publicly available programs that cover several important domains, such as JPEG, MPEG, GSM codecs, encryption, and PostScript rendering. Many of these applications are unoptimized versions derived from open-source programs that were not designed for the embedded domain.

- *Berkeley Design Technology, Inc.* is a commercial suite of DSP benchmarks, composed of a handful of simple computational kernels written in assembly (FIR and IIR filters, vector operations, Viterbi encoding, FFT, and so on). As such, BDTI is very specific for simple DSPs and has very limited applicability outside this domain.

- *Embedded Microprocessor Benchmark Consortium* is another commercial suite that contains several subdomains of benchmarks, including automotive, imaging, consumer, and telecommunications sections. EEMBC has evolved from a BDTI-like suite covering mostly simple kernels to a more comprehensive package containing a good variety of program complexity. EEMBC has a rigorous benchmarking certification procedure and allows both unoptimized (out-of-the-box) and optimized results to be published. The availability of optimized results (with C-level optimizations) is very important, as it enables evaluating how a processor performs on code written for it.

One interesting benchmarking domain that has emerged recently is benchmarking of embedded Java applications. As J2ME (*Java 2 Micro Edition*) becomes a popular platform for devices such as PDAs and cellular phones, an additional challenge in to evaluate how these devices perform on Java applications. Java benchmarking is complicated by the wide variation in Java execution techniques, which include factors such as the processor itself, the specific JVM, and transformations performed by the JVM (such as ahead-of-time compilation and just-in-time optimization).

Last, no commercial generic benchmark will ever beat a good ad hoc benchmark suite collected for the domain of interest. Developing an in-house benchmark suite (and having the opportunity to test processors against it during the selection process) is a very valuable asset that not many companies have. Unfortunately, it is also a very time-consuming effort, as it requires a good understanding of the various tradeoffs among benchmarks, applications, algorithms, and specific implementations. Ideally, we advocate that performance tracking on a robust benchmark suite should be raised to the same level of importance as defect tracking on a regression test suite. Unfortunately, the state of the industry is far from that.

10.3 Scalability and Customizability

We say that we *scale* or *customize* an instruction-set architecture when we specialize it for some particular use. In our usage, these terms have slightly different meanings. *Scaling* is adding, subtracting, or changing the parameters of "standard" parts of the architecture, such as adding more integer add functional units, removing a floating-point unit, changing the latency of a memory unit, or changing the number of ports in a register bank. *Customizing* is adding a particular piece of functionality to an ISA to accomplish a more specialized, narrow task than we think of a standard CPU as performing. The population count instruction, mentioned in Section 3.6, is a classic example of customization. These terms are frequently used interchangeably, and in any case the difference between them is subjective and sometimes difficult to determine. However, it is often instructive to think in terms of these two different things. Nonetheless, it is common to use the term *customization* as an umbrella for both, and we often do so here.

An ISA that readily admits these changes is *scalable* or *customizable.* There are a number of motivations for scaling or customizing, which correspond roughly to the four embedded optimization areas of performance, size, cost, and power.

- *Hardware performance* can improve an application or group of applications because the customized hardware fits the application better. It might offer ILP that is consistent with what is available in the application, or it might do certain critical things faster.

- *Hardware cycle time* could improve under customization because extraneous things on the critical paths of an implementation might be removed, or because functions less important to the application could take extra cycles in order to shorten the overall cycle time.

- *Die size and cost* can be smaller because of the removal of extraneous functionality, or because less important functionality can be built smaller than would be optimal.

- *Power usage* can be less for all of the reasons listed in the previous three points: customized hardware, cycle time changes, and removal of extraneous functions.

However, scaling and customizing have a number of costs, some of which are so severe that they make customization rare in the general-purpose computing world. Code incompatibility occurs when the changes are visible in the ISA, and programs must be recompiled to run on a new, customized processor. This disadvantage is unacceptable in many environments, though techniques that solve this problem are beginning to mature. Software toolchain development is expensive, and a new ISA suggests that a new toolchain will be required to use it. Third, user unfamiliarity with the visible aspects of the new ISA can cause the cost of using it to be severe. Finally, a customized processor might be used in fewer applications, thus lowering volumes and increasing manufacturing costs.

Sometimes these disadvantages are critical and can make customization impossible. When they can be overcome, it is often only with great difficulty. Nonetheless, there is a strong temptation to customize and scale in the embedded world because a processor very often runs one application or a small set of related applications all of the time. When that happens, customizing can yield a persistent gain. For example, a printer's CPU might perform image decompression, scaling, color space translation, and half-toning. Each of these algorithms operates on a similar data structure, and structurally they each do relatively similar things. However, a printer's CPU has no reason to be fast at 3D graphics, or linear programming, or database retrieval. Customizing for printer applications can produce all of the benefits listed above.

10.3.1 Scalability and Architecture Families

Customized ISAs are related to the base ISA as members of the same architecture family. Returning to our architecture-as-encoding metaphor, it is clear that both scaling and customizing an architecture will cause changes to compilers, to the architecture, and to the implementation. However, the degree and scope of customization can vary, and one would expect that large pieces of the compiler, the architecture, and the implementation could be reused across related ISAs. It would be unacceptable for a customized ISA to require new incompatible binaries, a new software toolchain, and entirely new hardware implementations. This is the wrong approach to the entire subject of customization, and we do not think in those terms. Within the broader scheme of an architecture family, our goal is to produce some meaningful leverage and commonality.

The challenge and the "Holy Grail" of customizability is to build a scalable and customizable framework in which we can describe a family of different ISAs (see Figure 10.7). This framework should have two crucial properties. First, all programs should run as well as possible, given the constraints of the given family member's architecture. Second, new toolchains must be produced quickly, and users should feel very little difference, if any, between the toolchain for one family member and that of another.

Within any such framework there will be many hardware components that naturally scale by making straightforward adjustments to the compiler, architecture, and implementation. Some typical examples include register banks, functional unit types and latencies, clusters, memory bandwidth, and interconnectivity. Register banks can have different numbers of registers, different-sized registers, and different numbers of read or write ports. Functional units can be added or removed. Typically, we think of scaling with respect to "normal" integer and floating-point units, but if we customize by adding more exotic functional units these too may be scaled. In each case, not only may functional units be added but replicated as well, yielding not only a variety of functional units but often several of the same kind. Memory bandwidth and cache structure (levels, structure, access patterns, line widths) can be varied. Hardware latencies for all of these factors can change within the framework. The number of clusters can change. Last, the interconnectivity among all of these components can be made richer or poorer.

If a hardware design group knows that it is designing within a scalable, customizable framework, the components will likely be designed in a somewhat different way

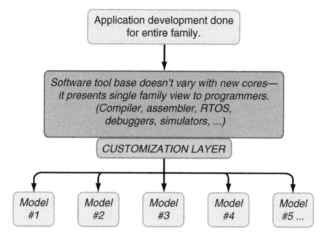

FIGURE 10.7 In a family approach to customized processors there is a lot of commonality among members of the family. Application development can be done once, with little or no change required other than recompiling to run the code correctly and with good performance on a new family member, even though the new core is object-code incompatible with the old one. Sometimes additional work is desirable in some routines to take advantage of the customization, however. This new work may take the form of changed compiler command-line switches, changes in unrolling amounts or the addition of pragmas, or (in the worst case) rewriting of some critical routines.

from how they would be designed to implement a one-of-a-kind ISA. Many of the aforementioned components are already usually designed as parameterizable libraries, but knowing that scaling is to be a major part of the design process there can and should be far more emphasis on parameterizable design. In that way, the NRE costs can be minimized for each new design. Similarly, functional units and register banks can be designed with the idea that they will be "tiled"; that is, several of them can be laid out in silicon with very little wasted space. All of this brings the advantages of lower cost and faster design, as well as better resultant designs.

The same lessons go for software as for hardware. One of the temptations most difficult to avoid in constructing a scheduler is building in target-dependent code. Starting with a retargetable compiler, or engineering a compiler from the beginning to target multiple implementations, may seem much more expensive but pays off in supporting implementation flexibility (and last-minute engineering changes) during the development cycle.

10.3.2 Exploration and Scalability

It only makes sense to scale extensively when there is a payoff in doing so. A key technology used in building scalable systems is *exploration*, the process of considering what properties would be desirable in an ISA and finding the custom ISA within the ISA framework that best matches those properties. The properties in question might be performance on important applications, or groups of applications, or they might be such constraints as power, cost, area, and meeting real-time guarantees.

We can distinguish between two different methodologies in finding a custom ISA family member: *analysis* and *exploration*. In an analytic methodology, the requirements are analyzed (either by some automated tool or by a human designer) and the design is customized (again either in some automated way or by hand) to fit that analysis. As a simple example, suppose we build a tool that calculates the maximal computational requirements of loops. If we want to build a processor customized for a single application that is dominated by a single loop, we can allow this tool to tell us what the mix of functional units should be. As another example, consider a tool that measures register pressure within an application and then suggests what the size of a register bank should be. Both of these analytic tools are practical, and both would most logically be built within a compiler. Analytic tools also have intuitive appeal, as they perform some sort of theoretical reduction or analysis of the application.

In our experience, however, finding a good scaling or customization is practical only through an exploration tool that searches for it. This is the case for two different reasons. First, the number of parameters an analytic technique must consider is quite large, and their interaction is very complex. Second, many aspects of customization are difficult to characterize in such simple terms in the first place, calling into question the value of any analytic formula. It thus becomes difficult to capture analytically enough of the key properties to make the entire job practical this way, though some pieces may yield to the analytic approach.

In principle, exploration is a simple process. The loop shown in Figure 10.8 outlines the process, in which we assumed that we are given an application to customize. To customize we repeatedly select a new trial ISA and evaluate it according to the desired criteria (which may be performance on that application, or power consumption running that application, or some other metric). Then we select the next trial ISA, usually letting the results of that exploration guide the selection. Most of the standard search techniques (e.g., Monte Carlo, genetic algorithms, and so forth) can be brought to bear on this problem.

The application we customize to should characterize the workload of the processor as faithfully as possible. Given that workload, we can carry out the evaluation by first compiling the application for the target processor. Having done that, we simulate the application or statically measure its performance to the best of our ability (if performance is our goal). If performance is not our only goal, or not a goal at all, we measure whatever other properties (e.g., power, area, cost) are important by other means, usually via a static model. Although what we have just described sounds straightforward enough, it turns out that the exploration process is difficult, as described in Section 10.3.7.

10.3.3 Customization

Everything we have said so far applies more to scaling than to true customizing; that is, adding special instructions or functional units that carry out some "exotic" functionality. Generally, when the compiler can recognize the special functionality exploring

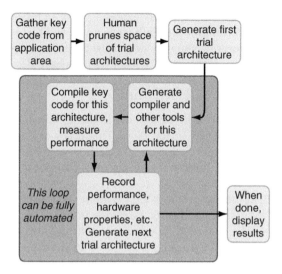

FIGURE 10.8 Automatic customization. Several research groups advocate an automated approach to customization, based on a loop similar to that the figure describes. Although many of the techniques have matured (retargetable compilers, architecture space exploration, and so on), full automation in a realistic environment is a distant goal.

ISAs for good use of this functionality can be straightforward, as is also the case when the programmer can "instruct" (via explicit description) the compiler in the use of the special functionality. In each of these cases, there are many subtleties that involve the capabilities of the compiler (dealing with this in detail is beyond the scope of this book).

The simplest case, however, is that of adding a special instruction (again, a good example is population count). In that case, the programmer can write the code to use a function that performs only that, and a compiler designed to deal with functions of that nature can treat it as if it were just another primitive operation such as multiplication or negation. More complex cases will imply an "end-of-world" situation, wherein the compiler can schedule on either side of the complex function but has to regard the function itself as a barrier. The compiler cannot move operations from one side of the function to the other because it does not know all effects of the function. Merging each of these cases into exploration can be practical once the compiler issues have been taken care of.

Customized Implementations

In addition to customizing an ISA, we may also customize its hardware implementation in ways that are not architecturally visible. In that case, we might have considerations very similar to some of the items cited previously. Typically, the techniques for performing such a customization are in the domain of microarchitecture or hardware design. However, the exploration techniques described previously can apply to this situation as well. Since we are considering highly exposed VLIW architectures, the gap between the ISA and the implementation is usually very small, and this is not as great a consideration as it might be for, say, superscalar architectures. Nonetheless, customization in cache structure, for example, is very like what we have been describing.

10.3.4 Reconfigurable Hardware

We saw in Section 6.2 that using FPGAs or similar technology it is possible to build hardware that can be changed in the field. This offers several advantages: lowered design cost (the same hardware designs can be leveraged across many uses), potentially less silicon (the same hardware can perform different things at different times), and so on.

In addition, field programmability is a capability that resonates well with customization. There are several customization scenarios in which reconfigurable hardware is appealing. For example, one could wait until a product is later in the development cycle before fixing the customized hardware. (Somehow, the psychology of design verification and regulatory clearance allows "software" to change after approval much more than hardware. Reconfigurable hardware sits between those two, and gets a lot of benefit from its software half in designers' minds.) As a second example, one could change a customization after the product is in the marketplace. Finally, one could repeatedly "recustomize" the same hardware as its use changes, even on a routine-by-routine basis, thus allowing hardware that is not only customized but customized to different things at different times (this is called "dynamic reconfigurability" in the field).

Certainly, there are problems that map well onto configurable hardware with convincing performance advantages over conventional software/hardware solutions. However, the cost of using configurable hardware, even when it works well, is likely to be high. A very active research community has been promising this vision for years (and we hope they continue to, since this is an important topic), but as of 2004 FPGAs unit cost is still significantly more expensive than the cost of an equivalent custom-logic circuit at similar performance and they cannot reach the performance of the hardware typically used in compute-intensive embedded environments at any reasonable cost.

On the other hand, reconfigurable hardware has been successful in building hardware simulation platforms and prototypes. Especially in full-custom or ASIC designs, an FPGA-based simulator can afford software teams the opportunity to work with "real" hardware (i.e., merely 10 to 100 times slower than the actual device) much earlier than would otherwise be possible. In addition, FPGAs are very effective in low-volume products, where the large NRE of ASIC development gets amortized over a small number of parts, effectively swamping unit cost considerations. Because of the growing NRE costs of deep submicron processes, we are seeing fewer and fewer products with volumes high enough to justify full ASIC development.

Using Programmable Logic

Customizing an instruction set with programmable logic involves two primary considerations. First, we need to identify sections of code or computation that could be encapsulated in programmable logic and encapsulate it as hardware (or compile it into hardware). Manufacturers of programmable logic supply tool sets geared toward taking simple computations (for example, at the expression level, or perhaps much more complex) and producing the appropriate array design, complete with debuggers, simulators, and so on. Then, we need to rewrite the code in such a way that the rest of the code — the part that has not been encapsulated — can interact with it correctly and efficiently.

The first step can be difficult, but FPGA manufacturers have made tremendous progress in providing tools that make this process tolerable. However, the second step is often fatal. This is because the interaction between the programmed logic and the rest of the processor invariably involves overhead. When the complexity of the customized portion is small enough to be done efficiently, the frequency of its interaction with the rest will typically increase, and the overhead thus involved is likely to be significant. Doing this in programmable hardware should be contrasted with customized instructions designed into the ISA and hardware in the first place. In that case, the customized hardware will be faster than the programmable version, and there is only the usual interaction overhead, as with any instruction. Alternatively, when the interaction is small, it is because there is a much more significant division between the customized functionality and the rest of the computation, and the associated software problem is often severe.

10.3.5 Customizable Processors and Tools

As mentioned previously, a customized processor only makes sense when the many barriers of object code incompatibility, user and developer unfamiliarity, and cost have been overcome. Here we discuss many of the technical challenges in building a customized processor.

Describing Processors

To explore a processor space, and to specify a chosen processor, there must be some language (see Figure 10.9) by which a human developer or an automated system can describe the processor. With the initial requirement, the subject of customizable processors is already in a quagmire: languages to describe computer systems, at any level, are about as old as programmable computers themselves, and except for some very low-level hardware description languages and some behavioral languages (especially VHDL and Verilog) there has been little popular acceptance of any choice. For a given instance of a processor, this is not terrible state of affairs. In the customized processor field, however, everything should be keyed off some formal description of a processor. With a fixed processor, one could write, say, an assembler. If one is producing customized processors within some framework, one wants an *assembler generator*, a tool that will read the description of a processor and produce an assembler for that processor. The same should then be true of compilers, debuggers, simulators, analyzers, and so on. In a good customization system even an assembly language manual and other documentation will be automatically produced, driven by the formal processor description.

Controversy: Customized Processors in FPGAs?

Now that the number of gates available in an FPGA allows an entire ambitious core to fit on a programmable chip, many researchers advocate building and shipping commercial processors, or processor cores, entirely out of reconfigurable logic. This would certainly be desirable, were it practical, in that the plasticity of the core would allow future improvements in customization, response to changes in usage patterns, and so on. Altera's *Nios* solution takes exactly this approach, shipping a soft processor core built on an FPGA substrate.

In fact, reconfigurability might be the key technology in performing customization on a per-application basis, rather than on a per-domain basis. The problem with customizing per-application is that with so fine-tuned a design there is little room for application change. Because it takes at least six months to ship even a synthesized core, there is no room for the often-significant application changes that invariably occur during the period right before the product ships (two of the authors of this book have painful personal experience with this issue). The usual remedy is to customize only to the extent that applications in the domain (e.g., printing, communications) run well. However, doing the entire core in an FPGA might be the perfect solution to application customization.

But is it practical? The trend is going in that direction, but there are still serious barriers of speed and cost. The speed gap between a fully customized design and one embodied in an FPGA is narrowing, but it is still significant enough to eat up much (if not all) of the advantage that comes from customization. The gap narrows significantly, however, when FPGAs are compared with nonconfigurable synthesized logic.

Xilinx's high-end VirtexIIPro series of FPGAs try to have the best of both worlds by incorporating FPGA cells and up to four hard PowerPC cores onto a single chip. However, these hard cores, while fast, suffer the same lack of configurability any hardwired implementation suffers (one cannot rewire the hard core to support new operations or change bus widths).

The second major barrier, perhaps more severe, is that of cost. Obviously, for low-volume designs FPGAs have a big advantage in cost, since their volumes are amortized over the full run of an FPGA, not just the particular design in question. However, for a design with high volumes FPGAs are not even close to practical.

Although there are not yet any popularly accepted architecture description languages, they all have much in common. Each must support specification of architectural elements such as functional units and registers, latencies, instruction encodings, interconnect topology, and memory elements. Through clever encoding, some of these can be hidden or implied (e.g., an instruction description implies the existence of registers or memories for its operands and a functional unit that performs the underlying operations). Sometimes description languages go considerably beyond this and allow functional behavior to be included, an important capability for simulation and compiling.

```
# The multiplication instruction from StrongARM.
OPERATION mul

SYNTAX "mul" ^ cond_names[cond] reg_names[rn]^"," reg_names[rm]^","
           reg_names[rs];

CODING cond 00000000 rn ---- rs 1001 rm;
TRANS
# get EX, Mult resources, release ID, reads sources, allocates dest
# mRF is a combined model for register file and forwarding paths

e_id_ex: {ex_buffer = mEX[], !id_buffer, v_rm = *mRF[rm], v_rs = *mRF[rs],
dst_buffer = mRF[rn], mlt_buffer = mMult[], v_iflag = *mCPSR[]}
               eval_pred(pred, cond, v_iflag); #evaluate predicate

# predicate true, gets BF, releases EX, compute

e_ex_bf: {pred>0, bf_buffer = mBF[], !ex_buffer};
               v_rn = v_rm * v_rs;

# gets WB, release BF, Mult, updates result
   e_bf_wb: {wb_buffer = mWB[], !bf_buffer, !mlt_buffer,
               *dst_buffer = v_rn, !dst_buffer};

# release BF and retire

e_wb_in: {!wb_buffer};

# predicate false, simply go through the pipeline, do nothing

e_ex_bf_null:   {pred==0, bf_buffer = mBF[], !!ex_buffer, !!dst_buffer};
e_bf_wb_null:   {wb_buffer = mWB[], !!bf_buffer, !!mlt_buffer};
e_wb_in_null:   {!wb_buffer};

# branch taken, flush this

e_ex_in:        {*mReset[], !!ex_buffer, !!dst_buffer, !!mlt_buffer};
```

FIGURE 10.9 **The description of the *mul* operation in the StrongARM architecture.** This is written in the architectural description language used in the Mescal system at Princeton University. It is part of a three-level machine description framework containing the Mescal Architecture Description Language (MADL), the peripheral annotations, and a C++ template library. The main reference for the system is Qin and Malek [2003].

10.3.6 Tools for Customization

Tools for customizable processor families are one of the most active research areas in embedded processing. A full survey might find 100 or more projects and at least two startup companies (Tensilica and ARC) active in 2004. These vary across a wide spectrum, from realistic engineering to pushing the research boundaries. It is difficult to identify an area of progress that could solve the most difficult problems or lead to broadly accepted, highly automated tools on the order of *lex* or *yacc*, but developers have distributed many commercial and public-domain systems and the field will undoubtedly progress.

Although they can be difficult engineering challenges, most of the tools necessary for a customizable processor family are straightforward in concept. Sadly, even for these more straightforward tools, especially in a commercial environment, the engineering effort can be daunting. These might be described as the typical "small matter of software" (for the uninitiated, this is a phrase used sarcastically by good programmers in the face of the many people who believe that if they can describe a process they can easily write code to implement it). And as we will see shortly, retargetable compilers represent an Olympic-class research and building effort.

For tools other than the compiler, there is an important principle that must be followed in designing a customizable family of processors: the run-time architecture and other non-ISA aspects of the family should stay constant among family members to the extent possible. This is, for most tools, a far more important factor in managing the engineering effort of customizability than dealing with changes in the ISA.

Assemblers must map the usual assembly language abstractions into machine language, following an object format (such as ELF). They must deal with abstractions such as symbol mapping, relocation, error checking, handling of immediates, conditional assembly, and macro facilities. Most of these are unchanged in a retargetable assembler, with the twist that the user-level language must be keyed off the machine description (perhaps invoking another customizable tool, an automatic ISA manual generator). As code is emitted, the assembler uses the machine description to determine what the final code will be. In a customizable system, *linkers* and *loaders* also just have to do what they normally do, but must be plastic enough to understand the description of the system and do their jobs correctly given such a description.

Debuggers also do not pose particular challenges beyond a somewhat greater engineering effort (which is bad enough!). The debugger must have a way of evaluating the stack of a paused program in order to determine the boundaries of procedure calls, the parameters passed to procedures, and the current values of registers saved within a procedure call frame.

In addition, the run-time code provides mechanisms for directly calling native procedures from within the debugging environment. Neither of these is particularly sensitive to changes in the processor instruction set. This situation highlights the extent to which the run-time architecture and other non-ISA aspects of the customizable family should stay constant among family members.

Unlike the other tools, however, debuggers have a significant range of how heavyweight they must be to handle a range of possible code optimizations. The system must handle the full range of the architecture family, and thus a debugger for even a simple member of the family might be a large piece of code if the family permits architectures for which much more complex code transformations are necessary (for example, if the architecture family could have both simple RISC instantiations and complex VLIW ones).

The operating system can present significant engineering challenges in customized families as well. Operating systems typically separate implementation-specific code from general code. Memory management, for example, can be implemented with a small machine-specific kernel, interfacing with the underlying memory management hardware. All higher-level memory functionality (e.g., paging) can then be implemented with architecture-independent code. This dictates that members of a single architectural family should implement a common memory management architecture.

Context switching can present larger problems. Although context switch code could be automated to key off machine descriptions, it might be too difficult to make it worth implementing, and typically this is code worth tuning and getting to be as tight as possible in any case. Finally, exceptions and interrupts should be identical between family members, except that the state save/restore code is processor specific. This, however, is essentially the code needed to perform processor swaps, and thus it adds little additional effort.

Customizable Compilers

The most significant piece of engineering required to have a scalable and customizable toolchain is the compiler. Here we mean "engineering" in the pioneering sense — of moon shots and heart transplants, not the snobbery of "just" engineering. This problem is at the forefront of compiler research.

Many retargetable compilers have been built, but very few are of commercial quality and do a good job of finding ILP on entire families of processors. The one we are most familiar with is the Multiflow compiler, which is an ancestor of the VEX compiler used in this book. That compiler, which first started generating correct code in 1985, was built to be retargetable from the very start, in that it had to support three different VLIW models that issued 7, 14, and 28 operations per cycle. The Multiflow compiler was licensed to many different computer companies upon the demise of Multiflow Computer in 1990. Its retargetability is legendary: anecdotally, its descendants have been said to have been the first code generators for both the Alpha and the IPF processors, and have been said to have generated the reported Pentium SPECmarks over a period of years, in addition to many other accomplishments. To have been that versatile while being a product-quality robust compiler is very remarkable. All that said, however, the compiler was first engineered to be scalable within the family of Multiflow machine models. The other retargetings involved an engineering effort that would probably be unacceptable for use within families, or in a production customization environment. Two other well-known retargetable compilers that generate significant ILP are the SGI Pro-64 (the lead designer of which was John Ruttenberg, who was also the force behind the building of the Multiflow compiler) and the Trimaran research infrastructure (which sprang from efforts at the University of Illinois, under Wen-mei Hwu, and HP Labs under VLIW pioneer Bob Rau). From a compiler's perspective, customization in the instruction set can occur in various ways.

1. Scaling operations; that is, adding or removing high-level operations present in the described existing repertoire of the customizable family. Multiply-add operations or floating-point operations might fall into this class.

2.   Supporting various sets of computational resources and their connectivity. For example, latency constraints that must be adhered to, register sizes, the cluster architecture, and so on.

3.   The introduction of new machine-dependent operations. A *population count* or *find first zero* might be in this class.

So what is the problem? Compiler writers implementing an ambitious ILP compiler must make a huge number of small choices. Do we schedule this type of thing ahead of that? Is it worth doing this when it puts more pressure on the registers? Should we instantiate this operation this way or that? There are literally hundreds of places in the compiler where, in the course of generating code, little decisions must be made that resemble these. For many of the decisions, the desirable answer can only be known when the architecture is fixed.

Consider, then, the group of decisions that should change when the family member changes. The compiler writer must find some way of leaving these decisions unbound, pending presentation of the actual CPU it is generating code for. There is a big engineering difference between simply deciding to do something one way versus leaving latitude for different decisions at different times. Similarly, when things scale and customize, the compiler itself has to be scalable (that is, generate the code that takes advantage of the number, sizes, and capabilities in the architecture) and customizable (that is, generate code for special operations). When latitude is left, compiler writers think of the latitude as a "switch," which may or may not be exposed to the compiler user as a compiler switch. If it is not exposed, the compiler must have some way of determining what setting to use (otherwise, it is left to the user).

As the combinations of possible switch settings mount, the engineering complexity of using the switches soars. The switches are not independent, and figuring out how to set a switch depends not only on the architecture but on how the other switches are set. Some decisions involve what order to do things in (this is the legendary phase-ordering problem). Building a compiler in which the phases are not predetermined is a challenge. If the switch settings are instead left to the user, history has shown that few users will read the meaning of and set the switches.

This does not even address the question of allowing users to add custom operations to the ISA. As we have said repeatedly, building a commercial-grade compiler that finds a lot of ILP is a significant engineering challenge that has only been accomplished a few times. Adding a great deal of plasticity to it could properly be regarded as a terrifying prospect.

Given these challenges, it is not surprising that even the retargetable compilers that find a lot of ILP are reasonably limited in their repertoire, generally requiring the architecture to match the precepts of the compiler designers. When the architecture strays significantly from that, it is not a matter of changing a table and resetting the switches. Usually, the engineering involves understanding the compiler in detail and changing parts of the compiler that were not written to be changed. When the distance is great enough, starting from scratch begins to make sense.

10.3.7 Architecture Exploration

Although the exploration process depicted in Figure 10.8 seems straightforward, there are difficulties at nearly every step, and these vary across many technical and social barriers.

Difficulty Characterizing Workload This should be easy in an embedded system. After all, it has been built to perform one specialized thing over and over again. Sadly, although embedded workloads *are* easier to characterize than general-purpose workloads, the characterization task itself remains complicated. Two different things make characterization difficult.

First, the idea of having in hand, well in advance, the application that will run on the processor is only a dream. Due to the typical design, verification, and regulatory clearance cycles, there is a long period of time (often years) between the final selection of an ISA and the shipment of a product incorporating the embedded core you designed. During this time the application suppliers usually feel free to change the application at will, being motivated by changes in market condition, emerging or changed standards, improved algorithms, or even caprice. Worse yet, in many environments applications can even change long after the product is shipped. This is now common because of the prevalence of flash and other nonvolatile memory.

Second, just as ISAs can be changed to suit an application, the application can be changed to suit the ISA. A typical scenario has the application programmer looking at the derived custom ISA and saying "What?! You're willing to give me two integer multipliers? If I had known that, I would have inverted those two loops and rewritten that second computation. By the way, if I do that, 16-bit multiplies will suffice just fine. I won't need 32 bits." No known automation can begin to capture this process. The important lesson of this is: *An exploration system must have the interactive services of an application domain expert.*

Difficulty Writing Retargetable Tools As described previously, these tools are difficult to write. The fact that building a retargetable high-performance compiler is a state-of-the-art research endeavor certainly is a barrier to exploration. Without a compiler like that, exploration is a self-delusional activity. The absence of a compiler to measure the actual performance of a candidate architecture has been a constant self-delusion throughout the history of computing.

Fast Measurement of Performance To judge the quality of a trial ISA, either a fast simulator or an analytic performance measurer is required. A technique for fast simulation that has lately become popular is what we call *compiled simulation* (described more fully in Section 6.3). A normal simulator, which we might analogously call an interpreted simulator, works by simulating in software the mechanism of the instruction issue and execute model embodied in the ISA. That is, it fetches operations one by one and then simulates the abstract behavior of the hardware, at least on the ISA level, that carries out the instructions. An even more elaborate and accurate form of simulation actually mimics the exact behavior of the underlying hardware. For the purpose of exploration, these two methodologies are slow and slower. Compiled simulation works instead by taking the application and statically translating it into a new program, in C, that mimics the behavior of that program running on the trial processor and reports on its characteristics as desired. This new program is then compiled and run on any system that can run a compiled C program. This has the advantage that instead of contemplating each operation one at a time (for the millions or billions of operations executed) and going through a full fetch-execute process for each we simply run this new program. By eliminating the constant fetch-execute cycles, simulation is usually sped up by a factor between 5 and 10. It has the further advantage that only part of the application has to be treated this way if the rest (including the OS port) can run on the host.

Even fast simulation would not suffice for a completely automated system, though. There, an analytic approximation of quality is likely to be the only practical possibility.

Dealing with the Complexity

Mitigating these problems requires a different view of how to explore. To solve the problem of late-emerging code, we never design an ISA for a completely narrow application. Instead, we try to capture a range of important applications or application types that would likely be similar to those that would run on the product. Thus, we customize less than is possible, in order to maintain future usability. We have noticed something that is quite fortunate: most applications in a given embedded area have enough commonality that one can gain from customizing for them all simultaneously (we say we customize for a domain rather than an application). Were this not true, customization would be a much less interesting area.

To solve the problem of the algorithm designer's skill in matching the application to the ISA, we can make the application writers be part of the team in doing the customization. To contemplate doing that, one needs to accept a painful fact:

> *Fully automated customization (i.e., without human intervention) is probably not realistic, and will not be for a very long time.*

The problem, as we said, is that the algorithm changes the programmer makes can dwarf the gains due to customization, and thus cutting the programmer out of the loop probably does not make sense. There is one subtle aspect to this: if time-to-market were practically affected in a major way by adding the programmer to the loop, there would be an argument for leaving them out. However, it takes years to produce the SoC and the product it goes into. Adding a few weeks to perform customization effectively probably is not a bad cost, given the results.

Other Barriers to Customization

In addition to the difficulties previously explored, there are other, smaller, more subtle barriers.

- *Management often sees customization as a liability.* Whereas designers and engineers find that customization adds significant challenge and stimulation to their jobs, management often sees it as fragile and incomplete, as well as a difficult thing to sell.

- *Toolchain maintenance is much more difficult.* There must be one instance of the toolchain per architectural family member, and thus storage, distribution, documentation, and other problems are more difficult. Worse still, quality control involves checking the correct behavior of M toolchains against N test programs (thus, M*N runs). In general, toolchain maintenance in this environment is an unsolved problem.

- *It is easy to overestimate the effort developers will spend on optimizing code.* Customization is a performance issue, and a key aspect of performance is programmer tuning of the code, especially for ILP, using techniques such as those described earlier in this chapter. It is easy to overestimate the effort users will put into this process, or any other labor-intensive aspect of customization. Just getting programmers to use simple pragmas, often necessary for good ILP performance, can be difficult to impossible.

- *Subtle forms of compatibility get in the way.* Programmers inevitably do not like the look and feel of new toolchains, however well engineered they are. Libraries change, the way you add assembly language inlining changes, and so on. Human nature is to want to go with the familiar.

Wrapping Up

Customization is an opportunity, and it is potentially a key embedded technology. It is also an important and spirited research field. What it is not, to any significant degree, is a commercially viable technology, and highly automated customization is even further away. We do not see that picture changing anytime soon.

10.4 Further Reading

Kernighan and Ritchie [1978] wrote the definitive book on the original C programming language, or "K&R C." The first C standardization effort, ANSI/ISO X3.159 (or "ANSI C," completed in 1989) was documented by the second edition of Kernighan and Ritchie [1989]. ISO/IEC standard 9899:1999(E) records the result of the second standardization effort (Kernighan and Ritchie do not have plans for a third edition).

The C++ programming language is best introduced by its creator, Bjarne Stroustrup [1997]. For more formal and in-depth explanations of the C++ language, programmers can consult the *C++ Annotated Reference Manual*, by Ellis and Stroustrup [1997].

Sun, in conjunction with Addison-Wesley, publishes an entire Java series of books about Java and its related technologies. The original language is described in *The Java Programming Language* by Arnold, Gosling, and Holmes [2000]. The JVM is documented in *The Java Virtual Machine Specification* by Lindholm and Yellin [1999], and JNI is described by Liang [1999].

Matlab is a product of Mathworks (their web site is *http://www.mathworks.org*). DSP/C is best explored by visiting the related web site at *http://www.dsp-c.org*. The ACE CoSy compilers can be found at ACE's web site at *http://www.ace.nl*.

An excellent set of essays on software engineering in general, and on techniques such as those related in Section 10.2, can be found in Jon Bentley's books *Programming Pearls* [2000] and *More Programming Pearls: Confessions of a Coder* [1988]. His essays on "The Back of the Envelope" are not to be missed.

The loop-oriented optimizations performed by high-performance (vectorizing) compilers are ably described by Wolfe, Ortega, and Shanklin [1996] and by Kennedy and Allen [2002].

For commercial forms of reconfigurable computing, see the Xilinx (*http://www.xilinx.com*) and Altera (*http://www.altera.com*) web sites. Tensilica can be found at *http://www.tensilica.com*, and ARC's web site is *http://www.arc.com*.

The critical technology for the software side of scaling and customizability is sophisticated architecture description. Figure 10.9 shows the MADL language, which is described in Qin and Malek [2003]. Other well-known systems of machine description languages include that by Halambi et al. [1999], Pees et al. [1999], Bradlee et al. [1991a and 1991b], and Kastner [2000].

10.5 Exercises

1. In a fixed-point format, define what happens if the radix point is further to the right of the LSB, and why this is an uninteresting format.

2. Take the FIR filter example in Figures 10.1, 10.2, and 10.4. Using all of the languages of the examples (C, C++, Java, Matlab), compute the running time for each of the languages. Compare and comment on the run-time overhead of each of the languages, and its appropriateness for an embedded system.

3. Using the settings described in Appendix A about how to change machine resources and the FIR example, change the number of memory accesses and the number of multiplication units, and plot the performance variations each configuration reaches.

4. Repeat the previous exercise. By reducing the available VEX registers, find the minimum number of registers necessary to avoid significant performance degradation.

5. A large fraction of system code spends most of its time in *memmove()*, which is a routine that safely copies a sequence of bytes from one location to another. Using C, write a correct *memmove()* version first with support for unaligned pointers (i.e., pointers do not have to be aligned to 4-byte or 8-byte boundaries)

and ensuring you support overlapping source and destination. Time your version of the code and compare it to the system *memmove()* by embedding it in your own microbenchmarks (e.g., small block moves, large block moves, and aligned, unaligned, and mixed cases for source and destination).

6. Using the *memmove()* of the previous exercise, optimize the code using C (hint: you can take advantage of possible alignment if you know about it). Repeat the timing experiments.

7. Repeat the previous exercise using inline assembly language code for your desktop.

8. Repeat the exercise using the VEX toolchain, trying to exploit the ILP available in the target machine.

9. Build a table that describes what happens to the radix point of a fixed-point representation when you multiply two fixed-point numbers. Consider all reasonable locations of the radix point. Does signedness/unsignedness of the representation matter? Repeat the exercise for a unit that squares a fixed-point value.

10. Using the "Eliminate redundant loads" example (in Section 10.2.2), repeat the experiments described in the text with the VEX toolchain and verify the results. Double the width of the VEX target and report what changes in IPC, operations per iteration, and overall performance.

11. Using the "Localize variables" example (in Section 10.2.2), quantify the effects of localizing the global variable on the VEX toolchain. Perform a back-of-the-envelope reason check this makes sense of your results. Confirm that by statically analyzing the code emitted by the compiler.

12. Using the "Specialize code" example (in Section 10.2.2), quantify the effects of specializing the FIR filter routine using the VEX toolchain. Perform a back-of-the-envelope reason check that makes sense of your results. Confirm this by statically analyzing the code emitted by the compiler.

13. Use table lookup and memoization example (in Section 10.2.2) and a version of the color- conversion routine of your choice (for example, the one provided with the imaging pipeline code described in Chapter 11), quantify the effects of memoizing the color conversion routine using the VEX toolchain and a real picture as your input data. Perform a back-of-the-envelope reason check that makes sense of your results.

14. Write a C routine that implements the "Find first one" operation (finds the index of the least significant bit at 1 within a register). Test it on a vector of random numbers of length 1000. Using the VEX capability for adding custom operations, add a "Find first one" operation and quantify the benefits of using the assembler intrinsics support.

15. Try optimizing the C implementation of the "Find first one" operation by using any or all of the following tricks: lookup tables, partial lookup tables, sequence of comparisons, and sequence of bitwise masking operations. Plot the results of the various C versions and compare them against one another in terms of code size and data size.

16. Build and optimize a C implementation of the "Population count" operation, considering the following tricks: looping based on the data value, summing up the bits in the value, exploiting the expression $x\&(x-1)$, and table lookup. Compile and time each of your versions on a general-purpose processor.

17. You have been assigned to write a linker and a loader for a customizable family of architectures. Write an essay about what you think it will change from family member to family member that will require the tools to change. How can you capture this variation by providing some plasticity in the tools?

18. Using one of the applications of Chapter 11, explore the space of VEX implementations (execution resources, registers, memory, caches) to find "the best" implementation. Note: maxing out every resource is not "the best," but you have to find what gives the most "bang for the buck" while yielding high performance.

11

Application Areas

There are no such things as applied sciences, only applications of science.

—Louis Pasteur, *French biologist and bacteriologist*, 1822–1895

The set of examples that comprise this chapter illustrate how embedded processing is practiced. Whereas the first ten chapters of our book discussed many different slices or aspects of embedded computing, this chapter presents systematic views of entire embedded computing devices. Our book would be incomplete without these examples, which show how engineers have successfully "put it all together" in the real world.

We begin with two areas described in detail, including code examples: digital printing/imaging and telecommunications. The last section includes textual descriptions but no code for other embedded application areas, including digital video, automotive systems, hard disks, and networking.

11.1 Digital Printing and Imaging

Digital imaging represents the set of technologies used to capture, transform, store, and render representations of images in a numerical (digital) form. Traditional *letterpress* printing (and its modern equivalents) for books has been used since its invention by Johannes Gutenberg in 1450, making digital imaging a very recent development indeed. The major technology developments that led to the mass diffusion of digital imaging are all clustered in the early 1970s. Boyle and Smith (Bell Labs) invented a charge-coupled device (CCD) that could digitally capture images, microprocessors became mainstream, computers could be coupled to *drum scanners* to acquire images, and manipulation tools such as *Photoshop* (originally developed for the production of the first *Star Wars* movie) were made available for desktop publishing users.

Printing digital images remained difficult until the 1980s, when affordable *non-impact* digital printing devices (devices that do not require a physical *master*) became available, in the form of *laser* and *inkjet* printers. These days, digital printing devices are ubiquitous and have reached quality levels that rival professional equipment. Indeed, even the most traditionally conservative parts of the publishing and commercial printing worlds are starting to embrace digital technology, and a growing fraction of printed matter (about 5%) is today being printed by digital (not offset) devices.

In the consumer domain, printing devices have evolved from a simple peripheral for a computer to a first-class citizen in the consumer and professional digital imaging worlds. With the rapid diffusion of digital still cameras (DSCs), consumers now want to print high-quality digital pictures directly from their camera (or storage media, the "digital film") without having to go through their personal computer. Most printer manufacturers targeting the consumer space now offer devices with standalone printing capabilities (so-called *direct photo* printers), some of them even including more complex user interfaces and small screens for previews (see Figure 11.1).

Unlike printers designed to be driven by a computer, *direct photo* printers cannot rely on the computer to perform the processing required to generate high-quality output. Direct photo printers need to embed the entire imaging pipeline, starting from a digital photo on the storage media (typically JPEG) and ending at the bits that drive the ink nozzles. The following sections describe an example of the typical software algorithms we may find in such an embedded pipeline, as well as some of the optimizations we can think of applying when targeting an embedded VLIW engine.

The electronic platforms for imaging devices usually contain a combination of a microcontroller and programmable and nonprogrammable accelerators. The microcontroller (often a medium-/high-speed scalar RISC processor, such as a member of the MIPS or ARM family) is responsible for overall task coordination, user interfaces, managing

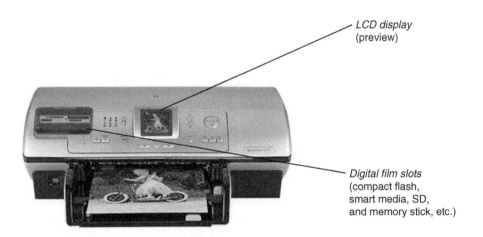

LCD display
(preview)

Digital film slots
(compact flash,
smart media, SD,
and memory stick, etc.)

FIGURE 11.1 **Example of a *direct photo* printer.** The HP Photosmart 8450.

job queues and peripherals, and noncritical parts of image processing. VLIW engines are likely to be used as programmable accelerators for the computing parts of the processing pipeline that do not have fine-grain real-time requirements and require built-in flexibility. Nonprogrammable engines (e.g., ASICs or FPGAs) are very commonly deployed to implement standardized stages of the imaging pipeline (for example, JPEG encoding/decoding) and the input/output stages of signal manipulation (for example, the demosaicing in a digital camera or the final bit-shuffling to the printing heads in an inkjet printer).

11.1.1 Photo Printing Pipeline

In this section we present the basic phases that comprise a typical printing pipeline (see Figure 11.2). Note that the ordering of the stages we present is not the only possible alternative. For example, it is possible to interchange scaling and color space conversion with similar results (subtle differences).

JPEG Decompression

Almost every digital camera can save pictures using the JPEG compressed format. JPEG is a standard for *lossy* image compression, which preserves good perceived quality while

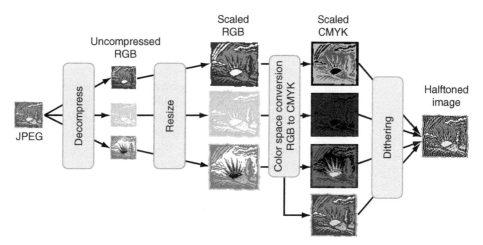

FIGURE 11.2 **Visual representation of a typical imaging pipeline in a *direct photo* printer.**
The diagram exemplifies a sequence of phases that start from JPEG and produce a dithered representation amenable to be transferred to print nozzles. Note that the order of the phases can change depending on implementation constraints. For example, the color space conversion could also operate from YUV to CMYK without passing through RGB. As color space conversion is more computationally costly than scaling, this step would take place before scaling. However, if the printer also enables a direct RGB uncompressed feed, other constraints might alter the pipeline from what we describe. Likewise, many algorithms exist for scaling (such as bilinear interpolation) and dithering (although we use Floyd-Steinberg in the example, what is used in practice is a range of fiercely defended and diverse proprietary techniques).

achieving good compression ratios (ratios of 10:1 to 20:1 are not uncommon). Storing compressed images yields much better utilization of nonvolatile storage (digital film, in either flash memory or disk storage). This storage accounts for a significant fraction of the retail cost of a digital camera.

A JPEG image typically stores "full" color information at 24 bits per pixel, which provides three 8-bit levels (and thus 256 levels) to the three major color components. Other compression formats, such as GIF, use 8-bit-per-pixel color maps (i.e., every pixel selects from a limited palette of 256 colors). The 16 million colors we can achieve with 24 bits per pixel and excellent compression ratios make JPEG a good compromise for digital cameras, leading to wide adoption of JPEG by camera manufacturers.

As a consequence, the first operation a printer needs to perform is *JPEG decompression*. To understand the decompression steps, it is necessary to first understand the basic JPEG compression strategy. A detailed description is beyond the scope of this book, and some of the relevant literature is reported in the "Further Reading" section.

Although nothing in JPEG addresses color spaces explicitly, the practice is to convert to luminance-chrominance color spaces. Starting from an RGB image (captured by the camera), the first step converts it to a luminance-chrominance color space (such as *YUV* or *YCbCr*) and then *downsamples* the components by collapsing (averaging) together groups of neighboring pixels. The idea behind downsampling is that the human eye is more sensitive to luminance (grayscale intensity) than to chrominance (color components), and thus it is common to reduce the color components by a factor of 2^1 or 4. For each of the individual components, the pixels are then grouped in 8×8 square blocks, and each block is transformed through a *discrete cosine transform* (DCT), which extracts the frequency components of the 8×8 blocks. Perceptual studies have shown that the eye is most sensitive to the low-frequency (high energy) components, and thus we can dedicate fewer bits to the high-frequency values of the transformed representation. Hence, we can use a nonuniform *quantization table* that divides and rounds the frequency components, so that the higher-frequency coefficients get quantized more coarsely. Quantization achieves the largest compression gain (as well as the largest loss of information) of all JPEG stages. Finally, quantized coefficients are encoded with a lossless technique (such as Huffman encoding) and emitted according to the file format standard.

If we work our way backward, decompression implies Huffman decoding, dequantization, *inverse discrete cosine transform* (IDCT) of each 8×8 block, and color space conversion back to RGB. Of these steps, the IDCT is usually the most computationally intensive part of the pipeline.

Scaling

Once the image is decompressed and in the RGB space, the next step is to scale the picture to the printer output resolution, which is typically much higher than the capture

---

1. For example, in the YCbCr space a typical resampling divides the Cb and Cr component in half, and is indicated as *4:2:2* format, or *4:1:1* when the downsampling is by one-fourth.

resolution. For example, assume we want to print a 10-inch by 7-inch enlargement on a 1200-dpi printer (12000 × 8400 pixels), starting from a picture taken on a 4.3M-pixel camera (2400 × 1800 format). This combination requires scaling the image by a factor of 5 linearly.

Scaling is a form of interpolation, for which there is a very wide set of techniques, ranging from simple pixel replication to very complex model-based algorithms that predict the value of the missing pixels. Scaling is a difficult problem, because we are really trying to "make something up" that is not in the original image. In practice, the majority of the algorithms in printers use a variation of *bilinear interpolation*, whereby we assign the value of each pixel based on its immediate neighbors. (Typically, we consider four neighboring pixels: two in the horizontal and two in the vertical direction.) More complex techniques use a larger set of neighbors, or try to ensure that image *edges* (abrupt spatial variations of the pixel intensity) are sharply preserved and not smoothed by a simple averaging operation.

Color Space Conversion

Color space conversion converts input colors (typically, RGB) to the colors the output device can render (typically, cyan-magenta-yellow, CMY). Intuitively, the difference between the two (see Figure 11.3) is that the RGB space represents a set of *additive* coordinates [i.e., colors are generated by adding various combinations of light wavelengths so that if we maximize all values the resulting pixel (255,255,255) is *white*], whereas the CMY space is *subtractive* [i.e., colors are created by overlapping pigments that absorb certain light wavelengths while reflecting the rest, so that the pixel

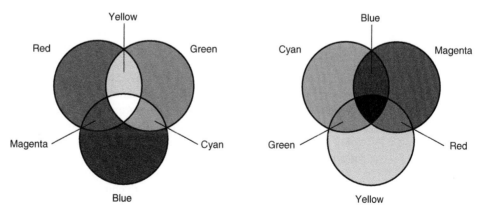

FIGURE 11.3 Color spaces. These two pictures show *additive* (RGB, left) and *subtractive* (CMY, right) color spaces. Intuitively, the combination of the primary additive colors appears *white* (for example, in a monitor), whereas the combination of the primary subtractive colors appears *black* (for example, in printed media).

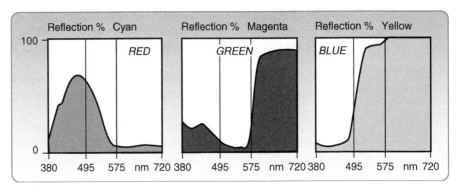

FIGURE 11.4 Reflectivity of CMY inks. As we can see, the frequency response of primary inks is far from being ideal with respect to what the human eye perceives as R, G, and B. This is what complicates the color space conversion algorithms, and the entire area of color management systems. Note that the magenta ink responds in both the red and blue portions of the visible light spectrum. (source: Kipphan [2001].)

(255,255,255) is *black*]. On a very first approximation, the simplest conversion from RGB to CMY is straightforward (the following assumes 8 bits/pixel):

```
cyan = 255 - red;
magenta = 255 - green;
yellow = 255 - blue;
```

In reality, to even hope to get colors that look remotely similar the transformation needs to the strongly nonlinear, which implies complex computations. This is because the reflectivity response of the individual inks is strongly nonlinear, as indicated in Figure 11.4.

In practice, most systems use a form of three-dimensional interpolation that converts the coordinates of a point in the "cube" of the RGB space to the closest point in a "cube" of the CMY space. Similar considerations apply if the conversion is from a luminance-chrominance space (YUV) to CMY. The conversion is usually implemented through a set of lookup tables that represents a quantized transformation of the cube vertices (see Figure 11.5). The color transformation tables are normally computed based on the color profiles of the input and output devices, and their generation involves complex mathematics. Fortunately, most of this computation can be performed off-line and hardcoded in a set of lookup tables for the most frequent combinations of device pairs.

The final steps of color space conversion for a printer target involve *black extraction*,[2] which is the process of extracting the fourth component (black, or *K*) of the CMYK space and some form of *device correction*, such as *gamma correction* (again, often implemented

---

2. Sometimes called *undercolor removal* (UCR).

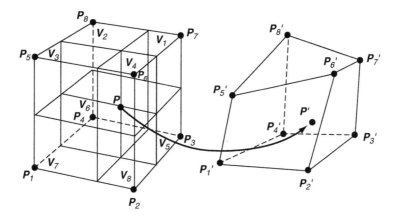

FIGURE 11.5 Example of cube transformation for color space conversion.

with a set of lookup table accesses). The simplest way of extracting the black component is by factoring out the common part of cyan, magenta, and yellow as follows:

```
black = min(cyan,magenta,yellow);
cyan = cyan - black;
magenta = magenta - black;
yellow = yellow - black;
```

To compensate for the nonlinear behavior of individual inks, normally the extraction of the K component is also implemented through a lookup table access.

Dithering

Dithering, also called *halftoning* or *color reduction*, is the process of rendering an image on a display device that can represent fewer colors than the number of colors in the original. The term *color resolution* (or *color depth*)[3] describes the number of individual different colors a device can directly produce. For example, an 8-bit/pixel monitor can represent 256 levels per color. Standard consumer-grade four-color inkjet printers can represent just two levels (*on* or *off*) per color, whereas mid-range color lasers can go up to eight or 16 levels. High-end color printers (used for example in medical imaging or professional prepress proofing) can reach resolutions of 512 to 2048 levels. Dithering trades spatial resolution for color resolution, decreasing the effective number of pixels while increasing the perceived levels of colors.

Traditionally, analog printing processes use dots of varying size to dither an image. Digital printing processes can approximate this technique by grouping the

---

3. Not to be confused with *spatial resolution*, which is the spatial level of detail in a digital image, represented in pixels.

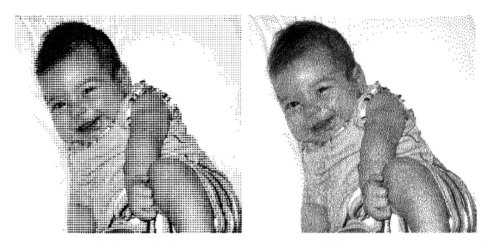

FIGURE 11.6   Dithering. The image on the left shows an example of clustered-dot dithering (using a "screening" mask, such as that normally found in newspapers or magazines). The image on the right shows dispersed-dot dithering (such as that most digital printers produce).

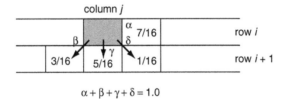

$$\alpha + \beta + \gamma + \delta = 1.0$$

FIGURE 11.7   Floyd-Steinberg dithering. The quantization error of every pixel is distributed among the neighbors in fractions of 7/16, 5/16, 3/16, and 1/16, as expressed by the α, β, γ, and δ parameters.

highest-resolution pixels the device supports into larger blocks and then filling the blocks with a varying number of individual dots (of the same size). The former method falls into the category of *clustered-dot* dithering, whereas the latter falls into *dispersed-dot* dithering.[4] Figure 11.6 shows an example of the different visual effects of the two forms of dithering.

Among the various dispersed-dot dithering schemes, one of the most commonly implemented algorithms is Floyd-Steinberg's *error diffusion*, invented in 1975. The idea behind error diffusion is rather simple: every time we quantize a value (to the nearest match the device can render) we distribute the quantization error over the neighboring pixels we have not yet considered. In particular, the Floyd-Steinberg technique establishes a distribution scheme (see Figure 11.7) that heuristically produces visually

4. In some literature, "clustered-dot" dithering is also called *amplitude modulated* (AM), and "dispersed-dot" dithering, *frequency modulated* (FM).

pleasing results. The following algorithm assumes that we can access two rows of the image at a time. As we describe in the following section, better approaches exist for more realistic (row-by-row) implementations.

```
void fsdither(char *Output, const char *Input)
{
    int i,j;
    for (i = 0; i < length; ++i) {
        for (j = 0; j < width; ++j) {
            int x = Input[i][j];
            int q = Output[i][j] = x > 127 ? 255 : 0;
            int error = x - q;
            Input[i][j+1]   += error * 7/16;
            Input[i+1][j-1] += error * 3/16;
            Input[i+1][j]   += error * 5/16;
            Input[i+1][j+1] += error * 1/16;
        }
    }
}
```

11.1.2 Implementation and Performance

In this section, we present some of the implementation guidelines for the key algorithms that constitute a typical imaging pipeline, as well as some performance measurements we can extract by using the VEX tool set. We also describe some of the key areas of performance improvement for an ILP target, by applying several of the tuning techniques we discussed in the previous chapter.

As for any benchmarking activity, the starting point and main work tool is profiling. Figure 11.8 shows the function-level profile for the imaging pipeline benchmark. This already represents a reasonably optimized version of the code, from which most of the inefficiencies were removed. For example, we manually unrolled the individual color components in the dithering and color space conversion routines so that we could take advantage of a large register set and replace memory accesses with accesses to "named" registers.

As we can see, only four functions (*dither*, *rgb_to_cmyk*, *interpolate_x*, and *interpolate_y*) contribute to about 85% of the execution time. This is a fairly ideal benchmarking situation. The fact that most of the execution time is concentrated on a handful of relatively simple functions implies that we can spend all of our optimization development effort on these, hopefully obtaining a large return on our investment.

Loop fusion (sometimes called *jamming*) is a transformation that increases ILP in the imaging pipeline. It consists of merging multiple separate innermost loops to form a single larger innermost loop. The advantage of fusing loops consists in removing the intermediate memory references (at the expense of more register pressure) and potentially exposing interloop ILP opportunities. In particular, we can easily combine the color space conversion and dithering loops, as Figure 11.9 indicates. To quantitatively

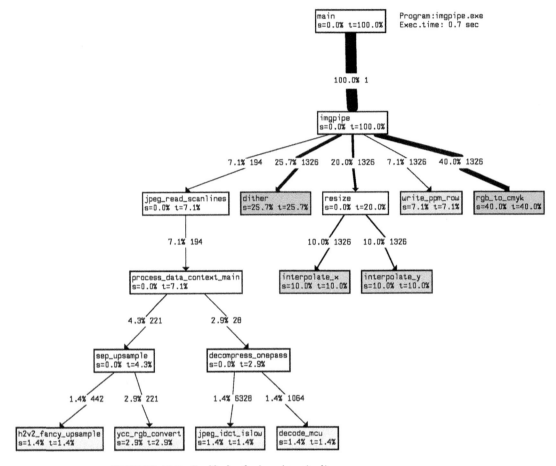

FIGURE 11.8 Profile for the imaging pipeline.

understand the benefits of fusion, we can look at the static scheduling for the individual inner loops (ignoring looping overhead) for various machine widths.

- For *width* = *1* (i.e., scalar), *csc* + *dither* takes 817 cycles, and *jammed* takes 773 cycles. This means that we save ∼ 6% operations (IPC is 1.0 for both).

- For *width* = *4* (i.e., default VEX), *csc* + *dither* takes 292 cycles (IPC = 2.8), and *jammed* takes 232 cycles (IPC = 3.33), with a saving of 26%.

- For *width* = *8*, *csc* + *dither* takes 170 cycles (IPC = 4.8), and *jammed* takes 129 cycles (IPC = 6.0), with a saving of 32%.

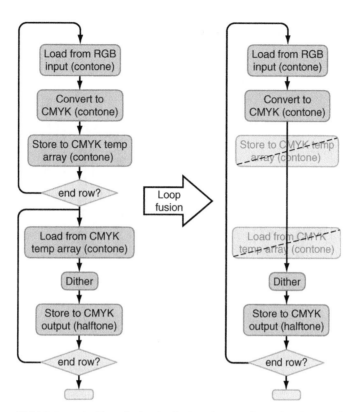

FIGURE 11.9 Loop fusion in the imaging pipeline. The chart on the left shows the original version (separate loops) of the code. The chart on the right shows the code after loop fusion. *Jamming* the two loops allows us to remove the load/store operations on the temporary array of contone CMYK data, and to eliminate the temporary array itself. This temporary array existed only due to the separation of the algorithm into individual routines operating row by row. Compilers can perform this transformation under ideal conditions, but the absence of perfect alias information forces compilers to optimize conservatively. Developers often have to perform jamming manually.

These examples show the increasing benefits of loop fusion as we increase the ILP. Whereas the advantage is marginal for a scalar target (6% is caused by the load/store elimination), wider machines see nonlinear improvements of 26% and 32% due to the fact that we have exposed a larger amount of parallelism. The utilization of the machine increases accordingly, and enables us to use about 75% (IPC = 6.0) of an 8-wide machine, whereas an implementation with separate loops reaches only about 60% utilization (IPC = 4.8). Loop fusion is not always beneficial (for example, it increases register and instruction cache pressure), but it is an important weapon to keep in a developer's arsenal.

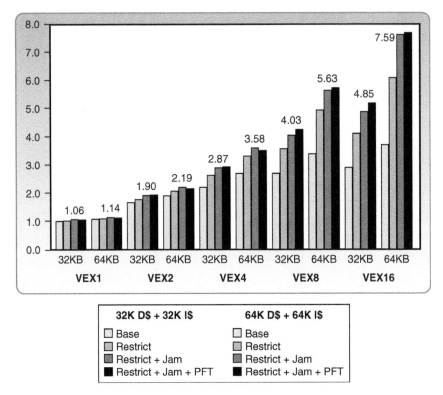

FIGURE 11.10 **Experimental results for the imaging pipeline benchmark.** The graph shows the performance (speedup) of several VEX configurations (1 to 16 units) and caches (32 KB and 64 KB) on the imaging pipeline versus a baseline of a RISC-like VEX configuration (1 unit). As we can see, we can reach ~50% utilization of a 16-unit VLIW machine (an impressive 7.6x speedup), but in order to do so we need to apply specific source-level tuning and ensure that the memory hierarchy is properly sized.

Figure 11.10 shows a more complete set of experiments in which we measure the overall performance (compared to a scalar RISC-like baseline, with 32 KB of instruction and data caches) of the imaging pipeline benchmark at varying width and optimization combinations. For this specific set of experiments we chose to evaluate the benefits of using alias annotation (*restrict*), loop fusion (*jam*), automatic compiler-driven data prefetching (*pft*), and a more aggressive (64 KB, instruction and data cache) memory hierarchy.

The first important observation from the chart is that *none* of these optimizations and code restructuring has any relevant effect on the performance of a scalar machine (the leftmost set of bars, indicating gains in the range of 8 to 14%, even with a double-size cache). This is a pitfall for developers: without exploring more of the design space (and particularly the ILP dimension), software developers will rarely dedicate much effort to performance tuning, and will not see the benefits of important features such as the C99 *restrict* keyword.

As we move to higher levels of ILP in the target machine, the benefits of a more tuned implementation and of compiler hints become evident. Additionally, the gains are not constant, but increase on wider machines. For example, the use of *restrict* yields a 19% improvement for a 4-wide machine, a 32% improvement for an 8-wide, and a 43% improvement for a 16-wide. Although these specific numbers apply only to the imaging benchmark, this trend is common to many applications with similar characteristics and shows the value of providing better alias information to the compiler. Note that the advantage is even larger (24% for 4-wide, 47% for 8-wide, 64% for 16-wide) when we model a better memory system (64-KB caches), because the fraction of time spent performing computation grows. The graph also shows the overall benefits of loop fusion, which confirms the trend we already discovered by a static analysis of the schedules of inner loops (see Figure 11.9).

Finally, the rightmost bar in each set shows the effect of automatic compiler-driven data prefetching. In this case, performance is not always positively affected by prefetching. In narrow machines (width of 2 to 4), adding prefetching can sometimes hurt performance, since (in VEX) prefetch operations compete for issue slots with memory operations and may occasionally lengthen the schedule. In wider machines (width of 8 to 16), the advantage of adding prefetches starts appearing as the competition for memory issue slots diminishes. Here, we observe improvements in the range of 1 (for 64-KB caches) to 6% (for 32-KB caches).

Summary

As we have seen through these simple VEX experiments, imaging applications represent a good target for ILP-based acceleration, and only moderate amounts of performance tuning are necessary to achieve good resource utilization of a VLIW execution engine. However, some code restructuring, as well as the introduction of compiler hints, are required. Overall, our experiments show that we can get to more than 90% of utilization of a 4-way processor, and approximately 50% net utilization of a 16-wide machine (assuming appropriate scaling of memory bandwidth and cache size). These results demonstrate that we can reach excellent levels of performance and utilization — even for aggressive ILP targets — starting from fully portable C code that does not contain processor-specific modifications. Although better utilization levels are achievable through manual assembly language encoding, it is important to remember the advantages of working with a high-level language implementation in terms of development cost (and time-to-market), flexibility, and ability to leverage the same code base for product variants and successive generations.

11.2 Telecom Applications

Telecommunications ("telecom") applications have a very long history that dates back to the nineteenth century (precisely, to 1876, when Alexander Graham Bell connected a battery-powered microphone and speaker, thus inventing the telephone). The use of electromagnetic waves (wireless radio) for communication was demonstrated a few years after, when Guglielmo Marconi succeeded in sending a long-wave signal from England to Canada. Since then, telephony has taken on a "universal" nature, first through analog networks and switches and then through the conversion to digital technologies in the 1970s. The 1990s saw the spectacular rise (and in some cases, fall) of businesses around data and voice conversion, including a revolution in cellular telephony.

The following sections cover a very small example of a single telecom application: voice encoding and decoding. In addition to technical difficulties, telecom systems carry a huge burden in maintaining backward compatibility. Many of today's "standards" evolved from decisions made decades ago, in regimes with very different technology and reliability constraints. Telecom systems must also take into consideration the variety of individual appliances and infrastructure. To make things worse, very strict reliability requirements and high availability (continuous operation) are mandatory for the regulated parts of the telecom world.

11.2.1 Voice Coding

The foundation of any telecom application is the concept of encoding voice. Human voice comes into the system as an analog signal, roughly in the 300- to 3,400-Hz range (note that this is much smaller than the audible range, normally 20 to 20,000 Hz). If we simply apply the Nyquist sampling frequency, we see that we have to sample roughly at 8 KHz (every 125 ms) to preserve a voice signal. By quantizing (for digital transmission) at 8 bits/sample, we can see that 64 Kbit/s of bandwidth are sufficient to digitally transmit voice. What we just described is the simplest form of digital encoding, *pulse code modulation* (PCM).

Historically, audio encoding techniques have been grouped in three different classes: *waveform*, *voice*, and *hybrid* codecs[5] (see Figure 11.11 and Table 11.1).

Waveform Codecs

Waveform codecs, such as the PCM example, attempt to preserve the signal waveform without paying any attention to its content. In other words, they are not dedicated to speech and do not try to exploit specific features of voice signals. Usually, they work on individual samples and their quality can be measured by objective metrics such as *signal-to-noise ratio* (SNR). Some of the more advanced waveform codecs use nonlinear approximations of the waveform. The problem with linear coding is that small-amplitude sections (silent) have poorer resolution than large-amplitude (loud) signals. The answer is a set of techniques called *companding*, wherein a coding scheme uses more bits or values for smaller-amplitude signals. (The two best-known schemes are μ-*law* and *A-Law*; see Figure 11.12.) Waveform coding schemes, such as ADPCM (*adaptive differential*

---

5. Note that the term *codec* is commonly used to describe the encoder-decoder combination, when no distinction needs to be made between the individual components.

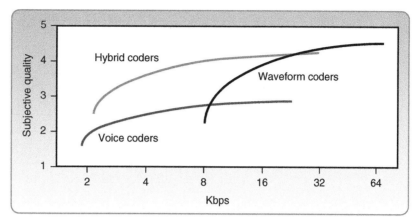

Score	Quality	Description of impairment
5	Excellent	Imperceptible
4	Good	Just perceptible, not annoying
3	Fair	Perceptible and slightly annoying
2	Poor	Annoying but not objectionable
1	Bad	Very annoying and objectionable

FIGURE 11.11   Voice coders. Qualitative classification of the three basic classes of voice coders indicating bandwidth requirements (*x* axis, in Kbit/s) versus quality. The quality (*y* axis) is measured in MOS (*mean opinion scores*), which is a perceptual assessment of a typical voice signal encoded and decoded with a given system.

Coding technique	Sampling rate	Typical bitrate	Typical application
Linear PCM	44.1 KHz	1.2 Mb/s	Music CD (16-bit stereo)
µ-law/A-law PCM	8 KHz	64 Kb/s	Telephony (8-bit mono)
ADPCM	8 KHz	16–32 Kb/s	Telephony
CELP family	8 KHz	4–16 Kb/s	Cellular and VoIP

TABLE 11.1   Coding techniques.

pulse code modulation) are commonly used to compress the PCM stream. ADPCM adds an adaptive component, which automatically finds the right companding thresholds, as well as a differential component, which encodes only the changes between neighboring samples.

Vocoders

Vocoders are filters that synthesize voice based on a model of human speech. During the encoding phase, a vocoder analyzes the speech signal (typically in PCM form) using the

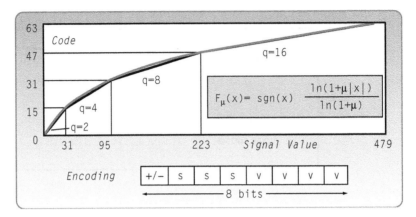

FIGURE 11.12 Companding is a technique that breaks the dynamic range of a signal into segments and assigns different quantization parameters to each. For example, μ-law in the United State is obtained by assigning μ = 255 in the equation shown. The 8-bit encoding scheme identifies the sign, the segment (*s*), and the value in the segment (*v*). A-law is a similar companding scheme used outside the United States with a better dynamic range. Note that, sadly, the difference in standards means that international communication always requires a quantization conversion.

underlying model, extracts the parameters, and transmits them together with accessory information (such as tables) necessary to decode them. The decoder uses the parameters and the tables and resynthesizes the speech waveform. Unlike the waveform codecs, there is no absolute quantitative metric for a vocoder, and subjective measurements (such as MOS, *mean opinion scores*) are commonly adopted. Most of the common vocoders are based on a variation of *linear prediction coders* (LPCs), as we describe in the following.

Hybrid Coders

As the term implies, hybrid coders combine linear waveform approximation and synthesized voice, hoping to incorporate the best of both. *Frequency-domain* hybrid coders divide the input into frequency bands that are then quantized independently. *Time-domain* hybrid coders are usually LPC based and include an adaptive component based on *vector quantization* of the input signal (for example, the *code-excited LPC* or CELP family). The ACELP system (*algebraic code-excited linear predictor*, Figure 11.13) is a hybrid coder employing a codebook that uses feedback to continuously analyze and predict the voice input. It uses a linear prediction scheme that extracts a set of parameters used as multiplicative coefficients for an auto-regressive polynomial interpolation of the z-transform of the signal. This is a form of *vector quantization* in which the parameters are used to modulate a set of vectors (called the *codebook*). The codebook and the parameters can be used to regenerate the voice waveform starting from a white-noise signal that "excites" the decoder. Given that the codebook could be shared by different fragments, the coder only needs to transmit the codebook once, along with a set of *{parameter, codebook pointer}* pairs for each fragment. Unlike the other methods we described, linear predictors are *adaptive filters* whose behavior changes over time.

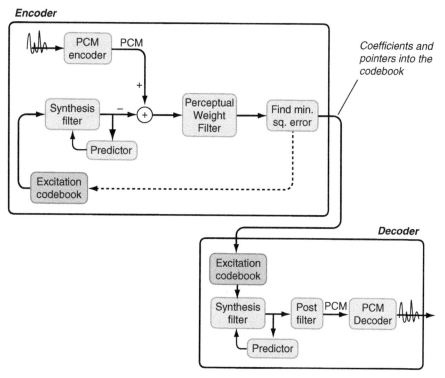

FIGURE 11.13 **Conceptual block diagram of a CELP (*code-excited linear predictor*) encoder-decoder system.** A linear-prediction filter uses an autoregressive model (AR; i.e., all poles) as a first good approximation of a speech fragment (typically in the order of 20 ms), so that it can predict the current sample as a linear combination of the past p samples (p being the order of the filter) starting from a white-noise source. When used in combination with *vector quantization* the samples actually represent coefficients for a set of vectors adaptively computed based on *a priori* knowledge of the characteristics of the signal. Practical implementations add several degrees of complexity, such as gain control, long-term prediction (to model pitch), and low-delay enhancements.

11.2.2 Multiplexing

Once we encode a voice signal into digital bits, the problems appear in how we transmit multiple voice channels over a physical medium, such as a wireless connection. There are three basic dimensions we can control: time, frequency, and encoding. These correspond to the three basic multiplexing techniques: TDMA (*time-divided multiple access*), FDMA (*frequency-divided multiple access*), and CDMA (*code-divided multiple access*).

- *FDMA* is based on *frequency partitioning*: each channel operates in a fixed radio frequency, rather like a broadcast radio or television station. FDMA was used in the early analogue mobile telephony systems and is considered obsolete today (except for legacy support).

- *TDMA* is based on *time-slot partitioning*: the compound signal is divided in short bursts of time, each of which is assigned to an individual channel. TDMA is the basis for the GSM (*Global System for Mobile* telecommunication) cellular network worldwide.

- *CDMA* is based on *direct sequence spread-spectrum* encoding,[6] in which the compound signal is generated at a much higher frequency by assigning a specific code to each channel. Each code modulates the way transmitter and receiver interpret the aggregate channel, so that a receiver sees the output of a transmitter using a different channel as random noise but sees the output of a transmitter using the same code as a correlated waveform it can decode. CDMA is the basis for the PCS (*Personal Communication System*) cellular network in the United States.

11.2.3 The GSM Enhanced Full-rate Codec

As an example of a complete vocoder, we concentrate our attention on the *GSM enhanced full-rate* (EFR) codec, a standard published by ETSI, for which documentation and sources are publicly available and whose use is not covered by proprietary licenses. The EFR encoder takes a 13-bit PCM input (either directly or through a μ-law/A-law converter) and produces GSM-encoded blocks of 456 bits with a frequency of 22.8 Kbit/s. The inverse EFR decoder produces blocks of 160 samples in 13-bit uniform PCM format. The basic scheme is an algebraic code-excited linear prediction (ACELP), including support for discontinuous transmission (DTX), voice activity detection (VAD), and comfort noise insertion (generation of artificial noise at the receiver when speech is absent).

Implementation and Performance

In this particular implementation of the GSM vocoder (see Figure 11.14) the code was written as a reference specification by ETSI and its inner workings are based on a standardized library of basic operations that guarantees "bit exactness" with respect to the specification. Although a complete rewrite of the code is likely to yield better performance, it may create conformance issues in the corner cases, and thus many designers start from the reference specification and optimize it. Unfortunately, the reference specification is not a good match for a VLIW (or any other ILP-style microprocessor) target. This is largely due to the complexity of the library of basic operations, which makes frequent use of global variables (to propagate overflow and carry conditions).

A straightforward ("base") compile-and-run of the GSM coder from the reference code reaches an IPC of only 1.46 (1.22 including cache stalls) for a standard 4-wide VEX configuration. Given that all basic functions are small and (with the exception of overflow

---

6. There is also a spread-spectrum technology based on frequency hopping, whereby the code rapidly switches the frequency at which a channel operates. Frequency hopping is used in some military applications, and relatively slow frequency hopping is used in Bluetooth and Wi-Fi. Both forms of spread-spectrum encoding have desirable channel sharing, multipath tolerance, and noise rejection characteristics compared to TDMA and FDMA.

CDMA, TDMA, 2.5G, and 3G?

Proponents of CDMA and TDMA have fought a long-standing battle since the introduction of CDMA in 1989, but no study has definitively shown the superiority of one method over the other. Although CDMA theoretically claims a 10x improvement in bandwidth efficiency over TDMA, there have been no deployments that substantiate the claim, and the higher cost of the equipment is a potential problem in times of economic downturns. On the other hand, known problems of TDMA (such as the fixed time slot, which creates all sorts of complications during cell roaming) have caused several standards bodies (such as ITU, the International Telecom Union, and ETSI, the European Telecom Standard Institute) to agree on two variations of CDMA for the third generation (3G) of mobile communication. These 3G systems provide digital data rates up to 2 Mbit/s (enough to view TV-quality video in real time).

Note that as we all wait for widespread deployment of 3G infrastructure other initiatives have emerged to add packet data over existing standards, such as GPRS (*Generalized Packet Radio Service*, 10 to 20 Kbit/s), a higher-speed variant called EDGE (*Enhanced Data Rate for GSM Evolution*, up to 60 Kbit/s), and *i-mode* (introduced by NTT and DoCoMo in Japan). This hybrid combination of existing voice networks and data add-ons is usually referred to as 2.5G ("Generation 2 and 1/2"), and it is becoming a good testbed to really understand consumer demand, usage patterns, market sizes, and business opportunities.

3G has begun deployment in the United States under the technical acronym CDMA2000 and marketing names such as Sprint's Express Network. European deployment of 3G, under the technical standard called UMTS, started in 2003. The adoption of 3G terminals and multimedia messaging services has been much slower than hoped, despite the very expensive license fees that the providers had to pay to win the 3G spectrum auctions arranged by many European governments.

---

and carry generation) free of side effects, we can attempt a full inline and see whether this transformation increases the ILP. In order to remove the overflow/carry generation overhead (which is likely to kill any compiler optimization), we can analyze the source code of the encoder and generate a specialized version of the basic operations for the (very few) cases in which overflow and carry are indeed used in the computation of the algorithm.

This optimized version (see Figure 11.15) of the code (*opt*) is indeed much faster (approximately four times) than the "base" run. This factor of 4 speedup is caused both by an increase of ILP, which now reaches an IPC of 2.49 (2.26 with cache effects), and by a significant reduction of the executed operations. The latter comes from inlining and the elimination of global variables and reduces the operations by a factor of 2.13.

At this point one might think that we have nearly exhausted the opportunities for improvement, short of rewriting the entire code. This is probably true, if we assume a fixed target machine. However, analysis of the execution profile shows that the heaviest functions by far are a handful of basic operations, among which are saturated addition,

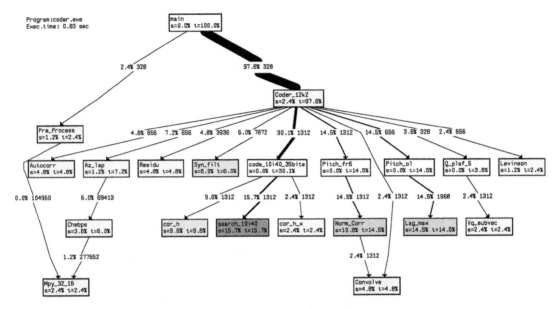

FIGURE 11.14   Profile for the GSM EFR encoder (*asm* version).

subtraction, multiplication, and shifts. Table 11.2 shows the fraction of total time spent in the top eight basic operations.

Depending on our target architecture, we can consider adding a small set of customized instructions to simplify the execution of some of the most important basic operations, while keeping the benefits of preserving the investment in the code base and its successive developments. This is something that could be done within industrial environments such as the Tensilica Xtensa processor core or the HP/ST Lx (ST200) family.

In this specific case, we have experimented with the set of customized instructions summarized in Table 11.3. This set of custom instructions (*asm*) yields another factor of 2.8 in performance improvement, as well as a factor of 3.3 in reduction of executed operations. Note that in this case the largest benefit comes from the reduction of operations, whereas the ILP diminishes slightly (IPC is 2.22, or 1.92 including cache effects). Figure 11.14 shows the execution profile of the *asm* version of the EFR encoder for a sample voice input.

Figure 11.15 sums it all up, by showing a set of experiments for varying machine widths and cache configurations. The three code versions correspond to those described previously (*base* for out-of-the-box ETSI code, *opt* for fully inlined basic operations, and *asm* for a processor with an augmented set of custom instructions). We can see that, even for a scalar machine, custom instructions give the largest benefit (8.6 times faster than a base configuration, and still about three times faster than an optimized version). As we described, this is largely due to the fact that the reference code was written assuming

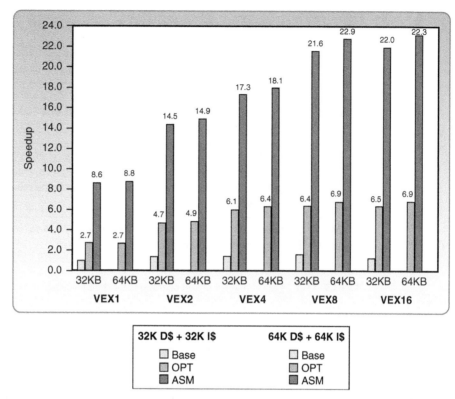

FIGURE 11.15 **Experimental results for the GSM EFR encoder.** The graph shows the performance (speedup) of several VEX configurations (1 to 16 units) and caches (32 Kbyte and 64 Kbyte) on the GSM EFR encoder versus a baseline of a RISC-like VEX configuration (1 unit). Unlike the imaging pipeline (see Figure 11.10) for the EFR, adding special DSP instructions is what yields larger speedups (roughly 4×) and enables the compiler to discover ILP.

L_mac	23%
L_add	18%
L_mult	15%
mult	4%
L_shl	3%
L_msu	2%
round	2%
L_sub	2%

TABLE 11.2 Usage of basic operations in the EFR coder.

MULT	Performs the fixed-point multiplication of *arg1* by *arg2* and gives a 16-bit scaled (shifted left by 15) result.
LMULT	Return the 32-bit result of the multiplication of *arg1* times *arg2* with one shift left.
LADD (LSUB)	32-bit addition (subtraction) of the two 32-bit variables with overflow and saturation control. The result is set at *0x7fffffff* when overflow occurs or at 0x80000000 when underflow occurs.
LSHL (LSHR)	Arithmetically shift left (right) the 32-bit input *arg1* of *arg2* positions. Zero fill the least significant bits of the result. If *arg2* is negative, arithmetically shift *arg1* right (left) by *–arg2* with sign extension. Saturate the result in case of underflows or overflows.
LMAC (LMSU)	Multiply *arg1* by *arg2* and shift the result left by 1. Add (subtract) the 32-bit result to *arg3* with saturation and return a 32-bit result.

TABLE 11.3 The set of customized operations for the EFR benchmark.

that the target hardware would efficiently execute the set of basic operations. However, if we want to preserve bit-exactness, it is likely that some subset of nonstandard saturating operations is necessary to realize these levels of improvement.

In this specific example, the addition of custom instructions also increases the compiler's chances of finding ILP. As we observe from the graph, the performance increase of the base code is pretty much flat if we increase machine resources. For the optimized code base, it flattens at 4-wide (and the incremental improvement between 2-wide and 4-wide is less than 50%). With custom instructions we can successfully exploit up to eight units.

Finally, we observe that cache effects are minimal for the vocoder benchmark. Most of the code fits in a 32-KB instruction cache, and a 16-KB data cache exhibits enough locality to capture most of the data accesses (a 64-KB cache confers small marginal benefits).

11.3 Other Application Areas

In this section we cover some of the other important application areas in the embedded domain. For these, we briefly describe the context and only present a descriptive view of some of the techniques involved. We do not cover any experimental evaluation, nor do we discuss details of the use of VLIW or DSP technologies. The goal of the following discussion is to paint a broad-brush picture of the complexity of some other relevant applications, for which readers can find similarities and differences with the two examples we described in Sections 11.1 and 11.2. Several implementations at various levels of optimization are available in the public domain and can be used as a basis for experimentation and analysis with VEX tools.

11.3.1 Digital Video

Under the term *digital video* we group the technologies necessary to encode, decode, transport, and deliver audio and video content. In this section, we deal largely with the consumer aspects of digital video, which are more relevant to the embedded domain than professional-grade devices. Video servers, broadcasting, multicasting, streaming video, and video-on-demand are similarly important areas. However, they mainly involve agglomerates of general-purpose computing clusters and large-scale networks, and hence they are less appropriate subjects for the scope of this book.

Although video appears to the eye to be continuous, all video technologies (including the original motion pictures on film stock) are built up of discrete sequences of still images. The key to achieving the illusion of continuous motion is the "flicker fusion" rate, which is the rate at which the eye perceives a sequence of images to be one continuous moving image. For most people, 50 frames (still images) per second (fps) is sufficient, which is why the North American television standard (NTSC) specifies a rate of 60 fps and the European television standard (PAL) specifies a slightly slower rate of 50 fps. However, it turns out that the eye can still be fooled in a number of ways: photographic film stock is shot at the low rate of 24 fps, but the projector flashes each frame of film *twice*, rendering an effective rate of 48 fps and fooling the eye into the illusion of smooth motion. Many video systems perform a similar optical trick called *interlacing*, where each frame is divided into two *fields* consisting of the odd- and even-numbered horizontal lines of the original image. By showing alternating fields, these systems can halve their frame rate and bandwidth requirements with a small perceived sacrifice in quality.

Audio and video are naturally analog signals, and thus need to be encoded before we can manipulate them digitally. As we saw in Section 11.1, still images are normally represented through their primary colors (red, green, blue). The frames of a moving image are represented similarly. Most of the video standards, however, favor a luminance-chrominance representation (YCbCr), wherein the luminance represents the intensity of the image (i.e., its brightness as if it were a grayscale image) and the chrominance represents the color components (i.e., its chromaticity, often expressed as *hue* and *saturation*). Another important difference with the still image domain concerns resolution: whereas devices capable of capturing and transforming still images of 4 to 8M pixels are today common, digital video resolutions are much lower. For example, the CCIR-601 standard — which regulates broadcast-quality digital video (most of the digital content we see) — has a relatively small (720 × 480) resolution. Even the highest-resolution North American HDTV broadcast has a maximum resolution of 1900 × 1080 pixels, interlaced for a frame rate of 30 fps. The illusion of motion and of high resolution comes from the rapid sequencing of multiple frames. In many video streams, neighboring frames are largely identical except for a few small changing elements. All video encoding schemes exploit this redundancy across frames, transmitting some (smaller) representation of the difference between frames.

Most of the standard video-encoding techniques are defined by the *Moving Picture Experts Group* (MPEG), an international organization of experts that develops and maintains standard specifications. Three of the most widely known video formats are MPEG-1 (ISO/IEC 11172), MPEG-2 (ISO/IEC 13818-2), and MPEG-4 (ISO/IEC 14496).

MPEG-1 and MPEG-2

Adopted in 1992 and 1994, respectively, MPEG-1 and MPEG-2 are audio/video standards that combine spatial and temporal compression techniques. MPEG-1 is optimized for low bit rates (352×240 resolution, 30 fps, and about 1.5 Mbit/s of bandwidth) and MPEG-2 for high bandwidth (the "main profile" is 720×480, 30 fps, 2 to 6 Mbit/s, and is extensible to 12 to 20 Mbit/s for high-definition formats). Other enhancements of MPEG-2 over MPEG-1 include multiple multiplexed video streams, interlaced frame encoding, improved error correction, and new audio schemes (including multichannel audio and surround sound). Apart from these minor differences, the two encoding schemes are very similar. A spatial DCT-based compression scheme (similar to JPEG) encodes some of the individual frames (*intracoded frames* or *I-frames*). I-frames are subdivided in 8×8 blocks, each of which is filtered through a DCT. The DCT coefficients are then quantized (the main compression step) and Huffman-encoded (see Figure 11.16). A temporal interpolation scheme encodes the remaining frames based on the difference with the neighboring frames (*predicted frames*, or *P-frames*, and *backward-predicted*

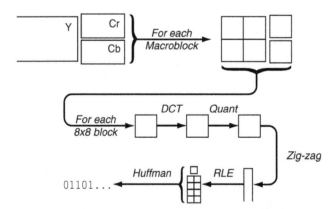

FIGURE 11.16 **Block diagram of I-frame compression.** Macroblocks (consisting of 16×16 pixels or four 8×8 blocks) are broken down into their luminance (Y) and chrominance (Cr and Cb) components, and each of them is passed through a DCT filter followed by a quantization step. The quantized DCT coefficients are scanned with a zig-zag "radial" path so that the DC components are traversed first and the high-frequency coefficients last. This sequence of coefficients is then run-length encoded (RLE), so that contiguous blocks of zeros get compacted away. The final step is a lossless Huffman coding of the resulting bit stream.

frames, or *B-frames*). I-frames, B-frames, and P-frames are interleaved with a predefined sequence, such as:

```
IBBPBBPBBPBBI... (12 frames between two I-frames)
```

In order to encode a P (or B) frame, the technique breaks down the image in chunks of 16×16 macroblocks and, in the luminance component of each macroblock, searches for the most similar one (*reference*) in a neighboring frame and in a neighboring area of the frame. This scheme is called *motion estimation*, as it relies on spatial and temporal motion locality properties to identify where similar parts of the image are most likely to be found in the same area of the picture in neighboring frames. Once a similar macroblock is found, only the differences are encoded and transmitted, together with the motion vector that identifies the reference macroblock (see Figure 11.17).

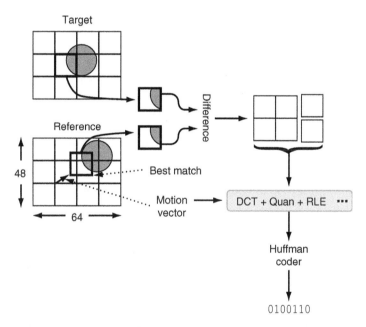

FIGURE 11.17 **Block diagram of P-frame compression.** Predicted frames are compressed through *motion estimation*. For each *target* macroblock in the predicted frame we search its neighborhood in the *reference* frame, and identify the macroblock with the smallest difference (normally computed as the order-1 norm, or *sum of absolute differences* of all pixels). The difference between reference and target is then processed in the same way as we described for an I-coded frame (Figure 11.16), but the number of bits required to transmit it is smaller, due to the reduced information content (at the limit, if the two macroblocks are identical, the information content of the difference is null). In addition, the decoder also needs to transmit the *motion vector* (i.e., the coordinates of the two-dimensional vector that represents the translation between the reference and the target macroblocks).

MPEG-4

Adopted in 1999,[7] MPEG-4 goes beyond simple audio and video compression and introduces support for synchronized overlays (such as text and graphics), metadata (for example, to store the story database of a movie), and object recognition (to augment motion estimation) such as separate background/foreground processing. In addition to MPEG standards, there are many proprietary formats, such as Apple QuickTime, Microsoft Windows Media, Real Video, and Motion JPEG (commonly adopted by the limited video functionality of several digital cameras). MPEG-4 is likely to replace (or be integrated with) many of these.

So far, we have described only video encoding. All video standards also include a separate section ("layer") that describes how to encode the sound channel associated with the video. Most of the audio compression schemes exploit psychoacoustic principles to eliminate the frequency components that are almost imperceptible to the human ear. This happens when low-amplitude (weak) sounds at a certain frequency occur very soon after a high-amplitude (strong) sound at a neighboring frequency. This is the principle behind "perceptual subband coding" schemes, such as that adopted by the popular MPEG-2 Layer 3 scheme (MP3), which achieves compression ratios of about 8 to 10.

In terms of computational complexity, digital audio and video are some of the most demanding applications in the embedded arena. If we combine the computational requirements with continuously changing standards, the cost pressure of consumer electronics, and the market dominance of a few large players we can see how challenging the development of a digital video device is. The firmware of a digital video player/recorder (encoder and decoder) can approach a million lines of code, and is distributed across legacy microprocessors, custom accelerators, and DSPs. A typical SoC includes microprocessors, accelerators, DSPs, and ASIPs, as well as nonprogrammable accelerators for the heaviest tasks (motion estimation for the recorder).

11.3.2 Automotive

The automotive domain is distinctively different from the other areas we have presented so far, largely because of the *safety-critical* nature of the electronics involved in it. Another significant difference in the automotive world is the intrinsic distributed nature of the processing taking place (see Figure 11.18), given the presence of distributed sensors and actuators (engine, vehicle, tires, environment, and entertainment) and the various interacting subsystems (engine control unit, safety, vehicle stability, information, and entertainment). Modern luxury automobiles contain hundreds of processors today, and this number will only increase. We can distinguish four primary categories in automotive electronics.

---

7. If you wonder what happened to MPEG-3, it was abandoned when it became evident that small changes to MPEG-2 (a new *profile*) would capture the major MPEG-3 driver (HDTV), and that legacy compatibility concerns would overwhelm any other technical consideration.

Body electronics (security, climate, seats, smart cards and smart keys, roof and doors, locks, onboard networks, and so on)

Chassis systems (cruise control, assisted steering and braking, safety airbags, and so on)

Powertrain electronics (engine and transmission control, injection/ignition, emission management, and so on)

FIGURE 11.18 **Example of three automotive electronics subsystems** (source: Siemens VDO Automotive website, *http://www.siemensvdo.com*).

- *Powertrain electronics* include engine control units (ECUs), transmission, and emission control.

- *Chassis systems* include controllers for braking (such as ABS), steering, traction, and wheels.

- *Body electronics* include controllers for the car security systems and locks (e.g., keyless entry), ignition, and interior climate control (air conditioning).

- *In-car computing* (sometimes also called *information systems*) includes devices such as telemetry (collision distance detectors), GPS navigation systems, multimedia controls for the entertainment/information system, and user interface (monitor lights, warnings, and so on).

In the following sections, we discuss some of the distinguishing features of the most critical automotive systems (such as ECUs or braking systems), without going into detailed description of the involved algorithms (well covered by textbooks on automatic control).

Fail-safety and Fault Tolerance

For many years microprocessors and microcontrollers have been the cornerstone of automotive electronics, and they are usually paired with a mechanical or hydraulic backup system to provide safety. We call this a *fail-safe* system, wherein a failure of an electronic component (such as the ABS control) falls back to a mechanical system that can operate correctly without the aid of the electronics. This is changing now, as vehicles shift to brake-by-wire and turn-by-wire systems, wherein electronic components must be fault tolerant or "fault functional" (continuing to operate safely in the presence of a known fault). Automotive engineers implement fault tolerance through *redundancy*, whereby a second processing unit (or a component of the same processing unit) validates every computation result and takes corrective actions when a fault is detected. In the modern era of mixed electronic and mechanical control, some electronic systems are also designed with mechanical backups, whereby the electronic system disables itself in the event of a fault.

Engine Control Units

The processing and sensing necessary for controlling an engine (primarily, fuel injection) are highly distributed. Consequently, a variety of processors contribute to a vehicle engine control unit (ECU), ranging from very simple 4-bit/8-bit microcontrollers (e.g., thermostat control) to 32-bit RISC processors dedicated to the coordination of the various functions.

A typical ECU manages the engine cycle. In terms of computational complexity, this means generating the right controls for the fuel injectors and the spark plugs of each cylinder in time for the engine to rotate at the appropriate RPM speed. At 6,000 RPM (which is close to the limit of many cars), the engine cycle is about 20 ms. At 3,000 RPM (typical revolution speed of a four-cylinder vehicle driving at about 120 Km/h), an ECU has to handle ~100 spark events per second and ensure that the running of the engine is smooth in the presence of a variety of external factors that can cause misfires.

The two main functions provided by an ECU are *injection* and *ignition*. Injection consists of regulating the fuel/air ratio that is injected into each cylinder at every revolution. Ignition is the process of firing the spark plugs with a timing that is carefully synchronized with the position of the piston. The ECU has to control injection and ignition in such a way as to optimize an objective function that accounts for fuel consumption, exhaust gas emission, pollution control rules, torque, and power delivery. Many of these dimensions push in opposite directions, and thus the ECU heuristics attempt to find a good compromise (see Figure 11.19).

The computation involved in controlling an engine at this speed is rarely a problem for modern microprocessors. As we mentioned, real-time deadlines are on the order of 10 ms, meaning that we can spend about 1M instructions of a 100-MHz processor for every engine cycle. This allows for rather complex control algorithms and indicates that the challenges are not of a computational nature, but instead involve component cost and reliability as well as accuracy and quality of the control algorithms themselves.

Finally, an interesting recent evolution of ECUs is related to the rapid adoption of flash/EEPROM memories to store the ECU program and static data. The fact that ECUs can now be reprogrammed on-the-fly reduces the expensive and time-consuming process of diagnosing and repairing a faulty ECU. At the same time this opens up a new set of problematic issues related to the appearance of after-market "code patches" that enable final users to change the factory-programmed behavior of the ECU.

In-vehicle Networking

The presence of a highly distributed electronics system and the need to have the individual subsystems communicate with one another puts a lot of pressure on the

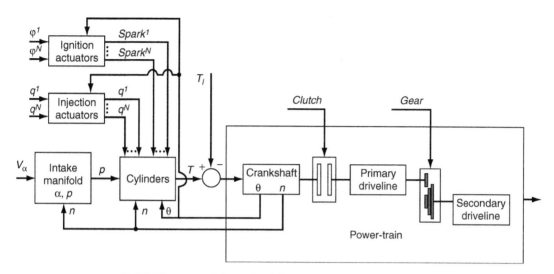

FIGURE 11.19 **Schematic of the ignition/injection control problem.** The four basic components of the system are the *manifold*, the *cylinders*, the *actuators*, and the *power-train* subsystem. The throttle valve controls the pressure in the manifold (*p*) through an electrical control (V_α). The engine produces a torque (*T*), as the cumulative torque from all cylinders, which in turn depends on a combination of the air-fuel mix inside the cylinder as well as the timing of the ignition command. The ECU task consists of generating the ignition signals for the sparks and the injection signal that determines the amount of fuel in each cylinder. The control system uses a crankshaft angle sensor to synchronize with the motion of the cylinders. The dynamics of the power-train system depend on the engine torque, the load torque (T_l), and the position of clutch and gear selector. Modern control systems use hybrid (continuous-discrete) approaches that model each component and apply standard control algorithms combined with heuristics to optimize the various situations that can occur (such as cutoff and idle speed control).

communication infrastructure. Traditionally, cars implemented point-to-point wiring among the various modules, wherein each individual signal used its own dedicated channel. Considering that a high-end vehicle contains close to 5 Km and 100 Kg of wires, it is easy to see that this results in a very inefficient, bulky, expensive, and difficult-to-maintain wiring harness.

For this reason, automotive companies are pushing strongly for a set of multi-plexed serial data bus standards that reduce the number of in-vehicle wires. Some of the emerging standards include various classes of bus protocols, distinguished by speed and functionalities. *Low-speed* networks (class A) cover throughput up to about 10 Kbps and are used for devices such as the entertainment system, the car computer, or other simple sensors. *Medium-speed* networks (class B) are in the range 10 to 125 Kbps and transport various diagnostics information, such as speed, faults, or emission data. *High-speed* networks (class C, up to 1 Mbps or greater) are used for all real-time control functions (ECU, vehicle control, steer/brake by wire).

From this description, it should be clear that modern automobiles are heterogeneous distributed computing systems, involving a wide variety of subdisciplines, including fault tolerance, networking, and real-time control.

11.3.3 Hard Disk Drives

Modern disk drives (see Figure 11.20) are marvels of integration and miniaturization, and each of them constitutes an embedded system in its own right. Designers of disk drives must solve a number of problems in diverse fields, including mechanical engineering, electrical engineering, materials science, and computer science.

From a purely physical perspective, disk drives come in a wide variety of shapes and sizes. The primary determinant of disk size is diameter. For example 5¼" disk drives are barely still in production today, with the bulk of the market consisting of 3½" drives for desktop systems and 2½" or smaller drives for laptop systems. Surprisingly small drives are commercially available. Many drives have been built to fit PCMCIA slots, and IBM's MicroDrive fits into a CompactFlash format. Disk drives include both a disk housing

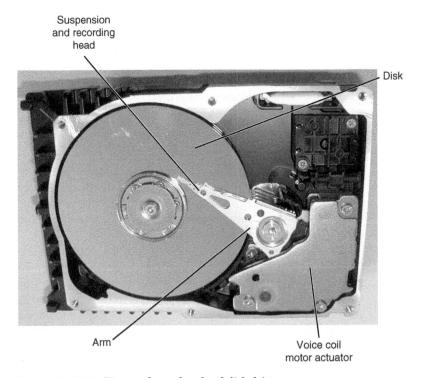

FIGURE 11.20 Picture of a modern hard disk drive.

(inside which live the disk surfaces) and a circuit board that both powers and controls the device.

A disk drive consists of one or more *platters*, which are disk-shaped pieces of aluminum that have been coated with a magnetizable material. A platter typically has two usable *surfaces*, and each surface is divided into circular *tracks*. Each track consists of many linear *sectors*, wherein a sector typically stores a power of 2 bytes (sector sizes of 512 bytes are prevalent). The *capacity* of the disk is the product (suitably multiplied) of these quantities. Manufacturers distinguish between *formatted* (or user-usable) capacity and *unformatted* capacity, which also counts the storage "wasted" in order to make the disk usable (for example, each sector has a header used by the drive to synchronize to the disk surface and correctly follow the track). Manufacturers also refer to the *areal density* (bits per unit area) of a disk drive, which is a function of the *linear density* (bits per inch linearly along a single track) and the *tracks per inch* (radially, how many tracks can be placed next to each other in one inch) of the disk.

The disk *head* is the electromagnetic device that reads or writes data on the magnetizable surface of the disk. Modern disks have separate heads for reading and writing. Today's read heads are called "magnetoresistive" or "giant magnetoresistive" (giant refers to the resistance, not the size of the head), whereas the write heads use a technology called "thin-film inductor." Heads are mounted on a larger piece of material called a *slider* (which is something of a misnomer, as the slider does not actually touch the disk surface while the disk is operating; it instead floats on a cushion of air). Each slider is mounted on an *arm*, and the head-slider-arm assembly is called an *actuator*. The actuators are grouped together with a single pivot, so that the heads move in concert over their respective surfaces. A *voice coil motor* moves the actuators to place each head over a track. Tracks on different surfaces are inscribed so that a single pivot position lines up with a track on each surface. The set of such tracks is called a *cylinder*.

Most modern disks rotate at 5,400 RPM, although models with 7,200 RPM are used for high-performance applications and devices that rotate as fast as 15,000 RPM are commercially available.

The circular geometry of a disk means that tracks near the outside edge of the disk are longer than those near the center. Drive manufacturers exploit this fact with a technique called *zoned bit recording*, whereby tracks near the edge of the disk contain more sectors. With zoned bit recording, each sector has roughly the same linear dimension, so that about the same area of magnetizable material is used. Interestingly, hard disks rotate at a constant angular velocity (unlike compact discs or DVDs, which vary their rotational speed to maintain a constant *linear* velocity) and thus the disk electronics must operate at higher frequency when reading or writing the outer sectors of the disk. This also means that the bandwidth of a disk is higher when accessing the outer tracks.

A disk drive is a random-access device, but the physical nature of access means that there are two delay factors involved in accessing data. The *seek time* of a disk drive is the time to move the heads from one set of tracks (cylinder) to another. As of this writing, typical mean seek times for disk drives are between 8 and 10 ms, with high-performance drives seeking as quickly as 4 ms. The *rotational latency* is the time after the seek has completed, wherein the drive waits for the desired sector to pass under

Spindle speed (RPM)	Average latency (half rotation) (ms)	Typical current applications
3,600	8.3	Former standard, now obsolete
4,200	7.1	Laptops
4,500	6.7	IBM Microdrive, laptops
4,900	6.1	Laptops
5,200	5.8	Obsolete
5,400	5.6	Low-end IDE/ATA, laptops
7,200	4.2	High-end IDE/ATA, Low-end SCSI
10,000	3.0	High-end SCSI
12,000	2.5	High-end SCSI
15,000	2.0	Top-of-the-line SCSI

TABLE 11.4   Spindle speed, rotational latency, and current applications. (source: *http://www.pcguide.com.*)

the head. Rotational latency is strictly a function of drive rotation speed. Table 11.4 lists RPM, average rotational latency, and the current types of drives that correspond to those parameters.

There are at least four computationally intensive areas related to disk drives: controlling the disk motors, decoding (and encoding) the data stream, scheduling the requests for data, and managing the disk (which, paradoxically, includes operating system software that also attempts to schedule requests for data).

Motor Control

There are two motors in a disk drive assembly: the spindle motor (which spins the disks) and the voice coil motor (which positions the heads over the tracks). Managing the voice coil motor includes two major modes that correspond to accessing data and seeking. In *track-following mode*, the controller adjusts the head position to follow the track as the disk rotates. Unlike the academic ideal, tracks vary in their radial distance from the center of rotation of the disk (this happens for a variety of reasons, including manufacturing variances, eccentric spindle rotation, and external shock). To determine where the head is located relative to the center of the track, each disk sector includes "servo fields" that are slightly radially offset from the center of the track. By measuring the signal strength as the head passes over the servo fields, the controller can determine how far the head has strayed from the center of the track and adjust the voice coil motor appropriately. Such *closed-loop control* is standard in modern devices, although early disk drives used *open-loop control* where no feedback was available.

The other mode for the voice coil controller is *seek mode*, wherein the controller rapidly moves the head to another track. Seeking is divided into many phases, including accelerating the actuators, decelerating them, stopping them, and then waiting for the heads to stabilize or *settle* before switching into track-following mode.

The task of the spindle motor controller is easier: maintain the rotational velocity of the disk at its designed speed. Just starting the disk spinning can involve some complexity, as friction is nontrivial. Once the disk is spinning, maintaining the specified velocity requires monitoring and a feedback loop, as the performance of the spindle motor will change as it and the disk warm up.

The Agere VC2100 and the ST L7250 chips are examples of disk controller chips combining spindle control and voice coil motor control into a single device. Each has interfaces to drive the voice coil motor, including a 14- or 15-bit digital-to-analog converter (DAC), a separate interface that drives the spindle motor (including three-phase power to the motor), and a variety of control and monitoring interfaces.

Data Decoding

Data on the surface of the disk are encoded by magnetizing the disk surface. One can think of a sector as consisting of a number of magnets placed in a straight line. When writing data, the write head changes the orientation of each magnet so that either its north pole or its south pole lies in the direction the head moves relative to the disk surface. Recall that when two magnets are placed with one of their north poles touching the other's south pole they combine to form a single effective magnet with the same orientation as the two original magnets. This means that only *changes* in magnetic polarization are visible along the length of the sector. When reading data, the read head senses these changes in magnetic polarization and translates the changes back into a data stream.

So much for the easy description. One might be tempted to use one magnet per bit, encoding the bit in the polarization of that magnet. It turns out that there are more efficient ways of encoding bits in the sequence of magnetic polarizations that work out to better (less) than one magnet per bit. These encodings are beyond the scope of this book. It also turns out that very long sequences of magnets with the same orientation are bad, because the read circuitry needs to have some idea of where the magnetic boundaries occur so that it can "clock" the magnetic domains as they pass by. With a very long run of identically oriented magnets, the hardware runs the risk that its clock will get out of sync with the magnetic domain boundaries on the disk surface. Thus, when a change finally does occur the hardware will have lost count and will then infer the wrong data value. To prevent this, efficient coding schemes always include at least one magnetization change every 10 or so magnets, so that the hardware clock and the magnetization domains stay synchronized.

Intersymbol interference further complicates the job of the decoder. Because the magnetic domains are packed so closely in a sector, adjacent domains affect each other. (More precisely, one can view the effect of a single domain as looking like a Gaussian, or bell-shaped curve. Unfortunately, the width of the Gaussian is wider than one bit time.) A technique called PRML (partial response, maximum likelihood) and refinements on PRML are used to remove the effects of intersymbol interference. PRML uses a particular coding system when writing data, and combines a filter with a Viterbi decoder when reading the data back. The coding system constrains the valid set of possible bit patterns in such a way that the Viterbi decoder can compare those possible bit patterns with the analog signal values received from the read head and choose the most likely one of those patterns to have produced the observed waveform. The filtering and Viterbi decoding functions of PRML turn out to be ideal for implementation on a DSP architecture.

Manufacturers of disk drive chip sets currently offer separate read-channel or read/write channel devices for processing the data received from or sent to disk heads. The latest chips (announced but not yet given part names as of this writing) in both the ST and Agere product lines claim to support perpendicular recording, presumably where the magnetic domains are oriented perpendicularly to the disk surface. No commercial disk systems use perpendicular recording as of this writing, but the never-ending quest for increased areal density suggests that this technique will be adopted soon.

Disk Scheduling and On-disk Management Tasks

Above the control and data levels of the disk, the electronics on the disk perform a variety of other functions. Today's disks come in two major flavors: IDE and ATA (integrated device electronics and advanced technology attached, both anachronistic names from the early years of the PC era). These are the bargain-price disks found in most PCs, whereas SCSI (small computer systems interface) disks are the disk of choice in high-performance applications. A third standard, serial ATA, is just beginning to emerge as we write this book. At a minimum, the drive electronics must interface to one of these disk interface standards.

Most disks now include hardware sector or track *caches*, which record the results of recent requests and can answer a repeated request immediately if the controlling computer re-requests a sector. Going one step further, some disks also *prefetch* into the cache, attempting to anticipate the next user request. Prefetching an entire track is the most common way to perform this. If the user has requested a particular sector on a disk, it is a reasonable guess that they will also be interested in other sectors on the same track as the requested sector. Depending on the application, this *track-buffering* technique can pay off handsomely in request latency.

By far the most computationally interesting and intensive higher-level disk management task is *disk scheduling*. The SCSI protocol supports split transactions in a way similar to the way SoC buses support them (see Chapter 6). This allows for multiple outstanding requests for data (either reading or writing), in which the user places requests for additional sectors before the first request has been fulfilled. In SCSI terminology this is "command queueing and reordering" (IDE/ATA drives support only a single request at a time).

Disk scheduling is a computational variant of the NP-complete traveling salesman problem (TSP). At its basic level, disk scheduling is complicated because of the balance between seek time and rotational latency (these two delays have been roughly balanced for all of the history of disk drives). If either factor were much larger than the other, a trivial algorithm would suffice. The balance induces a two-dimensional structure to the problem that makes it look like the TSP. The problem is not exactly a TSP because of the repetitive nature of the geography (if you miss a sector this pass, it will come around in the next pass, but your overall latency increases drastically).

NP-completeness alone should be enough to occupy any scheduling algorithm, but other considerations apply. A scheduling algorithm must operate *on-line* (as in real applications, requests for data are continually arriving). A scheduling algorithm should also be *fair*, so that no request "starves" because a sequence of later, more convenient, requests are served. And it would be useful to support *priority*, so that a real-time request could be prioritized over a request that can tolerate delay. On-line operation and fairness are issues today. Unfortunately, no current disk drive protocol supports the notion of priority.

Disk Scheduling and Off-disk Management Tasks

Although not strictly part of the disk embedded system, many of the tasks performed by the disk drive complicate the job of the operating system or user programs. We have already mentioned the disk scheduling problem. Most operating-system device drivers also attempt to schedule disk drive requests. This leads to second-guessing. The SCSI interface allows the OS to place multiple requests, but it does not allow the OS to specify the order in which they will be served by the drive. Unfortunately, the host processor is likely to have more computational power than the embedded disk controller, and the host processor may also be restricting the visible requests to a subset it has sent to the controller. Thus, the controller will not have as good information to work with.

For the OS to perform its own scheduling, it must have some idea of the physical structure of the disk. Unfortunately, this information is not readily available through the existing interfaces. In fact, addressing limitations in the IDE/ATA interface cause such disk drives to lie about their number of heads, sectors, and tracks (the "logical" geometry differs from the "physical" geometry). Operating systems end up empirically measuring the latency with which requests are answered and inferring physical geometry from these results. Further, disk drives perform "defect mapping," in which sectors with manufacturing defects are remapped by the controller to a set of "spare" sectors that are more or less nearby. Defect mapping means that the seek time and rotational latency to access a particular sector may be different from what might be guessed from the expected geometry of the disk.

Before closing this section on disk drives, we observe two trends that will change how disk drives are built and used. First, the SoC revolution has begun to affect disk drives as well. Both Agere and ST have announced SoC product lines for disk controllers (called TrueStore and Nova, respectively), and these SoCs integrate most of the functions described previously onto a single chip (for analog noise reasons, the preamplifier associated with the drive heads remains a separate component). Second, there are a number of new disk drive interface standards (FibreChannel exists already, Serial ATA is just emerging, and Infiniband is under development), some of which look like networking protocols and make the potential of NASDs (network-attached storage devices) real. Such standards will free the disk drive from the constraints of processor or file-server boxes, making them standalone embedded devices in their own right.

11.3.4 Networking and Network Processors

Computer networks move data among computers, typically from a single source to a single destination—like a universal digital postal system. The 1990s saw the transformation of the networking world from a few isolated corporate and academic islands into the highly interlinked Internet of today.

Computer networks are structured like mathematical graphs, consisting of nodes linked by node-to-node edges.[8] Endpoint or leaf nodes, reachable by only a single link, are user devices such as computers. Interior nodes make up the networking infrastructure and include a wide variety of devices with names such as routers, switches, hubs, gateways, firewalls, access points, VPN (virtual private network) boxes, and modems (these last in at least three flavors: dial-up, DSL, and cable).

Such a graph-structured topology lends itself to distributed administration. Any individual or organization that wishes to join the world-wide network need only connect its network at one point to enable connectivity to the rest of the world. However, different entities view the network in different ways. Network infrastructure suppliers see their networks in terms of "core" and "edge" routers. The former have relatively small numbers of ports and huge aggregate bandwidth. They are sometimes referred to as "backbone" routers. The latter tend to have more ports with somewhat lower aggregate bandwidth. They interface to the customers of the network providers, which tend to be smaller (lower-tier) network providers or corporate customers. Corporate networks tend to be organized into "internal" and "external" divisions, with a relatively open internal network surrounded by gateways and firewalls that restrict traffic to and from the big, bad outside world (picture a walled city in medieval style). Individuals typically pay for some sort of access on a service basis (the phone company, cable company, or wireless services company provides or supports network access).

Network links are usually described in terms of *bandwidth*, or the number of bits the link can move per second. Table 11.5 lists a number of common link speeds for a variety of links. Note the wide variety of link types: services that run over twisted-pair copper phone lines (dial-up and ADSL), services that run over broadcast coaxial cable (cable modems), wireless services (wireless and cellular data), and high-performance links that require carefully managed copper or fiber-optic wiring.

Networking nodes (henceforth generically termed "routers" for the sake of discussion) are excellent examples of embedded equipment. Historically, many routers were based on general-purpose computers with multiple network interfaces, but over time purpose-built devices have come to dominate the networking market. Today's consumer-electronics routers are smaller, have fewer parts (and fewer moving parts such as fans

---

8. Broadcast networking technologies, such as the original Ethernet, were more common in an earlier era in which both wiring and electronics were far more precious. Today's wired networks are built almost exclusively from point-to-point links and multiway switches. For most intents and purposes, network designers think in terms of graphs with simple point-to-point edges. Even today's wireless networks, which are intrinsically broadcast media because of the shared medium of radio frequencies, are treated logically as point-to-point networks.

Type of link	Link type	Bandwidth
Home service	Dial-up	Up to 56 Kbps
	ADSL	Up to 2.4 Mbps
	Cable modem	Up to 30 Mbps
Wireless data	802.11b ("Wi-Fi")	11 Mbps
	802.11a and 802.11g	54 Mbps
Cellular data	GPRS	115 Kbps
	EDGE	384 Kbps
	3G 1xRTT	144 Kbps
	3G 1xEV	Up to 5 Mbps
Ethernet (wired, office, or home data)	10M	10 Mbps
	100M	100 Mbps
	1G ("gigabit Ethernet")	1 Gbps
	10G	10 Gbps
Corporate data (typically copper cable)	T1	1.544 Mbps
	T3	43.232 Mbps
Corporate and network provider (typically fiber-optic cable)	OC-3	155.52 Mbps
	OC-12	622.08 Mbps
	OC-48	2.488 Gbps
	OC-192 or "10G"	10 Gbps
	OC-768 or "40G"	40 Gbps

TABLE 11.5 Examples of communication links and their associated bandwidth. Note that these are the peak bandwidth each type of link can deliver ("guaranteed not to exceed"). Actual performance of shared media (wireless, cellular, and cable modems) can be much lower.

or drives), and have higher reliability than desktop and notebook computers. Larger-scale corporate and network infrastructure routers may require fans, rack mounting, and computer-room installation (and thus be similar in physical requirements to server computers), but they remain special-purpose machines. And while managing a router often seems to require knowledge of the black arts, the majority of this task is configuration and reconfiguration to track topological changes. Firmware upgrades are not uncommon for routers. Such updates can either support new functionality or patch security holes.

Networking is often described in terms of seven layers of protocols, the so-called "ISO/OSI networking stack." In theory, each layer defines and solves a problem using the layer below it (independently of the layers above it). In practice, protocols deployed in real systems span multiple layers of the OSI stack. For example, the MAC (medium access control) layer of many networking protocols is considered a mixture of physical and data-link layer protocols. The TCP/IP header, the basis of the Internet, combines aspects of the network and transport layers. From bottom to top, the seven layers are:

- *Physical layer*: The physical layer defines physical and electrical characteristics of data links. These include the size and shapes of connectors and cables, and the voltages and timing used to encode data in electrical signals (or the wavelengths and timing used to encode data in optical signals).

- *Data link layer*: This layer handles issues associated with a single link, independent of network topology. This includes access control, which deals with how the endpoints share the medium over which signals propagate. This can also include various low-level signals, such as flow control between the endpoints of a link.

- *Network layer*: This is the first layer that considers communication as a network problem rather than a link-level problem. It defines the space of network addresses and supports routing individual packets.

- *Transport layer*: The transport layer includes error checking, error correction, and flow control. It provides an end-to-end data stream abstraction rather than one based on individual packets.

- *Session layer*: The session layer groups multiple related connections (typically from a single user). While this was less relevant in the early Internet, recent "multimodal" connection services that combine voice, video, and data have made session-layer protocols more important in recent years.

- *Presentation layer*: Presentation has to do with aspects of data formatting, including how characters are represented as bytes. The extension of the ASCII (American Standard Code for Information Interchange) to Latin-1 (adding additional characters for Western European variants) and later to Unicode (a 16-bit representation capable of representing virtually all written languages) is a good example of a presentation-level issue.

- *Application layer*: The application layer includes everything else above the networking stack. Examples include file transfer protocols such as FTP and HTTP; mail protocols such as SMTP, POP, and IMAP; and the network time protocol, NTP.

Some commercial terms — such as "layer-2 switch," "layer-3 switch," and "layer-7 switch" — refer to routers that operate at the data link, network, and application levels, respectively. Until relatively recently, most network infrastructure worked at layer 3 and below, with transport layer and higher issues typically being handled by the computing devices at the endpoints of the network. Layer 7 switches require much more processing and code than lower-level switches. They appear to find most use in Web- or general network-based services (caching, firewalls, and load balancing across a farm of servers). Beyond this, many research projects have proposed "active" or "intelligent" networks whose routers run general-purpose code, but the adoption of such techniques remains open.

The workload on a modern router can be computationally impressive. Consider a single 100-Mb Ethernet link. Ethernet packets vary in size from a minimum of 64 bytes to a maximum of about 1500 bytes. Using the 64-byte minimum size, this gives a worst case of about 200,000 packets per second, or about 5 microseconds of time to process each packet. For modern general-purpose processors, that leaves time for thousands of computational cycles and tens of memory accesses. The former is ample; the latter is constrained (especially if the processor must both move the packet and access-memory-based routing tables to make a routing decision). However, this is just for a single 100-Mb link. Link speeds in core routers are hundreds of times faster, and routers can have many ports. The product of high-bandwidth links with many ports quickly scales past what the memory and I/O buses of a modern processor can support, forcing designers to consider alternatives.

Router construction techniques have varied over time. One high-performance technique splits the design into per-link *line cards* that communicate through a shared *core* or *switch fabric* (this can be seen as a descendant of designs that plugged multiple interface cards into the bus of a single general-purpose machine). Such designs concentrate more processing power in each line card, but they also require building a distributed system wherein physically separated components cooperate to perform the overall task.

At a lower design level, some sort of processing element must make routing decisions. Many designs split the work between ASICs and programmable processors whereby the ASICs move data and the programmable processors (relieved of data-movement responsibilities) focus on routing tables and decisions. More recently, FPGAs have seen wide use in high-end routers, as their reconfigurability allows quicker time-to-market in low-volume, high-margin designs. Even more recently, a number of vendors have introduced *network processor* chips, which are SoCs that are purpose-built for communication routing applications. One can see a computational evolution in the transition from ASICs to FPGAs to network processors, wherein improvements in transistor density allow increasingly programmable solutions. Network processors are the most recent, programmable, and general-purpose component used to build routers, although their feasibility for backbone or "core" routers remains to be demonstrated.

Network Processors

Some network processors might better be described as router-on-a-chip designs. Figure 11.21 shows the top-level diagram of the Intel IXP1200 network processor, the first of a family of network processors Intel introduced in 2001. The design includes a number of high-bandwidth interfaces: to SRAM, to SDRAM, to the PCI bus of a host CPU, and to the proprietary IX bus (where communication devices such as Ethernet or ATM

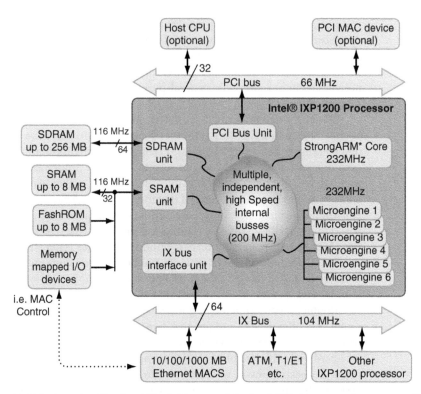

FIGURE 11.21 **Top-level block diagram of the Intel IXP1200 network processor.** The IXP should be considered an SoC integrating six programmable microengines, a StrongARM control processor, and numerous high-performance memory and I/O interfaces (SRAM, SDRAM, IX bus, and PCI bus) into a single device. (source: *Intel IXP1200 Network Processor Family: Hardware Reference Manual*, part number 278303008).

interfaces can be attached). There are also seven different processor cores integrated into one chip: six "microengines" that perform header processing and a single StrongARM embedded controller core (which manages the rest of the components on the chip). In a manner similar to the processor-plus-ASIC designs, the microcontrollers can instruct a programmable DMA engine to move packets between the IX bus and the memories, while at the same time the microengine performs header processing. The system is designed to be used in a store-and-forward manner, in which each packet is stored in its entirety in memory (i.e., the SRAM or SDRAM) when it arrives, and is then written back out to the correct interface (possibly with changes to its header) when it is sent on its way. With about 6 Gbits/s bandwidth to the network interfaces and another 9 Gbits/s bandwidth to off-chip memory, a single IXP1200 can handle multiple gigabit-speed links, and comes close to being able to handle 10-G (OC-192) links. However, the lack of a high-speed path to link to a switch fabric or other IXPs (the path to the PCI bus is much slower and not directly connected to the high-speed on-chip buses) makes it difficult to combine multiple IXP chips to build a larger router.

The IXP1200 is designed to take advantage of the independence of routing decisions across packets, using multiprocessing and multithreading. In addition to the hardware parallelism in having six microengines, each microengine hosts four hardware threads. The threads cooperatively share the hardware of that engine, which means that software must explicitly yield before another thread can run. Multithreading increases the utilization of each microengine, allowing an engine to switch to a different thread after it launches a long-latency operation. Each thread is individually programmable (although all threads on a microengine share a single, 1- or 2-Kbyte program store), allowing them to divide work homogeneously or heterogeneously depending on the workload. The collection of microengines and threads allows the IXP to process up to 24 packets simultaneously.

Figure 11.22 shows the block diagram of a single microengine in the IXP1200 architecture. Readers should find Figure 11.22 familiar. It resembles Figure 1.3 (which depicts a traditional DSP) in style and layout. In particular, the architecture diagram depicts individual multiplexers, special-purpose register files, and limited connection pathways. The architecture of an IXP1200 microengine might be a textbook study in violating our VLIW design maxims. There are condition code registers (which evaporate upon thread switch). There are many nonaddressable or partially addressable storage spaces (in particular, the load and store register banks). ALU operands get their left and right operands from separate register banks. Many instructions rely on information from previous instructions to do their work. For example, the 32-bit ALU result is often used as a control parameter for the memory read/write operations, and the only way to shift by a variable amount is to use a register specifier from the previous instruction.

On the other hand, the IXP1200 microengine does a good job of "exposing power" in its memory interfaces. The programming model gives control over the load and store buffer mechanisms to the programmer, architecturally exposing the memory-address and memory-data registers hidden in many general-purpose processors (these are called "read transfer" and "write transfer" register banks in the diagram). There are separate instructions for access to off-chip SDRAM, off-chip SRAM, on-chip (shared) scratch-pad RAM, and the transmit/receive FIFOs in the IX bus unit. This gives the programmer or compiler direct control over what gets loaded and stored, in what transfer size, and in what order (including parallel access to different banks or addresses of memory).

Nothing in the foregoing description makes it easy to program or compile to an IXP. Although the IXP architecture does have a C compiler for the microengines, as of this writing it supports only a limited subset of C-standard language constructs. The assembler is similarly quirky. It has many features like those of a linear assembly optimizer, giving users the option of hand allocating registers or using one of two different built-in (and syntactically incompatible) register allocators. The exposed load and store mechanisms of the IXP beg for effective compiler optimizations. There has been some impressive research work in compiling to IXP microengines using a domain-specific functional programming language front end coupled to an optimizing back end

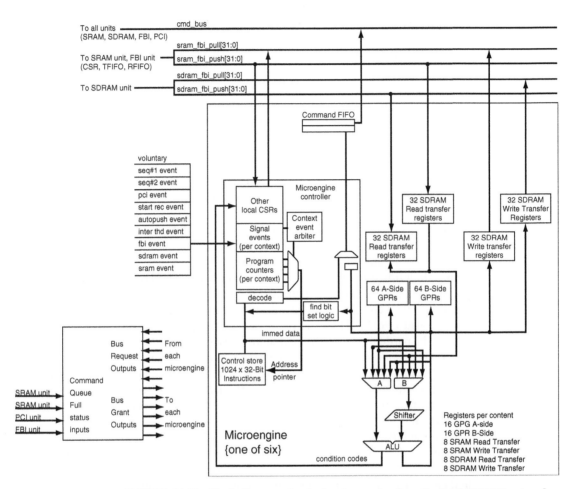

FIGURE 11.22 **Block diagram of a single microengine from the Intel IXP1200 network processor.** Note the DSP-like features: exposed multiplexers, separate register banks, and limited connections between parts. (From the *Intel IXP1200 Network Processor Family Hardware Reference Manual.*)

(which uses integer linear programming to solve the register allocation problem), but this approach remains some distance from the programming mainstream.

Intel's IXP architecture has enjoyed enough commercial success to justify a second generation of products. The second-generation IXP2400 series of processors benefits in the usual way from Moore's law: higher clock rates and larger memories (and more microengines per chip). Intel has also dropped the proprietary IX bus in favor of LVDS (low-voltage differential signaling) ports, which are used to interface to a variety of electrical and optical physical interfaces. Most intriguingly, Intel has added a cryptography-related block to one variant of the architecture, allowing a new set of firewall, VPN (virtual private network), and other security-related features to be performed by IXP processors.

The Intel IXP architecture goes the farthest in the direction of multiprocessor and multithreaded parallelism, but network processor products from other manufacturers have similar characteristics. The Motorola (formerly C-Port before acquisition) C-5 network processor might be better characterized as a *line card on a chip*, in that it is designed with a separate *fabric* interface that can be used to interface it with another C-5 network processor or to a centralized fabric chip that connects many C-5 network processors into a larger system. However, in other respects the C-5 is very similar in structure to the IXP, having a number of high-bandwidth interfaces to physical network interfaces, memory, 16 *channel processors*, and a separate *executive processor* for system maintenance. Unlike the threaded design of the IXP microengine, each channel processor looks more like an ASIC-plus-processor design, with a MIPS-based programmable core supported by a stream-oriented set of bit- and byte-oriented programmable special-purpose processors.

We began this book with the assertion that the VLIW hammer is the right one for the embedded processing nail. We stand by this assertion, but we would be demagogues rather than scientists if we claimed that VLIW is right for all embedded applications. The particular case of network processing has virtual independence across packets but a computationally narrow memory-access-dominated decision path for each packet. Intriguingly, there *is* ILP to be found in packet processing code, and especially in systems that integrate many levels of processing into a single device. However, a single ILP-oriented, wide-issue VLIW is probably not the best answer for this case. For routing, the high-throughput, latency-tolerant, multiprocessor-based approach taken by network processors seems well suited.

11.4 Further Reading

It would be beyond the scope of this book to provide an exhaustive coverage of the application areas for embedded VLIW architectures. In this section we provide some pointers to readers as a starting point for investigation of areas of interest more deeply, but we do not expand the discussion to the depth of the other chapters.

Digital Imaging

An authoritative reference for digital imaging, color, and printing in general is the book by H. Kipphan [2001], an invaluable source of information for print media technologies and related manufacturing processes. An excellent reference for in-depth analysis of dithering techniques is the book by R. Ulichney [1987]. For more information on the JPEG standard, the ISO JPEG web site (at *http://www.jpeg.org*) and the Independent JPEG Group web site (at *http://www.ijg.org*) are good places to start, together with the book by Pennabaker and Mitchell [1993] and a lighter but excellent introduction to the subject in Wallace's CACM paper [1991]. On a more general introduction to the topic of data compression, a good reading is also *The Data Compression Book*, by Nelson and Gailly [1995]. For a much deeper look at color science, a "classic" is the book by Wyszecki and Stiles [2000]. A field related to digital imaging, in which many concepts overlap, is computer graphics, for which the book by Foley, Van Dam, Feiner, and Hughes [Foley et al., 1995] provides a good introduction, as well as the excellent book by Bhaskaran and Konstantinides [1997]. The book by Rao and Yip [1990] provides an in-depth look at the DCT. Finally, the algorithm for radial interpolation used in the application example is based on a technique described in [Vondran and Desoli, 2000].

Telecom

Understanding telecommunications problems implies understanding communications theory, for which the seminal work by Claude Shannon [1948] is always the place to start. For a good academic-style coverage of digital signal processing (and processing of speech signals), the "classic" textbooks of Oppenheim and Schafer [1975] and Rabiner and Schafer [1978] provides excellent references. We also recommend Makhoul's [1975] tutorial as a lighter overview of linear prediction techniques. More modern updates include the books of O'Shaughnessy [1987] and Klejin and Palwal [1995]. Additionally, the "laboratory textbook" of Barnwell, Nayebi, and Richardson [Barnwell et al., 1996] provides a more practical point of view.

For a more detailed reference to the algorithm described in Section 11.2, ETSI (the European Telecommunication Standard Institute) publishes a set of documents that contains in-depth descriptions and reference C-code implementation of the relevant standards [ETSI, 2000a and b]. Many DSP companies also routinely publish how to optimize important algorithms on their platform, as the work by Wang and Fu [2000] shows for the TI C6x DSP family.

Digital Video, Automotive, Networking, and Storage

- *Digital Video*: Among the variety of textbooks that cover the area of digital video, we recommend the books by Wang, Ostermann, and Zhang [Wang et al., 2002] and the book by Telkap [1995]. A more practical set of information about digital video is covered by Watkinson [2000] and Jack [2001]. For a deeper dive into motion analysis, we also suggest the book by Sezan and Lagendjik [1993]. The book by Haskell, Puri, and Netravali [Haskell et al., 1997] provides specific information on MPEG-2. See also the lighter paper by Gall [1991].

- *Automotive*: Many automotive problems can be described in terms of hybrid systems, for which readers can find a good collection of perspectives in the book edited by Alur, Henzinger, and Sontag [Alur et al., 1996]. The analysis, design, and control of hybrid systems is a very important problem that because of the real-time fault-tolerant nature of the domain emphasizes the verification aspects, as presented by Nelson [1990] and the work by Lala and Harper [1994]. A good summary of the challenges and opportunities in digital control of automotive hybrid systems is presented in the Proceedings of the IEEE paper by Balluchi et al. [2000].

- *Network Processors*: The best way to learn about network processors is probably by looking at the reference manual for a commercial product, such as the Intel IXP or the Motorola C-Port. An overview of the Intel IXP is also available in the paper by George and Blume [2003] and the paper by Adiletta et al. [2002] published in a special issue of the *Intel Technical Journal* entirely dedicated to network processors. Likewise, the white paper by C-port founder Husak [2000] is a good place to start. An excellent overview of network processor research challenges is the MICRO-34 tutorial presentation by Mangione-Smith and Memik [2002]. Finally, a recommended book on the subject is the collection edited by Crowley et al. [2003].

- *Disk Drives*: The technology behind hard disk drives has evolved so rapidly that the most reliable sources of information are likely to be product-oriented web sites, such as PcGuide, which contains extremely deep and accurate descriptions of modern PC hardware. For a more scientific approach to the problem, we suggest the modeling paper by Ruemmler and Wilkes [1994] and the later overview on performance issues by Ng [1998]. The paper by Siegel and Wolf [1991] takes a more theoretical approach to the coding problem. The papers by Cidecyan et al. [1992], Lyi and Tomizuka [1999], Abidi [1994], Abramovitch and Franklin [2002], and Andrews et al. [1996] provide further information on the various aspects of disk drive design and scheduling algorithms for data access and allocation.

11.5 Exercises

1. Using the VEX tools, modify the imaging pipeline benchmark so that color space conversion happens before upscaling (note that the color space conversion now needs to operate on three components and the scaling on four components). Is the new version of the algorithm slower or faster? Can you see visual differences for large scaling factors? How does the profile of the application change?

2. Using the VEX tools and the imaging pipeline benchmark, change the scaling algorithm to implement pixel replication, instead of bilinear interpolation. Compare the execution performance of the two implementations. Can you see visual differences for large scaling factors?

3. Using the VEX tools and the imaging pipeline benchmark, change the color space conversion algorithm to implement tri-linear interpolation instead of the (proprietary) radial interpolation technique. Compare the performance of the two implementations. What is the primary effect that causes performance variations?

4. Using the VEX tools and the imaging pipeline benchmark, change the halftoning algorithm to random dithering. Compare the performance of the two implementations and describe the visual differences.

5. Using the VEX tools and the EFR benchmark, determine the smallest I-cache/D-cache sizes that provide a good performance tradeoff (less than 10% degradation from the ideal cache case). Repeat the same for the imaging pipeline benchmark. Compare and contrast the two applications.

6. Using the VEX tools and the EFR benchmark, model a noncached machine wherein code fits in instruction memory but we need to explicitly wait for several cycles for data accesses. Experiment within the 5- to 10-cycle range (hint: you need to tell the compiler that the load latency grows). Compare the performance with respect to cache cases (smaller hit latency, longer miss latency) for both the EFR benchmark and the imaging benchmark.

7. Using publicly available resources and the VEX toolchain, compile and simulate an MPEG-2 encoder and decoder program on a sample video. Profile the code and identify the most important routines.

8. Using the encoder example from the previous exercise, experiment with a set of custom-defined instructions that can speed the code up (hint: one of the most important encoding routines is motion estimation, which requires computing a sum of absolute differences).

9. The effective resolution of a DVD player is 720×480. HDTV's resolution will go up to 1920×1080, which is a factor of 6.0 more pixels. Assuming an MPEG-2 compression standard, what is the required capacity of a HD-DVD disk to store a 120-minute movie?

10. One of the issues a designer of a reliable system has to face is failure detection. Academic models assume that components cease to operate when they fail (*fail stop*). In the real world, components can fail without being aware that they have failed. Describe the ways in which a component can fail without indicating that it has failed. Discuss how you might engineer a system to tolerate such failures.

11. Consider a six-cylinder, four-stroke engine running at 4500 RPM. How many interrupts per second (assuming one interrupt per revolution) can you expect in the engine control unit? If you have a 100-MHz processor, how many operations can you afford to run in the algorithm that determines when to fire the spark plug?

12. For the degenerate case in which seek time is much larger than disk rotational latency, devise an optimal disk-scheduling algorithm. Devise another algorithm for the opposite case (seek time much shorter than rotational latency). By "devise" we mean describe your algorithm in text and argue why it is optimal.

13. Many database system integrators use only a fraction of the available hard disk space on the disk they install. Name two reasons this should be the case.

14. For a 2½" diameter hard disk, assume that the radius of the innermost track is 0.25 inch. What is the ratio of the number of sectors of the outermost track and the innermost track?

The VEX System

I hate books; they only teach us to talk about what we don't know.

— Jean-Jacques Rousseau, *Swiss-born French philosopher, political theorist*, 1712–1778

This appendix describes the VEX (VEX stands for "VLIW example") system that accompanies the book and is used for the examples throughout the book. VEX includes three basic components:

1. *The VEX Instruction Set Architecture*: VEX defines a 32-bit clustered VLIW ISA that is scalable and customizable to individual application domains. The VEX ISA is loosely modeled on the ISA of the HP/ST Lx (ST200) family of VLIW embedded cores. Scalability includes the ability to change the number of clusters, execution units, registers, and latencies. Customizability enables users to define *special-purpose* instructions in a structured way.

2. *The VEX C Compiler*: The VEX C compiler is a derivation of the Lx/ST200 C compiler, itself a descendant of the *Multiflow* C compiler. It is a robust, ISO/C89 compiler that uses *trace scheduling* as its global scheduling engine. A very flexible programmable machine model determines the target architecture. For VEX, we selectively expose some of the parameters to allow architecture exploration by changing the number of clusters, execution units, issue width, and operation latencies without having to recompile the compiler.

3. *The VEX Simulation System*: The VEX simulator is an architecture-level (functional) simulator that uses *compiled simulator* technology to achieve a speed of many equivalent MIPS. The simulation system also comes with a fairly complete set of POSIX-like *libc* and *libm* libraries (based on the GNU *newlib* libraries), a simple built-in cache simulator (level-1 cache only), and an API that enables other plug-ins used for modeling the memory system.

The following sections cover each of the components in detail, and provide usage examples for what we envision are the most common uses of them — as well as what is needed for some of the book's exercises. More detailed reference documentation for the tools is available at this book's web site at *http://www.vliw.org/book*.

A.1 The VEX Instruction-set Architecture

For the purpose of this book, VEX only defines an ISA in terms of the *visible architecture*; that is, the syntax, semantics, and constraints of operations. Because VEX is a flexible architecture, we can distinguish two types of constraints: the set of rules all implementations have to obey (such as the base ISA, register connectivity, memory coherency, architecture state) and the set of rules of a specific VEX instance (such as the issue width, the number of clusters, the mix of functional units, latencies, and custom instructions).

VEX models a scalable technology platform for embedded VLIW processors that allows variation in issue width, the number and capabilities of structures such as functional units and register files, and the processor instruction set. In the spirit of statically scheduled VLIW architectures, the compiler is responsible for schedule correctness. In addition to basic data and operation semantics, VEX includes features that provide the compiler greater flexibility in scheduling multiple concurrent operations. These include a complete exposure of all architecture latencies and resource constraints.

- Parallel execution units, including multiple integer ALUs and multipliers

- Parallel memory pipelines, including access to multiple data memory ports

- Architectural support for data prefetching and other locality hints

- A large architecturally visible register set

- Partial predication through *select* operations

- An efficient branch architecture with multiple condition registers

- Encoding of long immediate operands within the same instruction

This section specifies the structure and behavior of the VEX architecture, and excludes most implementation and microarchitecture details except those embodied in VEX.

VEX defines a parametric space of architectures that share a common set of application and system resources, such as registers and operations. A VEX instance (that is, an individual processor) implements a variation of the base architecture, which we obtain by specializing the set of customizable parameters, such as the issue width, the number and mix of functional units, and so on. The most basic unit of execution in VEX is an *operation*, similar to a typical RISC-style instruction. An encoded operation is called a *syllable*, and a collection of syllables issued in a single cycle and executed in VLIW mode as an atomic unit is called an *instruction*.

Why VEX?

Among the proliferation of various VLIW embedded and DSP processors, no dominant embedded VLIW architecture had emerged as we were writing this book. For a while, we considered creating a fictional ISA for the book examples, but no tools would have been available for it, and we believe that hands-on experience is a fundamental component in the process of learning this complex field.

At the same time, the HP/ST Lx (ST200) architecture had been announced and two of the writers were heavily involved in its design and development. Lx is a very clean new architecture, with no legacy to support, robust tools, and extensive scalability and customizability features, and seemed to be close to the ideal target we were aiming for. So, we decided to start from the Lx architecture, remove some of the engineering tradeoffs of a real product, and simplify the ISA to better match our tutorial requirements. What we then called "VEX" was born.

The VEX compiler is derived from the Lx compiler, which is itself a descendant of the *Multiflow* compiler. We believe that the VEX compiler combines the robustness of an industrial compiler with the flexibility of a research platform. Using VEX, you can compile complex programs and at the same time experiment with new architecture ideas, custom instructions, and scalability. We also decided to make the VEX compiler only available in binary form. With this limitation, we see it more as a platform for embedded VLIW research than for VLIW compiler research, which is already well covered by other compilation environments such as Trimaran (see *http://www.trimaran.org*) or SUIF (see *http://suif.stanford.edu*).

The VEX C compiler is limited in many ways: it only targets C (sorry, no C++, no Java), it concentrates on acyclic scheduling (no software pipelining), it only supports partial predication (no full predication), and its only region shape is a *trace* (no superblocks nor treegions). For those who find these limitations too constraining, one important concept to take away from this book is that *in the design of a new architecture the available compiler technology has to be considered a fundamental component of the technology portfolio*. This is what we can make available. We have built interesting and commercially viable VLIW processors with it, and it is our firm belief that these are very valuable tools for understanding the space of embedded VLIW architectures.

A.1.1 VEX Assembly Language Notation

To understand the assembly language notation for a VEX operation, consider the following example:

```
c0 cmpne $b0.3 = $r0.4, $r0.5
;;
```

The cluster identifier *c0* denotes the cluster upon which the operation is to be executed (0 in this case). The destination operand(s) are given by a list to the left of the "=", whereas the source operands are listed to the right of the "=". In this case, the

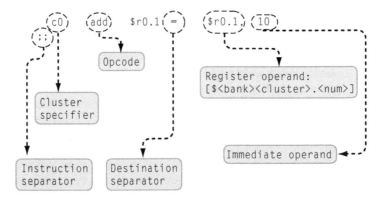

FIGURE A.1 **Anatomy of the assembly language notation for a VEX instruction.** The VEX assembly language is fairly straightforward, with destination registers separated by an "=" sign from source registers, to avoid ambiguity. The only notational complication comes from the clustered nature of VEX, and operations need to explicitly identify the executing cluster and the location of the operand.

only destination operand is *branch register #3* of *cluster 0,* and the source operands are *general-purpose registers #4* and *#5* of *cluster 0.* In general, the cluster identifier is optional where registers are used as operands, in that they uniquely identify the cluster upon which the operation is to be executed. The instruction separator (";;") indicates the end of a group of operations issued in the same cycle. Figure A.1 shows a more detailed breakdown of the notation for a VEX instruction.

Instructions that include multiple operations simply list each operation on a separate line, with a double semicolon as a separator of instructions. For example, the following assembly language listing shows two instructions, the first with two parallel operations and the second with three.

```
    c0 add $r0.13 = $r0.3, $r0.0    # instr 0, op 0
    c0 sub $r0.16 = $r0.6, 3        # instr 0, op 1
;; ### end of first instruction

    c0 shl $r0.13 = $r0.13, 3       # instr 1, op 0
    c0 shr $r0.15 = $r0.15, 9       # instr 1, op 1
    c0 ldw.d $r0.14 = 0[$r0.4]      # instr 1, op 2
;; ### end of second instruction
```

A.1.2 Clusters

VEX is a *clustered* architecture (see Figure A.2). It provides scalability of issue width and functionality using modular execution clusters. A cluster is a collection of register files and a tightly coupled set of functional units. Functional units within a cluster directly access only the cluster register files, with only a few exceptions. VEX clusters are architecturally visible and the code contains explicit cluster assignments (to choose the

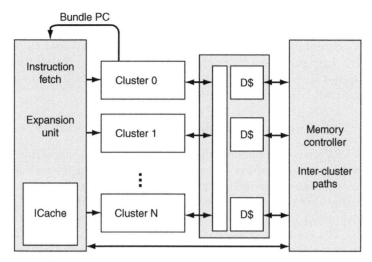

FIGURE A.2 **Structure of a VEX multicluster implementation.** At the multicluster level, VEX defines the infrastructure to fetch and decode instructions, to sequence programs, to access memory, and to move data across clusters.

execution cluster for an operation) and explicit intercluster copy operations (to move data across clusters). Intercluster copy operations may require more than one cycle (pipelined or not) and may consume resources in both the source and the destination cluster. Because we can associate data cache ports and/or private memories with each cluster, VEX allows multiple memory accesses to execute simultaneously. Clusters obey the following set of rules. This diagram shows that there can be multiple data cache blocks, attached by a crossbar to the different clusters and allowing a variety of memory configurations.

- A single cluster can issue multiple operations in the same instruction.

- Clusters can have different widths and different operation mixes.

- Not all clusters have to support the entire VEX ISA.

- Units within a single cluster are indistinguishable. In other words, a cluster can only execute a finite set of simultaneous operations, but these operations do not have to be assigned to particular units within the cluster. The hardware decoding logic assigns operations to units within a cluster.

By convention, VEX clusters are numbered from zero. Control operations execute on cluster 0, which is — in this sense — a "special" cluster that must always be present in any VEX implementation.

At the architecture level, *functional units are only connected to register files* and not to other functional units. The details of microarchitecture bypassing (forwarding) are not exposed at the architecture level but translate into shorter producer-consumer latencies of the bypassed operations. Functional units and register files within a single cluster are fully interconnected. In other words, it is always possible to write the result of a functional unit to a register in the same cluster without passing through intermediate storage. Functional units and register files in different clusters may have limited connectivity. VEX only guarantees the minimal functionality to move data between general-purpose register files in different clusters. Note that some functional units (such as the branch unit) may read registers from other clusters.

A.1.3 Execution Model

A VEX architecture issues multiple operations in an instruction in a single cycle, and these operations are executed as a single atomic action. Instructions are executed strictly in program order, but within an instruction *all operands are read before any results are written*. For example, it is possible to swap the value of a pair of registers in a single instruction. Instructions cannot contain sequential constraints among their operations.

The execution model treats instructions as atomic units. An exception caused by an instruction may not affect the execution of any instruction issued earlier, and must prevent the instruction that is generating the exception from modifying the programmer visible state. The execution behavior is that of an *in-order* machine: each instruction executes to completion before the start of the next one. In other words, all syllables of an instruction start together and commit their results together. Committing results includes modifying register state, updating memory, and generating exceptions.

Operations may have architecturally visible non-unit latency (*non-uniform assigned latencies — NUAL —* model). Not all operations are required to have the same latency, and the compiler has to schedule the code while obeying latency constraints. Operations may have a different latency, depending on the functional unit or the source/destination register pair. If the hardware can complete an operation in the same number of cycles (or fewer) than assumed by the compiler, no stalls or interlocks are required. If an operation requires longer than the assumed latency, the hardware stalls execution until the architectural assumptions hold again (cache misses and branches fall into this category). In this sense, VEX is a *less-than-or-equal — LEQ —* machine (see Sections 3.2.2 and 5.4.3 for details). When the hardware does not provide support to check for latency violations, the behavior of a code sequence that violates latency constraints is undefined.

Each VEX instance imposes limits on the number and type of operations that fit in a single instruction. When it is not possible to fill every available operation "slot," the VEX encoding scheme ensures that no space is wasted. VEX encodes operations in 32-bit *syllables* that include two reserved bits for sequencing and cluster encoding.

- The *instruction-stop bit* (set in the last syllable of an instruction) indicates the end of an instruction and is used by the sequencing logic to identify the execution boundaries within a cycle.

- The *cluster-start bit* (set in the first syllable of a cluster within an instruction) indicates the beginning of the section of the instruction corresponding to a new cluster. Syllables of an instruction are required to be sorted in cluster order, from low to high addresses. The cluster-start bit is used by the dispersal logic to route the proper section of the instruction to the corresponding cluster.

A.1.4 Architecture State

The architecturally visible state consists of the collection of the state of all architecturally visible *containers*. VEX containers include general-purpose registers, branch registers, control registers, and in general any nonvolatile and addressable storage element. VEX containers obey the following constraints.

- All architecturally visible containers must be individually addressable. In other words, no architecturally visible element can be implicitly part of a larger container without an operation that allows it to be individually addressed.

- Architecturally visible containers are never overwritten by operations that do not explicitly specify the container among their destinations. Containers may not be implicitly overwritten (this would be an example of a *hot spot*).

- The architecture implementation must provide a "copy" mechanism to move data to and from any architecturally visible container.

All VEX operations operate on 32-bit containers, and do not include specific support for non 32-bit values. For example, the memory architecture widens smaller accesses (8- and 16-bit) to 32-bit containers. Larger data types (e.g., 64-bit) are accessed with multiple 32-bit memory operations. Operations on smaller data types require the compiler to execute the proper sign/zero extensions. Note that although they may appear as an exception to the previous rule, single-bit branch/select registers are actually a concise representation of the 32-bit integer values 1 and 0. Operations that manipulate branch registers must perform the proper conversions when moving values between general-purpose registers and branch registers.

A.1.5 Arithmetic and Logic Operations

VEX supports a "traditional" set of RISC-style integer operations. Less traditional operations include *shift-and-add* (for efficient address computations), *select* (for partial predication), logical *and/or* operations (for control-flow simplification), *min/max* operations, and a rich set of *integer multiplication* operations. The version of VEX that accompanies the book focuses on *integer* operations, and does not include any specific hardware support for floating point, which is emulated through a library of intrinsics derived from the public-domain *SoftFloat*[1] package.

Tables A.1 through A.3 outline the VEX arithmetic and logical operations with a brief description of each. In Table A.2 we show the rich set of multiplication operations VEX supports, as often required in DSP-like algorithms. In the tables, we use the notations *s1* and *s2* to indicate a source general-purpose register, *t* for a target general-purpose

---

1. *SoftFloat* was written by John R. Hauser at the International Computer Science Institute (ICSI), in collaboration with the University of California at Berkeley. See *http://www.cs.berkeley.edu/~jhauser/arithmetic/softfloat.html* for more information.

Operation	Description
ADD t=s1,{s2|im}	Add
ADDCG t,b=b,s1,s2	Add with *carry* and *generate carry*
AND t=s1,{s2|im}	Bitwise AND
ANDC t=s1,{s2|im}	Bitwise complement and AND
DIVS t,b=b,s1,s2	Division step with *carry* and *generate carry*
MAX t=s1,{s2|im}	Maximum signed
MAXU t=s1,{s2|im}	Maximum unsigned
MIN t=s1,{s2|im}	Minimum signed
MINU t=s1,{s2|im}	Minimum unsigned
OR t=s1,{s2|im}	Bitwise OR
ORC t=s1,{s2|im}	Bitwise complement and OR
SH1ADD t=s1,{s2|im}	Shift left 1 and add
SH2ADD t=s1,{s2|im}	Shift left 2 and add
SH3ADD t=s1,{s2|im}	Shift left 3 and add
SH4ADD t=s1,{s2|im}	Shift left 4 and add
SHL t=s1,{s2|im}	Shift left
SHR t=s1,{s2|im}	Shift right signed
SHRU t=s1,{s2|im}	Shift right unsigned
SUB t={s2|im},s1	Subtract
SXTB t=s1	Sign extend byte
SXTH t=s1	Sign extend half
ZXTB t=s1	Zero extend byte
ZXTH t=s1	Zero extend half
XOR t=s1,{s2|im}	Bitwise exclusive OR

TABLE A.1   Integer arithmetic operations in VEX.

register, *b* for a branch register (source or destination), and *im* to indicate a source immediate (constant). VEX operations are semantics based and format independent, and the same opcode is used regardless of the type of operands and results. For example, VEX uses *add* for additions between registers, or between register and immediates.

Operation	Description
MPYLL t=s1,{s2|im}	Multiply signed low 16 × low 16 bits
MPYLLU t=s1,{s2|im}	Multiply unsigned low 16 × low 16 bits
MPYLH t=s1,{s2|im}	Multiply signed low 16 × high 16 bits
MPYLHU t=s1,{s2|im}	Multiply unsigned low 16 × high 16 bits
MPYHH t=s1,{s2|im}	Multiply signed high 16 × high 16 bits
MPYHHU t=s1,{s2|im}	Multiply unsigned high 16 × high 16 bits
MPYL t=s1,{s2|im}	Multiply signed low 16 × 32 bits
MPYLU t=s1,{s2|im}	Multiply unsigned low 16 × 32 bits
MPYH t=s1,{s2|im}	Multiply signed high 16 × 32 bits
MPYHU t=s1,{s2|im}	Multiply unsigned high 16 × 32 bits
MPYHS t=s1,{s2|im}	Multiply signed high 16 × 32, shift left 16

TABLE A.2 Multiplication operations in VEX.

Examples

The following example shows how to use *select* operations in a simple if-conversion (note that the VEX compiler would recognize this as *min* and *max*).

```
## Implements:
##              if (x > 10) t = 10;
##              if (x < 0) t = 0;
## where x is in $r0.1 and t is in $r0.2
##
   c0 cmpgt $b0.0 = $r0.1, 10
   c0 cmplt $b0.1 = $r0.1, 0
;;
   c0 slctf $r0.2 = $b0.0, $r0.2, 10
;;
   c0 slctf $r0.2 = $b0.1, $r0.2, 0
;;
```

The following example shows how to efficiently use the extensive multiplication repertoire in VEX (assumes a two-cycle multiplication).

```
## Implements:
##      int t = ((short)a)*((short)b) + (a»16)*(b»16)
## where a is in $r0.1, b in $r0.2 and t in $r0.3
```

Operation	Description
CMPEQ {t|b}=s1,{s2|im}	Compare (equal)
CMPGE {t|b}=s1,{s2|im}	Compare (greater equal - signed)
CMPGEU {t|b}=s1,{s2|im}	Compare (greater equal - unsigned)
CMPGT {t|b}=s1,{s2|im}	Compare (greater - signed)
CMPGTU {t|b}=s1,{s2|im}	Compare (greater - unsigned)
CMPLE {t|b}=s1,{s2|im}	Compare (less than equal - signed)
CMPLEU {t|b}=s1,{s2|im}	Compare (less than equal - unsigned)
CMPLT {t|b}=s1,{s2|im}	Compare (less than - signed)
CMPLTU {t|b}=s1,{s2|im}	Compare (less than - unsigned)
CMPNE {t|b}=s1,{s2|im}	Compare (not equal)
NANDL {t|b}=s1,s2	Logical NAND
NORL {t|b}=s1,s2	Logical NOR
ORL {t|b}=s1,s2	Logical OR
SLCT t=b,s1,{s2|im}	Select *s1* on true condition
SLCTF t=b,s1,{s2|im}	Select *s1* on false condition

TABLE A.3 Logical and select operations in VEX.

```
##
    c0 mpyll $r0.4 = $r0.1, $r0.2
    c0 mpyhh $r0.5 = $r0.1, $r0.2
    xnop 1
;;
    c0 add $r0.3 = $r0.4, $r0.5
;;
```

The following example shows how to efficiently use the logical operation repertoire in VEX to implement complex conditional expressions (assumes a two-cycle compare-to-branch delay and a two-cycle memory load). Note the use of speculation (ldw.d) to enable the manipulation of memory operations in conditionals.

```
## Implements:
##    if ((a > 0 || d < 0) && *pb > c)
##       goto LABEL;
```

```
## a in $r0.3, pb in $r0.4, c in $r0.5, d in $r0.6
##
   c0 cmpgt $r0.13 = $r0.3, $r0.0
   c0 cmplt $r0.16 = $r0.6, $r0.0
   c0 ldw.d $r0.14 = 0[$r0.4]
;;
   c0 orl $r0.13 = $r0.13, $r0.16
;;
   c0 cmpgt $r0.14 = $r0.14, $r0.5
;;
   c0 andl $b0.0 = $r0.13, $r0.14
   xnop 1
;;
   c0 br $b0.0, LABEL
;;
```

A.1.6 Intercluster Communication

VEX uses a pair of *send* and *receive* operations to implement intercluster communication. Send/receive operations specify a source/destination register pair and an intercluster path identifier. A *send* operation places the source register value on the specified intercluster path. The corresponding *receive* operation, which must be issued in the same instruction, retrieves the data from the specified intercluster path and stores it in the destination register. The immediate operand enables a large number of microarchitectural paths.

Table A.4 shows the basic intercluster operations VEX supports. For convenience and readability, VEX assembly language usually represents pairs of *send/receive* operations with the macro *mov*, as the example shows.

The following code shows a simple example of an instruction that issues two intercluster copy operations in parallel.

```
## Copy reg.3 of cluster 0 to reg.4 of cluster 1
## Copy reg.1 of cluster 2 to reg.7 of cluster 3
## (in the same instruction)
##
   c1=c0 mov $r1.4 = $r0.3
   c3=c2 mov $r3.7 = $r2.1
;;
```

Operation	Description
SEND s1, im	Send \<s1\> to the path identified by \<im\>
RECV t = im	Assigns the value from the path identified by \<im\> to \<t\>

TABLE A.4   Intercluster operations in VEX.

A.1.7 Memory Operations

VEX is a *load/store* architecture, meaning that only *load* and *store* operations can access memory, and that memory operations only target general-purpose registers (e.g., there are no *memory-to-memory* operations). The version that accompanies the book uses a *big-endian* byte-ordering model. Memory accesses in VEX are restricted to native alignment (i.e., *0 mod 2* for short, *0 mod 4* for int, *0 mod 8* for double). Misaligned accesses cause a nonrecoverable trap.

VEX only supports a *base-plus-offset* addressing mode, wherein the base may be any general-purpose register but the offset must be an immediate. For example, the following examples represent a subset of the supported load operations.

```
## int a[]; t = a[10] (a in $r0.2, t in $r0.1)
   c0 ldw $r0.1 = 40[$r0.2]
;;

## short a[]; t = a[10] (a in $r0.2, t in $r0.1)
   c0 ldh $r0.1 = 20[$r0.2]
;;

## char a[]; t = a[10] (a in $r0.2, t in $r0.1)
   c0 ldb $r0.1 = 10[$r0.2]
;;
```

VEX supports speculative execution of memory *load* operations. Control speculation occurs when the compiler moves a load operation before a controlling branch in the original program order. VEX supports this form of speculation through *dismissable load* operations. A *dismissable load* (sometimes called *silent load*) ignores nonrecoverable exceptions and thus guarantees that *correct programs run correctly*. On the other hand, programs that rely on the generation of nonrecoverable exceptions may not be compatible with the VEX speculation model. VEX also supports the concept of explicit memory prefetching, through a *prefetch* operation.

When multiple memory accesses are allowed, VEX guarantees coherency between the memory structures, including caches and local memories. A VEX implementation may introduce stall cycles in order to provide this guarantee. Users are responsible for guaranteeing coherency beyond the uniprocessor model.

Table A.5 shows the repertoire of VEX memory operations, including possible modifiers (represented as *{.modifier}*). VEX supports two flavors of memory modifiers: dismissable (*.d*) to indicate speculative operations and optional *locality hints* (*.s* for "streaming" accesses and *.l* for "local" accesses, whose precise meaning and implementation is left to the end user).

The semantics of dismissable load operations are somewhat subtle. A dismissable load must return exactly the same value as a corresponding conventional load if such a load could be executed. When a conventional load would suffer a nonrecoverable exception, the dismissable load must return a 0. Thus, the correct behavior of dismissable loads is tightly coupled with the processor exception model.

Operation	Description
LDW{.d}{.s}{.l} t = im[s]	Load word
LDH{.d}{.s}{.l} t = im[s1]	Load halfword signed
LDHU{.d}{.s}{.l} t = im[s1]	Load halfword unsigned
LDB{.d}{.s}{.l} t = im[s1]	Load byte signed
LDBU{.d}{.s}{.l} t = im[s1]	Load byte unsigned
STW{.s}{.l} im[s1] = s2	Store word
STH{.s}{.l} im[s1] = s2	Store halfword
STB{.s}{.l} im[s1] = s2	Store byte
PFT{.s}{.l} im[s1]	Prefetch

TABLE A.5   Memory operations in VEX.

Access hints are performance enhancement hints, and a VEX implementation may choose to ignore them. The VEX memory system may use different caching methods and/or memory structures, depending on the access hint. For example, cache lines loaded by addresses tagged with spatial-only locality may be flagged to be replaced sooner than others.

Prefetch operations are also defined as hints to the underlying memory system. The intended behavior is to cause the requested data to be loaded into the local data cache (or prefetch buffer) if not already present. A legal, but not very interesting, implementation of prefetch is a *nop*. Semantically, a prefetch operation is indeed equivalent to a nop (it is not allowed to modify the programmer visible state or to cause an exception). Properly implemented prefetch operations may be used to reduce cache miss rates by loading data into the cache in advance of a load or store operation, without stalling execution. The following code shows an example of a dismissable load.

```
## Implements:
##    if (p != 0) *p += 2
## With p in $r0.1, 2-cycle load, 2-cycle compare
##
   c0 cmpne $b0.0 = $r0.1, 0
   c0 ldw.d $r0.2 = 0[$r0.1]
      xnop 2
;;
   c0 add $r0.2 = $r0.2, 2
   c0 br $b0.0, L1
;;
```

```
    c0 stw 0[$r0.1] = $r0.2
;;
L1:
```

A.1.8 Control Operations

VEX supports a simple statically predicted branch architecture, in that branches are not considered the most critical operations for the typical media-processing embedded applications. The VEX compiler uses profiling and static branch prediction extensively to linearize the predicted paths, which coincide with the *fall-through* paths. To remove microarchitecture dependences from the ISA level, VEX does not expose branch delay slots. The assumption is that the microarchitecture quashes the necessary instructions in the pipeline following a taken branch. In this way, it is possible to apply *dynamic branch prediction* schemes when they prove to be effective. VEX branches execute in two phases.

1. *Prepare the condition*, specifying the branch through a comparison or logical operation, in advance of the control flow change point and store it in a set of single-bit *branch registers*.

2. *Execute the branch* based on one of the condition registers as the very last action of an instruction.

The presence of multiple branch registers allows the compiler to start preparing multiple conditions before executing the first branch. All compare and logical operations can target either a branch or a general register for flexibility. The delay between the generation of a condition and its use in a branch is exposed to the compiler. Only *cluster 0* supports the execution of branch operations. However, all clusters can execute compare/logical operations and write the condition result to their own branch registers. In a multi-cluster organization, branches execute on *cluster 0* but can read conditions from other clusters.

VEX specifies branch target addresses in two alternative ways: through a relative displacement from the program counter or through the content of a special register (the *link register*) for indirect jumps. A simplifying assumption in VEX is that branch displacements are wide enough to reach the entire *text* section, and thus we do not distinguish between *short* and *long* branches. VEX support for *call* operations is limited to a simple *branch-and-link* operation, which saves the return pointer to the special *link register*. The software is responsible for all other calling conventions (save and restore registers, manage the stack), as we describe in Section A.2. Table A.6 lists the VEX control operations. In addition to the standard notations, we also use *off* to indicate a PC-relative code offset, and *lr* for the VEX link register (*$l0.0*).

Finally, a special operation is the multicycle nop control (*xnop*). In VEX, *xnop* operations take an argument and define the number of cycles the machine must wait before issuing the next instruction. This can be implemented in various ways: with a separate operation (very inefficient), with a few bits in each instruction (good to cover small

Operation	Description
GOTO off	Unconditional relative jump
IGOTO lr	Unconditional absolute indirect jump to link register
CALL lr = im	Unconditional relative call
ICALL lr = lr	Unconditional absolute indirect call to link register
BR b, off	Conditional relative branch on true condition
BRF b, off	Conditional relative branch on false condition
RETURN t = t, off, lr	Pop stack frame (t = t + off) and *goto* link register
RFI	Return from interrupt
XNOP n	Multicycle nop (advance the pipeline for *n* cycles)

TABLE A.6   Control operations in VEX.

latencies), or completely ignored for a microarchitecture with a scoreboarded register file. The compiler can optionally be instructed to emit explicit *nop* operations (empty instructions) with the *-fno-xnop* flag.

Examples

The following example shows how to use a combination of compare and logical operations to simplify control flow and to start the preparation of multiple branches with multiple condition registers.

```
## Implements:
##              if (a || b) { [Block 1] };
##              if (a > 0 && b < 0) { [Block 2] } ;
## where a is in $r0.1 and b is in $r0.2
##
   c0 orl $b0.0 = $r0.1, $r0.2
   c0 cmpgt $r0.3 = $r0.1, 0
   c0 cmplt $r0.4 = $r0.2, 0
;;
   c0 andl $b1.0 = $r0.3, $r0.4
;;
   c0 br $b0.0, L1 ## L1 starts [Block 1]
;;
   c0 br $b1.0, L2 ## L2 starts [Block 2]
;;
   ## Continue with the fallthrough path
```

In the multicluster case, two identical branch syllables are encoded in the instruction. The first (in cluster 0) provides the branch target. The second (in the condition cluster) provides the branch condition. For example, the following code sequence branches on a condition on cluster 2.

```
##
## Generate condition on cluster 2
##
    c2 cmplt $b2.0 = $r2,1, $r2.0
        xnop 1
;;
##
## Branch on c1.0 (also uses a syllable on c1.2)
##
    c0 br $b2.0, L2
;;
```

A.1.9 Structure of the Default VEX Cluster

The default VEX cluster (supported by the default tool configuration) has two register files, four integer ALUs, two 16 × 32-bit multiply units, and a data cache port (see Figure A.3). The cluster can issue up to four operations per instruction. The register

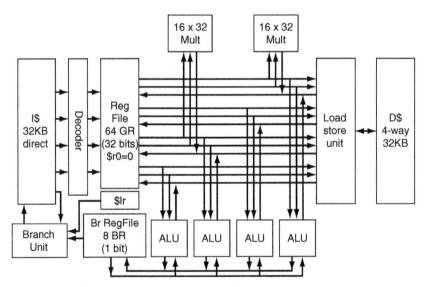

FIGURE A.3 Structure of the default VEX cluster. What the VEX default configuration implements is a 4-issue cluster that loosely resembles the HP/ST ST220 VLIW processor core. The cluster includes 4 integer units, 2 multipliers, a load-store unit, and a control unit. VEX allows extending the cluster by changing the issue width, the number of clusters, as well as other architecture parameters.

set consists of 64 general-purpose 32-bit registers (GRs) and eight 1-bit branch registers (BRs). In addition to base computational resources, the default VEX cluster also contains a control unit (branch unit) for program sequencing.

Note that without changing the base instruction set the cluster organization could be significantly altered, with no impact on the software. For example, we could produce a cluster with two integer ALUs and one multiply unit. Similarly, the functionality of the cluster could be expanded with additional special-purpose operations. The default VEX clusters contain *memory*, *integer*, and *branch* functional units.

- *Memory units* perform load, store, and prefetch operations. There are as many units as data cache memory ports connected to the cluster. Each memory unit is associated with an access to the memory system.

- *Integer units* execute the common set of integer, compare, shift, and select operations on registers or immediate operands.

- *Branch units* execute control operations based on the conditions stored in branch registers, such as conditional branches, unconditional jumps, direct and indirect calls, and returns.

Given the restriction that only four syllables may be used to encode the operations for the cluster, at most four operations may be issued in a single instruction.

Register Files and Immediates

VEX operands can be *general-purpose* registers (GR), *branch* registers (BR), *link* registers (LR), or *immediates* (constants).

- *General-purpose registers* are a set of 64 32-bit general-purpose registers, including one special register: *register #0* wired to the constant 0. The software conventions of the VEX RTA (see Section A.2) define other usage rules for other VEX registers.

- *Branch registers* are a set of eight 1-bit registers written by compare/logical operations and read by conditional branches. In addition, branch registers are used as conditions for select operations and store the carry bit for the operations that manipulate carries.

- *Link register* supports for procedure calls, returns, and indirect jumps.

- *Immediate operands* encode compile-time and load-time constants. VEX instructions encode the necessary immediates without requiring extra operations. VEX supports three types of immediates: *branch offsets* (24-bit for branch operations) fit in a single syllable, *short immediates* (9-bit for all operations) fit in a single syllable, and *long immediates* (32-bit for all operations) draw bits upon one adjacent extension syllable in the same cluster and instruction. Immediate extensions are decoded in the same instruction as the operation that reads them, and carry no performance penalty.

A.1.10 VEX Semantics

This section describes the semantics of the VEX operations using the syntax of C preprocessor macros. This set of macros is very similar to what, for example, the VEX compiled
simulator emits to implement VEX operations. The description only covers the architectural state changes of each operation without considering the exception behavior.
The description of the computational operations is self-explanatory. The description of
memory operations uses the set of `sim_mem_access_safe*()` utilities to mimic the
behavior of *speculative* memory accesses that silently dismiss nonrecoverable exceptions. The description of control operations uses the `goto_instr(x)` utility to indicate
changes in control flow, and the `next_instr()` utility to indicate the address of the
instruction following the current. Note that the *link register* used for system calls and
indirect jumps is always explicitly named, in that the VEX ISA prohibits "invisible" side
effects of operations on architecturally visible states.

```
/* Memory Macros and Operations */
#define UINT8(s) ((s) & 0xff)
#define INT8(s) (((signed) ((s) << 24)) >> 24)
#define UINT16(s) ((s) & 0xffff)
#define INT16(s) (((signed) ((s) << 16)) >> 16)
#define UINT32(s) ((unsigned) (s))
#define INT32(s) ((signed) (s))
#define MEM8(a) (*((volatile unsigned char*)(a)))
#define MEM16(a) (*((volatile unsigned short*)(a)))
#define MEM32(a) (*((volatile unsigned*)(a)))
#define MEMSPEC8(a) sim_mem_access_safe8(a)
#define MEMSPEC16(a) sim_mem_access_safe16(a)
#define MEMSPEC32(a) sim_mem_access_safe32(a)

#define LDBs(t,s1) t = INT8(MEMSPEC8(s1)) /* speculative */
#define LDB(t,s1) t = INT8(MEM8(s1))
#define LDBUs(t,s1) t = UINT8(MEMSPEC8(s1)) /* speculative */
#define LDBU(t,s1) t = UINT8(MEM8(s1))
#define LDHs(t,s1) t = INT16(MEMSPEC16(s1)) /* speculative */
#define LDH(t,s1) t = INT16(MEM16(s1))
#define LDHUs(t,s1) t = UINT16(MEMSPEC16(s1)) /* speculative */
#define LDHU(t,s1) t = UINT16(MEM16(s1))
#define LDWs(t,s1) t = INT32(MEMSPEC32(s1)) /* speculative */
#define LDW(t,s1) t = INT32(MEM32(s1))
#define STB(t,s1) MEM8(t) = UINT8(s1)
#define STH(t,s1) MEM16(t) = UINT16(s1)
#define STW(t,s1) MEM32(t) = UINT32(s1)

/* Computational and Logical Operations */
#define ADD(t,s1,s2) t = (s1) + (s2)
```

```
#define AND(t,s1,s2) t = (s1) & (s2)
#define ANDC(t,s1,s2) t = ~(s1) & (s2)
#define ANDL(t,s1,s2) t = ((((s1) == 0) | ((s2) == 0)) ? 0 : 1)
#define CMPEQ(t,s1,s2) t = ((s1) == (s2))
#define CMPNE(t,s1,s2) t = ((s1) != (s2))
#define CMPGT(t,s1,s2) t = (INT32(s1) > INT32(s2))
#define CMPGE(t,s1,s2) t = (INT32(s1) >= INT32(s2))
#define CMPLT(t,s1,s2) t = (INT32(s1) < INT32(s2))
#define CMPLE(t,s1,s2) t = (INT32(s1) <= INT32(s2))
#define CMPGTU(t,s1,s2) t = (UINT32(s1) > UINT32(s2))
#define CMPGEU(t,s1,s2) t = (UINT32(s1) >= UINT32(s2))
#define CMPLTU(t,s1,s2) t = (UINT32(s1) < UINT32(s2))
#define CMPLEU(t,s1,s2) t = (UINT32(s1) <= UINT32(s2))
#define MOV(t,s1) t = s1
#define MPYL(t,s1,s2) t = (s1) * INT16(s2)
#define MPYH(t,s1,s2) t = (s1) * INT16((s2) >> 16)
#define MPYHS(t,s1,s2) t = ((s1) * INT16((s2) >> 16)) << 16
#define MPYLU(t,s1,s2) t = (s1) * UINT16(s2)
#define MPYHU(t,s1,s2) t = (s1) * UINT16((s2) >> 16)
#define MPYLL(t,s1,s2) t = INT16(s1) * INT16(s2)
#define MPYLH(t,s1,s2) t = INT16(s1) * INT16((s2) >> 16)
#define MPYHH(t,s1,s2) t = INT16((s1) >> 16) * INT16((s2) >> 16)
#define MPYLLU(t,s1,s2) t = UINT16(s1) * UINT16(s2)
#define MPYLHU(t,s1,s2) t = UINT16(s1) * UINT16((s2) >> 16)
#define MPYHHU(t,s1,s2) t = UINT16((s1) >> 16) * UINT16((s2) >> 16)
#define NANDL(t,s1,s2) t = (((s1) == 0) | ((s2) == 0)) ? 1 : 0
#define NOP() /* do nothing */
#define NORL(t,s1,s2) t = (((s1) == 0) & ((s2) == 0)) ? 1 : 0
#define ORL(t,s1,s2) t = (((s1) == 0) & ((s2) == 0)) ? 0 : 1
#define OR(t,s1,s2) t = (s1) | (s2)
#define ORC(t,s1,s2) t = (~(s1)) | (s2)
#define SH1ADD(t,s1,s2) t = ((s1) << 1) + (s2)
#define SH2ADD(t,s1,s2) t = ((s1) << 2) + (s2)
#define SH3ADD(t,s1,s2) t = ((s1) << 3) + (s2)
#define SH4ADD(t,s1,s2) t = ((s1) << 4) + (s2)
#define SHL(t,s1,s2) t = (INT32(s1)) << (s2)
#define SHR(t,s1,s2) t = (INT32(s1)) >> (s2)
#define SHRU(t,s1,s2) t = (UINT32(s1)) >> (s2)
#define SLCT(t,s1,s2,s3) t = UINT32(((s1) == 1) ? (s2) : (s3))
#define SLCTF(t,s1,s2,s3) t = UINT32(((s1) == 0) ? (s2) : (s3))
#define SUB(t,s1,s2) t = (s1) - (s2)
#define SXTB(t,s1) t = UINT32((INT32((s1) << 24)) >> 24)
#define SXTH(t,s1) t = UINT32((INT32((s1) << 16)) >> 16)
#define XOR(t,s1,s2) t = (s1) ^ (s2)
```

```
#define XNOP(n) /* do nothing */
#define ZXTB(t,s1) t = ((s1) & 0xff)
#define ZXTH(t,s1) t = ((s1) & 0xffff)

/* Carry Manipulation */
#define ADDCG(t,cout,s1,s2,cin) { \
    t = (s1) + (s2) + ((cin) & 0x1); \
    cout =   ((cin) & 0x1) \
            ? (UINT32(t) <= UINT32(s1)) \
            : (UINT32(t) <  UINT32(s1)); \
}
#define DIVS(t,cout,s1,s2,cin) { \
    unsigned tmp = ((s1) << 1) | (cin); \
    cout = UINT32(s1) >> 31; \
    t = cout ? tmp + (s2) : tmp - (s2); \
}

/* Basic Control Operations */
#define goto_instr(X) /* jumps to the instruction at address "x" */
#define next_instr() /* address of the instr following address "x" */

#define BR(b1,off) if (b1 == 1) goto_instr(off)
#define BRF(b1,off) if (b1 == 0) goto_instr(off)
#define GOTO(off) goto_instr(off)
#define IGOTO(lr) goto_instr(lr) /* "lr" is the link reg (l0)*/
#define CALL(off,lr) { lr = next_instr(); goto_instr(off); }
#define ICALL(off) { lr = next_instr(); goto_instr(s1); }
#define RETURN(sp,off,lr) { sp += off; goto_instr(lr); }
```

A.2 The VEX Run-time Architecture

The VEX *run-time architecture* (RTA) defines the common software conventions necessary to compile, link, and execute a VEX program. In other systems, the RTA is sometimes also called the *application binary interface* (ABI). VEX applications run in a 32-bit environment and use the ILP32 data model in which integers, longs, and pointers are 32 bits. Within this specification, *halfword* refers to a 16-bit object, *word* refers to a 32-bit object, and *doubleword* refers to a 64-bit object.

In the following we focus on an RTA model well suited to embedded systems, in that it is restricted to a *single statically bound nonrelocatable* load module. This model does not support dynamically linked libraries, allows the use of absolute addresses, and does not use function descriptors or a global data pointer. Other models are possible with VEX but are outside the scope of this book.

A.2.1 Data Allocation and Layout

This section describes how to access and lay out various types of data objects in the VEX world. All VEX items greater than 8 bytes must be aligned on a 16-byte boundary. Smaller data items must be aligned on the next larger power-of-2 boundary. In other words, 1-byte objects have no alignment restrictions; 2-byte objects have to be aligned *0 mod 2*; objects of sizes 3 and 4, *0 mod 4*; objects of sizes 5 to 8, *0 mod 8*; and so on.

- *Global variables*: Common blocks, dynamically allocated regions (such as objects returned by *malloc()*), and external data access are made with an *absolute address*.

- *Local static data* accesses are made with an *absolute address*.

- *Local memory stack variables* accesses are relative to the stack-pointer register. Stack frames must always be aligned on a 32-byte boundary. That is, the stack-pointer register must always be aligned on a 32-byte boundary.

- *Constants and literals* may be placed in the text or data segments.

Table A.7 lists the fundamental scalar data types supported by the VEX architecture (values expressed in bytes).

Type	C	Size	Align	Hardware representation
Integral	char signed char	1	1	signed byte
	unsigned char	1	1	unsigned byte
	short signed short	2	2	signed halfword
	unsigned short	2	2	unsigned halfword
	int, signed int long, signed enum	4	4	signed word
	unsigned int unsigned long	4	4	unsigned word
Pointer	any-type * any-type (*)()	4	4	unsigned word
Floating point	float	4	4	IEEE single precision
	double	8	8	IEEE double precision

TABLE A.7 Scalar data types in VEX.

Aggregate data types (structures, unions, and arrays) assume the alignment of their most strictly aligned component. The size of any object, including aggregates and unions, is always a multiple of the object's alignment. An array uses the same alignment as its elements. Structure and union objects can require padding to meet size and alignment constraints. An entire structure or union object is aligned on the same boundary as its most strictly aligned member; an array object is aligned on the same boundary as its element type. Each structure member is assigned to the lowest available offset with the appropriate alignment. This may require internal padding, depending on the previous member. A structure's size is increased, if necessary, to make it a multiple of the alignment. This may require tail padding, depending on the last member. Figure A.4 shows the layout of typical structures and bit fields.

A.2.2   Register Usage

VEX registers are partitioned into the following classes.

- *Scratch registers* may be destroyed by a procedure call. The caller must save these registers before a call if needed (also called *caller saves*).

- *Preserved registers* must not be destroyed by a procedure call. The callee must save and restore these registers if used (also called *callee saves*).

- *Constant registers* contain a fixed value that cannot be changed.

- *Special registers* are used in the call/return mechanism.

Tables A.8 and A.9 show a description of the register usage in VEX. Note that VEX defines a *user mode* (in which all registers are available) and a *kernel mode* (in which only a subset of registers is available). The kernel mode is useful for reducing the overhead of context switches that do not require the entire set of registers offered by the processor.

A.2.3   Stack Layout and Procedure Linkage

The memory stack in VEX is used to spill registers and pass parameters. It is organized as a stack of procedure frames, beginning with the main program's frame at the base of the stack and continuing toward the top of the stack with nested procedure calls. The frame for the currently active procedure is at the top of the stack. The memory stack begins at an address determined by the operating system, and grows toward lower memory addresses. The stack pointer register always points to the lowest address in the current frame on the stack.

Each procedure creates its frame on entry by subtracting its frame size from the stack pointer, and removes its frame from the stack on exit by restoring the previous value of the stack pointer, usually by adding its frame size. Not every procedure needs a memory stack frame. However, every nonleaf procedure needs to save at least its return link. A procedure frame (see Figure A.5) consists of three regions.

1. *Local storage*: A procedure may store local variables, temporaries, and spilled registers in this region.

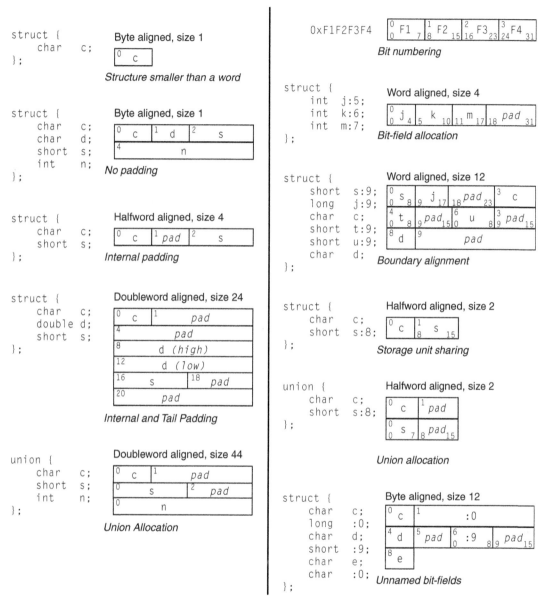

FIGURE A.4 **Layout of typical structures and unions (left) and bit fields (right) in VEX.**
The figure refers to a big-endian byte-ordering model. Bit numbering is left-to-right for
LSB-to-MSB bits.

Register	Class	Usage (user mode)	Use (kernel mode)
General registers (cluster 0)			
$r0.0	Constant	always zero	always zero
$r0.1	Special	stack pointer	stack pointer
$r0.2	Scratch	struct return pointer	struct return pointer
$r0.3–$r0.10	Scratch	argument/return value	argument/return value
$r0.11–$r0.15	Scratch	temporaries	temporaries
$r0.16–$r0.56	Scratch	temporaries	(unavailable)
$r0.57–$r0.63	Preserved	temporaries (callee save)	
$l0.0	Special	link register	link register
General registers (other clusters)			
$ri.0	Constant	always zero	always zero
$ri.1–$ri.56	Scratch	temporaries	(unavailable)
$ri.57–$ri.63	Preserved	temporaries (callee save)	
Branch registers (cluster 0)			
$b0.0–$b0.3	Scratch	temporaries	temporaries
$b0.4–$b0.7	Scratch	temporaries	(unavailable)
Branch registers (other clusters)			
$bi.0–$bi.7	Scratch	temporaries	(unavailable)

TABLE A.8   Register usage in VEX.

2. *Outgoing parameters*: Parameters in excess of those passed in registers are stored in this region. A procedure accesses its incoming parameters in the outgoing parameter region of its caller's stack frame.

3. *Scratch area*: A 16-byte region provided as scratch storage for procedures called by the current procedure, so that each procedure may use the 16 bytes at the top of its own frame as scratch memory.

The stack pointer must always be aligned at a 32-byte boundary (i.e., stack frame sizes are a multiple of 32 bytes), and programs may not write below the stack pointer. Most procedures have a fixed-size frame. The VEX compiler determines the size required

Cluster 0	
$r0.0	Constant register 0; if written to. It represents a *bit bucket* (written values are discarded).
$r0.1	The *stack pointer* holds the limit of the current stack frame, which is the address of the stack's bottommost valid word. At all times, the stack pointer must point to a 0 mod 32 aligned area. The stack pointer is also used to access any memory arguments upon entry to a function and is preserved across any functions called by the current function.
$r0.2	*Struct return pointer register*. If the function called returns a struct or union value larger than 32 bytes, the register contains, on entry, the appropriately aligned address of the caller-allocated area to contain the value being returned. Scratch otherwise.
$r0.3–$r0.10	*Argument and return values* up to 32 bytes are passed in these registers. Arguments beyond these registers appear in memory (see Section A.2.3). Within the called function, these registers are scratch registers.
$r0.11–$r0.56	Scratch registers (caller saves) with no specific role in the calling sequence.
$r0.57–$r0.63	Preserved registers (callee saves) with no specific role in the calling sequence.
$10.0	*Link register* to store the return address on entry to a procedure. Branch operations read it for indirect local jumps, returns, and indirect function calls.
$b0.0–$b0.7	Scratch registers (caller saves) with no specified role in the calling sequence.
Other clusters	
$ri.0	Constant register 0. If written to, it represents a *bit bucket* (written values are discarded).
$ri.1–$ri.56	Scratch registers (caller saves) with no specific role in the function calling sequence.
$ri.57–$ri.63	Preserved registers (callee saves) with no specific role in the calling sequence.
$bi.0–$bi.7	Scratch registers (caller saves) with no specified role in the calling sequence.

TABLE A.9 Detailed register usage in VEX.

for each region, pads the local storage area to a multiple of 32 bytes, creates the frame by subtracting a constant from the previous stack pointer, and removes the frame by adding the same constant to the stack pointer before returning.

Procedure Linkage

VEX defines the following types of calls.

- *Direct calls* made directly to the entry point of the target procedure

- *Indirect calls* made through a function pointer that points to the address of the function entry point for the target function

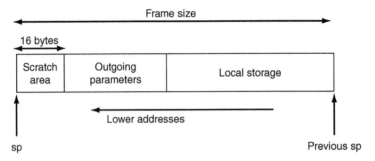

FIGURE A.5 **The VEX procedure frame.**

- *Special calls* made through a special calling convention negotiated between the compiler and the run-time system (e.g., *intrinsics* calls)

For all calls, the compiler has to keep the values that live across the call alive in scratch registers by saving them into preserved registers or on the memory stack. It must set up parameters in registers and memory, and then issue the call operation, assuming that the call displacement field is sufficiently wide to reach any target. The call operation saves the return link in the link register.

At *procedure entry*, the compiler allocates a frame on the memory stack, if necessary. Then, if it is a nonleaf procedure, it must save the return link in the memory stack frame, together with any preserved registers that will be used in this procedure.

At *procedure exit*, the compiler is responsible for restoring the return link and any preserved registers that were saved, as well as for deallocating the memory stack frame (if created). Finally, the procedure exits by branching through the link register with the *return* instruction. After the call, any saved values must be restored.

Parameters are passed in a combination of general registers and memory (see Figure A.6). The first 32 bytes of the parameter list are passed in registers, and the rest of the parameters are passed on the memory stack, beginning at the caller's stack

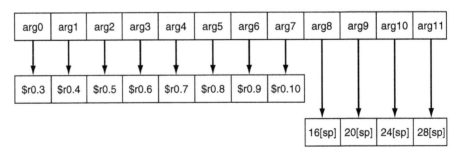

FIGURE A.6 **Parameter passing in VEX.**

pointer plus 16 bytes. The caller uses up to eight general registers for parameters. To accommodate variable argument lists, there is a fixed correspondence between an argument's position in the parameter list and the register used for general register arguments. This allows a procedure to spill its register arguments easily to memory before stepping through the argument list with a pointer.

Parameters are first allocated on a conceptual argument list, which is then mapped to a combination of registers and the memory stack. The argument list begins at relative address 0, and is allocated toward increasing addresses. Each parameter begins on a 4-byte boundary. Each 4-byte unit in the argument list is called an *argument slot* (named *arg0*, *arg1*, *arg2*, and so on). Parameters may use more than one argument slot, and are aligned and padded within the argument list according to the following rules.

- Small integral scalar parameters (smaller than 4 bytes) are padded on the left to a total width of 4 bytes and placed in the next available argument slot.

- 32-bit integral scalar pointers and single-precision floating-point parameters are placed in the next available argument slot.

- Double-precision floating-point scalar parameters are aligned to an 8-byte boundary (possibly leaving an argument slot empty) and placed in the next two consecutive argument slots.

- Aggregates up to 4 bytes in size are padded to 4 bytes and placed in the next available argument slot.

- Aggregates larger than 4 bytes are padded to a multiple of 4 bytes, aligned to an 8-byte boundary (possibly leaving an argument slot empty), and placed in as many argument slots as needed.

The first eight argument slots (32 bytes) in the argument list are passed in registers, according to the previous rules and are associated one-to-one with the procedure arguments. If an aggregate parameter straddles the boundary between *arg7* and *arg8*, the part that lies within the first eight slots is passed in registers, and the remainder is passed in memory. The remainder of the parameter list, beginning with *arg8*, is passed in the outgoing parameter area of the memory stack frame. Parameters are mapped directly to memory, with *arg8* placed at location *sp+16*, *arg9* at *sp+20*, and so on.

A function with variable arguments may assume that the first eight variable arguments can all be found in the argument registers. It may then store these registers to memory, using the 16-byte scratch area for *$r0.7*–*$r0.10*, and using up to 16 bytes at the base of its own stack frame for *$r0.3*–*$r0.6*. This arrangement places all variable parameters in one contiguous block of memory. Return values follow rules similar to arguments.

- Integral and floating-point values up to 4 bytes are returned in *$r0.3*. For smaller integers, the content of the upper bits must be zero-filled (if unsigned) or sign-extended (if signed) to 4 bytes.

- 64-bit floating-point values are returned in *$r0.3* and *$r0.4*.

- Aggregates smaller than 32 bytes are padded to a multiple of 4 bytes and returned in successive general registers beginning with *$r0.3*.

- Return values larger than 32 bytes are returned in a buffer allocated by the caller. A pointer to the buffer is passed to the called procedure in *$r0.2*.

A.3 The VEX C Compiler

The VEX development system (sometimes referred to as the *VEX toolchain*) includes the set of tools that allows C programs compiled for a VEX target to be simulated on a host workstation. The center of the VEX toolchain is the Multiflow/VEX C compiler. The VEX toolchain is mainly intended for architecture exploration, application development, and benchmarking. It includes a very fast architectural simulator that uses a form of binary translation to convert VEX assembly language files to native binaries running on the host workstation. The translator annotates the binaries to collect execution statistics and includes an (optional) cache simulator to collect D-cache and I-cache data. Figure A.7 shows the overall structure of the VEX toolchain.

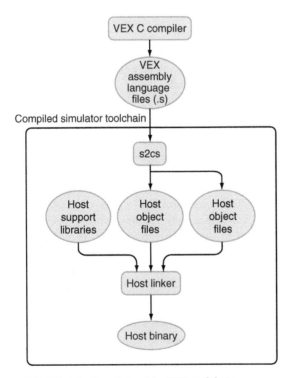

FIGURE A.7 Structure of the VEX toolchain.

A command-line interface controls the toolchain. The first-level C compiler driver (*cc*) hides all steps involved in getting from a C program to a VEX "executable." The toolchain directory tree looks like a standard compiler development tree, with a */bin* directory containing tools, a */lib* directory for libraries, a */usr/include* directory for headers, and so on.

The VEX *compiled simulator* uses a binary translator to generate an executable binary for the host platform that contains the operations for simulating a program compiler for VEX. For example, assuming we want to compile two files *file1.c* and *file2.c* into a Linux binary *a.out*, the set of commands to issue is:

```
$[1] <vex>/bin/cc -c file1.c
$[2] <vex>/bin/cc -c file2.c
$[3] <vex>/bin/cc -o a.out file1.o file2.o
```

Command 1 causes the following steps to be executed.

```
<vex>/bin/cc # cc shell
  <vex>/lib/rcc # "real" cc driver
    <vex>/lib/cpp <cpp_flags> file1.c file1.i # C preprocessor
    <vex>/lib/ccom <ccom_flags> file1.i file1.s # C compiler
    <vex>/lib/as <as_flags> # Assembler driver
      <vex>/lib/s2cs <s2cs_flags> file1.s file1.cs.c # Compiled Simulator
      <host>/cc -c file1.cs.c # Host C compiler
      <host>/mv file1.cs.o file1.o # Move host object file
```

Command 2 causes the equivalent sequence on *file2.c*. Command 3 causes the following steps to be executed.

```
<vex>/bin/cc # cc shell
  <vex>/lib/rcc # "real" cc driver
    <vex>/bin/ld <ld_flags> file1.o file1.o -o a.exe # Linker driver
      <host>/cc   -o a.exe # Linux C linker/loader
                <vex>/lib/crt0.o # VEX C run-time initialization
                file1.o file2.o  # Application object files
                <vex>/lib/libc.a # VEX C library
                libcache.sl       # Cache simulation library
                ldcs.a            # Simulation support library
                <host>/libc.so.6 # Linux C library
```

Once steps 1 through 3 are complete, we obtain a host executable binary *a.out* that can be executed simply by invoking it. The file *a.out* contains the compiled simulator image of the user application compiled for VEX and converted back into host object format. The image also contains various simulation helper functions, and the D-cache/I-cache simulators. According to compile-time flags, the user can select different levels of accuracy for the simulation.

- The *default mode* produces an executable that reproduces the correct behavior, and collects standard additional timing information for a set of default architecture parameters. The executable includes instrumentation code that counts execution statistics and optionally invokes the I-cache and D-cache simulators. This mode can be used to benchmark applications and to evaluate the benefit of code transformations and compiler optimizations. Execution statistics are emitted in text form in files called *ta.log.###*, which are emitted at program exit.

- When compiled with *profiling flags* (*-mas_G*) the executable includes instrumentation code that collects execution statistics and emits a file that can be interpreted by *gprof* to visualize profile data. This mode uses the native profiling support in the host C compiler to emit calls to the profiling routines at every routine entry point. At program exit the profile data is emitted so that *gprof* correctly interprets *simulated time*.

In default compilation mode, the intermediate steps are hidden to the user, and intermediate files (stored temporarily in the */tmp* directory) are removed after compilation, or on errors. To keep intermediate files, it is necessary to add the *–mas_g* and *–ms* flags to the compilation. Table A.10 lists the relevant file suffixes generated by the VEX toolchain.

A.3.1 Command Line Options

The *cc* program is the driver for the VEX C compiler. It supports the C language, as defined by Kernighan and Ritchie in *The C Programming Language* [1989], and the ISO C89 standard. A compilation command looks like

```
cc -o outputfile source1 source2 . . . sourceN,
```

where *outputfile* is the name of the object file (or executable file) you wish to create, and *source1* through *sourceN* are C source files and compiled object modules. The C compiler determines how to process these files on the basis of their file names, as follows.

- Files whose names end with *.c* are taken to be C source programs. They are preprocessed, compiled, and assembled, and each object program is left on the file whose name is that of the source with .o substituted for .c. The .o file is normally deleted. By default, .c files are compiled as ISO/ANSI C.

- Files whose names end with *.s* are taken to be assembly source programs and are preprocessed and assembled, producing an .o file.

- Files whose names end with *.i* are taken to be compiler source programs and are not preprocessed.

Optimization is in effect by default. For more information about optimization, see the options below. The following options (grouped by category) are interpreted by *cc*.

File type	Description
file.c	C source file.
file.i	C preprocessed file, normally removed. Temporarily stored by the *rcc* driver as */tmp/cpp####.*
file.s	VEX assembly file, normally removed. Temporarily stored by the *rcc* driver as */tmp/com####.*
file.cs.c	VEX compiled simulator translated file, normally removed. Temporarily stored by the *as* driver as */tmp/csim####.c.*
file.o	Host object file containing the compilation of the CS translated file. Permanently saved for the link step for compilations with the *–c* flag.
a.out	Host executable image containing the binary representing the user application and the simulation routines.
ta.log.###	Output of the simulation, containing simulation and cache statistics.
gmon.out gmon-nocache.out gmon-icache.out gmon-dcache.out	Output of the simulation when compiled with profiling flag on (-*mas_G*). Each of the "gmon-" files contains the *gprof* database, for cumulative data, execution data (*nocache*), instruction, and data cache only (*icache*, *dcache*).
database.ifprob	Output of the VEX compiler when compiling for profile data collection for profile-based optimization (-*prob_gen*).
ifprob.out ifprob.###	Output of the simulation when collecting profile data for profile-based optimization (-*prob_gen*).

TABLE A.10 File types in the VEX toolchain.

Output Files

This set of options determines which stages the compiler will execute, and which files it will leave after finishing.

-o output   Give the name output to the executable file produced by the loader, rather than the default name *a.out*. If this option is used, and the file *a.out* already exists, it will be left undisturbed.

-c   Suppress the loading phase of the compilation. Do not delete the *.o* files produced by the assembler. These files may be loaded by *cc* or *ld* at a later time.

-S   Compile the named C programs and leave the assembler language output on corresponding files suffixed *.s*. No *.o* file is produced.

-E	Run only the standard preprocessor on the named C programs, and send the result to the standard output. (See "Preprocessing.")
-M	Run only the standard preprocessor on the named C programs, requesting it to generate makefile dependences and send the result to the standard output. (See "Preprocessing.")

Preprocessing

Before compiling the program, the compiler invokes the standard GNU C preprocessor (*cpp*), which provides features such as macro expansion and conditional compilation. The options in this set control *cpp*. Note that when using the K&R mode (*–KR* switch) the preprocessor is invoked with the *–traditional* switch, whereas the default mode of the preprocessor is invoked when using the ANSI mode of the compiler (default, or *-mfansi* switch).

-Dname=def **-Dname**	Define the name to the preprocessor, as if by #*define*. If no definition is given, the name is defined as *1*.
-Uname	Remove any initial definition of name.
-Idir	#*include* files whose names do not begin with / are always sought first in the directory of the file argument, then in directories named in *-I* options, then in directories on a standard list.
-C	Prevent the preprocessor from eliding comments. Normally, the preprocessor replaces all commands (i.e., all characters falling between /* and the next */) with a single space.
-E	Run only the standard preprocessor on the named C programs, and send the result to the standard output.
-M	Run only the standard preprocessor on the named C programs, requesting it to generate makefile dependences, and send the result to the standard output. Dependences are generated by analyzing the program's #*include* statements.

Optimization

This set of options determines how the compiler will optimize your program. Optimization is in effect by default (i.e., *-O2* compilation). We only give rough definitions of the different optimization types. Each successive option provides additional optimizations in addition to those performed at the previous levels. By default, the option *-O2* is in effect, which will provide good performance for most C programs. The *-O4* and *-H** options should be used with care and on the basis of experimentation. In any large program, a few routines may benefit from these optimization levels. They should not be used for programs as a whole. For most compilations, you will not need to specify this option. The more aggressive loop unrolling options (*-H2* through *-H4*) should only be used for routines for which experimentation has shown that they are effective.

These will typically be routines whose execution time is dominated by relatively simple loops. Note that the VEX system does not currently support source-level debugging. Although the compiler would correctly generate a STABS directive when invoked with a -g flag, the VEX simulator would ignore them.

-O	Equivalent to -O2. This option is in effect by default.
-On	This series of options controls which optimizations the compiler performs, as follows:

> **-O1** All scalar optimizations
>
> **-O2** Minimal loop unrolling and trace scheduling compilation
>
> **-O3** Basic loop unrolling and trace scheduling compilation
>
> **-O4** Heavy loop unrolling (see -H4)

-Hn	This series of options controls loop unrolling. They override the loop unrolling that is implicitly requested by the -On optimization options.

> **-H0** No unrolling
>
> **-H1** Basic unrolling
>
> **-H2** Aggressive unrolling
>
> **-H3** Heavy unrolling
>
> **-H4** Very heavy unrolling

-lb_limit n	Set the "loop branch limit" to n. The compiler ceases to unroll any loop when the unrolled loops body has n internal branches. Branches to code outside the loop body are not counted, and therefore do not inhibit unrolling. That is, -lb_limit puts an implicit limit on loop unrolling, supplementing the explicit limit provided by any source code directives or command line options. By default, the loop branch limit is 0. Branches internal to a loop inhibit loop unrolling.
-fexpand-div	Instruct the compiler to replace call to library intrinsics with inline assembly for integer divide and remainder functions. A single 32-bit division gets expanded to about 60 assembly language operations and yields significant code expansion and compile slowdown. To be used with caution (only when division performance is important).
-fno-xnop	Do not emit xnop instructions, but emit explicit nop instructions instead.
-fmm=<mmf>	Read machine description parameters (latency, resources, and so on) from file <mmf>.

-autoinline   Enables automatic function inlining. Automatic inlining attempts to inline functions in the same module until an inlining "budget" is reached. The compiler also emits the code for the function being inlined, assuming that the assembler and the linker will remove unused functions.

-mincode   Turns on a set of flags aimed at minimizing code size of the generated object file. This set of flags usually adversely affects performance and should be used with caution.

-prefetch   Turns on automatic prefetch insertion.

-cache_hints   Interprets cache locality hints and emits the corresponding memory instructions.

Profiling

The compiler supports profile-based optimization with a three-step compilation process. The options controlling profiling are:

-prob_gen   The compiler annotates conditional branches with code that counts execution statistics (taken/not-taken branches). During this process, it saves the profile information in a file stored in the *database.ifprob* directory, corresponding to the name of the module. The module name and the profile directory can be changed through internal compiler options. When the executable is generated, the loader links in a module that contains the routine to dump the profile information. When the executable is run, the exit routine dumps the profile information in a file named *ifprob.out*, in the directory in which the executable is run. If *ifprob.out* already exists, the compiler attempts to generate a file named *ifprob.nnn*, where *nnn* is an increasing number until no file with such a name exists.

-prob_use   The compiler looks for a file called *ifprob.out* in the *database.ifprob* directory. If such a file exists, the compiler assigns branches the probability that has been computed in the previous profile run(s), and uses it to guide the selection of traces during trace scheduling. It is wise to use the same compiler options (except *–prob_gen/-prob_use*) in both steps of the compilation, to avoid mismatches between branches and profile information. Also note that the compiler uses line numbers to maintain branch information, and hence it is possible for the profile information to be imprecise, in particular when multiple branches map to the same source line number. This may happen, for example, in the presence of large preprocessor macros. In the cases where the compiler detects inconsistencies in the profile information, it emits a warning.

-pg   Generate extra code to write profile information suitable for the analysis program *gprof*.

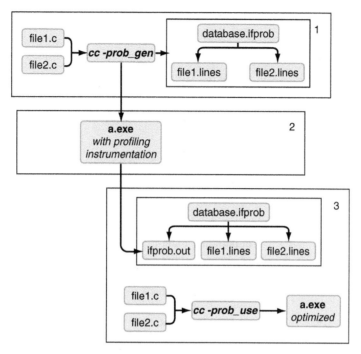

FIGURE A.8   The three steps of profile-based compilation. (See also Figure 7.2.)

A typical profile-based compilation involves the following steps (see Figure A.8).

1. Compile with the *-prob_gen* flag, so that the compiler can instrument the code to count branch probability. This information is saved in the *database.ifprob* directory

2. Run with significant data set, collect the branch statistics, and emit them in a file at the end of the first run (usually *ifprob.out*).

3. Recompile with the *-prob_use* flag, after having copied the *ifprob.out* file to the *database.ifprob* directory.

With the *-prob_use* flag, the VEX compiler uses collected data to pick traces. As we saw in the compiler chapter, trace scheduling favors more probable traces. Code compaction happens on linear paths, and off-trace paths may be penalized by compensation code. Profiling can have significant impact on performance.

Language Definition

These options control certain extensions to the language. By default, the C compiler obeys the ISO/ANSI C definition.

-K+R	Use the language definition given by Kernighan and Ritchie ("traditional" C).
-mfansi	Use the ANSI/ISO C language definition. This is the default.
-mfinline	Allow the Multiflow language extension to manually control inline expansion.
-c99inline	Allow C99-style *inline* keywords to manually control inline expansion.
-funsigned-char	Treat *char* as unsigned (default is signed).
-align n	This option indicates that all data items larger than *n* bytes obey their optimal alignment, where *n* is 1, 4, or 8. For example, the option *-align 1* means that any data object may start at any address (i.e., the program does not obey any alignment restrictions). By default, alignment is eight, stating that the program always observes optimal alignment. When accessing data items whose native alignment is larger than the "forced" alignment, the VEX compiler generates a sequence of extract/merge operations to ensure that the accesses are properly aligned, resulting in a performance loss.

Libraries

These options let you link C programs with various subprogram libraries, in addition to the standard libraries. Libraries that are distributed as part of the VEX compiler are located in the directory *<vex_tree>/lib*.

-l*nnn*	Links with the library file named lib*nnn*.a. The loader will search for this file in any directories specified with the *-L* option and in the directories *<vex_tree>/lib* and *<vex_tree>/usr/lib*. Libraries are searched in the order in which they appear on the command line. Therefore, they should normally appear at the end of any *cc* command. This flag is passed directly to the loader.
-L*dir*	Library archives are sought first in directories named in *-L* options and then in directories on a standard list. This flag is passed directly to the loader.

Passing Options to Compile Phases

This group of options allows you to pass options from the *cc* command to the preprocessor (*cpp*), loader (*ld*), or assembler (*as*). Note that any file name or option that *cc* does not recognize is automatically passed to the loader. Any manual entry for the GNU C preprocessor lists the available *cpp* options.

-mp*nnn*	Pass the option *–nnn* to the c preprocessor (*cpp*).
-ma*nnn*	Pass the option *-nnn* to the assembler (*as*).

-ml*nnn*	Pass the option *−nnn* to the linker/loader (*ld*).
-Wa,\<options\>	Pass comma-separated *\<options\>* to the assembler.
-Wl,\<options\>	Pass comma-separated *\<options\>* to the linker/loader.
-Wp,\<options\>	Pass comma-separated *\<options\>* to the C preprocessor.

Terminal Output and Process Control

This group of options controls the terminal output of the compiler.

-w	Suppress warning diagnostics from the compiler.
-mv	Display a banner line, including the version number.
-mve	Display a banner line, including the version number of the compiler, and terminate. Do not proceed with compilation.
-d	Show all invocations of the compiler phases and run the compiler.
-dn	Show all invocations of the compiler phases and do nothing.
-ms	Compile the named programs, leave the assembly language output on corresponding files suffixed *.s*, and continue to generate *.o* files normally. By default, *cc* deletes any *.s* files it creates.
-temp=*directory*	Create temporary files used during compilation in *directory*, rather than in /tmp (the default). An error occurs if *directory* is missing, if the given path is not the name of the directory, or if the given path is not writable.
-S	Only compile to the assembler level, leave the assembly language output on corresponding files suffixed *.s*, and stop.
-help │ --help	Show help message for basic options.
--license	Show VEX license.

Other Options

The following set of options controls the compiled-simulator invocation

-mas_g	Compile the named programs, and leave the intermediate files used in the compiled simulator step in *.cs.c*, then continue to generate *.o* files normally. By default, *cc* deletes any *.cs.c* file
-mas_t	*-mas_t* enables the collection of compiled simulator run-time statistics, I-cache simulation, and D-cache simulation when a program is executed. Statistics appear in the *ta.log.nnn* file at the end of the program execution.

It is also possible to individually turn on part of the simulation statistics:

-mas_ti   collects I-cache simulation data

-mas_td   collects D-cache simulation data

-mas_G   Turn on *gprof*-style collection of profiling data. The *gprof* tool produces an execution profile of programs in which the effect of called routines is incorporated into the profile of each caller. Profile data is taken from the call graph profile file (*gmon.out* default).

-mas_d   Show internal assembler steps.

-mld_d   Show internal linker steps.

The following options control miscellaneous configuration and diagnostics for the VEX compiler.

-fmm=<mm_file>   Reads the machine model configuration file from *<mm_file>*.

-fmmdump   Dumps (to *info_file*) the current machine model configuration, which could be used to produce a machine model file to pass to the *-fmm=<file>* option.

-fdraw-dag=<n>   Emits to the *DAG file* (default, *DAG.vcg*) the VCG representation of the DAG for trace number *<n>* of the last procedure in the compilation unit.

-fdag-file=<fname>   Sets the *DAG file* to *<fname>*.

-fdraw-cfg   Emits the control flow graph (basic blocks) for every procedure of the compilation unit. The graphs are emitted to files named *GRAPH<procname>.vcg*.

A.3.2 Compiler Pragmas

This section discusses the set of compiler *pragmas* available in the VEX system. Pragmas are hints, directives, and assertions the programmer can pass to the compiler to improve performance.

Unrolling and Profiling

Unrolling pragmas control the loop optimization heuristics applied by the compiler. The loop optimization phase of the compiler consists of two successive phases: *first unrolling* (whereby the loop induction variables are transformed so that all iterations can be executed in parallel) and *second unrolling* (whereby the loop induction variables are not transformed). In most cases, the first unrolling phase is sufficient to achieve the desired behavior, and the second unrolling phase should be used with caution. Profiling pragmas control the way the compiler picks traces when no profiling information is available.

Pragma	Description
#pragma unroll_amount(n1,n2)	Specifies the amount of unrolling the compiler must perform in the first (*n1*) and second (*n2*) unrolling phases for the loop. This pragma applies to the following loop. The statement immediately following the pragma must be a loop statement (*for*, *while*, or *do*). The compiler flags a syntax error if the pragma precedes any other statement. This pragma takes precedence over command line flags.
#pragma precondition_amount(n)	Specifies the amount of preconditioning the compiler must perform for the loop. This pragma applies to the following loop. The value *n* must be compatible with the unrolling amount specified for the loop. It is only legal to specify a preconditioning value that is an integer multiple of the unrolling amount. The statement immediately following the pragma must be a loop statement (*for*, *while*, or *do*). The compiler flags a syntax error if the pragma precedes any other statement. This pragma takes precedence over command line flags.
#pragma trip_count(n)	Specifies the estimated number of iterations of the loop, and is used to guide compiler heuristics. This pragma applies to the following loop. The statement immediately following the pragma must be a loop statement (*for*, *while*, or *do*). The compiler flags a syntax error if the pragma precedes any other statement. This pragma takes precedence over command line flags.
#pragma if_prob(n1,n2)	Specifies the probability of the following branch. The two parameters specify the number of times the following branch is executed (*n2*) and the number of times the following branch is taken (*n1*). The compiler computes the taken-branch probability as *n1/n2*. The statement immediately following the pragma must be an *if* statement. The compiler flags a syntax error if the pragma precedes any other statement.

The following example shows how to tell the compiler to unroll a loop four times (using the first unrolling phase), to precondition the loop to four iterations, and to use a typical trip count of 1000 iterations for the compiler heuristics.

```
void loop_pragmas(int N, int a[], int b[] int c[])
{
    int i;
    #pragma unroll_amount(4,1)
    #pragma precondition_amount(4)
    #pragma trip_count(1000)
    for(i=0;i<N;++i) {
        a[i] = b[i] * c[i];
    }
}
```

The following example shows how to tell the compiler that a branch is biased to be taken 20 times over 100 executions (i.e., a 20% taken probability).

```
int if_pragmas(int a, int b)
{
    #pragma if_prob(20,100)
    if (a>b)
        return foo(a + b);
    else
        return bar(a - b);
}
```

Assertions

Assertions give the compiler more information about the program being compiled. Note that assertions are not hints, and the compiler trusts the programmer about their validity. If the asserted condition can be false, it is possible for the compiler to generate code that would produce unexpected results. Assertions are valid in the current scope, are not propagated to other scopes, and should be used with extreme caution.

Pragma	Description
#pragma assert_eq(exp1,exp2,n) **#pragma assert_ne(exp1,exp2,n)**	Assert equality (*assert_eq*) and inequality (*assert_ne*) of the two C expressions, *exp1* and *exp2*, modulo *n*, in the current scope.
#pragma assert_lt(exp1,exp2) **#pragma assert_le(exp1,exp2)** **#pragma assert_gt(exp1,exp2)** **#pragma assert_ge(exp1,exp2)**	Assert less-than (*assert_lt*), less-equal-than (*assert_le*), greater-than (*assert_g*), or greater-equal-than (*assert_ge*) of the two C expressions, *exp1* and *exp2*, modulo *n*, in the current scope.

The following example asserts that the pointers *p* and *q* are aligned *0 mod 4* in the function *foo()*.

```
foo(char *p, char *q, int N)
{
    int i;
    #pragma assert_eq(p,0,4)
    #pragma assert_eq(q,0,4)
    for(i=0; i<N; i++)
        *p++ = *q++
}
```

Memory Disambiguation

Given two memory references to arbitrarily complex address expressions A and B, the compiler applies a set of techniques that try to answer the question "Can the addresses

A and B ever be the same?" This set of techniques falls into the category of *memory disambiguation*. There are three possible answers to the previous question: *yes*, when the compiler can definitely establish that A and B alias; *no*, when the compiler can definitely establish that A and B never alias; and *maybe*, when the compiler cannot establish the alias relationship between A and B. In its default operation mode, the compiler has to treat *maybe* memory dependences as potential aliases, and the scheduler uses this information to limit code motion.

The compiler supports a set of pragmas to force the scheduler to alter this default behavior and to ignore some of the memory dependences. Note that like assertions the *#pragma ivdep* directive is *not a hint* and the compiler trusts the user on the truth of the assertion. If indeed some memory dependence may exist in the loop, it is possible for the compiler to generate code that would produce unexpected results. The *ivdep* pragma is only valid for the following loop, and should be used with extreme caution.

Pragma	Description
#pragma ivdep	Forces the compiler to treat all "maybe" memory aliases as "no" memory aliases in the following loop. This pragma applies to the following loop. The statement immediately following the pragma must be a loop statement (*for*, *while*, or *do*). The compiler flags a syntax error if the pragma precedes any other statement.
#pragma restrict	Implements a variation of the C99 *restrict* keyword in the form of a pragma. It is a type-annotation pragma and applies to the following declaration (or *typedef*). It instructs the compiler that pointers with a *restrict* type point to memory areas that cannot overlap.

The following example shows the usage of the *ivdep* pragma. The use of *ivdep* indicates to the compiler that no alias exists in the following loop. In this particular example, this means that the user wants to inform the compiler that the vectors a[], b[], and c[] point to distinct memory areas that do not overlap (at least for the first N elements). The compiler will use the information to reorder the memory accesses, so that, for example, it is legal to load a new value of b[] before writing the new value of a[]. Obviously, if the two arrays a[] and b[] ever overlap (i.e., the *ivdep* was asserted incorrectly), the code generated by the compiler will produce unexpected results.

```
void loop_with_ivdep_pragma(
    int N, int a[], int b[], int c[])
{
    int i;
    #pragma ivdep
    for(i = 0;i < N; ++i) {
        a[i] = b[i] * c[i];
    }
}
```

The following example shows the usage of the *restrict* pragma.[2] The use of *restrict* indicates to the compiler that no alias exists for pointers declared with a *restrict* type. In this particular example, this means that the user wants to inform the compiler that the vectors a[], b[], and c[] point to distinct memory areas that do not overlap (at least for the first N elements). The compiler will use the information to reorder the memory accesses, so that, for example, it is legal to load a new value of b[] before writing the new value of a[]. Obviously, if the two arrays a[] and b[] ever overlap (i.e., the *ivdep* was asserted incorrectly), the code generated by the compiler will produce incorrect results.

```
#pragma restrict
typedef r_int int;

void loop_with_restrict_pragma(
    int N,
    r_int a[],
    r_int b[],
    r_int c[])
{
    int i;
    for(i=0;i<N;++i) {
        a[i] = b[i] * c[i];
    }
}
```

The VEX compiler also supports a limited form of the ISO-C99 *restrict* keyword for pointers. The *restrict* keyword has effects similar (with different syntax) to the *restrict* pragma described previously. For example, the following loop generates equivalent annotations, through the use of the C99 syntax.

```
void loop_with_c99_restrict(
    int N,
    int * restrict a,
    int * restrict b,
    int * restrict c)
{
    int i;
    for(i=0;i<N;++i) {
        a[i] = b[i] * c[i];
    }
}
```

---

2. Note that the VEX compiler predates the C99 *restrict* keyword. The *restrict* pragma substantially implemented the same concept, with a different technique. The VEX compiler supports both ways.

Cache Control

The VEX compiler supports a set of pragmas that allow programmers to attach certain attributes to C data types. The compiler attaches the attributes to the data type and maintains them during the compilation process through the final code generation back end. The machine-specific back end is responsible for interpreting the type attributes and for generating the proper actions. The basic concept behind VEX type attributes is that they represent *hints to the compiler* and *never impact the correctness of the program*. In this way, the back end is free to ignore them if it chooses to do so, or if the particular compilation target lacks hardware support for implementing the behavior suggested by the hint.

These type attributes influence data cache accesses and enable the user to manually force a compiler-directed data prefetching. VEX memory operations include two qualifiers that specify *streaming* accesses (i.e., accesses to objects that only exhibit *spatial locality*) and *local* accesses (i.e., accesses to objects that exhibit a strong temporal locality). The following pragmas control the prefetching algorithm and the replacement policy of the cache.

Pragma	Description
#pragma lmb	Attaches a *spatial locality* attribute to the following type definition or variable declaration. The statement immediately following the pragma must be a type declaration (*typedef*) or variable declaration. The compiler flags a syntax error if the pragma precedes any other statement. In case of a type declaration, the attribute applies to all variables of the same type. In case of a variable declaration, the attribute applies to the declared variable only.
#pragma stream	Attaches a *temporal locality* attribute to the following type definition or variable declaration. The statement immediately following the pragma must be a type declaration (*typedef*) or variable declaration. The compiler flags a syntax error if the pragma precedes any other statement. In case of a type declaration, the attribute applies to all variables of the same type. In case of a variable declaration, the attribute applies to the declared variable only.
#pragma prefetch(num)	Attaches a *prefetch* attribute to the following type definition or variable declaration. The statement immediately following the pragma must be a type declaration (*typedef*) or variable declaration. The compiler flags a syntax error if the pragma precedes any other statement. In case of a type declaration, the attribute applies to all variables of the same type. In case of a variable declaration, the attribute applies to the declared variable only. The value *num* indicates the prefetch distance (expressed in multiples of D-cache lines).

Note that type annotation pragmas always refer to the physical memory storage implied by the definition/declaration. The following construct

```
#pragma stream
typedef int stream_int;

stream_int *p;
```

defines a *stream_int* type derived from the basic type *int*, tagged with a *streaming* attribute, and declares a pointer *p* pointing to data of type *stream_int*. In other words, the pragma will affect all accesses through *p* (such as **p*) but not the accesses to set or read the value of *p* itself. If the desired behavior is to have the pointer *p* itself be tagged with the *spatial locality* attribute, we need the following statements.

```
#pragma stream
typedef int *stream_int_ptr;

stream_int_ptr *p;
```

Finally, if we want both *p* and **p* to be tagged with the *spatial locality* attribute, we can use the following combination.

```
#pragma stream
typedef int stream_int;

#pragma stream
typedef stream_int *stream_int_stream_ptr;

stream_int_stream_ptr *p;
```

Similarly, it is possible to annotate types with a *prefetch* attribute, as in the following example.

```
#pragma prefetch(1)
typedef int pft1_int;
```

One way of using the *prefetch* attribute to operate fine-grain prefetch control is in a *cast* operator, as the following example (multiplication of a vector by a constant) shows.

```
for(i=0;i<10000;i++) {
    ((pft1_int *)c)[i] = ((pft1_int *)a)[i] * k;
}
```

This example suggests to the compiler that it add a prefetch operation to the accesses of the arrays *c[]* and *a[]* in the loop. The parameter *1* to the prefetch pragma indicates that the amount to prefetch is *one* D-cache line. If the size of a D-cache line is (for example) 32 bytes, the compiler will emit one prefetch operation for the line containing *(int)c+i+32* and one prefetch operation for the line containing *(int)a+i+32* at each loop iteration. In this case if the strides taken by *i* are smaller than the prefetch distance, adding the prefetch will cause the values of *c[]* and *a[]* to be loaded in the cache long before their use, in this way avoiding a potential cache miss.

A.3.3 Inline Expansion

Inline expansion is an optimization that replaces calls to functions by the function itself. It is beneficial because it eliminates the overhead required to make a function call, and it allows optimizations to take place that would otherwise be inhibited by function calls (such as *loop unrolling*). For example, the two pieces of code following show a simple example of manual inline expansion.

```
int f1(int x,int y,int q)
{
    int z = mac(x,y,q);
    return z * 2 + 4;
}

int mac(int a,int b,int c)
{
    return a*b + c;
}
```

```
int f1(int x, int y, int q)
{
    z = x * y + q;
    return z * 2 + 4;
}
```

The code on the left calls the function mac. This involves some overhead for saving and restoring registers. Inline substitution, performed "by hand" on the right, eliminates the overhead for calling mac by rewriting the calling program so that the definition of mac is substituted "inline."

The mechanics of actual inline expansion are significantly more complex. When the compiler performs inline expansion, it guarantees that the expansion will not affect the program's behavior at all. In particular, this means that static and external variables will behave correctly, and that local variable names within the expanded function will not conflict with variables in the calling function.

A function that is expanded inline disappears completely into the function that calls it, and this has consequences for both debugging and profiling. Calls to inlined functions do not appear in profiles produced by *gprof*. Most debugging tools cannot set breakpoints within inlined functions.

The VEX-compiler supports two methods of user-controlled inlining.

Multiflow-style Inlining

This inline facility in the VEX compiler (triggered by the *-mfinline* flag) extends the syntax of C,[3] and it is based on the concept of an *inline module*. An inline module is a group of functions that can be substituted inline. Functions to be inlined need to be enclosed in an *inline declaration*. The compiler does not generate code or storage for an inline declaration. Therefore, inline expansion can only take place after the function being expanded has appeared within an inline declaration. The compiler inlines all

---

3. Note that the VEX compiler predates the C99 *inline* keyword, which is more user friendly, but also more limited than the *inline module* concept.

functions in an inline module that are declared with the *inline* attribute. For example, the following code expands all calls to the function *mac()* within the function *f()*.

```
inline_declare {
inline_module maclib {
    inline int mac(int a,int b,int c) {
        return a*b + c;
    }
}}

inline_module maclib {
    inline int mac(int a, int b, int c) {
        return a*b + c;
    }
}
inline_use maclib;
int f(int x, int y, int q)
{
    int z = mac(x,y,q); /* this call is inlined */
    return z * 2 + 4;
}
```

C99-style Inlining

This inline facility resembles the *inline* hint in C99.[4] All functions in scope marked with *inline* are considered candidates for inlining. This mode is triggered by the *-c99inline* flag. The following example implements the same inlining functionality of the *mac()* function within *f()*.

```
inline int mac(int a, int b, int c) {
    return a*b + c;
}

int f(int x, int y, int q)
{
    int z = mac(x,y,q); /* this call is inlined */
    return z * 2 + 4;
}
```

Finally, note that the *-autoinline* flag of the VEX compiler uses the same mechanisms in a transparent way, and is equivalent to performing the following (with all functions of *hello.c* marked as *inline*).

---

4. For readers more familiar with the GNU C (*gcc*) compiler, C99 inline hints are very similar to what *gcc* supports.

```
inline_module hello_1234 {
    inline_declare {
        inline_module hello_1234 {
            #include "hello.c"
        }
    }
    #include "hello.c"
}
```

A.3.4 Machine Model Parameters

The version of the VEX compiler that accompanies the book supports a limited form of dynamic reconfigurability. The VEX compiler optionally parses a configuration file passed through the *-fmm=<mm_file>* option. For example, the command

```
<vex>/bin/cc hello.c -fmm=config.mm
```

reads in the configuration from the *config.mm* file. The configuration file syntax is a free-format list of *<directive, property, value>* tuples. The *<property>* fields are machine-model specific strings and have to match those used in the default machine description (Section A.6 specifies the VEX-specific configuration properties.) The *<value>* field is an integer value. The currently supported *<directive>* commands are:

- *CFG*: To set a configuration option. Currently, only *Debug* and *Dump* are supported. *Debug* sets the "verbosity" level of compiler messages when parsing the configuration file. *Dump* instructs the compiler to dump the variables that can be reconfigured with their value, in a format that can be reread by the compiler itself.

- *RES*: To set the size of a machine resource. This can be used to set the quantity of resources available in a single instruction. For example: 4 multipliers, 8 issue slots, 3 memory ports, and so on.

- *DEL*: To set the delay of a computation machine element. This can be used to modify the issue-use delay of an operation (number of instructions between the issue of an operation and the instruction where a consumer of any output can be scheduled).

- *REG*: To set the number of registers of a register bank machine element. Note that registers in a bank can only be reduced from the statically compiled value, and that lower bounds mandated by the RTA must be obeyed (see Section A.2) for the banks that participate in the calling convention.

For example, the following is a legal configuration file.

```
CFG: Debug     1 ## Verbose compilation
RES: Alu.0     2 ## 2 ALUs on cluster 0
RES: Memory.0  1 ## 1 Mem port on cluster 0
DEL: AluR.0    3 ## 3-cycle integer ops on cluster 0
```

```
DEL: CmpGr.0   3 ## 3-cycle compare ops on cluster 0
REG: $r0      32 ## Use 32 general purpose registers
REG: $b0       2 ## Use 2 branch registers
```

A.3.5 Custom Instructions

The VEX compiler includes a limited form of support for user-defined operations at the C language level through _asm*() intrinsics. Because these intrinsics map directly into VEX intermediate-level operations (and ultimately assembly language operations), they are limited to operations that have no side effects, do not access memory, and do not modify any hidden state. When the user inserts a call to _asm() in a C program with the proper parameters, the compiler schedules the operation and allocates the registers. In this way, the user can refer to C variables for operands and destinations. The compiler interprets calls to _asm*() in a special way. The implicit function prototypes for the intrinsics (included in the *vexasm.h* header) are:

```
/* From "<vex>/usr/include/vexasm.h" */

typedef unsigned int                     __vexasm1;
typedef struct {unsigned int n0,n1;}     __vexasm2;
typedef struct {unsigned int n0,n1,n2;}  __vexasm3;
typedef struct {unsigned int n0,n1,n2,n3;} __vexasm4;

void      _asm0(int opcode, ...);
__vexasm1 _asm1(int opcode, ...);
__vexasm2 _asm2(int opcode, ...);
__vexasm3 _asm3(int opcode, ...);
__vexasm4 _asm4(int opcode, ...);
```

The first argument (*opcode*) is a numeric identifier for the operation. The other (optional) arguments after *opcode* represent the values read by the operation (with a limit of eight). Currently, _asm*() calls can only represent operations with zero to four return values. Taking the address of an _asm*() function is illegal. The following is an example of _asm*() usage.

```
#include <vexasm.h>

void foo(int *c, int *a, int *b, int size)

{
    int p;
    for (p = 0; p < size; p++) {
        *c++ = (int)_asm1(0x12,*a++,*b++);
    }
}
```

In this example, we are calling the intrinsic number 0x12 with two arguments for all elements of an array and storing its result in a third array. If, for example, the intrinsic

0x12 implements the "average" function, we can write the code in a more readable form, such as:

```
#include <vexasm.h>

#define AVG(a,b) ((int)_asm1(0x12,(a),(b)))

void average (int *c, int *a, int *b, int size)
{
    int p;
    for (p = 0; p < size; p++) {
        c++ = AVG(*a++,*b++);
    }
}
```

This produces the following code for the loop body (for a one-cluster VEX, unrolled twice). The highlighted instructions are those the compiler produces to map the _asm1() intrinsic calls. As we can see, the compiler schedules the code around the intrinsic calls and performs the usual optimizations (including loop unrolling) and register allocation tasks.

```
L0?3:
        c0    cmplt $b0.0 = $r0.5, 1
        c0    ldw.d $r0.3 = 0[$r0.2]
        c0    cmplt $b0.1 = $r0.5, $r0.0
        c0    add $r0.5 = $r0.5, 2
;;
        c0    ldw.d $r0.7 = 0[$r0.4]
;;
        c0    ldw.d $r0.8 = 4[$r0.2]
        c0    add $r0.2 = $r0.2, 8
        c0    brf $b0.0, L1?3
;;
        c0    ldw.d $r0.9 = 4[$r0.4]
        c0    add $r0.4 = $r0.4, 8
;;
        c0    asm,18 $r0.3 = $r0.3, $r0.7
;;
        c0    stw 0[$r0.6] = $r0.3
        c0    brf $b0.1, L1?3
;;
        c0    asm,18 $r0.8 = $r0.8, $r0.9
;;
        c0    stw 4[$r0.6] = $r0.8
        c0    add $r0.6 = $r0.6, 8
        c0    goto L0?3
;;
L1?3:
```

In terms of resource usage, the compiler built-in assumption is that an _asm*()_ operation occupies a number of issue slots that is the maximum of the number of output registers it produces (with a minimum of one) and half the number of input registers it consumes (with a minimum of one). This default can be overridden with a compiler configuration file, as described in Section A.3.4. The VEX compiler implicitly assumes two groups of _asm_ intrinsics: _group A_ (with _asm_ opcodes from 0 to 63) has a default latency of one cycle, and _group B_ (with _asm_ opcodes from 64 to 127) has a default latency of two cycles. Default latencies can be changed by providing a machine-model configuration file to the compiler, as described in Section A.3.4.

A.4 Visualization Tools

Many of the VEX tools are capable of emitting graph information that is compatible with the VCG (_Visualization of Compiler Graphs_)[5] tool. The compiler can emit the following information in VCG form.

- Control flow graphs (see Figure A.9) for each of the procedures of a compilation unit, through the _-fdraw-cfg_ command line option.

- DAGs (see Figure A.10) for each of the individual traces of the first procedure of a compilation unit, through the _-fdraw-dag=<trace_num>_ and _-fdag-file=<name>_ command line options.

- Compacted schedules (see Figure A.11) in VCG form can be produced from any VEX assembly language file by using the _schplot_ utility (in _<vex>/bin/schplot_).

- To visualize (for comparison, see Figure A.12) profiling information, the VEX distribution includes the _rgg_ utility (in _<vex>/bin/rgg_) that converts the standard _gprof_ output into a VCG call graph (see Figure A.13).

Visualization tools are often a very useful instrument in the development of tuned applications. In particular, profiling visualization is an invaluable tool to help determine where to spend time in the source-level optimization of a complex application. Profiling is usually necessary regardless of the target architecture style. For machines with ILP like VEX, once the most important routines are isolated DAG visualization helps the fine-tuning of the implementation. For example, it easily shows if we are successful in removing dependences. By turning a "deep" DAG into a "shallow" DAG, we can immediately see that we have exposed a larger amount of ILP.

---

5. VCG stands for "Visualization of Compiler Graphs," and is a tool (designed primarily by George Sander and used in the ESPRIT project #5399 COMPARE) that generates and displays a layout of graphs as they occur typically in compiler construction. See Sander [1995].

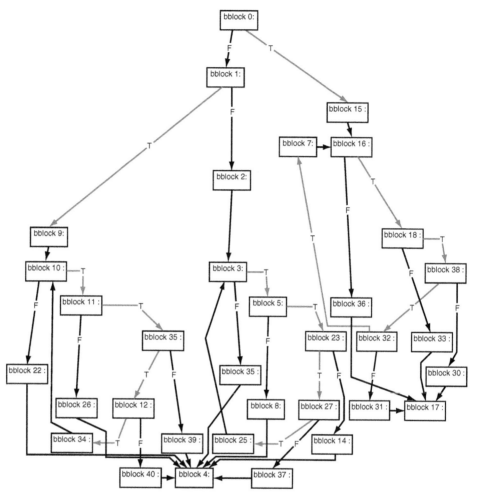

FIGURE A.9 Example of control flow graph visualization. Nodes are basic blocks of a function, and edges are control flow links (branches). The VEX compiler also emits the individual operations within each block (omitted from this picture for simplicity). The control flow graph can be emitted at various stages, before and after optimization.

A.5 The VEX Simulation System

The VEX simulator uses a so-called *compiled simulation* technique, based on the principles described in Chapter 6. The compiled simulator (CS) translates the VEX binary to the binary of the host computer by first converting VEX to C and then invoking the host C compiler to produce a host executable.

In addition to the standard semantics of the instructions, CS also emits instrumentation code to count cycles (and other interesting statistics), as well as code to dump

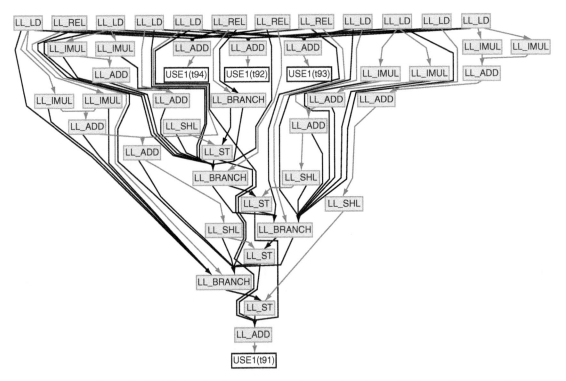

FIGURE A.10 Example of DAG visualization. As one would expect, nodes are VEX operations and edges are dependence graphs. The description allows turning on and off edge types (flow, anti, constraints, and so on) for easier visualization of complex DAGs.

the results to a log file at the end of the simulation (the log file is named *ta.log.###*). Timing instrumentation is turned on with the *-mas_t* flag passed to the compiler driver (or *-mas_ti* and *-mas_td* for finer grain control; see the section on compiler flags). By default, CS also performs a simple one-level cache simulation.

CS operates on each of the individual VEX assembly language (*.s*) files corresponding to the compilation units of a program and translates them back to C by implementing the VEX operation semantics and the calling convention (ABI), and introducing the appropriate instrumentation code. The CS-generated C files are then compiled with the host platform C compiler (e.g., *gcc* for Linux) and linked with the support libraries that deal with the instrumentation. During linking, the CS *ld* wrapper ensures that the right libraries are linked in the right order, and performs the necessary "magic" (such as wrapping system functions so that they do not cause problems) for the binary to execute correctly.

By default, VEX links in a simple cache simulation library, which models an L1 instruction and data cache. The cache simulator is really a trace simulator, which is embedded in the same binary for performance reasons but only communicates with the VEX execution engines through simple events that identify memory locations, access

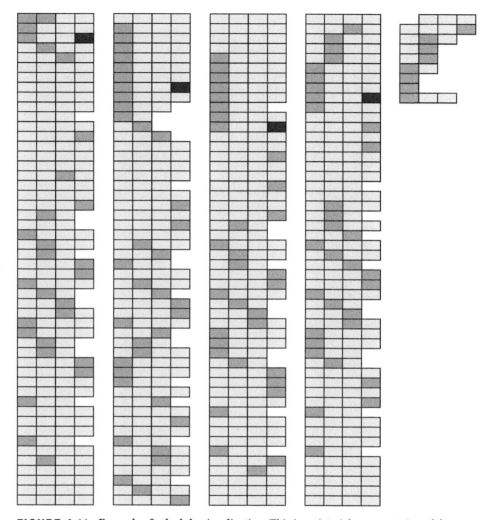

FIGURE A.11 **Example of schedule visualization.** This is a pictorial representation of the scheduled VEX assembler output. Although its primary use is largely decorative (or educational), it also provides a quick visual impression of the utilization of the machine in a given trace.

types, and simulation time. If desired, the default cache simulation can be replaced by a user-defined library that overrides the event-handling routines.

A.5.1 *gprof* Support

The VEX simulator includes "simulated" support for *gprof* when invoked with the -*mas_G* option. Unlike *gprof* running in the host environment, the VEX *gprof* instrumentation only adds time to the simulation. It is *noninvasive* as far as the simulation itself is concerned, and it is *not based on statistical PC sampling*. At the end of simulation,

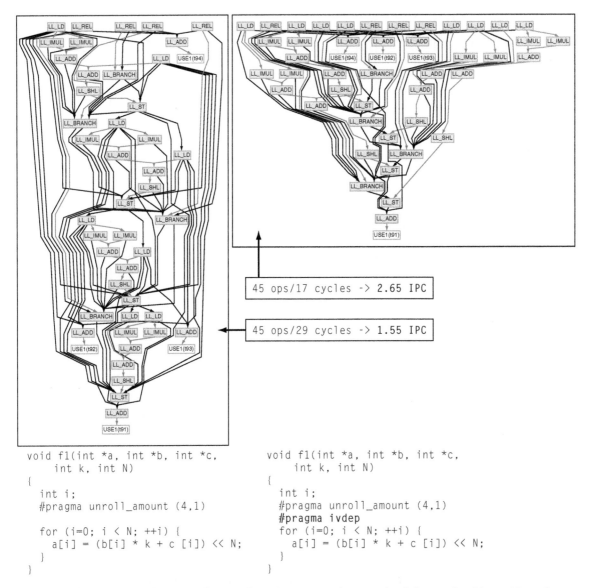

```
void f1(int *a, int *b, int *c,
     int k, int N)
{
  int i;
  #pragma unroll_amount (4,1)

  for (i=0; i < N; ++i) {
    a[i] = (b[i] * k + c [i]) << N;
  }
}
```

```
void f1(int *a, int *b, int *c,
     int k, int N)
{
  int i;
  #pragma unroll_amount (4,1)
  #pragma ivdep
  for (i=0; i < N; ++i) {
    a[i] = (b[i] * k + c [i]) << N;
  }
}
```

FIGURE A.12 DAG visualization and ILP. Both DAGs represent the same simple loop code with or without the *#pragma ivdep* (no induction variable dependences). Just looking at the DAGs, it is obvious that the version on the right exposes a much higher degree of ILP (the DAG is "shallow"). In fact, this corresponds to a 70% increase in performance (from IPC of 1.55 to 2.65) for a default VEX machine.

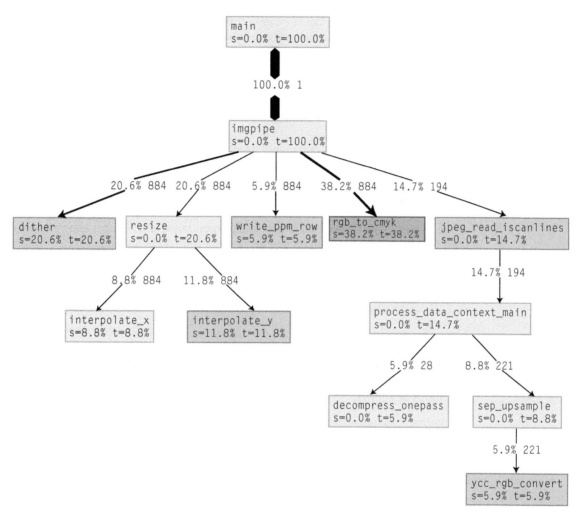

FIGURE A.13 **Example of visualization of a profiled call graph.** The *rgg* utility emits a graph representation of the function-level call graph. Each node in the graph corresponds to a procedure, and each edge to a procedure call. Nodes are labeled with relative execution times for themselves (*s* = %) and for the descendent subgraph (*t* = %), and are color coded for importance. Edges are labeled with execution counts and with relative execution time, and have a thickness based on their importance. For example, the *write_ppm_row* function is called 884 times by *imgpipe* and amounts to 5.9% of execution time (all in the function itself) of the execution under test.

four files are emitted: *gmon.out* containing profile data that include cache simulation, *gmon-nocache.out* containing profile data that does not include cache simulation (i.e., assumes perfect caches), and *gmon-icache.out* and *gmon-dcache.out* containing data for, respectively, I-cache-only and D-cache-only statistics (this requires using the built-in cache simulator). Programmers can compare the two files to identify the parts of an application that put particular pressure on the D-cache or on the I-cache subsystems. To visualize profile data, users can run the *<vex>/bin/rgg* utility that converts *gprof* data into a call graph compatible with the format of the graphical interface *vcg* (also distributed as *<vex>/bin/xvcg*).

Note that the compiler also supports the *-pg* option to emit the *gprof* instrumentation part of the VEX code itself. Unlike the instrumentation emitted with *-mas_G*, this instrumentation is invasive, and models what would be necessary to do for a nonsimulated target.

Profiling flags are most commonly used in conjunction with timing flags (*-mas_t*). If the profiling flag is turned off without the timing flag, the *call tree* is emitted at exit, but no timing information is available in the *gmon.out* files.

Note that *gprof* profiling and *profile-based optimization* are two completely separate and distinct features not to be confused. Profile-based optimization (triggered by *–prob_gen* and *–prob_use* flags) is a two-step compilation process that allows the compiler to collect branch profile data to drive optimizations in a second phase. Profiling with *gprof* (triggered by the *–mas_G* flag), on the other hand, collects routine-level profile data for analysis (and there is currently no feedback path to the compiler).

A.5.2 Simulating Custom Instructions

The VEX compiled simulator parses and converts the code produced by the compiler from *_asm*()* calls (see Section A.3.5) but knows nothing about the semantics of the operations themselves, which must be provided by the end user. To be able to simulate a user-defined library, the simulator defines a standard interface for *_asm*()* type operations as follows:

- For each *asm* operation, it produces a call to the function *sim_asm_op*()* with the proper arguments. The symbols *sim_asm_op0* — *sim_asm_op4* are reserved and cannot be used in the user program.

- The prototypes for the *sim_asm_op** symbols are:

```
typedef unsigned int                      __vexasm1;
typedef struct {unsigned int n0,n1;}      __vexasm2;
typedef struct {unsigned int n0,n1,n2;}   __vexasm3;
typedef struct {unsigned int n0,n1,n2,n3;} __vexasm4;

void      sim_asm_op0(int, ...);
__vexasm1 sim_asm_op1(int, ...);
__vexasm2 sim_asm_op2(int, ...);
__vexasm3 sim_asm_op3(int, ...);
__vexasm4 sim_asm_op4(int, ...);
```

Users must provide an implementation of *sim_asm_op*()* for the opcodes used in the program, compile it with the host compiler, and link the object file to the executable. Otherwise, a link error will be generated. A sample implementation of the *sim_asm_op1()*

function for the previous example might look as follows.

```
#include <stdarg.h>
#include <stdio.h>

extern unsigned int sim_asm_op1(
    unsigned int opcode,
    ...)
{
    va_list ap;
    unsigned int t, s1, s2;
    va_start(ap, opcode);

    switch(opcode) {

    case 0x12: /* AVG(s1,s2) */
        s1 = va_arg(ap, unsigned int);
        s2 = va_arg(ap, unsigned int);
        t = (s1 + s2) / 2;
        break;

    default:
        _linux_fprintf(stderr,
            "Error: opcode %d not supported\n",
            opcode);
        _linux_exit(1);
    }
    return t;
}
```

If we write the *sim_asm_op1()* implementation in *asmlib.c*, a sample compilation and simulation sequence to be able to test the file *average.c* is:

```
1. Compile the VEX with the _asm() calls:
      <vex>/bin/cc -c average.c

2. Compile (natively) the asm library
      gcc -c asmlib.c

3. Link (with the VEX compiler) the 2 parts together
      <vex>/bin/cc -o average average.o asmlib.o

4. Run the average binary
```

A.5.3 Simulating the Memory Hierarchy

As mentioned previously, the VEX simulator links a simple cache-simulation library by default, which only models a (configurable) L1 instruction and data cache. In addition,

VEX also contains a basic software development kit (SDK) to replace the built-in cache library with a set of user-defined functions. The SDK is in the form of a set of headers for the API that the VEX simulator expects when running VEX code. Because of the way in which dynamically linked libraries work, the default functions can be overridden by linking a natively compiled library that redefines them. Users must redefine *initialization* and *finalization* routines (called at the beginning and end of the simulation), as well as *data tracing* functions for each of the memory access types. The *tracing* functions are called at every data memory access (or simulated instruction cache line fetch), but do not affect the execution of the program semantics. In this way, the redefined routines can implement arbitrary behaviors, while preserving the correct program execution. Time is accounted for separately in the execution engine and in the cache simulation model.

Simulating instruction caches is a particularly challenging task in a compiled simulator, especially if we want to be able to link with modules compiled for the simulation host. In this case, we cannot build a simulated VEX memory model but have to keep the one the host mandates. VEX models instruction caches by simulating a dynamic loader that assigns addresses to every compilation unit as soon as one of its functions is loaded. This deviates from a statically linked model but still provides significant instruction cache behavior.

A.6 Customizing the VEX Toolchain

The idea behind VEX is to provide a flexible environment for architecture exploration of VLIW architectures. As such, it allows users to selectively change the compiler target and many of the simulation parameters. The VEX compiler, in addition to the standard compile-time options (flags), optionally reads a compile-time configuration file where it is possible to define machine resources such as number and latency of functional units and number of registers for each architected register file. The compiled simulator also optionally reads a configuration file whereby users can specify execution-time parameters, such as clock and bus cycles; cache parameters (size, associativity, refill latency); and various advanced options. Finally, VEX includes an extension mechanism by means of which it is possible to introduce user-defined custom instructions (also known as *assembly language intrinsics*). VEX *intrinsics* are modeled as black boxes, and thus they need to be explicitly instantiated (through a special naming convention) in the C sources. Once the compiler recognizes the intrinsics, it optimizes around them, and performs scheduling and register allocation for them like any other operation.

The following sections describe in some detail the three configuration options in VEX. Note that all VEX tools come with a default configuration, outlined in Table A.11.

A.6.1 Clusters

By default, the VEX compiler generates code for a one-cluster VEX architecture. The option *-width n* changes the number of clusters to *n*, which must be 1, 2, or 4.

Parameter	Description	Default	How to change
Clusters	VLIW clusters (fully interconnected groups of units and register files)	1	Compile time flag: *-width <n>* option (only 1, 2, and 4 clusters allowed)
Issue width	Total number of operations in a VLIW instruction (cycle)	4 per cluster	Compile-time machine model
Integer ALUs	Units for integer operations, comparisons, shifts	4 per cluster, 1-cycle latency	Compile-time machine model
Integer MULs	Units for integer multiplications	2 per cluster, 2-cycle latency	Compile-time machine model
Integer registers (GRs)	General-purpose registers	64 per cluster, 32 bits	Compile-time machine model (GRs can only be decreased)
Branch registers (BRs)	Branch condition and predicate registers	8 per cluster, 1 bit	Compile-time machine model (BRs can only be decreased)
Link register	Address for indirect branches	1 in cluster 0, 32 bits	Cannot be changed
Memory load	Units to load from mem	1 per cluster, 3-cycle latency	Compile-time machine model
Memory store	Units to store to mem	1 per cluster, 1-cycle latency	Compile-time machine model
Memory pft	Units to prefetch mem	1 per cluster	Compile-time machine model
Copy units	*Src/dst* for intercluster copy operations	1 *src* + 1 *dst* per cluster, 1 cycle	Compile-time machine model

TABLE A.11 VEX default parameters.

A.6.2 Machine Model Resources

Here we describe the properties relevant to the VEX-specific machine description. Most of these should be supported with the compiler producing correct code. They are classified as follows.

- *Computational machine elements*: properties for *DEL* directives

- *Register bank machine elements*: properties for *REG* directives

- *Machine resources*: properties for *RES* directives

Note that some of these properties are cluster specific. The following example shows properties for cluster 0 (suffix *.0*). To get the same properties for the other identical clusters, replace prefix/suffix accordingly (for example, *DEL:CmpGr.1* is for cluster 1, *RES:Alu.2* is for cluster 2, and so on).

Computational MEs can be used in a DEL directive:

```
AluR.0          Integer Op, Immediate on Src1
Alu.0           Integer Op, Immediate on Src2
CmpGr.0         Compare to general register / select
CmpBr.0         Compare to branch
Select.0        Select
Multiply.0      Multiply
Load.0          Load Word to GR
LoadLr.0        Load Word to LR
Pft.0           Prefetch
Asm1L.0         User-defined asm, Group A, 1 Slot
Asm2L.0         User-defined asm, Group A, 2 Slots
Asm3L.0         User-defined asm, Group A, 3 Slots
Asm4L.0         User-defined asm, Group A, 4 Slots
Asm1H.0         User-defined asm, Group B, 1 Slot
Asm2H.0         User-defined asm, Group B, 2 Slots
Asm3H.0         User-defined asm, Group B, 3 Slots
Asm4H.0         User-defined asm, Group B, 4 Slots
CpGrBr.0        Copy GR to BR
CpBrGr.0        Copy BR to GR
CpGrLr.0        Copy GR to LR
CpLrGr.0        Copy LR to GR
Spill.0         Spill (Store)
Restore.0       Restore GR (Load)
RestoreLr.0     Restore LR (Load)
```

Register bank MEs can be used in a REG directive:

```
$r0             General Purpose Register Bank
$b0             Branch Register Bank
```

Machine resources can be used in a RES directive:

```
Global Resources
IssueWidth      Total issued operations (> 0)
MemStore        Total Store Ops (> 0)
MemLoad         Total Load Ops (> 0)
Cluster Resources
Alu.0           Integer ALU slots (>= 2)
AluR.0          Integer ALU slots - imm. on src1 (>= 2)
Mpy.0           Multiply slots (> 0)
CopySrc.0       Copy-Source slots (> 0)
CopyDst.0       Copy-Dest slots (> 0)
Memory.0        Memory load slots (> 0)
```

A.6.3 Memory Hierarchy Parameters

The built-in cache simulator in the compiled simulator currently supports a method to set most of the relevant parameters for the simulated memory and bus. The method to instruct the compiled simulator about the configuration parameters is through a configuration file consisting of *<property> <value>* pairs. An example follows.

```
CoreCkFreq            500
BusCkFreq             200
lg2CacheSize          15 # (CacheSize = 32768)
lg2Sets               2  # (Sets = 4)
lg2LineSize           5  # (LineSize = 32)
MissPenalty           25
WBPenalty             22
lg2StrSize            9  # (StrSize = 512)
lg2StrSets            4  # (StrSets = 16)
lg2StrLineSize        5  # (StrLineSize = 32)
StrMissPenalty        25
StrWBPenalty          22
lg2ICacheSize         15 # (ICacheSize = 32768)
lg2ICacheSets         0  # (ICacheSets = 1)
lg2ICacheLineSize     6  # (ICacheLineSize = 64)
ICachePenalty         30
NumCaches             1
StreamEnable          FALSE
PrefetchEnable        TRUE
LockEnable            FALSE
ProfGranularity       1.000000
```

Table A.12 outlines the individual parameters in detail.

The compiled simulator looks for a file named *vex.cfg* in the invocation directory and parses it according to the previously outlined syntax if the file is present. Alternatively, it is possible to use the environment variable *VEXCFG* to pass the name of the simulation configuration file.

A.7 Examples of Tool Usage

This last section lists some sample use of the VEX tools to cover the most likely scenarios for software development, experimentation, and architecture exploration through the VEX tool set. The examples assume familiarity with the Linux operating system and command line shells. All examples assume that the VEX toolchain is installed in */home/vex*.

A.7.1 Compile and Run

The first example is a simple compile-and-run sequence of a program consisting of two compilation units, *file1.o* and *file2.o*, and the math library (*-lm*), instructing

CoreCkFreq	The frequency of the core clock, in MHz
BusCkFreq	The frequency of the bus clock, in MHz
lg2CacheSize	The log2 of the data cache size in bytes (e.g., 10 => 1 KB)
lg2Sets	The log2 of the data cache associativity (e.g., 2 => 4-way set associative)
lg2LineSize	The log2 of the data cache line size in bytes (e.g., 8 => 64 KB)
MissPenalty	The stall penalty of a data cache miss in core cycles
WBPenalty	The stall penalty of a data cache writeback in core cycles
PrefetchEnable	Enable prefetching (TRUE or FALSE)
NumCaches	Number of caches in the architecture
StreamEnable	Enable the stream buffer (TRUE or FALSE)
lg2StrSize	The log2 of the stream buffer size in bytes (e.g., 10 => 1 KB)
lg2StrSets	The log2 of the stream buffer associativity (e.g., 2 => 4-way set associative)
lg2StrLineSize	The log2 of the stream buffer line size in bytes (e.g., 8 => 64 KB)
StrMissPenalty	The stall penalty of a stream buffer miss in core cycles
StrWBPenalty	The stall penalty of a stream buffer writeback in core cycles
g2ICacheSize	The log2 of the instruction cache size in bytes (e.g., 10 => 1 KB)
lg2ICacheSets	The log2 of the I-cache associativity (e.g., 2 => 4-way set associative)
lg2ICacheLineSize	The log2 of the I-cache line size in bytes (e.g., 8 => 64 KB)
IcachePenalty	The stall penalty of an instruction cache miss in core cycles

TABLE A.12 Parameters for the built-in VEX cache simulator.

the compiler to maximize optimization (-O4) and do not remove the assembly language file (-ms).

```
## Compile individual modules
/home/vex/bin/cc -ms -O4 -c file1.c
/home/vex/bin/cc -ms -O4 -c file2.c

## Link (with math library)
/home/bin/cc -o test file1.o file2.o -lm

## Run the program
./test
```

This command sequence, in addition to any side effect (such as terminal output) the execution of *test* produces, generates two VEX assembly language files (*file1.s* and *file2.s*), two host (Linux) object files containing the compiled version of the CS-instrumented VEX assembly language files (*file1.o* and *file2.o*), a host-executable file containing the instrumented version of the executable compiled simulator for the code (*test*), and a simulation logfile (*ta.log.000*) containing the statistics corresponding to the simulation of the execution of *test* on the default VEX platform.

The assembly language files are useful for checking the static behavior of the compiler, and can be analyzed with the *pcntl* utility (which collects static compile information from a VEX assembly language file). For example, if we invoke

```
## Analyze file1.s
/home/vex/bin/pcntl file1.s
```

we obtain a breakdown of every function in the assembly language file and every compilation *trace* per function, with the vital statistics (instructions per cycle, number of scheduled cycles, number of scheduled operations and nops, number of copies for a multicycle configuration, and so on). The listing also includes cumulative statistics that can be used as a first approximation to evaluate the effectiveness of code reorganizations or different combinations of compiler flags.

```
Procedure: rgb_to_cmyk_and_dither::
Trace    IPC Cycles   Oper   Copy    Nop
-------------------------------------------
    3   1.58     12     19      0      1
    1   3.33    232    773      0      0
    7   1.00      1      1      0      0
    6   1.00      1      1      0      0
    5   1.00      1      1      0      0
    4   0.50      2      1      0      0

Operations  = 796
Instructions = 249
Reg. moves   = 0
Nops         = 1
Avg ILP = 3.19679
```

The simulation output file, as described, contains a set of self-explanatory statistics, such as cycles (total, execution, stalls, operations, equivalent time), branch statistics (executed, taken, conditional, unconditional), instruction memory statistics (estimated code size, hits/misses), data memory statistics (hits/misses, bus conflicts, copybacks), bus statistics (bandwidth usage fraction), cumulative figures (overall IPC with and without accounting for stalls), and simulation statistics (simulation time, equivalent MIPS speed). The output of a simulation run is the primary tool in guiding experimentation.

A.7.2 Profiling

A common use of the VEX tools is with the *gprof* profiling tool. By using the example of Section A.7.1 we can insert profiling instrumentation (at the simulation level) through the *-mas_G* flag as follows.

```
# Compile individual modules with CS profiling
/home/vex/bin/cc -ms -mas_G -O4 -c file1.c
/home/vex/bin/cc -ms -mas_G -O4 -c file2.c

## Link (with math library)
/home/bin/cc -mas_G -o test file1.o file2.o -lm

## Run the program
./test
```

The run of the profiled CS binary, in addition to the standard simulation output, also produces a set of data files for *gprof*, including *gmon.out* (containing the data for the overall execution), *gmon-nocache.out*, *gmon-icache.out*, and *gmon-dcache.out* (containing, respectively, the data for the execution assuming infinite caches, the instruction cache only, and the data cache only). The latter three are particularly useful in identifying pathological situations that affect the instruction or data caches for a specific benchmark. By running the standard *gprof* utility on the instrumented binary, we can obtain individual statistics from the *gmon*.out* files.

```
# Get overall execution statistics
gprof test gmon.out

# Get execution statistics assuming infinite caches
gprof test gmon-nocache.out

# Get execution statistics on instruction cache
gprof test gmon-icache.out

# Get overall execution on data cache
gprof test gmon-dcache.out
```

In addition to the *gprof* data files, an instrumented profiled run also produces a flattened version of the function profile, with statistics for the number of cycles spent in the instruction and data cache for each executed function.

```
Flat profile (cycles)
    Total        D-cache      I-cache   Function
  142934306      20005200      983340   rgb_to_cmyk
   89338101      23394096      622665   dither
   41688760       3077172      400635   interpolate_x
   34709205      12166200      238410   interpolate_y
```

```
24579498        1818396         57375   write_ppm_row
10075928        1472580         22005   ycc_rgb_convert
 5548602         510300         21600   jpeg_idct_islow
 3494605         963936         52740   h2v2_fancy_upsample
 2743026         192132         53595   decode_mcu
 1350417          43092          3915   jpeg_fill_bit_buffer
  671699          17028        248625   decompress_onepass
  167867          81000         44325   imgpipe
  131632          38232         69615   process_data_context_main
  109835          47520         14850   sep_upsample
   69817           9828          2340   jpeg_huff_decode
   69082          36540         15165   jpeg_read_scanlines
     ...             ...          ...   ...
```

Finally, it is possible to produce a graphical representation of the call graph (as described in Section A.4) with the *rgg* tool.

```
# Generate visual call graph, excluding cache effects
# and filtering out functions taking less than 1%

/home/vex/bin/rgg test -m gmon-nocache.out -m 0.01
```

A.7.3 Custom Architectures

The support for customization in VEX is present at three levels.

1. *Custom instructions*: Inserted through *_asm()* intrinsics and simulated through a custom host-level library

2. *Custom clusters, resources, and latencies*: Controlled through a compile-time configuration file (*-fmm=<machine-model>*)

3. *Custom memory architecture*: Wherein simple deviations from the default model are captured through the CS configuration file (*vex.cfg*) and complex memory architectures require writing a user-level instrumentation routine

As we described in Section A.3.5, we can instantiate custom instructions simply by including the *vexasm.h* header file and by using the *_asm(...)* syntax. This instantiates a "black-box" assembler of instructions the compiler schedules based on the resource pattern and delay information we define. Additionally, the compiler requires a separate simulation library that contains the helper code to implement the semantics of the custom instruction. If our simulation library is named *asmlib.c*, the following command sequence compiles our canonical example.

```
# Compile (VEX compiler) individual modules
/home/vex/bin/cc -ms -O3 -c file1.c
/home/vex/bin/cc -ms -O3 -c file2.c
```

```
# Compile (host compiler) simulation library
gcc -c asmlib.c

## Link (with math library and assembler library)
/home/bin/cc -o test file1.o file2.o -lm asmlib.o
```

If we want to instruct the compiler to target a custom machine model, we can pass the *-fmm=<machine-model>* flag during the compilation phase, or we can use the *-width <clusters>* to model a clustered architecture. A common experiment (for example, to create a reference baseline) is to model a single-issue RISC-like target, which we can do simply by creating a *risc.mm* file containing the following directives (limit issue slots to one operation, reduce registers to 32)

```
RES: IssueWidth 1
REG: $r0 32
```

and passing the right flags to the compiler:

```
# Compile modules with "risc" machine model
/home/vex/bin/cc -ms -O3 -fmm=risc.mm -c file1.c
/home/vex/bin/cc -ms -O3 -fmm=risc.mm -c file2.c
```

At the other end of the extreme, we can try to model a very wide architecture (4 clusters, 32 issue slots, 32 memory operations, 32 multipliers, 32 send/receive paths), which will most likely provide an upper bound to performance. To this aim, we can generate a *verywide.mm* configuration file containing

```
RES: IssueWidth 32
RES: MemLoad 32
RES: MemStore 32
RES: MemPft 32
RES: Alu.0 32
RES: Mpy.0 32
RES: CopySrc.0 32
RES: CopyDst.0 32
RES: Memory.0 32
RES: Alu.1 32
RES: Mpy.1 32
RES: CopySrc.1 32
RES: CopyDst.1 32
RES: Memory.1 32
RES: Alu.2 32
RES: Mpy.2 32
RES: CopySrc.2 32
RES: CopyDst.2 32
RES: Memory.2 32
RES: Alu.3 32
```

```
RES: Mpy.3 32
RES: CopySrc.3 32
RES: CopyDst.3 32
RES: Memory.3 32
```

and invoking the compiler with the proper flag:

```
# Compile modules with "risc" machine model
/home/vex/bin/cc -ms -O3 -fmm=verywide.mm -c file1.c
/home/vex/bin/cc -ms -O3 -fmm=verywide.mm -c file2.c
```

Finally, when we invoke the CS-generated binary, we can also change the run-time simulation statistics by writing a *vex.cfg* file for CS. At simulation time, we can change cache configuration, core and bus frequency, and in general any parameter that does not require recompilation. For example, if we want to model a machine with a 64-KB data cache (4-way), 16-KB instruction cache (2-way), 1-GHz core clock, and 200-MHz memory bus clock we can write a *vex.cfg* file containing

```
CoreCkFreq           1000
BusCkFreq            200
lg2CacheSize         16 # 64KB dcache
lg2Sets              2  # 4-way dcache
lg2ICacheSize        14 # 16KB icache
lg2ICacheSets        1  # 2-way icache
```

Then, we can simply invoke the simulation of our benchmark

```
## Run the program
./test
```

and look at the *ta.log.<nnn>* output file to analyze the statistics corresponding to the new configuration defined in *vex.cfg*.

As we have seen, the VEX tools are a flexible framework that allows experimenting with a variety of configuration parameters, both at compile time and at simulation time. In Chapter 11 we showed some of the more advanced uses of VEX on a few important application domains. In this section, we covered some of the basic uses of the tools that will enable users to apply VEX to the applications of their interest.

A.8 Exercises

1. Using a benchmark program (with input data) of your choice, test the effect of VEX optimization flags (from *-O1* to *-O4*, *-H1* to *-H4*, *-mincode*, *-autoinline*) on performance and code size. In particular, measure static code size (simply count assembler instructions of each compilation unit) and dynamic code size (using the simulation statistics) and discuss the effects of the different optimization strategies.

2. Construct a simple loop example in which you cannot use the *ivdep* pragma (because of loop-carried dependences) but in which you can selectively use the *restrict* pragma/keywords. Measure static and dynamic performance, and show that indeed the compiler would generate incorrect code when using *ivdep*.

3. Implement, in C, an integer matrix multiplication routine (for square matrices, using the prototype below). Test the effect of the VEX unrolling and restrict pragmas/keywords by measuring the static performance (schedule length of the innermost loop) and the dynamic effects. Observe and plot the trend for different matrix sizes (from 10 to 1000) and cache sizes.

```
void matmult(int result[], int a[], int b[], int N);
```

4. Using the matrix multiplication code of the previous exercise, plot the control flow graph of *matmult()* and identify the loops. In addition, plot the data dependence graph of the innermost loop (hint: how do you identify the trace number corresponding to the innermost loop?) for the version with and without the *restrict* hints, and comment on the differences.

5. Using the matrix multiplication code of the previous exercise, collect static and dynamic execution statistics for different machine configurations by varying the issue width between 1 and 8 and experimenting with several combinations of VEX execution units and register bank sizes. Chart the results and discuss the performance/cost tradeoffs.

6. Repeat the experiment of the previous exercise by selecting two combinations of execution units, and vary the cache memory parameters. Experiment with both instruction and data caches that are in the range 4 to 64 KB, have 1- to 4-way associativity, and have 4- to 64-Byte line sizes. Discuss the performance tradeoffs of the various memory configurations.

APPENDIX **B**

Glossary

Here we collect terms whose meanings are particularly useful to readers of this book, or whose terminology is used inconsistently in the community. This is not meant to be a comprehensive glossary.

ABI (application binary interface). A set of software standards that describe how programs should interface with each other, with libraries, and with the operating system. Analogous to the way an ISA is a contract between hardware and software, an ABI is a contract between user programs and the run-time system.

Absolute address. An address within the process' address space that is computed as an absolute number, without the use of a base register.

ACM (Association for Computing Machinery). A professional organization for the area of Computer Science. See *http://www.acm.org*. See also IEEE.

AGU (address generation unit). The functional unit in a microprocessor responsible for generating memory addresses. Normally, it includes a simple ALU for base + offset computation, pre- and post-increments, and similar operations.

Altivec. PowerPC's micro-SIMD extension to support superword and subword parallelism.

ALU (arithmetic and logic unit). The computational unit of a CPU (central processing unit) of a microprocessor that performs operations such as addition, subtraction, multiplication, bit-wise logical (AND, OR, NOT, XOR), and comparison (greater than, less than, equal). ALUs can also support address computations, although a separate AGU is sometimes used for that purpose. The bit width of the "natural" ALU data is usually the same as that of the machine datapath and is what is used to identify the "size" of a processor (32-bit, 64-bit), regardless of the width of other processor buses.

ARM (advanced RISC machine). Originally Acorn RISC machine, a family of 32-bit RISC microprocessors used in a variety of embedded applications. At the writing of this book, ARM is by far the most widely used 32-bit embedded processor core. The ISA is simple and fairly orthogonal, like many other RISC processors, and includes a basic form of predication implemented as a 4-bit instruction field specifying a combination of processor status flags to be used as a predicate for the current instruction. The ISA has 27 registers (16 available for general-purpose use). One peculiarity of the ISA is that the program counter is exposed in R15, which somewhat simplifies assembly language programming but creates all sorts of headaches for the compiler and the microarchitecture. ARM2 (ARM1 was never released) was the original Acorn RISC machine, designed by Acorn Computers Ltd. ARM3 added cache multiprocessing support. ARM6 was the first embeddable core with an additional MMU for virtual memory. The ARM7 is a low-power, reduced-size variation of the ARM6 and one of the most widely used cores for embedded applications. The ARM7TDMI includes the Thumb ISA 16-bit extension to reduce code-size requirements for low-end highly cost-sensitive embedded applications. Finally, the ARM9 is the latest member of the family, together with its variations such as the ARM9J, to include the *Jazelle* instruction set extension for efficient Java execution. More recently, Intel has taken over the DEC StrongARM line of ARM-compatible processors, with the SA-100, SA-1100, and the Xscale implementations.

ASIC (application-specific integrated circuit). An integrated circuit designed to perform a particular function by defining the interconnection of a set of basic circuit building blocks drawn from a library provided by the circuit manufacturer. The individual gates and wires of an ASIC are normally synthesized from a high-level RTL description of the circuit (written in Verilog or VHDL). The gate-level description is then mapped to a technology-specific library of cells, which are placed and routed to get the final description ready for the manufacturing process at the silicon foundry.

ASIP (application-specific instruction-set processor). A (usually small) programmable core integrated in an SoC and dedicated to a few specific functions (for example, audio decoding). ASIPs try to strike a balance between programmability and low cost by providing a platform on which multiple related applications and different generations of an application can be mapped onto the same ASIP. Use of ASIPs is very common in telecom, networking, and audio-video consumer products.

Assertion. A test programmers embed in a program to detect potential error conditions. Assertions are used for debugging.

Athlon. AMD's 7th-generation x86-compatible processor (1999); also called K7.

ATM (automated teller machine). First deployed in the 1970s, these embedded machines automate many common banking tasks such as withdrawing cash, making deposits, and viewing balances.

ATM (asynchronous transfer mode). A networking protocol based on fixed-size, 53-byte cells and virtual circuits. Used today mostly at the data link layer.

Automaton. A finite-state machine designed to sequence through a known set of states, according to a set of rules that govern the state transactions. Automata theory studies ways to apply automata to different fields, as well as techniques to optimize the mapping, implementation, and execution of automata-based algorithms. Synonym: finite-state machine.

b (bit). The basic unit of information. Sometimes abbreviated "b."

B (byte). By convention, a group of eight bits that can represent one of 256 values. Sometimes abbreviated "B."

Back end. The part of a software system that performs the final stages of the process the system implements. In compiler terminology, it identifies the last phases of the compiler that schedule operations to optimize machine resources and generate final assembled code.

Base + offset addressing. An instruction-set architecture trait whereby memory operations specify both a base and an offset as part of the operation itself. This implies the presence of a dedicated AGU that pipelines a scaled addition before the memory access itself. An alternative to base + offset addressing (for example, in Intel's IPF) is direct addressing (memory is only accessed directly through a register) paired with post-increment modifiers.

BDTI (Berkeley Design Technology, Inc.). A consulting company that publishes one of the well-known embedded benchmark suites. See *http://www.bdti.com.*

Binding. The process of resolving a symbolic reference in one module by finding the definition of the symbol in another module and substituting the address of the definition in place of the symbolic reference. The linker binds relocatable object modules, and the dynamic loader binds executable load modules. Modules are searched in a certain binding order, so that a definition of a symbol in one module has precedence over a definition of the same symbol in a later module.

Bit rate. A data rate expressed in bits per second, commonly used when discussing digital sampling and transmission rates of audio and video signals. For example, high-quality compressed digital audio requires a stream of about 120 Kb/s. Digital video at QCIF (320 × 280) quality starts at about 1.5 Mb/s.

BLAS (basic linear algebra subroutine) libraries. A set of libraries that implement a common set of vector and matrix operations.

Bluetooth. A communication protocol based on radio links for short-range ("personal area") networking of a variety of "personal" devices, such as mobile phones, digital cameras, printers, and handheld devices. Originally intended as a replacement for cables, Bluetooth has grown into the Personal Area Networking (PAN) space.

Byte code. An "architecture-neutral" object file format consisting of a sequence of opcode/data pairs. Byte code programs are supposed to be passed to interpreters that by fetching, decoding, and executing the byte code pairs effectively run the program. Unlike fully bound machine code, byte code is theoretically independent of the target architecture, and the dependences are kept in the interpreter. For execution speed, byte code programs can be translated directly into target machine instructions, either statically ("ahead-of-time") or dynamically ("just-in-time"). For example, most Java compilers generate byte code, which is what normally gets distributed in class (or jar) files.

CAD (computer-aided design). Software-based tools that allow design of other systems, particularly those related to mechanical engineering.

CAGR (compound annual growth rate). The growth rate that best fits an exponential curve, expressed as an annual percentage growth.

CFG (control flow graph). A graph describing the ways the program counter might traverse a procedure. Nodes in the graphs are basic blocks (maximal straight-line segments of instructions). Edges represent control transitions (typically branches).

Checkpointing. The act of saving the state of a computation (program, simulation, and so on) so that it is possible to restore that state later (for example, after a crash or after a failed speculation).

CISC (complex instruction-set computer). An instruction-set architecture style wherein the semantics of instructions include several sequential operations, including memory accesses, address computations, and ALU operations. The idea behind CISC was to "narrow the semantic gap" between instruction set and languages by attempting to raise the complexity of individual instruction to match common language constructs (e.g., string operations and looping constructs). The Motorola 680x0 family and the Intel x86 family are examples of CISC instruction sets (the classification makes less sense with modern microarchitectures that use many RISC and ILP concepts while preserving a visible CISC instruction set).

CMOS (complementary metal-oxide semiconductor). The currently dominant semiconductor implementation style. CMOS uses two transistors per inverter and was originally adopted because of its low switching current.

COMA (cache-only memory architecture). A distributed shared-memory style in which there is no "main memory" in the system, only a collection of caches associated with all of the processing nodes in the system. See also NUMA.

Code bloat and code explosion. Negative side effects of some compiler optimizations that cause the size of the generated code to grow. A controlled amount of code growth ("bloat") is usually acceptable and often beneficial because it enables aggressive optimizations such as function inlining and speculative code motions. The innovators of ILP-oriented region scheduling compilation coined the term *code explosion* to describe excessive code size growth from optimizations. Large code expansion can cause negative side effects on instruction cache performance. Modern compilers are engineered to balance the benefits of code-expanding optimizations with the costs of large code size.

CODEC (coder/decoder). Any software algorithm or dedicated device that implements the functionality needed for analog-to-digital conversion of signals, and *vice versa.*

Co-design. The process in which both the hardware and the software components of an embedded system are considered together during the design phase. By using co-design techniques, designers can make global decisions about the partitioning of the system in its hardware and software parts.

Compensation code. Some region schedulers, such as trace schedulers, make code motions that could lead to incorrect behavior on some code paths in order to increase performance. Extra code, called compensation code, is then placed on those paths to ensure correct behavior. Most compensation code is simply copies of operations that should have been executed but are not on that path in the new schedule.

Compiler phase. A major transformation or analysis step in a compiler. Transformation phases modify the internal representation of the program, whereas analysis phases collect useful data for other transformation phases, without changing the intermediate representation. Individual phases may require multiple "passes" over every operation in the intermediate representation.

Conditional move. A conditional move operation replaces the value of its destination register with its source only if a condition is true. It is equivalent to the C statement *if (cond) dest = src;.*

Cydrome. One of two ILP-oriented mini-supercomputer startups founded in the 1980s to build machines in the VLIW style. Started in 1984, it designed and built a CPU (the Cydra 5) especially oriented toward efficient modulo scheduling. Its technology had a great influence on the IPF, more than 10 years after its death in the late 1980s.

DAG (directed acyclic graph). A directed graph (consisting of nodes connected by directed edges) that does not contain cycles. In other words, there is no path from a node back to itself. DAGs are commonly used in compiler back ends to represent the data flow of acyclic code regions during the scheduling phase.

Data flow. Architecture style wherein the execution of each individual computation is triggered directly by the availability of the required operands and not by an explicit sequencing of steps (which is what von Neumann architectures do). Data flow implicitly defines parallelism at the finest grain. Although it did not succeed in its purest form (including the use of data-flow languages) it is implemented — in a very restricted form — in most out-of-order superscalar microarchitectures.

Datapath. The fully connected collection of processor ALUs, registers, and communication paths. Datapaths are normally characterized by their bit width (16-bit, 32-bit,

64-bit). Processors can include different datapaths (it is common to have completely separate integer and floating-point datapaths) as well as different width datapaths (a 32-bit machine, with a 32-bit integer datapath, may include a 64-bit floating-point datapath).

DAXPY. The name of a subroutine (part of the BLAS library) that computes a linear combination of vectors $y = a * x + y$. The "D" refers to double-precision; "A," "X," and "Y" come from the variable names; and "P" refers to "plus."

DEC (Digital Equipment Corporation). A pioneering computing company of the minicomputer age, DEC merged with Compaq in the late 1990s, which then merged with HP in 2001.

Disambiguation. A set of compiler techniques used to answer the question "Could these two computed memory references refer to the same location?"

Dismissable. The property of an operation that because it is executed speculatively can safely *dismiss* exceptions if they get generated.

Dithering. A technique used to quantize digital data (such as images and audio) so that fewer bits per unit (pixel or audio sample) are necessary to represent the signal. It is commonly used when generating data to be printed to match the capability of the output device and the print media. It is also common in computer graphics to enhance the visual quality of colormap-based images (by interleaving pixels of different colors the human retina interpolates as a shade that does not exist in the palette).

DMA (direct memory access). A system organization wherein a peripheral writes directly into the main memory, without processor involvement. DMA is typically performed by a DMA engine, which is programmed by the processor but as a separate hardware task.

DMMU (data memory management unit). A separate MMU for data access. See also IMMU.

DRAM (dynamic random-access memory). The densest type of main memory used in computer design. DRAM cells store bit values using a small amount of charge in a capacitor. Because the capacitor leaks, every cell in the DRAM must periodically be "refreshed" by reading and rewriting its value. DRAM is implemented using different process technology from processing elements, and thus the two cannot easily be integrated on the same chip.

DTMF (dual-tone multi-frequency). The name of the system of touch-tones used by the telephone system. Each digit (in addition to the star and octothorpe keys) corresponds to a unique pair of tones.

Dynamically linked library (DLL). A library that is prepared by the linker for quick loading and binding when a program is invoked, or while the program is running. A DLL is designed so that its code can be shared by all processes bound to it.

ECC (error correction codes). A system that stores a value using specially-coded extra bits, so that if a limited number of bits are randomly corrupted, the error can be detected, and in some cases, the original value can still be retrieved from the overall (partially corrupted) value. Parity is one of the simplest forms of ECC, providing indication that a single bit has been corrupted. More sophisticated types of ECC include CRC (cyclic redundancy checks) and the encodings used for data transmission and storage.

ECL (emitter-coupled logic). A semiconductor implementation style. ECL historically enjoyed performance advantages (and power disadvantages) compared to CMOS, but the gap has closed as CMOS techniques have been continually improved.

EDA (electronic design automation). Software tools that help in designing hardware. While there is a large space of EDA companies, the three giants in the fields are Cadence, Mentor Graphics, and Synopsys.

EEMBC (Embedded Microprocessor Benchmark Consortium). A consortium that maintains and publishes an embedded benchmark suite. See *http://www.eembc.org*.

EEPROM (electrically erasable programmable read-only memory). A form of memory that most closely resembles a ROM in operation, but that can be erased and rewritten at somewhat high cost and low speed. In contrast, a PROM can be written just once but not erased and an EPROM is typically erased by exposing its circuits to ultraviolet light.

Endianness. A convention (part of the run-time architecture, or ABI) that establishes the order of individual bytes within a multibyte memory representation. Big-endian means that bytes are ordered such that the most significant byte has the lowest address (and little-endian the other way around). The term comes from Swift's *Gulliver's Travels* via the famous paper "On Holy Wars and a Plea for Peace" by Danny Cohen, USC/ISI IEN 137, April 1980: "The Lilliputians, being very small, had correspondingly small political problems. The Big-Endian and Little-Endian parties debated over whether soft-boiled eggs should be opened at the big end or the little end."

EPIC (explicitly parallel instruction computing). An architectural style coined by Intel to describe the Itanium Processor Family; EPIC shares many defining characteristics with VLIW.

EPROM (erasable programmable read-only memory). See EEPROM.

Equals machine. A VLIW machine whereby the results of an operation commit at exactly the scheduled latency. The TI C6x architecture is an example of an equals (EQ) machine. See also Less-than-or-equals machine.

Exception. Exceptions are "exceptional" events that may occur as the result of the execution of a particular instruction. They are used to signal unusual conditions that have to be treated separately, such as a miss in the TLB or a division by zero. Unlike interrupts, exceptions are synchronous. Other books [notably Hennessy and Patterson (2003)] use *exception* as an umbrella term for both synchronous exceptions and asynchronous interrupts. Synonyms: *fault* (deprecated) and *trap*. *Trap* is also used to mean a control flow instruction that changes the privilege level of the executing process and jumps to a new piece of code.

Execution time. The time during which a program is actually executing, not including the time during which it and its DLLs are being loaded.

Fab. Short form of "fabrication facility," a manufacturing plant for semiconductor wafers.

FFT (fast Fourier transform). An efficient variant of the DFT (discrete Fourier transform) algorithm, the FFT transforms spatial or temporal data into a frequency-space representation. The FFT has *O(nlogn)* execution time.

FIFO (first-in, first-out). A queuing structure (hardware or software) which corresponds intuitively to a pipeline.

FIR (finite impulse response). One of the two major families of digital filtering algorithms. An FIR filter has the property that the output value at a particular point depends directly on a certain range of the input, and not on previous output values of the filter. See also IIR.

FPGA (field-programmable gate array). A gate array in which the connections among individual logic elements can be programmed into the device after it has been manufactured. Typical logic elements include a collection of simple logic gates, a small lookup table implemented with memory blocks, a flip-flop register, and the fabric to connect them. The programmable logic is normally stored in memory cells, which can be reprogrammed multiple times simply by downloading a new configuration from a host computer (in a few seconds).

Full predication. A predication strategy that requires architectural support in the form of a *predicate register file* and predicate register specifiers in all operations. Hardware that supports full predication must conditionally execute all predicated operations, based on the value of the included predicate.

Function pointer. A reference or pointer to a special descriptor that uniquely identifies the function. In the simplest case, the descriptor is simply the address of the function. In a DLL, the function descriptor contains the address of the function's actual entry point as well as the pointer to the linkage table.

GPRS (general packet radio service). A data service built on top of GSM cellular telephone service. GPRS is a step toward 3G wireless service and is sometimes described as a "2.5G" service.

GSM (global system for mobile communications). The standard for cellular telephone service in the entire world except for the United States and China.

Handheld personal computer. A small, general-purpose, programmable, battery-powered computer capable of handling most personal-productivity and media applications. The device can be operated comfortably while held in one hand. A palmtop is usually loaded with an operating system such as PocketPC or PalmOS and can be synchronized with other computing devices, such as a desktop PC. Synonyms: personal digital assistant (PDA), pocket computer, palmtop.

Hard coding. Programming jargon that specifies the despicable practice of writing constant values directly into a program, possibly in multiple places, where they cannot be easily modified. Changing something hard coded requires recompilation and sufficient understanding of the implementation to be sure that the change will not introduce inconsistency that will cause the program to fail. Its counterpart in hardware design is the term *hardwiring*.

Hard macro. In ASIC terminology, a hard macro is a preverified placed-and-routed block that can be used as a component in a design. Hard macros tend to be tied to a given technology, process, and vendor. Examples of common hard macros include microprocessor cores, memory and register files, and speed and/or area.

HPL ("HP Laboratories" or "HP Labs"). The research and development laboratories of the Hewlett Packard Company.

IBURG. A technique initially published by Fraser, Hanson, and Proebsting [1992] to automatically generate the code for a tree parser starting from a tree grammar in which each rule is annotated with its cost. IBURG derivatives are commonly used in compilers to build the instruction selection phases that choose the right sequence of instructions corresponding to the high-level constructs of the target program. The underlying technique behind IBURG is a bottom-up rewriting system (BURS) based on dynamic programming to minimize the cost function based on the cost of the individual rules.

IEEE (The Institute of Electrical and Electronics Engineers). A professional organization offering a variety of programs, services and standards in the area of electrical engineering and computer science. See *http://www.ieee.org*. See also ACM.

If-conversion. The set of techniques that converts control dependences into data dependences. These techniques eliminate *if* instructions in a program by transforming the code so that execution proceeds along both branches of the *if* and then the right result of the computation of the two branches is selected based on the original *if* condition. Note that if-conversion is independent from the architecture support necessary to efficiently implement it (such as full or partial predication).

IIR (infinite impulse response). One of the two major families of digital filtering algorithms. The output value of an IIR filter depends not just on the local range of input but also upon the previous outputs of the filter. This feedback loop makes each filter output value depend on all prior input values, hence the "infinite" in the name.

ILP (instruction-level parallelism). A form of uniprocessor parallelism in which performance is improved via the parallel execution of independent operations within a single program flow-of-control. The most common architectural design styles that embody ILP are superscalar and VLIW.

IMMU (instruction MMU). A separate MMU for instruction access. See also DMMU.

Inlining. The act of replacing a function call with an instance of the function's body. Actual argument expressions are substituted for formal parameters, usually as part of a high-level, machine-independent optimizer in a compiler. Inlining is an enabling optimization (i.e., it improves the effectiveness of other optimizations) because it increases the likelihood that a compiler will spot redundancies and optimization opportunities. If done carelessly (for example in case of recursions) inlining may cause code size to increase exponentially.

Instruction opcode. A mnemonic acronym used in assembly language to represent a machine operation.

Instruction scheduling. The compiler phase that orders instructions on an ILP architecture in an attempt to reduce the execution time (or optimize other target metrics such as code size and energy consumption).

Instrumentation. The act of interspersing extra operations inside a program to monitor the program behavior itself. It can be done automatically by a tool (for example, the compiler can insert profiling instrumentation) or by the programmer in an *ad hoc* manner (for example, when inserting timing annotations).

Intel 80x86. The generic description for the family of Intel microprocessors that include the 8086, 8088, 80186, 80286, 80386, 80486, Pentium, Pentium Pro, Pentium II, Pentium III, and Pentium 4. The abbreviation x86 is also used to identify non-Intel compatible processors from other vendors, such as AMD or Cyrix. The x86 family dramatically evolved over time. The 186 was a 16-bit processor with no virtual memory. The 286 added virtual memory. The 386 was the first processor to have 32-bit addressing and multitasking support. The 486 added an optimized on-chip instruction and data cache. The Pentium added minimal superscalar support, with two in-order integer pipelines and integrated floating-point support. The Pentium Pro, II, and III implemented a completely new microarchitecture that executes out-of-order micro-operations a front-end engine generates starting from the original x86 instructions. Successive generations, including the Pentium 4, add further ILP support.

Interrupt. Arises as a result of events external to the instruction stream of the processor. Examples include I/O (disk ready, serial port ready, mouse, keyboard). Unlike exceptions, interrupts are normally asynchronous. A special type of interrupt is the *non-maskable interrupt* (NMI), which cannot be masked (turned off) by setting hardware registers. Typical examples of NMIs include reset and power-off.

IP (intellectual property) block. An IP (intellectual property) block is a logic component that can be assembled together with other IP blocks and custom circuitry to implement a given system in ASIC or FPGA technology. It is the hardware equivalent of a software library implementing a well-defined function. IP blocks are a fundamental concept for the electronic design automation (EDA) industry, as they represent the basic unit for *reuse*. While in theory IP blocks ought to be independent of technology, processes, and vendors, the practice is still lagging behind because of the wild incompatibility across interconnection standards. IP blocks can include peripherals (e.g., UARTs), bridges (e.g., PCI) and CPU cores (e.g., ARM7) and can be made available as hard cores (tied to a specific VLSI process) or soft cores (synthesizable Verilog/VHDL code).

IPC (interprocess communication). A mechanism for processes to communicate with each other. An IPC protocol is expressed as a set of programming interfaces (APIs) that enable the creation, execution, termination, and communication of concurrent processes running on a single computer (or on multiple computers connected by a network). Examples of IPC mechanisms include POSIX-style fork/wait primitives, pipes and name pipes, message queues, sockets, semaphores, and shared memory.

ISA (instruction-set architecture). The "contract" that needs to be understood in order to write legal programs for a given processor architecture. Parts of a processor that are left to the implementation — such as number of functional units, cache size, and cycle speed — are not part of the ISA.

Java. A simple, object-oriented, distributed, interpreted, robust, secure, architecture-neutral, portable, multithreaded, dynamic, general-purpose programming language developed by Sun Microsystems in the mid 1990s. Java supports a platform-independent programming paradigm, in which an intermediate representation (called byte code) is shipped to an interpreter that executes it. In this way, the target dependences are constrained in the interpreter and not embedded in the program. The execution of Java is based on an underlying virtual machine (the JVM, or Java virtual machine). Java as a language uses many of the concepts of C++, such as overloading and inheritance, and simplifies some of the programmer's tasks (for example, it has automatic garbage collection).

JPEG (Joint Photographic Experts Group). JPEG is the name of the committee that designs and standardizes techniques for compression of digital images. The widely known JPEG standard is a DCT (discrete cosine transform)-based technique to compress color images. Contrary to popular belief, JPEG (and its video counterpart) does not define a file format (that would be JFIF) but only the methods to compress and decompress the images.

LALR (look-ahead left-to-right) Parser. The "best practice" family of parsing algorithms. LALR parsers run efficiently and are capable of parsing most context-free languages.

Leak. An incorrect management of resources in a program that occurs when resources are not properly released after the program stops using them. Because of the way in which program scopes work in many languages, failing to free resources makes them "leak out."

Over time, long-running programs with leaks will exhaust their memory. For example, a common leak is the so-called "memory leak," which causes a program to consume all available memory over time. Programming environments (such as Java) that support automatic garbage collection attempt to provide a standard means of freeing unused resources based on their usage pattern, and independently of what the programmer writes in the code.

Less-than-or-equals machine. A VLIW machine whereby the results of an operation commit between the time the operation issues and the scheduled latency of the operation. Most VLIW architectures use less-than-or-equals (LEQ) execution models. See also Equals machine.

Link time. The time during which a program or DLL is processed by the linker. Any activity taking place at link time is static.

Linux. Open-source implementation, written from scratch, of a UNIX-like operating system kernel. Originated and coordinated by Linus Torvalds, it is today packaged in an ample variety of commercially supported distributions (themselves released under open-source licenses). Linux is quickly becoming the OS of choice for servers. The authors' (and Torvalds') preference for the pronunciation of "Linux" (a very controversial matter) is *līnuks*.

Load module. An executable unit produced by the linker (either a main program or a DLL). A program consists of at least a main program and may also require one or more DLLs to be loaded to satisfy its dependences.

MAC (multiply-accumulate) instruction. An instruction that typically performs an operation of the form $a+=b*c$. A MAC fuses a traditional multiplication operation with an addition (accumulation) operation into a single instruction.

Mathematical relation. For any set S, a relation R is a subset of $S \times S$. Equivalently, R can be seen as a map from $S \times S$ to {0,1}.

MAX (multimedia acceleration extensions). The media-oriented, micro-SIMD extensions to the HP PA-RISC architecture.

Memoization. A technique to optimize functions by caching the results corresponding to a given input parameter set of the function. If the function is successively called with the same parameter set, it simply returns the cached value instead of recomputing it.

MESI (modified, exclusive, shared, invalid, or "messy"). An acronym for the states of a directory-based, shared memory cache-coherence protocol.

Microcontroller. A microprocessor designed for embedded applications, and historically built onto a single chip. Microcontrollers are often used in *controlling* workloads, and often use 8-bit or 16-bit architectures.

Microkernel. A style for designing operating systems that offloaded many former kernel functions to user processes, leaving only a reduced (or "micro") kernel running in privileged mode. Mach was the first microkernel operating system. Early microkernels were criticized for the performance penalties associated with crossing multiple protection domains to handle OS responsibilities, but more recent microkernel OSs have addressed this problem.

Middleware. Software (used in distributed computing) that spans heterogeneous machines running different operating systems but that still provides useful collaboration across programs running on different platforms.

MIPS. A speed unit (*million instructions per second*) used to rate processors. Sometimes also called "meaningless indication of processor speed" to indicate the questionable value of marketing-driven benchmarking of processors. Given the ambiguity of the metric (what is an "instruction"?), for many years the unit of 1 MIPS was considered the speed of the DEC VAX 11/780, and other processors were measured through the *Dhrystone* benchmark. Today, standards-setting bodies such as SPEC periodically release benchmark suites that better represent the typical workload one can expect to run on a modern processor.

MIPS [company] (microprocessor without interlocked pipeline stages). The name of one of the RISC workstation processors, based on a research processor from Stanford University.

Misprediction. When an implementation uses branch prediction, it speculates about the direction of branches, allowing the pipeline to continue processing operations along the predicted path. A misprediction occurs when the prediction turns out to be incorrect. Correctly handling it requires squashing the incorrectly speculated operations.

MMU (memory management unit). A hardware unit that translates virtual memory addresses to physical memory addresses. MMUs can support virtual memory (VM) and also distributed shared virtual memory.

MMX (matrix math extensions or multimedia extensions). The media-oriented, micro-SIMD extensions to the x86 architecture.

Modulo scheduling. The first production-quality compiler technique for software pipelining. Pioneered by Bob Rau and his colleagues, and central to the Cydrome machines they later developed.

MOPS. Million of operations per second. For architectures (such as VLIWs) where operations and instructions do not coincide, we need to distinguish between the speed of the machine in terms of executed instructions (see MIPS) and of executed operations.

MPEG (Moving Picture Experts Group). A consortium of partners organized as an ISO committee that generates standards for digital audio and video compression. MPEG-1, MPEG-2, and MPEG-4 are some of the standards supported by MPEG.

MSB (most significant bit). The bit at index $n - 1$ in an *n-bit* value, which corresponds to the greatest-valued position in the word (2^{n-1} for an unsigned value).

MTU (maximum transfer unit). In networking (and in particular on Ethernet), the largest size packet that a network element can support with having to break the packet into smaller pieces.

Multiflow Computer. One of two ILP-oriented minisupercomputer startups founded in the 1980s to build machines in the VLIW style. Started in 1984, it designed and built CPUs that issued 7, 14, or 28 operations, and delivered a VLIW-oriented trace-scheduling-based compiler technology that is still in common use in the computer industry in 2005, 15 years after the company's death.

Multithreading. An architectural or implementation technique that shares hardware at a fine grain among multiple threads. Each thread looks like an independent computation and holds the illusion that it runs alone on the processor. Variants of multithreading include vertical (in which different threads use different execution resources), horizontal (in which threads use different cycles on the machine), and simultaneous (in which different threads can execute on different functional units in the same machine cycle).

Mux (multiplexer). A hardware unit that chooses among different input lines to produce a single output line. Often, the output line has higher bandwidth than the input lines, and thus the multiplexer can "interleave" the input values on the output.

Name space. A set of shorthand representations of other objects, wherein equality is the same for names as for objects. For example, a file system provides a name space in which no two files have the same name.

NaN (not-a-number). A range of values specified by the IEEE floating-point specification that indicate that an error occurred during computation (for example, division by zero). NaNs occupy a large encoding space, allowing them in principle to hold some debugging information about the nature of their cause. NaNs come in two flavors: signaling NaNs raise exceptions as soon as they are generated, whereas nonsignaling NaNs are treated like normal "values" and propagate in a "sticky" manner to all dependent computations that use them.

NaT (not-a-thing). An additional architecture bit used for speculative operations in the IPF architecture. A dismissable load will produce a NaT value if it would have caused an exception. Compilers performing speculation will transform a load in the original program into a speculative dismissable load and a nonspeculative check instruction that verifies that the speculatively loaded value is a thing.

NRE (nonrecurrent engineering). The set of expenses that only occur once in the design (or development) of a product. This is in contrast to per-part, or unit, cost.

Operation. An operation is an atomic action, in general considered roughly equivalent to a typical instruction of a traditional 32-bit RISC machine.

OS (operating system). The low-level software responsible for managing resources on a processor. Among other things, operating systems manage I/O, memory layout and protection, and processes. The operating system is one of the first pieces of code to run when a system boots.

Overlapped execution. This occurs when operation A, which was launched earlier, is still executing while operation B is executing.

Own data. Data belonging to a load module that is referenced directly from that load module and that is not subject to the binding order. Typically, own data is local in scope.

Parallel execution. Operations A and B are being executed at the same time. This requires multiple functional units.

Parallel issue. Operations A and B are released to the execution hardware at the same time. This does not require multiple functional units, but it does require some sort of queuing support to allow the issuing to happen.

Parallelism. The property that two operations or tasks can execute at the same time without interfering with each other. Parallelism offers the opportunity to speed up a computation, at the cost of worrying about interference.

Partial predication. A predication strategy that relies on *conditional move* and *select* operations. Whereas the code transformation steps for full and partial predication are very similar, the final code generated for partially predicated architectures contains normal operations, augmented by conditional moves and selects.

PC (program counter). The register that holds the address of the instruction currently being executed.

PCMCIA (Personal Computer Memory Card International Association). A standard for credit-card-sized expansion cards for notebook computers. PCMCIA cards have been used to add a removable modem, Ethernet networking, wireless networking, CD/ROM interfaces, and disk drives to notebook computers. PCMCIA was renamed "PC cards."

PC-relative addressing. Code that uses its own address (commonly called the program counter, or PC) as a base register for addressing other code and data.

PDA (personal digital assistant). See hand-held computer.

Phase ordering. The sequence in which compiler phases are invoked. Sometimes compiler phases have contrasting goals (e.g., register allocation and code scheduling), and thus it is important to invoke them in the right order and/or to insert heuristics so that one phase does not harm its successors and does not undo the transformations its predecessors just did. Finding the optimal phase ordering is a complex — and still unsolved — problem.

PIC (position-independent code). Code that executes correctly regardless of where it is placed in memory (for example, it uses relative, not absolute, branches). PIC does not require relocation. This term has a dual meaning. First, position-independent code is designed so that it contains no dependence on its own load address. Usually, this is accomplished by using *pc*-relative addressing so that the code does not contain any absolute addresses. Second, it implies that the code is also designed for dynamic binding to global data. This is usually accomplished using indirect addressing through the linkage table.

PID (position-independent data). Analogous to PIC, but for data. PID accesses to global variables need to go through indirect references to linker-generated tables via a dedicated "global pointer" register.

Pipeline. A sequence of hardware units that collaborate sequentially to produce a result. Each unit performs its part of the task, and then passes the work on to the next unit in assembly-line style. A pipelined functional unit will generally have a slightly longer latency than a combinatorial functional unit executed in the same technology, but the pipelined unit will be able to launch more operations per unit of time.

Pipelining. A pipelined functional unit can typically begin execution of one operation per cycle, but takes some number of cycles before the result of that operation becomes available. A pipelined datapath overlaps various phases of the execution of an instruction by operating on multiple instructions in assembly-line style. For example, a traditional single-issue RISC pipeline might have separate phases for instruction fetch, decode/register fetch, execution, memory access, and register writeback. Up to five instructions can be in the pipeline at one time. Complications occur when multiple instructions of various types can be in flight, or when control instructions or exceptional conditions change the flow of control in the program.

POS (point-of-sale) terminal. A device used in retail sales, most commonly for charging credit and debit card transactions.

Position-independent code (PIC). See PIC.

POSIX (portable operating system interface for UNIX). A standard that defines a common and portable API that should work on all UNIX systems. See *http://www.pasc.org*.

Pragma (#*pragma*). A way of adding extra-linguistic information to a program that will be compiled. Pragmas typically do not obey the syntax of the language being used, and refer to implementation or system features that are not normally modeled by the language.

Precomputation. A technique that trades space for time by computing values and storing them in a table, allowing them to be accessed rather than recomputed when they are needed. Depending on the size of the table and the complexity of the computation, precomputation can provide performance and cost improvements.

Preconditioning. A technique applied to unrolled counted loops that removes loop-index tests from the unrolled body of the loop. By performing some number of loop iterations in a prologue, the preconditioning code can ensure that the iteration count of the loop is a multiple of the unrolling amount that has been applied. Then there is no need for the internal loop-index branches in the body of the loop, because they will never be executed.

Predication. A technique for transforming control dependence into data dependence. Predication has two major variants: *partial predication* (which can be added to an unpredicated architecture with small additional cost) and *full predication* (which requires building an architecture from a clean start).

Prefetching. A technique that attempts to reduce the time a processor spends waiting for instructions or data to be retrieved from memory. Modern processors automatically prefetch instructions following the one currently being executed into a fetch window, by trying to predict the direction of branches. Data prefetching is usually triggered by compiler-inserted operations that try to predict regular accesses through large data structures.

Preserved register. A register guaranteed to be preserved across a procedure call. Synonym: *callee-save register.*

Profile. A set of statistics indicating where a program spends its time. Profiles take a variety of forms, including call graph profiles, control-flow-graph profiles, and node, edge, and path profiles. Profiles can also include statistics about other hardware events (such as cache misses).

Program invocation time. The time during which a program or DLL is loaded into memory in preparation for execution. Activities taking place at program invocation time are generally performed by the system loader or dynamic loader.

Quicksort. A fast sorting algorithm, notable because it was the first such algorithm to show $O(n \log n)$ expected-case running time.

Reentrant. A piece of code designed to be invoked simultaneously by multiple different processes. For example, operating system kernel code must often be written in a reentrant manner, because of interrupts and context switches.

Retargetable. Used to describe a compiler that has been designed to support many different computer architectures. Adapting such a compiler to a new architecture is called "retargeting."

RISC (reduced instruction-set computer). An architectural style named and popularized in the 1980s. RISC hallmarks include orthogonal 32-bit instruction encodings, simple operation semantics, and load/store architecture.

RTL (register transfer level). A term used both for code that describes hardware (e.g., code written in VHDL or Verilog) and for the resulting representation after that code has been compiled into a logical representation.

Scan chain. A circuit design methodology that links the registers of a chip so that they can be read out sequentially, like a gigantic shift register. Scan chains allow debugging and testing of the chip.

Scheduling. The fundamental ILP-oriented optimization, scheduling groups parallel operations to form instructions.

Scratch register. A register that is not preserved across a procedure call. Synonym: *caller-save register.*

Scratch-pad memory. A small, fast, on-chip memory. Many embedded processors include scratch-pad memory that is as fast as the first-level cache and integrated into the processor core. For embedded systems with multiple cores, memories that are shared between processors for communication and synchronization purposes are sometimes also called scratch-pad memories.

SCSI (small computer systems interface). An I/O standard for interfacing to peripherals, and in particular hard disks. Used more for server than for desktop (and never in notebook) applications, the SCSI standard has higher bandwidth and a more sophisticated transaction model than other hard disk interfaces.

SDRAM (synchronous DRAM). A dynamic memory that also incorporates a synchronous interface, meaning that it includes a set of latches controlled by a clock signal. This means that it can be clocked along with other components on the memory bus and that it allows more advanced functionality than normal DRAM, such as pipelining of accesses.

Select. A conditional select operation selects between two inputs based on a condition, and then sets the output to the selected input. It is equivalent to the C statement *if (cond) dst = src1; else dst = src2;*, or more briefly, *dst = cond ? src1 : src2;*.

SIMD (single instruction, multiple data). A style of multiprocessing initially named and promoted during the 1980s, in which a single control unit drives many functional units in lock-step fashion. SIMD multiprocessors are no longer constructed (the cost of long wires to the control unit now outweighs the transistor savings from having a single control unit). Micro-SIMD operations are part of virtually all general-purpose processors, and are effective at accelerating a variety of media-related codes.

SMP (symmetric multiprocessing). A style of multiprocessing in which all processors are peers in the construction of the machine, having the same access to memory and communications links.

SMTP (simple mail transfer protocol). The low-level protocol behind electronic mail.

SoC (system-on-a-chip). An integrated circuit that includes multiple functions on a single die. Many SoCs integrate a processor, memories, and peripherals into a single chip.

Soft macro. In ASIC terminology, a soft macro is a preverified synthesizable block that can be used as a component in a design. Soft macros are not usually tied to a given technology, process, or vendor, but need to be synthesized and processed by a CAD back end (place-and-route) for each design in which they are included. Because of this, soft macros are flexible but sometimes not optimized for speed and/or area. Compare and contrast with hard macros.

Software pipeline. An instruction-scheduling technique that overlaps multiple iterations of a loop into a single densely-scheduled *kernel* of code. Software pipelining improves throughput (loops completed per cycle) while not paying particular attention to latency (time to finish a single loop). Software pipelines typically require prologue and epilogue code before and after the loop to allow the kernel to execute legally, although some hardware constructs (such as rotating predicate registers) can reduce or remove prologue and epilogue code.

SoPC (system-on-a-programmable-chip). An integrated circuit that is like an SoC, but also integrates programmable logic. The programmable logic (typically based on FPGA technology) allows "late" customization or reprogramming of the chip after it has shipped.

SPEC (Standard Performance Evaluation Corporation). A nonprofit organization that publishes benchmarks used in the microprocessor and Java spaces.

Speculation. An implementation and architectural technique that allows a processor to "guess" a value that will be available in the future (such as a branch condition or the fact that a load and a store do not address the same memory location) and then execute as if the value were known. If the value is guessed correctly, the machine continues executing normally, and benefits from not having stalled to wait for the value to become available. If the value is guessed incorrectly (misspeculation), the machine must reset its state, squashing any operations that were executed based on the incorrect guess.

Speculative operation. A speculative operation (also known as "eager") is an operation executed prior to the resolution of the branch under which the operation would normally execute. Special attention must be paid to speculative memory load operations to handle the possible resulting exceptions. Speculative memory load operations are sometimes called "dismissable," as any exception deriving from the operation has to be ignored ("dismissed") by the system.

Spill. An operation performed by a register allocator when it runs out of registers to hold values for a computation. The code to save and restore the value is called "spill code."

SRAM (static random-access memory). SRAM is fast but large RAM. A typical SRAM cell requires four to six transistors, and thus it is much larger than a DRAM cell (but can produce a value more quickly). SRAMs are built using the same technology as processors, and thus the two can easily be included in the same chip.

SSE (streaming SIMD extensions). Additional extensions to the x86 architecture that give more control over the memory hierarchy and add micro-SIMD instructions that manipulate floating-point data types.

Static binding. A binding that takes place at link time rather than program invocation or execution time.

Sub-word. A piece of a register that is smaller than a full word. Used mostly with respect to sub-word parallelism, in which a word-sized register is treated in a micro-SIMD manner as multiple independent sub-words by a micro-SIMD functional unit.

Superblock. A form of region used for region scheduling. Superblocks are like traces, except that they can have no side entrances. The only entrance to a superblock must be its first block.

Supercomputing. The "high end" of computing. Supercomputers are machines whose price/performance is not competitive with regular machines but whose absolute performance far exceeds those of regular machines. The VLIW mini-supercomputer startups Multiflow and Cydrome paradoxically offered supercomputer performance at minicomputer prices.

Superpipelining. An implementation technique that pipelines operations below the length of the shortest-latency operation. That is, in a superpipelined design all operations require more than a single cycle to complete.

Superscalar. An implementation technique that allows architectures to support ILP in a backward-compatible manner. Superscalar implementations still require optimizing compilers to achieve much ILP, but their hardware must dynamically find the ILP.

Superword. An architectural unit larger than the native word width of a machine. VLIWs can support superword operations by grouping operations on adjacent lanes.

Synthesizable. A level of hardware design that is not bound to a particular implementation technology. Synthesizable designs are more easily ported to new technologies, but they tend to achieve lower performance and lower density (higher area) than more customized designs.

TCP/IP (transmission control protocol/internet protocol). The Internet Protocol is the basis of the modern Internet, and provides addressing for all hosts and routing within the network. Transmission Control Protocol provides a reliable, stream-oriented communication abstraction between two hosts that is layered on top of the Internet Protocol. In practice, their implementation and packet formats are bound together, so it is common to see the pair described as TCP/IP.

Timestamp. A data value that represents time. Many algorithms rely on timestamps to ensure correctness in sorting out values generated in a distributed manner.

TLB (translation lookaside buffer). A cache of virtual-to-physical page mappings. See also MMU.

Toolchain. The set of software associated with constructing and compiling to an embedded processor. A toolchain includes a compiler as its primary component but also includes a vast array of other tools, including assemblers, linkers, loaders, and binary editing utilities.

Trace scheduling. The first region-scheduling technique proposed. A trace is a path through the CFG of a procedure. A trace scheduler treats all operations on the trace as if they all occurred in a single basic block, reordering operations to produce a compact schedule. As part of the reordering, maintaining program semantics may require generation of *compensation code.*

Trampoline code. Small fragments of code the compiler inserts when it needs to "bridge" code fragments that cannot be easily modified (for example, because they were already compiled). A common case occurs for dynamically linked libraries, or to reach jump targets that extend beyond the range an individual branch can reach. Synonym: *stub.*

Treegion. A region used in region scheduling that has a single entry point but may include multiple acyclic paths through the CFG that originate at the entry point.

Trip count. The number of times a loop iterates. Often deducible from or recorded in profile information.

TTL (transistor-transistor logic). An implementation style for digital logic, built from bipolar transistors. TTL was the technology behind the first widespread development of digital integrated circuits in the 1960s. TTL was almost entirely replaced by CMOS in the 1980s.

UART (universal asynchronous receiver/transmitter). A common block that interfaces between a parallel I/O bus and a serial interface. UARTs are an early version of hardware IP, as they were available as single chips in the MSI era.

UDP (user datagram protocol). An unreliable datagram communication protocol, built on top of the Internet Protocol.

UML (unified modeling language). A standard method for modeling and describing object-oriented code. UML diagrams follow a set of conventions for depicting classes and the various relationships (inheritance, delegation, and so on) among them.

Unicode. A 16-bit character set that can represent most human character sets. Unicode uses "visual identity" to reduce the number of characters represented, and thus identical characters in Chinese and Japanese (for example) do not receive separate codes. Unicode can be efficiently and backward-compatibly embedded into programs based on the ASCII or ISO Latin 1 character sets using an encoding called UTF.

Varargs. Support for functions with a variable number of arguments ("variadic functions"). ABI standards for *varargs* are notoriously difficult to implement.

Vectorizable. Code that is amenable to transformation into a form that can run quickly on a vector computer. In practical terms, vectorizable code tends to be loop oriented, with array accesses that can be analyzed easily at compile-time.

Verilog. A hardware description language, probably the most commonly used, for ASIC design. Verilog's syntax gets its inspiration from the C language and is very well supported by most CAD, simulation, and synthesis tools. Compare with VHDL.

Versioning. Building different versions of the same function, some of which perform better on a restricted set of inputs. Synonym: *function specialization.*

VEX branch registers. The VEX base model contains a set of eight 1-bit registers encoding the condition for conditional branches and carry bits. For branch operations, they store the trigger condition (output of a compare operation) for a branch. The value stored in a branch register is a concise representation of the 32-bit integer values 1 (true) or 0 (false).

VEX control registers. One of a set of special registers maintained by the hardware (or operating system or user) with special semantics and often requiring special access.

VEX dispersal. The operation of extracting and routing the syllables of one bundle stored in the I-cache line to the proper slots in the bundle buffer. To avoid using I-cache space for empty syllables, only nonempty syllables are stored in the I-cache lines. Hence, it is necessary to "disperse" the syllable of each bundle to the full-size bundle buffer.

VEX general-purpose registers. The set of directly addressed fixed-point registers. The VEX base model contains one general-purpose register file per cluster, organized as a bank of 64 32-bit registers. The compiler is responsible for explicitly scheduling data transfers among general-purpose registers residing in different clusters.

VEX instruction. Implementation's natural execution unit, consisting of multiple operations issued during the same cycle and executed in parallel. An instruction is encoded in multiple syllables that are always issued and executed in parallel.

VEX syllable. Encoded component of an instruction that specifies one operation to be executed by the machine functional units. Syllables consist of register and/or immediate fields and opcode specifiers. A VEX instruction may contain multiple syllables, each 32 bits wide. The syllable is also the indivisible unit for instruction compression/dispersal.

VGA (video graphics array). The display card in a computer. VGA also refers to the standard connector for analog display connections.

VHDL (Very High-Speed Integrated Circuit Hardware Description Language). A hardware description language commonly used in the design of ASICs and well supported by CAD and synthesis tools. VHDL uses a syntax and many language concepts that were derived from the ADA language.

Virtual machine. A technique whereby one machine simulates or emulates the execution of another machine. Hardware support may or may not aid the emulation. VM was pioneered by IBM in the 1970s and has enjoyed a resurgence as a concept through the popularity of Java.

VLSI (very large-scale integration). A semiconductor technology allowing hundreds of thousands of transistors to be integrated on a single die. Predecessors of VLSI included MSI (medium-scale integration, 100 to 10,000 transistors) and LSI (large-scale integration, 10,000 to 100,000 transistors). The community stopped adding superlative acronyms at the VLSI stage (imagine "extra-super-giant-scale integration") over a decade ago.

VM (virtual memory). A technique that allows the operating system to place the pages associated with a process anywhere in memory, while providing the program with the illusion that its pages are laid out contiguously (or in whatever manner the program expects). The program sees *virtual addresses.* The hardware and operating system conspire to translate virtual addresses into *physical addresses* through a number of mechanisms. VM allows processes to operate without interfering with each other, and it also allows various protections to be enforced by the hardware and OS.

Vocoder. A technique for compressing human speech. For example, common cellular phones use advanced vocoder techniques.

W (Watt). A unit of power, or energy per second, corresponding to 1 J/s (Joule per second) or 1 VA (Volt Ampere).

C

APPENDIX

Bibliography

Abidi (1994). A. A. Abidi, "Integrated Circuits in Magnetic Disk Drives," *Proceedings of the 20th European Solid-State Circuits Conference*, pp. 48–57, 1994.

Abramovitch and Franklin (2002). D. Abramovitch and G. Franklin, "A Brief History of Disk Drive Control," *IEEE Control Systems Magazine*, vol. 22, no. 3, pp. 28–42, June 2002.

Accetta et al. (1986). M. Accetta, R. Baron, D. Golub, R. Rashid, A. Tevanian, and M. Young, "MACH: A New Kernel Foundation for UNIX Development," Technical Report, Computer Science Department, Carnegie-Mellon University, 1986.

ACE CoSy compilers (2004). At ACE Associated Computer Experts/ACE Associate Compiler Experts/ACE Consulting. Web site at *http://www.ace.nl*.

Adiletta et al. (2002). M. Adiletta, M. Rosenbluth, D. Bernstein, G. Wolrich, and H. Wilkinson, "The Next Generation of Intel IXP Network Processors," *Intel Technology Journal*, vol. 6, no. 3, pp. 6–18, Aug. 2002.

Aerts and Marinissen (1998). J. Aerts and E. J. Marinissen, "Scan Chain Design for Test Time Reduction in Core-Based ICs," *Proceedings of the 1998 International Test Conference*, pp. 448–457, Oct. 1998.

Aho et al. (1986). A. V. Aho, R. Sethi, and J. D. Ullman. *Compilers: Principles, Techniques, and Tools*. Reading, MA: Addison-Wesley, 1986.

Aho et al. (1989). A. V. Aho, M. Ganapathi, and S. W. K. Tjiang, "Code Generation Using Tree Matching and Dynamic Programming," *ACM Transactions on Programming Languages and Systems*, vol. 11, no. 4, pp. 491–516, Oct. 1989.

Aiken and Nicolau (1988). A. Aiken and A. Nicolau, "Optimal Loop Parallelization," *Proceedings of the SIGPLAN 1988 Conference on Programming Language Design and Implementation*, pp. 308–317, June 1988.

Albert (1999). E. Albert, "A Transparent Method for Correlating Profiles with Source Programs," *Proceedings of the 2nd Workshop on Feedback-Directed Optimization*, In Conjunction with the 32nd Annual International Symposium on Microarchitecture, pp. 33–39, Nov. 1999.

Albonesi (1998). D. H. Albonesi, "The Inherent Energy Efficiency of Complexity-Adaptive Processors," *Proceedings of the 1998 Power-Driven Microarchitecture Workshop* in conjunction with the *25th Annual International Symposium on Computer Architecture*, pp. 107–112, June 1998.

Aldworth (1999). P. J. Aldworth, "System-on-a-Chip Bus Architectures for Embedded Applications," *Proceedings of the 1999 International Conference on Computer Design*, pp. 297–298, 1999.

Allard et al. (1964). R. W. Allard, K. A. Wolf, and R. A. Zemlin, "Some Effects of the 6600 Computer on Language Structures," *Communications of the ACM*, vol. 7, no. 2, pp. 112–119, Feb. 1964.

Allen and Kennedy (2001). J. R. Allen and K. Kennedy. *Optimizing Compilers for Modern Architectures: A Dependence-Based Approach.* San Francisco, CA: Morgan Kaufmann Publishers (an imprint of Elsevier), 2001.

Allen et al. (1983). J. R. Allen, K. Kennedy, C. Porterfield, and J. Warren, "Conversion of Control Dependence to Data Dependence," *Proceedings of the 10th ACM Symposium on Principles of Programming Languages*, pp. 177–189, 1983.

Almasi (2001). G. Almasi, "MaJIC: A Matlab Just-In-Time Compiler," Ph. D. Thesis, University of Illinois at Urbana-Champaign, 2001.

Altera Corporation (2004). Web site at *http://www.altera.com.*

Alur et al. (1996). R. Alur, T. A. Henzinger, and E. D. Sontag (eds.), *Hybrid Systems III: Verification and Control, Lecture Notes in Computer Science 1066.* Berlin, New York: Springer-Verlag, 1996.

Analog Devices (2004). Web site at *http://www.analogdevices.com/processors.*

Anderson et al. (1997). J. M. Anderson, L. Berc, J. Dean, S. Ghemawat, M. Henzinger, S.-T. A. Leung, D. Sites, M. Vandevoorde, C. Waldspurger, and W. E. Weihl, "Continuous Profiling: Where Have All the Cycles Gone?" Technical Note 1997-016. Digital Equipment Corporation, Systems Research Center, Palo Alto, CA, July 1997.

Andrews et al. (1996). M. Andrews, M. A. Bender, and L. Zhang, "New Algorithms for the Disk Scheduling Problem," *Proceedings of the 37th Annual Symposium on the Foundations of Computer Science*, pp. 550–559, Oct. 1996.

ANSI (1989). C89 Standard ANSI/ISO X3.159, 1989.

Appel (1998a). A. W. Appel. *Modern Compiler Implementation in C.* New York: Cambridge University Press, 1998.

Appel (1998b). A. W. Appel. *Modern Compiler Implementation in Java.* New York: Cambridge University Press, 1998.

Appel (1998c). A. W. Appel. *Modern Compiler Implementation in ML.* New York: Cambridge University Press, 1998.

Appel and George (2001). A. W. Appel and L. George, "Optimal Spilling for CISC Machines with Few Registers," *Proceedings of the SIGPLAN 2001 Conference on Programming Language Design and Implementation*, pp. 243–253, May 2001.

ARC International (2004). Web site at *http://www.arc.com.*

ARM (1995). Advanced RISC Machines Ltd., "An Introduction to Thumb," Technical Report, 1995.

Arnold et al. (2000). K. Arnold, J. Gosling, and D. Holmes. *The Java Programming Language*. 3d ed. Reading, MA: Addison-Wesley, 2000.

Arvind et al. (1980). Arvind, V. Kathail, and K. Pingali, "A Data Flow Architecture with Tagged Tokens," Technical Report TM 174, Laboratory for Computer Science, Massachusetts Institute of Technology, 1980.

Asanovic (2000). K. Asanovic, "Energy-Exposed Instruction Set Architectures," *Proceedings of the Work in Progress Session, 6th International Symposium on High-Performance Computer Architecture*. Jan. 2000.

Ashenden (2001). P. J. Ashenden. *The Designer's Guide to VHDL*. 2d ed. San Francisco, CA: Morgan Kaufmann Publishers (an imprint of Elsevier), 2001.

Athanas and Silverman (1993). P. M. Athanas and H. F. Silverman, "Processor Reconfiguration Through Instruction-Set Metamorphosis," *IEEE Computer*, vol. 26, no. 3, pp. 11–18, March 1993.

August et al. (1998). D. I. August, D. A. Connors, S. A. Mahlke, J. W. Sias, K. M. Crozier, B. Cheng, P. R. Eaton, Q. B. Olaniran, and W. W. Hwu, "Integrated, Predicated, and Speculative Execution in the IMPACT EPIC Architecture," *Proceedings of the 25th Annual International Symposium on Computer Architecture*, pp. 227–237, July 1998.

Bala and Rubin (1995). V. Bala and N. Rubin, "Efficient Instruction Scheduling Using Finite State Automata," *Proceedings of the 28th Annual International Symposium on Microarchitecture*, pp. 46–56, Dec. 1995.

Bala et al. (2000). V. Bala, E. Duesterwald, and S. Banerjia, "Dynamo: A Transparent Dynamic Optimization System," *Proceedings of the SIGPLAN 2000 Conference on Programming Language Design and Implementation*, pp. 1–12, May 2000.

Balarin et al. (1999). F. Balarin, M. Chiodo, P. Giusto, H. Hsieh, A. Jurecska, L. Lavagno, A. Sangiovanni-Vincentelli, E. M. Sentovich, and K. Suzuki, "Synthesis of Software Programs for Embedded Control Applications," *IEEE Transactions on Computer-Aided Design of Integrated Circuits and Systems*, vol. 18, no. 6, pp. 834–849, June 1999.

Ball (1998). S. Ball. *Debugging Embedded Microprocessor Systems*. Boston: Newnes, 1998.

Ball (2003). S. Ball. *Analog Interfacing to Embedded Microprocessors*. 2d ed. Boston: Newnes, 2003.

Ball and Larus (1992). T. Ball and J. R. Larus, "Optimally Profiling and Tracing Programs," *Proceedings of the 19th SIGPLAN-SIGACT Symposium on Principles of Programming Languages*, pp. 59–70, Feb. 1992.

Ball and Larus (1994). T. Ball and J. R. Larus, "Optimally Profiling and Tracing Programs," *ACM Transactions on Programming Languages and Systems*, vol. 16, no. 4, pp. 1319–1360, July 1994.

Ball and Larus (1996). T. Ball and J. R. Larus, "Efficient Path Profiling," *Proceedings of the 29th Annual International Symposium on Microarchitecture*, pp. 46–57, Dec. 1996.

Balluchi et al. (2000). A. Balluchi, L. Benvenuti, M. DiBenedetto, C. Pinello, and A. Sangiovanni-Vicentelli, "Automotive Engine Control and Hybrid Systems:

Challenges and Opportunities," *Proceedings of the IEEE*, vol. 88, no. 7, pp. 888–912, July 2000.

Banerjia (1998). S. Banerjia, "Instruction Scheduling and Fetch Mechanisms for Clustered VLIW Processors," Ph. D. Thesis, Department of Electrical and Computer Engineering, North Carolina State University, 1998.

Barnwell et al. (1996). T. P. Barnwell, K. Nayebi, and C. H. Richardson. *Speech Coding: A Computer Laboratory Textbook*. New York: John Wiley and Sons, Inc., 1996.

Barr (1999). M. Barr. *Programming Embedded Systems in C and C++*. Sebastopol, CA: O'Reilly & Associates, 1999.

Barr (2003). M. Barr, "Embedded Systems Bibliography," Online at *http://www. netrino.com/Publications/Bibliography/*, June 2003.

Beck et al. (1993). G. R. Beck, D. W. L. Yen, and T. L. Anderson, "The Cydra-5 Minisupercomputer: Architecture and Implementation," *The Journal of Supercomputing*, vol. 7, no. 1–2, pp. 143–180, May 1993.

Bentley (1988). J. Bentley. *More Programming Pearls: Confessions of a Coder*. Reading, MA: Addison-Wesley, 1988.

Bentley (2000). J. Bentley. *Programming Pearls*. 2d ed. Reading, MA: Addison-Wesley, 2000.

BDTI (2002). Berkeley Design Technology, Inc, "Summary of DSP Books and Significant Research Articles." Web site at *http://www.bdti.com/faq/1.htm*.

Bhaskaran and Konstantinides (1997). V. Bhaskaran and K. Konstantinides. *Image and Video Compression Standards: Algorithms and Architectures*. 2d ed. Boston: Kluwer Academic Publishers, 1997.

Bhavnagarwala et al. (2001). A. J. Bhavnagarwala, X. Tang, and J. D. Meindl, "The Impact of Intrinsic Device Fluctuations on CMOS SRAM Cell Stability," *IEEE Journal of Solid-State Circuits*, vol. 36, no. 4, pp. 658–665, April 2001.

Blaauw and Brooks (1997). G. A. Blaauw and F. P. Brooks. *Computer Architecture: Concepts and Evolution*. Reading, MA: Addison-Wesley, 1997.

Bradlee et al. (1991a). D. G. Bradlee, S. J. Eggers, and R. R. Henry, "Integrating Register Allocation and Instruction Scheduling for RISCs," *Proceedings of the 4th International Conference on Architectural Support for Programming Languages and Operating Systems*, pp. 122–131, April 1991.

Bradlee et al. (1991b). D. G. Bradlee, R. R. Henry, and S. J. Eggers, "The Marion System for Retargetable Instruction Scheduling," *Proceedings of the SIGPLAN 1991 Conference on Programming Language Design and Implementation*, pp. 229–240, June 1991.

Briggs (1992). P. Briggs. "Register Allocation via Graph Coloring," Ph. D. Thesis, Rice University, 1992.

Brooks et al. (2000). D. Brooks, V. Tiwari, and M. Martonosi, "Wattch: A Framework for Architectural-Level Power Analysis and Optimizations," *Proceedings of the 27th Annual International Symposium on Computer Architecture*, pp. 83–94, June 2000.

Brown et al. (1992). S. D. Brown, R. J. Francis, J. Rose, and Z. G. Vranesic. *Field-Programmable Gate Arrays*. Boston: Kluwer Academic Publishers, 1992.

Buchholz (1962). W. Buchholz (ed.). *Planning a Computer System: Project Stretch.* New York: McGraw-Hill, 1962.

Burger and Austin (1997). D. Burger and T. M. Austin, "The SimpleScalar Tool Set, Version 2.0," Technical Report CS-TR-97-1342, University of Wisconsin-Madison, June 1997.

Calder et al. (1997). B. Calder, M. Jones, D. Lindsay, J. Martin, M. Mozer, and B. Zorn. "Evidence-based Static Branch Prediction Using Machine Learning," ACM Transactions on Programming Languages and Systems, vol. 19, no. 1, Jan. 1997.

Callahan et al. (1991). D. Callahan, K. Kennedy, and A. Porterfield, "Software Prefetching," *Proceedings of the 4th International Conference on Architectural Support for Programming Languages and Operating Systems*, pp. 40–52, April 1991.

Capitanio et al. (1994). A. Capitanio, N. Dutt, and A. Nicolau, "Partitioning of Variables for Multiple-Register-File Architectures via Hypergraph Coloring," *Proceedings of the IFIP WG10.3 Working Conference on Parallel Architectures and Compilation Techniques*, pp. 319–322, Aug. 1994.

Cavanagh (1984). J. J. F. Cavanagh. *Digital Computer Arithmetic: Design and Implementation.* New York: McGraw-Hill, 1984.

CDC (1980). Control Data Corporation, "CDC Advanced Flexible Processor Microcode Cross Assembler (MICA) Reference Manual," Technical Report, CDC, Publication No. 77900500, April 1980.

Cesario et al. (2002). W. Cesario, A. Baghdadi, L. Gauthier, D. Lyonnard, G. Nicolescu, Y. Paviot, S. Yoo, A. A. Jerraya, and M. Diaz-Nava, "Component-Based Design Approach for Multicore SoCs," *Proceedings of the 39th Design Automation Conference*, pp. 789–794, June 2002.

Chaitin (1982). G. J. Chaitin, "Register Allocation and Spilling via Graph Coloring," *Proceedings of the 1982 SIGPLAN Symposium on Compiler Construction*, pp. 98–101, June 1982.

Chandy and Misra (1979). K. M. Chandy and J. Misra, "Distributed Simulations: A Case Study in Design and Verification of Distributed Programs," *IEEE Transactions on Software Engineering*, vol. 5, no. 5, pp. 440–452, Sept. 1979.

Chang et al. (1991a). P. P. Chang, N. J. Warter, S. A. Mahlke, W. Y. Chen, and W. W. Hwu, "Three Superblock Scheduling Models for Superscalar and Superpipelined Processors," Technical Report CRHC-91-25, Center for Reliable and High-Performance Computing, University of Illinois at Urbana-Champaign, Oct. 1991.

Chang et al. (1991b). P. P. Chang, S. A. Mahlke, W. Y. Chen, N. J. Warter, and W. W. Hwu, "IMPACT: An Architectural Framework for Multiple-Instruction-Issue Processors," *Proceedings of the 18th Annual International Symposium on Computer Architecture*, pp. 266–275, May 1991.

Chang et al. (1995). P. P. Chang, N. J. Warter, S. A. Mahlke, W. Y. Chen, and W. W. Hwu, "Three Architectural Models for Compiler-Controlled Speculative Execution," *IEEE Transactions on Computers*, vol. 44, no. 4, pp. 481–494, April 1995.

Chang et al. (1999). H. Chang, L. Cooke, M. Hunt, G. Martin, A. McNelly, and L. Todd. *Surviving the SoC Revolution: A Guide to Platform-Based Design.* Boston: Kluwer Academic Publishers, 1999.

Chaoui et al. (2000). J. Chaoui, K. Cyr, J.-P. Giacalone, S. de Gregorio, Y. Masse, Y. Muthusamy, T. Spits, M. Budagavi, and J. Webb, "OMAP: Enabling Multimedia Applications in Third Generation (3G) Wireless Terminals," Texas Instruments Technical White Paper SWPA001, Dec. 2000.

Charlesworth (1981). A. E. Charlesworth, "An Approach to Scientific Array Processing: The Architectural Design of the AP-120B/FPS-164 Family," *IEEE Computer*, vol. 14, no. 9, pp. 18–27, Sept. 1981.

Chekuri et al. (1996). C. Chekuri, R. Johnson, R. Motwani, B. K. Natarajan, B. R. Rau, and M. Schlansker, "Profile-Driven Instruction Level Parallel Scheduling with Application to Super Blocks," *Proceedings of the 29th Annual International Symposium on Microarchitecture*, pp. 58–67, Dec. 1996.

Chen and Baer (1994). T.-F. Chen and J.-L. Baer, "A Performance Study of Software and Hardware Data Prefetching Schemes," *Proceedings of the 21st Annual International Symposium on Computer Architecture*, pp. 223–232, April 1994.

Chinnery and Keutzer (2002). D. Chinnery and K. Keutzer. *Closing the Gap Between ASIC & Custom: Tools and Techniques for High-Performance ASIC Design*. Boston: Kluwer Academic Publishers, 2002.

Cho (2001). S. Cho, "Power Management of iPAQ," Technical Report, Information Sciences Institute, University of Southern California, 2001. On web site: *http://www.pads.east.isi.edu/presentations/misc/sjcho-pm-report.pdf*.

Choi et al. (2001). Y. Choi, A. Knies, L. Gerke, and T.-F. Ngai, "The Impact of If-Conversion and Branch Prediction on Program Execution on the Intel Itanium Processor," *Proceedings of the 34th Annual International Symposium on Microarchitecture*, pp. 182–191, Dec. 2001.

Chou and Roy (1996). T.-L. Chou and K. Roy, "Accurate Power Estimation of CMOS Sequential Circuits," *IEEE Transactions on Very Large Scale Integration (VLSI) Systems*, vol. 4, no. 3, pp. 369–380, Sept. 1996.

Christensen (1997). C. M. Christensen. *The Innovator's Dilemma: When New Technologies Cause Great Firms to Fail*. Cambridge, MA: Harvard Business School Press, 1997.

Cideciyan et al. (1992). R. D. Cideciyan, F. Dolivo, R. Hermann, W. Hirt, and W. Schott, "A PRML System for Digital Magnetic Recording," *IEEE Journal on Selected Areas in Communications*, vol. 10, no. 1, pp. 38–56, Jan. 1992.

Cody et al. (1985). W. J. Cody, J. T. Coonen, D. M. Gay, K. Hanson, D. Hough, W. Kahan, R. Karpinski, J. Palmer, F. N. Ris, and D. Stevenson, "A Proposed Radix- and Word-length-independent Standard for Floating-point Arithmetic," *SIGNUM Newsletter*, vol. 20, no. 1, pp. 37–51, Jan. 1985.

Cohen (1978). D. Cohen, "A Methodology for Programming a Pipeline Array Processor," *Proceedings of the 11th Annual Workshop on Microprogramming*, pp. 82–89, Nov. 1978.

Colwell and Steck (1995). R. P. Colwell and R. L. Steck, "A 0.6-μm BiCMOS Microprocessor with Dynamic Execution," *Proceedings of the International Solid-State Circuits Conference*, pp. 176–177, 1995.

Colwell et al. (1987). R. P. Colwell, R. P. Nix, J. J. O'Donnell, D. B. Papworth, and P. K. Rodman, "A VLIW Architecture for a Trace Scheduling Compiler," *Proceedings of the 2nd International Conference on Architectural Support for Programming Languages and Operating Systems*, pp. 180–192, Oct. 1987.

Colwell et al. (1988). R. P. Colwell, R. P. Nix, J. J. O'Donnell, D. B. Papworth, and P. K. Rodman, "A VLIW Architecture for a Trace Scheduling Compiler," *IEEE Transactions on Computers*, vol. 37, no. 8, pp. 967–979, Aug. 1988.

Colwell et al. (1990). R. P. Colwell, W. E. Hall, C. S. Joshi, D. B. Papworth, P. K. Rodman, and J. E. Tornes, "Architecture and Implementation of a VLIW Supercomputer," *Proceedings of the 1990 International Conference on Supercomputing*, pp. 910–919, Nov. 1990.

Conte and Gimarc (1995). T. M. Conte and C. E. Gimarc (eds.). *Fast Simulation of Computer Architectures*. Boston: Kluwer Academic Publishers, 1995.

Conte et al. (1996). T. M. Conte, S. Banerjia, S. Y. Larin, K. N. Menezes, and S. W. Sathaye, "Instruction Fetch Mechanisms for VLIW Architectures with Compressed Encodings," *Proceedings of the 29th Annual International Symposium on Microarchitecture*, pp. 201–211, Dec. 1996.

Cooper and Torczon (2004). K. D. Cooper and L. Torczon. *Engineering a Compiler*. San Francisco, CA: Morgan Kaufmann Publishers (an imprint of Elsevier), 2004.

Cordan (2001). B. Cordan, "Configurable Platform-Based SoC Design Techniques," *Parts I and II, EE Design*, March 12 and March 20, 2001.

Cordan (2001b). B. Cordan, "Configurable Platform-Based SoC Design Techniques," *Part II, EE Design*, March 20, 2001.

Cover and Thomas (1991). T. M. Cover and J. A. Thomas. *Elements of Information Theory*. New York: Wiley Interscience, 1991.

Crowley et al. (2003). P. Crowley, M. A. Franklin, H. Hadimioglu, and P. Z. Onufryk. *Network Processor Design: Issues and Practices, Volume I*. San Francisco, CA: Morgan Kaufmann Publishers (an imprint of Elsevier), 2003.

Culler et al. (1998). D. E. Culler, J. P. Singh, and A. Gupta. *Parallel Computer Architecture: A Hardware/Software Approach*. San Francisco, CA: Morgan Kaufmann Publishers (an imprint of Elsevier), 1998.

Dasgupta (1979). S. Dasgupta, "The Organization of Microprogram Stores," *ACM Computing Surveys*, vol. 11, no. 1, pp. 39–65, March 1979.

Davidson (1971). E. S. Davidson, "The Design and Control of Pipelined Function Generators," *Proceedings of the 1971 International Conference on Systems, Networks, and Computers*, Jan. 1971.

Davidson et al. (1975). E. S. Davidson, L. E. Shar, A. T. Thomas, and J. H. Patel, "Effective Control for Pipelined Processors," *Proceedings of the 15th IEEE Computer Society International Conference*, pp. 181–184, Feb. 1975.

Dehnert and Towle (1993). J. C. Dehnert and R. A. Towle, "Compiling for the Cydra 5," *The Journal of Supercomputing*, vol. 7, no. 1–2, pp. 181–227, May 1993.

Dehnert et al. (1989). J. C. Dehnert, P. Y.-T. Hsue, and J. P. Bratt, "Overlapped Loop Support in the Cydra 5," *Proceedings of the 3rd International Conference on Architectural Support for Programming Languages and Operating Systems,* pp. 26–38, April 1989.

DeHon (1996). A. DeHon. "Reconfigurable Architectures for General Purpose Computing," Ph. D. Thesis, AI Laboratory, Massachusetts Institute of Technology, 1996.

Dennis and Misunas (1974). J. B. Dennis and D. P. Misunas, "A Preliminary Architecture for a Basic Data-flow Computer," *Proceedings of the 2nd Annual International Symposium on Computer Architecture,* pp. 126–132, Dec. 1974.

Design and Reuse (2004). Web site at *http://www.design-reuse.com.*

Desoli (1998). G. Desoli, "Instruction Assignment for Clustered VLIW DSP Compilers: A New Approach," Technical Report HPL-98-13, Hewlett-Packard, Feb. 1998.

DSP Group (2004). Web site at *http://www.dspg.com.*

DSP/C (2004). Web site at *http://www.dsp-c.org/.*

Ebcioğlu and Altman (1997). K. Ebcioğlu and E. R. Altman, "DAISY: Dynamic Compilation for 100% Architectural Compatibility," *Proceedings of the 24th Annual International Symposium on Computer Architecture,* pp. 26–37, June 1997.

Economides (2004). Nick Economides, web site at *http://www.stern.nyu.edu/networks/site.html.*

EE Times (2004). Web site at *http://www.eet.com.*

Eichenberger and Davidson (1995). A. E. Eichenberger and E. S. Davidson, "Stage Scheduling: A Technique to Reduce the Register Requirements of a Modulo Schedule," *Proceedings of the 28th Annual International Symposium on Microarchitecture,* pp. 338–349, Nov. 1995.

Eichenberger and Davidson (1996). A. E. Eichenberger and E. S. Davidson, "A Reduced Multipipeline Machine Description that Preserves Scheduling Constraints." *Proceedings of the SIGPLAN 1996 Conference on Programming Language Design and Implementation,* pp. 12–22, May 1996.

Ellis (1985). J. R. Ellis, *"Bulldog: A Compiler for VLIW Architectures,"* Ph.D. Thesis, Yale University, 1985.

Ellis and Stroustrup (1990). M. A. Ellis and B. Stroustrup. *The Annotated C++ Reference Manual.* Reading, MA: Addison-Wesley, 1990.

Embedded Linux Consortium (2004). Web site at *http://www.embedded-linux.org.*

Embedded Processor Watch (1998–2004). Web site at *http://www.mdronline.com/publications/e-watch.html.*

Embedded Systems Programming (2004). Web site at *http://www.embedded.com.*

Emer and Clark (1984). J. S. Emer and D. W. Clark, "A Characterization of Processor Performance in the VAX-11/780," *Proceedings of the 11th Annual Symposium on Computer Architecture,* pp. 301–310, Jan. 1984.

Emmelmann et al. (1989). H. Emmelmann, F.-W. Schroeer, and R. Landwehr, "BEG – A Generator for Efficient Backends," *Proceedings of the SIGPLAN 89 Conference on Programming Language Design and Implementation,* pp. 227–237, July 1989.

ETSI (2000a). ETSI EN 300 723 V6.1.1 (2000-11). Digital Cellular Telecommunications System (Phase 2+); Enhanced Full Rate (EFR) Speech Processing Functions; General

Description (GSM 06.51 version 6.1.1 Release 1997). European Telecommunications Standards Institute, Nov. 2000.

ETSI (2000b). ETSI EN 300 724 V8.0.1 (2000-11). Digital Cellular Telecommunications System (Phase 2+) (GSM); ANSI-C Code for the GSM Enhanced Full Rate (EFR) Speech Codec (GSM 06.53 version 8.0.1 Release 1999). European Telecommunications Standards Institute, Nov. 2000.

Fan et al. (2002). X. Fan, C. S. Ellis, and A. R. Lebeck, "Synergy Between Power-Aware Memory System and Processor Voltage Scaling," Technical Report CS-2002-12, Department of Computer Science, Duke University, Nov. 2002.

Faraboschi et al. (1998). P. Faraboschi, G. Desoli, and J. A. Fisher, "Clustered Instruction-Level Parallel Processors," Technical Report HPL-98-204, Hewlett-Packard, 1998.

Faraboschi et al. (2000). P. Faraboschi, G. Brown, J. A. Fisher, G. Desoli, and F. Homewood. "Lx: A Technology Platform for Customizable VLIW Embedded Processing," *Proceedings of the 27th Annual International Symposium on Computer Architecture*, pp. 203–213, June 2000.

Farkas et al. (1995). K. I. Farkas, N. P. Jouppi, and P. Chow, "Register File Design Considerations in Dynamically Scheduled Processors," DEC/WRL Research Report 95/10, Digital Equipment Corporation, Western Research Laboratory, Nov. 1995.

Farkas et al. (1997a). K. I. Farkas, P. Chow, N. P. Jouppi, and Z. Vranesic, "Memory-System Design Considerations for Dynamically-Scheduled Processors," DEC/WRL Technical Report 97/1, Digital Equipment Corporation, Western Research Laboratory, Feb. 1997.

Farkas et al. (1997b). K. I. Farkas, P. Chow, N. P. Jouppi, and Z. Vranesic, "The Multicluster Architecture: Reducing Cycle Time Through Partitioning," *Proceedings of the 30th Annual International Symposium on Microarchitecture*, pp. 149–159, Dec. 1997.

Fauth et al. (1995). A. Fauth, J. Van Praet, and M. Freericks, "Describing Instruction Set Processors Using nML," *Proceedings of the 1995 European Conference on Design and Test*, pp. 503–507, March 1995.

Fernandes et al. (1997). M. Fernandes, J. Llosa, and N. Topham, "Using Queues for Register File Organization in VLIW Architectures," Technical Report ECS-CSG-29-97, Department of Computer Science, University of Edinburgh, Feb. 1997.

Fernandes et al. (1998). M. M. Fernandes, J. Llosa, and N. Topham, "Partitioned Schedules for VLIW Architectures," *Proceedings of the 12th International Parallel Processing Symposium*, pp. 386–391, March 1998.

Fisher (1979). J. A. Fisher. "The Optimization of Horizontal Microcode Within and Beyond Basic Blocks: An Application of Processor Scheduling with Resources," Ph. D. Dissertation, Technical Report COO-3077-161, Courant Mathematics and Computing Laboratory, New York University, New York, Oct. 1979.

Fisher (1980). J. A. Fisher, "2^n Way Jump Microinstruction Hardware and an Effective Instruction Binding Method," *Proceedings of the 13th Annual Workshop on Microprogramming*, pp. 64–75, Nov. 1980.

Fisher (1981). J. A. Fisher, "Trace Scheduling: A Technique for Global Microcode Compaction," *IEEE Transactions on Computers*, vol. 30, no. 7, pp. 478–490, July 1981.

Fisher (1983). J. A. Fisher, "Very Long Instruction Word Architectures and the ELI-512," *Proceedings of the 10th Annual International Symposium on Computer Architecture*, pp. 140–150, June 1983.

Fisher (1993). J. A. Fisher, "Global Code Generation for Instruction-Level Parallelism: Trace Scheduling-2," Hewlett-Packard Laboratories Technical Report HPL-93-43, 1993.

Fisher and Freudenberger (1992). J. A. Fisher and S. M. Freudenberger, "Predicting Conditional Branch Directions from Previous Runs of a Program," *Proceedings of the 5th International Conference on Architectural Support for Programming Languages and Operating Systems*, pp. 85–95, Sept. 1992.

Fisher and Rau (1991). J. A. Fisher and B. R. Rau, "Instruction-level Parallel Processing, *Science*, vol. 253, pp. 1233–1241, Sept. 1991.

Fisher et al. (1981). J. A. Fisher, D. Landskov, and B. D. Shriver, "Microcode Compaction: Looking Backward and Looking Forward," *Proceedings of the 1981 National Computer Conference*, pp. 95–102, May 1981.

Fisher et al. (1996). J. A. Fisher, P. Faraboschi, and G. Desoli, "Custom-Fit Processors: Letting Applications Define Architectures," *Proceedings of the 29th Annual International Symposium on Microarchitecture*, pp. 324–335, Dec. 1996.

Flautner and Mudge (2002). K. Flautner and T. Mudge, "Vertigo: Automatic Performance-Setting for Linux," *Proceedings of the 5th Symposium on Operating Systems Design and Implementation*, pp. 105–116, Dec. 2002.

Fleischmann (2001). M. Fleischmann, "Longrun Power Management," White Paper, Transmeta Corporation, Jan. 2001.

Flinn and Satyanarayanan (1999). J. Flinn and M. Satyanarayanan, "Powerscope: A Tool for Profiling the Energy Usage of Mobile Applications," *Proceedings of the 2nd IEEE Workshop on Mobile Computer Systems and Applications*, in conjunction with the 3rd USENIX Symposium on Operating Systems Design and Implementation, pp. 2–10, Feb. 1999.

Flynn (1995). M. J. Flynn. *Computer Architecture: Pipelined and Parallel Processor Design*. Boston: Jones and Bartlett Publishers, 1995.

Foley et al. (1995). J. D. Foley, A. van Dam, S. K. Feiner, and J. F. Hughes. *Computer Graphics: Principles and Practice in C*. 2d ed. Reading, MA: Addison-Wesley, 1995.

Fraser et al. (1992a). C. W. Fraser, D. R. Hanson, and T. A. Proebsting, "Engineering a Simple, Efficient Code-Generator Generator," *ACM Letters on Programming Languages and Systems*, vol. 1, no. 3, pp. 213–226, Sept. 1992.

Fraser et al. (1992b). C. W. Fraser, R. R. Henry, and T. A. Proebsting, "BURG – Fast Optimal Instruction Selection and Tree Parsing," *SIGPLAN Notices*, vol. 27, no. 4, pp. 68–76, April 1992.

Freeman and Soete (1997). C. Freeman and L. Soete. *The Economics of Industrial Innovation*. 3d ed. Cambridge, MA: MIT Press, 1997.

Free Software Foundation GCC (2004). Web site at *http://www.gcc.gnu.org*.

Fu et al. (1992). J. Fu, J. Patel, and B. Janssens, "Stride Directed Prefetching in Scalar Processors," *Proceedings of the 25th Annual International Symposium on Microarchitecture*, pp. 102–110, Dec. 1992.

Fujimoto (1990). R. M. Fujimoto, "Parallel Discrete Event Simulation," *Communications of the ACM*, vol. 33, no. 10, pp. 30–53, Oct. 1990.

Gajski et al. (1994). D. Gajski, F. Vahid, S. Narayan, and J. Gong. *Specification and Design of Embedded Systems*. Englewood Cliffs, NJ: Prentice Hall, 1994.

Gajski et al. (2000). D. Gajski, J. Zhu, R. Domer, A. Gerstlauer, and S. Zhao. *SpecC: Specification Language and Methodology*. Boston: Kluwer Academic Publishers, 2000.

Gallagher et al. (1994). D. M. Gallagher, W. Y. Chen, S. A. Mahlke, J. C. Gyllenhaal, and W. W. Hwu, "Dynamic Memory Disambiguation Using the Memory Conflict Buffer," *Proceedings of the 6th International Conference on Architectural Support for Programming Languages and Operating Systems*, pp. 183–193, Oct. 1994.

Ganssle and Barr (2003). J. Ganssle and M. Barr. *Embedded Systems Dictionary*. Lawrence, KS: CMP Books, 2003.

George and Blume (2003). L. George and M. Blume, "Taming the IXP Network Processor," *Proceedings of the SIGPLAN 2003 Conference on Programming Language Design and Implementation*, pp. 26–37, May 2003.

Gloy and Smith (1999). N. Gloy and M. D. Smith, "Procedure Placement Using Temporal-Ordering Information," *ACM Transactions on Programming Languages and Systems*, vol. 21, no. 5, pp. 977–1027, Sept. 1999.

Goldberg (1996). D. Goldberg, "Computer Arithmetic," in J. L. Hennessy and D. A. Patterson, *Computer Architecture: A Quantitative Approach*. 2d ed. pp. A1–A77, San Francisco, CA: Morgan Kaufmann Publishers (an imprint of Elsevier), 1996.

Goldschmidt and Hennessy (1993). S. Goldschmidt and J. L. Hennessy, "The Accuracy of Trace-Driven Simulations of Multiprocessors," *Proceedings of the 1993 ACM SIGMETRICS Conference on Measurement and Modeling of Computer Systems*, pp. 146–157, June 1993.

Goodman (1983). J. R. Goodman, "Using Cache Memory to Reduce Processor-Memory Traffic," *Proceedings of the 10th Annual International Symposium on Computer Architecture*, pp. 124–131, June 1983.

Goodwin and Wilken (1996). D. W. Goodwin and K. D. Wilken, "Optimal and Near-Optimal Global Register Allocation Using 0-1 Integer Programming," *Software — Practice and Experience*, vol. 26, no. 8, pp. 929–965, Aug. 1996.

Govil et al. (1995). K. Govil, E. Chan, and H. Wasserman, "Comparing Algorithms For Dynamic Speed-Setting of a Low-Power CPU," *Proceedings of the 1st Annual International Conference on Mobile Computing and Networking*, pp. 13–25, Dec. 1995. Also Technical Report TR-95-017, International Computer Science Institute (ICSI), Berkeley, CA, 1995.

Graham et al. (1982). S. L. Graham, P. B. Kessler, and M. K. McKusick, "Gprof: A Call Graph Execution Profiler," *Proceedings of the 1982 SIGPLAN Symposium on Compiler Construction*, pp. 120–126, June 1982.

Grehan et al. (1998). R. Grehan, R. Moote, and I. Cyliax. *Real-Time Programming: A Guide to 32-Bit Embedded Development.* Reading, MA: Addison-Wesley, 1998.

Grunwald et al. (2000). D. Grunwald, P. Levis, K. Farkas, C. Morrey, and M. Neufeld, "Policies for Dynamic Clock Scheduling," *Proceedings of the 4th Symposium on Operating System Design and Implementation*, pp. 73–86, Oct. 2000.

Gupta et al. (1991). A. Gupta, J. Hennessy, K. Gharachorloo, T. Mowry, and W.-D. Weber, "Comparative Evaluation of Latency Reducing and Tolerating Techniques," *Proceedings of the 18th Annual International Symposium on Computer Architecture*, pp. 254–263, April 1991.

Gwennap (1995). L. Gwennap, "Intel's P6 Uses Decoupled Superscalar Design," *Microprocessor Report*, vol. 9, no. 2, pp. 9–15, Feb. 1995.

Gwennap (1996). L. Gwennap, "Digital 21264 Sets New Standard," *Microprocessor Report*, vol. 10, no. 14, pp. 11–16, Oct. 1996.

Gyllenhaal and Hwu (1996). J. C. Gyllenhaal and W. W. Hwu, "HMDES Version 2.0 Specification," Technical Report IMPACT-96-3, Center for Reliable and High-Performance Computing, University of Illinois at Urbana-Champaign, 1996.

Hadjiyiannis et al. (1997). G. Hadjiyiannis, S. Hanono, and S. Devadas, "ISDL: An Instruction Set Description Language for Retargetability," *Proceedings of the 34th Conference on Design Automation*, pp. 299–302, June 1997.

Hajj et al. (1998). N. B. I. Hajj, G. Stamoulis, N. Bellas, and C. Polychronopoulos, "Architectural and Compiler Support for Energy Reduction in the Memory Hierarchy of High Performance Microprocessors," *Proceedings of the 1998 International Symposium on Low Power Electronics and Design*, pp. 70–75, Aug. 1998.

Halambi et al. (1999). A. Halambi, P. Grun, V. Ganesh, A. Khare, N. Dutt, and A. Nicolau, "Expression: A Language for Architecture Exploration Through Compiler/Simulator Retargetability," *Proceedings of the 1999 Conference on Design Automation and Test in Europe*, pp. 485–490, Jan. 1999.

Harvard Machine SUIF (2004). Web site at *http://www.eecs.harvard.edu/hube/research/ machsuif.html.*

Hashemi et al. (1997). A. H. Hashemi, D. R. Kaeli, and B. Calder, "Efficient Procedure Mapping Using Cache Line Coloring," *Proceedings of the SIGPLAN 1997 Conference on Programming Language Design and Implementation*, pp. 171–182, May 1997.

Haskell et al. (1997). B. G. Haskell, A. Puri, and A. N. Netravali. *Digital Video: An Introduction to MPEG-2.* London: Chapman & Hall, 1997.

Hauser and Wawrzynek (1997). J. R. Hauser and J. Wawrzynek, "Garp: A MIPS Processor with a Reconfigurable Coprocessor," *Proceedings of the 5th IEEE Symposium on Field-Programmable Custom Computing Machines*, pp. 24–33, April 1997.

Havanki (1997). W. A. Havanki, "Treegion Scheduling for VLIW Processors," MS Thesis, Department of Electrical and Computer Engineering, North Carolina State University, Raleigh, NC, July 1997.

Havanki et al. (1998). W. A. Havanki, S. Banerjia, and T. M. Conte, "Treegion Scheduling for Wide Issue Processors," *Proceedings of the 4th International Symposium on High-Performance Computer Architecture*, pp. 226–276, Feb. 1998.

Henderson (2000). Rebecca Henderson testimony in the Microsoft antitrust proceedings, April, 2000. On Web site *http://www.usdoj.gov/atr/cases/f4600/4644.htm*.

Hennessy and Patterson (2003). J. L. Hennessy and D. A. Patterson. *Computer Architecture: A Quantitative Approach*. 3d ed. San Francisco, CA: Morgan Kaufmann Publishers (an imprint of Elsevier), 2003.

Hill et al. (1999). M. D. Hill, N. P. Jouppi, and G. Sohi. *Readings in Computer Architecture*. San Francisco, CA: Morgan Kaufmann Publishers (an imprint of Elsevier), 1999.

Hinton et al. (2001). G. Hinton, D. Sager, M. Upton, D. Boggs, D. Carmean, A. Kyker, and P. Roussel, "The Microarchitecture of the Pentium 4 Processor," *Intel Technology Journal*, Q1, Feb. 2001.

Hong et al. (1998). I. Hong, D. Kirovski, G. Qu, M. Potkonjak, and M. Srivastava, "Power Optimization of Variable Voltage Core-Based Systems," *Proceedings of the 35th Conference on Design Automation*, pp. 176–181, May 1998.

Hanono and Devadas (1998). S. Hanono and S. Devadas, "Instruction Selection, Resource Allocation, and Scheduling in the AVIV Retargetable Code Generator," *Proceedings of the 35th Design Automation Conference*, pp. 510–515, June 1998.

Husak (2000). D. Husak, "Network Processors: A Definition and Comparison," C-Port White Paper, Motorola, 2000.

Hwu and Chang (1989). W. W. Hwu and P. P. Chang, "Achieving High Instruction Cache Performance with an Optimizing Compiler," *Proceedings of the 16th Annual International Symposium on Computer Architecture*, pp. 242–251, April 1989.

Hwu and Patt (1987). W. W. Hwu and Y. N. Patt, "Checkpoint Repair for High-Performance Out-of-Order Execution Machines," *IEEE Transactions on Computers*, vol. 36, no. 12, pp. 1496–1514, Dec. 1987.

Hwu et al. (1993). W. W. Hwu, S. A. Mahlke, W. Y. Chen, P. P. Chang, N. J. Warter, R. A. Bringmann, R. G. Ouellette, R. E. Hank, T. Kiyohara, G. E. Haab, J. G. Holm, and D. M. Lavery, "The Superblock: An Effective Technique for VLIW and Superscalar Compilation," *The Journal of Supercomputing*, vol. 7, no. 1–2, pp. 229–248, May 1993.

IBM (1998). International Business Machines (IBM) Corporation, "CodePack: PowerPC Code Compression Utility User's Manual Version 3.0," IBM Technical Report, 1998.

IBM (2004). IBM CoreConnect bus architecture. Web site at *http://www.chips.ibm.com/ products/coreconnect*.

IEEE (1990). IEEE 610.12-1990, *IEEE Standard Glossary of Software Engineering Terminology*. Institute of Electrical and Electronics Engineers, 1990.

IEEE (1995). IEEE 1394-1995, *IEEE Standard for a High Performance Serial Bus — Firewire*. Institute of Electrical and Electronics Engineers, 1995.

Impact Research Group (2004). Web site at *http://www.crhc.uiuc.edu/Impact*.

Intel (2001). Intel Corporation, *Intel IXP1200 Network Processor Family Hardware Reference Manual*. Dec. 2001.

Intel (2004). Intel Corporation, PCA (Intel Personal Internet Client Architecture) developer's Web site at *http://www.intel.com/pca/*.

ISO (1999). C99 Standard ISO/IEC 9899, International Organization for Standardization, 1999.

ISO JPEG (2004). Web site at *http://www.jpeg.org*.

Jack (2001). K. Jack. *Video Demystified: A Handbook for the Digital Engineer*. 3d ed. Eagle Rock, VA: LLH Technology Publishing, 2001.

Jacobs et al. (1982). D. Jacobs, J. Prins, P. Siegel, and K. Wilson, "Monte Carlo Techniques in Code Optimization," *Proceedings of the 15th Annual Workshop on Microprogramming*, pp. 143–148, Oct. 1982.

Jas and Touba (1998). A. Jas and N. A. Touba, "Test Vector Decompression via Cyclical Scan Chains and its Applications to Testing Core-Based Designs," *Proceedings of the 1998 IEEE International Test Conference*, pp. 458–464, Oct. 1998.

Jas et al. (2000). A. Jas, B. Pouya, and N. A. Touba, "Virtual Scan Chains: A Means for Reducing Scan Length in Cores," *Proceedings of the 18th IEEE VLIS Test Symposium*, pp. 73–78, April 2000.

Jefferson (1985). D. R. Jefferson, "Virtual Time," *ACM Transactions on Programming Languages and Systems*, vol. 7, no. 3, pp. 404–425, July 1985.

Jefferson and Sowizral (1982). D. R. Jefferson and H. Sowizral, "Fast Concurrent Simulation Using the Time Warp Mechanism, Part I: Local Control," Rand Note N-1906AF, The Rand Corporation, Dec. 1982.

Johnson (1991). M. Johnson. *Superscalar Microprocessor Design*. Englewood Cliffs, NJ: Prentice Hall, 1991.

Johnson and Schlansker (1996). R. Johnson and M. Schlansker, "Analysis Techniques for Predicated Code," *Proceedings of the 29th Annual International Symposium on Microarchitecture*, pp. 100–113, Dec. 1996.

Jolly (1991). R. D. Jolly, "A 9-ns 1.4 Gigabyte/s, 17-Ported CMOS Register File," *IEEE Journal of Solid-State Circuits*, vol. 26, no. 10, pp. 1407–1412, Oct. 1991.

Jouppi (1990). N. P. Jouppi, "Improving Direct-Mapped Cache Performance by the Addition of a Small Fully-Associative Cache and Prefetch Buffers," DEC/WRL Technical Note TN-14, Digital Equipment Corporation, Western Research Laboratory, March 1990.

Jouppi and Wall (1989). N. P. Jouppi and D. W. Wall, "Available Instruction-Level Parallelism for Superscalar and Superpipelined Machines," DEC/WRL Research Report 89/7, Digital Equipment Corporation, Western Research Laboratory, July 1989.

JPEG Group (2004). Web site at *http://www.ijg.org*.

Kailas et al. (2001). K. Kailas, A. Agrawala, and K. Ebcoiglu, "CARS: A New Code Generation Framework for Clustered ILP Processors," *Proceedings of the 7th International Symposium on High-Performance Computer Architecture*, pp. 133–146, Jan. 2001.

Kahan (2004). W. Kahan. Web site at *http://www.cs.berkeley.edu/~wkahan*.

Kahan (1983). W. Kahan, "Mathematics Written in Sand—the HP-15C, Intel 8087, etc.," *1983 Statistical Computing Section of the Proceedings of the American Statistical Association*, pp. 12–26 (a retyped version is available at *http://www.cs.berkeley.edu/~wkahan/MathSand.pdf*).

Kandemir et al. (2000). M. Kandemir, N. Vijaykrishnan, M. J. Irwin, and W. Ye, "Influence of Compiler Optimizations on System Power," *Proceedings of the 37th Conference on Design Automation*, pp. 304–307, June 2000.

Kastner (2000). D. Kastner, "TDL: A Hardware and Assembly Description Language," Technical Report TDL1.4, Saarland University, 2000.

Kathail et al. (1994). V. Kathail, M. Schlansker, and B. R. Rau, "HPL PlayDoh Architecture Specification: Version 1.0," Technical Report HPL-93-80, Hewlett-Packard Laboratories, March 1994.

Kemp et al. (1998). T. M. Kemp, R. K. Montoye, J. D. Harper, J. D. Palmer, and D. J. Auerbach, "A Decompression Core for PowerPC," *IBM Journal of Research and Development*, vol. 42, no. 6, pp. 807–812, Nov. 1998.

Kernighan and Pike (1999). B. W. Kernighan and R. Pike. *The Practice of Programming*. Reading, MA: Addison-Wesley, 1999.

Kernighan and Ritchie (1978). B. W. Kernighan and D. M. Ritchie. *The C Programming Language*. Englewood Cliffs, NJ: Prentice Hall, 1978.

Kernighan and Ritchie (1988). B. W. Kernighan and D. M. Ritchie. *The C Programming Language*. 2d ed. Englewood Cliffs, NJ: Prentice Hall, 1988.

Kipphan (2001). H. Kipphan. *Handbook of Print Media: Technologies and Production Methods*. New York: Springer-Verlag, 2001.

Klaiber and Levy (1991). A. C. Klaiber and H. M. Levy, "An Architecture for Software-Controlled Data Prefetching," *Proceedings of the 18th Annual International Symposium on Computer Architecture*, pp. 43–63, April 1991.

Klaiber (2000). A. Klaiber, "The Technology Behind Crusoe Processors," White Paper, Transmeta Corporation, Jan. 2000.

Klejin and Paliwal (1995). W. B. Klejin and K. K. Paliwal (eds.). *Speech Coding and Synthesis*. Burlington, MA: Elsevier, 1995.

Kogge (1972). P. M. Kogge. "Parallel Algorithms for the Efficient Solution of Recurrence Problems," Ph. D. Thesis, Stanford University, Dec. 1972.

Kogge (1973). P. M. Kogge, "Maximal Rate Pipelined Solutions to Recurrence Problems," *Proceedings of the 1st Annual Symposium on Computer Architecture*, pp. 71–76, 1973.

Kogge (1977). P. M. Kogge, "The Microprogramming of Pipelined Processors," *Proceedings of the 4th Annual International Symposium on Computer Architecture*, pp. 63–69, March 1977.

Kozuch and Wolfe (1994). M. Kozuch and A. Wolfe, "Compression of Embedded System Programs," *Proceedings of the 1994 IEEE International Conference on Computer Design*, pp. 270–277, Oct. 1994.

Labrousse and Slavenburg (1990). J. Labrousse and G. A. Slavenburg, "A 500 MHz Microprocessor with a Very Long Instruction Word Architecture," *Proceedings of the IEEE International Solid-State Circuits Conference*, pp. 44–45, Feb. 1990.

Lala and Harper (1994). J. H. Lala and R. E. Harper, "Architectural Principles for Safety-Critical Real-Time Applications," *Proceedings of the IEEE*, vol. 82, no. 1, pp. 25–40, Jan. 1994.

Lam (1988). M. S. Lam, "Software Pipelining: An Effective Scheduling Technique for VLIW Machines," *Proceedings for the SIGPLAN 1988 Conference on Programming Language Design and Implementation*, pp. 318–328, June 1988.

Lam and Wilson (1992). M. S. Lam and R. P. Wilson, "Limits of Control Flow on Parallelism," *Proceedings of the 19th Annual International Symposium on Computer Architecture*, pp. 46–57, April 1992.

Lampson (1983). B. W. Lampson, "Hints for Computer System Design," *Proceedings of the 9th ACM Symposium on Operating Systems Principles*, pp. 33–48, Oct. 1983.

LANCE Retargetable C Compiler (2004). Web site at *http://www.icd.de/es/lance/lance.html*.

Landskov et al. (1980). D. Landskov, S. Davidson, B. Shriver, and P. W. Mallett, "Local Microcode Compaction Techniques," *ACM Computing Surveys*, vol. 12, no. 3, pp. 261–294, Sept. 1980.

Lanneer et al. (1995). D. Lanneer, J. Van Praet, A. Kifli, K. Schoofs, W. Geurts, F. Thoen, and G. Goossens, "Chess: Retargetable Code Generation for Embedded DSP Processors," in P. Marwedel and G. Goossens (eds.). *Code Generation for Embedded Processors*. Boston: Kluwer Academic Publishers, pp. 85–102, 1995.

Lapinskii et al. (2002). V. S. Lapinskii, M. F. Jacome, and G. A. De Veciana, "Cluster Assignment for High-Performance Embedded VLIW Processors," *ACM Transactions on Design Automation of Electronic Systems*, vol. 7, no. 3, pp. 430–454, July 2002.

Larin and Conte (1999). S. Y. Larin and T. M. Conte, "Compiler-Driven Cached Code Compression Schemes for Embedded ILP Processors," *Proceedings of the 32nd Annual International Symposium on Microarchitecture*, pp. 82–92, Nov. 1999.

Larus (1993). J. R. Larus, "Efficient Program Tracing," *IEEE Computer*, vol. 26, no. 5, pp. 52–61, May 1993.

Larus (1999). J. R. Larus, "Whole Program Paths," *Proceedings of the SIGPLAN 1999 Conference on Programming Language Design and Implementation*, pp. 259–269, May 1999.

Le Gall (1991). D. Le Gall, "MPEG: A Video Compression Standard for Multimedia Applications," *Communications of the ACM*, vol. 34, no. 4, pp. 46–58, April 1991.

Lee (1994). R. Lee, "Multimedia Enhancements for PA-RISC Processors," *Proceedings of Hot Chips VI*, pp. 183–192, Aug. 1994.

Lee (1995). R. Lee, "Accelerating Multimedia with Enhanced Microprocessors," *IEEE Micro*, vol. 15, no. 2, pp. 22–32, April 1995.

Lee (2002). E. Lee, "Embedded Software," in M. Zelkowitz (ed.). *Advances in Computers, Volume 56*. London: Academic Press, 2002. Also at web site *http://www.ptolemy.eecs.berkeley.edu/publications/papers/02/embsoft/embsoftwre.pdf*.

Lee et al. (1995). M. T.-C. Lee, V. Tiwari, S. Malik, and M. Fujita, "Power Analysis and Low-Power Scheduling Techniques for Embedded DSP Software," *Proceedings of the 8th International Symposium on System Synthesis*, pp. 110–115, Sept. 1995.

Lefurgy et al. (1997). C. Lefurgy, P. Bird, I.-C. Chen, and T. Mudge, "Improving Code Density Using Compression Techniques," *Proceedings of the 30th Annual International Symposium on Microarchitecture*, pp. 194–203, Dec. 1997.

Lefurgy et al. (1999). C. Lefurgy, E. Piccininni, and T. Mudge, "Evaluation of a High Performance Code Compression Method," *Proceedings of the 32nd Annual International Symposium on Microarchitecture*, pp. 93–102, Nov. 1999.

Leupers (1997). R. Leupers. *Retargetable Code Generation for Digital Signal Processors*. Boston: Kluwer Academic Publishers, 1997.

Leupers (2000). R. Leupers, "Instruction Scheduling for Clustered VLIW DSPs," *Proceedings of the 2000 International Conference on Parallel Architectures and Compilation Techniques*, pp. 291–300, Oct. 2000.

Leupers and David (1998). R. Leupers and F. David, "A Uniform Optimization Technique for Offset Assignment Problems," *Proceedings of the 11th International Symposium on System Synthesis*, pp. 3–8, Dec. 1998.

Leupers and Marwedel (1997). R. Leupers and P. Marwedel, "Time-Constrained Code Compaction for DSPs," *IEEE Transactions on Very Large Scale Integration (VLSI) Systems*, vol. 5, no. 1, pp. 112–122, March 1997.

Leupers and Marwedel (2001). R. Leupers and P. Marwedel. *Retargetable Compiler Technology for Embedded Systems: Tools and Applications*. Boston: Kluwer Academic Publishers, 2001.

Li and John (2003). T. Li and L. K. John, "Run-Time Modeling and Estimation of Operating System Power Consumption," *Proceedings of the 2003 ACM SIGMETRICS Conference on Measurement and Modeling of Computer Systems*, pp. 160–171, June 2003.

Liang (1999). S. Liang. *Java Native Interface: Programmer's Guide and Specification*. Reading, MA: Addison-Wesley, 1999.

Liao et al. (1995). S. Liao, S. Devadas, K. Keutzer, S. Tjiang, and A. Wang, "Code Optimization Techniques for Embedded DSP Microprocessors," *Proceedings of the 32nd Conference on Design Automation*, pp. 599–604, Jan. 1995.

Liao et al. (1996). S. Liao, S. Devadas, K. Keutzer, S. Tjiang, A. Wang, G. Araujo, A. Sudarsanam, S. Malik, V. Zivojnovic, and H. Meyr, "Code Generation and Optimization Techniques for Embedded Digital Signal Processors," in G. de Micheli and M. Sami (eds.), *Hardware/Software Co-Design*. Boston: Kluwer Academic Publishers, 1996.

Lindholm and Yellin (1999). T. Lindholm and F. Yellin. *The Java Virtual Machine Specification*. 2d ed. Reading, MA: Addison-Wesley, 1999.

LinuxDevices.com (2004). Web site at *http://www.linux.devices.com*.

Lions (1996). J. Lions. *Lions' Commentary on UNIX*. 6th ed. San Clemente, CA: AnnaBooks (RTC Books), 1977.

Lipasti and Shen (1996). M. H. Lipasti and J. P. Shen, "Exceeding the Dataflow Limit Via Value Prediction," *Proceedings of the 29th Annual International Symposium on Microarchitecture*, pp. 226–237, Dec. 1996.

Liu and Layland (1973). C. L. Liu and J. W. Layland, "Scheduling Algorithms for Multiprogramming in a Hard-Real-Time Environment," *Journal of the ACM*, vol. 20, no. 1, pp. 46–61, Jan. 1973.

Llosa and Freudenberger (2002). J. Llosa and S. M. Freudenberger, "Reduced Code Size Modulo Scheduling in the Absence of Hardware Support," *Proceedings of the 35th Annual International Symposium on Microarchitecture*, pp. 99–110, Nov. 2002.

Llosa et al. (1995). J. Llosa, M. Valero, E. Ayguadé, and A. González, "Hypernode Reduction Modulo Scheduling," *Proceedings of the 28th Annual International Symposium on Microarchitecture*, pp. 350–360, Dec. 1995.

Llosa et al. (1996). J. Llosa, A. González, M. Valero, and E. Ayguadé, "Swing Modulo Scheduling: A Lifetime-Sensitive Approach," *Proceedings of the 1996 International Conference on Parallel Architectures and Compilation Techniques*, pp. 80–86, Oct. 1996.

Llosa et al. (1998). J. Llosa, M. Valero, E. Ayguadé, and A. González, "Modulo Scheduling with Reduced Register Pressure," *IEEE Transactions on Computers*, vol. 47, no. 6, pp. 625–638, June 1998.

Lowney et al. (1993). P. G. Lowney, S. M. Freudenberger, T. J. Karzes, W. D. Lichtenstein, R. P. Nix, J. S. O'Donnell, and J. C. Ruttenberg, "The Multiflow Trace Scheduling Compiler," *Journal of Supercomputing*, vol. 7, no. 1–2, pp. 51–142, May 1993.

Luk and Mowry (1996). C.-K. Luk and T. C. Mowry, "Compiler-Based Prefetching for Recursive Data Structures," *Proceedings of the 7th International Conference on Architectural Support for Programming Languages and Operating Systems*, pp. 222–233, Oct. 1996.

Luk and Mowry (1998). C.-K. Luk and T. C. Mowry, "Cooperative Prefetching: Compiler and Hardware Support for Effective Instruction Prefetching in Modern Processors," *Proceedings of the 31st Annual International Symposium on Microarchitecture*, pp. 182–194, Nov. 1998.

Macii et al. (1998). E. Macii, M. Pedram, and F. Somenzi, "High-Level Power Modeling, Estimation, and Optimization," *IEEE Transactions on Computer-Aided Design of Integrated Circuits and Systems*, vol. 17, no. 11, pp. 1061–1079, Nov. 1998.

Magnusson (1997). P. S. Magnusson, "Efficient Instruction Cache Simulation and Execution Profiling with a Threaded-Code Interpreter," *Proceedings of the 29th Conference on Winter Simulation*, pp. 1093–1100, Dec. 1997.

Magnusson et al. (2002). P. S. Magnusson, M. Christensson, J. Eskilson, D. Forsgren, G. Hållberg, J. Högberg, F. Larsson, A. Moestedt, and B. Werner, "Simics: A Full System Simulation Platform," *IEEE Computer*, vol. 35, no. 2, pp. 50–58, Feb. 2002.

Mahlke et al. (1992). S. A. Mahlke, D. C. Lin, W. Y. Chen, R. E. Hank, and R. A. Bringmann, "Effective Compiler Support for Predicated Execution Using the Hyperblock," *Proceedings of the 25th Annual International Symposium on Microarchitecture*, pp. 45–54, Dec. 1992.

Mahlke et al. (1993). S. A. Mahlke, W. Y. Chen, R. A. Bringmann, R. E. Hank, W. W. Hwu, B. R. Rau, and M. S. Schlansker, "Sentinel Scheduling: A Model for Compiler-Controlled Speculative Execution," *ACM Transactions on Computer Systems*, vol. 11, no. 4, pp. 376–408, Nov. 1993.

Mahlke et al. (1995). S. A. Mahlke, R. E. Hank, J. E. McCormick, D. I. August, and W. W. Hwu, "A Comparison of Full and Partial Predicated Execution Support for ILP Processors," *Proceedings of the 22nd Annual International Symposium on Computer Architecture*, pp. 138–150, May 1995.

Makhoul (1975). J. Makhoul, "Linear Prediction: A Tutorial Review," *Proceedings of the IEEE*, vol. 63, no. 4, pp. 561–580, April 1975.

MAME (2003). MAME: Multiple Arcade Machine Emulator. Web site at *http://www.mame.net*.

Mangione-Smith and Memik (2001). W. H. Mangione-Smith and G. Memik. "Network Processor Technologies," tutorial presented at the 34th Annual International Symposium on Microarchitecture. Web site at *http://www.cares.icsl.ucla.edu/pres.html*, Dec. 2001.

Matlab (2004). Mathworks. Web site at *http://www.mathworks.org.*

Martin and Chang (2003). G. Martin and H. Chang (eds.). *Winning the SoC Revolution: Experiences in Real Design.* Boston: Kluwer Academic Publishers, 2003.

Maurer and Wang (1991). P. M. Maurer and Z. Wang, "Techniques for Unit-Delay Compiled Simulation," *Proceedings of the 27th Conference on Design Automation,* pp. 480–484, Jan. 1991.

May (1987). C. May, "Mimic: A Fast System/370 Simulator," *Proceedings of the SIGPLAN 1987 Symposium on Interpreters and Interpretive Techniques,* pp. 1–13, July 1987.

McConnell (2004). S. McConnell. *Code Complete.* 2d ed. Redmond, WA: Microsoft Press, 2004.

McFarling (1989). S. McFarling, "Program Optimization for Instruction Caches," *Proceedings of the 3rd International Conference on Architectural Support for Programming Languages and Operating Systems,* pp. 183–191, April 1989.

Mescal (2004). Web site at *http://www.gigascale.org/mesc.*

Microprocessor Report (1996). S. Przybylski, "SDRAMs Ready to Enter PC Mainstream," *Microprocessor Report,* vol. 10, no. 6, pp. 17–23, May 1996.

MIPS Technologies, Inc. (2004). Web site at *http://www.mips.com.*

Mittal et al. (1997). M. Mittal, A. Peleg, and U. Weiser, "MMX Architecture Overview," *Intel Technology Journal,* 3rd Quarter, 1997.

Montanaro et al. (1996). J. Montanaro, R. T. Witek, K. Anne, A. J. Black, E. M. Cooper, D. W. Dobberpuhl, P. M. Donahue, J. Eno, W. Hoeppner, D. Kruckemyer, T. H. Lee, P. C. M. Lin, L. Madden, D. Murray, M. H. Pearce, S. Santhanam, K. J. Snyder, R. Stephany, and S. C. Thierauf, "A 160-MHz, 32-b, 0.5-W CMOS RISC Microprocessor," *IEEE Journal of Solid-State Circuits,* vol. 31, no. 11, pp. 1703–1714, Nov. 1996.

Moon and Ebcioğlu (1992). S.-M. Moon and K. Ebcioğlu, "An Efficient Resource-Constrained Global Scheduling Technique for Superscalar and VLIW Processors," *Proceedings of the 25th Annual International Symposium on Microarchitecture,* pp. 55–71, Dec. 1992.

Moon and Ebcioğlu (1997). S.-M. Moon and K. Ebcioğlu, "Parallelizing Nonnumerical Code with Selective Scheduling and Software Pipelining," *ACM Transactions on Programming Languages and Systems,* 19(6), pp. 853–898, Nov. 1997.

Morgan (1998). R. Morgan. *Building an Optimizing Compiler.* Boston: Butterworth-Heinemann, 1998.

Motorola (2001). Motorola, Inc., "C-Port Network Processors Reference Manual," distributed by Freescale Semiconductor, 2001. Web site at *http://e-www.motorola.com.*

Motwani et al. (1995). R. Motwani, K. V. Palem, V. Sarkar, and S. Reyen, "Combining Register Allocation and Instruction Scheduling," Technical Report CS-TN-95-22, Department of Computer Science, Stanford University, Aug. 1995.

Mowry (1994). T. C. Mowry. "Tolerating Latency Through Software-Controlled Data Prefetching," Ph. D. Thesis, Computer Systems Laboratory, Stanford University, March 1994.

Mowry and Gupta (1991). T. C. Mowry and A. Gupta, "Tolerating Latency Through Software-Controlled Prefetching in Shared-Memory Multiprocessors," *Journal of Parallel and Distributed Computing*, vol. 12, no. 2, pp. 87–106, June 1991.

Mowry et al. (1992). T. C. Mowry, M. S. Lam, and A. Gupta, "Design and Evaluation of a Compiler Algorithm for Prefetching," *Proceedings of the 5th International Conference on Architectural Support for Programming Languages and Operating Systems*, pp. 62–73, Sept. 1992.

Muchnick (1997). S. S. Muchnick. *Advanced Compiler Design and Implementation.* San Francisco, CA: Morgan Kaufmann Publishers (an imprint of Elsevier), 1997.

Müller (1993). W. Müller, "Employing Finite Automata for Resource Scheduling," *Proceedings of the 26th Annual International Symposium on Microarchitecture*, pp. 12–20, Dec. 1993.

Müller et al. (2003). W. Müller, W. Rosenstiel, and J. Ruf. *SystemC: Methodologies and Applications.* Boston: Kluwer Academic Publishers, 2003.

Nelson (1990). V. P. Nelson, "Fault-Tolerant Computing: Fundamental Concepts," *IEEE Computer*, vol. 23, no. 7, pp. 19–25, July 1990.

Nelson and Gailly (1995). M. Nelson and J.-L. Gailly. *The Data Compression Book.* 2d ed. New York: M&T Books, 1995.

Ng (1998). S. W. Ng, "Advances in Disk Technology: Performance Issues," *IEEE Computer*, vol. 31, no. 5, pp. 75–81, May 1998.

Nicolau and Fisher (1981). A. Nicolau and J. A. Fisher, "Using an Oracle to Measure Potential Parallelism in Single Instruction Stream Programs," *Proceedings of the 14th Annual Workshop on Microprogramming*, pp. 171–182, Dec. 1981.

Nohl et al. (2002). A. Nohl, G. Braun, O. Schliebusch, R. Leupers, H. Meyr, and A. Hoffmann, "A Universal Technique for Fast and Flexible Instruction-Set Architecture Simulation," *Proceedings of the 39th Conference on Design Automation*, pp. 22–27, June 2002.

OCB (2000). OCB Development Working Group, "Virtual Component Interface Standard," Virtual Sockets Interface (VSI) Alliance, Nov. 2000.

Oppenheim and Schafer (1975). A. V. Oppenheim and R. W. Schafer. *Digital Signal Processing.* Englewood Cliffs, NJ: Prentice Hall, 1975.

Orfanidis (1995). S. Orfanidis. *Introduction to Signal Processing.* Englewood Cliffs, NJ: Prentice Hall, 1995.

O'Shaughnessy (1987). D. O'Shaughnessy. *Speech Communications: Human and Machine.* Reading, MA: Addison-Wesley, 1987.

Özer et al. (1998a). E. Özer, S. W. Sathaye, K. N. Menezes, S. Banerjia, M. D. Jennings, and T. M. Conte, "A Fast Interrupt Handling Scheme for VLIW Processors," *Proceedings of the 1998 International Conference on Parallel Architectures and Compilation Techniques*, pp. 136–141, Oct. 1998.

Özer et al. (1998b). E. Özer, S. Banerjia, and T. M. Conte, "Unified Assign and Schedule: A New Approach to Scheduling for Clustered Register File Microarchitectures,"

Proceedings of the 31st Annual International Symposium on Microarchitecture, pp. 308–316, Dec. 1998.

Palacharla et al. (1997). S. Palacharla, N. P. Jouppi, and J. E. Smith, "Complexity-Effective Superscalar Processors," *Proceedings of the 24th Annual International Symposium on Computer Architecture*, pp. 206–218, May 1997.

Panda et al. (1999). P. R. Panda, N. D. Dutt, and A. Nicolau. *Memory Issues in Embedded Systems-on-Chip: Optimizations and Exploration*. Boston: Kluwer Academic Publishers, 1999.

Patel and Davidson (1976). J. H. Patel and E. S. Davidson, "Improving the Throughput of a Pipeline by Insertion of Delays," *Proceedings of the 3rd Annual International Symposium on Computer Architecture*, pp. 159–164, 1976.

Patterson (1985). D. A. Patterson, "Reduced Instruction Set Computers," *Communications of the ACM*, vol. 28, no. 1, pp. 8–21, Jan. 1985.

PC Guide (2004). The PC Guide web site at *http://www.pcguide.com*.

Pees et al. (1999). S. Pees, A. Hoffmann, V. Zivojnovic, and H. Meyr, "LISA – Machine Description Language for Cycle-Accurate Models of Programming DSP Architectures," *Proceedings of the 36th Conference on Design Automation*, pp. 933–938, June 1999.

Pennebaker and Mitchell (1992). W. B. Pennebaker and J. L. Mitchell. *JPEG Still Image Data Compression Standard*. New York: Van Nostrand Reinhold, 1992.

Pering and Broderson (1998). T. Pering and R. Broderson, "Dynamic Voltage Scaling and the Design of a Low-Power Microprocessor System," *Proceedings of the 1998 Power-Driven Microarchitecture Workshop*, pp. 74–79, held in conjunction with the *25th Annual International Symposium on Computer Architecture*, June 1998.

Pettis and Hansen (1990). K. Pettis and R. C. Hansen, "Profile Guided Code Positioning," *Proceedings of the SIGPLAN 1990 Conference on Programming Language Design and Implementation*, pp. 16–27, June 1990.

Pfister (1982). G. F. Pfister, "The Yorktown Simulation Engine: Introduction," *Proceedings of the 19th Conference on Design Automation*, pp. 51–54, Jan. 1982.

Pillai and Shin (2001). P. Pillai and K. G. Shin, "Real-Time Dynamic Voltage Scaling for Low-Power Embedded Operating Systems," *Proceedings of the 18th Symposium on Operating Systems Principles*, pp. 89–102, Oct. 2001.

Pinter (1993). S. S. Pinter, "Register Allocation with Instruction Scheduling: A New Approach," *Proceedings of the SIGPLAN 1993 Conference on Programming Language Design and Implementation*, pp. 248–257, June 1993.

Playstation 2 Linux Community. Web site at *http://www.playstation2-linux.com*.

Podlesny et al. (1997). A. Podlesny, G. Kristovsky, and A. Malshin, "Multiport Register File Memory Cell Configuration for Read Operation," U.S. Patent No. 5,657,291, Sun Microsystems, Inc., Aug. 12, 1997.

Poppeliers and Chambers (2003). J. C. Poppeliers and S. A. Chambers. *What Style is It?: A Guide to American Architecture*. Rev. ed. New York: John Wiley, 2003.

Proebsting and Fraser (1994). T. A. Proebsting and C. W. Fraser, "Detecting Pipeline Structural Hazards Quickly," *Proceedings of the 21st SIGPLAN-SIGACT Symposium on Principles of Programming Languages*, pp. 280–286, Feb. 1994.

Przybylski (1990). S. Przybylski. *Cache and Memory Hierarchy Design: A Performance-Directed Approach.* San Francisco, CA: Morgan Kaufmann Publishers (an imprint of Elsevier), 1990.

Przybylski (1996). S. Przybylski, "SDRAMs Ready to Enter PC Mainstream," *Microprocessor Report,* vol. 10, no. 6, pp. 17–23, May 1996.

Qin and Malik (2003). W. Qin and S. Malik, "Flexible and Formal Modeling of Microprocessors with Application to Retargetable Simulation," *Proceedings of the 2003 Conference on Design, Automation and Test in Europe,* pp. 556–561, March 2003.

Rabbah and Palem (2003). R. M. Rabbah and K. V. Palem, "Data Remapping for Design Space Optimizations of Embedded Memory Systems," *ACM Transactions on Embedded Computing Systems,* vol. 2, no. 2, pp. 186–218, May 2003.

Rabiner and Schafer (1978). L. R. Rabiner and R. W. Schafer. *Digital Processing of Speech Signals.* Englewood Cliffs, NJ: Prentice Hall, 1978.

Raghunathan et al. (1998). A. Raghunathan, N. K. Jha, and S. Dey. *High-Level Power Analysis and Optimization.* Boston: Kluwer Academic Publishers, 1998.

Rao and Yip (1990). K. R. Rao and P. Yip. *Discrete Cosine Transform: Algorithms, Advantages, Applications.* Boston: Academic Press, 1990.

Rashinkar et al. (2001). P. Rashinkar, P. Paterson, and L. Singh. *System-on-a-Chip Verification: Methodology and Techniques.* Boston: Kluwer Academic Publishers, 2001.

Rau (1993). B. R. Rau, "Dynamically Scheduled VLIW Processors," *Proceedings of the 26th Annual International Symposium on Microarchitecture,* pp. 80–92, Dec. 1993.

Rau (1994). B. R. Rau, "Iterative Modulo Scheduling: An Algorithm for Software Pipelining Loops," *Proceedings of the 27th Annual International Symposium on Microarchitecture,* pp. 63–74, Nov. 1994.

Rau and Fisher (1993). B. R. Rau and J. A. Fisher, "Instruction-Level Parallel Processing: History, Overview, and Perspective," *The Journal of Supercomputing,* vol. 7, no. 1–2, pp. 9–50, May 1993.

Rau and Glaeser (1981). B. R. Rau and C. D. Glaeser, "Some Scheduling Techniques and an Easily Schedulable Horizontal Architecture for High Performance Scientific Computing," *Proceedings of the 14th Annual Workshop on Microprogramming,* pp. 183–198, Oct. 1981.

Rau et al. (1982). B. R. Rau, C. D. Glaeser, and R. L. Picard, "Efficient Code Generation for Horizontal Architectures: Compiler Techniques and Architectural Support," *Proceedings of the 9th Annual International Symposium on Computer Architecture,* pp. 131–139, 1982.

Rau et al. (1989). B. R. Rau, D. W. L. Yen, W. Yen, and R. A. Towie, "The Cydra-5 Departmental Supercomputer: Design Philosophies, Decisions, and Trade-Offs," *IEEE Computer,* vol. 22, no. 1, pp. 12–26, 28–30, 32–35, Jan. 1989.

Rau et al. (1992). B. R. Rau, M. Lee, P. P. Tirumalai, and M. S. Schlansker, "Register Allocation for Software Pipelined Loops," *Proceedings of the SIGPLAN 1992 Conference on Programming Language Design and Implementation,* pp. 283–299, June 1992.

Razdan and Smith (1994). R. Razdan and M. D. Smith, "A High-Performance Microarchitecture with Hardware-Programmable Functional Units," *Proceedings of the 27th Annual International Symposium on Microarchitecture*, pp. 172–180, Nov. 1994.

Reshadi et al. (2003). M. Reshadi, P. Mishra, and N. Dutt, "Instruction Set Compiled Simulation: A Technique for Fast and Flexible Instruction Set Simulation," *Proceedings of the 40th Conference on Design Automation*, pp. 758–763, June 2003.

Riseman and Foster (1972). E. M. Riseman and C. C. Foster, "The Inhibition of Potential Parallelism by Conditional Jumps," *IEEE Transactions on Computers*, vol. 21, no. 12, pp. 1405–1411, Dec. 1972.

Rosenberg (2001). L. H. Rosenberg, "Verification and Validation Implementation at NASA," *CrossTalk: The Journal of Defense Software Engineering*, vol. 14, no. 5, pp. 12–15, May 2001.

Rotenberg et al. (1996). E. Rotenberg, S. Bennett, and J. E. Smith, "Trace Cache: A Low Latency Approach to High Bandwidth Instruction Fetching," *Proceedings of the 29th Annual International Symposium on Microarchitecture*, pp. 24–35, Dec. 1996.

Roy and Johnson (1997). K. Roy and M. C. Johnson, "Software Design for Low Power," *Low Power Design in Deep Submicron Electronics: Proceedings of the NATO Advanced Study Institute*, pp. 433–460, Aug. 1997.

Ruemmler and Wilkes (1994). C. Ruemmler and J. Wilkes, "An Introduction to Disk Drive Modeling," *IEEE Computer*, vol. 27, no. 3, pp. 17–28, March 1994.

Ryu et al. (2001). K. K. Ryu, E. Shin, and V. Mooney. "A Comparison of Five Different Multiprocessor SoC Bus Architectures," *Proceedings of the 2001 Euromicro Symposium on Digital Systems Design*, pp. 202–211, Sept. 2001.

Sanchez and Gonzales (2000). J. Sanchez and A. Gonzales, "Instruction Scheduling for Clustered VLIW Architectures," *Proceedings of the 13th International Symposium on System Synthesis*, pp. 41–46, Sept. 2000.

Santhanam et al. (1997). V. Santhanam, E. H. Gornish, and W.-C. Hsu, "Data Prefetching on the HP PA-8000," *Proceedings of the 24th Annual International Symposium on Computer Architecture*, pp. 264–273, May 1997.

Sazeides and Smith (1997). Y. Sazeides and J. E. Smith, "The Predictability of Data Values," *Proceedings of the 30th Annual International Symposium on Microarchitecture*, pp. 248–258, Dec. 1997.

Schlansker and Rau (2000). M. S. Schlansker and B. R. Rau, "EPIC: An Architecture for Instruction-Level Parallel Processors," Technical Report HPL-1999-111, Hewlett-Packard Laboratories, Feb. 2000.

Schlansker et al. (1994). M. S. Schlansker, V. Kathail, and S. Anik, "Height Reduction of Control Recurrences for ILP Processors," *Proceedings of the 27th Annual International Symposium on Microarchitecture*, pp. 40–51, Nov. 1994.

Schneck (1973). P. B. Schneck, "A Survey of Compiler Optimization Techniques," *Proceedings of the 1973 ACM/CSC Annual Conference*, pp. 106–113, Aug. 1973.

Schorr (1971). H. Schorr, "Design Principles for a High-Performance System," *Proceedings of the 1971 International Symposium on Computers and Automata*, pp. 165–192, April 1971.

Schreiber et al. (2000). R. Schreiber, S. Aditya, B. R. Rau, V. Kathail, S. Mahlke, S. Abraham, and G. Snider, "High-Level Synthesis of Nonprogrammable Hardware Accelerators," *Proceedings of the 2000 IEEE International Conference on Application-Specific Systems, Architectures, and Processors*, pp. 113–126, July 2000.

Schumpeter (1962). Joseph A. Schumpeter. *Capitalism, Socialism, and Democracy.* New York: Perennial, 1962.

Schwartz (1966). J. T. Schwartz, "Large Parallel Computers" *Journal of the ACM*, vol. 13, no. 1, pp. 25–32, Jan. 1966.

Scientific Computing on the Sony Playstation 2. Web site at *http://www.ncsa.uiuc.edu/Projects/AllProjects/Projects95.html.*

Semeraro et al. (2002). G. Semeraro, G. Magklis, R. Balasubramonian, D. H. Albonesi, S. Dwarkadas, and M. L. Scott, "Energy-Efficient Processor Design Using Multiple Clock Domains with Dynamic Voltage and Frequency Scaling," *Proceedings of the 8th International Symposium on High-Performance Computer Architecture*, pp. 29–42, Feb. 2002.

Semiconductor Industry Association (SIA) (2003). Web site at *http://www.sia-online.org.*

Sezan and Lagendijk (1993). M. I. Sezan and R. L. Lagendijk (eds.). *Motion Analysis and Image Sequence Processing.* Boston: Kluwer Academic Publishers, 1993.

Shannon (1948). C. E. Shannon, "A Mathematical Theory of Communication," *Bell System Technical Journal*, vol. 27, pp. 379–423; 623–656, July/Oct. 1948.

Shaw (2001). A. C. Shaw. *Real-Time Systems and Software.* New York: John Wiley & Sons, 2001.

Siegel and Wolf (1991). P. H. Siegel and J. K. Wolf, "Modulation and Coding for Information Storage," *IEEE Communications Magazine*, vol. 29, no. 12, pp. 68–86, Dec. 1991.

Silberschatz et al. (2002). A. Silberschatz, P. B. Galvin, and G. Gagne. *Operating System Concepts.* 4th ed. New York: John Wiley & Sons, 2002.

Simon (1999). D. E. Simon. *An Embedded Software Primer.* Reading, MA: Addison-Wesley, 1999.

Siska (1998). C. Siska, "A Processor Description Language Supporting Retargetable Multi-pipeline DSP Program Development Tools," *Proceedings of the 11th International Symposium on System Synthesis*, pp. 31–36, Dec. 1998.

Sites and Agarwal (1988). R. L. Sites and A. Agarwal, "Multiprocessor Cache Analysis Using ATUM," *Proceedings of the 15th Annual International Symposium on Computer Architecture*, pp. 186–195, May 1988.

Smith (1982). A. J. Smith, "Cache Memories," *ACM Computing Surveys*, vol. 14, no. 3, pp. 473–530, Sept. 1982.

Smith (1985). B. Smith, "The Architecture of HEP," in J. S. Kowalik (ed.). *Parallel MIMD Computation: The HEP Supercomputer and its Applications.* Cambridge, MA: MIT Press, 1985, pp. 41–55.

Smith (1991). M. D. Smith, "Tracing with Pixie," Technical Report CSL-TR-91-497, Computer Systems Laboratory, Stanford University, Nov. 1991.

Smith and Pleszkun (1988). J. E. Smith and A. R. Pleszkun, "Implementing Precise Interrupts in Pipelined Processors," *IEEE Transactions on Computers*, vol. 37, no. 5, pp. 562–573, May 1988.

Smith et al. (1989). M. D. Smith, M. Johnson, and M. A. Horowitz, "Limits on Multiple Instruction Issue," *Proceedings of the 3rd International Conference on Architectural Support for Programming Languages and Operating Systems*, pp. 290–302, April 1989.

Srivastava and Eustace (1994). A. Srivastava and A. Eustace, "ATOM: A System for Building Customized Program Analysis Tools," *Proceedings of the SIGPLAN 1994 Conference on Programming Language Design and Implementation*, pp. 196–205, June 1994.

Stallings (2004). W. Stallings. *Operating Systems: Internals and Design Principles.* 5th ed. Upper Saddle River, NJ: Pearson/Prentice Hall, 2004.

Stanford SUIF Compiler Group (2004). Web site at *http://suif.stanford.edu.*

Steinke et al. (2001). S. Steinke, R. Schwarz, L. Wehmeyer, and P. Marwedel. "Low Power Code Generation for a RISC Processor by Register Pipelining," Technical Report 754, University of Dortmund, Department of Computer Science XII, 2001.

Stone (1967). H. S. Stone, "One-Pass Compilation of Arithmetic Expressions for a Parallel Processor," *Communications of the ACM*, vol. 10, no. 4, pp. 220–223, April 1967.

Storer and Szymanski (1982). J. Storer and T. Szymanski, "Data Compression via Textual Substitution," *Journal of the ACM*, vol. 29, no. 4, pp. 928–951, Oct. 1982.

Stroustrup (1997). B. Stroustrup. *The C++ Programming Language.* 3d ed. Reading, MA: Addison-Wesley, 1997.

Su et al. (1994). C.-L. Su, C.-Y. Tsui, and A. M. Despain, "Low Power Architecture Design and Compilation Techniques for High-Performance Processors," *Proceedings of IEEE COMPCON*, pp. 489–498, March 1994.

Sudarsanam et al. (1997). A. Sudarsanam, S. Liao, and S. Devadas, "Analysis and Evaluation of Address Arithmetic Capabilities in Custom DSP Architectures," *Proceedings of the 34th Conference on Design Automation*, pp. 287–292, June 1997.

Tanenbaum (2001). A. S. Tanenbaum. *Modern Operating Systems.* 2d ed. Upper Saddle River, NJ: Prentice Hall, 2001.

Tanenbaum and Woodhull (1997). A. S. Tanenbaum and A. Woodhull. *Operating Systems: Design and Implementation.* 2d ed. Upper Saddle River, NJ: Prentice Hall, 1997.

Target Compiler Technologies (2004). Web site at *http://www.retarget.com.*

Tekalp (1995). A. M. Tekalp. *Digital Video Processing.* Upper Saddle River, NJ: Prentice Hall, 1995.

Tensilica, Inc. (2004) Web site at *http://www.tensilica.com.*

Terechko et al. (2001). A. Terechko, E. Pol, and J. van Eijndhoven, "PRMDL: A Machine Description Language for Clustered VLIW Architectures," *Proceedings of the Conference on Design, Automation, and Test in Europe*, p. 821, March 2001.

Terechko et al. (2003). A. Terechko, E. Le Thénaff, and H. Corporaal, "Cluster Assignment of Global Values for Clustered VLIW Processors," *Proceedings of the 2003*

International Conference on Compilers, Architectures and Synthesis for Embedded Systems, pp. 32–40, Oct. 2003.

Texas Instruments. Web site at *dspvillage.ti.com*.

Thoen and Catthoor (2000). F. Thoen and F. Catthoor. *Modeling, Verification, and Exploration of Task-Level Concurrency in Real-Time Embedded Systems*. Boston: Kluwer Academic Publishers, 2000.

Thomas and Moorby (1998). D. E. Thomas and P. R. Moorby. *The Verilog Hardware Description Language*. 4th ed. Boston, MA: Kluwer Academic Publishers, 1998.

Thorlin (1967). J. F. Thorlin, "Code Generation for PIE (Parallel Instruction Execution) Computers," *Proceedings of the 1967 AFIPS Conference*, vol. 30, pp. 641–643, April 1967.

Thornton (1964). J. E. Thornton, "Parallel Operation in Control Data 6600," *Proceedings of the 1964 AFIPS Fall Joint Computer Conference*, no. 26, part 2, pp. 33–40, 1964.

Thornton (1970). J. E. Thornton. *Design of a Computer: The Control Data 6600*. Glenview, IL: Scott Foresman and Co., 1970.

Tiwari et al. (1994a). V. Tiwari, S. Malik, and A. Wolfe, "Compilation Techniques for Low Energy: An Overview," *Proceedings of the 1994 International Symposium on Low-Power Electronics and Design*, pp. 38–39, Oct. 1994.

Tiwari et al. (1994b). V. Tiwari, S. Malik, and A. Wolfe, "Power Analysis of Embedded Software: A First Step Towards Software Power Minimization," *IEEE Transactions on Very Large Scale Integration (VLSI) Systems*, vol. 2, no. 4, pp. 437–445, Dec. 1994.

Toburen et al. (1998). M. C. Toburen, T. M. Conte, and M. Reilly, "Instruction Scheduling for Low-Power Dissipation in High Performance Microprocessors," *Proceedings of the 1998 Power-Driven Microarchitecture Workshop*, pp. 14–19, held in conjunction with the *25th Annual International Symposium on Computer Architecture*, June 1998.

Todd and McNelly (2001). L. Todd and A. McNelly, "The Transition to System-on-a-Chip," Technical Report, Cadence Design Systems Inc., Feb. 2001.

Tokoro et al. (1977). M. Tokoro, E. Tamura, K. Takase, and K. Tamaru, "An Approach to Microprogram Optimization Considering Resource Occupancy and Instruction Formats," *Proceedings of the 10th Annual Workshop on Microprogramming*, pp. 92–108, Oct. 1977.

Tomasulo (1967). R. M. Tomasulo, "An Efficient Algorithm for Exploiting Multiple Arithmetic Units," *IBM Journal of Research and Development*, vol. 11, pp. 25–33, Jan. 1967.

Top 500 Supercomputer Sites, (2004). Web site at *http://www.top500.org*.

Touzeau (1984). R. F. Touzeau, "A Fortran Compiler for the FPS-164 Scientific Computer," *Proceedings of the 1984 SIGPLAN Symposium on Compiler Construction*, pp. 48–57, June 1984.

Traub et al. (1998). O. Traub, G. Holloway, and M. D. Smith, "Quality and Speed in Linear-Scan Register Allocation," *Proceedings of the SIGPLAN 1998 Conference on Programming Language Design and Implementation*, pp. 142–151, May 1998.

Trimaran (2004). Web site at *http://www.trimaran.org*.

Tullsen and Eggers (1993). D. M. Tullsen and S. J. Eggers, "Limitations of Cache Prefetching on a Bus-Based Multiprocessor," *Proceedings of the 20th Annual International Symposium on Computer Architecture*, pp. 278–288, May 1993.

Tullsen et al. (1995). D. M. Tullsen, S. J. Eggers, and H. M. Levy, "Simultaneous Multithreading: Maximizing On-Chip Parallelism," *Proceedings of the 22nd Annual International Symposium on Computer Architecture*, pp. 392–403, May 1995.

uCdot Embedded Linux Developer Forum (2004). Web site at *http://www.ucdot.org.*

uClinux Embedded Linux/Microcontroller Project (2004). Web site at *http://www. uclinux.org.*

Uhlig and Mudge (1997). R. A. Uhlig and T. N. Mudge, "Trace-Driven Memory Simulation: A Survey," *ACM Computing Surveys*, vol. 29, no. 2, pp. 128–170, June 1997.

Ulichney (1987). R. Ulichney. *Digital Halftoning.* Cambridge, MA: MIT Press, 1987.

Vondran and Desoli (2000). G. L. Vondran and G. Desoli. "Radial and Pruned Radial Interpolation," U.S. Patent Number 6,040,925. March 2000.

VSI (Virtual Socket Interface) Alliance (2004). Web site at *http://www.vsi.org.*

Wallace (1991). G. K. Wallace, "The JPEG Still Picture Compression Standard," *Communications of the ACM*, vol. 34, no. 4, pp. 30–44, April 1991.

Walls and Williams (2000). C. Walls and S. Williams, "Multicore Debug Sought in SoC Design," *EE Times*, March 2000.

Wang and Fu (2000). M. Wang and X. Fu, "GSM Enhanced Full Rate Speech Coder: Multichannel TMS320C62x Implementation," Texas Instruments Application Report, SPRA565B, Feb. 2000.

Wang et al. (2000). Z. Wang, K. Pierce, and S. McFarling, "BMAT: A Binary Matching Tool for Stale Profile Propagation," *Journal of Instruction-Level Parallelism*, vol. 2, May 2000.

Wang et al. (2002). Y. Wang, J. Ostermann, and Y.-Q. Zhang. *Video Processing and Communications.* Upper Saddle River, NJ: Prentice Hall, 2002.

Warter et al. (1993). N. J. Warter, S. A. Mahlke, W.-M. W. Hwu, and B. R. Rau, "Reverse If-Conversion," *Proceedings of the SIGPLAN 1993 Conference on Programming Language Design and Implementation*, pp. 290–299, June 1993.

Waser and Flynn (1982). S. Waser and M. J. Flynn. *Introduction to Arithmetic for Digital Systems Designers.* New York: Holt, Reinhart, and Winston, 1982.

Watkinson (2000). J. Watkinson. *The Art of Digital Video.* 3d ed. Burlington, MA: Focal Press, 2000.

Weiss and Smith (1987). S. Weiss and J. E. Smith, "A Study of Scalar Compilation Techniques for Pipelined Supercomputers," *Proceedings of the 2nd International Conference on Architectural Support for Programming Languages and Operating Systems*, pp. 105–109, Oct. 1987.

Wess and Gotschlich (1997). B. Wess and M. Gotschlich, "Optimal DSP Memory Layout Generation as a Quadratic Assignment Problem," *Proceedings of the 1997 International Symposium on Circuits and Systems*, vol. 3, pp. 1712–1715, June 1997.

Winegarden (2000). S. Winegarden, "Bus Architecture of a System on a Chip with User Configurable System Logic," *IEEE Journal of Solid-State Circuits*, vol. 35, no. 3, pp. 425–433, March 2000.

Wittig and Chow (1996). R. Wittig and P. Chow, "OneChip: An FPGA Processor with Reconfigurable Logic," *Proceedings of the IEEE Symposium on FPGAs for Custom Computing Machines*, pp. 126–135, April 1996.

Wolfe (2001). A. Wolfe. Emerging Applications for the Connected Home. Micro-34 Keynote Speech, Dec. 2001, Austin, TX. Available at *http://www.microarch.org/micro34/talks/Wolfe-Keynote.PDF*.

Wolfe (1995). M. Wolfe. *High Performance Compilers for Parallel Computing*. Redwood City, CA: Pearson Education (Addison-Wesley), 1995.

Wolf (2001). W. Wolf. *Computers as Components: Principles of Embedded Computing Systems Design*. San Francisco, CA: Morgan Kaufmann Publishers (an imprint of Elsevier), 2001.

Wolf (2002). W. Wolf. *Modern VLSI Design: System-on-Chip Design*. 3d ed. Upper Saddle River, NJ: Prentice Hall, 2002.

Wolfe and Chanin (1992). A. Wolfe and A. Chanin, "Executing Compressed Programs on an Embedded RISC Architecture," *Proceedings of the 25th Annual International Symposium on Microarchitecture*, pp. 81–91, Dec. 1992.

Wong (2002). W. Wong, "JIT Speeds Simulation," *Electronic Design*, Sept. 2002.

Wu and Larus (1994). Y. Wu and J. R. Larus, "Static Branch Frequency and Program Profile Analysis," *Proceedings of the 27th Annual International Symposium on Microarchitecture*, pp. 1–11, Nov. 1994.

Wyszecki and Stiles (2000). G. Wyszecki and W. S. Stiles. *Color Science: Concepts and Methods, Quantitative Data, and Formulae*. 2d ed. New York: John Wiley & Sons, 2000.

Xilinx, Inc. (2004). Web site at *http://www.xilinx.com*.

Yeh and Patt (1991). T.-Y. Yeh and Y. N. Patt, "Two-level Adaptive Training Branch Prediction," *Proceedings of the 24th Annual International Symposium on Microarchitecture*, pp. 51–61, Sept. 1991.

Yi and Tomizuka (1999). L. Yi and M. Tomizuka, "Two-Degree-of-Freedom Control with Robust Feedback Control for Hard Disk Servo Systems," *IEEE/ASME Transactions on Mechatronics*, vol. 4, no. 1, pp. 17–24, March 1999.

Young (1997). C. Young, "Path-based Compilation," Ph.D. Thesis, Harvard University, Oct. 1997.

Young and Smith (1994). C. Young and M. D. Smith, "Improving the Accuracy of Static Branch Prediction Using Branch Correlation," *Proceedings of the 6th International Conference on Architectural Support for Programming Languages and Operating Systems*, pp. 232–241, Nov. 1994.

Young and Smith (1999). C. Young and M. D. Smith. Static Correlated Branch Prediction, *Transactions on Programming Languages and Systems*, vol. 21, no. 5, pp. 1028–1075, Sept. 1999.

Young et al. (1995). C. Young, N. Gloy, and M. D. Smith, "A Comparative Analysis of Schemes for Correlated Branch Prediction," *Proceedings of the 22nd Annual International Symposium on Computer Architecture*, pp. 276–286, May 1995.

Zalamea et al. (2001). J. Zalamea, J. Llosa, E. Ayguadé, and M. Valero, "Modulo Scheduling with Integrated Register Spilling for Clustered VLIW Architectures,"

Proceedings of the 34th Annual International Symposium on Microarchitecture, pp. 160–169, Dec. 2001.

Zeng et al. (2002). H. Zeng, X. Fan, C. Ellis, A. Lebeck, and A. Vahdat, "Ecosystem: Managing Energy as a First Class Operating System Resource," *Proceedings of the 10th International Conference on Architectural Support for Programming Languages and Operating Systems*, pp. 123–132, Oct. 2002.

Zhang et al. (1997). X. Zhang, Z. Wang, N. Gloy, J. Chen, and M. Smith. System Support for Automatic Profiling and Optimization, ACM SIGOPS Operating Systems Review, *Proceedings of the Sixteenth ACM Symposium on Operating Systems Principles*, Volume 31, Issue 5, October 1997.

Zhou and Conte (2002). H. Zhou and T. M. Conte, "Code Size Efficiency in Global Scheduling for ILP Processors," *Proceedings of the 6th Annual Workshop on the Interaction between Compilers and Computer Architectures*, in conjunction with the *8th International Symposium on High-Performance Computer Architecture*, pp. 79–90, Feb. 2002.

Zhou et al. (2001). H. Zhou, M. D. Jennings, and T. M. Conte, "Tree Traversal Scheduling: A Global Scheduling Technique for VLIW/EPIC Processors," *Proceedings of the 14th Annual Workshop on Languages and Compilers for Parallel Computing*, pp. 223–238, Aug. 2001.

Ziv and Lempel (1977). J. Ziv and A. Lempel, "A Universal Algorithm for Sequential Data Compression," *IEEE Transactions on Information Theory*, vol. 23, no. 3, pp. 337–343, May 1977.

Ziv and Lempel (1978). J. Ziv and A. Lempel, "Compression of Individual Sequences via Variable-Rate Coding," *IEEE Transactions on Information Theory*, vol. 24, no. 5, pp. 530–536, Sept. 1978.

Zivojnovic et al. (1995). V. Zivojnovic, S. Tjiang, and H. Meyr, "Compiled Simulation of Programmable DSP Architectures," *Proceedings of the 1995 IEEE Workshop on VLSI Signal Processing*, pp. 187–196, Sept. 1995.

Zyuban and Kogge (1998). V. Zyuban and P. Kogge, "The Energy Complexity of Register Files," *Proceedings of the 1998 International Symposium on Low-Power Electronics and Design*, pp. 305–310, Aug. 1998.

Index

Printed and bound by CPI Group (UK) Ltd, Croydon, CR0 4YY

03/10/2024

01040339-0011